Scenarios for Writing

Scenarios for Writing

ISSUES, ANALYSIS, AND RESPONSE

GREGORY R. GLAU
Arizona State University

CRAIG B. JACOBSEN
Chandler-Gilbert Community College

MAYFIELD PUBLISHING COMPANY
Mountain View, California
London • Toronto

For Courtney—I love you.

—G. R. G.

For Laura, with love.

—C. B. J.

Library of Congress Cataloging-in-Publication Data
Glau, Gregory R.
    Scenarios for writing : issues, analysis, and response / Gregory R. Glau, Craig B. Jacobsen.
        p. cm.
    Includes bibliographical references and index.
    ISBN 1-55934-983-2
    1. English language—Rhetoric. 2. Narration (Rhetoric) 3. Report writing. I. Jacobsen, Craig B. II. Title.
    PE1408.G5588 2000

                                                                        00-056837

Manufactured in the United States of America
10   9   8   7   6   5   4   3   2   1

Mayfield Publishing Company
1280 Villa Street
Mountain View, California 94041

Sponsoring editor, Renee Deljon; developmental editor, Rick Roehrich; production editor, Lynn Rabin Bauer; manuscript editor, Beverley J. DeWitt; art director, Jeanne Schreiber; design manager and cover designer, Susan Breitbard; text designer, Ellen Pettengell; cover images: college students photo © David R. Swanson/Liaison Agency, chalk outline photo VCG/FPG International; art editor and illustrator, Amy Folden; photo researcher, Emma Ghiselli; manufacturing manager, Randy Hurst. The text was set in 10/12 Meridian Roman by G&S Typesetters and printed on 45# Chromatone Matte by Banta Book Group. Scenarios in this book may resemble actual events but, unless otherwise indicated, any resemblance to actual events or to persons living or dead is purely coincidental.

Acknowledgments and copyrights continue at the back of the book on pages 497–499, which constitute an extension of the copyright page.

Preface

Scenarios for Writing is a rhetoric-reader with sequenced collaborative and individual assignments focused on issues of the day. More than any other composition textbook currently available, this book brings rhetorical situations to life, offering students immediate, identifiable audiences and purposes for their writing. Dedicated to improving students' academic, civic, and general communication skills, Scenarios for Writing offers an approach that seamlessly integrates practice in reading, thinking, listening, speaking, and writing. Teachers and students have told us how much they like this book's distinctive approach; we invite you to read on and discover what makes Scenarios so different, engaging, and effective.

A UNIQUE APPROACH

Scenarios for Writing is different from other rhetoric-readers in a number of ways. The primary difference is found in the narrative "scenarios" that lie at the center of the work students do in chapters 4 through 9. Practical tools for the composition classroom, these short narratives dramatize contemporary issues and establish contexts for rhetorical analysis and interaction. Presenting composites of real-life events and interest groups—such as those students themselves, or their families, friends, or coworkers might encounter—the scenarios grab students' attention, make the issues understandable, and encourage empathy with the people involved. The flexible assignment sequences that follow the scenarios invite students to work collaboratively and individually as they aim to resolve the central dilemma. The readings and the writing and speaking assignments that accompany each scenario stress the multiple perspectives inherent in any issue, so students gain practice in thinking about and communicating from varied, often conflicting, perspectives that combine group and individual interests. Finally, each scenario chapter culminates with academic essay options.

The scenarios chapters, then, provide a central problem to solve, a basic structure for students' work, a range of flexible sequenced assignments, and initial research sources; however, the specific interest groups, processes, and outcomes that individual classes bring to life are left for individual groups of students and teachers to decide. The scenarios are, in this sense, student- and class-driven, and so will be different every time they're used. But what is constant is that students, as members of interest groups interacting with other competing interest groups, learn to approach issues from multiple perspectives and to communicate with immediate audiences and purposes in mind. Throughout the process of working with the scenarios, students constantly develop new ways of solving rhetorical problems related to clearly defined rhetorical situations.

OVERALL ORGANIZATION

Scenarios for Writing is divided into two parts and includes three appendixes. Part I: Student Guidebook, includes three chapters, each covering a different aspect of college reading, writing, and research and providing "Applying What You Read" activities. Chapter 1 grounds students in an understanding of the rhetorical situation, discusses the recursive nature of writing and the different stages of the writing process, and helps students analyze their own writing processes. Chapter 2 moves students into discussions of various aspects of college reading and writing and the specific work they'll do in the scenarios chapters. Chapter 3 covers research strategies and writing from sources, including evaluating and acknowledging sources.

Part II: The Scenarios, opens with an introduction that serves as a bridge between the book's two parts, preparing students to apply the advice found in part I to the rhetorical work the scenarios require in part II, and detailing how the scenarios chapters work. Six scenarios, each in its own chapter, follow the introduction: Chapter 4, Online Education: Who Needs the Classroom, Anyway?; Chapter 5, Student Privacy: Bad Times at Westwood High; Chapter 6, Guns for Sale: Recycling Your Police Department's Weapons; Chapter 7, Suburban Sprawl: The Future of Saguaro Flats; Chapter 8, Pornography on the Internet: Cyberporn at Your Local Library?; and Chapter 9, Living Wills: Decisions about Life and Death. Readings ("Resources") help to inform students about the scenarios' central and related issues. Three appendixes appear at the end of the text: Appendix A, Preparing a Writer's Portfolio; Appendix B, Extending the Scenarios to Your Community: Service Learning; and Appendix C, Documenting Your Sources.

A CLOSER LOOK AT THE SCENARIOS CHAPTERS

Although the specific structure of each of the scenarios chapters (chapters 4–9) varies slightly, their overall framework and apparatus are consistent. "First Impressions" open each scenario chapter. This feature presents three to five images related to the issue at the center of the chapter's scenario, followed by questions that prompt students' initial thinking, discussion, and writing. A brief discussion of the central issue comes next, immediately preceding the actual scenario (the two- to three-page narrative account of a timely situation that calls for rhetorical action on the part of a number of interest groups). Details about the interest groups and options for involvement follow the scenario and precede the chapter's "Resources"—the collection of readings that can serve as an initial set of sources. "Questions for Discussion and Writing" follow every reading and lend themselves, if desired, to additional collaborative and individual work.

A sequence of activity and assignment options follows the readings: "Taking Action," a collaborative project; "Speaking Your Piece," an opportunity for the group to speak about its position publicly; and "Individual Writing: Essay Options," each chapter's culminating set of optional academic projects. "For Further Research and Writing" discussions suggest ways for students to widen the focus of each scenario. In addition, "Applying What You Read" and "For Example" boxes appear throughout the text.

FEATURES SUMMARY

Scenarios for Writing is a different kind of rhetoric-reader, one that brings rhetorical situations and issues of the day to life by offering

- Six scenarios that are relevant to students' everyday lives, current issues dramatized in narrative form and appropriate for rhetorical analysis and response.
- Flexible assignment sequences that combine collaborative and individual work and that culminate in academic writing (research-based persuasive essays).
- More than 50 diverse reading selections that enrich students' understanding of the scenarios' central issues—each accompanied by "Questions for Discussion and Writing."
- Seamless integration of reading, research, thinking, listening and speaking, and writing activities.
- Consistent emphasis on persuasion and negotiation within the context of various, often competing, points of view.
- Three chapters of rhetorical instruction in Part I: Student Guidebook.
- Photos followed by questions opening each chapter ("First Impressions") in part II.
- Three appendixes that complement students' scenarios work: appendix A on constructing portfolios, appendix B on extending the scenarios to service-learning projects, and appendix C on documenting sources.

ACKNOWLEDGMENTS

We'd like to thank the following colleagues who listened, read parts of, made suggestions about, or otherwise were involved in *Scenarios for Writing:* Linda Adler-Kassner, Steve Beatty, Dan Bivona, Debra Black, Dan Breazeale, Rea Busker, Laura Bush, Sharon Crowley, Frank D'Angelo, Sarah Duerden, Heidi Ernst, Steve Farmer, Jeanne Garland, Amy Glau, Tracy Glau, Kohl Glau, Rob Glau, Maureen Daly Goggin, Peter Goggin, Matt Golosinski, Babs Gordon, Nancy Gutierrez, Chris Helfers, Rita Hendin, Tiffany Johnson, Kate Mohler, Patricia Murphy, Camille Newton, Jeanne Olson, Charlotte Person, Deirdre Pettipiece, John Ramage, Duane Roen, Michael Stancliff, Dave Sudol, Marilyn Terreault, Judy Van, Jackie Wheeler, and Dena Zingales.

Thanks, also, go to all the reviewers: George Bebensee, University of Kentucky; Suzanne Bordelon, University of Alaska, Fairbanks; Stuart Brown, New Mexico State University; Rich Bullock, Wright State University; Deborah Burns, Merrimack College; Ann M. Feldman, University of Illinois at Chicago; Marguerite Helmers, University of Wisconsin, Oshkosh; Rebecca Jackson, New Mexico State University; David Kann, California Polytechnic State University, San Luis Obispo; Margaret Lindgren, University of Cinncinnati; Alan Meyers, Harry S. Truman College; John Ramage, Arizona State University; Susan A. Schiller, Central Michigan University; Julie Segedy, Chabot College; and Matt Smith, Chattanooga State Technical Community College. Particular thanks go to the many students whose insights, experience, and candid comments helped shape this book. Their collaboration has been invaluable.

We also would like to thank Tom Broadbent, who saw the initial promise of this text; Rick Roehrich, as good a developmental editor as there is; Beverley DeWitt, who did an outstanding job of copyediting the text; and Lynn Rabin Bauer, who's done a wonderful job as production editor.

More than "special thanks" go to Renee Deljon, who worked with us on this project for three years and always was supportive, helpful, thoughtful and—most important—constantly worked to help us construct the best possible text.

Brief Contents

Contents

*"Questions for Discussion and Writing" follow each reading.

PART I

 Student Guidebook

CHAPTER 1

The Rhetorical Situation and Your Writing Process

Our goal is to help you learn to write successfully. Writing is not mysterious: it is a process that can be learned and mastered. During college and later, in your professional life, you'll be called on again and again to write. In college, you write reports, term papers, and essay exams. You write letters home and e-mail messages to friends. In your professional life, you'll write memos, reports, and summaries. Often this writing requires that you collaborate with classmates or colleagues. The keys to writing successfully are understanding what the situation calls for and having a writing process that helps you meet those expectations. Accordingly, in this first chapter we focus on

- How writing depends on what is called the rhetorical situation—the occasion for writing, the purpose for writing, the topic, the audience, and the writer.
- How your own writing process may vary depending on the rhetorical situation in which you write.
- The recursive (nonlinear) nature of writing.
- How to use the activities in the writing process—which include prewriting, drafting, and revising—to compose writing that suits the rhetorical situation.
- Learning what you think through the process of organizing and composing academic compositions.

THE RHETORICAL SITUATION

Think of writing as a series of choices. When you sit down to write anything, you make dozens, hundreds, or thousands of choices. You decide what you want to say and how to begin. You choose every word, and you decide where sentences will begin and end and the form they'll take. You decide when to finish a paragraph and begin a new one. Often when we write we make these decisions without much thought. But even the simplest piece of writing can demonstrate how important the rhetorical situation is. Think of a grocery list, for example. If you are shopping for yourself, simply writing "cereal" on your list might be enough of a reminder. If someone else is doing the shopping, however, you might want to be more specific, to ensure that you get the kind of cereal you want. Recognizing who will use your list shows an awareness of audience—one aspect of the rhetorical situation. Knowing that your reader will need more information, you add detail to your list, writing "plain instant oatmeal." The result is that your audience is more likely to understand what you want, and you are more likely to get it.

The grocery list demonstrates simply how the rhetorical situation works. Now let's take a closer look at its elements: the occasion for writing, the purpose, the topic, the audience, and the writer. If you were to analyze the rhetorical situation in our example, you might find this:

Occasion: a dwindling food supply

Purpose: to remind the shopper of what is needed

Topic: items needed from the grocery store

Audience: the person doing the shopping

Writer: you

Simple enough, but the rhetorical situation affects all of the decisions you make as you write: the form in which you choose to write (a list), what you include on the list (items needed from the hardware store don't belong on a grocery list), how much detail to provide (the shopper might not know your favorite cereal), and even the care you take to write legibly or how much you abbreviate.

You understand the rhetorical situation better than you realize. In fact, you make decisions based on it whenever you communicate—whether in spoken or written form. You probably speak differently to your mother than you do to your younger brother or sister. This is a reflection of your understanding of audience, and the way in which you wish to present yourself to different audiences. You probably do different things with your words, depending on the situation: you inform (to answer a question, for example), you persuade, you question, you propose solutions. This is a reflection of your understanding of your rhetorical purpose.

One of the keys to successful writing is the ability to analyze the rhetorical situation and to make conscious writing decisions based on that

BOX 1.1   APPLYING WHAT YOU READ
Considering Your Rhetorical Situation

Letters are a good tool for understanding the rhetorical situation. A letter has a clearly defined audience and purpose, and it follows a familiar form. Spend a few minutes writing a letter to your closest friend, describing something embarrassing that happened to you recently. Write the letter as if you were going to mail it. Write with confidence that nobody but your intended audience (your closest friend) will read it.

Stop after you've written the first few paragraphs of the letter. Turn the page over and begin a second letter to your grandmother in which you describe the same incident. Again, approach the letter as if you were really going to send it, and assume that your grandmother will be your only reader. Write the first few paragraphs.

Now, compare the two letters. Did you:

- Make different word choices in the two letters, perhaps using slang in one but not in the other?
- Include more details in one letter than the other because one of your target audiences already knew something about the incident or the people involved?
- Include fewer details in one letter than the other to make the incident you were describing seem somehow different or less embarrassing?
- Use a different tone in the two letters, perhaps reflecting the relationship between you and your audience?
- Pay closer attention to spelling, grammar, and even your handwriting in one of the letters?

What other differences and similarities did you notice? Your instructor may ask you to discuss your findings with your classmates.

analysis. It's not enough simply to write down whatever words come to your mind. Instead, carefully plan your writing to address the requirements of the rhetorical situation.

As a student, you might have difficulty writing in college classes because you sometimes only vaguely sense the rhetorical situation in which you find yourself. You don't know, for instance, who might be your audience other than your instructor, or you don't have a real purpose for writing anything, or the details of the writing occasion are fuzzy. We find that asking students to address real-life problems and issues that provide authentic rhetorical situations helps. Identifying concrete issues to contend with, a genuine writing situation, and a specific audience for whom to write makes your research and writing more valuable—and lets you shape your writing to the rhetorical situation. Box 1.1: Considering Your Rhetorical Situation gives you a chance to practice making effective rhetorical choices.

Whether or not you think consciously about your purpose, audience, or situation when you write, these elements are part of the rhetorical situation, and they influence the decisions you make as you write. Although you already instinctively understand the rhetorical situation, you probably haven't given it much thought before now. A deeper understanding of the elements that make up the rhetorical situation will help you to analyze the circumstances in which you are asked to write. Such an analysis can go a long way toward writing success.

You can think of the elements of the rhetorical situation in terms of questions you might ask about it:

- *Occasion:* What is prompting you to write? In college writing, the occasion might be a term paper assignment from your history instructor. Professionally, you might be asked to write a portion of your company's annual report or a memo supporting the purchase of certain equipment.

- *Purpose:* What are you trying to accomplish by writing? A writing task can have more than one purpose. Your history term paper might have as part of its purpose the comparison of two time periods covered in the course, but a second purpose might be to demonstrate your understanding of the material. In an annual report you might wish to inform investors in a general way about your area of the company, and you might also want to portray your department's contributions in the best possible light.

- *Topic:* What are you writing about? Your topic might be assigned to you (for example, a comparison of ancient Athens and colonial America), or you might be allowed to choose your own (the historical treatment of women by society, perhaps). In either instance, the focus—the level of detail—is often yours to determine. Should you write only about democracy in ancient Athens and colonial America, or should you broaden the comparison? Should you examine the historical treatment of women in Western cultures, or should you also include Eastern societies?

- *Audience:* For whom are you writing? To achieve your purpose, you must understand your reader. For example, if you want to persuade someone to learn a musical instrument, it might help to know what objections he or she might have so that you can address them. It's also important to provide the right amount of information for the reader, yet we are often forced to speculate on what our audience knows and values. The form in which you write as well as the content of your writing will depend on your audience. You might be comfortable scribbling a note to your best friend in pencil on scratch paper, but you probably wouldn't write to the president of your company in that manner.

- *Writer:* What do you—the writer—bring to the task? For example, how much do you know about the subject? If you're writing about a familiar topic, you might not need to do much research. On the other hand, writing about something you know very little about might demand a great deal of study. Also consider how your reader will perceive you. Generally you want to present yourself as reasonable, knowledgeable, and intelligent.

It's critical to understand how the aspects of the rhetorical situation drive all of your writing activities. In part II of this book, you'll encounter scenarios that prompt you to write. The rhetorical situation for each of these writing projects will influence how you approach them. For example,

- Your purpose for writing, your audience, and the topic itself will affect how much research you do before you begin to write.
- Your audience and what they already know about your topic will influence, to some extent, the length of your composition by defining the amount of information you need to supply.
- Your prior knowledge of the topic will influence how much time you'll need for research.
- The occasion, purpose, and audience will influence the form in which you'll write (such as a formal letter, a memo, or a proposal).
- The purpose, topic, audience, and even you, the writer, will influence the organization of your composition.

Box 1.2: Composing a Practice Letter lets you put your understanding of the rhetorical situation into action.

YOUR WRITING PROCESS

The term *writing process* is probably one you already know. In fact, there is no single writing process. Each of you has developed your own way of composing—a way of recording ideas on paper in a coherent form. This process has evolved during your education and will continue to develop throughout your life. This process changes, at least to some extent, to reflect your rhetorical situation.

Each writing task—that is, every situation in which you are asked to write—influences how you go about composing what you want to say. Think for a moment of the various aspects of any writing task: you have a purpose for writing, and you write to a specific audience in a particular context at a certain time and place. All of these elements of the rhetorical situation influence your writing process—they determine the information you include, the words you choose to convey it, and the structure in which you present it.

BOX 1.2 APPLYING WHAT YOU READ
Composing a Practice Letter

Now that you understand a bit more about the rhetorical situation, let's put what you've learned to work. Let's suppose that your car needs three hundred dollars in repairs, but you're short of money this month. This is your *occasion* for writing. Because your Aunt Rebecca has helped you in the past, you decide to write to her to try to borrow some cash to fix your car. This makes your aunt your *audience* and borrowing money your *topic.* Your letter must focus on your *purpose,* which is to persuade Aunt Rebecca to send you the money. You won't write about school, or work, or your personal problems unless they have some relation to your purpose.

In the past, Aunt Rebecca has helped you by lending you money for school, but she probably doesn't want to become your personal banker. Think about the person with whom you're trying to communicate. What is the best way to convince Aunt Rebecca? Who is she, and what strategies might persuade her to send you a check? And how should you—the *writer*—present yourself? As desperate and pitiful? As hardworking but beset by unexpected problems? What words and information will you include in your letter to characterize yourself?

Spend a few minutes writing a draft of a letter asking Aunt Rebecca for money. You know that you need the money for car repairs, but you must decide how to explain what's wrong with your car (and how much information Aunt Rebecca needs to have), how much money to ask for, and how to approach your aunt. Should you be formal or informal? How should you begin your letter? Should you write your letter by hand or on a computer?

Share your draft with several of your classmates, and read theirs as well. Compare what each of you said about the following:

- Why you need the money and when you need it.
- How much money you need.
- How, and when, you propose to pay the money back.
- Your relationship with Aunt Rebecca. For example, does she like you? If so, your tone will be different than if she has never met you. Did you repay the money you borrowed from her earlier? If you did, you can write more confidently this time, can't you?

In your small group, determine which of the strategies seemed the most convincing. Consider how you might rewrite your draft to make a more compelling argument. After you've shared your letters, your instructor may ask each group to report to the class.

Personalizing the Writing Process

There is no single best way to write. Your writing process is a unique reflection of your experiences and personality. That said, there are ways in which you can approach writing that will help you make the most of your efforts. Although they may employ these approaches differently, successful writers generally make use of a multiple-step writing process that includes some or all of these activities:

Prewriting	Revision
Organizing ideas	Editing
Drafting	Proofreading
Peer review	Publishing

Incorporating these activities into your writing process is a matter of trial and error, of discovering which approach works best for you.

The Recursive Nature of Writing

The writing process may appear pretty straightforward: you do some prewriting (called invention work, because it gets you started) to develop some ideas, you organize those ideas, you write about them in a form that seems to suit your purpose and audience, you have others read and comment, and then you revise and edit your work. A final proofreading and you're finished, right? Well, writing is a bit more complex than that.

Think back to the idea of the rhetorical situation, and how any piece of writing involves several elements: you're writing for a particular purpose, you have in mind a specific audience under certain circumstances, and each aspect of your rhetorical situation influences the writing decisions you make. As you write, you move back and forth from your text to, say, your purpose for writing, to make sure that each part of the text suits your purpose . . . or you move from your text to thinking about your audience, continually checking the text to ensure that it suits the needs of that audience. This back-and-forth flow can be described as *recursive:* the writing activity re-occurs as you re-think, re-examine, and re-write.

Writing is a complex activity. It is rarely a neat, straightforward, linear process in which you know exactly what you want to say before you begin. Even if you're working on something as simple as the grocery list mentioned earlier, which is a fairly linear writing project, you may go back to the list to add and change things, perhaps to insert more information so that you'll get the brand of cereal or the specific kind of cookies you want. Someone may cross out an item on the list and scribble additions sideways on the paper. Whoever goes to the store might revise the list by arranging the items in some kind of order, perhaps in the sequence in which the products are displayed in the store or with frozen food items last on the list. In any case, you construct the list in a recursive manner that circles back on itself several times.

The same thing happens when you take on a more extensive writing task. You begin with some ideas and jot them down as you prewrite. These notes lead to other, perhaps more detailed and developed ideas. You might decide to eliminate or change some of your earlier ideas. The writing process is rarely sequential but instead recursive, with a back-and-forth flow.

You might add something here and change something there as the piece of writing develops and grows. As you continue to draft and revise, you shuttle back to prewriting to generate more ideas. As you return again and again to one or another aspect of the process, you see that the steps aren't really separate from one another. You see that the writing process doesn't follow a neat, straight path. You see that writing is nonlinear.

As you write, you are not only working on the writing task at hand, but you are also refining your writing process. Through practice, you discover what works for you and what doesn't. You find that strategies that work in one situation can be used in other, similar situations. Your writing process is never perfected. It evolves as you change and discover new approaches.

ELEMENTS OF THE WRITING PROCESS

Writing is a series of decisions that your writing process helps you make—you learn as you write. Understanding the steps that make up the writing process will help you decide how best to take advantage of them.

Prewriting

The Greek philosopher Aristotle defines rhetoric as "the ability, in each [particular] case, to see the available means of persuasion" (*Aristotle* 36). Writers often begin to gather all of their "available" ideas through what is called *invention work,* in which they extract ideas on their topic from their mind and put them down on paper. Invention activities help you formulate and understand your ideas through the process of writing them down. Such writing also helps you see how your ideas connect to one another.

Prewriting consists of activities that help you begin the writing process. You start simply by thinking about the writing task at hand, letting it come into focus. It can be helpful to do some of this "thinking" on paper, by jotting down what you already know about the subject, as well as any questions you might have or might expect your reader to have. Prewriting can be an excellent way to overcome the writer's block brought on by a blank piece of paper.

There are a number of prewriting activities. It is up to you to determine the one(s) that work best by trying several to see which ones produce the most useful information. And, as is the case in other aspects of the writing process, your rhetorical situation helps determine the prewriting activities you might find useful: for a letter to your grandmother, jotting down a few ideas might help you begin, whereas for a formal report to the president of your company, you'd make extensive notes and perhaps support them with documentation.

Try these activities to help you begin:

Television violence

- "Action" shows—guns, police, car chases
- Cartoon violence: does the coyote still get smashed all the time while the roadrunner gets away?
- Don't they have some rating system on TV now? I don't remember seeing any rating information.
- What about the local news? Someone's always getting into a car crash.
- Or someone gets shot—how many guns <u>do</u> we have in this country?
- Sports—think of hockey on TV! Even professional basketball, the way they fly around and hit the floor
- And what's football but a contact sport?
- Does slapstick comedy count, where someone falls down and it's supposed to be funny?
- Where in our society does all this violence come from?

FIGURE 1.1 *Brainstorming*

- *Brainstorming:* Quickly list as many ideas about your topic as you can think of, without worrying about writing complete sentences or determining the value of any of them. Brainstorming gives you a chance to amass a body of raw material. Some of it might be inferior. Some of it will probably be interesting but not quite right for your paper. The rest of it, developed, supported, and connected, will provide a basis for drafting your writing project. Figure 1.1 shows the types of ideas someone brainstorming about violence on television might jot down.

- *Freewriting:* Write about a topic for a set period of time, say five minutes, without stopping. Don't pause if you run out of things to say—even if that means writing "I can't think of anything else to write about." Try to pour out onto the page everything that you can call to mind about your topic: thoughts, questions, connections, concerns, anything. The point of freewriting is to get something on paper that can be shaped later. See Figure 1.2 for an example of freewriting on the topic of television violence.

- *Idea mapping* (sometimes called *clustering*): When making an idea map, you begin by writing your topic in the center of a blank

Violence on television

Okay, I have to get down what I know about violence on television, and keep writing all the time. I can't even lift up my pen, I have to keep writing. What was that show we watched last night, something about cops and there was a car chase. Big wreck. Sirens, flashing lights, an ambulance. What else, what else? And right after that, a shootout, right downtown, on the local news. Two or three people hurt, badly. Why is the news always bad? But then, even in the sports part of the news, there was that hockey player who was really hurt. Wow—think of the violence in sports and I wonder why they always focus on that: sure, you get the scores, but there's <u>always</u> some player who gets hurt, no matter what sport it is.

I can't think of anything else, I can't . . . I wonder if there are still a lot of cartoons with violence? I haven't watched cartoons in years, but boy, they <u>used</u> to have the action and the characters would be squashed or blown up . . .

FIGURE 1.2 *Freewriting*

sheet of paper. Circle it and draw a line outward to another circle in which you write a word or idea associated with the topic. Extend your web out to another word or idea associated with the second. For example, to prepare an idea map about violence on television, you might begin with the words "television violence." Your second bubble might contain the words "kids and violence." Your third, following this trail of associations, might contain "violent cartoons." The lines between idea bubbles should indicate relationships. Whenever you exhaust one line of thought, you go back to an idea for which you have additional thoughts. In the end, you should have a fairly extensive web (Figure 1.3).

Different types of prewriting have different advantages. Some people find an approach that works well for them and stick with it; others use different approaches to match the kind of writing they're doing or the topic. There's no reason you can't combine prewriting activities; for example, you can freewrite and then use an informal structure like clustering to organize your thoughts.

Analyzing the rhetorical situation—commenting in writing on your thoughts about the occasion, purpose, topic, audience, and writer—can

FIGURE 1.3 *Idea Mapping or Clustering*

be one effective use of prewriting. Remember that everything you do in your writing involves making conscious choices about all aspects of the writing process. This means considering your occasion for writing (why bother to write at all?); your purpose (what you're trying to accomplish); your topic (what you already know about the topic and what aspect or perspective you'd like to focus on); your audience (what they already know and what information you need to supply); and you, the writer (what you bring to the situation). By consciously thinking about all aspects of a writing situation, you'll learn several things:

- You'll gain a better sense of your own writing process.
- When you face similar writing situations in the future, you'll already be familiar with what's difficult for you and what's not (so

you'll know where you might need to spend more time) and what's effective and what's not (so you'll have an idea of how to improve).

- You'll know how to analyze the situation you face.
- You'll know how to determine which rhetorical appeals and strategies (discussed in chapter 2) might work best in particular writing situations.

Writing about your approach to writing can also help you clarify your writing process. Box 1.3: Examining Your Writing Process provides questions to guide your exploration.

Organizing Ideas

Once you've generated raw material through your invention activities, you should begin to think about the structure of your paper. A few short, simple sentences that briefly summarize your central points can help give you a sense of where you are going and how you expect to get there. Later, when you begin drafting, you may find the structure of your paper changing. A brief summary that reminds you where you intended to go can be helpful.

Thinking about organizing your ideas doesn't mean constructing an outline before you begin drafting your paper. Doing so would mean you already knew everything you wanted to say before you began putting your ideas on paper, whereas the very act of putting those thoughts on paper is a way to understand what you think. Instead, consider those few short, simple sentences that briefly summarize your central points as only a beginning. You can rearrange later, after you have a draft. Think of your organizing activity as a predraft, something to guide your thinking as you compose the first formal draft.

Writing as Learning You often learn from what you write and how you write. Writing words on paper may lead to a new perspective or may force you to address an argument that opposes your position. It's a good idea to begin writing without a final conclusion in mind, but rather to accept that you'll learn and change your views as you compose. Be open to changing your focus a bit, to wrestling in writing with the beliefs you began with.

There are many ways in which to organize a paper. How you do so depends on your rhetorical situation: your purpose, your audience, and the context in which you're writing. Think back to the letters, class papers, or work documents you've written: in some, you probably got right to the point and wrote as little as possible. In others, you may have spent some time introducing the problem or issue before proposing your solution. In still others, you might have touched on some personal issues before getting to the heart of your document. The form you used and how you organized your words depended on the rhetorical situation in which you found yourself.

BOX 1.3 APPLYING WHAT YOU READ
Examining Your Writing Process

Take a few minutes to think about how you've approached writing tasks in the past, and write a few paragraphs describing how you normally proceed. These questions might help you to examine your writing process:

- When you have something to write, how do you begin? Do you brainstorm or make lists or outlines before you begin writing full sentences and paragraphs?
- At what time of day do you like to write? Why?
- Is there a particular place in which you like to do your writing? Do you have physical requirements for comfort, noise level, or setting?
- Do you have any rituals about writing—say, a favorite pen or coffee in a particular mug?
- Do you write on a computer, in pencil, or with a pen?
- How many drafts do you usually write? Do you prefer to write just one draft, to be done with it?
- How extensive are your revisions? Do you simply proofread for misspelled words, or are you willing to make substantial changes, such as moving paragraphs?
- What do you do when your papers are returned with a grade and perhaps also with written comments?
- Do you ever ask other people to read and comment on your writing before you finish with it? What kinds of comments are most helpful?
- How do you know when you're finished writing?
- Is your writing process affected by the amount of time you have to complete an assignment?
- What is the hardest part of your writing process? Why? The easiest? Why?
- What have you learned about writing from your earlier writing experiences?

Take the time to delve into the physical and mental aspects of your writing process. We often don't recognize our trouble spots until we see them on paper. If you like to write in a room full of people, with the radio and television on and the phone ringing, but readers often comment that your writing is fragmented, that observation might tell you something.

Once you've written a description of your writing process, share it with a few of your classmates in a small group. Discuss what your processes have in common and why you think these similarities exist. Were you taught to write the way you do, or did you develop your process on your own? What part of your writing process would you like to change? What part of it seems to work best? Your instructor might ask groups to share their comments with the rest of the class.

Aristotle's Organizational Scheme   One way to organize your paper so that you can incorporate the research you've collected is to use a model developed by the Greek philosopher Aristotle. This organizational scheme includes answering possible objections to your ideas (discussed in detail under "Anticipating and Answering Objections" later). Aristotle observed that the most effective examples of discourse have five main parts:

1. An introduction (*introductio*), which introduces the topic by set-ting the stage and includes the main point.
2. A narration (*narratio*), which describes what is at stake in the dis-cussion—what the main issues are and why the topic is impor-tant. (This is often combined with the introduction.)
3. The confirmation (*confirmatio*) or main body of the statement, which includes the writer's explanation of why the argument is valid, as well as evidence to support the claim(s) made in the text.
4. A refutation (*refutatio*), which answers possible objections to the claim(s).
5. A conclusion (*peroratio*), which pulls everything together and of-ten contains a call for action on the part of the reader (or listener).

Aristotle's model is only one of many ways in which to organize your ideas. It allows you to combine your ideas and research into broad cate-gories; then you can make connections, move ideas around, and provide support.

Other Organizational Approaches   You can also organize a research paper by beginning with a list of problems and issues, along with the strengths and weaknesses of each. Or you might begin by addressing the possible objections to your own position (in essence, reversing Aristotle's confirmation and refutation sections). By identifying and eliminating, at the outset, any objections to your position, you indicate to your audience that you have a strong position. Beginning with the ideas that are simplest to understand and then moving to the more complex ideas is another way to organize information.

Anticipating and Answering Objections   Because people hold differing points of view on most issues, especially civic issues, you should plan to acknowledge and attempt to come to terms with other views as you or-ganize your ideas. Answering objections is something you do all the time. Have you ever asked, say, to borrow the family car, and when your mom and dad said no, you somehow talked them into letting you take it after all? You probably convinced them by answering their objections. When they told you why they objected ("You never put gas in it" or "You stayed out too late the other night" or "All your friends leave their trash in the backseat"), you had an answer for them.

Think about the last time you went to a movie with friends: did every-one immediately agree to see the same film? Probably not. More likely, someone suggested a film, and someone else said she heard it was really bad. Then another friend suggested a different film, and someone else chimed in with what he'd heard or read about it, and so on. In this way, you and your friends came to a collective decision that everyone could live with. You agreed as a group to see a particular film.

The same holds true when a group tries to decide where to go for dinner or lunch, or where to go on a family vacation. You're more successful in getting your view across when you attempt to work with the others involved. This is what we mean when we say you must answer objections: you must work with others to understand their positions and then come to terms with them.

Answering an objection doesn't mean simply disagreeing with it or stating simply that it is wrong. Rather, it involves providing evidence to support your contention that the objection is incorrect. If your parents object to loaning you the car because "You never put gas in it," simply answering "Yes, I do" is not an effective response. It makes more sense to say, "Well, I did put gas in the car just last week—here's the receipt. And remember when we all went to Trader Joe's on Sunday? I dropped you off so I could go and get gas. And today," you might add as you open your wallet, "I've set aside fifteen dollars to buy gas." Our point is that you can't answer an objection simply by denying it; rather, you need to supply facts and examples to support your point of view.

Here are some other ways of responding to objections to your ideas:

- Agree with the objection, but then shift to a different point of view: "I agree with you on that, but if we look at it from this perspective, we see that. . . ."
- Agree in part with the objection: "Yes, although that might be true under those conditions, it's more important that we look at. . . ."
- Refute the objection with facts or figures: "Although it might appear that this proposal would be expensive, it would actually save us money. Here's how it. . . ."
- Answer the objection head-on: "That objection is simply wrong." Then support your assertion with facts.
- Refute the objection as flawed in some way: "The responses might appear to be positive, but the results of the survey you mentioned were misleading (or outdated or inaccurate) because. . . ."
- Characterize the objection as minor: "In the big scheme of things, what you're suggesting really isn't much of a problem because. . . ."

In many writing situations, your ideas will be on public display for others to read and to criticize. You must be prepared to enter into a thoughtful, reasoned discussion about the issues and problems inherent in your topic. You must respect the views of others while supporting your own.

Drafting

Once your prewriting work has helped you put some of your ideas on paper and you've thought about the organizational scheme that might best serve your purpose, you're ready to make your first attempt to express your ideas in coherent form. This is called a first version or a first draft. Don't worry about spelling or editing at this point. Concentrate instead on the larger structural issues—on organization. This is your opportunity to expand your ideas, to flesh them out. In essence you're writing to see how much you have to say about the ideas you've generated in prewriting. Remember that drafting is an exploratory process. In your first draft you explore what you want to say, how much you know about your topic, what research you might need to do to support your position, and whether your topic is worth pursuing.

The more you develop your early draft, the better. It's easier to reorganize and expand ideas you've already recorded in writing than it is to generate a new set of ideas. Consider what you want your composition to do: most often, you want to make a point. The drafting process will help you determine what you want to say, and also what evidence will effectively support that thesis.

As you compose, stop occasionally and reread your work, pretending that you're coming to it for the first time. Is the explanation that you just inserted as clear as it should be? Does the example you just added do a good job of illustrating the point you're making? Because drafting is an exploratory process, you must evaluate—as you write—how effectively your evidence is working. Allow yourself to recognize that what you thought was a good example doesn't really do the job; you need to find something better. Be open to revising as you draft—because you're learning what you think as you write.

Many writers make the mistake of stopping too soon when drafting. They think that a few paragraphs provide enough of a start. In your initial draft, try to write as much as possible. You can always remove sections and add detail and support later, but a full-length draft, even one that requires significant revision, is the best head start you can give yourself in the writing process.

This initial drafting process is also a good time to consider the rhetorical purpose of each paragraph. Ask yourself: Why am I including this information? Where do I need additional examples to show what I mean? Where do I need more evidence (facts, testimony)? Where can I use a visual aid? How does this section support my main idea?

Peer Review

After you've completed your first or second draft, you may ask someone to read what you've written. An outside reader often provides the critical perspective you need to identify the things you've overlooked. As a way of testing a writing's effectiveness, good peer reviewers read from the perspective of the target audience. They offer you specific advice on ways for improving your draft, rather than vague generalities. For example, an unhelpful peer reviewer might tell you, "Your paper is good." A helpful reviewer would say, "Your opening paragraph is especially effective. I was interested from the start and wanted to read on because I was anxious to see how you would support your assertions. I think that you need to do that more. The third paragraph makes me want to say, 'prove it.' Do you have any research to back up what you say?"

See the difference? Of course you enjoy hearing that your paper is "good," but you need to know why the reviewer thinks it's good. A good reader—an effective peer reviewer—pays attention to the reactions the material creates and then explores—and explains to the writer—how it does this. If you are reading for a friend or classmate and you find yourself particularly interested in what is being said, examine what in the paper has created that interest. Is it the examples? Is it the tone the writer sets, or the rhythm of the sentences? The ability to tell the writer specifically what works, what doesn't, and why makes you a valuable resource for the writer.

Effective techniques for conducting peer review include these approaches:

- Instructors ask students to pair up with a classmate and exchange drafts. The partners read through their classmate's text and mark in the margins any suggestions they have, indicate where they found the writing confusing, and note where more support is needed. Partners then read each other's comments, and the reviewer explains his or her comments to the writer. This combination of written and oral commentary lets the writer question the reviewer about comments that might be misunderstood. It also allows the reader to question the writer ("What did you mean here . . . ?") as the text is being developed.

- Students pair up, and each reads his or her paper to the partner, who listens and takes notes. When you read your paper aloud, you'll find that you skip over many of the mechanical problems that can get in the way of reading silently. This is especially true in an early draft, when you're concentrating more on the content than on the mechanical aspects of the paper. Usually, a paper must be read through two times for the listener to really understand it; often the listener follows along with a copy of the text. The listener then indicates where the text needs more information, where it isn't clear, and so on.

- Students, in pairs, read each other's papers: student A reads student B's paper aloud, while student B listens. Then student B reads A's paper aloud. Hearing someone else read your paper often helps you spot areas that are confusing or undeveloped.

- Your instructor may tell you exactly what to focus on as you read and comment on your classmates' papers. It can also be useful for student writers to indicate at the top of their draft what they'd like their classmates to focus on and respond to: for example, "Please tell me if my main point is clear and how to improve my organization."

When you and your classmates discuss issues and when you read each others' writing, you are testing your ideas. Back-and-forth discussions of this sort are part of writing's social process, which allows each of you to have an impact on what the other thinks. In other words, your classmates serve as a sounding board for your ideas. They can offer criticism about parts of your writing that might be confusing, they can ask you for more information if you did not explain things as well as you might have, they can request clarification about your ideas and concepts, and they can indicate where you need more outside research to strengthen your position. In essence, you serve as a living audience for one another, always with the goal of improving your writing.

As you consider the comments of peer reviewers, remember that the final responsibility for your writing task belongs to you. Your readers may offer you suggestions, but how you implement them is your choice. Pay close attention to your reviewers' observations, especially if their comments are well supported.

Revision

Once you have completed a first draft, you need to assess its merits. Some writers confuse revision with simple proofreading—they think revision involves only correcting spelling and mechanical errors. The true meaning of revision, however, has to do with re-envisioning or re-seeing your own writing.

Let's consider what it means when "re-" precedes a term:

Redo means to do something again.

Reevaluate means to reconsider or rethink something.

Renew suggests making something new, perhaps even better.

Redesign means to revise in appearance or content.

Reorganize means to organize again or anew.

Adding "re-" to any term indicates a major adjustment. We encourage you to view revision as a re-envisioning of your work—and an opportunity to make extensive adjustments if they're needed.

You can reexamine your text after you've completed a draft or two, when you have a clearer idea of what you want to say. Drafting can help you understand and clarify your position. We often find after a draft or two that our main idea appears at the conclusion of our text. When we revise the draft, we begin the new version with our concluding paragraph and ideas.

To revise effectively you have to see your writing from a fresh perspective. We're often too close to our writing to see it objectively and to judge what should be kept, what should be taken out, and what should be moved or developed further. To become a good reviser, you must become a good reader. To read your own writing effectively, assume that you know little about the subject and that you're reading the text for the first time. Read through your draft as someone who is new to it would. As you read, ask yourself these questions:

- Which terms don't I completely understand? Mark the terms so that you can provide clear explanations for them when you revise your text.

- Which statements or sections are confusing or unclear? Work to clarify these sections when you revise your composition.

- Does the organizational scheme make sense? Do the ideas follow a logical pattern? Does it make sense to present my case chronologically? If so, make sure that your ideas are arranged in their order of occurrence (first this happens, and then this, and so on). Or can I make a stronger case by beginning with the least important idea and moving toward the most important point? If so, make sure your ideas appear in that sequence. As you revise, arrange your thoughts and ideas so that they build on one another.

- What parts of the paper require additional evidence to support the points I'm making? Where is the text unconvincing? Plan to add facts or testimony or statistical evidence to support your position when you revise.

- What questions do I have after reading the text? Answer these questions as you revise.

- Which parts of my text are especially strong? Use these sections as models for revising other, weaker parts of your text.

Before composing additional drafts, it helps to set your writing aside for a time. Let your ideas evolve for a day or two if possible. This often strengthens your critical perspective.

When you return to your draft, try to see it as a member of your target audience might. What do you find compelling? What is confusing? What requires still more explanation? Is your writing accomplishing everything it might? As you revise and revise again, remember that the effects of revision are cumulative. Each draft should improve your composition, moving you closer to achieving the purpose of your writing task. As you approach a finished product, you can begin to focus more on spelling, grammar, and mechanics.

Editing

Think of editing as your final chance to examine each of your sentences and their structure. When you revise, you consider your text as a whole. Editing asks you to examine it as smaller units—sentences. When you proofread your text (the subject of the next section), you'll examine it in even smaller units—words.

You edit your work to achieve clarity and to eliminate errors of grammar, usage, and style. When you edit, ensure that each of the points you make supports your thesis, that your sentences are well structured, and that your ideas are clear and explicit. This is your opportunity to fine-tune your work. Editing is like tightening the nuts and bolts of the structure you're constructing through your writing.

To edit your text, read through it and think of *clarity*. Don't worry about the strength of your arguments or whether you have provided sufficient evidence. Instead, watch for places where the writing doesn't make sense, where an awkward phrase or a misused word distracts you from what you're reading. Be on the lookout for sentences that are unclear, that wander, or that are garbled and for points that do not support your main idea. Editing represents an opportunity to refine and polish what you've written. Complete this crucial step in your writing process with care.

Proofreading

Finally, after you've written, reviewed, revised, and edited your work so that you're satisfied with it, read through it carefully to ensure that your grammar, punctuation, and spelling are correct. There's not much point in doing any of this until the very end of your writing process. If you are tempted to omit proofreading, however, remember that spelling and grammar errors can damage the way your writing is received. What will your readers think if they find the word "t3he" in your writing? Although it's tempting to rely on spell-checking software, remember that these programs check only to see if the word you've used is a word. They don't ensure that the word you've used is the one you want. For example, "The man approached me in a threatening manor" is a very different sentence than "The man approached me in a threatening manner." The first sentence means that the approach was made in a big, scary house. The second means that the approach was done in an intimidating way. Such spelling errors can change the meaning of your writing.

Proofreading your own writing can be difficult. Because you know what you want to say, you tend to skim rather than pay close attention. There are a number of strategies that address this tendency. Perhaps the simplest is to read the last sentence of your draft, then the second to last, and so on, until you reach the first sentence. This helps you see what is really there. This strategy is especially effective for finding run-on sentences and sentence fragments.

Publishing

When you've corrected the errors you found during proofreading, it's time to produce your document. Keep in mind that your presentation can have an important effect on your reader. An essay in support of a scholarship application won't be as effective if you choose a typeface so small and faint that your reader has to hold the page up to the light to read it. The format of your writing should reflect the hard work you've put into composing it.

In academic situations, your instructor often tells you what format is required. Follow the instructions carefully. Use a standard business font, such as Times Roman, throughout your paper. Limit the number of fonts you use, unless you want your paper to look like a ransom note. Again, think about your audience. If your instructor is reading twenty or thirty essays, how might you make your paper inviting to the eye?

Often, the nature of the writing demands a specific format. Business letters require particular elements in particular places. Memos generally follow a standard format. Footnotes, endnotes, and parenthetical citations require very specific formats. Most academic writing—the kind you do in college—requires research, which means indicating where all of your information came from. (There's more on this in chapters 2 and 3 and appendix C.)

MOVING TO CHAPTER 2

In this chapter we examined how the rhetorical situation affects each aspect of your writing process. Chapter 2 helps you learn how writing for a public audience defines your writing goals and the types of writing you'll do. We focus on the strategies you can use to convince an audience, and the reading and research that you draw on to support your claims. In college writing, as well as in the writing you'll do in your career, your audience will rarely be convinced unless you provide sufficient research—facts, data, testimony, and other evidence—to show that your position or proposal is the best approach.

Work Cited

Aristotle on Rhetoric. Trans. George A. Kennedy. New York: Oxford UP, 1991.

CHAPTER 2

College Writing and Critical Reading

In chapter 1, you learned about the rhetorical situation: how it influences each aspect of your construction of any written piece—and especially how it affects your writing process. You saw that the steps of that process are recursive and are shaped by the rhetorical situation in which you compose. We also hope that you're beginning to understand that you can learn from the writing you do, through the process of doing it.

In this chapter you'll think about the discourse communities you belong to and how your writing becomes public in some of those communities. You'll learn that your readers require thoughtful, reasoned essays and how different types of writing require differing approaches and strategies. You'll also start to learn how your writing task influences your reading strategies, as well as how to incorporate the research you find into your writing. This chapter should help you:

- Understand what public discourse is and the ways in which it differs from more private methods of communication.
- Understand the types of writing assignments you'll work with in part II of the text.
- Learn how to construct effective, persuasive texts through the use of rhetorical appeals and strategies.
- Examine your reading process to see how your rhetorical situation and the kind of writing you plan to do affect it.
- Learn how to use a journal for personal as well as research purposes.

PUBLIC DISCOURSE AND DISCOURSE COMMUNITIES

During the course of our daily activities, we all move between a number of groups or communities. We interact with family members and friends, with classmates, and with coworkers. The language we use differs for each group—just as your letter to Aunt Rebecca would be different if it were addressed to your best friend . . . or to a relative you'd never met. Your language, your choice of subject, and the form of your writing change when you address different people or different communities. We call these groups discourse communities. They can be identified at least partly by the language(s) they use. In this case, we don't mean language in the sense of, say, Spanish or English. Rather, we mean the particular or specialized language spoken by members of a specific group or community. In a sense, the various discourse communities you belong to can be defined somewhat by the language members use to communicate with other members. Do you greet your friends one way ("Hi ya, dude!"), your classmates another ("Did you get your homework done?"), and your grandmother another way ("It's good to see you, Grandma!")? You likely use different words, tones, and emphases for different audiences. These groups represent different discourse communities.

The academic communities you become a part of during your college work are also discourse communities. For example, sociologists use different words than do, say, psychologists. During your college career, you will join one or more discourse communities, at least in part by learning to speak their languages.

Whenever any of us engages in public discourse, we need to keep in mind the various groups or communities that will read or listen to our texts. We must ensure that the language we use and the types of arguments we make are understood by these groups and will be convincing to them. Our goal is to get the group we're communicating with to agree with what we have to say. We can help those other interested parties to identify with our position.

Identifying with another means recognizing that we share some common ground, that we can understand one another. Identifying with someone means viewing an issue or a problem from that person's perspective. You can, for example, identify with the concerns and problems of another student because you're also a student. We can identify with other drivers, say, because we also have to get around on the interstates and freeways.

When applied to your writing, this concept means that the better you're able to identify the common ground you share with members of your audience, the easier it will be to persuade them of the validity of your ideas for solving a problem. This is the goal of public discourse. Taking part in public discourse does not mean arguing or trying to sway others to accept your position as the only possible solution. Rather, it means working with others, from a common perspective and through language all can understand, to come to some amicable and workable solution. This is how we solve problems.

At the same time, it is not necessary in argumentative writing that your reader agree completely with you. Rather, it's important that he or she can recognize and understand your position. At times, your reader might say, "Yes, I agree completely with you and will do exactly as you suggest." More often, however, your reader will respond, "I now have a better understanding of your position. I don't agree completely with everything you've written, but you've provided enough supporting evidence for me to understand that you've made a rational argument. I can see your point of view."

We have seen the ways in which the discourse community for which you're writing affects your writing process. Now, we examine the role your purpose in writing plays.

THE AIMS AND TYPES OF WRITING

All writing responds to a particular rhetorical situation: that situation determines what you want your writing to accomplish in the specific situation for your specific audience. Your aim or purpose may be to inform, to analyze, or to persuade. You may construct other types of writing in your college classes and later, in your career. We look at a selection of writing types in this section.

Informative Essays

The writer of an informative essay provides information or otherwise expands the reader's knowledge. An informative essay doesn't include personal opinion; instead, it presents information without trying to sway the readers. When you write an informative essay, provide your readers with enough information to allow them to make a decision about or come to an understanding of an issue.

Begin the informative essay by considering your audience: What information do they need to make an informed decision about this issue? What might they already know? In what form should the information be presented? Might visual aids help your audience better understand the information? What facts or statistics might increase your readers' comprehension?

Process or Instructional Essays

A process or instructional essay explains how to do something: you can liken it to a set of instructions. This essay might explain how to change the oil in your car, it could contain step-by-step instructions for writing a software program, or it might provide a detailed plan for exploring San Francisco's Golden Gate Park.

When you write a set of instructions, consider your audience and what they might already know about the subject. Focusing on these characteristics encourages you to provide the kind of information your audience needs to understand the steps of the process you're explaining.

A set of instructions must be complete; it must also be clear. This means anticipating questions your readers might have. It may also mean providing visual aids to help your readers understand. If you are providing a step-by-step guide for exploring Golden Gate Park, for example, a map of the park would be a useful aid. Explain the process in a logical, straightforward manner, giving instructions in order, from beginning to end.

As we noted in chapter 1, Aristotle defines rhetoric as "the ability, in each [particular] case, to see the available means of persuasion" (*Aristotle* 36). Although a process or instructional essay may not seem "persuasive," in fact you must persuade your reader that the approach you outline is correct, that he or she will be able to complete the task successfully by following your plan.

Take care to provide everything your reader might need to know to complete the task you outline in a process or instructional essay. Review your essay carefully to determine whether anything is missing that might help your reader. Would illustrations enhance the discussion? Would additional data or statistics be useful?

Proposal Essays

A proposal offers a specific plan for resolving a deficiency or a problem or outlines how some task might be accomplished.

When you suggest to a friend that the two of you see a certain movie, you're making a proposal: you provide information about the movie you're proposing and give reasons for seeing it rather than some other film.

Proposals are often made in response to a problem:

- The company you work for needs more computers; someone proposes the purchase of a certain type and brand.

- There are numerous accidents on a stretch of highway; you propose measures to make the road safer.

- Several faculty members at your college are proposing that it should offer courses over the Internet. In fact, they're suggesting that students should be able to earn a bachelor's degree without setting foot on campus. Other faculty members are against the proposal, citing concerns about the costs, the logistics of offering online degrees, and whether it's possible to ensure that an online degree is the equivalent of an on-campus degree. You propose a plan for developing an online degree program.

An effective proposal essay provides enough detail so that readers can understand why the proposal is being made. Then it demonstrates how best to resolve the issue.

Evaluation Essays

In an evaluation essay the writer explains the benefits and weaknesses of an idea, a program, a product, or some other topic. The writer demonstrates what is good or effective or logical about the idea or item— and what perhaps isn't so good or workable. An evaluation essay also addresses other issues, such as whether the cost is acceptable.

You exercise your skill for evaluation as you make everyday decisions. Why do you choose to eat at one restaurant rather than another: cost? quality or quantity of food? ambience? Why do you select one book over another: author? length? subject?

Any evaluation necessarily involves criteria, the basis on which the evaluation is made. Evaluations, then, usually begin with an explanation of the criteria on which they are based. Consider the following:

Look for these features when selecting a backpack for hiking . . .

The best DVD players should have these capabilities . . .

To solve college-level mathematics problems, you'll need a calculator that can . . .

Selection of the criteria on which an evaluation is based is, of course, critical. You must explain in your essay how each criterion relates to the item being evaluated. You must also state the basis for judging whether the item meets each criterion. You already do this whenever you buy anything as you weigh the item's cost against its perceived value. You ask questions about quality, warranty, durability, and functionality. You measure the item against what you expect it to be able to do.

If you were evaluating a backpack, for instance, one of your criteria might be the overall weight it can carry effectively. You might evaluate and compare the following characteristics for each of the backpacks you're considering: the reputation of the manufacturer, the strength and durability of the material from which the backpack is made, the size of the pockets, and the construction of the frame.

To compose an evaluation for the best calculator to use in a college mathematics class, your criteria might include the processing speed of the calculator, the screen size and capabilities, and the comprehensiveness of the user's manual.

Evaluations are also often written in response to proposals. In these cases, they address why the proposal should be accepted or implemented. Here are some examples:

- There are various ways to make our highways safer (for example, changes in speed limits, more police patrols, barriers between roadways). An evaluation of a proposal to improve highway safety would investigate how successful the proposed solution might be.

- There are various ways to stop plagiarism in college writing classes (for example, the instructor can examine all student drafts or ask for copies of all sources). An evaluation essay on this subject would explain how effective each of the proposals might be.
- There are countless computer systems and software. An evaluation of a proposed purchase would explain how well the configuration would meet the company's needs.

Analytic Essays

In an analytic essay, the writer carefully examines an issue. In many ways such writing is persuasive. An analytic essay often focuses on broad issues, and the writer works to understand and explain the issues.

To analyze commonly means to take something apart to better understand it. (You could, for example, take apart a bicycle's gears to help you understand how its gear and chain system function.) In writing, analysis means examining and explaining all aspects of an issue. Your purpose in writing an analytic essay is to present the issue so that your readers will understand it. For example, an analytic essay might examine any of these issues:

- In what ways does violence on television or in the movies affect how people behave?
- Why do students bring weapons to school?
- In what ways are politicians and the political process in this country becoming more corrupt?
- Why are symbols so important to human beings?

Analytic essays require thorough documentation: writers of analytic essays support their arguments by incorporating into their essays material they borrow (properly identified) from other writers, testimony from experts in the field, or facts or statistical data that strengthen the position they take. An analytic essay always includes a works-cited list, which provides full citations for all the sources used in the essay. The works-cited list also gives readers a good starting point for further research on the topic, helping them find every source that the writer of the analytic essay consulted.

Persuasive Essays

A persuasive essay is successful when it convinces its audience that the writer's viewpoint—among many viewpoints—is the correct one. Such an essay seeks to persuade the audience to do what the writer asks of it. Your audience might have a variety of viewpoints; as a persuasive-essay writer, your job is to convince them of the validity of yours.

When you construct a persuasive essay, you must ask yourself questions like these: What information does my audience need to be convinced that my position is sound? What facts, data, evidence, or testimony can I provide to convince them to act in the way I want them to? How can I address ideas that are counter to my own, to successfully convince my audience that my position is strong?

You convince an audience by providing solid supporting evidence in a way that appeals to that audience—regardless of the type of essay you're writing. That is, your audience must understand your argument and see how your evidence supports your position. You can best accomplish those goals through what the Greek thinker Aristotle called rhetorical appeals.

THE POWER OF RHETORICAL APPEALS

Often you write to convince someone to accept your views concerning an issue. You might even wish to move your audience to take action. To argue persuasively, you must appeal to something that your audience values.

Much of the writing you'll do in college—and most of what you'll write as you work through the scenarios in part II of this text—is persuasive: you're trying to convince your reader of something. More than 2,300 years ago Aristotle identified three kinds of appeals that make up an effective argument: logos, pathos, and ethos. Here are some simple explanations of these rhetorical appeals:

Logos is the traditional name for appeals to reason or logic. A logical argument appeals to the mind. It proposes a logical position and supports that position with facts and data as evidence. Logos is also concerned with the formal logic of a statement: Does it make sense? Does one part follow another in a logical manner? Does the evidence supplied support and strengthen the point being made?

Pathos is the traditional name for an appeal to emotions or values. Think of pathos as ways for moving an audience to do what you'd like them to do: change their position, agree with you, or take action. Ask yourself: How might I involve my audience with this issue? What kinds of emotions or values might move them on a "gut level"? Greed, fear, anger, guilt, and sympathy can all be powerful persuasive devices.

Ethos describes an appeal based on the authority and credibility of the source—the writer's ethical qualifications. It involves answering questions like these: Why should someone believe me? Have I done enough research to present my issue with authority? Do I possess special credentials or experience that qualifies me as an expert? Am I a reasonable and well-informed commentator?

Using Appeals

You might not know it, but you already use these rhetorical appeals. Here's an example. Let's say that you want to invite a classmate to lunch. If you were to use a logos appeal, you might say, "Let's have lunch together. It will give us a chance to talk about the group project." It makes sense—is logical—to use the opportunity of having lunch together to get some coursework done. Logos, effectively applied, helps your audience realize that your argument makes good sense.

If you were to use a pathos appeal, you might say, "Please have lunch with me—I hate to eat alone." Here, you're hoping that your classmate will feel some sympathy for you and will be moved to take action, namely, to join you for lunch. Pathos can be very effective in motivating behavior. Although people generally like to think they are motivated by cold logic and careful reasoning, emotions and values often override good sense. We've all done things we knew weren't sensible because we "felt" they were right. Indiscriminate use of pathos can leave your audience feeling manipulated, though, which can cause resentment that hurts your argument.

An ethos appeal might draw on your own authority gained through experience. You might say, "Let's eat at Mama's Pizza. I ate there last week, and it was terrific." In this case you're hoping that your classmate has faith in your endorsement. Your ethos appeal might be strengthened if your classmate had enjoyed a meal at another restaurant you had suggested. Conversely, if you recommended a restaurant that your classmate dislikes, that might hurt your ethos appeal. Ethos may be the most critical of the appeals: if you lack credibility, no amount of logos or pathos will make people believe you.

Of course, rhetorical appeals are subtler than these examples. When Aristotle identified logos, pathos, and ethos appeals, he also wrote that rhetoric is finding possible ways to persuade an audience. How might you use the art of rhetoric—Aristotle's "means of persuasion"—to determine the best way to convince someone that your position on an issue is correct? Analyzing the rhetorical situation can help you to see the means of persuasion that are available to you.

Here's an example: Let's say you want to borrow some more money from your Aunt Rebecca, this time for extra books and supplies that you'd like to have. Your instructors don't require these items, but you think having them would help you in your classes. How might you frame a request for money to buy things you really don't need?

The occasion is clear—you have a desire to purchase educational materials but lack the funds. Your purpose is pretty obvious—you want the cash. This dictates that your topic will be money for your education.

You've known Aunt Rebecca all your life, and you know that, although she supports your education, she might be skeptical about anything she thinks is "extra." To get what you want, you'll have to ask for it in just the right way.

Selecting an Appeal Type

Consider the rhetorical appeals available to you: which type might convince Aunt Rebecca? You might make sure she knows that:

- You've always made regular payments on the other loans you've received from her. This is both a pathos appeal (you know she values repayment) and an ethos appeal (your payment record indicates that you're trustworthy). You're using the rhetorical strategy of *illustration* (see the next section for a discussion of these strategies) as you point out your payment record to Aunt Rebecca.

- You now have a part-time job, so you'll be able to repay the loan easily. This is a logos appeal (you demonstrate that you have a source of repayment) that might also be an ethos appeal (you're responsible enough to hold down a job while you're a student). Here, you might also draw on the rhetorical strategy of *cause and effect:* having a job allows you to earn the money to repay the loan. At the same time, Aunt Rebecca might worry that your schoolwork will suffer because you have a job. You might attempt to assure her that working doesn't interfere with your studies, perhaps by *explaining* (another rhetorical strategy) how you structure your time.

- You'll receive higher grades in your classes if you have additional books and supplies. This is something of a pathos appeal because you know that Aunt Rebecca wants you to do well in school. You hope that telling your story (using the rhetorical strategy of *narration*) will help Aunt Rebecca understand your situation and regard you with sympathy.

If you know that Aunt Rebecca has been swayed in the past mostly by cold reason and facts, you might concentrate on making more logos than other kinds of appeals. If you know that she never lends money to nieces and nephews who fail to make regular payments, you'd focus on your ethos—your character—and on how much sense it makes to loan you money because you've always repaid her.

RHETORICAL STRATEGIES

You use rhetorical strategies to help make rhetorical appeals. Understanding the rhetorical situation and the rhetorical strategies available to you can make a big improvement in your writing. As you work with these tools, you'll see that the elements of the rhetorical situation (occasion, purpose, topic, audience, and writer) combine with types of rhetorical appeals and rhetorical strategies in almost limitless combinations. This is what makes each person's writing unique. The way in which you convey information is as individual as the relationship between you and your audience.

Once you know what you want to accomplish with your writing—what you want your composition to do (to explain, to inform, to persuade, and so on)—you next consider the ways in which you might achieve your goal.

We've discussed the ways in which the decisions you make and the rhetorical situation can guide your use of tone, information, and even word choice. In particular, an accurate analysis of the rhetorical situation and your writing task can help you select the most effective rhetorical strategies for achieving your purpose.

As with the various aspects of the rhetorical situation, rhetorical strategies work together and in combination with one another—you don't select and use only one of them in a particular composition. Just as you wouldn't base every writing decision on only one aspect of the rhetorical situation, you wouldn't rely exclusively on one strategy. A blending of strategies or of elements from different strategies is most effective.

You see these rhetorical strategies in action all the time. For example, if you were to watch national news coverage of a hurricane that had come ashore in a populated area, you might see a number of these strategies at work:

Explanation: The television reporter provides a broad overview of what has happened: basic information concerning the size of the storm, where and when it hit, and how much damage it caused. To give you a sense of the scope of the disaster, television news might show video taken from a helicopter flying over the damaged areas.

In your writing, it's unwise to rely solely on explanation—unless explaining is your only purpose. When you explain something that has happened, you are often also trying to achieve other purposes. For example, you might explain to your dad in some detail that small accident you had with the family car . . . but you also want your dad to understand that you're not a reckless driver. You might explain to a significant other why you forgot his or her birthday . . . but you also want that person to forgive and forget. You'd draw on other rhetorical strategies to help you achieve your other purposes.

Illustration: A televised report on a hurricane might provide a smaller scale illustration or example of the destruction by presenting the impact the storm had on one family. The camera might show the members of that family picking through their scattered belongings. An illustration like this gives a more focused view than does the big picture, which can be overwhelming.

You provide illustrations or examples all the time, to demonstrate and explain what happened. Your teachers may remind you to "show, not just tell." When you tell, someone might not understand, but if you can show—especially if you can provide several examples—your audience should more easily understand.

As you explained your fender bender to your dad, perhaps you tried to illustrate exactly what had happened by diagramming the accident scene. When you explained why you forgot that birthday, you might have provided examples of all the other times you didn't forget ("Remember two years ago when you wanted that new coat, and I surprised you by bringing it to you at work?").

Cause and effect: On the television news, you might see a story explaining why the storm was so large or why it caused an unusual amount of damage. This cause-and-effect explanation helps you understand the origins of the situation.

Are you starting to see how these strategies work with one another and how you use them in various rhetorical situations? Can you hear yourself saying, "Dad, what really caused the accident was how fast that other driver pulled out from the curb. . . ."? Or, "I sure hope you understand why I forgot your birthday. It wouldn't have happened if only I'd written it in my daily planner. Next year I'll be sure to do that. . . ."?

Comparison and contrast: Hurricane coverage might include a comparison to a similar storm thirty years ago or a contrast with the relatively quiet hurricane season last year. You might, for example, use a contrast strategy with your father: "Boy, this small dent won't cost nearly as much to repair as that accident you had in January."

Process analysis: Television coverage might include a computer-generated model showing how a hurricane is generated over warm ocean waters.

Classification: You might learn from the news reporter that hurricanes are classified according to their size, wind speed, and potential damage, as a way of trying to predict how they will behave.

Narration: You might hear a story about how a brave police officer put herself at risk to rescue people in danger. Anecdotes and stories can help an audience better understand events that are not part of their personal experience.

Definition: Coverage might include an explanation of the differences between a tropical storm and a full-fledged hurricane.

Each of these strategies can be employed to inform people about a hurricane. There are many ways of reaching the same goal. If you look back at what you've read in this chapter, you can see a number of these strategies at work.

None of these strategies is necessarily better than the others; the strategies function in different ways. *Definition,* for example, helps your reader understand the essentials (what makes a storm a hurricane). *Comparison and contrast* can be useful in associating unfamiliar information with something your reader may already be familiar with. If your audience is familiar with tornadoes, for example, you might help them understand hurricanes by first explaining how they are like tornadoes (comparison) and then showing how they are different (contrast). You are probably more familiar with these strategies than you realize. You use them regularly to help convey information. When you write, rhetorical strategies help you bridge the gap between what you know and what you want your reader to learn and to believe.

Think back to the letter you wrote to your Aunt Rebecca in chapter 1. You probably drew on several rhetorical strategies as you tried to convince her to lend you the money you needed. You *explained* your situation and probably provided some *illustrations* of what you needed the loan for. Perhaps you also discussed the *cause* of your financial difficulty and the positive *effect* the loan would have. You might have used several rhetorical strategies to achieve your purpose. Your choice of which rhetorical strategies to use was determined by your rhetorical situation.

Rhetorical strategies are some of the strongest tools you have as a writer. They represent different ways of organizing and presenting information, and they depend on your rhetorical purpose. Sometimes the strategy you select is dictated by the person to whom you are writing: a teacher, for example, might ask you to *compare* two works of literature, or an employer might ask you to *illustrate* several sales techniques. More often, though, writers make conscious choices about the information they include, how they organize their data, where they use examples and illustrations, whether statistics will help make their case, and whether to employ visual aids. If you think of rhetorical strategies as tools, you know that you'd use a shovel for a different task than you'd use a rake; you'd use a hoe for a different purpose than you might a saw; and that, although both a lawnmower and a line trimmer will cut grass and weeds, you'd select the first for cutting large areas and the trimmer for tidying the edges. As a child, you quickly found that a fork was the perfect utensil for eating potatoes, but it didn't work very well for cereal; instead, you chose a spoon. Effective writing requires that you consider all the rhetorical tools available to you to determine which will best help you achieve your goals as you write. Don't limit yourself by considering only one rhetorical tool.

We're now going to move from thinking about writing strategies to looking at techniques for acquiring the information you'll include in your

---

✳ **BOX 2.1   APPLYING WHAT YOU READ**

How Do You Read?

It's often worthwhile to think about your own reading habits and to compare them with what others do. Take a moment to jot down on a piece of paper your answers to these questions:

- What do you like to read?
- What do you dislike reading?
- How do you read a magazine article (and what do you like to read in magazines)?
- How do you read a newspaper article (and what do you like to read in newspapers)?
- Do you read an Internet text differently than you read a magazine or a newspaper? In what ways?
- How do you read a college textbook? In what ways is this reading different from the way in which you read a magazine or newspaper?
- How do you read longer, more complex nonfiction (such as a history of the Vietnam War)?
- What strategies do you use to help you understand and retain what you've read?
- What do annotating and summarizing mean to you?

Share your comments with several of your classmates in a small group. How do your responses compare with theirs? Your instructor might ask you to share your group's responses with the rest of the class.

---

writing: reading and thinking critically and recording the information you uncover.

READING AND THINKING CRITICALLY

When you begin any writing project, whether during your college career or in your professional life, you rarely have all the information you need. Finding the information and data to support your arguments is called research—which is the subject of chapter 3. But research nearly always involves reading: finding relevant books and articles in the library, searching the Internet, and then doing more reading and searching to understand the information you've collected. Before we look at reading critically, it may be useful for you to assess your reading habits, using the questions in Box 2.1: How Do You Read?

Reading critically does not mean reading to criticize the text. Instead, it means reading to question the text, to make connections to what you've learned from other articles and books, and to think about how the information can help you as you construct your writing projects.

Reading critically means being an active reader, working with the text rather than assuming that you understand an article simply because you've read it. Reading critically means questioning, challenging, and engaging the text as you work your way through it. Reading critically involves asking yourself questions like these:

- What is the writer's thesis? What kind of evidence does the writer provide to support that thesis? How credible are the writer's facts and other statistical information? How can I tell? Why should I believe this text?

- What relevant issues does this writer ignore or pay little attention to? What does that tell me about this text?

- In what ways does the writer present evidence? Is that presentation effective?

- Does the text document the sources of all facts and figures?

- Does the writer provide examples or illustrations to clarify the text?

- How does this article relate to other texts I've read? Do the facts in this one support or contradict those in the others? In what ways?

- Does the writer acknowledge and explain other points of view?

Considering differing points of view will help you to think critically. Thinking critically means thinking in a thoughtful manner. When you think and write about issues—those in the scenarios in part II of this book, those presented in the texts you read, or the problems you encounter in life—you want to:

- Examine each issue fully: What is its relevant history and background? What effect has it had? How does it involve me personally? What might change the situation for the better? What is really at stake? Thinking critically about something means not considering it in black-and-white or simplistic terms, but instead examining it from all viewpoints. This doesn't mean accepting all perspectives as correct. It simply means recognizing their validity.

- Interpret and analyze the facts and other information regarding the issue: What is valid and what is tangential? What facts are vital to understanding the issue?

- Ask probing and substantial questions, questions that cannot be answered without careful analysis.

- Consider several possible solutions to the problem, even if you don't agree with all aspects of those solutions. Considering solutions is not the same as accepting or recommending them. The key to solving a complex problem is considering all possible ways of solving it. Because solutions usually come with a price, it's important to determine and articulate the advantages of one solution (even with its weaknesses) over the others.

- Take all the information, facts, data, and ideas you've collected and construct an effective and persuasive text that accurately outlines your thoughts concerning the issue.

One way to improve your critical thinking is to work with others: hear their perspectives, listen to their points of view, and consider their ideas. Involvement with others to address complex ideas and issues forces you to abandon any simplistic notions you might have about those issues. You learn how to understand the problems involved and how to cooperate with others to find a workable solution. This kind of activity teaches you to identify the right questions—questions that lead to an honest and open discussion of what is important.

Prereading Strategies

Before you begin to read any text, think about your purpose: are you reading for entertainment, for general information, or for some other reason (perhaps you're looking for specific facts or statistics)? Like the prewriting strategies that you use to begin your writing process (brainstorming, clustering, and others), prereading strategies help you become engaged with the text. Consciously thinking about how you want to read a particular text gives you a plan of action to follow when you begin reading.

Examine a text before you begin reading it. Note its physical characteristics, including whether it contains headings that indicate its outline, whether boxes display information or graphics, whether bulleted lists highlight information, and so on. These elements can tell you a lot about the text and the author, and some help you to better understand what you're reading.

Think about the title and what it tells you about the text. The title is intended to summarize the essence of the text—while capturing your interest and arousing your curiosity. Some titles provide a lot of information for predicting what is in the text. That makes your reading easier. Next, skim the text for a quick overview: read the first and last paragraphs and perhaps material that is highlighted in some way (boxes, headings, bold-faced or italicized terms or phrases).

Before you begin reading, consider what you want your reading to accomplish: What might you learn from this text? What information in the text (including facts, statistics, testimony) might you use in your own writing? What does the text provide that makes sense to you, and how do you feel about the issues it covers? How might you use this information to support your own position on an issue? Does the text include anything that contradicts your ideas? What in this text connects to other things you've read?

✳ **BOX 2.2   FOR EXAMPLE**
  Annotating a Reading

She saw the ad on the Internet	Ira Doreen Donovan, an <u>elementary school teacher</u> in Miami, was 31 credits shy of a master's degree in special education when she saw an <u>on-line advertisement</u> for Columbia State University. After sending $800 as the first payment on a $2,000 de-
All she was asked to do was to summarize?	gree, Ms. Donovan received a textbook to <u>summarize</u> and send back for grading.
Then she got an MA and a PhD? and a great GPA without doing any of the work?	Believing this was the first step of several, she was shocked when shortly after, a certificate not only for a <u>master's</u> but a <u>doctorate</u> arrived at her home. Along with the degrees came transcripts awarding her a <u>3.9 grade point average</u> for classes never taken and credit for a <u>completed thesis</u> and <u>dissertation</u>.
I'd feel foolish, too.	"I called the school and told them if this degree isn't worth the paper it's printed on, I don't want to pay for it," Ms. Donovan said. "This degree mill made me look like a fool."

Annotating for Active Reading

One way to read any text more effectively is to interact with it by annotating as you read: Underline the text and indicate in the margins what strikes you as significant. List questions you have next to specific paragraphs. Respond to the ideas in the text with your comments and ideas. It's also useful to underline the main point or thesis of the reading. Being an active reader helps you make the text yours, for a better understanding of the writer's perspective. Making the text yours is the first step in incorporating what you learn from a text into your own writing.

Here's an example: suppose your instructor asks you to read the article "Technology: Easy Degrees Proliferate on the Web" by David Koeppel as an assignment. To better understand the article, you decide to annotate it. Box 2.2: Annotating a Reading illustrates what your comments might look like and what you might underline in the first few paragraphs of Koeppel's article. (The complete article appears in chapter 4 of this text.)

Being an active reader doesn't mean simply highlighting sections of text with a yellow marker. Rather, it involves interacting with the text: questioning, commenting, making marginal notes about ideas the text presents, and noting connections between this text and others you've read. Jotting down questions and underlining passages help you become actively involved in understanding the text. These activities also help you remember what you're reading.

Writing Effective Summaries

Many writers also find summarizing useful. A summary condenses the information that an article contains, often into just a few sentences. Summarizing requires that you note only the most important information from the article. Composing a summary that captures the essence of an article or essay can help you to understand what you have read.

One effective way to begin writing a summary is to outline what you're reading. An outline essentially lists the main points of a piece of writing, forming the basis for a summary. A summary of David Koeppel's first few paragraphs (in Box 2.2) might read like this:

> Koeppel provides the example of a woman who summarized a text and received an MA and a PhD for doing so. "Diploma mill" is right. This woman received a refund, but others didn't—and they didn't receive an education, either.

What is important about summarizing is capturing the essence of the piece you're reading. When you begin composing your own text, you can quickly identify the highlights of the article from your summary and incorporate them into your writing. For instance, to cite Koeppel's article as one of several you'd read that reported on distance learning, you might use your summary to write:

> In the *New York Times,* David Koeppel notes that, at least for some people, getting a college education means mailing a check, doing a little work, and waiting for your degree to arrive. Others, though, receive neither the degree nor an education. . . .

Just as there are strategies to use before you read and things you can do as you read to help you comprehend the information, there are ways to increase your understanding when you've completed your reading. We call these postreading strategies.

Postreading Strategies

Once you've worked your way through an article, annotated it, and summarized its main points, it's time to look over your notes and think about what your reading has taught you. Spend a few minutes reviewing your annotations and summary: What's the main thing you learned from the text? What new ideas did you gather from this reading? Did you learn anything that surprised you? How does the information in this reading relate to other articles you've read? What questions do you still have about this reading? How might you answer those questions? Will this reading be an effective source for your writing project? What information can you extract from this reading to support your writing?

Now that you've thought about ways for reading and working with a text, let's consider what you might do with the information you discover through your reading. We suggest collecting the information in a journal.

A WRITER'S JOURNAL

As you read, it's important to keep tabs on the notes, annotations, and summaries you create. A good place to record such information is in something called a writer's journal. Notes and other information from your journal may become the basis for group and individual writing projects. Recording your ideas on paper moves them from your mind to written form—and helps you learn what you really think. As writing theorist Peter Elbow suggests, "Meaning is not what you start with but what you end up with . . . [so view] writing not as a way to transmit a message but as a way to grow and cook a message" (15).

Once you've recorded your ideas and questions on paper or electronically, you can refer to and expand on them as you continue your research. A journal allows you to keep track of various pieces of information and to better understand how they relate to one another. It's important to record your ideas, responses, and questions systematically because, for a writing project of any depth, it's difficult (if not impossible) to keep everything in memory.

When you've completed the reading your instructor asks you to do or you feel you need to do, made notes in your journal, and perhaps summarized what you've read, you'll have some information with which to begin your writing. The reading and the journal writing you've done, then, serve as the foundation both for further research and for the writing you'll construct.

From Writer's Journal to Research Journal

A writer's journal can contain reading notes, summaries, and perhaps also personal reflections, but why not also use it to record anything and everything that comes to mind as you work on a writing project? You can use your journal to keep track of the research you gather for each writing project and to note your questions and concerns as you solve writing problems. Your writer's journal can become the repository for just about everything that comes to mind during the course of each writing project.

A writer's journal should be a flexible space. Its contents and format can vary to suit the project you're involved with and your purpose. Your rhetorical situation affects the materials you collect, the notes you take, and the summaries you write. Select a journal format that allows you to store pictures, add pages, and insert dividers. As you read and gather information, keep in mind your audience and your purpose for writing. What kind of information will help you as you compose? What information will help you get your message across to your intended audience?

Some writers use what Anne Berthoff calls a dialectical journal, in which you reserve one page for your notes and observations and use the facing page to question and to comment on your notes (Enos 549–52). In this way, the two pages "speak" to each other. For an example of what a dialectical journal might look like (again, based on the first few

✳ **BOX 2.3 FOR EXAMPLE**
Using a Dialectical Journal

Check other sources to see if they agree. Are there many such stories?

Wonder if these degrees "count" out there in the world, in the job market. Who decides, anyway, if a college degree is valid or that one is better than another?

Koeppel illustrates his ideas about distance learning with one example of a woman working on her MA. She summarized a text and received "certificates" for both her MA and PhD.

paragraphs of David Koeppel's newspaper article), see Box 2.3: Using a Dialectical Journal.

From time to time, your instructor might ask you to reflect on the work you've done. If you keep careful journal notes on your process and progress, you'll have a rich resource for those reflections. See appendix A for more on this subject.

Ways to Use Your Journal

To summarize, you can use your journal in a number of ways:

- To jot down notes and ideas about the issues you consider critical to your writing project. It is your research log.
- To record questions as they come up (and the answers you discover). Your journal is a good place for summarizing the essence of what you've read.
- To list questions for further research and to note ideas suggested by your instructor and classmates as they read what you've written.

- To reflect on your writing progress and process, as you work your way through your writing projects.
- To begin to "wallow in complexity" by wrestling in writing with an issue.

We borrowed the expression "wallowing in complexity" through the act of writing from John Ramage and John Bean (22). By wrestling in writing with an issue or a problem, you begin to complicate your thinking about it, to view it from a different perspective, as if through someone else's eyes. There are always several ways of looking at an issue. Keep others' perspectives in mind.

MOVING TO CHAPTER 3

In this chapter, we've focused on the kinds of writing you'll do in part II of this text and elsewhere, the rhetorical strategies you can employ to construct effective texts, and how your writing is grounded in the reading you do. Learning to read critically and thoughtfully and then recording in some form the information—the research—you collect during your reading is the basis for all the academic writing you'll do in college.

In chapter 3, we discuss how to integrate research into your writing. We show you how to evaluate sources and how to use the information you find to make your writing strong.

Works Cited

Aristotle on Rhetoric. Trans. George A. Kennedy. New York: Oxford UP, 1991.

Elbow, Peter. *Writing without Teachers.* New York: Oxford UP, 1973.

Enos, Theresa, ed. *A Sourcebook for Basic Writing Teachers.* New York: Random, 1987.

Ramage, John D., and John C. Bean. *The Allyn and Bacon Guide to Writing.* 2nd ed. Needham Heights, MA: Allyn, 2000.

CHAPTER 3

 Incorporating Research into Your Writing Process

In chapter 2, we discussed the kinds of papers you'll write in part II of this text. We saw that the proper use of rhetorical appeals and strategies can make your arguments more convincing. We also reviewed the ways in which your rhetorical situation influences how you find and read research information. Finally, we investigated a number of ways for recording the research data you locate.

In this chapter, we look at how you put into practice much of what you've learned. Our focus is on researching information, evaluating the information you find, and then using that information to support the positions you take in your writing. Our purpose here is to help you learn:

- Researching skills for various research sites: your library, the Internet, and others.
- How to evaluate the sources you discover.
- How to gather and use information effectively, both as background for your writing projects, as well as to provide evidence that will support your arguments.

But why do you need research? Isn't your personal opinion enough to convince your audience?

In this country, we are all free to express our opinions openly. In fact, we value our right to speak freely and independently. And often, especially in informal conversation, your opinion might be all it takes to sway others to agree with your suggestion: to go to a certain movie, for example, or to eat lunch at a particular cafe.

In writing, though, and especially in the kinds of writing you'll do in college or in your professional life, your personal opinion is often not sufficient to sway your audience. At least some in your audience are likely to have views that differ from your own. In fact, the give-and-take of academic discussion, in which each side expresses its views and then is questioned by others with (somewhat) opposing positions, is designed to help everyone understand all relevant perspectives.

Most college writing or speaking assignments require that you support your position with facts and examples: without them, why should your audience believe you? To assemble these facts and examples—your evidence—you must conduct research. You use what you learn from your research to support the positions you maintain in your writing. Even though you might be a good writer and your reader might be inclined to accept your arguments on their own merit, you'll be more effective if you can quote others who support your positions, especially if you:

- *Cite those who are experts in their fields:* Remember Aristotle's notion of ethos—that we believe someone when we trust them, when they are a credible witness? If you had a problem with your car, whose opinion would you be more likely to believe: the professional mechanic who regularly works on your car or a friend of yours who rides a bicycle everywhere? Would you be more likely to trust your chemistry professor's explanation of a complex chemical reaction or your roommate's?

- *Provide facts that support what you say:* Facts or statistics add credence to your position, especially when you present them clearly and understandably. Presenting data in graphical form (in a chart, a graph, or a table) can help your audience understand them.

- *Demonstrate that the solution you suggest has been successful elsewhere:* Illustrations and examples show your audience what others have done when faced with similar problems.

You already know how to research a number of topics—even if you haven't called what you did research. For example, have you ever repeated what you had read in a film review when you and a friend were deciding which movie to see? You were using text-based research. Have you ever mentioned someone else's opinion of a restaurant or a band to influence a friend to eat at that restaurant or see that band? You were using an aspect of "field research" called interviewing. Even though you didn't conduct a formal interview (you may have "interviewed" the person you quote over the telephone or through e-mail), the result was the same: you relied on another person's or group's opinion to try to influence someone else. Before buying something, have you purchased a magazine or a shopper's guide to learn about the product? That's a form of research. Before making a purchase, have you compared prices or checked product assessments on the Internet? That too is research.

RESEARCH STRATEGIES AND YOUR RHETORICAL PURPOSE

Your rhetorical purpose determines where you look for information and the kinds of information you search for. Your audience, your purpose, and the setting or context that surrounds your writing determine the kind of research that will serve you best. Each type of source has its advantages (articles in academic journals are usually well researched; the Internet offers a huge and expanding range of information) and weaknesses (some academic journal articles are difficult to read; anyone can post to a Web site, so you must evaluate all Internet sources for reliability and integrity).

Let's consider some research examples. Suppose that your college sociology instructor asks you to briefly define the words *social behavior*. You might begin with the definition provided in your textbook, and you might also look up the words in a dictionary. That might be enough research for the brief definition you were asked to provide.

If your sociology instructor asked you, instead, to outline the history of social behavior, you might begin by examining library texts that focus on social behavior. Your search might lead to academic journals—which contain articles written by scholars and researchers—to see what information you might find there. You could begin with the same definitions of the term that you identified in your simpler search, but you'd also look for examples that show how social behavior has changed over time. You'd need more than a dictionary definition to complete this assignment.

Let's take the assignment a step further: you might instead be asked to describe a specific kind of social behavior; in that case you'd look for facts and statistics about that type of behavior, rather than simple definitions. Or you might be asked to compare one kind of behavior with another (how teenage males behave when they're in groups, for example, versus how they behave when they're alone). In this instance, you'd look not for definitions or statistics, but for examples of male teenage behavior. In your college library, you might find examples (and perhaps photos) of such behavior in popular magazines and newspapers. To learn why such behavior occurs, you might search for studies of male teenage behavior that have been published in academic journals and books.

So far, these examples have centered on textual material—the kind we usually think about when we hear the word *research*. In addition to text-based research, however, your instructor might also ask you to observe and then question some of your friends about their behavior in various situations. Instead of reading a text to find information, you are making direct observations.

For instance, your sociology instructor might ask you to examine how a small group of your friends (males and females together) behave in various situations (in a nice restaurant, in a fast-food restaurant, at the mall, and in a classroom). Your instructor might also ask that you speculate why your friends behave as they do in those different settings.

To complete the assignment, you might observe your friends, take notes on their behavior, and then discuss with them why they acted as they did. This is called field research. In field research you move out of the library and into the world, where you can observe, ask questions, conduct surveys, and interview people.

Essentially, then, to conduct research is to find information that will serve your purpose at a particular time and place, and for a specific situation.

At one time, academic research was restricted to printed texts: students would go to the library and read books and journal articles about the topic they were researching. Today, for some projects, students might also read articles in newspapers and popular magazines; conduct interviews; make personal observations; ask people to complete questionnaires and surveys; and, of course, search the Internet.

The Internet

Today, when we think of "research," the first thought that may come to mind is to search the Internet: pull up a few Web pages, print them, and your research is complete. However, in college writing and in the writing you'll do later in your professional life, Web-based research is rarely sufficient for a project of any depth—you might find some information, but perhaps not enough or the right kind; or the information you find might lack credibility. And although there is a lot of information on the Web, only a fraction of the material that is available in a library can be found there. Consider Internet research as a supplement to library research, rather than a replacement for it. Ironically, because it's easy to download information from the Internet, you can experience "information overload": you can collect huge amounts of information that is related only tangentially to your topic. Research consists of more than simply finding and printing Web pages. It absolutely means carefully evaluating the information you find (because anyone can post a Web page, you could find yourself citing information posted by a ten-year-old "authority").

Developing your personal research skills will serve you well in your college classes and after graduation. "Surfing the Web" for information may seem easy, but there are no shortcuts to conducting effective research. Because they must be thoroughly and carefully evaluated, Web sites can require even more research effort than does text-based information.

Conducting searches on the Internet (and in the library) will help sharpen your research skills. The search strategies you use on the Web and in the library are often similar—and transferable. For example, you've probably clicked on the Search button in Netscape Navigator or Microsoft Internet Explorer and used a search engine to look for something on the Web. A search engine is a software program that electronically looks for what you specify. You also probably quickly learned that different search engines locate different information—that Google (www.google. com) gives you different results than does Yahoo! (www.yahoo.com)—and that both return somewhat different information than a search using a browser like Netscape (www.Netscape.com). You might also have used a meta-search engine, such as Dogpile (www.dogpile.com), which scans several search engines at the same time.

The Library

You can conduct research at many libraries in the same way you do on the Internet: libraries provide various search engines, and you select the one that will best meet your needs. To search popular magazines, for instance, you look through one library database; another database focuses on academic journals, and still another helps with newspapers. For example, many libraries offer search engines called UnCover and EBSCO-host; the two produce different search results. Once you understand the concept of search engines, you can conduct wide-ranging searches on the Internet and in your college library.

Although libraries don't supply hypertext links as does the Internet, did you know that they offer a similar feature? Here's a research hint: whenever you find a book in your college library, spend a few minutes to examine the other texts that surround the one you just located. Books about the same topic are shelved together. This means that once you find one book on the topic you're researching, you'll be faced by many others. Because you're standing right there, it's easy for you to take your research further. If you were looking for books on the history of the Confederacy, for instance, you'd find a number of such texts—all with their own perspectives and information—near each other on your library's shelves.

Using Your Research Skills

As we mentioned, the type of research you might conduct for any writing project depends on your rhetorical situation. Here's a more detailed example of the kinds of issues and problems you'll face in the scenarios you'll find in part II of this text, and of the steps you might take to complete a specific writing assignment.

Suppose that a controversy erupted on your campus when a student hung a large Confederate flag in his dorm room window. Everyone who passed by could see it. The school newspaper has been full of letters denouncing the flag—some see it as a racist symbol—and it has also printed a letter from the student, who claims it's his constitutional right to display the flag. In your college history class, your instructor asks you to write a paper about this controversy: does a student's right to free speech protect his or her ability to display the Confederate flag on school property?

Identifying the questions you need to answer is the first step in careful research. Begin by constructing a list of your questions. Start with the who, what, when, where, how, and why questions that a reporter might ask. For your history class paper, you might include these questions:

Who is involved?

- Does a student, or anyone, have the right to display anything he or she chooses in a dorm room window? Does the school have any say in the matter?
- Would it matter if others on campus could not see the offensive flag?
- Does it matter who is offended? What if only one person complains about the flag? What if five hundred people complain about it?

What is happening?

- Have other schools had similar problems? How did they address them?
- Does it matter what is displayed? What if someone displayed a Claude Monet painting? A magazine foldout of a nude woman? A nude man? A picture of his or her mother? A four-letter word, in large letters? A huge picture of his or her own face? A religious symbol?

When did the problem begin?

- Is this a new problem? Have there been similar instances in the past at this school?
- Does it matter if the flag had been displayed for some time before anyone complained? Why?

Where is the problem?

- Is the flag clearly visible to anyone passing by, or is the flag displayed in a window that is difficult for most passersby to see?
- Does the flag's location matter? Why or why not?
- Who owns or controls the dorm room window in which the flag is displayed?

How should the problem be handled?

- If the school administration has the power to control what someone displays in his or her dorm room window, what makes you think the administration will stop there? Might it also want to read student e-mail or electronically bug the bathrooms and the cafeteria?
- If the school can control the dorm windows, can it also control what goes on inside the dorm rooms? That is, can the school

control whether males and females share a dorm room only during certain hours? Can the school ban alcohol from dorm rooms?

Why is this a problem?

- How do you judge the level of offensiveness of the flag? Would it matter if some people were very offended, but others couldn't care less? Why?

- What rights do students have, and what rights don't they have? How might a specific response (forcing removal of the flag, for example) infringe on those rights?

Once you've identified some basic questions that you'd like to explore, consider the kind of research that might help you learn more about the controversy surrounding the Confederate flag. To find answers to your questions, you might decide to try several different approaches. When you do research, you can't always know in advance where you'll locate the information you need. In this instance, you might find that reading about the history of flag display is interesting, but it doesn't help your search. Or you might find that you get more usable and reliable information by reading about similar cases in law journals than you do by interviewing students on your campus. You often must try several different research approaches because you can't know in advance which will be the most productive.

To begin your history paper, you might examine the Constitution of the United States and its discussion of free speech. Part of your paper might focus on whether you think the Constitution applies in this case. Because the Constitution doesn't contain language addressing the issue of displaying a flag that others object to, you also might try to learn if anyone has published an article that makes such a connection. That would mean looking for sources beyond the Constitution—called secondary sources—that discuss whether the right of free speech is protected in other instances involving flags.

PRIMARY RESEARCH AND SECONDARY SOURCES

Research that you originate is called primary research. Primary research includes the interviews you conduct, the observations you make, and the surveys you distribute and tabulate—you are the research source. Because you conduct the research yourself, you have direct, personal knowledge gained from your own work. If you interview the student who has the flag hanging in his dorm window, you have conducted primary research. If you cite what someone wrote about the situation (in a letter to the editor in your campus newspaper, for example), you are using a secondary source.

Use of secondary sources means citing information from research others have conducted: texts written by other people, facts identified by others, and statistics tabulated by others.

When you conduct primary research, you know the questions you asked, you know what you observed, and you know how you collected and tallied any statistical information. But when you use secondary sources—reports of work that others have done—it's important to think about how reliable those sources might be and what biases the writers might have.

EVALUATING SOURCES FOR BIAS

When using a secondary source, you must analyze it carefully: Who wrote it? Where it was published? What ax might the writer have to grind? It's important that you screen all secondary sources for biases and prejudices of any kind, so that you can understand any you find and explain them to your readers. As a writer, you are responsible for the integrity of your sources—primary as well as secondary.

With print-based sources, the material is in front of you. A careful examination of it can allow you to discover biases the writer or publication might have; other articles in the same issue might indicate a magazine's point of view. For example, if you were researching the Confederate flag issue, and you discovered a journal called *Restore the Confederacy,* you could examine the articles in several issues (and the editorials if the magazine publishes them), to get a sense of the magazine's overall point of view. In this case, the journal's title provides a hint. If you found an author who'd written several magazine pieces that all focused on how the flag makes a racial statement, you could read those articles and gain a good sense of her position.

It's important to remember that just because a source appears to be biased or has a unique point of view does not mean that you can't use the information that source contains. It does mean that you need to inform your readers of any biases you identify. You must make certain that your readers receive all relevant information, for only then will your writing truly inform.

For example, in preparation for writing about the displaying of the Confederate flag in the dorm room window, you might interview some of the students on your campus. If you interviewed the roommate of the person displaying the flag, it would be important for your readers to know that your source was that roommate. If you interviewed the person who made the original complaint about the flag, shouldn't your readers also be given that information? With any research you do, you must inform your readers of any biases in the sources that you use for research.

You also want to consider the source of the information you find. The National Association for the Advancement of Colored People (NAACP), for

example, is likely have an entirely different perspective on the Confederate flag issue than might the American Civil Liberties Union (ACLU).

It's also important to learn to read statistics with a grain of salt—that
is, to really analyze what you're reading rather than accepting the information at face value. Here's an example. A recent study of Arizona residents found that fewer people were exercising: the number of adults
indicating that they engaged in physical activity during their leisure time
had dropped from about 76 percent in 1994 to less than 49 percent in
1998. "Arizonans place 1st as couch potatoes," read the headline in the
state's largest newspaper, the *Arizona Republic,* and the Arizona Department of Health Services said the results indicated an "epidemic" of inac-
tivity (qtd. in Wilson).

Those results sound bad, don't they? But what a reader had to dig a
little to learn, reporter Steve Wilson notes, was that the study was based
on a series of random phone calls placed throughout the day . . . when
people who were out exercising were less likely to be at home to answer
the phone.

Carefully evaluate all the information you collect, as well as its source,
before you accept it as true. Begin with this premise: just as you have various purposes for the papers you write in your college classes (to inform,
to persuade, and so on), other writers have various purposes for the texts
they compose and for publishing their work in the venue in which it appears. There are no hard-and-fast rules for separating all facts from all
opinions, but there are questions you can ask to understand the potential
for bias in your research sources. These questions will serve you well for
almost any kind of research you conduct. Box 3.1: Beginning Your Evaluation provides some questions to help you in your investigation. The following sections address specific types of research sources.

Newspapers

Newspapers usually try to do what their name suggests: they provide
coverage and some analysis of the news. They also have editorial pages,
where opinions are expressed; usually it's clear whether what you're reading is a news item or an editorial. Most newspapers take care to report the
facts and statistics they include in their news articles accurately. As you'd
expect, editorials might use facts and statistics in a way that helps support
the point the writer is trying to make.

Most newspapers have a particular political slant, which is obvious
in their editorials, but it is also evident in *how* various news events are
portrayed. If you examine newspapers from several large cities (your college library will have copies), such differences might be readily apparent.
Select an issue in the news (political issues are useful to focus on) and
compare how each newspaper covers it. Suppose, for instance, that the
president just made a major speech, or dedicated a national monument,
or signed a bill into law. You'll find that newspapers that generally support

BOX 3.1 FOR EXAMPLE

Beginning Your Evaluation

Here are some questions to ask about secondary source material. They will help you to identify and perhaps to understand an essay's biases:

- What is the writer's point of view or position on the issues being discussed? Is the writer trying to mislead me in some way? How?
- Does the writer seem to present all pertinent information, or do some data appear to be missing? Do I fully understand the points the writer is making, or am I left with questions?
- If this writer quotes other authors, where were their comments published? What can I learn from those sources that might indicate whether this author is credible?
- Is the writer trying to influence my point of view in some way, or is the writer simply presenting facts?
- Can I discover anything about the writer's political (or other) views? Does the article or book or Web site contain any clues to the writer's beliefs, perspectives, or background?
- Can I learn anything from the publication itself? Are most of the articles written to persuade? Or are they written to inform? Even articles in what is nominally a newsmagazine (such as *Time*) might contain editorial comments.
- How thorough is the documentation? Does the piece supply the sources the writer used to support his or her position? When a writer cites sources, you can examine them yourself for bias; if the sources are not supplied, how do you know the information in the article is accurate? A well-documented essay carries more weight than one built only on opinion.
- Do the texts of this publisher include a statement of editorial goals that indicates a particular point of view?

the president will give such an event more coverage than will newspapers that oppose most of the president's policies. Supportive papers might place more emphasis on the event—by running more pictures of it or by including other articles discussing or analyzing it, for example—than will those newspapers whose editors don't agree with the president. In other words, a newspaper can support the political views of its editors by covering the news in ways that are intended to reinforce those views.

You also can often learn something about a newspaper piece by considering where it originates: articles in local papers that are reprinted from nationally recognized newspapers or from national news bureaus usually are clearly identified. A newspaper with a long history (such as the *New York Times*) generally can be considered reliable. You can also ask questions like these about local papers: What do I know about this newspaper? What kind of a reputation does it have? How do others, who have lived in this city for a long time, describe it? If you were reading two essays, and one quoted extensively from the *New York Times* while the other quoted only from a supermarket tabloid, which essay would carry more weight? Do you think that *USA Today* might present more of a national perspective than, say, your local paper?

Magazines

Magazines come in many varieties. For a quick indication of a magazine's purpose and focus, consider its name. What does the magazine's title tell you? For example, you would expect *Time* and *Newsweek* to focus on news, which means they are fact based; you would expect *People* to focus on personalities and human interest stories. What might be the focus of a magazine called *George*? How might you find out?

You can also get a sense of a magazine's purpose and audience by examining the articles it publishes:

- Does the magazine focus on news items? If so, do its articles focus on national issues, regional concerns, or human interest stories?

- Does the magazine publish "fluff" pieces—features without much textual information but perhaps with lots of pictures?

- What do you already know about the magazine? What kind of a reputation does it have?

- What kind of article might this magazine publish on the Confederate flag issue, do you suppose? That is, do you think it would be more likely to publish a news item, something with a lot of photos (and little real information), or a profile of the people involved? Would this magazine be likely to print a detailed history of incidents involving flag displays, perhaps documenting the legal background of such displays? Or would it publish a large photograph of the flag and only brief interviews with a few students?

- What does the magazine tell you about the author of each article? You can often gain a sense of what a magazine piece is trying to accomplish by reading what the magazine says about the piece's author: What else has he or she published (other works are often listed at the end of the article)? What issues is the author interested in? (Someone who focuses exclusively on ethical issues, for instance, might be a better source for your research than someone who's never written about ethics.)

- How current is the magazine? This is especially important when you're researching topical issues.

Journals

Journals are a major source of communication and information transfer within professional and scientific fields: attorneys read law journals, physicians read medical journals, and composition teachers read journals about literature and about writing.

Because journals have an academic readership (many are published at universities), journal articles are always thoroughly researched and documented. This doesn't necessarily mean that such articles present only unbiased facts; rather, it means that journal articles often provide a survey of what has already been published about a specific topic and then use that information to support the claims the article makes.

A law journal, for example, might publish an article about a student's constitutional right to display a Confederate flag in his dorm window. That article would outline and explain other, similar cases, and perhaps it would quote from rulings made by judges in those instances. A writer using this article for research draws on the information it presents to support his or her legal opinion about such a display.

Many academic journals carry no advertising; this sends the message that advertising revenue does not influence what they publish. Most academic journals are "peer reviewed," which means that scholars or experts in the field read and approve each article before it's published. "Approval" doesn't mean that the reviewers agree with the author; instead, it means that they believe the findings and conclusions in the article are based on solid research meeting academic standards.

You can get a good sense of the editorial standards of almost any journal by reading its publication requirements, which are usually listed in the front of the journal. There you'll learn which topics the journal covers, what its article requirements are (the specific academic areas in which the journal publishes articles), and sometimes how many people peer-review an article before publication (when a journal asks for three copies of any submission, that probably means each article will have three reviewers).

Books

Books are valued as research resources in college writing because they contain information that is generally accurate. Although books are frequently written to persuade, the process of writing a book is so complex and lengthy that it used to be safe to assume that every fact or statistic had been thoroughly checked. However, with the advent of publishing by computer, this is no longer always the case. With cost constraints and the acceleration of the publishing process, editorial standards have declined, and some inferior books are published. Therefore, you can't assume that something is accurate simply because you read it in a book. You must evaluate the book and its author carefully before incorporating the information it contains into your research.

You can gain a sense of the quality of a book by asking questions such as these:

- How thoroughly researched is the information in the book? If the author cites facts, statistics, and data, are the sources of that information well documented? Could you go to those sources and examine them yourself, if you wished? Check at the end of each chapter or in the back of the text to see if there's a list of works cited.

- Where were the author's secondary sources published? Remember that established national publications such as the *Los Angeles Times,* for example, are generally more reliable than smaller, more obscure publications.

- Who published this book? What other books has this publisher produced? If you find that this publisher produces only texts that favor a return of the Confederacy, you should note that bias when you cite the text in your essay about the Confederate flag.

Internet Sources

The Internet contains a huge amount of research information, and much of it—especially that provided by the government—can be considered reliable. Because anyone can create and maintain a Web page, however, it's important that you learn how to evaluate Internet sources.

The Internet should never be your only research source. Instead, it should supplement other kinds of research, especially library research. Just as you would not rely solely on personal interviews to prove a point, you should not rely solely on a single source for all of your research.

The Internet contains hypertext links: click on a word and you're electronically sent ("linked") to another Internet location. This capability opens up a myriad of avenues for further research, but it also means you have to carefully and critically evaluate Web sites. Hyperlinks take you places, to more information, but don't necessarily help you understand or analyze what you find there. Materials published on the Internet can appear professional and unbiased, but information that would allow you to evaluate the credibility of the Web page is often lacking. Questions to ask when evaluating an Internet site include:

- *Who created the site?* Was it an individual, a company, an organization, a government agency? If you learn that you're examining a personal Web site, its level of reliability is completely different from that of a Web site sponsored by, say, a government agency or a university. As you probably know, the Web suffix generally indicates the source of the Web site:

  .edu indicates an educational institution: www.asu.edu, for instance, is the Web address for Arizona State University.

  .com indicates a for-profit company: www.cnn.com is the Web address for the Cable News Network.

  .org indicates an organization: www.pbs.org is the Web address for the Corporation for Public Broadcasting.

- *How current is the posting on the site?* Often, Web sites include their "publication date," which tells you the last time the Web site owner modified something on the site. This gives you some sense of how up-to-date the information is.

- *What links does the site contain?* Often, following some of the links provides a good deal of information about the credibility of the Web site. (You'd be suspicious, for example, if you followed the links from an apparently unbiased Web site and they all took you to extreme right- or left-wing organizations' Web sites.)

- *Who appears to be the target audience for this site?* Determining to whom the site appeals might give you a sense of its purpose.

- *How is the information presented?* Are biases apparent, or does the site appear to be strictly informational? More important, are all sides of an issue represented?

- *What kind of documentation is supplied?* Remember that in an academic journal article, all statistics, quotations, and paraphrases are documented. Does this Internet site make undocumented statements?

Network Solutions assigns most domain names, and it offers a "Who Is Who" lookup for nearly all except personal sites on the Web. This search will tell you a lot about the creator of any Web page. It not only identifies who "owns" the domain name but also provides e-mail contact information. The address for Network Solutions is http://www.networksolutions.com/. If the Web page you're looking for is not listed, then you know it is a personal page (Sherman).

ACKNOWLEDGING YOUR SOURCES

In most of the writing you do in college, you're expected to provide accurate and complete citations for all outside sources you use. Once you leave college and work professionally, you'll also be expected to provide sources for the information in your correspondence, memos, and other writing. Citing the information you use from other sources serves several purposes:

- It lets your reader know that the information comes from someone other than you.

- Citing respected sources provides evidence that your position is well-founded and that your arguments are supported by the findings of qualified others. Demonstrating that your solution to a problem has proved effective elsewhere, in one or more similar situations, adds to your credibility. Citing facts and statistical information supporting your position makes you more convincing.

- Proper citations also allow your readers to verify your sources. They can then refer to the same articles, books, or Web pages you consulted to learn more about the subject.

As a writer and speaker, you already know the basics of citing a source: suppose that you want to see a particular movie and you invite some friends, but they aren't interested. You might tell them about a review you've read or mention that another friend has seen the film and liked it. Either way, you're using an outside authority to help make your case, to convince your friends that your view has validity.

This is why documenting your sources is so important. If you can cite someone your reader respects as an authority on the issue you're discussing, your position will have more credibility. In the movie example, if you repeat what someone whose opinion your friends respect thought about the movie, won't your friends be more likely to be convinced than if you simply say, "Well, I heard the movie was good"? If you can cite facts you located in the *San Jose Mercury News,* and add statistics from the *Harvard Business Review,* you'll be more likely to convince a reader than if you simply write, "Well, I once heard that. . . ."

Quoting and Paraphrasing

Once you have information that supports the point you're making, or that illustrates an idea you're explaining, or that is evidence for your position, you need to decide how to present that information. Although some data lend themselves to a visual presentation (a chart, table, graph, or photo), most of what you'll use will be text: something someone wrote. To incorporate textual information from other writers into your writing, you can either quote your source directly or paraphrase the information—that is, put it into your own words.

How do you decide which method is most effective for a particular piece of information? As with everything else, consider your rhetorical situation: your purpose, your audience, the occasion for writing, the topic, and you, the writer. In an informal composition, it might be better to put the information you're borrowing from a outside source into your own words. After all, when you write a letter to Aunt Rebecca or a memo to a coworker, you probably don't quote others directly. That is, you wouldn't write something like this to your aunt:

> I got an estimate to fix my car. The mechanic wrote: "Our estimate for the tune-up is $95. Our estimate for new brakes (front) is $155. Our estimate for a new turn signal module is $172."

Instead, you'd write something like this:

> Joe at the car repair place tells me it'll cost about $425 to fix my car. . . .

In addition to thinking of your situation and whether the writing you're doing is formal or informal, consider what you're trying to accomplish and what your audience needs to know. Aunt Rebecca probably just needs to know the total amount of money you want to borrow, and then she'll decide whether to make the loan. If you were submitting an insurance claim for this work, however, do you think your insurance company would be satisfied with a lump-sum amount? They'd insist on the exact figures, and they probably would want a copy of the estimate as calculated by the repair shop.

What if you were writing a memo about computer supplies to your employer? In some instances, all you'd need to indicate is that next month's budget will be about $500 higher than last month's because supply costs have increased. In other cases (perhaps when the actual budget is being prepared), you'd be expected to supply detailed dollar amounts for each item or category.

In your academic writing, think about what your source information should do and how it can most effectively achieve that purpose. What does your audience need? Will the source have more ethos and be more believable if you use an exact quotation? Or might the data that your audience needs be more effectively presented in a graph than in the dry prose the source uses to convey it? Or would the information be clearer if you expressed it in your own words?

Although there is no exact rule of thumb, generally the more formal your writing situation, the greater the need to use direct quotations. The quotations you use should be brief, and you should place them into context. Introduce quotations carefully. At the same time, take care not to rely too heavily on quotations; research material should support the points you're making, not overwhelm them.

Whether you paraphrase a source—restate what you read in your own words—or quote the source directly, you need to indicate where the material came from. For example, suppose you read an article in the *New York Times* by Morgan Kohl titled "Humans and Outer Space: The Costs." On page 15 of the newspaper you find the statement: "NASA reports that it will cost $20 billion to put humans onto Mars." If you quote this sentence, you might write:

> *New York Times* reporter Morgan Kohl explains that "NASA reports that it will cost $20 billion to put humans onto Mars" (15).

If you restate this information in your own words—paraphrase it—you still must cite your source:

> According to Morgan Kohl in the *New York Times,* a NASA report indicates American taxpayers will have to spend $20 billion to put human beings onto Mars (15).

Whether you quote directly or paraphrase your source, you always must indicate where the information came from. Refer to Appendix C: Documenting Sources for more information on how to cite sources properly.

Avoiding Plagiarism

Whenever we write, we want to show that our texts are well researched. We do so by attributing ideas and words that come from other writers to those writers. That is, we want our readers to distinguish the words and ideas that are our own from those we've borrowed from other sources. By providing such information to our readers, we are being academically honest. We are also giving our readers the opportunity to go to those sources and read them.

It's difficult to understand why some students present other writers' ideas and words as their own. It would seem that students would want to show their instructors how much research work they've done. One way to do that is to cite everything that is not your work.

At first glance, it might seem easier to plagiarize, because you wouldn't have to spend time working on your writing. In fact, it's more difficult to plagiarize than to write your own material. The effort and energy it takes to change at least some words to disguise the plagiarism would be better spent on legitimate work.

Sometimes, of course, students plagiarize unintentionally because they don't understand how to use and attribute sources properly. The rules on citing are quite easy to follow: anytime you use someone else's ideas or words, you need to indicate in your text where they came from. Whether you quote someone directly or paraphrase the words of a writer or speaker, you must let your reader know that those thoughts did not originate with you. It doesn't matter if the ideas came from a book, a magazine, a newspaper, or a Web site: attribute everything that is not your own work to its original author. If you're ever unsure whether you're plagiarizing something, ask your instructor.

Now that you've thought about some of the research questions you might ask and considered ways in which to evaluate your research sources, let's look at how best to put those sources to work. What do you do with the information you find?

INTEGRATING RESEARCH INTO YOUR WRITING

Information and quotations from your research should be incorporated into your text in a way that strengthens and supports your argument. Facts and statistical information that support a point you are making must be blended into your text. Suppose you want to suggest that young men and women don't vote in national elections for reasons other than a distaste for politics. To support your conclusion, you plan to cite the results of a *Washington Post* opinion survey about voting preferences. How would you incorporate the *Post* data into your text?

One effective way to use the *Washington Post* survey results is to first make your point, then provide the survey results, and then explain how

BOX 3.2   FOR EXAMPLE
Integrating Statistics into Your Text

If you were writing an essay suggesting why young men and women don't vote in national elections, this is how you might cite survey information that appeared in an article on page 12 of the *Washington Post:*

> Although many older people complain that today's young people don't vote because they're "turned off by politics," the real reasons that today's youth are not involved are much more complicated. Certainly some teens have been discouraged by political events and politicians, but the *Washington Post* recently reported that there are several reasons for their lack of interest.
>
> *Washington Post* reporter Amy Graves asked 535 teenagers if they planned to vote in the next presidential election, and, if they did not, why they would not vote. Her results might surprise you. Of the teenagers who said they didn't plan to vote:
>
> - 22 percent said they didn't have the time to make an informed decision.
> - 15 percent felt their one vote wouldn't mean anything in a large election, such as one for the presidency.
> - 10 percent didn't care or used the word "apathetic."
> - 5 percent weren't registered and could not vote.
> - only 3 percent said they were "discouraged" by recent political events. (Graves 12)
>
> Therefore, contrary to the popular notion that teens are discouraged by politics in this country, in reality there appear to be several reasons for their lack of interest. Not all of these reasons may be valid, of course, so let's explore them in more detail. . . .

the survey results support your point. Your text might read like the example in Box 3.2: Integrating Statistics into Your Text.

It's important to use quotations and paraphrases in ways that allow your readers to follow your argument clearly and easily. Take care to blend quotations into your text; they shouldn't interrupt the flow of your writing. Lead into each quotation by explaining why you're including it—how it's related to the point you're making. Follow the quote with an explanation of the role it plays in supporting your argument. Box 3.3: Integrating Quotations and Paraphrases into Your Text shows ways of doing this.

You can use the same structure whenever you employ facts, examples, or data from other sources to support and strengthen your argument. The careful use of sources clarifies your argument and makes it more compelling. Depending on the information you provide and the way in which you use it, it may take several paragraphs to explain your research and then to demonstrate the ways in which it supports the point you're making. Use sources to support all parts of your argument.

BOX 3.3   FOR EXAMPLE

Integrating Quotations and Paraphrases into Your Text

Let's assume that your instructor asked you to read a newspaper article titled "Technology: Easy Degrees Proliferate on the Web" by David Koeppel. (You'll find the full text in chapter 4.) You plan to cite in your own paper the example that Koeppel reports in paragraphs 1 and 2 of his article. First, introduce the data, perhaps in this way:

> David Koeppel reports that, at least for some students, getting an online education is not exactly a rigorous process.

Let's assume that you then wish to paraphrase Koeppel's first paragraph and quote from his second. You could blend his words with your own in this manner (the "(1)" at the end of the third sentence indicates that the information is from page 1 of Koeppel's article):

> . . . Koeppel tells the story of Ira Doreen Donovan, an elementary school teacher, who sent a partial payment of $800 to Columbia State University and in turn was sent a textbook she was to summarize. She did so but was "shocked when shortly after, a certificate not only for a master's but a doctorate arrived at her home. Along with the degrees came transcripts awarding her a 3.9 grade point average for classes never taken and credit for a completed thesis and dissertation" (1).

Finally, show how the Donovan story supports your argument. Your finished paragraph might look like this:

> David Koeppel reports that, at least for some students, getting an online education is not exactly a rigorous process. Koeppel tells the story of Ira Doreen Donovan, an elementary school teacher, who sent a partial payment of $800 to Columbia State University and in turn was sent a textbook she was to summarize. She did so but was "shocked when shortly after, a certificate not only for a master's but a doctorate arrived at her home. Along with the degrees came transcripts awarding her a 3.9 grade point average for classes never taken and credit for a completed thesis and dissertation" (1). Sadly, there are many such incidents in which the online college gets the money but the student gets only a grade and no education.

There are various documentation styles for citing quotations and other information. The Modern Language Association (MLA) provides a common format used in the humanities; many of the behavioral sciences use a format developed by the American Psychological Association (APA). We've provided more information on proper citation format in Appendix C: Documenting Sources. Your instructor will tell you which format to use in your class.

No matter which citation method you're asked to follow, the main idea is the same: to give your readers complete source information (including the author's name, when and where the document was published, the page number where you found the quotation, and other relevant data) for any quotations you use or paraphrases you create. This provides your readers with the opportunity to use your sources in their own research.

MOVING TO PART II: THE SCENARIOS

As with any writing you compose, the way in which you read and conduct research is controlled by your rhetorical situation: your audience, your purpose, and the context that surrounds the reading. What questions are you asking? What kinds of information are you looking for? How will you use that information to persuade your audience?

We've discussed several strategies—annotating, summarizing, keeping a journal—to help you accomplish your reading goals and use the information you find to compose persuasive texts. You construct persuasive texts by providing the data, facts, testimony, and other evidence that your audience requires, and by incorporating that information in a sound organizational plan that your audience can understand.

In Part II: The Scenarios, you'll take what you've learned in these early chapters and apply the concepts to solving the kinds of problems you'll confront in real life.

Works Cited

Sherman, William L. (U of Northern Colorado). "WWW Source Evaluation Tip." E-mail to Writing Program Administrators Listserv. 9 Mar. 2000.

Wilson, Steve. "Read Stories Based on Statistics with Grain of Salt." *Arizona Republic* 29 Jan. 2000: A2.

PART II

The Scenarios

In part II of *Scenarios for Writing,* we provide a structure within which you and your classmates are asked to grapple with simulated real-life issues and problems. As you develop and present your views on how best to address these problems, you'll engage in a variety of activities that are intended to help you better understand and improve your writing process. We call our presentations of these issues and problems *scenarios.*

WHAT ARE SCENARIOS?

What characteristics do these scenarios—really, brief stories—share? All have three main elements:

- *Change, recent or impending:* Each scenario in this text involves a modification of the status quo. Without change, there are no new problems to solve.

- *Multiple constituencies:* The change that forms the basis for a scenario must affect more than two interested and involved parties, each with its own perspective on the issues. (A dispute between a pair of neighbors, for example, wouldn't become a scenario.) The change might affect some constituencies in a positive way and others negatively.

- *A public or civic focus:* Public problems call for open discussion (and perhaps debate) among the interested groups. This give-and-take may take place in writing (in the press, for example) or orally, at open meetings.

Each scenario in the chapters that follow outlines a problem—a change involving multiple, public constituencies—that becomes apparent as you read the story: Perhaps guns and other weapons begin to appear at a local high school, and students, parents, and administrators must decide how to respond. Perhaps a proposed land development might severely alter the lifestyles of the people who live in a small, rural community. Perhaps there is a move to limit Internet access at the local library, where just about anyone can access and download what some term "pornography." Because many of the issues in the scenarios are public in nature, part II in a way represents a return to the origins of rhetoric, when citizens (unfortunately, only males in those days) discussed and debated public and civic problems and issues.

We don't provide solutions for the questions these scenarios raise. Rather, we ask you to develop your own. Proposed solutions are never "right" or "wrong"; there is no single solution for the issues these scenarios present. Instead, any proposal will have multiple positive and negative aspects. All our classes develop distinct and different ideas for how best to solve the problems and issues we ask them to confront.

WHY USE SCENARIOS?

In Part II: The Scenarios, stories anchor each chapter, forming the impetus for writing assignments and other activities. We've used this approach for a number of reasons:

- Stories catch our interest more quickly than does instructional text. Because of that, we believe you'll find the scenarios interesting and enjoyable to read.

- The narrative format enables you and your classmates to understand the issues quickly and, because we ask you to become actively involved in each scenario, to easily take on the role of one of the interested parties. By assuming the role of someone affected by the scenario, you become involved in working (in collaboration with your classmates) to solve the problems and issues the scenario presents. You and several of your classmates will decide together how the scenario affects you, including your reasons for having the concerns you do; the ideas you have for solving the problem; and the effect(s) your proposed solution might have on your group, as well as on the other groups affected by the situation.

- You should find it easy to sympathize and empathize with the (fictitious) people in each story because each scenario addresses public, civic, or ethical issues and problems of the kind you and your families may one day face.

- You'll learn that gathering information, discussing research, and working as a member of a small group of classmates enhances the work you do on your own. As a group you can gather more information than any of you would if you worked alone. Collaboration also helps you to better understand your research, because you share and discuss what you find with your classmates. And because group activities are designed so that each member is responsible for some part of the group assignment, no one member has to carry the rest of his or her group by doing the lion's share of the work.

- The scenario approach involves you in knowledge making—not just in knowledge finding and knowledge presenting. By working with your classmates to determine the best solution or solutions to a given set of issues and problems, you construct a new way of addressing the developments outlined in each scenario. This is knowledge creation. (You also discover information in your research, and you may present your solution in writing and orally if your instructor asks you to do so.)

- Each scenario asks you to work collectively toward a consensus on the best solution(s) to a particular problem at a particular moment in time for a specific group of people. This approach simulates the way in which social and other problems are addressed in life. If you had a personal problem, you might work with family members to solve it; if you had a business problem, you'd collaborate with your coworkers; if there were a problem in your neighborhood, you might get together with your neighbors to decide what to do; if your city or town faced a difficulty of some sort, you'd work with the other residents of your community to solve it.

In addition to working with your classmates to discover possible solutions to the problems you'll explore, you'll also have the opportunity to express your own position. At the end of each scenario, you'll construct an individual writing assignment. You work toward the construction of this assignment as you participate in the group activities addressing the scenario: as you discuss and determine what your group believes, as you conduct research and share information, and as you compose a collaborative group statement and perhaps share an open discussion with everyone in your class. By the time your instructor asks you to compose your individual writing, you'll be well prepared to do so.

WORKING WITH THE SCENARIOS

As you begin reading through a scenario, think about how the elements of the rhetorical situation—occasion, purpose, topic, audience, and writer—interact. Paying close attention to the circumstances in the scenarios will make your writing decisions easier. The techniques you learned in part I of this text should inform your interaction with each scenario. You'll draw on your understanding of what a rhetorical situation is, ways to conduct research and critically read the sources you find, your writing process, and how to evaluate and use your research in your text to support your position.

Each scenario provides an authentic *occasion* for writing: problems and issues that might affect you and your classmates. For the first few activities in each scenario, your instructor will ask you to work with several of your classmates, as a member of one of the groups involved with the scenario, to consider all aspects of the problem or issue your group faces.

The Collaborative Statement

Working through the various stages of the writing process, your group then composes a collaborative statement outlining what it thinks about the problems facing it in the scenario. Your group addresses its statement to the individual or group it believes has the ability to resolve the problem. To prepare the collaborative statement, you and the other members of your group:

1. Read about and discuss the issues presented in the scenario.
2. Work with invention activities (including brainstorming, free-writing, and clustering) to help you understand the problems and issues.
3. Compose a first draft of a collaborative statement.
4. Work to revise that draft so that it clearly articulates your message.
5. Share your draft with other groups, so all can make suggestions.
6. Read additional sources on the issue, and complete more invention activities to further clarify your ideas.

7. Revise your draft until you're satisfied that it's ready for editing and publishing.

For this collaborative writing, you have a specific *purpose:* to inform your audience of your group's thinking about the scenario, or to propose a solution to some of the problems you face, or to persuade your audience to help modify the situation, or to explain what others have done in similar circumstances. You draw on your knowledge of rhetorical strategies and appeals to compose a statement that delivers your message to a particular *audience,* for a specific purpose. As you work to capture your ideas on paper, you should begin to clarify what you really think, as well as ways in which you feel the problem represented in a scenario should be solved. In other words, you clarify your ideas about the issue through the process of writing about them.

Research—and the Readings

To offer context and background information for each scenario, we provide a range of readings related to that scenario's subject; we've also followed each reading with questions about the text. These questions will help you and your classmates understand the readings and think about how they relate to other texts you've read and discussed. We've selected readings that provide the same type of information you'd look for if you really were involved in the scenario; they are taken from a range of sources, including newspapers, magazines, journals, books, and the Internet. Evaluate and use the information and data in these readings to support your group's position and to construct your individual writing projects. Your instructor may ask you to read all or only some of the readings.

As you work with the readings, you'll use the research tools you've already learned, including summarizing, paraphrasing, and annotating. You'll evaluate the readings for credibility. If you keep a writer's journal, you might record the details of what you read, the ways in which ideas connect and support one another, the questions that arise, and any visual aids your research uncovers (such as graphs, drawings, and photographs). The information you record in your journal can serve as research for your compositions, as you integrate what you learn from those readings into your writing, to support your thesis.

The Open Meeting

Your instructor might ask you and your classmates to follow your collaborative written statement with an "open meeting" in which each group presents its ideas orally and, perhaps, questions members of the other groups. These open discussions can help you further clarify your thinking and better understand the problems and issues the scenario portrays.

Individual Writing

When you've completed your collaborative work, you next construct an individual writing assignment; your instructor will select the assignment you are to focus on from the options offered for each scenario. This is your opportunity to use all of what you've learned to this point in the scenario: you can draw on your readings, discussions, collaborative writing, and journal writing (and perhaps a whole-class open meeting) to compose your individual paper. At the end of each scenario, there are suggestions for further writing and research.

Because much of what you do as you work through a scenario depends on collaborating effectively with your classmates, let's discuss how you can best do that.

WORKING TOGETHER EFFECTIVELY

The first step toward group or collaborative work is to discuss and share. When you collaborate or work together in class, you share some of your ideas and writing with your classmates. Later, you might have the opportunity to present your ideas to the entire class.

Listen, Speaking, Collaborating

Listening, speaking, and collaborating in a classroom setting might seem simple enough. But think critically about each of these terms, and consider how the rhetorical situation influences how we define them:

- *Listening:* What does it mean to really listen? Is simply hearing the words enough, or does listening mean making an effort to understand what the speaker is saying? Do you listen in different ways to different people? Why? In what ways? How can you indicate to the speaker that you fully understand what he or she is saying? What activities (such as taking notes) might help you become a better listener?

- *Speaking:* What does it mean to fully and clearly explain something to another person? How can you know if your listener understands what you're saying? Is speaking the same as writing, but in oral form? How do you translate ideas expressed on paper into something a listener can grasp? How do you clearly put into words the ideas in your mind?

- *Collaborating:* The word *collaborate* means to work together, but what activities does that include? Does collaboration imply an equality among those involved? Does it mean that each must do his or her share of the work? How do you know whether someone is carrying his or her full load? What steps can you take to ensure that a small group functions as it should?

Cooperative Learning

Here's an example of how these activities—listening, speaking, and collaborating—interact with one another. Much of the initial work you'll do for each scenario requires that you work in small groups, each representing an interested party—someone who has a stake in the issues involved.

If you've been involved in such group activities in the past, you might have found your experiences productive and helpful. Perhaps you found group work both useful and informative, especially when collaboration generated more information than each group member might have found alone. Did you notice, however, that sometimes not everyone in a group did an equal amount of the work?

The group work in which you'll participate as you engage the scenarios might not be the same as what you've undertaken in the past. Our approach is modeled on "cooperative learning." When we ask you and your classmates to perform a cooperative activity, we mean that you collaborate or work together toward a common goal. Each member of the group has a specific role to play and activities for which he or she is responsible.

Suppose that your group is asked to collect information on an issue that your class is investigating: one member might locate relevant information in the college library, another student might collect information from the Internet, and still another might interview several people. Then each of you shares with the others the information you've collected. Each group member must be actively involved if you are to complete your assigned task.

You contribute to your group in several ways. You conduct research, and you report the results of that research to the group. Whenever you are asked to participate in a group activity, each of you is assigned a specific role:

- *Task manager:* The task manager keeps the group focused and ensures that it is ready to report its findings when called on to do so.
- *Recorder:* The recorder writes down decisions made by the group.
- *Speaker:* The job of the speaker is to report the group's findings to the entire class. Often, the recorder creates a written document containing the group's main points; the speaker then elaborates on and explains those main points to the rest of the class.
- *Questioner:* The questioner, or devil's advocate, deliberately questions what the group is doing and the decisions the group makes, to help ensure that it stays on the right track.

At times, your instructor may combine some of these roles (especially in smaller groups). In other situations, your teacher may assign more than one student to each role, especially if you're working on a more complex activity.

For some scenarios, you might be asked to assume a role that's antithetical to your feelings about the issue or problem. If this happens, it's important to realize that you can learn a lot by being part of a group with which you don't completely agree. To study an issue from a new or different perspective or to promote a solution with which you don't fully agree often helps you to truly understand your own thinking. When you adopt a position that appears to be opposed to what you believe, you can stretch your thinking—you can grow and change.

Composing a Group Statement

As part of the group work, each group is asked to outline its views about the issues and problems each scenario presents in a brief statement. These statements—usually only two pages in length—can take a variety of forms, including a letter to the editor, a guest editorial for the local newspaper, or a statement to the government agency that might solve the problem. Constructing these collaborative statements helps you clarify your ideas.

One effective approach to constructing a group statement is for each group member to compose his or her own statement, listing the most important issues and problems. Then, working collectively, group members draw on the individual comments to construct a group statement.

Another effective approach for putting together a group statement is to take the notes each group member has made (from readings and discussions), designate one group member to record the group's ideas, and then collaboratively compose an initial draft of what your group thinks. This might seem somewhat hectic the first time you try it, with several group members offering suggestions on what to write and how to write it, but, if you give the process some time, you'll find that working together is an interesting and useful way to get your collective ideas onto paper.

Once you have a first draft of your collaborative statement, each group member should read through it, marking any sections that are unclear. Work together to clarify those parts. Next, each group member should read the statement once more, this time looking for places in the text where an argument might require more evidence. Then, again working together, decide which of the pieces of evidence gathered during your research (facts, data, testimony, statistics) might provide additional support for the points you're trying to make. The idea is to read through and carefully revise your draft several times, to ensure that your group's ideas are expressed as clearly as possible.

Your instructor may ask you to read and comment on each others' papers (your group statements or your individual assignments). Working together in that way gives you the chance to help your classmates become better writers: by acting as a real reader and indicating where in the text you need more information, where you find the writing confusing, or where additional elaboration might be useful, you can help your classmates improve their composition.

Speaking at an Open Meeting

Once each group has constructed and revised its written statement, your instructor may ask you to participate in an open meeting in which group members present their ideas to the entire class. In such a meeting, instructors might allow groups to question one another. This kind of oral give-and-take helps you continue to clarify your ideas; it also helps you learn to answer objections to your group's position.

If your instructor asks your group to participate in an open meeting, your group must adapt its written statement for oral presentation. Speaking to a group is not the same as reading a written statement aloud. An oral argument differs from a written presentation in two ways: you must anticipate questions from your audience, and you must make all connections explicit.

When you speak to a large group, your listeners can ask questions about what you've said. It's important to anticipate the questions your audience might ask (some may be difficult to answer) so that you are prepared with appropriate responses.

In an open meeting, you scrutinize the presentations of others, and they pay close attention to your presentation. They might have questions about statements you make, or they might disagree with an assertion you make. Prepare yourself by trying to anticipate your audience's reaction:

- What questions do you think they might have?
- What in your statement might be confusing?
- How might you make your points more clearly?
- Are you providing enough support for your proposed solution?

As you listen to the other speakers, take notes. Keep track of any questions you have or any points you'd like to challenge later. How do the other groups' positions affect yours? Where do you agree and disagree? You might think that you'll remember your questions, but it's always best to take careful written notes.

When ideas are presented in writing, the reader can review earlier passages to clarify what the writer said, but, in a spoken presentation, the listener does not have this same opportunity. Therefore, the speaker must make each connection explicit, so that listeners can readily follow along and understand what is being said. In an open meeting, your group's presenter must be organized and logical, just as your written group statement must be organized and logical.

Give your spokesperson an opportunity to practice in front of the group so that group members can offer advice and ask questions. You might ask one or more members to play the role of devil's advocate, taking an op-posing view for the purpose of identifying possible flaws in your speaker's position. You should be critical but supportive; in this way you can iden-tify flaws in the presentation while the speaker practices his or her delivery.

LOOKING FOR SCENARIOS IN YOUR OWN LIFE

Now that you understand the concept behind the scenario approach—a simulation of active participation in solving real-life problems and is-sues—keep your eyes open for scenario-like situations in your personal or academic life, in your community, or at work. Then apply what you're learning as you work through the scenarios to solving *real* problems, to finding the best solutions for *real* issues.

Think about the places in your life where you might find scenario-like situations:

- *Professional/work life:* One of our scenarios focuses on a library in a small town—and whether its computers should be monitored or censored in some manner. The librarians and others who work at the library have a stake in the issue, as do the library's patrons—including students and children who both need access to informa-tion.

    In your own work environment, there might be potential con-flicts that require groups to work together to search for an ac-ceptable resolution. For example, you might face a change in working conditions, in which you (and your fellow workers) must interact with the owners of the firm, perhaps a labor union, gov-ernment agencies, and others. Or you might encounter some other sort of change in the workplace (a different manufacturing arrangement, new cubicles for office staff, or a change in insur-ance options) that would require various groups to work together to find and implement the best solution.

- *Community life:* One scenario in this text asks if it is acceptable for a community to resell the firearms it confiscates if it uses the funds it collects for worthwhile purposes. Does your community do this? Should it?

    Life in your town is constantly in flux: construction of new roads or freeways, modifications in community services, perhaps a pro-posed new power plant nearby, changes in methods for disposal of hazardous waste, a proposal to alter how your local government functions, or plans to construct a huge "superstore" down the street from where you live.

- *Academic life:* In this text, one scenario focuses on a move to dis-tance learning at a college. Do online classes (or does pursuing an online degree) provide the same educational benefits as the traditional model? What should a college education consist of? Is a degree from an online college "worth" as much as a degree from a traditional institution? Why or why not?

What changes are there in your personal education world? Have changes recently been made at or are they proposed for your campus community? Is there a proposal to build a new dorm? Have new restrictions on bicycles on campus been posted? Are there policy changes at the campus day care center? The health center? Are there recycling issues? Safety concerns? Student protests of some kind? A change in the way the administration enforces some of its rules? A proposal to eliminate an important or popular degree program?

- *Personal life:* One of our scenarios centers on a changing situation at a local high school, where weapons begin to appear. Have there recently been changes at your siblings', cousins', or children's schools? Another of the scenarios centers on quality-of-life issues, as well as property rights. What is occurring in your neighborhood? Are your general living conditions deteriorating in some way? What about your quality of life?

Appendix B offers another approach for extending the skills you'll develop as you work with the scenarios in part II. The concept of service learning benefits your community as it helps you expand and enhance your thinking and writing abilities.

GETTING STARTED

Now it's time to become involved: to read, discuss, research, and work to solve the problems the scenarios in chapters 4–9 present. One bit of advice: pretend that you really belong to the group you're assigned to and participate actively. You'll find that you learn a lot while your writing improves.

CHAPTER 4

Education Today

WHO NEEDS THE CLASSROOM, ANYWAY?

Netscape: Online college degrees – online degree programs at Canyon College

Back | Forward | Reload | Home | Search | Netscape | Images | Print | Security | Shop | Stop

Go To: http://www.canyoncollege.edu/   What's Related

WebMail | Contact | People | Yellow Pages | Download | Mac Guru Brian

Earn your online college degrees at Canyon College.

Enroll today in any number of
online degrees or online courses and certificate programs !

View the online college degrees and courses offered by Canyon College by selecting a link below.

- List of Online Degrees
- Business Administration
- Psychology
- Health Care Administration
- Counseling
- Social Work
- Theology
- Divinity
- List of Online Courses

- List of Online Certificate Programs
- Legal Nurse Consultant
- Travel Agent Training
- Holistic Nursing and Wellness Counseling
- Hypnosis
- Case Management
- Paralegal Training
- Grief Counseling
- Continuing Education Courses

Canyon College offers a unique opportunity for students to earn their Bachelors, or Masters in any one of the online college degrees offered and in the convenience of their home or office! Students may also earn an online Associates degree in Business Administration.

- Associates - ABA
- Bachelors - BBA, BS, BA
- Masters - MBA, MS, MA

Students may also take individual online courses in a wide range of disciplines. Canyon College also offers continuing education courses online.

As with other online colleges which offer online degrees and courses, Canyon College offers you a truly online experience. Enroll today to start in any one of the online college degrees or courses offered above and earn your college credits online. Start your college degree online today and earn your Associates, Bachelors or Masters degree from the comfort of your home or office!

◆ **FIRST IMPRESSIONS** ◆

Be sure to look at and think about the photographs that introduce this chapter. Then spend a few minutes jotting down answers to these questions:

- Do you think you could effectively learn in the environment suggested by the first photograph—working on a laptop computer while sitting under a tree? Or is the more traditional method more effective for you, as portrayed in the second photograph? Why?
- The advertisement lists a number of degree programs that can be completed over the Internet. Are there classes or degrees that should not be offered over the Internet? Why or why not?
- The photograph of the University of Phoenix portrays a modern, businesslike environment, while the photograph of a more customary campus portrays a different atmosphere. Which do you prefer? Why?
- How do you define a "college education"? Do you think in terms of number of credit hours, or subjects studied, or selecting a major, or knowledge gained, or skills demonstrated, or what?
- How do you see your own college education? What do you hope to gain from attending college?
- What is your initial reaction to the concept of "distance learning"?
- Would you want to take an online class? Why or why not?
- What might be the benefits of taking a college class over the Internet? The problems?

Your instructor might suggest that you use your responses to these questions as a starting point for discussion. Hold onto them because they'll help you in the other activities in this scenario.

Throughout the country, colleges and universities are undergoing dramatic change. The days of college campuses lined with red brick buildings covered with ivy, where full-time students live in dormitories and earn their degrees before heading out into the working world, seem to be far behind us. Many students are commuters, fitting their schooling into a tight schedule already filled with family and work. Often these students reverse the traditional college track: they've been in the working world and are coming back to college, either for the degree they never earned or for another one to further their career goals. These students don't live on campus; they stop there before or after work.

Increasingly, colleges and universities have tried to accommodate nontraditional students by offering more classes early in the morning or late in the evening, opening branch campuses in locations convenient to these students, and delivering classes through what is known as distance education. Through some form of distance education, colleges bring class materials to their students, rather than insisting that students come to campus.

The traditional college course is taught in a classroom, where students and instructor meet regularly. In contrast, courses offered through distance education might never require that students and instructor be in the same place at the same time.

In the past, distance learning has often meant correspondence courses: students mailed in their assignments; and lectures, if any, were provided on videotape or audiotape. In many communities, college courses, and particularly community college courses, are offered through public access television stations.

Today, distance education often means courses taught over the Internet. Instructors and students exchange assignments and homework via e-mail or through a Web site. Discussions, if they occur, might take place in an online chat room or through an electronic bulletin board to which students post their questions or comments.

Technological advances are only one factor at play in the creation of online classes. As college degrees become a prerequisite for more careers, most people find they need a degree to advance. This demand has increased enrollments at many colleges and universities, and it has even spurred the creation of for-profit colleges such as DeVry and the University of Phoenix. Harcourt Publishing has formed a distance-learning subsidiary, Harcourt Learning Direct. Arizona's Rio Salado Community College does not have a single classroom: all of its classes are offered electronically— over the Internet, on CD-ROMs, and so on. Some have decried these changes as a relaxation of academic standards or a packaging of education as a product to be sold rather than a process to undertake.

Your own college might offer courses over the Internet. Perhaps you have not given it much thought, but such classes raise a number of issues:

- *Convenience:* If you can complete assignments at any time, it might be easier to fit school into your already full schedule.

- *Quality of instruction:* Is there something important lacking when courses are taken out of the classroom? Is there anything that might make a distance-learning class better than a traditional one?

- *Learning styles:* Some people learn better at their own pace with an instructor who acts simply as a guide. Others might need the structure of regular class meetings to keep them on track.

- *Access:* People with mobility difficulties or those who live in isolated areas might find Internet-based coursework the only practical way to earn a degree.

Online classes offer economic benefits to the schools as well. Such courses don't require additional classroom space, a scarce commodity on many campuses. Part-time faculty who teach online courses don't need office space (they can work from home). Of course, online classes can require a substantial commitment of funds for the technology needed, and instructors often require training before they can teach these classes.

As with many new ideas, faculty, administrators, students, and even alumni have mixed reactions to the prospect of moving education onto the Internet. What if there were a proposal to begin offering some online courses at your college or university? Imagine that you attend a school that has decided to make such a change. The college's chancellor has announced that the school will move some of its classes onto the Internet as a first step toward offering complete degree programs through distance learning. The announcement comes as a bit of a surprise to the campus community, and it means a number of important changes and adjustments. Some members of the campus community find the idea exciting; others find it frightening. Imagine that:

- You are a student who might like to take at least some of your classes online. Do you worry that you won't learn as much as you would in a traditional classroom? Are you comfortable enough with your computer skills to take an online class? Would it concern you if you took a class where the only way to reach your teacher was through e-mail?

- You have been teaching for fifteen years, and you have worked hard to improve the way in which you teach your students. Would you see the addition of Internet classes as an intriguing challenge to your skills, a possible compromise of educational standards, or an unwelcome addition to your workload? Why?

- You graduated from college thirty years ago, and you look back on your classroom experiences as an important part of your education. Do you think that those experiences could be duplicated in an online chat room? Do you want your alma mater to move into the future or stay grounded in its traditions?

- As an administrator, you would have to work out the logistics of making the move to online education happen. What resources does the college have already? What would it need to acquire? Do you see the move to distance learning as a lowering of academic standards or as a way to encourage more students to take your college's courses?

The scenario that follows examines some of the issues that new technologies have introduced into higher education. Although computers in the classroom have caused some debate, the prospect of students being able to earn a degree without setting foot on a campus raises questions about what a college education should be. Our current models for higher education go back centuries, and although there have been changes, none have been so drastic as the possibility of virtual colleges.

Although this scenario takes place at a small college, the questions that the situation raises apply to any institution that is considering Internet classes, whether it is a large university, a small college, or a community college. The particulars will be different everywhere because the needs of the campus population will help shape the decisions that are made, but the central questions about what makes a college education and whether the Internet can provide it remain the same.

You and your classmates will form teams that represent the various constituencies involved in shaping online education. You'll work, by yourself and in collaboration, on tasks that you might face if you encountered this situation at your own school.

Like all of our scenarios, this one provides a launching point for further research, discussion, and writing—in this case, about the intersection of technology and education, both in the classroom and outside of it. As you read and write, keep your eyes open for aspects of the discussion that you might explore further.

We provide you with an array of sources that discuss and comment on online education. These selections should give you a sense of some of the issues involved, and they let you sample what has already been said on the subject. There is much more information available, as you'll find when you do your own research.

THE SCENARIO

The Chancellor Makes an Announcement

Hearthwood College is a small, four-year school located not far from Pittsburgh, Pennsylvania. When Hearthwood was founded in the late nineteenth century, it was situated deep enough in the wooded hills that the trip to the city took nearly half a day. Things have changed, and the city's suburbs now surround Hearthwood's once-rural campus. Although most of the school's students live on or near campus, a growing number are commuters who stop for a class or two in the evenings after work. They are earning their degrees while working and raising families. Hearthwood recognizes the importance of this growing element of its student population, and the administration has responded by offering more classes in the evenings, and even some very early in the morning and on Saturdays.

Meanwhile, the campus is also experiencing something of a space crisis. There are only five classroom buildings, and as the student population has grown, finding space for all of the classes has become an increasing headache. Hearthwood faces some hard choices. Building more classroom space would be costly because most of the land around the campus is occupied. Constructing a new building would mean sacrificing part of Hearthwood Green, the only sizable plot of land left on campus. For years the Green has been a free-speech area, as well as the spot for the annual homecoming rally. Tearing up the Green would be unpopular, to say the least, among both students and alumni.

But this September, during Hearthwood's fall convocation ceremony, Chancellor Beatrice Dunwald stunned the gathered students and their families. After finishing her customary welcoming remarks, she departed from the speech she'd used every semester for the past four years:

> As we begin this new century, Hearthwood College must move forward without losing touch with our past. The past ten years have seen great changes in the college and the community around us, and we must recognize those changes and adjust to them. We must act rather than react, if we are going to continue our proud tradition. We must have a plan for our future.
>
> You all know that Hearthwood strives to be at the forefront of educational innovation. As of this fall, all of the dormitory rooms are wired for Internet access, every student has a free e-mail account, and the college Web site offers students access to their schedules and grades. Our plan is to take things a step farther. At the start of school next fall, Hearthwood College will begin offering classes on the Internet. These classes might never physically meet, but they will offer students the high-quality education that has always been associated with Hearthwood. We believe that such a move is not only inevitable, but also desirable. It will help alleviate our crowding problems, it will allow students more flexible scheduling, and it will keep our college at the forefront. In addition to our traditional programs, our long-term goal is to offer full degree programs in many majors online.
>
> I know that the transition might be difficult or even frightening, and so I want us all, the whole campus community, to collaborate actively. Together we can make Hearthwood an even greater school than it already is!

With that, Chancellor Dunwald left the podium. Since then, the campus has been abuzz with speculation and debate about her announcement. Students, faculty, administrators, and alumni have mixed feelings about the idea and plenty of questions. What classes will be offered online? Who will teach them? Can anyone take them? Will some classes be offered only online? Won't it be too easy to cheat? A joke makes the rounds about earning a degree without ever getting out of your bathrobe. What if you can't afford a computer? Is this online approach really necessary? Will tuition be cheaper for online classes? If an online course is just as good, why go to class at all?

As the spring semester starts, these questions hang in the air. Chancellor Dunwald asks faculty, administrators, alumni, and students to enter into a discussion of the plan, with that conversation to begin in the pages of the *Hearthwood Herald*, the daily campus newspaper. All perspectives are invited, and all suggestions are welcome.

ENTERING THE SCENARIO: WHAT MAKES A COLLEGE EDUCATION?

Now that you've been introduced to the scenario, your instructor will place you in a group with several of your classmates. These groups represent the various people—constituencies—who are concerned with how to move Hearthwood into online education. It's not necessary that your group come to a complete consensus about how you feel. In most situations people have mixed feelings. Your task is to represent what you think would be the real concerns of people in your group. To start, read all of the group descriptions that follow to get a sense of the issues involved, paying closest attention to the description of the group to which you've been assigned. The next step involves "fleshing out" your group description and your group's perspective based on how you and the members of your group feel about online education.

Hearthwood College Students

Hearthwood College attracts students from a wide range of backgrounds. Some are traditional students—recent high school graduates who live in dormitories, attend school full-time, and see the campus as the center of their academic and social lives. A sizable minority, though, are nontraditional students. These students range in age from their early twenties into their seventies. Most are part-time students supporting themselves and, sometimes, their families. They take classes when they can, knowing that it will take them much longer than four years to earn a degree.

These two groups of students are very different. The traditional students come to Hearthwood from as far away as Montana, and they come for the experience as much as the education. The nontraditional students are mostly locals who attend the college because it is close to their homes. For the traditional students, online classes simply mean not having to get up early to get to class. For many of the commuter students, however, online classes mean being able to have dinner with their families or not having to hire a babysitter. Still, despite their differences, these two groups of students share a desire to get the most out of their education.

Probably only a few of you in the student group are willing to sacrifice quality for convenience, and many of you might wonder whether something might not be missing from the educational experience when it moves online. And be honest: Are a few of you wondering whether you are self-motivated enough to get everything done without the requirement of regular classroom attendance? Do some of you worry that a degree from a virtual university won't carry as much weight with potential employers once you've graduated and are looking for a job?

Hearthwood's Faculty

Like those of the students, the faculty group's reactions to the chancellor's announcement are mixed. Some look forward to teaching an online class; others are skeptical.

Because your own education occurred almost entirely in the classroom, many of you might worry about how tried-and-true methods of teaching will migrate to the Internet. After all, conducting an online discussion is a very different thing than running a classroom exchange. Some of you, frankly, might be frightened by the idea. Perhaps you aren't comfortable using computers for anything other than word processing, and even that is often frustrating. You wonder what advantages online classes offer you.

Others in your group might suspect that cheating would be rampant in an online structure. How could you know who was really doing the work on the other end?

You've also heard "horror stories" from colleagues who've taught online classes: stories about students who continue to ask for help electronically long after the course has concluded; students who submit papers or ask questions in a random fashion, forcing the teacher to deal with a number of subject areas at the same time; and more.

What concerns some of you isn't the idea of offering a few classes online. That seems to make sense, and many classes would translate quite well. Your concern involves the practicality of offering a full degree online. How can students do chemistry experiments online? Would you trust your life to a heart surgeon who had received her degree online? How do you answer a student's questions online?

Your concerns go well beyond simple conservatism or fear of change. Some of you might wonder if a move toward Internet education isn't a sign that college degrees are being packaged for delivery, just like any other product. Once that happens, won't those degrees devalue as colleges compete with one another to see which can offer a degree at the least cost? Most of you went into teaching because you enjoy the process—including the face-to-face interaction with students. You now worry that the process will be changed forever.

Parents of Hearthwood Students

In many cases, especially for traditional students, parents are the ones who, every semester, write the checks to pay Hearthwood's tuition bills. How might members of this group feel about the chancellor's ideas?

Some of you might have college degrees and fond memories of your educational experiences; others might never have attended college. Collectively, what do you think a college education should consist of? How can you ensure that your sons and daughters get good value for your tuition dollars? Are you concerned that an Internet degree won't be worth the paper it's printed on?

On the other hand, flexible course scheduling might mean that your son or daughter could more easily hold down a job while taking classes, and so pay for more of his or her educational expenses.

The College's Administrators

The deans, department chairpersons, and other administrators will have to deal with the nuts and bolts of the changes to online instruction. They are the ones who will decide which courses are offered online, who teaches them, and how they are structured.

As a member of this group, you already have your hands full trying to coordinate all the activities of a busy campus. Hearthwood's aggressive move to computerize over the past few years means that the college probably has much of the computing power it needs for online instruction. The school doesn't, however, have enough trained faculty or support staff with the knowledge and experience to offer classes online.

You and the other members of the administration might see the move to Internet classes as a double-edged sword: it might help alleviate some of the overcrowding issues, but it will likely create a whole new set of problems.

On the plus side, such a move should help increase the prestige of Hearthwood, reflecting well on the administration. On the minus side, however, there are untold problems and risks in such a move.

Members of the Hearthwood Alumni Association

The Hearthwood Alumni Association (HAA) is a strong presence in campus affairs. You are a loyal and vociferous bunch, and many of you contribute substantial amounts of money to the college. As a group, HAA holds fund-raisers, helps to organize Homecoming Week and its large rally on the Green, and volunteers in various capacities on campus. HAA members work closely with corporate recruiters to arrange job interviews for graduating Hearthwood seniors.

Your central concern is that Hearthwood maintain its strong reputation and that it continue to offer a valuable educational experience. Like all of the other groups, you might be split in your feelings about the chancellor's plan. You like the idea of Hearthwood being on the cutting edge of new technology, but some of you might mutter disparaging comments about "Hearthwood-dot-com."

PARTICIPATING WITHIN YOUR HEARTHWOOD GROUP

Now that you've read the scenario and the group descriptions, you're ready to participate actively. Your instructor will ask you, along with your classmates, to role-play as a representative of the group you've joined. To role-play, you put yourself in the place of someone in that group, and explore how you think you might feel if you were that person. Remember that the group descriptions are merely starting points. They should help you get into character, but there are many more issues involved than those raised in the brief descriptions. Use the questions in Box 4.1: Your Initial Discussion about Hearthwood to focus the group discussion.

As was clear in the group descriptions, no group is likely to be completely unified. Group members will express a range of opinions, often as a result of diversity in their backgrounds and experiences. A student who is attending school at night while working and raising a family will likely feel differently about the chancellor's proposal than will a nineteen-year-old traditional student. A parent who had a good educational experience when she attended college might feel differently about Internet classes than a parent who's recently taken some distance-learning classes. Before beginning your group discussion, read Box 4.2: Representing the Range of Opinion for suggestions your group can apply to encourage members to explore their positions.

TAKING A POSITION: WRITING TO THE *HEARTHWOOD HERALD*

The first writing task of this scenario asks your group to compose a collaborative guest editorial for the campus newspaper, in which your group expresses its view on the chancellor's plan. This editorial (limited to two pages in length) is a chance for your voice to be heard in the debate about online education. Your audience will be the readers of the *Hearthwood Herald,* which includes pretty much everyone on campus. Within that audience, you are particularly interested in influencing the chancellor because she will have a hand in making many of the most important decisions.

Later, as you continue to work with this scenario, you will compose an individual writing assignment, so think of this collaborative editorial as a first step in determining your own ideas about online education.

RESOURCES: EDUCATION.COM?

Before joining the debate on an issue, it's wise to have some idea of what has already been said and written about it. Before your group writes its editorial for the campus newspaper, your instructor might ask you to

BOX 4.1 APPLYING WHAT YOU READ
Your Initial Discussion about Hearthwood

Working with the other members of your group, discuss and record what you think about these issues:

- What are the five most serious concerns your group has with the changes planned for Hearthwood?
- Which of the other groups are most likely to share some of your viewpoints on Hearthwood?
- What kinds of classes should be offered online? Why?
- What types of resistance to your position might you expect? How might you respond to this resistance?
- Think about the practicalities of putting classes and degree programs online: Who might gain from this change? Who might suffer? In what ways?
- Is anything lost or gained in taking a class online? What?
- What issues in this scenario do you find especially interesting? What issues concern your group more than they do the other groups? What issues are you and members of your group least interested in?

When you're done, your instructor might ask you to share your comments with the rest of your class.

do some research into online education at other institutions, to learn how they've resolved the issues that now face Hearthwood College. You might also want to interview professors and administrators at your college, to find out how they would make some of the decisions outlined in this scenario.

Our readings provide a sampling of what others have to say about the distance-education debate. The writers represented here examine many of the same questions that you're now exploring in this scenario. Although they don't always agree, these readings might offer insights or perspectives that you and your group haven't thought of. The scope and details of an issue become clear through the process of exploration: by discussion with peers and through research. Keep in mind the reading strategies you learned earlier (prereading, annotating, summarizing, and so on), and make use of them to interact actively with these readings.

Walt Whitman is, of course, a well-known poet. You might wonder why we begin this chapter's readings with one of his short poems—but we expect that you'll enjoy making connections between what Whitman has to say and your educational experiences.

No matter which interested party you represent, you'll learn from Robert Cwiklik's report of what education might look like in the future—and will have a chance to consider how that future fits into your educational plans. Jamie P. Merisotis and Jody K. Olsen outline the current

BOX 4.2 APPLYING WHAT YOU READ
Representing the Range of Opinion

To help your group generate a fuller range of ideas, each group member should adopt the persona, or role, of a person who would belong to the real group. For example, one member of the faculty group might represent an assistant professor who is anxious to try online teaching; another might represent a full professor known for his dynamic classroom presence who is skeptical of the supposed benefits. Still another might adopt the persona of an instructor who fears and resents the intrusion of technology into the educational process.

For the first part of this activity, brainstorm with your group members a list of all the positions that might exist within your group. Then assign these positions to various group members.

Now, think about the position you're representing. How would someone in your position feel? What are the implications of this change for someone like you? How might it affect your life? Are you in favor of the proposed change at Hearthwood? Against it? Ambivalent? Can you see the positive aspects of a move to online education? The problems?

Finally, as a group, generate a list of the concerns, advantages, and observations that your members have identified. Everyone should keep a copy of this list: it's valuable invention work that all can draw on later in the scenario, and it will serve as research for individual writing projects.

When you're done, your instructor might ask you to share your "personas" with other members of the class.

debate on distance learning, and it's only right that their discussion takes place in an online forum.

If you represent the interests of students, you'll find that writer David Koeppel brings home the debate on distance education with specific examples: stories about real people who have pursued an education online. Faculty and administrator groups will be especially interested in the analyses presented by Pamela Mendels and Dan Carnevale, as they highlight problems associated with online learning, and in the revolutionary proposal reported by Jodie Morse for a free online university. James Perley and Denise Marie Tanguay take these concerns to a higher level in their look at accreditation, or what constitutes a college class. Finally, Steven Crow responds to a number of questions and concerns, arguing that online education can be equivalent to the more traditional model.

The selections that follow will also help you as you complete the writing tasks later in this scenario, and they might provide you with avenues to pursue in your own research. You'll be asked to draw on the information in these readings for the collaborative statement your group will compose and, later on, for your individual writing. Given your initial discussion with the members of your group, think about how your group will react to each of these readings:

- What points made in these selections reinforce what you discussed within your group?
- Which of these pieces offer evidence (facts, statistics, testimony, and so on) that might undermine your position? How might you respond to such evidence?
- Are there any examples or precedents in the readings that you might cite to support your position?
- What most interests you about these readings? Which readings move you to reconsider your own ideas about education?

As you read these selections, note anything you think might be useful to you as you participate in your group discussion about whether and how Hearthwood should move into Internet education.

◆ READINGS

※ When I Heard the Learn'd Astronomer
Walt Whitman

When I heard the learn'd astronomer,
When the proofs, the figures, were ranged in columns before me,
When I was shown the charts and diagrams, to add, divide, and
    measure them,
When I sitting heard the astronomer where he lectured with much
    applause in the lecture-room,
How soon unaccountable I became tired and sick,   5
Till rising and gliding out I wander'd off by myself,
In the mystical moist night-air, and from time to time,
Look'd up in perfect silence at the stars.

◆ QUESTIONS FOR DISCUSSION AND WRITING ◆

1. Were you surprised that the first reading selection for this scenario was a poem? Why? What is your initial reaction to this short poem? What do you like or dislike about it?

2. In your college classes, do you ever feel like the speaker of this poem, who notes that when "shown the charts and diagrams" and while listening to "the astronomer where he lectured," the speaker "became tired and sick"? Why or why not? Do you think you might feel differently if you heard about and worked with those "charts and diagrams" in an online class? Why or why not?

3. Do you think that Whitman is saying that personal experience (looking "up in perfect silence at the stars") is as valuable—or perhaps even more valuable— than working with "charts and diagrams," or sitting "in the lecture-room"? Why or why not?

4. Do you think that either of the types of learning Whitman describes—sitting and listening to a lecture or looking at the stars yourself—can effectively be replicated in an online class? Why or why not?

5. Have you ever taken an Internet class? If so, what is your sense—now that you're in college—of whether an Internet class is a "real" college or university class? Can you provide details to compare the two types of classes? If you have not taken such a class, would you take one now that you've read a bit about them? Why or why not?

✳ A Different Course

FOR MANY PEOPLE, COLLEGE WILL NO LONGER BE A SPECIFIC PLACE, OR A SPECIFIC TIME

Robert Cwiklik

The Internet could unleash a new force into university life: star power.

Ten years from now, talented university professors may develop whole courses in the form of multimedia lessons distributed well beyond their host universities to masses of students over the Internet, says Jonathan Zittrain, director of Harvard's Berkman Center for Internet and Society. Such products, which Mr. Zittrain likens to "textbooks on steroids," could combine video lectures with coordinated demonstrations on virtual blackboards and create a new class of academic celebrities, with top professors building world-wide reputations.

Star teachers and pumped-up multimedia texts are just two aspects of the future that experts envision for higher education. Of course, the prognosticators differ on specific points in their forecasts. Some see the private sector muscling in on education; some envision a rethinking of the traditional campus; and most see the school library eclipsed by online stacks. But all these forecasts seem to revolve around one agreed-upon premise: In the future, geography is going to matter a lot less.

"Education will change from a place-centered enterprise to an 'education where you need it,'" says Douglas Van Houweling, chief executive of University Corporation for Advanced Internet Development, the Washington-based consortium of universities and private-sector partners established to implement Internet2, a project aimed at enhancing the capacities of the global computer network.

"A decade from now," says Dr. Van Houweling, "it wouldn't surprise me if the majority of education took place in people's homes, in people's offices, on the production line, wherever it is needed." 5

AT THEIR CONVENIENCE

Workers seeking advanced training but lacking the time to pursue on-campus studies, or undergraduates without the means or desire to live on-campus, would be able to tap into, say, a video of a professor's latest lecture "asynchronously"—meaning, not necessarily at the time it was delivered—from their home or workplace desktops.

Such access, while freeing students from rigid class schedules, would also enable them to rewind and review difficult points or fast-forward past obvious ones. And while the lecture runs in the top left corner of their computer screens, students could perhaps watch a graphical display of an important concept in a window on the top right—a combination virtual blackboard and slide projector. Meanwhile, on the bottom left, germane links to other lectures in the course, or in other courses, could be displayed. On the bottom right, students could perhaps monitor live commentary on the class from other students in a chat room, or compose an e-mail query to their instructor.

Glimpses of that vision can be found on the Internet today. Scores of universities now offer online courses that count toward degrees. Their efforts have generally been greeted with enthusiasm as ways of extending educational opportunities beyond the campus.

As a rule, Internet-based courses today aren't nearly as flashy as the predictions. Michael P. Lambert, executive director of the Distance Education and Training Council, a Washington nonprofit group that tracks such efforts, says that most online courses, while making use of e-mail and chat rooms, still amount to "glorified study guides" delivering lessons via pages and pages of plain text. Still, some of the advanced features experts envision are already showing up in universities' online offerings. For example, Stanford University, in Stanford, Calif., offers video lectures with synchronized slide demonstrations. Other advanced features are in the planning stages.

But schools may not be the only institutions delivering online education down the road. Because information technology makes it possible to deliver big chunks of the campus experience without the campus, private-sector players are already contending for a bigger slice of the shifting higher-education market. 10

Ten years down the road, "universities will not enjoy the monopoly they've had in the past," says Daniel E. Atkins, dean of the School of Information at the University of Michigan, in Ann Arbor. Apollo Group Inc., a Phoenix-based education holding company, already offers online accredited degree programs, mainly in business-related subjects, through its wholly owned University of Phoenix. And Kaplan Educational Centers, the standardized-test-preparation unit of *Washington Post* Co., recently announced plans to create an online law school, offering courses taught by teachers also employed at various brick-and-mortar law schools, with the goal of becoming fully accredited.

Both the University of Phoenix and the Kaplan efforts are aimed at working professionals. Some experts say private-sector initiatives in higher education will probably continue to focus on such students, leaving basic instruction in such academic strongholds as science and the humanities largely to universities. Chris Thomsen, director of a commission on technology and education at Stanford University, says that while it "may sound pretty naive," he sees "no threat" that corporations will eclipse universities in such traditional domains.

Mr. Zittrain, of Harvard, says that either of two possible new university models may emerge in response to marketplace changes ushered in by new technologies. On the one hand, elite universities could attempt to leverage their prestige into brand-name dominance of an exploding online market, overwhelming competitors of inferior cachet. That could lead to big changes in the traditional campus: Mr. Zittrain says that students, instead of attending classrooms for an academic year, may make single annual visits to campuses, perhaps a month long, to establish personal contacts with professors and classmates.

Even students who stay on campus year round could have a vastly different experience with teachers. Dr. Van Houweling's Internet2 project is working to enhance the Web's capacity to transmit, among other things, live multimedia productions online. As these enhanced capacities are rolled out over the next few years, he says, universities will increasingly import lectures from faculty all over the world "to get the best" available instruction in a given field.

"The way it feels to be on the campus will change," Dr. Van Houweling   15
says. "It won't any longer be dominated by the faculty who actually live on that campus."

GOING IT ALONE

Then there's another possible model: Mr. Zittrain says individual professors may try to offer their own courses over the Internet, separate from any single institution. Such a strategy, if successful, "could eliminate the university from the calculus," he says. For instance, he says, new accrediting methods could develop to give an online course by a professor with the stature of, say, Harvard Law School's Alan Dershowitz, the status of an accredited university course of today.

Naturally, there could be significant drawbacks to these scenarios. For instance, to the extent that the market power of top universities is driven by their very exclusivity, distribution of their courses over the Internet may threaten to "dilute it" in the eyes of many people, Mr. Zittrain says.

Professors as online celebrities may also pose a danger, says Paul Saffo, director of the Institute for the Future, a Palo Alto, Calif., research and consulting firm. "Does it set in motion a star-making machine that corrupts academia in the same way that TV corrupted football or baseball with outrageous salary differences?"

And what does that mean for professors who aren't stars online? Mr. Zittrain says that even if some instructors develop highly popular online course modules, he says, such offerings are "still going to require some intermediary" to interact with students—to respond to their e-mail queries and grade assignments and tests, among other things. But functioning as such an intermediary may involve "more craft and less art" than current modes of classroom instruction, he says.

Indeed, there are already shadows in the bright dawn of this new educational approach. Some professors are grousing that electronic courses consume a startlingly huge chunk of their time in responding to students' e-mailed queries—far more time, they suggest, than similar queries raised in a classroom, where an answer to one student may satisfy several others as well.

"TOO SIMPLISTIC"

To some, such complaints are just one example of why the Internet won't displace brick-and-mortar universities. The notion that Internet-based distance learning "will suddenly take over all of higher education is far too simplistic," says Robert McClintock, director of the institute for Learning Technologies at Columbia University in New York. He says the Internet will probably be a boon for continuing education, or professional-retraining initiatives, but argues that the full richness of a higher education can't be captured online.

"A great deal of pedagogy is in small groups in seminars," he says, and amounts to "conversation with a thoughtful person."

"That's not a commodity," he adds.

Some experts aren't swayed by such arguments. Mr. Thomsen of Stanford, for example, says collegiate chat rooms will offer ample opportunities for student-teacher interactions.

Mr. Zittrain says that watching old forms survive and new ones take root in academia's networked future "will be a kind of Darwinian experiment." But a consensus view already appears to be solidifying among experts about the probable fate of one current academic structure: the university library.

"Natural forces," such as the costs of maintaining huge collections of books and other documents, are driving a gradual conversion of these materials to digital form and the eventual development of an online "universal library," says Dr. Atkins of the University of Michigan, who is also director of the university's digital-library project. "In a decade," he says, "a threshold of collections with most everything you need will perhaps be available" online.

A universal online library would most likely be modeled on electronic commerce, Dr. Atkins says. A commercial service would probably search a network of individual online libraries to find the document sought, post terms and fees, and deliver it to the user.

But the universal library will also be a place "where knowledge work is done," says Dr. Atkins. For instance, he says tools are being developed to permit researchers to collaborate online, either in real time or asynchronously, with colleagues the world over, and to utilize sophisticated scientific instruments at remote locations, such as the Hubble Space Telescope, from their own desktops.

WEAKER CENTER

Indeed, just as the Internet may make access to instruction less campus-dependent, it could do the same for academic research, potentially diluting the power of big university research centers. "If the Net allows for rich collaboration without the need for geographic proximity, the university as a geographic center is weakened," says Mr. Zittrain.

But Dr. McClintock says an all-encompassing online library would 30 hardly eliminate the need for physical libraries, if only to house a collection of "canonical texts" required to verify digitized versions. These hard copies "may become sort of like the gold in Fort Knox," he says. "We may not want to consult it much, but we're all glad it's there."

Moreover, Dr. McClintock says that despite the potential power of an online library to foster learning and research collaboration, "a vital campus will still be important" for research and the generation of knowledge.

To illustrate this, Dr. McClintock says he likes to remind people that the Redmond, Wash., headquarters of Microsoft Corp.—symbol, to some, of the high-tech barbarians poised to storm academia's ramparts—resembles nothing so much as a campus. "And they call it that," he says.

◆ QUESTIONS FOR DISCUSSION AND WRITING ◆

1. What is your initial reaction to the quotation in paragraph 5 that says, "A decade from now, it wouldn't surprise me if the majority of education took place in people's homes, in people's offices, on the production line, wherever it is needed"? Do you agree or disagree? Why?

2. In paragraph 10, Cwiklik begins a discussion of how the private sector is entering the field of higher education, and, in paragraph 11, he discusses Kaplan Educational Centers' plan for an online law school. How do you feel about the private sector moving into public education? Do you think that such a move will make for better schools? Why? Would it matter to you if your degree came from a public college or university or from one operated by a major corporation? Why or why not?

3. Starting in paragraph 25, Cwiklik outlines how campus libraries are becoming virtual libraries, where "most everything you need will perhaps be available" online (paragraph 26). Does the concept of conducting *only* online research appeal to you? Why or why not? Do you think it would be easier, faster, or more reliable to conduct research online than to work in your own college or university library? Why or why not?

4. *Ethical question:* If you knew that a class offered through one of the avenues explored in these articles (on the Internet, for example) was bogus and that you'd receive a good grade just for paying the fee and buying the books, would you take the class? Why or why not?

 The "Effectiveness" Debate

WHAT WE KNOW ABOUT THE QUALITY OF DISTANCE LEARNING IN THE U.S.

Jamie P. Merisotis and Jody K. Olsen

The use of technology as a medium for delivering postsecondary education is rapidly gaining prominence and popularity, both in the U.S. and around the globe. Evidence of this increasing visibility of technology-based learning is everywhere. For example, a 1999 report from the International Data Corporation (IDC) estimates that 2.2 million college students in the U.S. will be enrolled in some form of distance education by 2002, up from approximately 710,000 in 1998. IDC's research estimates that 85 percent of two-year colleges in the U.S. and 84 percent of four-year colleges will offer distance learning courses by 2002.* Similarly, a report from the Campus Computing Project at the Claremont Graduate School found that one-third of all classes on college campuses used Internet resources in 1998, compared with only 15 percent in 1996.

THE "NO SIGNIFICANT DIFFERENCE" NOTION

But what is known about the effectiveness of this teaching and learning method? This question has become increasingly prominent as technology has made distance learning more common. At least one major web site, maintained by North Carolina State University's Thomas Russell, is dedicated to this. This site, *The No Significant Difference Phenomenon,* compiles various writings on distance learning. With few exceptions, the bulk

---

*In this article, distance education is understood to rely on a combination of technology, including television, videotapes, audiotapes, video conferencing, audio conferencing, e-mail, telephone, fax, Internet, computer software, and print.

of these writings suggest that the learning outcomes of students using technology at a distance are similar to the learning outcomes of students who participate in conventional classroom instruction. The "no significant difference" finding has become accepted as fact in the policy community, where at least some public officials have pronounced that the last college campus has been built.

A recent working paper from Indiana University's Center for Social Informatics challenges the "no significant difference" notion. The paper points out that "many authors in the distance education literature discuss only the positive aspects of computer-mediated distance education," and notes that students' potential problems with distance education is "a taboo topic in the discourse." The study investigates students' frustrations with a single web-based course. Their findings? Students faced several problems, including technical difficulties, lack of prompt feedback from the instructor, and ambiguous instructions (*see* www.slis.indiana.edu/CSI).

Even more compelling is a study completed by the U.S. Army Research Institute for Behavioral and Social Sciences. That study, entitled "Training Through Distance Learning: an Assessment of Research Findings," was published in October 1999, and reviews a broad array of literature on the effectiveness of distance learning. The report found the quality of the research on distance learning's effectiveness was quite weak.

WHAT'S THE DIFFERENCE?

That study strongly supports the findings of a 1999 report that examined the recent literature on distance learning's effectiveness. That report, entitled *What's the Difference? A Review of Contemporary Research on the Effectiveness of Distance Learning in Higher Education,* was published by The Institute for Higher Education Policy in Washington, DC, with support from the American Federation of Teachers and the National Education Association.

The *What's the Difference?* report (available at www.ihep.com) has served as a kind of lightning rod in the debate in the U.S. about the quality and effectiveness of distance learning. From April through October 1999, the report had been cited in major media, such as the Associated Press wire (which ran a lengthy story published in more than 300 newspapers), and the trade press and higher education magazines. The report was downloaded over 30,000 times (in pdf format) from the authors' web site.

Why such a fuss? The report, after all, is a pretty straightforward and frankly somewhat dull review of the available literature on the subject. The main conclusion of the report is that there is a relative paucity of original research dedicated to explaining or predicting phenomena related to distance learning. Despite the large volume of written material concentrating on distance learning, the amount of original research is quite limited. The study's analysis encompassed about 40 of these original works of research—a number far fewer than is often cited as "evidence" that there is no significant difference.

From this more limited group of original research, three broad measures of the effectiveness of distance education are usually examined. These include:

- student outcomes, such as grades and test scores;
- student attitudes about learning through distance education; and
- overall student satisfaction toward distance learning.

Most of these studies conclude that, regardless of the technology used, distance learning courses compare favorably with classroom-based instruction. For example, many experimental studies suggest that the distance learning students have similar grades or test scores, or have the same attitudes toward the course. The descriptive analyses and case studies focus on student and faculty attitudes and perceptions of distance learning. These studies typically conclude that students and faculty have a positive view toward distance learning.

A closer look at the research, however, suggests that it may not be prudent to accept these findings at face value. Several problems with the conclusions reached through this research are apparent. The most significant problem is that the overall quality of the original research is questionable and thereby renders many of the findings inconclusive.

QUALITY OF THE RESEARCH

The report's critique of the quality of the research makes four simple   10
points. First, much of the research does not control for extraneous variables and therefore cannot show cause and effect. Most studies of distance learning are designed to measure how a specific technology—the "cause"—effects some type of learning outcome or influences students' attitudes toward a course—the "effect." To accurately assess this relationship, other potential causes must not influence the measured outcomes. In almost all of the experimental research we reviewed, there was inadequate control of extraneous variables.

Second, most of the studies do not use randomly selected subjects; many rely instead on intact groups (such as an entire class of students) for comparison purposes. As a result, these studies run the risk of having several variables affect academic achievement or student satisfaction, instead of the technology itself used to provide the education at a distance.

Third, the study found questionable the validity and reliability of the instruments used to measure student outcomes and attitudes—such as questionnaires and surveys. And fourth, many studies do not adequately control for the feelings and attitudes of students and faculty—what the educational research refers to as "reactive effects"—which can sometimes skew findings by showing short-term or temporary benefits that are not sustained over the educational program.

GAPS IN THE RESEARCH

What is perhaps more compelling, however, is what the literature does not say about the effectiveness of distance learning. These gaps must be filled so that public-policy discussions about distance education can be based on accurate and adequate information.

One major gap in the research is a lack of studies dedicated to measuring the effectiveness of total academic programs taught at a distance. Virtually all of the comparative or descriptive studies focus on individual courses. That raises serious questions about whether an academic program delivered by technology compares favorably with an on-campus program. Government policies, such as student-assistance programs, are typically aimed at providing access to degrees or programs of study, not just single courses, making it especially important to fill this gap.

A number of studies showed that students in distance learning courses   15
tend to drop out of their courses before finishing at a higher rate than students in conventional classes. The issue of student persistence is important both because dropping out reveals a negative response to online learning, and because research surveys of students could be excluding these dropouts, causing a tilt in the student outcome findings toward those who are successful.

The research to date also does not consider how a student's learning style—how he or she processes information, for example—can influence the success of particular technologies. Our understanding of how the learner, the learning task, and specific forms of technology interact is, in fact, limited. We do know, however, that student characteristics, such as gender, age, and educational experience, make a big difference in levels of achievement and satisfaction for distance learners. Information about a student's preferred learning style could influence how a course is designed, including what type of technology is used.

So far, the research on distance education has no conceptual framework. Several researchers have lamented the lack of theory dealing with the interactions and interrelationships of variables contributing to the effectiveness of distance learning programs. Theory allows researchers to build on one another's work, which increases the likelihood of their addressing the most important questions in a field. For distance learning, there is a vital need to develop a more integrated, coherent, and systematic program of research based on theory.

Further, the research does not adequately assess the effectiveness of digital libraries. Many students, particularly those in remote locations, rely on digital "libraries" for access to bibliographies for different resources, as well as full texts. But can digital libraries provide adequate support? Anecdotal evidence suggests that the curriculum objectives of some distance learning courses have been altered because of the dearth of resources available.

REACTIONS TO THE REPORT

What's the Difference? obviously struck a chord with those interested in using technology in higher education. That chord, however, has not been entirely harmonious. Indeed, the reaction tells us much about how fractured the debate on distance learning in the U.S. has become.

Many college presidents, faculty, and administrators seemed intrigued by the conclusion that much of the research on distance education is of questionable quality, rendering its findings inconclusive. Several representatives from major online learning or software companies praised the work and said the findings merited further exploration. "The lack of relevant, quality research, when viewed with the speed in which distance learning is evolving, should be a concern to everyone," the chair of one of these companies wrote to the report's authors. "My only regret was the negative hyperbole and rhetoric that others used following the release of your report."

Not surprisingly, that "negative hyperbole and rhetoric" came from people who have a stake in distance education. In *Education Daily,* one attorney in Washington, D.C., who represents institutions that have distance learning programs, compared "critics" of online learning to those who bemoaned the introduction of books into the classroom three hundred years ago. Thomas Russell, producer of the *No Significant Difference* web site, was quoted in the media as saying that he agreed with the findings about the lack of research on the effectiveness of distance learning. But Russell also complained to the newsletter *Information Technology in Postsecondary Education* that the report "does a serious disservice to the thousands of dedicated and conscientious faculty who have worked in distance education over a great many years. These faculty are in the very best position to judge the efficacy and quality of such programs and do not deserve the implication, inherent in the report, that they are engaged in an activity which provides education of a lesser quality than that accepted by their profession."

LESSONS LEARNED

What's the Difference? is not the most important or influential report ever written on distance learning in higher education. It is probably not even the most important document published on the topic last year. But the report and the reaction to it have brought out into the open some of the key issues in the debate about distance education. *What's the Difference?*

also offers guidance on how to proceed as technology gains prominence in the teaching and learning process.

One of the things learned from researching and writing the report is that too much of the debate has taken place with an "us" versus "them" mentality. It is somewhat surprising to learn that those who use technology as a major teaching and learning medium see themselves as a community somehow separate and distinct from the rest of higher education. Certainly some level of advocacy and focus is appropriate—as evidenced by the balanced perspectives taken by this online journal—but this wholly separate identification reinforces the notion that what "we" do is more important or better than what "they" do. Much the same bunker mentality is evident among those faculty members who see distance learning as the latest pernicious administrative attempt to reduce or eliminate their influence on curriculum and pedagogy.

Yet almost half of all college courses use e-mail and other Internet resources. The reality is that technology is playing, and will continue to play, a critical role in teaching and learning. As a pedagogical tool, distance education probably leads to different educational outcomes than traditional classroom-based instruction—some better, some worse. The polar views expressed in many policy discussions—that there is "no significant difference" on the one extreme, and that distance learning is inherently inferior on the other—defy reason. The real debate needs to focus on identifying what approaches work best for teaching students, period.

Faculty also must be heard in this debate. The media and the policy-making community have so strongly identified professors as being "opposed" to distance learning that any serious attempt by faculty members to inform the debate is treated with suspicion and derision. This must change. Faculty must be at the forefront of understanding what works, and what does not work, because they are ultimately the arbiters of educational quality and effectiveness. Nothing can substitute for that experience, commitment, and knowledge.

Perhaps the most important lesson learned is that more research is needed. Coalitions of online-learning providers, faculty members, college administrators, and student leaders must work together to answer the questions the report raises and to fill in the gaps it identifies. More volleys in the acrid debates over online education are not needed; credible, broadly supported research is.

There is some danger that the innovations are advancing more rapidly than our understanding of their practical uses. Princeton historian Robert Darnton points to this common problem with new technologies in his essay in the March 18, 1999, issue of the *New York Review of Books*. Darnton observes that, since its inception, electronic publishing has passed through three stages: "an initial phase of utopian enthusiasm, a period of disillusionment, and a new tendency toward pragmatism." So far, we have heard a lot about the "utopian" possibilities. Now "pragmatism" needs to come to the fore to allow us to discuss the practical implications of distance learning as a tool to enhance teaching and learning. Joining in this pragmatic and ultimately crucial discussion must become the common goal of those with an interest in higher education's future.

◆ QUESTIONS FOR DISCUSSION AND WRITING ◆

1. All college classes should have some mechanism for assessing whether learning has taken place—that is, whether students have learned what the curriculum was designed to help them learn. In paragraph 8, Merisotis and Olsen suggest "three broad measures of the effectiveness of distance education": (1) student outcomes, (2) student attitudes about distance learning, and (3) student satisfaction with distance learning. As a student, do you think that these three areas can accurately reflect what you "got out of" a college or university course? Jot down your answers to these questions:

   - What "outcomes" do your present college classes have? What should you know or be able to do when you complete them?
   - Can "student attitudes" accurately measure the learning that takes place in a college class? Do you feel more "satisfied" with the classes in which you learned a lot—and have negative feelings about those classes in which you didn't learn as much?

2. Merisotis and Olsen note that "students in distance learning courses tend to drop out of their courses . . . at a higher rate than students in conventional classes" (paragraph 15). Why do you suppose that happens? In what ways might online courses be improved to aid retention?

3. Which of the articles you've read so far do you find the most persuasive? Why? Which data from the articles you've read do you find the most convincing? Why? If you had to argue for or against online education, what facts or figures or illustrations from these articles might you use in your statement?

✳ Technology

EASY DEGREES PROLIFERATE ON THE WEB

David Koeppel

Ira Doreen Donovan, an elementary school teacher in Miami, was 31 credits shy of a master's degree in special education when she saw an on-line advertisement for Columbia State University. After sending $800 as the first payment on a $2,000 degree, Ms. Donovan received a textbook to summarize and send back for grading.

Believing this was the first step of several, she was shocked when shortly after, a certificate not only for a master's but a doctorate arrived at her home. Along with the degrees came transcripts awarding her a

3.9 grade point average for classes never taken and credit for a completed thesis and dissertation.

"I called the school and told them if this degree isn't worth the paper it's printed on, I don't want to pay for it," Ms. Donovan said. "This degree mill made me look like a fool."

Columbia State returned her money, but others say they have not been so lucky.

After investigating 36 complaints, including one from Norway and one from Malaysia, the Louisiana Attorney General's office has filed for a preliminary injunction against Columbia, charging that it violates the state's Unfair Trade Practices Act and consumer protection laws. Last month the State of Illinois also filed suit seeking an injunction and restitution for consumer and the state.

Repeated calls to Columbia's office in Metairie, La., seeking comment were not returned.

The Internet has "rekindled the old-fashioned diploma mill," said Michael Lambert, the executive director of the Distance Education and Training Council, a recognized accrediting agency that has approved 65 on-line and home-study schools. "The Internet is a haven for these places."

Surfing the Web these days is like flipping through a virtual college catalogue. With its interactivity and accessibility, the Internet has sparked new interest in home-study programs, offering actual courses on line or just information.

Although many distance-learning schools have solid reputations and graduation requirements, hundreds of Web sites have popped up for schools charging between $200 and $7,000 for sheepskin that requires little or no work from students. Columbia, for instance, promises degrees within 27 days.

Elaborate home pages make schools look credible, Mr. Lambert said. The schools can operate in the anonymity of cyberspace, sometimes listing just an E-mail address or post office box. And on line, they can reach a global audience for minimal cost.

Eugene Sullivan, co-author with David W. Stewart and Henry Spille of "External Degrees in the Information Age," the American Council on Education's guide to correspondence programs, defines a diploma mill as an "organization that sells degrees without an academic base and without requiring sufficient academic achievement."

While perfectly legitimate schools might have an element or two of a diploma mill (say, credit for work experience), experts say there are multiple defining characteristics:

- The school emphasizes credit for work or life experience without appropriate mechanisms for assessing that experience in terms of college-level learning.
- Degrees are obtained in far less time than would be required at a legitimate institution. (A bachelor's degree typically takes four

years of full-time course work, a master's one to two years, a Ph.D. dissertation several years to research and write.)

- Tuition and fees are on a per-degree basis instead of per semester or course.

- School brochures list faculty members who neither teach nor provide other services, and there is virtually no interaction with faculty members.

- The school is not accredited by an agency approved by the Department of Education, the Council for Higher Education Accreditation or other legitimate institutions.

Accreditation, however, is voluntary.

"From my experience it's not the blatantly fraudulent schools that are the real threat," Mr. Stewart said. "It's the academic frauds that have a little substance that are the problem."

He was referring to schools that require students to perform some academic exercises like writing a paper or taking an exam—and some students might invest considerable effort—but their degrees are unacceptable to established colleges and universities and unimpressive to prospective employers.

But experts admit that most such institutions cater to people who   15
know exactly what they are getting into.

"Many people are well aware of what they are doing," Mr. Sullivan said. "They want a credential and they want to get it quickly. But others are busy people or foreign students who don't know much about higher education. They see these places as programs that fit their needs."

Joe Joyal of Atlanta said he had worked as an engineer for 20 years without a degree and applied to Columbia State for a joint bachelor's/master's degree in mechanical engineering. He received both degrees in under six months after summarizing two textbooks.

He said he suspected the degree was worthless but nonetheless listed it on his resume. Later he had second thoughts and took it off. He is pursuing a degree from an accredited distance-learning program. Columbia State claims in Internet advertising that it is accredited by the International Accrediting Association, a "fictitious school accrediting agency," according to the Louisiana Attorney General's complaint. The owner of Columbia, Ronald Dante, was sentenced in February in Los Angeles to five-and-a-half years in prison for operating fraudulent schools in California. He jumped bail and is being sought by United States marshals, according to Michelle Muth, a spokeswoman for the Federal Trade Commission. Columbia continues to operate.

Perhaps the largest crackdown on schools took place from 1981 to 1991, when Operation Dipscam (for diploma scam) put 50 out of business on charges ranging from mail or wire fraud to conspiracy. "Sometimes we'd find phony accreditations or that we were able to negotiate a degree for a lower price," said Allen Ezell, a former agent with the Federal Bureau of Investigation who oversaw Dipscam. "Some schools sent transcripts and diplomas to students for courses never taken."

States like New York and Illinois closely regulate academic institutions, requiring that they be authorized to operate. But many don't. Mr. Ezell said investigations often start by looking into schools incorporated in the states with the weakest laws, like Hawaii, Utah and Louisiana.

Hawaii has been wrangling with a few unaccredited schools lately. Its department of consumer affairs has sued Pacific Western and American State Universities, two distance-learning schools with offices there, for not making clear in advertisements that they are unaccredited. After agreeing to a settlement, American State decided to close. "The penalties were too substantial," the school's lawyer, Evan R. Shirley, said, specifically citing the requirement that every ad disclose its unaccredited status.

"My client never explicitly expressed wrongdoing," he added, "but a conclusion could be rationally made that there was wrongdoing."

Pacific Western's case is pending. Calls to its office and lawyers were not returned, but in answer to the complaint filed in circuit court in Honolulu, it denied allegations that it misleads consumers about its accreditation or suggests it is "somehow accredited or approved by the State of Hawaii to award academic degrees."

Another area of dispute that has caused considerable legal wrangling has been the similarity in names between accredited and unaccredited schools.

An unaccredited school called Washington University, which has an office in Bryn Mawr, Pa., but is incorporated in Hawaii and the British Virgin Islands, settled a suit in June filed by the more established Washington University of St. Louis. The suit charged that the unaccredited school infringed on its trademark and engaged in unfair competition.

The details of the settlement are confidential, but the consent judgment entered by the court told the school to come up with a new name, and one that separated the words "Washington" and "University" with a word of at least 10 characters.

Yil Karademir, who owns the unaccredited school, chose Washington International University. (Unaccredited schools tend to favor the word "International," as well as "America," "United" and "Pacific.")

The St. Louis school had complained that it had received inquiries from prospective students and alumni who were confused when they saw the other school's ads—not to mention being the target of protests from human-rights activists after a businessman linked to Myanmar's military dictatorship bought an honorary doctorate.

"What they do bears no resemblance to the education we provide," said Lori Fox, the associate general counsel for Washington University in St. Louis. "Are they a diploma mill? You'll have to draw your own conclusions."

Mr. Karademir said he is not running a diploma mill.

"We are a young university," he said. "We didn't even know about them when we chose the name three years ago. They're not exactly Harvard.

Calling us a degree mill is hitting below the belt in order to belittle and discredit us."

Mr. Karademir said his school is made up mostly of international students who are given academic credit for life experience, though he plans to add on-line courses in the fall. Washington International's Web site is extensive and promises to grant degrees in one year. "The academic comunity [sic] find our degree programs to be OUTSTANDING!" the Web site declares. "All Washington International University degrees are ATTESTED and sealed for authenticity by a Government appointed NOTARY!"

Costs range from $2,850 for a Bachelor of Science in business administration to $7,400 for a combination bachelor's and master's degree.

Meanwhile, the Pennsylvania Department of Education is investigating complaints about the school, according to Michelle Haskins, a department spokeswoman.

Last year, the Illinois Attorney General succeeded in shutting down 35 an on-line school, Loyola State University, for violating consumer protection laws by confusing students into thinking it was Loyola University of Chicago. Patricia Kelly, division chief of consumer protection in the Attorney General's office, said that Lorie LaFata, who ran the school, created dummy transcripts with fictional class names, codes and grades. Students would receive diplomas after paying $2,800. "We were able to see she was not offering what she promised," Ms. Kelly said.

In her settlement with the Attorney General's office, which had filed suit against her, Ms. LaFata agreed to pay restitution to the state and not to conduct business on the Internet for five years, including having a Web site.

"The state and I came to a good understanding," said Ms. LaFata, who offered that she had been a Columbia State student. "I did have to admit to wrongdoing. It was an awful time for me. I hope to leave that behind."

Richard Mitchell, president of the New Orleans Better Business Bureau, advises prospective students to do their own investigating before signing up with a distance-education school.

"Do some intelligent things like checking out a school with agencies that can give you more information," he said. "Don't just jump into a school because they have an impressive Web site. If you take time and do your homework, you can avoid a problem."

Mr. Lambert said it was easy for unsophisticated applicants to be 40 fooled. "In mixing dollars and dreams," he said, "it's many of the true innocents that get trampled on."

HOW TO CHECK SCHOOL CREDENTIALS

Surfing the Web for a home-study school? The Department of Education suggests that the first step is to check a school's accreditation—a process in which courses are reviewed, students surveyed and campuses inspected. For a list of agencies approved to accredit schools, write:

Department of Education Accreditation and Eligibility Determination Division, 6000 Independence Ave., S.W., Washington, D.C. 20202-5244; (202) 708-7417; www.ifap.ed.gov/scb.html/agenc.htm.

The Council for Higher Education Accreditation, an organization of colleges and universities, also approves accrediting agencies. Write: One Dupont Circle, N.W., Suite 854, Washington, D.C. 20036-1110; (202)955-6126; www.chea.org.

——————◆ QUESTIONS FOR DISCUSSION AND WRITING ◆——————

1. Now that you've read Koeppel's article, do you agree with his title? Why or why not?
2. *Ethical question:* In an employment interview, your prospective employer mentions that another job candidate has a degree from what you know to be a bogus online university. Do you mention what you know? Why or why not?
3. Starting in paragraph 12, Koeppel lists several "defining characteristics" that indicate when an online school might be a "diploma mill." These characteristics include giving credit to students for work and life experiences, accelerated degree completion, payment on a degree basis instead of a semester or per-course basis, little interaction with faculty members, and a lack of accreditation. Although lack of proper accreditation seems an obvious weakness, how do you feel about the other characteristics Koeppel lists?
   - What's wrong with giving college credit for work and life experiences?
   - What is the problem with getting a degree more quickly than at traditional colleges?
   - Why is paying for your degree all at once, rather than by semester or by course, an indication of a bogus degree?

❋ Study Finds Problems with Web Classes
Pamela Mendels

The online field trip to a virtual campus was marred by confusion. The assignments on the class Web site left students bewildered. The flood of messages to the class e-mail discussion list left many recipients feeling inundated. Technical problems interfered with work.

The result for the graduate students who enrolled in B555, the fictitious name of a real Web-based course offered by a university two years ago, could be summarized in one word: frustration.

And that, say researchers who have written a case study about the class, points to a need for a serious examination of what they call a taboo subject in academia: the problems with Web-based distance education.

Rob Kling, a professor at Indiana University in Bloomington and the study's co-author, said "there are a lot of good potentials" for technology in education. But, he added, "There are a lot of limitations and, further, it is neither simple nor cheap."

These are fighting words for techno-enthusiasts extolling the possibilities of new media and education. But they cannot be dismissed as coming from Luddites suspicious of technological innovation. Kling is a prominent professor of information systems and information science as well as a professor of computer science. His co-author and the study's investigator, Noriko Hara, is a graduate student interested in instructional uses of technology.

That may be the reason their paper, a working draft now being revised, is beginning to attract attention. Hara has received about 60 requests for copies of it, since word of the paper began circulating on education-related e-mail lists in August. And both she and Kling have been asked to present the paper at a conference next month on new media and learning.

William H. Dutton, a professor at the University of Southern California and one of the conference organizers, invited them because, he says, the often boosterish attitude toward Web-based education stands in marked contrast to the paucity of research into students' reactions to it. "There is a great deal of enthusiasm, but perhaps less of a critical perspective than there should be," he said.

The study in question is a limited one. The report looks at just one class—and a small one at that—so it is not a survey of distance education courses as a whole, and few if any generalizations can be drawn from it. But, Dutton said, such case studies are instructive because they raise questions that can prompt further research. He believes the findings will resonate with many people who have tried to teach online. "It forces people to deal with very real issues about the usability of current systems," he said.

B555 was offered by what the authors describe as a "major university" in fall, 1997. The study offers few identifying details, because the authors promised confidentiality to the students and their instructor.

But this much is known. The subject of the class involved the use of technology for teaching languages. Eight masters' degree students enrolled initially: five campus students and three off-campus students. Two of the long-distance students dropped the class because of problems with the technology.

The instructor, who was foreign-born, was a Ph.D. candidate who was asked to teach the course after its designer, a faculty member in her program, fell ill. The instructor had never taught a distance education course. She had, however, taken the class herself and had a hand in the design of the B555 Web site. The class never met face-to-face, but was conducted largely through e-mail discussion and assignments posted on a Web site.

Hara had begun the study expecting to hear a lot of enthusiasm for it. Instead, she said, she found frustration far beyond what one would expect in a small class. The amount of e-mail traffic generated by the class was one source of complaints, Hara found. In one typical week, for example, students received 35 messages about the class, which at the time they considered too cumbersome. One student quoted in the study commented that "just talking in conversation would be so much easier."

The students were not the only ones who felt the e-mail load was too great. "The instructor also commented that at the beginning of the semester she was spending all day doing nothing but reading and responding to e-mail messages," the study says. "Later in the semester, she was able to reduce the workload, but still spent a large chunk of time on this course."

Students were also frustrated by the potential for misunderstanding inherent in electronic communication. In one online chat session during a "virtual" field trip to a community Web site, a student wrote in a chat that she liked "calling rows," prompting another student to tell Hara that she assumed her classmate meant "calling role."

"Sometimes it's confusing, the teacher and half the students are non-   15
native speakers," the second student complained.

Confusion cropped up in other ways on the trip. One student failed to master commands necessary to make her words appear on the screen during the chat, despite having practiced using the technology. Another found the text conversation scrolled too quickly for her to absorb—and then disappeared. Over the course of the semester, students became flustered because they did not receive frequent or detailed enough responses by e-mail from their instructor. "One of the problems is that I'd like to have feedback. A kind of constant feedback," another student said.

Others failed to grasp what the teacher expected when she posted assignments. "I usually don't understand what she wants, either e-mail or from the Web site," one student told Hara.

Still another student was disoriented by the lack of visual cues that students receive from teachers in a classroom. He complained to Hara that he had received little response from the instructor about his contributions to the class e-mail discussion, and didn't know how to interpret this. In a traditional setting, he said, "You can tell from the classroom what the professor thinks about you from the body language and the way they talk."

Some people who have read the paper, however, think it unfairly criticizes Web courses. "I thought overall this was condemning distance learning in ways that distance learning does not deserve to be condemned," said Carrie Heeter, a professor of telecommunication at Michigan State University.

For example, she believes much of the frustration in the class stemmed   20
from human rather than technical problems. One example was the time the teacher failed to send out assignments according to her usual schedule. "That doesn't have to do with an online course. That's a professor not doing what they say they would," Heeter said.

In addition, she said, she believes some of the problems in the class could have been handled through technological tweaking. Bulletin boards devoted to specific class topics, for example, might have proved a more manageable form of discussion than e-mail lists.

Kling responds that to blame human or other problems for the frustration felt by the online students is to beg the question of what happens when universities transfer courses to the Web. There will always be bad teachers and institutional problems such as a graduate student being asked to teach a course he or she has not drawn up, Kling said. The question is, what happens when inexperienced teachers teach online?

However, Kling said the next version of the paper will make clear that the course instructor had a reputation for being a good classroom teacher. The problem, apparently, was that she had failed to receive adequate orientation in Web pedagogy.

Kling said if university administrators are going to push distance education, they must begin to recognize that teaching online is not the same as teaching in a classroom. Both teachers and students need to understand this and be better prepared to handle the differences, he said.

Kling believes that researchers have so far overlooked the thorny details of what is involved with online pedagogy, while extolling the educational potential of technology.   25

"The professional literature and even the scholarly literature about activities related to the use of computer networks tend to be upbeat, optimistic and at times even utopian," he said. He also noted that to look at the literature on the subject, one would not have "a clue that issues of the kinds we identified could happen, let alone be thought through and engaged."

Walter S. Baer, a senior policy analyst at the Rand Corp. who has written about the Internet and technology, agrees. He says the study is useful in pointing out problems that are hardly unique to B555. "I think similar frustrations are arising in many institutions around the country," he said.

◆ QUESTIONS FOR DISCUSSION AND WRITING ◆

1. Now that you have a sense of the problems that Mendels outlines in this article, to whom or what do you attribute those difficulties? Were the problems the teacher's fault, or were they caused by the technology?
2. Mendels lists a number of problems a researcher discovered about an online class, including:
   - Too much e-mail for both students and the instructor.
   - Misunderstandings in communication.
   - Technological problems.
   - A lack of visual clues some students needed to fully understand what the teacher wanted.

   If you were to redesign this course, what changes would you implement to eliminate the problems Mendels outlines?
3. If you had been a student in the course that Mendels describes, would you have dropped the class, or would you have done something to improve the situation? Why? What might you have done?

❊ Digital Dreamer

A SOFTWARE BILLIONAIRE HANDS OUT $100 MILLION
FOR A FREE ONLINE UNIVERSITY. BUT WILL IT MAKE
THE GRADE?

Jodie Morse

A yacht packed with vacationing millionaires off the coast of St. Bart's is an unlikely laboratory for social-policy reform. So perhaps it was the Caribbean sea breeze or the free-flowing 1945 Mouton-Rothschild that got Michael Saylor, the 35-year-old CEO of the high-tech company MicroStrategy, thinking about how to amend the inequities in higher education. He shared his thoughts over sea bass and chocolate soufflé. "And by the end of the evening," he recalls, "I knew I'd hit on the next big thing in education."

Back ashore last week, Saylor took his idea public, pledging $100 million to create a nonprofit "online Ivy League–quality university." And then came an even bigger revelation. He says it will allow everyone, from cabbie in Bombay to housewife in L.A., to earn a top-notch degree—for free. "If you put a professor's best performance of his life online, you can make something even better than Harvard," says Saylor, an M.I.T. graduate.

The number of schools granting online degrees has doubled in the past year, according to a study released last week. The distance-education craze has spawned cyber-only schools like Jones International University, whose Colorado-based operation offers online courses to 500 students in 30 countries. Traditional campuses are also getting wired. Stanford offers a virtual master's degree; the University of Chicago and Columbia, among others, have signed up with the Internet start-up UNext.com to create a for-profit online college. Saylor's announcement ups the ante considerably. He is banking on replacing the world's "10,000 average professors" with an all-star faculty (think Bill Clinton and Henry Kissinger), all of whom he expects to teach pro bono.

With warp speed, Saylor's proposal became the talk of the highest ivory towers. And the reactions were mostly of the unpublishable kind. "Saylor's naïveté is breathtaking," says David Noble, a history professor at Toronto's York University and a sharp critic of distance learning. "It's the quintessence of counterfeit education." Adds Carole Fungaroli, an English professor at Georgetown: "It's the same as sex on the Internet. You can get it online, but it's not as good as in person."

Scholarly studies on distance learning thus far are scant. But several high-profile distance ventures have flopped, and research has shown that chat-room courses tend to be more costly and have higher attrition rates than lecture-hall classes. And there's the prickly legal issue of ownership: who retains the rights to a Wordsworth lecture once it is let loose in cyberspace?

Saylor's stunning business record may help sway some critics. As the founder of MicroStrategy, he made his fortune—$10 billion on paper as of last week—by counseling clients like Victoria's Secret on how to mine their consumer data. Conceived 10 years ago by Saylor and an M.I.T. frat brother, the company has grown to 2,000 employees and $200 million in revenue. Lately, Saylor has been making his money by selling customers personalized weather, traffic and sports reports. A Roman Empire buff, he convenes a "university week" each summer for his employees, during which they take business tutorials, attend mandatory study halls and sit for finals that Saylor insists "people actually flunk." Even in conversation, he tends to lecture. In a two-minute riff, he alights on Henry Ford, Julius Caesar and *Star Trek,* comparing their missions to his own.

The inspiration for his latest project was closer to home. The son of an Air Force officer, Saylor attended college on a full scholarship and wants to make a comparable opportunity available to all. But his aims are not entirely altruistic. He has plans to pluck the brainiest students to go to work for MicroStrategy. His headline-grabbing announcement could also have a more immediate payoff. Saylor is recruiting investors for a second MicroStrategy stock offering, a period during which SEC rules forbid him to publicize his company.

At the very least, Saylor's ideas may light a fire under the academy, which has been queasy about entering the online arena. Back at the real Harvard, Gregory Nagy, a professor of classical Greek literature, has a virtual version of a course on heroism for his continuing-education students. And he runs late-night e-mail symposiums for his undergrads, while in his pj's. "Plato intended Socratic dialogues to be open-ended," says Nagy. "And the debate shouldn't stop when you leave the classroom." Saylor's solution to that problem is simple: lose the classroom.

◆ QUESTIONS FOR DISCUSSION AND WRITING ◆

1. What is your initial reaction to Michael Saylor's idea of an "online Ivy League–quality university"? Would you sign up for classes there? Why or why not?
2. Morse quotes the responses of people from traditional universities to Saylor's idea. Do you agree or disagree with their comments? Why?
3. Outline what you see as the benefits of Saylor's idea. Also detail what you see as potential problems with his concept.
4. Morse notes that "traditional campuses are also getting wired. Stanford offers a virtual master's degree; the University of Chicago and Columbia, among others, [are creating] a for-profit online college" (paragraph 3). If that's true, what could be wrong with Saylor's ideas?

✳ How to Proctor from a Distance

EXPERTS SAY PROFESSORS NEED SAVVY
TO PREVENT CHEATING IN ON-LINE COURSES

Dan Carnevale

Technology is offering students new and easier ways to cheat, especially in on-line courses. But the same technology is also giving professors easier ways to catch cheaters.

Back when distance education was conducted through correspondence, it wasn't easy to tell who had really written a paper or filled out a test form. Now that courses are on line, professors are using technology to identify students more reliably, although still not beyond the shadow of a doubt.

Colleges venturing into distance education face a great deal of apprehension among faculty members about the potential for cheating. Dees Stallings, director of academic programs at VCampus, a company that helps colleges set up on-line courses, says one of the first things he has to do when working with new professors is allay their fears of on-line cheating.

"Everybody's always concerned when they first get started," he says. "They'll ask things like, 'How do I know it's not Grover who's taking the course?'"

Measuring the extent of on-line cheating is difficult. No national data exist. Several colleges with extensive distance-education programs—including Michigan State University, Ohio University, the University of Texas System, Park College, and Pueblo Community College—report that they have had few, if any, cases where disciplinary action has been taken for cheating in on-line classes. More cheating is reported in traditional classrooms, officials say.

The potential for cheating in distance-education courses is about equal to that in traditional courses, Mr. Stallings says, but professors need a new savvy to detect and prevent cheating on line. Besides worrying about whether students are really who they say they are, faculty members are anxious about on-line term-paper mills and other digital aids to cheating.

Jeanne M. Wilson, president of the Center for Academic Integrity, which is affiliated with Duke University, says the growth of on-line education makes it harder to be sure that the student who gets the credit is the one who did the work. "If you don't ever meet the student, it's harder to evaluate the student's work."

Even students who sit in a lecture hall with hundreds of others can feel isolated and anonymous, she points out, adding that such anonymity prevents the creation of a bond between student and professor that might discourage cheating. On-line education only worsens that sense of isolation and anonymity, she says.

"It's kind of like the difference between living in a big city and living in a small town where everyone knows your folks and would tell them if you did something wrong," Ms. Wilson says.

To the contrary, argues Mr. Stallings, one of the benefits of an on-line   10
class is that almost all communication is in writing. "That really brings the
academic rigor up. This allows an instructor to get to know a student better than in an on-site class."

Some tactics that professors can use to prevent cheating include making an unexpected phone call to discuss a point further or to ask the student
how he or she found some piece of information. In addition, Mr. Stallings
says, a $20 camera can sit atop a student's computer and send the profes-
sor a stream of images of the student taking a test or discussing issues.

Still, he acknowledges, nothing is foolproof: "My girlfriend can still
hold up a cue card off camera."

The best way to prevent cheating during tests is to have proctors keep
an eye on students, Mr. Stallings says. If the students are too far away to
come to the main campus for exams, the professor can call a local college
or high school and ask someone to serve as proctor. In extraordinary
cases, an Army officer could supervise a test for a subordinate, or a priest
could keep watch while a parishioner takes a midterm exam.

It's up to the professor to be realistic about students' behavior and not
get mired in denial when evidence suggests that a student might be cheating, Mr. Stallings adds. "A professor can say, 'Darn, I taught that guy to
write in two weeks!'"

Darcy W. Hardy, director of the University of Texas's distance-educa-   15
tion component, called Telecampus, says the key to catching cheaters is to
know the students in the class. But instructors can't do that if a course has
a large enrollment, whether in the classroom or on line.

"I often tell people that if you really want to see distance education,
go to one of those lecture-hall classrooms," she says.

One way of getting a jump on plagiarizers is to ask every student to
write a 500-word essay at the beginning of the semester that can serve as
a kind of fingerprint of writing style. The topic isn't important—it can be
the student's summer vacation or the family cat—as long as the essay can
serve as a reference point to help a professor spot a paper that isn't an original work later in the semester.

"I guess that's kind of sneaky, but it gives the faculty the upper edge,"
Ms. Hardy says.

Professors can also use on-line chats and discussion boards to get to
know students better. Chats and discussions generate text that is recorded,
so an instructor can refer back to it after assignments are turned in.

"You can always have a ringer or a pigeon in any environment," Ms.   20
Hardy says. "If you can keep that up for a whole semester, you're doing
pretty good."

Whether a ringer or Grover, Ms. Hardy agrees that it's a little tougher
to catch cheaters on line. But if professors remain vigilant and take reasonable precautions, they'll probably be able to nab the offender, she says.

Luis Nazario, a composition professor at Pueblo Community College in
Colorado, says that during his six years of teaching on line, he has had three

instances of students trying to cheat. Each time, he could tell intuitively that the students had received some extra help when completing their assignments.

The best way to weed those students out, Mr. Nazario says, is through the proctored examinations that are required in the courses. "It's my chance to get even," he says.

Eventually, Mr. Nazario says, those students dropped out of the course.

Mr. Nazario also says he talks to his students over the phone at least   25
three times during the semester to discuss each student's progress, which helps him make sure these students are really who they say they are.

"Students are going to cheat in the classroom or out of the classroom," he says. "I'm more concerned with the ones I didn't catch."

Mr. Stallings, of VCampus, based in McLean, Va., has taught courses at several colleges and maintains that it should be no easier to succeed at cheating on line than in a traditional classroom—if the professor is as clever as the cheaters.

Professors can cut and paste just as well as students, he says, recalling that one of his students at Park College, in Missouri, turned in a paper that appeared to have been plagiarized. So Mr. Stallings copied a chunk of it into an on-line search engine and found the source, in the Library of Congress's on-line archives. The paper got an F.

"It took about five minutes," he says. "Everything is on a paperless, electronic form, so you can go out and find things easier than if it was typewritten."

Mr. Stallings adds: "I will never say it's virtually impossible to cheat in   30
virtual classrooms, but it's tough. You can't hide in cyberspace."

As a practical matter, he notes, virtual courses are most likely—at least for the time being—to attract continuing-education students, who he says are usually more ethical than traditional 19-year-old undergraduates.

When faced with a situation that may involve plagiarism, professors who teach on line and those who teach in the classroom should face the same burden of proof in undertaking an inquiry, says Ms. Wilson, of the Center for Academic Integrity.

Such charges, she notes, are usually evaluated like civil lawsuits—a weighing of a preponderance of the evidence—rather than a demand for proof beyond a reasonable doubt.

Inevitably, some cheaters are going to slip through the cracks.

"People are going to cheat on their income tax. They'll cheat on any-   35
thing," Ms. Hardy says. "Our job is to make that more difficult for them."

◆ **QUESTIONS FOR DISCUSSION AND WRITING** ◆
---

1. What is your immediate reaction to the methods Carnevale outlines for stopping online cheating? Are they necessary? Will they work? Why or why not?
2. *Ethical question:* Do you think college students are more likely to cheat in an on-line class than in a traditional classroom? Why or why not?

3. *Ethical question:* If you knew that a classmate was cheating, would you turn him or her in? Why or why not?
4. Carnevale quotes a professor who suggests that "continuing-education students . . . are usually more ethical than traditional 19-year-old undergraduates" (paragraph 31). Do you agree? Why or why not?

 ## Accrediting On-Line Institutions Diminishes Higher Education

James Perley and Denise Marie Tanguay

On-line instruction and distance education have swept through institutions of higher education with astounding speed. Now, commercial interests are avidly pursuing those developments, a reality that threatens to redefine higher education. While on-line *courses* offered by traditional institutions raise a number of questions about the equivalence and quality of offerings, and about faculty responsibility for the curriculum, totally on-line *institutions* raise questions about the meaning and preservation of higher education itself.

Such institutions raise the specter of a higher-education system that is nothing more than a collection of marketable commodities—a system that could turn out to be all but unrecognizable to the scholarly communities that invent and reinvent higher education on a daily basis.

Several indications of the new, commercially based enterprise have emerged in the past few years: the rapid, franchise-like expansion of the University of Phoenix, the establishment of Western Governors University, and the announcement of a new virtual university to be funded by the corporate parent of the publisher Harcourt Brace.

More than any of those developments, however, the decision of the North Central Association of Colleges and Schools to accredit Jones International University causes the greatest concern.

Why? Because it is inappropriate, if not impossible, to accredit an entirely on-line institution using traditional methods, in which faculty members and administrators work together on an extensive self-study process.

Consider just a few of the key issues: Can accreditors truly evaluate a university based solely on distance learning—with classrooms, libraries, and faculty members located somewhere in cyberspace—in the same way that they evaluate a traditional institution? Can we really call those institutions "colleges" or "universities" if they lack both a critical core of full-time faculty members and a system of governance by which the faculty is responsible for developing curricula and academic policy?

Can accreditors actually determine that new, on-line institutions meet the same basic criteria for quality—or, at least, equivalent criteria—that traditional accredited institutions must meet?

Neither the University of Phoenix nor Western Governors University raises the same questions about accreditation as a totally campus-free, on-line institution, such as Jones International. Phoenix has 81 campuses and offers only a portion of its programs on line. Western Governors markets on-line courses offered by traditional universities, and has a special accreditation status through a multiregional accrediting agency.

The fundamental difficulty with institutions that rely heavily, or exclusively, on distance education is that they are characterized by a practice called "unbundling." In that practice, course materials are prepared by a "content expert" and delivered by a "faculty facilitator," in a uniform manner, producing predictable and measurable "outcomes" that fit uniform assessment tools. Such a process of turning education into modular units represents a basic change in an essential characteristic of higher education.

The unbundling process removes the student from the content expert and packages the course material into discrete units—disrupting or precluding the critical interaction between students and faculty members over time. It destroys the ability of a faculty member to alter classroom content and process in response to students' reactions to the materials, or to consider the varying educational backgrounds and needs of individual students who are taking a specific course. In fact, we believe that the practice so alters the educational process that institutions offering only prepackaged or unbundled courses should not be accredited in the same way as traditional forms of higher education.

Three major features have characterized higher education in this country, have insured its quality, and have established its pre-eminent position in the world. Those features are what distinguishes higher education from other postsecondary endeavors, such as corporate training centers, proprietary trade schools, and continuing adult-education courses that do not lead to a degree. The three defining features are: a guarantee of academic freedom; the existence of a functioning system of collegial governance; and the presence of a group of scholars and students engaged not only in teaching and learning, but also in advancing the frontiers of knowledge.

Academic freedom assures the right of faculty members to fulfill their responsibility to teach and engage in research protected from inappropriate external pressures, which might constrain their thinking and debate. Because of that essential principle, faculty members in the United States are free to examine the controversial as well as the conventional in a search for truth. That, in turn, insures that faculty members have the ability to constantly improve their courses and teaching. That right and that responsibility are a vital component of the search for quality.

The fact that our system of higher education has protected the right of academic freedom—and allowed and encouraged multiple perspectives in every discipline to be developed, examined, and taught—has distinguished the high standards of intellectual debate in the United States from the "party line" mandates of the educational systems of some other countries.

tually enhance interaction. Their positive, firsthand experiences undercut simplistic denials of the effectiveness of distance education.

All that raises the question: Are those who oppose the accreditation of any virtual institution, regardless of its resources and performance, more concerned about quality, or about who defines it?

The A.A.U.P. and other groups and individuals expressing the greatest reservations about on-line institutions, as distinguished from on-line instruction, argue that on-line programs at traditional institutions draw upon proven methods of insuring quality that non-traditional institutions often lack. Faculty members are central to that process, those critics assert: Only full-time faculty members are fully effective mentors and teachers; only full-time faculty members can develop an effective curriculum and protect its integrity; only full-time faculty members, who are free to teach their own curriculum, can exercise academic freedom—and, thereby, provide the highest-quality learning experience for students.

At traditional institutions, faculty members are hired because they possess the requisite education and experience to fulfill those basic responsibilities. They design the curriculum and teach and evaluate it; they also hold themselves accountable to faculty governance, exercised through departments, colleges, and institution-wide curricular-review bodies.

But nothing inherent in an on-line institution demands radical redefinition of those traditional roles. At many institutions that use the Internet as a vehicle for instruction, the design, delivery, and evaluation of each course remain in the hands of a single faculty person, often full time. Faculty members control the learning environment; they use e-mail to lecture and encourage discussion on line, and to read, comment on, and grade papers. Faculty members might need help to master the technology and to design World-Wide Web sites, but the faculty-led classroom model is translated into the asynchronous environment of Internet instruction.

Of course, many on-line institutions, including Jones International, will not replicate every aspect of that model. Technology and the Internet enable a significant recasting of traditional educational processes and the role that faculty members play in those processes.

Jones International unbundles a faculty member's traditional role, placing various faculty responsibilities in the hands of several people. The institution hires content experts to work with its full-time instructional-design staff to create the degree requirements and the curriculum, and to evaluate their quality. The institution also employs mentors, skilled at facilitating learning on line, to teach and work directly with students. Full-time faculty members manage the quality of academic courses and programs by linking the content experts and the mentors, and supporting the professional-development needs of the mentors.

At the time of Jones International's accreditation review, more than 25 appropriately credentialed people—including faculty members from some of the top research universitites—had designed, delivered, and evaluated courses for the 65 enrolled students.

If we are to develop truly effective, interactive courses, we will always need such experts in various disciplines to create content and to be partners with those with technical expertise. We will always need mentors who work directly with students to stimulate the questioning, creativity, and critical thinking that we all value in higher education. We will always need trained individuals to develop a credible, fair system to evaluate learning.

In accrediting an on-line institution, therefore, we must find evidence that knowledgeable people in each field of study have defined the content of the curriculum. We must ascertain that the students' learning experience allows for effective interactions, both between faculty members and students, and among students. And we must be sure that a valid system for evaluating student achievement exists.

In other words, the capacity of an on-line institution to foster and protect faculty responsibilities will continue to be a key consideration in assuring the quality of an institution—and in granting accreditation.

◆ QUESTIONS FOR DISCUSSION AND WRITING ◆

1. Do you agree or disagree with Crow's position, as stated in the title of his essay, that "Virtual Universities Can Meet High Standards"? Why?
2. Now that you've read and thought about some of the issues in accrediting online colleges, do you believe that online college and university classes can offer students the same educational benefits as traditional classes? Why or why not?
3. Think about the articles your instructor asked you to read, and construct two lists: one that shows the benefits of distance-learning classes and another that lists their possible problems. Does this list change your mind about whether these types of courses ought to replace some of your traditional college or university classes? Why or why not?

TAKING ACTION
Writing a Guest Editorial for the Campus Paper

Now that you've read the selections in the Resources and perhaps done some outside research of your own, you have a grounding in the issues under discussion. The next step is to write that collaborative editorial for the campus newspaper expressing your group's feelings and ideas about the chancellor's plan.

The campus paper, the *Hearthwood Herald,* will publish these guest editorials daily as a way of generating a campuswide discussion. The chancellor has indicated her sincere interest in the suggestions and concerns of the campus community, and this is your group's chance to be heard.

The goal of your editorial should be to explain what your group believes is essential to the educational process, how this might be translated onto the Internet, and what the implications are for the chancellor's plan. Do you believe that any classes might be moved successfully to the Internet? Which ones? Why?

You can be fairly certain that the chancellor has some ideas of her own about how things should go. You'll need to support your assertions with evidence, even if that evidence consists only of examples from your own experience or data from your research.

The *Herald* insists that your guest editorial be brief: the newspaper imposes a maximum length of two pages. Get to your point, make it clearly, and support it briefly but strongly. Read some editorials in your own campus or local newspaper to get an idea of what editorials usually look like and how they sound. Remember that everyone on campus may read your comments, so think carefully about how you want to be perceived. Choose your words and your message accordingly.

Asking the Right Questions

It's often useful to start wrestling with a problem or issue that affects you, as the Hearthwood situation affects the groups in this scenario, by first discovering what you already know and what you'd like to learn more about. Begin with questions. Those questions will lead to other questions that will help your group determine the best solution for the problems the Hearthwood College scenario presents.

As you draft your editorial for the *Hearthwood Herald,* consider the scenario from a reporter's point of view, focusing on the who, what, when, where, and why of the scenario. As you write, try to answer the following questions:

- Based on what you've read, what perspectives might each of the other Hearthwood groups have? What are the strengths and weaknesses of those perspectives?

- Can you make your position stronger by aligning your group with others? Will it help to let *Hearthwood Herald* readers know that more than one group shares your ideas about some of the issues, problems, or possible solutions?

- What events in the Hearthwood College scenario can be controlled? How?

- What are some of the consequences to Hearthwood College students if Internet classes are implemented? To the administration? To the alumni? What specific effects will such classes have on the members of your group?

- What are the consequences if you do nothing to try to change the situation?

- How do the issues and problems in the Hearthwood College scenario relate to a broader national perspective on distance learning?

Which group you represent and the approach you decide to take will determine the position you propose. You might, for example, argue against any online or Internet classes, or you might urge restricting the extent to which such classes are offered: perhaps you'd suggest that large lecture classes might work as online courses, but smaller writing classes would not.

Constructing a Collaborative Text

Working with the members of your group, draft an editorial for the *Hearthwood Herald* that expresses your group's views on the benefits and problems you see with distance learning.

As we noted earlier, one way to start constructing your group statement is for each group member to compose his or her own statement, listing the most important issues and problems as he or she sees them. Then, working together, your group can draw on those initial comments to compose the group statement.

Another method for constructing your group's text is to start with the notes that each of you has made, designate one group member to record the group's ideas, and then collaboratively compose an initial draft of what your group thinks. At first, this process might be a bit hectic, with several group members offering suggestions on what to write and how to write it, but, with time, you'll find that working together is an interesting and useful way to get your collective ideas onto paper.

When you've completed a first draft of your collaborative text, each group member should read through the draft, marking any sections that are unclear. Work together to clarify those parts. Then, each group member should read the statement once more, this time looking for places in the text where your argument might need more evidence. Then, again working together, decide what pieces of evidence gathered during your research (facts, data, testimony, statistics) might provide additional support for your argument.

Your instructor might ask you to read and comment on the other groups' statements. Working together in that way gives you the chance to help your classmates become better writers, as you act as real readers for one another. Indicate the places in the text where more information is needed, or where the writing is confusing, or where some elaboration might help. Follow the procedure in Box 4.3: Using Your Classmates' Suggestions to apply the feedback you receive to improve your composition.

SPEAKING YOUR PIECE
Campus Open Forum

After the editorials in the *Herald* have been running for nearly a month, the chancellor decides that an open campus forum might help

BOX 4.3   APPLYING WHAT YOU READ
Using Your Classmates' Suggestions (Written Peer Review)

Once your group has completed a brief, collaborative text that outlines your message to the *Hearthwood Herald,* exchange your draft with that of another group. Read their editorial carefully, and make notes on (and indicate in the margins) its strengths and weaknesses.

What suggestions can you make on how the group might improve its ideas? What are the strengths of its draft? The weaknesses? Where was the editorial confusing? How might the group clarify its position? What suggestions might you offer to improve the editorial?

Once your group gets feedback from your classmates, work together as a group to revise your editorial to the *Herald.* What suggestions did you receive that make sense? Where does your text need clarification, or further explanation, or more evidence? What facts or other data have group members collected that you can add to your text, to make it more convincing?

everyone better understand the positions of the various groups. The campus community will meet in Hollice J. Peters Auditorium, and representatives from all groups will be invited to speak. The purpose of the forum is to exchange views. The chancellor has expressly asked each group to indicate which classes it thinks should be moved to the Internet first.

In addition to each group's delivering a prepared statement, there will be a chance for everyone to ask questions. To participate fully in the discussion, listen carefully to all questions so that you're sure what you're being asked. Feel free to take a moment to confer among yourselves before you answer. There's no reason that your group can't have more than one answer to a question, if you feel that your positions are diverse enough to warrant it.

Remember, as with your editorial to the *Herald,* this is a public forum. How you present yourself can reflect on the positions you are arguing. If your group is well prepared with both substantive questions and thoughtful answers, and if you are courteous to others, people are likely to look more favorably on your group's position.

From Written Preparation to Public Speaking

As you prepare for the forum, refer to your editorial. One purpose of the forum is to decide, specifically, which classes should be the first ones moved online. You should be prepared to offer your suggestions and to support them with good reasons. What is it about these classes that makes them compatible with teaching and learning on the Internet? How can they be structured to alleviate the concerns of the campus community?

For example, if some of the faculty members express concern that on-line classes might allow students to cheat more easily, how might the class you suggest be structured to reduce that risk? If the alumni worry that such classes will devalue a Hearthwood degree, what can you say to alleviate their concerns?

Speaking at the Campus Forum

In a full-class open meeting, representatives of each group will be allowed to state their groups' positions about online education at Hearthwood College. Each speaker will be given a time limit, as would be the case in a real public forum.

When all the groups have presented their statements on what Hearthwood should do, members of each group might be allowed to question members of the other groups. Your instructor may assign one or more students to act as moderators, to make sure everyone has the opportunity to get his or her point(s) across to the rest of the class.

INDIVIDUAL WRITING
Essay Options

So far in this scenario, you've worked with a group of your classmates to compose a group editorial and then to present your group's ideas in an open meeting. Now, your instructor will ask you to complete one or more individual writing assignments: an informative essay, a process essay, and/or a proposal essay. Although each assignment asks you to approach the subject of online education from a different perspective, they all require that you make use of the research, writing, and speaking you've done so far in this scenario. Be sure to look over and consider the notes you've taken, the group discussions you've had, and the statements and questions from the other groups during the campus forum. You might also need to do additional research to better understand the issues or to find support for something you want to say.

The Informative Essay

Before a college makes the decision to offer classes on the Internet, a lot of research needs to be done. Faculty, staff, and administrators must understand what an online education is, how it works, and what its strengths and weaknesses are. Because those involved have to understand all aspects of the situation, for this assignment we ask you to construct an informative essay that focuses on distance learning.

To compose a useful informative essay, you'll need to research the history and development of online education (a good starting point are the readings in this chapter). There's no sense in reinventing the wheel, so your research should focus on the challenges and successes experienced by other schools that offer online courses. You're writing for an audience of people who will construct and teach an online curriculum, so the purpose of your paper should be to provide them with an overview of what has been successful and what has failed in online education.

Take a look at the kinds of classes that have been offered and are being offered online. Which seem to work best? Why? How are they set up? Do some online classes "meet" in chat rooms, as one would in a classroom, to conduct discussions and share ideas? Are there deadlines throughout a semester, or are online classes self-paced, with students completing work when they can? Is there a difference in tuition costs? How are questions about cheating handled?

There is, of course, a lot of information about online education available on the Internet, but don't limit yourself to just searching Web sites for supporting information about online education. Many education journals have published articles about the subject, and even popular magazines and newspapers have covered it. Remember your audience and your purpose: to inform. You aren't trying to convince anyone that online education is good or bad; instead, you're simply trying to provide your audience with the information they need to move into Web-based teaching successfully.

The Process Essay

A process essay explains how to do something: you can liken it to a set of instructions. Both Hearthwood students and Hearthwood faculty will need training before online classes are offered. For this assignment, your focus is what students will need: How do they begin learning about online education? What do they need to know to succeed in a virtual classroom? Your essay will be included in the how-to section of the Hearthwood College Student Handbook, and it should help students make the adjustment to the new system.

When you are constructing a how-to essay, keep in mind that organization is critical. You want your reader to be able to receive the information in a way that makes sense. Place yourself in the position of students who might know the basics of computing and can get around online, but might be new to college and to the idea of online education. Where can they find the information they need before beginning an online class? How do they contact the instructor if they have problems or questions? What are the most important things they should remember when taking an online class?

It might help to begin by listing all the questions you think such students might have and using those questions to help you create a simple outline for your paper. When writing instructions, you need to anticipate follow-up questions because you won't be there to answer them in person. What questions will students have as they read your instructions? How can you make sure they are clear and complete?

The Proposal Essay

For this assignment, we ask you to construct a proposal essay, describing how a specific class (you select one) might be presented over the Internet. You might select a class you've taken recently or one you're enrolled in now, so that you're familiar with the kind of work and activities the class entails. Consider carefully whether a class might lend itself to online instruction before deciding on it.

Once you've chosen a class that seems suitable to you, you'll have to "translate" it into an Internet experience. In your proposal, try to answer some of these questions:

- Is contact with the instructor important in this class? If so, how will that contact take place? Will students have more than just e-mail contact with each other and with the instructor?
- How will class "discussions" take place? Are these an important part of the class you propose to put on the Internet?
- What is your plan for handling quizzes? Tests? Midterm and final examinations?
- How will students complete in-class writing assignments?
- What do you have to say about possible cheating? How will you ensure that students who receive credit for the class actually took the class?
- What classroom activities usually take place in this class? How can you translate them to an Internet setting?
- What classroom activities will not be possible on the Internet? Alternatively, what activities could be part of an online class that couldn't be done in a traditional classroom? How will these differences change the educational experience?
- In what ways can you ensure that the online class is as rigorous as the traditional class?

Remember that a proposal accounts for as many details as possible. It also anticipates difficulties with and objections to its approach.

To conclude this scenario, your instructor may ask that you follow the instructions in Box 4.4: Reflections on the Hearthwood College Scenario. The process of writing about ways in which your attitudes may have changed helps clarify your thinking.

BOX 4.4   APPLYING WHAT YOU READ
Reflections on the Hearthwood College Scenario

You've written, read, and discussed quite a bit about online education. Your knowledge of the subject has grown, and your views have become more complex. Look back at the first writing you did for this scenario, after you'd thought about the photographs that introduce this chapter and read the First Impressions questions. Then jot down your answers to these questions:

- Do you look at education and college life differently than you did when you first began thinking about them for this scenario? How so?
- Is there something in your initial writing that catches your attention now that really didn't seem to be important the first time around?
- In what ways might you modify your definitions of "college education" or "distance learning"?
- What have you learned about writing as you worked through the Hearthwood College scenario?

FOR FURTHER RESEARCH AND WRITING

The situation at Hearthwood College isn't an unusual one. More and more colleges and universities are looking at the Internet as a delivery tool for education. This brings up a number of issues that you might explore further.

One source of additional information is a weekly newspaper designed for college and university professors: the *Chronicle of Higher Education*. Both National Public Radio (NPR) and public television stations regularly cover educational issues and problems.

For further writing, consider these topics: Where are colleges heading? Will the future see the disappearance of the traditional college campus? Are schools such as Hearthwood an endangered species? Will technology replace the chalkboard with the virtual classroom?

You might instead want to look back for topics: Where did the traditional notions of a college education come from? Who decided that the liberal arts curriculum was a good idea? What is the purpose of the liberal arts curriculum? Given recent advances in technology, is liberal arts still a valid course of study?

Another possible avenue of research might focus on related questions: Does making college more accessible to all devalue a college degree? How important is a college degree? Are college degrees more or less mandatory for the current generation? What are students' attitudes toward their education? Your experiences working with this scenario might have raised other questions that you'd like to answer for yourself through research and writing.

You now have read, discussed, and written about some of the potential problems with and benefits of distance education. Each day, teachers, students, and administrators at colleges and universities around the country grapple with these types of problems. We hope that working through this distance-learning scenario has helped you improve how you read and write; we also hope that you better understand how to work effectively with others. The skills you used in this scenario will aid you in the work you've yet to do in this and your other college classes. Ultimately, these skills will also help you in your career.

CHAPTER 5

Student Privacy: Bad Times at Westwood High

FOURTH AMENDMENT

The right of the people to be secure in their persons, houses, papers, and effects, against unreasonable searches and seizures, shall not be violated; and no Warrants shall issue but upon probable cause, supported by Oath or affirmation, and particularly describing the place to be searched, and the persons or things to be seized.

◆ FIRST IMPRESSIONS ◆

Be sure to look at and think about the photographs that introduce this chapter. Then spend a few minutes jotting down answers to these questions:

- What is your initial reaction to the first photograph? Does it represent a potential threat to other students or an invasion of privacy? Why or why not?
- How would you apply the Fourth Amendment to the Constitution of the United States to using a metal detector at your high school? To searching student lockers or cars?
- Did you always feel safe at your high school? Why or why not?
- If you didn't feel safe at school, what might have made it a safer place for you?
- Did your high school have any security features (guards, a fence, metal detectors, other)? If so, describe them.
- When you think about "weapons on a high school campus," what comes to your mind?
- What were your high school's policies regarding guns on campus? Other weapons (knives, for example)? How were those policies enforced? Were they effective?
- When you were a high school student, did your school have the right to search your locker? Your backpack? Your car? If you were in high school today, how would you feel about such searches?
- Would you have been willing to give up some of your constitutional rights against illegal "search and seizure" to make your high school a safer place?

When you're done, your instructor may ask you to share your comments with your classmates.

Although tragic incidents that involve shootings at high schools make headlines, almost all of our schools are in fact safe for both students and teachers. But most people would argue that even a single weapon on a high school campus is one too many, and there are indications that more and more students are bringing weapons of some kind to school. Often, in the student's eyes, the weapon offers some measure of protection from other students with weapons.

Today's students fear weapons on campus. A survey of 1,200 fourteen-through eighteen-year-old students, reported by ABC News, indicated that the number who feel safe at school dropped from 44 percent in 1998 to 37 percent in 1999. The same survey reported that the percentage of junior high school students who feel safe on campus dropped from 44 percent to 33 percent in the same period. Students are afraid at least partly because of weapons on campus: although the number of students expelled for bringing a gun to school dropped 31 percent between 1997 and 1998, California and Texas each expelled more than 300 students for bringing guns on campus during the 1997–98 school year (ABC News.com). Nationwide, in the 1997–98 school year, nearly 4,000 students were expelled for bringing a gun onto a school campus.

An obvious way to stop students from bringing weapons onto campus is to install metal detection equipment and to introduce a mandatory search policy for all backpacks and bookbags. But there are personal rights concerns; and not every school wants to search its students, their lockers, and their backpacks. In New Mexico, for instance, one school simply bolted its lockers closed, so students must carry their backpacks all day long. In Buffalo, New York, a school now forces students to leave their bookbags in their lockers during the day; and, in Florida, one school simply banned bookbags and backpacks completely, so that school officials can see everything a student is carrying.

How safe is the high school you attended? If you have younger siblings or cousins, if you have children of your own, or if you plan to have children someday, what should be done to ensure their safety at school? What rights do students have under search-and-seizure laws? What responsibilities do school officials have for protecting their students?

What would your initial reaction be and what would you want to see done if:

- Someone was shot at your high school?
- The principal of your son's high school installed metal detectors at all school entrances?
- Violence was increasing at your daughter's school, including knife fights in the hallways?
- Each morning, the school administration searched the backpacks of every student?
- Your car was searched as you dropped off your brother at his high school?
- Drug dealers exchanged shots next to your cousin's school?
- Your best friend brought a gun to school, "for protection"?

Although our Westwood High School scenario is situated in a fictional high school near Seattle, Washington, the issues it addresses are found everywhere: weapons are a serious problem in today's high schools.

Pretend for a moment that you live in Winterhaven, Washington, home of the Westwood High School Wildcats. There have never been many problems on the Westwood campus, but last year, James Rowe, a Westwood sophomore, brought a gun to school. Rowe was showing the .25 automatic pistol to some friends in one of the restrooms, and he accidentally dropped it. The gun discharged without injuring anyone. A hall monitor saw James running away, and his gun was later found in a wastebasket. After a quick investigation, Rowe was suspended for two weeks.

In early April of last year, on the day Winterhaven received its final snowfall of the season, Christina Nelson, a Westwood junior, was stabbed outside the women's locker room. Nelson needed minor surgery but refused to identify her attacker, who was never apprehended.

A week after the stabbing, what the local paper described as a riot took place in the school cafeteria, but it was actually a fight between two student factions at Westwood. The sheriff's office suspected, but could never prove, that the fight was over drugs. Two Westwood students spent a night in the hospital; another, Terry Burton, spent two weeks in the hospital recovering from stab wounds. The knife used in the incident was never found.

Imagine that:

- You're a senior at Westwood, and you're proud of your school. After all, your baseball team won the state championship last year, and Westwood has a good academic reputation: more than 40 percent of your class has earned some scholarship money for college. Considering the incidents we just outlined, are you afraid to go to class? What should the police and school administration do, if anything, to make Westwood a safer place? What personal rights, if any, would you be willing to sacrifice if giving them up would make the campus safer? Do you think it's possible to make any school completely safe?

- Your child attends Westwood High. What would you like to see done to ensure the safety of all students at the school? What personal rights do you think your son or daughter should be willing to give up to ensure the safety of all students? Should students have to pass through metal detectors at school entrances? Should armed guards patrol the hallways? Should students allow their backpacks to be searched? Their cars?

- You're an underclassman at Westwood. Are you concerned about what might happen over the next several years, in terms of your safety on campus? How would you feel if your school were surrounded by a high fence, with armed guards at the gates?

- You're a member of Westwood High School's administration, so it's your responsibility to make sure that every student is safe on campus. How do you plan to do that? What options are you considering, and how do you plan to implement them? What responsibility does a school administration have to ensure the safety of its students? How can a high school administration balance safety concerns against the personal rights the Constitution guarantees all American citizens? How far should the school administration go to protect students from violence?

- You teach at Westwood High, so you find yourself in the middle of things: students on one side, the administration on the other, and parents somewhere in between. How do you respond to the recent campus problems? How would you feel working, as a colleague puts it, in an "armed camp"?

Questions such as these are being raised in many high schools around the country. In this scenario we'll ask you to consider some of the issues and problems that Westwood High School faces. We'll ask you and your classmates to address questions such as these:

- How does a school know that it has a problem with weapons on campus? What measures should it take to solve the problem? Should an isolated incident prompt safety measures, such as the installation of metal detectors at school entrances or armed guards in the hallways? Or should stringent safety measures be implemented only after a series of serious incidents?

- Once the school administration becomes aware of a problem with weapons on campus, how can it determine who is responsible? Should the majority of students be punished because of the bad deeds of a few?

- If those responsible for bringing weapons onto campus are caught, what should the penalty be? More and more school districts have what is called a zero-tolerance policy for weapons on school grounds: anyone caught with a weapon on campus is expelled immediately, often for as long as a year. Is this policy fair? Should the zero-tolerance policy apply to weapons other than guns and knives? Should a Swiss army knife or a pocket nail file qualify as a weapon? Should the zero-tolerance policy apply to a student who inadvertently brings a weapon onto campus? What if a student has a gun locked in the trunk of his car because he plans to do some target practicing with friends after school? Should he be expelled?

Although our scenario is set in the Pacific Northwest, the problem with weapons in school, especially in high schools, is one that concerns students, parents, and administrators nationwide. Individual schools must determine how to address local issues and problems, but the overriding goal is the same for everyone: how can we ensure that our schools are safe?

To work through this scenario, your instructor will ask you and your classmates to form groups. Each group will represent one of the parties that have a stake in what happens at Westwood High School. Your instructor will ask you to work in these groups, collaboratively and individually, on a number of exercises that will help you understand and ultimately address the issues and concerns you would experience if Westwood High were a real school.

This scenario provides a starting point for further research on and discussion of a range of topics: You might focus on why students feel the need to bring weapons onto campus. You might ask what the causes are for the seeming increase in violent behavior occurring in this country. You might explore the ways in which school punishments are determined and enforced. To help you get started, we provide readings from a variety of sources: newspapers, the Internet, government agency publications, journals, and so on. We've selected the kinds of readings you might find and use if you were actually involved in the Westwood High School scenario.

THE SCENARIO

Are Student Rights More Important than Group Safety?

As with any school, Westwood High School has had its share of bad days: a few years back, the basketball team lost the state championship on a controversial last-second free throw; two years ago a popular teacher was killed in a car accident; that same semester two students were suspended because they were caught plagiarizing a paper for their senior English class.

But lately things have become much worse for Westwood and its students, and now the school faces a new danger: weapons on campus.

Westwood High is in Winterhaven, Washington, a growing suburb about 20 miles east of Seattle. Fifteen years ago, Winterhaven was a quiet, small community of 6,500 residents, many of whom worked in the lumber industry, for Deadwood Timber and Sawmill. During the past decade, Winterhaven has been "discovered," and more and more Seattle residents have chosen to live and to raise their families here, even though they have to commute more than a half hour to jobs in Seattle.

Winterhaven's population has mushroomed to nearly 30,000, and, as with many cities and neighborhoods and schools, society's changing demographics have altered the nature of the community. School enrollments have increased dramatically, but the Winterhaven Valley Governing Council, which oversees Winterhaven County's entire school system, has been slow to fund the growth. Westwood High has been forced to rely on a number of portable classroom buildings; most classes are overcrowded, and not all students can fit into the cafeteria at the same time. Because of this, Westwood students are allowed to leave campus during the lunch period. The open campus, however, has created its own set of problems: the number of students trying to leave, eat, and return at the same time has filled Westwood's parking lots with confusion and speeding cars, and the number of fender benders on nearby residential streets has increased dramatically.

Over the past few years, the area surrounding Westwood High has slowly deteriorated: yards are overgrown, houses are shabby, streets are not maintained as well as they once were, and drug busts are becoming more prevalent (recently a suspected crack house was raided and closed down by the local sheriff, with help from Seattle's SWAT Team). The sheriff's office has stepped up its patrols, especially near the schools. But because Winterhaven is an unincorporated area, the town has to rely on the sheriff's department for protection, and these days, the sheriff's force is stretched pretty thin.

The worst of Westwood's bad days occurred just last spring: Jeremy Gordon, a Westwood junior and honor-role student, was shot and injured in the Westwood parking lot, allegedly by a nonstudent. No one was apprehended. There were rumors of a drug deal gone bad, but that was never proved, and over the summer Gordon's family moved away.

Because of increasing problems at the school, the Winterhaven Valley Governing Council assigned a new principal, who started work at Westwood High this fall. Dr. Michael Jensen's previous academic position had been as drug enforcement coordinator at what could be described as a troubled high school, where campus problems with drugs, alcohol, weapons, and violence were prevalent.

Such had not been the case at Westwood until early in the fall semester, when a small bag of crack cocaine fell out of a student's backpack as the student was searching for a book. The student was immediately referred to juvenile authorities but was back in school the next day.

Only a week after that incident, Donald Lowry, Jr., should not have been surprised when he found Principal Jensen going through his locker. But Don was shocked because he's attended Westwood since his freshman year, he is co-captain of the football team, and he carries a 3.8 GPA. Don Lowry is hardly the type of student whom anyone might suspect of doing something illegal.

"We got an anonymous tip, and we're looking for drugs, as you might expect," Dr. Jensen told Don, "or anything else that shouldn't be here."

"You've got to be kidding," Don replied. "You don't really expect to find anything in my locker, do you?"

"Well, we'll see," Dr. Jensen shot back. He continued his search but found nothing.

Don was outraged, and it didn't take long for everyone to hear what had happened. Soon there were more than fifty students gathered outside the principal's office, shouting, "We deserve privacy! We deserve trust!" After about fifteen minutes, this gathering was dispersed without incident, but the students remained upset about Dr. Jensen's actions.

The students, of course, complained to their parents, and soon letters and editorials began to appear in the student newspaper, the *Westwood Reporter,* and in the local paper, the *Winterhaven Times.*

As those involved tried to work things out, the situation worsened: four Westwood High students totaled a car as they left campus for lunch. No one was seriously hurt, but the sheriff determined that the driver had been drinking. The rumor was that one of the boys had been keeping a bottle or two of alcohol in his locker and shared it with his friends on their way to lunch. And worse, when the sheriff's deputy looked through the wrecked car, he found a .38 revolver and several rounds of ammunition.

Dr. Jensen and his administration immediately cracked down and searched the lockers of all of Westwood's 955 students. This is a partial list of what they found:

- One .38 Colt handgun (this student claimed he didn't know where the gun came from).
- Two pellet guns (both students claimed that the guns must have been planted in their lockers).
- Bags containing small quantities of marijuana in six lockers.
- Three cases of beer, scattered among sixteen lockers.
- Two foil-wrapped packages of crack cocaine.
- Four knives.
- Two clubs.
- Four bottles of hard liquor; seven bottles of wine.

Because possession of drugs or weapons on a school campus is a criminal matter, the local school board ceded authority to the Winterhaven Valley Governing Council. Dr. Jensen immediately announced that he would ask the Winterhaven Valley Governing Council to "approve my measures to ensure the safety of all Westwood High School students." Principal Jensen is proposing that:

- All cars coming onto campus be subject to search.
- All students and staff wear a photo ID badge at all times.
- School administrators search all bookbags every morning.
- Metal detectors be installed at all school entrances.

ENTERING THE SCENARIO: DEALING WITH THE CRACKDOWN

Now that you've read about the situation at Westwood High School, it's time for you to become actively involved. Your instructor will ask you to work with several of your classmates as a member of one of the groups affected by and interested in the situation at Westwood High. Although your main concern should center on how your group is affected by the principal's proposals, the descriptions that follow will help you understand the perspectives of all the groups involved in this scenario. These group descriptions are only a start; it is your group's job to continue to "flesh out" your group's description and perspectives based on how group members feel about student privacy and safety.

Members of the Senior Class

You and the other members of Westwood's senior class have been together for four years, and you have a good deal of school spirit and pride. You are disturbed by some of the recent events at Westwood. Because you expect to graduate next spring, the principal's ideas may not seem especially onerous—after all, your class will be affected for only one academic year. But you're proud of your high school and concerned that it may be turned into a walled fortress of some kind or, as one student described it, "a prison surrounded by a barbed-wire fence." At the same time, some members of your senior class might welcome improved security at the school and might suggest that the administration go even further in its efforts to improve safety.

Members of the Freshman, Sophomore, and Junior Classes

As a member of a group that has two or more years until graduation, you recognize that Dr. Jensen's actions—especially the proposed searches—will have a greater impact on you than on the senior class. What would your group like to see happen, to ensure the safety of all students while protecting personal privacy rights for members of your group?

As might members of the senior class, some of you might embrace the principal's ideas. You might be more willing than members of the other groups to allow backpack searches, car searches, and metal detectors at the school's entrances, as long as these measures increased your safety at Westwood High.

Members of the Westwood High School Administration

The members of the administration are responsible for the education of Westwood High School's students, as well as for their safety. Because school lockers are school property, your group argues that you can examine the contents of those lockers whenever you choose to do so.

You and the other members of the administration also believe that you must have the authority to extend your searches to other places where illegal drugs and dangerous weapons might be hidden, including backpacks, cars parked on campus, and perhaps even to visitors who come onto campus.

In fact, because school safety is a primary concern of the administration, you also want to explore other approaches. Some ideas that have been mentioned include security fencing around the campus, perhaps topped with razor wire; secured gates at each parking lot entrance; video surveillance cameras in the hallways and perhaps even in bathrooms; and drug-sniffing dogs in the hallways. And only last week, Dr. Jensen suggested that if his initial actions aren't effective, then armed guards should be hired (he proposes to use off-duty Sheriff's Department officers) to "patrol Westwood, both inside and outside, to make sure all students are safe. There will be no more drugs or violence at Westwood High School."

Several Parents, the More Active Members of the Parent-Teacher Association

As a parent, you wonder about the fairness of what is now called "the Lowry incident." Because nothing was found in Don Lowry's locker, you ask why this student, an outstanding and exemplary one, was singled out for such a search, and whether anonymous tips shouldn't be fully investigated before they're acted on. As a parent, you might argue that because you know your sons and daughters would never bring illegal drugs or weapons onto campus, they should never be searched, in any manner. You see the administration's actions as heavy-handed and arbitrary. Among your group of parents may also be those who feel that any and all searches or surveillance of students is acceptable if it keeps them safe and who agree in general with the school administration and its new ideas for improving school safety.

Westwood High School Faculty Members

You've taught at Westwood for some time now, and you enjoy your work, your colleagues, and the students. Recent events at Westwood and elsewhere trouble you, though, and you worry that something could happen in your classroom. You're concerned about the safety of everyone on campus, but you're not sure what role you should play. After all, you're an educator: you see campus safety as the responsibility of others. How much support should you give to Dr. Jensen's proposals? Are they appropriate? Do you think they will increase campus safety? Would you help implement his ideas—operating the metal detector, perhaps, or searching students' bookbags? Would you allow your car and bag to be searched whenever you enter campus? Would you agree to wear an ID badge whenever you are on campus? What are your views on the issue of campus safety?

JOINING AND NAMING YOUR INTEREST GROUP

Now that you've read through the scenario and met the interested parties, it's time for you to become actively involved. Your instructor will ask you to work with several of your classmates to take on the role of a student, a parent, a teacher, or a school administrator.

In this scenario, it's likely that there will be more than one group of parents, each with a different reaction to Dr. Jensen's ideas. The same is true for groups of students and, perhaps, teachers: different groups may feel differently about the principal's suggestions.

So that you can consider and understand the situation from your group's perspective, we ask that you really do pretend that you're a member of the group you represent. To determine how you collectively feel, you and the other members of your group can begin by discussing and answering questions such as these:

- Which issues in the Westwood High School scenario do you find especially interesting? What are some of the issues that might concern or affect your group more than they would concern members of the other groups?

- What other groups might share at least some of your beliefs and ideas? For example, in the Westwood situation, at least some students will recommend the same safety measures suggested by the other groups. Can those students ally themselves with a group of parents, perhaps, or even with the administration?

- Which groups might oppose your point of view? What objections might they have to your ideas? How might you counter those objections?

To deepen your involvement with the Westwood High scenario and your identification with your group, follow the instructions in Box 5.1: Naming Your Interest Group (page 148).

TAKING A POSITION: WRITING TO THE WINTERHAVEN VALLEY GOVERNING COUNCIL

The Winterhaven Valley Governing Council is an elected group that controls the funds for all of Westwood's schools, from kindergarten through the Westwood CC, the local community college. In Winterhaven County, all schools report to the council, and this group ultimately will decide which of Dr. Jensen's proposals, if any, they will fund.

For this scenario, the Winterhaven Valley Governing Council has asked all interested groups, including members of the school administration, to present in writing their views on Dr. Jensen's proposals. The council has asked that these statements be no longer than two pages.

RESOURCES: HOW DANGEROUS ARE OUR SCHOOLS?

With any issue, it's important to research what others have done in similar situations. Therefore, before you and the members of your group construct your statement to the Winterhaven Valley Governing Council, you'll find it useful to consider what other groups might have experienced as they confronted issues similar to those in this scenario. You also might want to conduct field research by interviewing the administrators and school board members who are responsible for a school's safety.

BOX 5.1   APPLYING WHAT YOU READ
Naming Your Interest Group

The names we used for the various interested groups at Westwood High School are simple, but they give you an idea of each group's perspective on the Westwood situation. To really become a part of the scenario, though, you and those in your group should give yourselves a name: an original name that helps to convey the image your group hopes to project. The name you give your group will help determine how others respond to your group's ideas, so consider the associations that are attached to words as you think about names. For example, a teachers' group that chooses the name Don't Search Us! presents itself differently than one that calls itself Teachers for a Safe School. A parents' group that uses a name like Hands Off Our Kids! comes across very differently from one called Concerned Westwood Parents.

If you're part of the group representing Westwood's administration, rather than choosing a name for your group, think about what kind of label might be appropriate for your group's approach to the Westwood situation. Do you see yourselves as conservative—and if so, how do you define the term? Do you view your ideas as progressive? What do you mean by that label? Or would you describe your group as reactionary? Liberal? Concerned? Thoughtful? Working with the members of your group, decide on one or more labels that accurately portray how you see yourselves, and define those labels so that the other groups will better understand your perspective.

Discuss with the members of your group some names of real groups and the feelings you associate with them. Then brainstorm a list of possibilities for your group. Once you've reached a consensus, share your group's ideas with the other groups.

The readings that follow provide you with background information on the larger issues, because the situation at Westwood High is typical of that at other schools and in other towns. The writers of these pieces explore a number of vital issues, and each has his or her own perspective. After each reading you'll find a series of questions that will help you think about the reading and better understand the issues involved.

Pulitzer Prize–winning cartoonist Steve Benson sets the stage for this set of readings with a provocative cartoon. Next we look at what the Fourth Amendment to the U.S. Constitution—one of the original amendments making up what is commonly called the Bill of Rights—says about protection of individuals against "unreasonable" searches. Michael Sniffen offers a number of statistics on crime—especially gang-related problems—in American schools, and Karen Peterson presents some startling statistics on guns in schools.

The federal government's *1999 Annual Report on School Safety* asserts, right at the start, that "the vast majority of America's schools are safe places." Not only does it provide a wealth of information to confirm that statement, but it also supplies data that could be used to refute it. All groups in the Westwood High scenario should find this report useful.

Many schools have zero-tolerance policies: any student caught with a weapon on campus is immediately expelled. Columnist E. J. Montini argues that such a solution is not right in all instances.

Both "State Urges Schools to Begin Random Search of Students' Lockers" and "Guards with Guns" propose possible ways to improve school safety—but all involve some loss of personal freedom. "Preventing School Violence: No Easy Answers" and "Personalization" outline methods school districts have implemented to make their schools safer. Groups in this scenario who are proposing alternate solutions to the problems at Westwood High School will find others' experiences informative.

Finally, all groups will learn something from the detailed data in R. Craig Sautter's essay, "Standing Up to Violence."

You'll also find the information in these readings helpful once you complete your group statement and begin to construct an individual writing project. Remember to interact actively with these readings and to implement the reading strategies you learned earlier (prereading, annotating, summarizing, and so on).

As you read these texts, think about how the group you represent might react and respond to the statements the authors make:

- What new ideas did you and the members of your group find in or generate from each reading, ideas you might use in your group's statement to the Winterhaven Valley Governing Council?

- From your group's perspective, what are the most important points each reading makes? If the points disagree with your perspective, how would you respond to them to strengthen your position?

- Are there issues or facts or data in any of the readings that might work against your group's position?

As you read, make note of anything in the readings that you think might improve or damage your group's position, so that you can incorporate the information into your group's written statement to the Winterhaven Valley Governing Council.

◆ READINGS

Life in the Classroom, *Steve Benson*

The Fourth Amendment to the Constitution of the United States

School Crime up 25%, *Michael J. Sniffen*

1 Million School Kids Toting Guns, *Karen S. Peterson*

1999 Annual Report on School Safety, U.S. Department of Education and U.S. Department of Justice

Growing Intolerant of Zeros, *E. J. Montini*

State Urges Schools to Begin Random Search of Students' Lockers, New York Times *Metropolitan Desk*

Preventing School Violence: No Easy Answers, *Lynne Lamberg*

Personalization, *Rebecca Martin Shore*

Guards with Guns, *Kevin Bushweller*

Standing Up to Violence, *R. Craig Sautter*

✳ Life in the Classroom

Steve Benson

Steve Benson, reprinted by permission of United Feature Syndicate, Inc.

─────────◆ **QUESTIONS FOR DISCUSSION AND WRITING** ◆─────────

1. What's your initial reaction to Benson's cartoon? Why do you suppose you feel as you do? What in the cartoon might trigger (no pun intended) your reaction?
2. Do you find this cartoon humorous or disturbing? Why?
3. Does cartoonist Benson make a good point or not? Why?

───

❊ The Fourth Amendment to the Constitution of the United States

The right of the people to be secure in their persons, houses, papers, and effects, against unreasonable searches and seizures, shall not be violated, and no Warrants shall issue, but upon probable cause, supported by Oath or affirmation, and particularly describing the place to be searched, and the persons or things to be seized.

─────────◆ **QUESTIONS FOR DISCUSSION AND WRITING** ◆─────────

1. In terms of high school students, how do you interpret this amendment to the Constitution? Does a search of a bookbag, for example, or a student's locker constitute an "unreasonable search and seizure"? Why or why not?
2. Do you think a school administration should have to obtain a search warrant before it is allowed to search a student's bookbag? Locker? Desk? Automobile? Clothing? Why or why not?
3. What constitutes "probable cause" when it comes to searching a student's backpack, locker, desk, or car?

───

❊ School Crime up 25%

MORE TEENS REPORT GANGS

Michael J. Sniffen

Nearly twice as many teenagers reported gangs in their schools in 1995 as they did in 1989, while the number of students victimized by violent crime increased nearly 25 percent, the U.S. government reported Sunday [April 1998].

President Clinton called the findings "unacceptable" and urged Congress to fight the trend by approving anti-gang and youth violence initiatives he offered a year ago, focusing on "what we know works—tough, targeted deterrence."

"Gangs, and the guns, drugs and violence that go with them, must be stopped from ever reaching the schoolhouse door," Clinton said.

Based on surveys of students ages 12–19, street gangs were spotted in schools by 28.4 percent of those questioned in 1995, compared with 15.3 percent in 1989, the Bureau of Justice Statistics and the National Center for Education Statistics reported.

Violent crime at school, such as physical attacks or a robbery by force, weapon or threat, was reported by 4.2 percent of students in 1995, up 23.5 percent from 3.4 percent six years earlier, the Justice and Education departments said. 5

Pascal Forgione Jr., U.S. Commissioner of Education Statistics, said that while relatively small, "this difference of 0.8 percentage points was statistically significant and represented an increase of about 270,000 students."

Forgione said that the gang increase came in every type of community. In central cities, students reporting street gangs rose to 40.7 percent from 24.8 percent; in suburbs, to 26.3 percent from 14.0 percent; and in non-metropolitan areas, to 19.9 percent from 7.8 percent.

Violence at school shocked the nation last month when two boys, ages 11 and 13, allegedly gunned down four students and a teacher at a rural middle school in Jonesboro, Ark. Classmate Melinda Henson said that Mitchell Johnson, 13, claimed to be part of a gang and wore something red "every day, because he was in the Blood Gang."

The survey found that gangs and violence went together. In 1995, 7.5 percent of all students who reported gangs in their schools also said they had fallen victim to violent crime there, compared with 2.7 percent of the students who reported no gangs in school.

Although citing changes in the six years between the two surveys, the report warned that the "reader should not assume . . . a stable trend between 1989 and 1995." 10

Indeed, government data show that violent crime by juveniles peaked in 1994 and has declined for two years since then. Arrests of teenagers for violent crimes dropped 2.9 percent in 1995 and 9.2 percent in 1996.

And gangs in schools also may be coming down from a peak of a few years ago. The National Center for Education Statistics pointed out that a different study found an even higher incidence of gangs in 1993 than the 1995 study did.

The 1993 study found 35 percent of students said "fighting" gangs were present in their schools. The government cautioned that "data from these two surveys cannot be compared directly due to different wording of the gangs question," but the differences could signal trends.

A coauthor of the report, Kathryn Chandler of the National Center for Education Statistics, cited another possible reason for the increase between 1989 and 1995 in gang reports.

"What we're seeing I think is that more people are aware nowadays of what a gang is," Chandler said. 15

The survey recorded a slight and statistically insignificant drop in students subjected to thefts and other property crime at school, dropping from 12.2 percent in 1989 to 11.6 percent in 1995.

When property crimes and violent crimes were combined, the overall victimization rate for students, those who suffered one or more crimes, remained nearly level at 14.5 percent in 1989 compared with 14.6 percent in 1995.

The survey also found that drugs were slightly more available. In 1995, 65.3 percent of students reported that marijuana, cocaine, crack, uppers or downers were available at school, compared with 63.2 percent in 1989.

The 1995 survey found that fewer than one in 1,000 students reported a gun to school authorities, but about one in 20 students said they saw another student with a gun at school. Among those who saw guns at school, 12.4 percent said they were victims of violent crime at school, compared with 3.8 percent of the students who did not see a gun at school.

There were no gun questions on the 1989 survey.   20

———————◆ **QUESTIONS FOR DISCUSSION AND WRITING** ◆———————

1. How effective are the presentations of statistical information in "School Crime up 25%"? Might there be a better, or a clearer, way to present this information? How?
2. *Ethical question:* Your seven-year-old son brought his pellet pistol to school, just to show it to a friend—but the friend reported your son to the principal's office. Following its policy, the school intends to expel your son for one year. How would you feel? What would you do?
3. As a parent, what would you expect your son's or daughter's school to do if a student brought a weapon into your child's classroom? That is, what steps would you expect the school to implement?
4. Sniffen speaks of gang activity in schools. What can you note about such activity in your own high school?
5. Although reporter Sniffen's article was published in 1998, his data are from 1995. Do you think the problems he reports on have worsened or improved since 1995? Why?
6. Referring to an earlier study, Sniffen reports in the final sentence of his article that "there were no gun questions on the 1989 survey." What can you infer from this statement?

✳ 1 Million School Kids Toting Guns

Karen S. Peterson

Nearly 1 million students carried a gun to school during the 1997–98 school year, and nearly half of them were armed six or more times, a key annual survey of kids said Thursday [June 1998].

But the PRIDE study of 154,350 students in grades 6–12 also showed the number of students bringing guns to school declined over the past five years, from 6% in 1993–94 to 3.8% in 1997–98.

The study, which also looked at drug use among the children, comes amid an increasing number of school shooting incidents around the country.

"With this volatile mixture of guns, bad attitudes and drugs, it only takes one student to create a national nightmare like Jonesboro, Ark., or Springfield, Ore.," said Thomas Gleaton, president of PRIDE. Students were killed by schoolmates at both locations.

PRIDE is a non-profit drug prevention program that has conducted the survey annually for the past 11 years.   5

Other findings:

- 64% of the 973,000 who carried guns used an illegal drug on a monthly basis.
- 51% of the students who carried guns to school said they had threatened to harm a teacher; 63% had threatened to harm another student.
- Of the students who carried a gun to school, 59% were white; 18% black; 12% Hispanic; 3% Asian and 3% Native American.

The survey found a connection between participation in school and after-school activities and a reduction in violent behavior and drug abuse.

Students who did not carry guns were 53% more likely to be involved in after-school programs and 34% more likely to participate in school activities.

◆ QUESTIONS FOR DISCUSSION AND WRITING ◆

1. What was your initial reaction to the headline "1 Million School Kids Toting Guns"? Do you feel the same or differently after reading the article? In what way(s)?

2. Do you think the headline writer is overdramatizing the information in Peterson's article? In what way?

3. Compare the statistical information in Peterson's text with the data provided by Michael Sniffen in "School Crime up 25%." What similarities can you find? Differences? What can you say about the overall trend of the data?

❋ 1999 Annual Report on School Safety

U.S. Department of Education and U.S. Department of Justice

INTRODUCTION

The vast majority of America's schools are safe places. In fact, notwithstanding the disturbing reports of violence in our schools, they are becoming even safer. But the fears of students, teachers and parents are real. And it is true that some schools have serious crime and violence problems. The *Annual Report on School Safety* is a guide for use in combating these fears and problems.

The 1999 edition of the *Annual Report* is designed to complement its predecessor. It presents an updated description of the nature and extent of crime and violence on school property. It shows what measures some schools have taken to prevent and address school violence, refining and revising the program information provided last year. And it captures the spirit of 54 communities around the country that have taken to heart one chapter in particular from last year's *Annual Report,* entitled *What Communities Can Do Through Collaboration.* This *Annual Report* is divided into four chapters: The Nature and Scope of School Violence; Safe Schools/Healthy Students—Collaboration in Action; Model Programs; and Resources.

Chapter 1 presents the nature and scope of school violence in the United States and abroad. The national perspective on school crime and safety issues examines data on homicides and suicides at school, injuries at school, crimes against students, crimes against teachers, weapons at school, the consequences of bringing firearms to school, and student perceptions of school safety. More detailed presentations of these and other related national data can be found in the *Indicators of School Crime and Safety, 1999* by the National Center for Education Statistics and the Bureau of Justice Statistics. This year, Chapter 1 also includes both an international perspective on school violence, comparing data across a number of different countries on feelings of safety, bullying and student behavior, as well as a discussion of hate crime and harassment legislation and related statistics.

CHAPTER 1: THE NATURE AND SCOPE OF SCHOOL VIOLENCE

The recent school shootings have drawn heightened public attention to school crime and safety. Unfortunately, public perceptions of school safety are often fueled by media accounts that play up tragic events and fail to provide a real understanding of the accomplishments of schools or the problems they face. The heightened public attention does provide an opportunity to closely examine what is happening in schools today. As we learn more, we can use that knowledge to fashion rational policies and strategies for preventing crime and increasing school safety.

Assessing the safety of our schools, on both national and international levels, is a complex undertaking. This report brings together, in one document, critical information gleaned from numerous surveys and reports. While we do not know as much about threats to school safety as we might like, this document is a starting point from which an initial assessment of school safety emerges. As more schools and jurisdictions collect data on school crime and safety issues, we will be able to eliminate information gaps. Readers should note that this report specifically addresses intentional injuries and crimes against students and teachers. A small amount of information on unintentional injuries and accidents is presented as well.

The first section of this chapter presents national data on school crime and youth violence. Data on international school crime and youth violence follow. The chapter concludes with information on hate crime and harassment.

Data used in this chapter are drawn from several different studies conducted by the Bureau of Justice Statistics, the Centers for Disease Control and Prevention, the National Center for Education Statistics, the National Institute of Child Health and Human Development, and the Survey Research Center of the University of Michigan. . . .

All the studies used nationally representative samples, except for the data source on school-associated violent deaths (which tracked all school-associated violent deaths in the country), and the data source for unintentional injuries (which used the school National Pediatric Trauma Registry to identify cases from 74 hospitals in 30 states). Data sources for the other studies varied. Some surveyed different populations of students, another surveyed teachers, and yet another surveyed other school staff. Definitions of crime, age groups analyzed, and time periods can vary from indicator to indicator. The reader should also note that definitions vary across studies. For example, "at school" and "away from school" may have different meanings, depending upon the study.

For a more complete understanding of most of the data in this report, see *Indicators of School Crime and Safety, 1999.* . . .

A NATIONAL PERSPECTIVE

Building on data provided in the *1998 Annual Report on School Safety,* this section provides a national picture of American schools and the amount of violence and crime experienced by those who work and learn there. Where possible, data are presented that update the *1998 Annual Report,* so that progress in combating school violence may be tracked and analyzed. Several data sources have been added to this year's *Annual Report.* . . .

TOTAL NUMBER OF STUDENTS, TEACHERS, AND SCHOOLS

	Total	Public	Private
Students	51,400,000	45,600,000	5,800,000
8th Grade	3,776,039	3,415,151	360,888
10th Grade	3,682,663	3,376,595	306,068
12th Grade	2,938,754	2,673,067	265,687
Teachers	3,100,000	2,700,000	400,000
Elementary Schools	64,800	48,000	16,800
Middle Schools[1]	14,000	14,000	—
High Schools	17,800	15,300	2,500
Other Schools[2]	12,400	4,000	8,400
Total Schools	109,000	81,300	27,700

[1] Due to the small number of private middle schools, they are not counted as a separate category.

[2] For private schools, these are combined schools that cross the elementary/secondary boundary.

Note: Number of students (public and private) are projected data from 1997–98. Number of public schools are from 1996–97; number of private schools are from 1995–96.

Source: Digest of Education Statistics, 1998 (May 1999, NCES-1999-036); Overview of Public Elementary and Secondary Schools and Districts, School Year 1997–1998 (October 1998, NCES 98-204); Public School Student, Staff, and Graduate Counts by State, School Year 1997–1998 (August 1999, NCES 1999-327); Private School Universe Survey, 1997–1998 (August 1999, NCES 1999-319)

This section attempts to address those questions at the heart of the school safety issue. Are most injuries that occur at school the result of violence? How much crime is occurring in our Nation's schools? Are schools more or less safe than in the past? Do students feel safe at school? What kinds of crimes are occurring? How likely is it that students or teachers will become the victims of school crime?

After a relatively quiet 1998–99 school year, we were subjected to a rude and tragic awakening after the shootings at Columbine High School. We were reminded once again that while homicides at school are extremely rare events, they do occur and they affect the perspective of all Americans, especially school children.

Homicides at school remain extremely rare events.

While multiple homicide events have captured headlines in recent years, there still exists a less than one in a million chance of suffering a school-associated violent death, but even that is too much.

- Preliminary data indicate that less than one percent of the more than 2,500 children nationwide who were murdered or committed suicide in the first half of the 1997–1998 school year (July 1, 1997–

December 31, 1997) were at school (on school property, at a school sponsored event, or on the way to or from school or a school sponsored event).

- For the complete school year, July 1, 1997 through June 30, 1998, there were 58 school-associated violent deaths (student and non-students) that resulted from 46 incidents. Forty-six of these violent deaths were homicides, 11 were suicides, and one teenager was killed by a law enforcement officer in the course of duty.

- Among the homicide deaths, 29 were single homicides, 14 were homicides in events with multiple victims, and three were part of a combination homicide/suicide. Among the homicide victims, 30 (65 percent) were male. Also, 34 (74 percent) were school aged children, six (13 percent) were school staff, and six (13 percent) were not affiliated with any school.

- Thirty-two (70 percent) of the homicides at school occurred on school property, one (2 percent) occurred at a school sponsored event, and 13 (28 percent) occurred in transit to or from school or a school sponsored event.

- Of the suicide deaths, eight were single suicides, and three were part of a combination homicide/suicide. Among the suicide victims, 10 (91 percent) were male, six (55 percent) were school aged children, one (9 percent) was school staff, and four (36 percent) were not affiliated with any school.

- Nine (82 percent) of the suicides occurred on school property. Two (18 percent) occurred in transit to or from school or at a school sponsored event.

The number of multiple victim homicide events at school has increased.

15

Although there were fewer school-associated violent death incidents in the 1997–98 school year (46 total) than in 1992–93 (55 total), the total number of multiple victim homicide events appears to have increased. . . . Multiple victim homicides include events where an offender fatally injured more than one victim. Combination homicide/suicides and multiple suicides are excluded from this count.

- Since the 1992–93 school year, there has been at least one multiple victim homicide event each year (except for the 1993–1994 school year). The number increased from two events in 1992–93 to five events in 1997–98.

Most injuries that occur at school are not the result of violence.

Among children (ages five through 18) who were admitted to a pediatric trauma unit or children's hospital for an injury sustained at school,

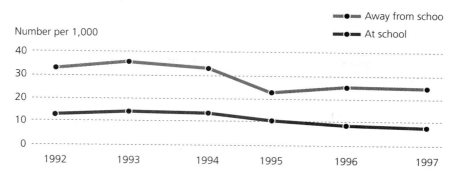

Number per 1,000

Legend: Away from school; At school

Note: Serious violent crimes include rape, sexual assault, robbery, and aggravated assault.

Source: U.S. Department of Justice, Bureau of Justice Statistics, National Crime Victimization Survey, 1992 to 1997.

FIGURE 1 *Serious Violent Crime against Students at and away from School: Number of Serious Violent Crimes against Students Ages 12 through 18 per 1,000 Students: 1992 to 1997*

90 percent were injured unintentionally through falls, sports, and school equipment (for example, wood shop equipment).

- Falls were the most common type of school injury, accounting for 43 percent of all admissions.

Despite recent occurrences, schools should not be singled out as especially dangerous places in the community. Most school crime is theft, not serious violent crime.

The nature of crime away from school is far more serious than at school. Thankfully, serious violent crime rates (as well as theft rates) are down both at school and away from school as compared with the 1993 data presented in last year's *Annual Report.* 20

- Students ages 12 through 18 were more likely to be victims of serious violent crime away from school than at school. In 1997, about 24 of every 1,000 students (ages 12 to 18) were victims of serious violent crimes away from school (a total of 635,900 serious violent crimes). In contrast, only eight of every 1,000 students were victims of serious violent crimes at school or going to and from school (201,800 total) (see figure 1).
- In 1997, there were 63 thefts for every 1,000 students (ages 12 to 18) at school. . . . Theft accounted for about 61 percent of all crime against students at school that year.

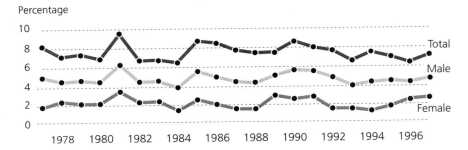

Percentage

Note: Examples of weapons are knives, guns, and clubs. "At school" means inside or outside the school building or on a school bus.

Source: University of Michigan, Survey Research Center, Institute for Social Research, Monitoring the Future Study, 1977 to 1997.

FIGURE 2 *Injuries at School with a Weapon: Percentage of 12th Graders Who Reported that Someone Had Injured Them with a Weapon at School during the Past 12 Months, by Sex: 1977 to 1997*

Students in school today are less likely to be victimized than in previous years.

Since 1993, the overall school crime rate for students ages 12 to 18 has declined as have rates of crime outside of school for this group.

- The overall school crime rate between 1993 and 1997 declined, from about 155 school-related crimes for every 1,000 students ages 12 to 18 in 1993 to about 102 such crimes in 1997. Crime victimization outside of school declined from about 139 crimes for every 1,000 students in this age group in 1993 to 117 such crimes in 1997. . . .

- In 1997, 5 percent of all 12th graders reported that they had been injured on purpose with a weapon such as a knife, gun, or club during the prior 12 months while they were at school, and 14 percent reported that they had been injured on purpose without a weapon. These numbers have remained fairly stable over the past 20 years (see figure 2).

Teachers are victims of crime at school as well.

As with student crime, most crimes against teachers are thefts. Teachers in urban schools are more vulnerable to crime at school than are suburban school teachers.

- On average, each year from 1993 to 1997 there were 131,400 violent crimes against teachers at school and 222,800 thefts from teachers at school, as reported by teachers from both public and private schools. This translates into a rate of 31 violent crimes

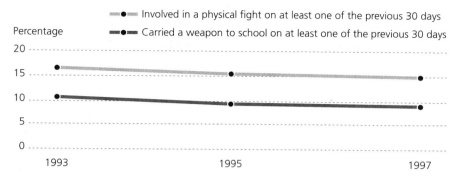

Note: Examples of weapons are knives, guns, and clubs. "On school property" was not defined for the questionnaire respondent.

Source: Centers for Disease Control and Prevention, Youth Risk Behavior Surveillance System.

FIGURE 3 *Weapon Carrying and Physical Fighting Trends: Percentage of Students in Grades 9 through 12 Who Reported Carrying a Weapon or Fighting on School Property on One or More of the Past 30 Days: 1993, 1995, 1997*

for every 1,000 teachers and a rate of 53 thefts for every 1,000 teachers.

- On average each year from 1993 to 1997, about 4 out of every 1,000 elementary, middle, and high school teachers were the victims of serious violent crime at school. . . .
- Teachers in urban schools (39 of every 1,000 teachers) were more likely to be victims of violent crime than were teachers in suburban schools (22 for every 1,000 teachers). . . .

Fewer students are carrying weapons and engaging in physical fights on school grounds. However, certain groups of students are at greater risk than others for these activities.

25

The presence of weapons and physical fights at school are dangerous and disruptive to the learning environment. Contrary to public perception, however, student weapon carrying and physical fighting have declined steadily in recent years.

- Between 1993 and 1997, there was a significant decrease in the percentage of high school students who carried a weapon (for example, a club, knife, or gun) on school property, and in the percentage of students in a physical fight on school property, on at least one of the 30 days preceding the survey (see figure 3).
- These declines were similar across sex, grade, and race/ethnic subgroups, but male students, younger students, and Black and Hispanic students were consistently more likely than their peers to engage in these behaviors.

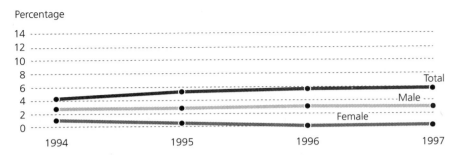

Percentage

Note: "To school" was not defined for the questionnaire respondent.

Source: University of Michigan, Survey Research Center, Institute for Social Research, Monitoring the Future

FIGURE 4 *12th Graders Carrying a Gun to School: Percentage of 12th Graders Who Reported Carrying a Gun to School at Least One Day in the Past Four Weeks, by Gender: 1994 to 1997*

- About 3 percent of 12th grade students reported carrying a gun to school at least one day during the previous 4-week period. This percentage remained fairly stable from 1994 to 1997 (see figure 4).

There are consequences for students who carry firearms to school.

- For the 1997–98 school year, States and territories reported that they had expelled an estimated 3,930 students for bringing a firearm to school. The number of expulsions declined from 6,093 for the 1996–1997 school year.

- In part, this decline is due to improvements in data collection and reporting. Therefore, caution should be used when interpreting these data.

- Fewer than half of the students expelled during the 1997–98 school year were referred for alternative placements. Students expelled for firearms often do not receive educational services through alternative programs or schools. Currently, very little is known about the number or nature of alternative programs. The U.S. Department of Education is conducting a survey of school districts to help provide better information about these programs and schools. Information from this study will be available in 2001.

Minority students and young students feel less safe at school than others.

- According to the 1998 National Assessment of Educational Progress (NEAP), higher percentages of Black and Hispanic 4th grade students reported feeling "very unsafe" at school (9 percent and 6 percent, respectively) than did White students at that grade level (2 percent).

- According to the 1998 NEAP, compared to 4th and 8th grade students, fewer 12th grade students reported feeling "very unsafe" at school, regardless of race.

AN INTERNATIONAL PERSPECTIVE

The U.S. is not the only country that confronts youth and school violence. While it is difficult to compare the U.S. to other countries on school safety and youth violence issues, several studies have been conducted across countries that provide comparable data on feelings of safety, bullying, and student behavior. The data from these studies are presented in this section.

The Third International Mathematical and Sciences Study (TIMSS)

TIMSS, conducted in 1995, consists of data from half a million students in 4th, 8th, and 12th grades in 41 countries. The eight countries that had data at all three levels were used in this report.

30

- Across several countries, older students were more likely than younger students not to have been threatened by another student. . . .

- While, overall, fewer 12th grade students (compared to 4th or 8th grade students) reported being threatened, U.S. 12th graders were more likely to have been threatened than 12th graders from other countries. . . .

The Health Behavior of School Children Study

This school-based research study, performed for the first time in the United States in 1997–98, has been conducted every four years by European countries since 1982. The research goal is to increase our understanding of health behaviors, lifestyles, and their context in young people, ages 11 to 15 years. The study provides data on 120,000 students from 28 countries for the 1997–98 school year. Fifteen countries included questions on injury and violence, six of which are used in this report. These countries were selected because their study methods and questions were similar to the United States. Data for 15-year-old students are presented because they are more closely related to the national data presented in the first section of this chapter.

- During the past 12 months, the majority of 15-year-old students across several countries (including the U.S.) have not been in a physical fight. . . .
- During the past 30 days, the majority of 15-year-old students across several countries (including the U.S.) did not carry a weapon for self-defense. . . .
- A substantial majority of 15-year-old students across many countries were not bullied at school. . . .

───────── ◆ **QUESTIONS FOR DISCUSSION AND WRITING** ◆ ─────────

1. The *1999 Annual Report on School Safety* is a detailed report that begins with this statement: "The vast majority of America's schools are safe places" (paragraph 1). If you were arguing that this statement is true, what statistical information would you point to in the report to support your position? What data would you select if you were trying to prove that this statement is inaccurate?
2. Do you agree or disagree with this comment (paragraph 19): "Despite recent occurrences, schools should not be singled out as especially dangerous places in the community. Most school crime is theft, not serious violent crime"? Why?
3. Which of the graphs presenting statistical information do you find the most persuasive? The least persuasive? Why? Overall, how effective is this report's presentation of data in graphs or charts?
4. Why do you suppose that more twelfth-grade males bring a gun to school than do twelfth-grade females (see Figure 4)?
5. The final section of this report (paragraphs 29–31) compares American information with international data. What strikes you as significant? Why?

✳ Growing Intolerant of Zeros

E. J. Montini

The mothers of Patrick DeTuro and Ryan McCoy were hoping the Deer Valley school board would take a moment during tonight's meeting to reverse its stiff-necked decision to expel their sons from high school.

But, no.

Last week, Maricopa County Superior Court Judge Roger Kaufman ordered the Deer Valley Unified School District to reconsider the expulsions. That could have happened at a meeting scheduled for tonight, but it won't.

Instead, the board supposedly has plans to discuss the issue at an executive session later in the week.

"The lives of these two boys have been on hold for a long time," Maria DeTuro told me. "We were hoping they would be back in school by now and this whole thing would have been forgotten. Now, we're hoping they'll get back in school after the Christmas vacation. It's all so sad and so unnecessary." 5

THE PLAN WAS . . .

On Oct. 8, [1998] Patrick DeTuro brought his mother's shotgun with him to football practice at Mountain Ridge High School in Glendale. Several players had planned to go out into the desert and shoot clay pigeons after practice. An assistant coach was to accompany them. Patrick was loaning the weapon to Ryan McCoy.

The boys met in the parking lot after school was out. The shotgun was in a plastic case, unloaded. Patrick handed the case to Ryan, who put it in the trunk of his car.

A security guard on campus watched the exchange, asked what was going on and reported the incident to the school principal.

Mountain Ridge has what it calls a "zero tolerance" policy concerning weapons on campus. The boys were immediately suspended, then expelled.

The circumstances weren't considered—such as the fact that no one was threatened and the unloaded gun was never removed from its case. The records of the boys weren't considered. 10

THE THOUGHT PROCESS

"Federal and state law says you should look at this on a case by case basis," said David William West, the boys' lawyer. "They didn't go through that thought process. These two young men don't have bad records. The red herring they throw at us is that anything short of expulsion will destroy the zero tolerance policy. Well, we support that policy."

The difference is how you enforce it.

Zero tolerance makes sense if it means every offense will be punished. It makes no sense at all if every offense is punished in the exact same way.

"This has been tough on the boys." Maria DeTuro said. "First, they have the school board do this to them. Then, they get a supportive ruling from a judge and still nothing changes. It doesn't give them much faith in the system."

Patrick, a sophomore, is working and taking correspondence courses. It's not the same. And it's not enough to keep up. Ryan, a senior, is to get a $40,000 Army Airborne scholarship upon graduation in June. The longer he's out of school, the more he is in danger of losing that. 15

"Our position is a simple one," attorney West said. "The next semester starts Jan. 5. We want a special hearing before school starts. What we're told is that people might not be around during the holidays. My answer is, that's fine, all the evidence is in and there's no disputing the facts. The board simply needs to sit down and use the discretion the judge found they never had used."

Judge Kaufman admonished the board for not considering all factors. But he also gave them an out. He said the case must be reviewed by Feb. 27, deep into the next semester. And even then, the board can come to the same conclusion.

"The only reason to do that would be spite," Maria DeTuro said.

She's right. District officials believe treating Patrick and Ryan worse than convicted criminals is necessary to maintain peace in schools. They say they want the other kids in the district to learn a lesson.

I'm sure they have.   20

Our only hope is that they unlearn it before they become grown-ups and ruin the lives of someone else's kids.

◆ QUESTIONS FOR DISCUSSION AND WRITING ◆

1. E. J. Montini outlines an incident where a student brought a gun to school and was expelled because of the school's zero-tolerance policy. Based on the information he provides, do you think the school did the right thing? Why?
2. Compare Montini's writing (which is a newspaper editorial) to Michael Sniffen's article (also from a newspaper). What differences do you see? Similarities?
3. *Ethical question:* A friend of yours brings a loaded gun to school "for protection." Would you turn him or her in to the school authorities? Why or why not?

❋ State Urges Schools to Begin Random Search of Students' Lockers

New York Times *Metropolitan Desk*

The State Attorney General, Peter G. Verniero, urged school officials today to start authorizing random searches of student lockers for drugs and weapons.

Speaking before a convention of the New Jersey School Boards Association at a hotel here, Mr. Verniero said drug abuse was a major problem in the state's schools, adding that one in five high school students had admitted using alcohol or drugs before class.

Mr. Verniero's office distributed a guidelines manual of more than 300 pages earlier this year advising school officials that current state laws make it legal for them to authorize such searches. But the Attorney General said today that many districts had not authorized the policy.

"Some educators, to their credit, will err on the side of not conducting a search out of fear of violating someone's rights," he said. "But on the other hand, if you've got reasonable suspicion for conducting a search, by all means you should conduct a search, because the bottom line is we want to prevent a tragedy from happening in the first place."

The School Search Policy Manual says that students' bags and lockers 5 may be searched if officials have reasonable grounds for suspecting wrongdoing, and that lockers may be inspected if the policy is announced at the start of the school year.

Mr. Verniero, who is the chairman of a national task force on violence among the young, said many state attorneys general were seeking to copy the New Jersey manual.

Several school officials said today they had never heard of the guidelines. Diane Cooper, the president of the East Orange Board of Education, said that she did not know that schools could adopt random search policies, but that she would ask her board to consider doing so to help counter a drug and gang problem.

Last year, she said, a high school student was suspended for a year after teachers found a knife in his knapsack. "We have been cautious in letting principals know that you do not infringe upon students' rights," she said. "Students have to feel that they are protected from unauthorized or unprovoked harassment."

Anne Thomas, a member of the Piscataway Board of Education, said her district did not have a random search policy and probably would not adopt one because drugs and weapons were not serious problems there.

Daniel Sooy, a board member for Mainland Regional High School in 10 Atlantic County, said that his district did not conduct random searches and probably would not, but that a search of high school girls' lockers two years ago turned up a large quantity of heroin. "We are very cautious of doing it," he said. "We have to have some very hard evidence. I think it's going a little too far if you do it without just cause."

He added, "I am wondering if we are getting too tight a society—if there are too many regulations."

◆ QUESTIONS FOR DISCUSSION AND WRITING ◆

1. As a parent, how would you respond to the suggestions made in "State Urges Schools to Begin Random Search of Students' Lockers," if they were put into effect at your daughter's school? Would you want the school to have some sort of "just cause" before searching your daughter's locker?

2. As a student, how would you respond to the ideas in this reading? Why? What alternatives could you offer?

3. *Ethical question:* You know someone at your high school who sells drugs and keeps them in his or her locker. Would you turn that person in? Would it matter what drug(s) he or she was selling? To whom the drugs were being sold? Whether this person was a friend of yours? Why?

✳ Preventing School Violence: No Easy Answers

Lynne Lamberg

Psychiatrists and other mental health professionals know how to identify and treat young people at risk for violent behavior, and they have a good handle on primary prevention of violence, too, presentations at the annual meeting of the American Psychiatric Association (APA) in Toronto, Ontario, in June and interviews afterward suggest. Implementing this knowledge is the tough part: that takes money, a network of support services, and physicians and others committed to voluntary service in their communities.

Last year, the National Institutes of Health budgeted only $10 million for research in childhood violence, said Harold Eist, MD, a psychiatrist practicing in Washington, D.C., and immediate past president of the APA. "This is a minuscule amount of money for this issue," Eist said in an interview. "It's as if Congress doesn't want to admit the seriousness of the problem.

"Violence is the leading public health problem in America," Eist asserted, "and we're doing virtually nothing about it."

WHENCE THE ESCALATION?

The bruises, black eyes, and bloody noses of playground clashes a generation or so ago now prompt nostalgia. In the 1997–1998 school year, children as young as 11 years old have gunned down classmates and teachers in mass shootings at schools in Pearl, Miss, West Paducah, Ky, Jonesboro, Ark, Edinburgh, Pa, and Springfield, Ore (JAMA. 1998; 279:1853), leaving 13 dead and 45 wounded, according to Ronald Stephens, EdD, executive director of the National School Safety Center, a nonprofit organization based in Westlake Village, Calif.

Such youngsters undeniably represent the far end of the violence spectrum, said Richard Harding, MD, APA vice president and clinical professor of pediatrics and psychiatry at the University of South Carolina School of Medicine, Columbia. In hindsight, signs of their disturbance may have been apparent, he said, but it takes a system sensitized to such signals to pick them up and to respond appropriately.

"Other children often distance themselves from peers who are irritable, angry, and talk of "blasting someone away' or other scary or extreme acts. Most children don't want to think about the things these children are thinking about," Harding said. "Yet they rarely report the danger to adults," he noted. "There's peer pressure not to tell."

The troubled youngster becomes increasingly isolated, Harding said, leaving him—the typical offender is male—with no counterbalance for his violent thoughts. He wants to make people pay attention to him. If he has seen enough examples of violence and bizarre behavior on television and in movies, video games, and comic books, Harding said, similar feats may seem a good way to impress others. Being kicked out of class may trigger an impulsive act of aggression.

"This is why locking up guns saves lives," Harding said. "If a person doesn't have ready access to a gun, the passage of time may permit him to reorganize and calm down."

"The recent school shootings are headline-grabbing events because of their rarity," Joan Kinlan, MD, a child and adolescent psychiatrist practicing in Washington, D.C., said at an APA workshop on violence. But the possibility of such violence in schools, she said, is appallingly common. In a national survey of nearly 22,000 students in public and private schools, nearly 13% of schoolchildren reported knowing another student who brought a gun to school in the 1995–1996 academic year (Students' Reports of School Crime. Washington, D.C.: US Dept of Education; 1998, publication NCES 98-241; available at: http://nces.ed.gov). The Centers for Disease Control and Prevention found that 7.6% of a representative sample of nearly 11,000 students in grades 9 through 12 reported carrying a gun during the 30 days preceding the survey (Youth Risk Behavior Surveillance–United States, 1995. MMWR. 1996:45 (SS-4): 1–86).

Some of those who carry guns belong to gangs. Others are those whom teachers would not suspect of violence. They often feel insecure, Kinlan said, and see the world as a dangerous place. They avoid fights. They are the ones who are bullied. "But because the gun is there," she said, "they may use it."

Stephens of the National School Safety Center said that from July 1, 1992, when the organization began keeping records, to July 1, 1998, there have been 226 school-associated violent deaths. Of these, 175 were shootings, 33 were stabbings or slashings, and the remainder were attributed to beatings, hangings, or asphyxiations. In the past school year alone, there were 40 violent deaths in the nation's schools.

The National Center for Education Statistics reported that 10% of US public schools experienced at least 1 serious violent crime in the 1996–1997 school year. These incidents included murder, rape or other type of sexual battery, suicide, physical attack or fight with a weapon, or robbery. There were nearly 190,000 physical attacks or fights without a weapon, as well as high numbers of thefts or larceny and vandalism (Violence and Discipline Problems in US Public Schools 1996–97. Washington, D.C.: U.S. Dept of Education; 1998, publication NCES 98-030; available at: http://nces.ed.gov.)

These statistics do not include other pervasive and disturbing events that create an atmosphere conducive to violence that occurs in schools on a daily basis, Kinlan said, citing "verbal harassment, graffiti in bathrooms that identifies kids by name, and sexual harassment of both boys and girls, such as butt holding and breast touching." A visitor to almost any public high school who spends just 5 minutes in the hall, she said, will see numerous examples of such violence.

Moreover, incidents of violence in schools probably are under-reported, according to Lois Flaherty, MD, clinical associate professor of psychiatry at the University of Pennsylvania School of Medicine, Philadelphia, and chair of the APA workshop on school violence. School administrators want to downplay violence, she said, and may not report such events as assaults on teachers and fights in lunchrooms.

Violence occurs most often in unstructured time, she said, when classes are changing, at lunchtime, recess, and dismissal, for example. Having clear rules for students about what is and is not acceptable behavior and having teachers who are viewed as fair and consistent, Flaherty said, help reduce violence.

CHILDREN NEED RULES, PROTECTION

Children who have witnessed violence or been victims of violence feel let down by the adult protective system, said Carl Bell, MD, chief executive officer of the Community Mental Health Council and professor of psychiatry and public health at the University of Illinois College of Medicine, both in Chicago. These children often have generalized anxiety and depression, he said at the APA workshop. They are afraid of being victimized again and may carry knives or guns to school for self-protection. "The solution is to reestablish the adult protective shield," he said in an interview. "The school must be clear about security. Children need to feel safe at school."

Some schools have eliminated lockers and even book bags, he said, providing 1 set of books to be used in class and another to be left at home. Others require that students use see-through book bags. Although some schools have used metal detectors at doors like those in airports, there are easy ways to stymie this system, he said: children may bring tin cups to set off the alarm, especially on test days, causing long delays. Handheld detectors may be more practical, he said, because they can be used for spot checks on, say, every second child or on different days of the week. Some schools employ uniformed security guards. Hallway cameras may serve as a deterrent. Signs can make the rules explicit, Bell said: "No guns; no alcohol; no fighting. Violators will be prosecuted. Do your part to make our school a safe place."

The school principal must make safety a prime mission, he said, by involving students and teachers in collaborative partnership to work toward their shared goal. In a mission-driven system, he said, students are asked to take personal responsibility for how they resolve conflicts with one another. Students who buy into the mission of keeping their school safe learn that it sometimes is necessary to snitch on someone whose behavior is subverting that goal.

Schools need gun safety drills, Bell said. "Ever school has procedures for a fire drill," he noted, "but few have plans for what to do if a student walks into school with a gun." Most, he said, have an "It won't happen here" mentality. Schools, he said, should adopt public address codes for emergencies like those hospitals use: "Mr Strong, report to the auditorium." Teachers should lock doors to their classrooms and stay with students until an all-clear signal sounds, not send students fleeing from the building. This tactic, he said, keeps them from becoming targets.

Students who are caught carrying weapons or are otherwise disruptive, Bell said, need counseling. They may need to go to an alternative school. They should not just be expelled and put on the street. "Behind all anger, usually, is some form of hurt," he said. "A child who tries to commit suicide," he noted, "gets a lot of attention. Disruptive children need intensive services, too. Schools need support from the social service system and the psychiatric system. Violent children may have treatable psychiatric illnesses." 20

SOME NEED IN-SCHOOL HELP

A contemporary approach to reducing youth violence is to reverse the traditional model of referring troubled youngsters out to treatment and bring both treatment and prevention services into the school. The mental health program affiliated with the University of Maryland School of Medicine, Baltimore, started in 1989 under Flaherty's direction, is an example.

According to its present director, Mark Weist, PhD, a clinical psychologist and associate professor in the Department of Psychiatry, the in-school program sees proportionally more youngsters with internalizing disorders such as depression and posttraumatic stress, while community mental health centers see proportionally more youngsters who had to act out to get treatment and have been diagnosed with disorders involving oppositional defiance, antisocial behavior, and conduct.

In some inner-city communities, the majority of children could benefit from some mental health services, Weist said in an interview. Studies show that fewer than one third of those who have such needs nationally receive appropriate services (Dryfoos JG. Full-Service Schools. San Francisco, Calif: Jossey-Bass; 1994; Adolescent Health. Washington, DC: Office of Technology Assessment; 1991). In-school programs, Weist said, not only minimize the stigma of seeking care, but also avoid financial, transportation, and other barriers, as well as long waiting lists and long intake procedures.

Kindergarten teachers, he said, can identify highly aggressive children, the ones at risk for later dropping out and engaging in violence and criminal behavior. "But schools often don't know what to do with these youngsters," he noted. Frequently the only way to get mental health services is to refer the child to special education, a cumbersome process that often leads to unwarranted labeling.

About one third of Baltimore's 183 schools now have expanded mental health services, provided by 5 separate programs. The one Weist directs serves 19 schools, offering brief focused intervention throughout the school years from providers with whom children feel comfortable. "After I'm finished wearing my clinician hat," said Weist, who spends part of his time working directly with high school students, "I can put on my mentoring hat." Students drop by his office for help with filling out college applications or studying for tests. In this context, he said, he continues to provide therapeutic services.

The program offers all students classroom training in ways to manage anger, develop cognitive skills, improve self-control, and reduce aggressive behaviors. Such programs also give youngsters the opportunity to talk about violence they've experienced. Having a classmate killed, for instance, understandably upsets the others. In this situation, Weist said, the mental health group forms a team, makes an announcement about what happened, asks for a moment of silence, and holds a series of meetings to let students know adults are concerned about them and are there to help them cope.

Without outside concern, Weist said, children may develop a sense that life is cheap, and whole communities may be numbed and feel beaten down by violence. Children who undergo traumatic experiences that are not processed, he noted, are more likely to become violent themselves.

Weist said the mental health program seeks parental consent for most of those who participate because the school wants the parents to become involved. In Maryland, youths over 16 years of age may independently receive mental health services. When substance abuse is involved, services may be provided to youths younger than 16 years without parental consent.

INVOLVE THE PARENTS

Paul Fink, MD, professor of psychiatry at Temple University School of Medicine, Philadelphia, Pa, speaking at the APA workshop on school violence, described a kind of psychological autopsy he conducts as the voluntary head of the Philadelphia health department's youth homicide committee. Annual reviews of the killings of all persons in the city under the age of 22 years, he said, showed that the earliest marker for killing or being killed was truancy.

This finding, he said, prompted lowering the threshold at which parents are brought into truancy court from 50 days to 25 days and increasing the court's sessions from twice a month to 4 days a week. Some 30,000 of the 215,000 students in the Philadelphia school system are absent on any given day, he said, and often parents are unaware that their children are skipping school. This year the court will handle 10,000 cases of youngsters absent from school 25 days or more, up from 2,000 when the cutoff was 50 days. The court also has been decentralized and moved into the community, holding sessions in schools. This raises the embarrassment for parents on the local level, Fink said, and also brings them into the school.

The committee found that ninth grade is a critical time: the majority of youngsters who murdered or were murdered had truancy problems or dropped out in that academic year. The transition to high school may be more perilous than previously suspected, Fink said, suggesting that a longer and more in-depth orientation period may prove a useful violence prevention strategy.

───────◆ **QUESTIONS FOR DISCUSSION AND WRITING** ◆───────

1. Author Lynne Lamberg cites psychiatrist Harold Eist as saying that "violence is the leading public health problem in America" (paragraph 3). Lamberg goes on to note that students a generation ago gave each other "bruises, black eyes, and bloody noses," while today's students are "gunn[ing] down classmates and teachers in mass shootings" (paragraph 4). Do you see a correlation between Eist's and Lamberg's statements? In what ways?

2. Throughout her article, Lamberg suggests that "troubled youngsters" are the cause of most violence in our schools. Based on your own educational experience, do you agree? What should schools do about such students?

3. What statistics in Lamberg's essay strike you as significant? What statistics or other data in her essay confirm other texts that you've read?

4. Lamberg suggests that providing mental health services to students would decrease the number of incidents of violence in our country's schools. Do you agree or disagree? Why?

───

 Personalization

WORKING TO CURB VIOLENCE IN AN AMERICAN HIGH SCHOOL

Rebecca Martin Shore

In many ways, Huntington Beach High School is the average American secondary school. It has neither the highest test scores in the district nor the lowest. It serves neither the most affluent community in the area nor the poorest. Its student body is roughly 34% minority. And, like many high schools in the country, Huntington Beach High experienced an increase in violence and suspendable behaviors over the last decade.

Administrators and staff members had begun taking the typical steps to curb unacceptable behaviors: establishing a stricter dress code, increasing the severity of punishment for misconduct, and discontinuing such school activities as dances and evening athletic events, at which disruptive behavior was exceeding the ability of supervisors to maintain a safe and secure environment.

However, four years ago the administration decided to take a different tack. Instead of asking the many to pay for the sins of the few, school officials launched a concerted effort to personalize the school experience for that small percentage of students who were engaging in disruptive behavior.

Some of the troublesome students were low achievers, some were members of minority groups, some came from low socioeconomic backgrounds, some had little or no parental support, some were flirting with gangs or had already become full-fledged members. Indeed, they represented a cross section of the school population; no single group was causing the problems, and thus no single group could be the target of the new strategy.

Staff members of Huntington Beach High school picked up the idea of personalization from Theodore Sizer, founder of the Coalition of Essential Schools, who views personalization as the single most important factor that keeps young people in school. When education is personalized, Sizer says, students are known by the adult professionals in the school. Huntington Beach staff members set out to test this theory.

The vice principal of supervision, the school psychologist, the school nurse, and the community outreach liaison all compiled "hot lists" of students whom they viewed as not on track to graduate because of behavior problems. Meanwhile, all Huntington Beach faculty members were asked to jot down the names of their "top 10" students—the ones who seemed to need extra attention— and the district office was asked to furnish a list of all Huntington Beach High School students who had received three or more F's on their latest report card. The names on the various lists were cross-referenced, and staff members started getting to know these youngsters by name.

First, an adopt-a-kid program was initiated, which matched adult volunteers on campus with one or two students of their choosing from the list. The adults were to listen, to provide information when needed, and to provide support or advice when asked. The adults met with the students before school, after school, over lunch, or—when appropriate—during class. To ensure frequent contact, several of the teachers appointed these students as their class aides. Others met with their students only a few times but nonetheless functioned as campus adults who knew the students by name and greeted them every time they saw them. Attempts were made to match students' learning styles with the adults' personality styles. This simple-to-implement program cost the school and its cash-strapped district nothing, since it relied on the effort of volunteers.

At the same time, the vice principal, the assistant principal, the school psychologist, the school nurse, the community outreach liaison, and selected staff members formed a group that met weekly to discuss the progress of students on the list. This group functioned much like a student study team, but its efforts were not limited to special education students. The weekly meetings enabled all staff members who dealt with student services to talk to one another and compare notes, thus ensuring that the left hand knew what the right hand was doing.

The principal instituted "most improved student" awards, which were given each quarter. Every teacher submitted the names of the boy and the girl who had shown the most improvement in that teacher's classes during the quarter. These students were then called out of class to receive their awards in person from the principal. They were given key chains with their names on them (provided by the Parent/Teacher/Student Association), certificates, and letters for their parents. The principal read the personal comments the teacher had written about these students. Many youngsters on the adopt-a-kid list received "most improved student" awards.

The administration maintained a "student of the month" program, which honored outstanding students by placing their names on the school marquee and in the principal's newsletter to parents. An "athlete of the month" program was begun as well. 10

A student forum was held twice each month in the principal's conference room, open to any student who wished to discuss a school activity or policy or to voice a complaint. The vice principal chaired the forum, demonstrating that students' ideas have value and ensuring that school officials would give them serious consideration.

The principal started a "green-ribbon campaign" to promote awareness of and to express a zero-tolerance attitude toward violence on campus. Every Tuesday throughout the school year, staff members and students wore little green ribbons (provided by the Parent/Teacher/Student Association) to show their antiviolence stance. The program was voluntary; students had to come to the office to request green ribbons. Yet, within a month, students were sporting green ribbons everywhere, from their hair to their shoelaces.

Over a period of about two months, the principal collected headlines from local newspapers that suggested an increase in violent acts within the community. He then assembled a panel composed of a juvenile court judge, a probation officer, a local detective, local police officers, and a Los Angeles mother whose son had been killed by gangland gunfire. Instead of packing all 2,050 students into the gym for the panel's presentation, he had students assemble with their English classes in the more intimate auditorium—roughly 250 students per period. In this setting, the students learned how the justice and penal systems deal with illegal and violent acts, and they were touched by the mother's personal account of the pain of senseless violence.

During the first year of the personalization effort at Huntington Beach High School, the student government spent a significant sum to provide each student with a folder— printed in school colors—containing school rules, regulations, and policies. The folders were distributed during physical education classes. But the vice principal noticed that trash cans outside the gymnasium were literally overflowing with these handsome folders at the end of the day on which they were issued.

Thus, during the first two weeks of the second year, administrators went to every English class to hand a folder to each student and to spend the period discussing the contents. Students were encouraged to ask questions about the source of each rule—whether from the education code, from district policy, or from school policy. For all intents and purposes, the administrative offices were shut down during this interval of visiting English classes, but not a single folder has been sighted in a trash can since.

Who's to say which of these initiatives was most influential in curbing violence and suspendable offenses at Huntington Beach High School? One thing is certain: the 1992–93 school year was different. The school had the lowest expulsion rate (only one student) and the lowest suspension rate in the entire district. Fifty-one percent of the students on "the list" improved their grade-point averages. At the same time, on the district's annual senior survey, seniors at Huntington Beach High gave their school the highest overall grade-point average of any senior class in the district. (There are six comprehensive high schools and one continuation school in the district.) This was a first for Huntington. Test scores also rose, probably a reflection of the greatly improved climate on campus. At the 1993 spring dance, which was held on a ship, the ship's personnel commented that Huntington students had been the best-behaved of all student groups using the ship that year.

During the 1993–94 school year, Huntington Beach saw a 47% decrease in suspensions over the previous year and "the list" was 51% shorter—even from the very first grading period. The adopt-a-kid program was expanded to include peer assistant leaders (PALS), to be sure that students at risk knew other students as well as adults. The improved climate on campus gave staff members the confidence to try block scheduling (which they later voted overwhelmingly to continue during the 1994–95 school year) and other progressive restructuring ideas. Under block scheduling, teachers see only 90 students a day (for longer periods of time), rather than dealing with 180 students a day in 50-minute periods. This allows teachers to work more closely with individual students, despite the large average class size of 39 at Huntington High. Student behavior at all school events, including graduation, was the pride of the district. And—to top off the 1993–94 school year—Huntington Beach High was named a 1994 California Distinguished School.

No frills. No new funds. No grants. Just some simple, low-cost efforts to personalize have yielded dramatic improvements at Huntington Beach High.

———————◆ **QUESTIONS FOR DISCUSSION AND WRITING** ◆———————

1. Do you think the ideas outlined in "Personalization" would work in other schools? Why or why not?

2. Shore lists a number of positive steps a school might take to improve its safety. Which of these actions seems most likely to work? Why? Which seems as if it might do little good? Why?

3. Which statistic or set of statistics from Shore's essay is the most impressive? Why?

4. Do you think the idea (described by Shore in paragraph 6) of identifying and then attempting to help students with "behavior problems" can be effective? Why or why not? How might you feel if you were one of these students?

5. Compare what Shore has to say about mental health problems with the way Lamberg describes the same kind of problems in "Preventing School Violence." Which information do you find more convincing? Why?

☀ Guards with Guns

Kevin Bushweller

In Baltimore, a middle school student shoots an unarmed school policeman with a .22 caliber pistol as the officer struggles to arrest him. A janitor nearby jumps on the boy and helps handcuff him, and the officer survives.

In Portland, Ore., a teenager walks into a city high school and shoots the first teacher he sees in the forehead with a pellet gun. She survives, but the incident frightens teachers and students.

Across the country, kids are bringing everything from butcher knives and pellet guns to automatic pistols and sawed-off shotguns to school every day, school security officials say. Some do it just to impress their friends; others actually use the weapons. Whatever the motivation, the widespread use of weapons by teenagers has prompted forceful responses from school districts. Some have put their resources into sophisticated security equipment . . . ; others have decided to build up their school security forces—or even, increasingly, to arm their security guards.

NO EASY ANSWER

To arm or not to arm? Deciding whether to give guards weapons is not easy. Some school districts were prompted to arm security guards years ago, and others are just now considering the step. Some worry that arming security guards turns the schools into armed camps, but proponents say the presence of the armed guards discourages students from bringing weapons to schools.

"There's no debate here," says Herbert Graham, director of policy and ₅ administrative services for the Los Angeles Unified School District. "Our officers are armed. It's a shame, but it's a necessary evil. We don't want to be in the situation where we have to confront an armed person without being armed."

In September and October of this school year, Graham says, school police seized approximately 300 weapons from students. About a third of the weapons were guns.

"Teachers don't confront armed suspects on the street," Graham says. "They shouldn't have to put themselves in that situation on campus."

And the rising tide of violence is not limited to big cities like Los Angeles: In Prince George's County, Md., a suburb bordering Washington, D.C., violence has quickly become a staple of life, both on the streets and in the schools. Last March, a 16-year-old boy walked into a chemistry class in a county high school one Friday morning, pulled a pistol out of his coat, and fired it at a student in the back of the room, missing him by inches, county police said. Later that month, one girl stabbed another girl in the stomach with a kitchen paring knife during a hallway brawl at a Prince George's high school.

Prince George's school police confiscated 27 handguns, six pellet guns, 12 BB guns, one starter pistol, and 159 knives from students on campus last year. Those are troubling numbers, school officials say, but the head of the school district police force says arming security guards is not the answer.

"I'm against it," says Peter Blauvelt, director of security for the Prince ₁₀ George's County schools. "There will be times when it's justified to use the weapons. That jeopardizes lots of innocent kids. People who carry guns think they have the ultimate answer to every problem. You can handle these situations unarmed."

In most cases, Blauvelt says, school security officers are able to confiscate weapons before they're used because kids tell teachers or police who is bringing them to school. The students, he says, will always be the best source of information about weapons.

The debate about arming security guards has reached even rural areas like Columbus, Miss., which has 5,900 students in its 15 schools. Larry Johnson, director of security for the Columbus schools, says he researched what other school systems were doing with their security guards and found an increasing number of them were arming officers. The schools that didn't have armed guards, he says, usually had security fences around the buildings.

Last fall—concerned that it was only a matter of time before the crime problems outside school walls became a problem inside—Johnson recommended arming the five security officers who patrol the district's schools. The school board voted to allow the officers to be armed only for special events such as football games and dances.

"They're not armed during school hours, but I believe that will eventually happen," Johnson says. "We've come to that day."

Some Columbus community leaders, however, are worried about arming police officers, even for special, after-school events. "I don't want someone armed walking around the school setting," Bernard Buckhalter, president of the Columbus-Lowndes County NAACP, told the Associated Press. "That is dangerous. I'm concerned that an innocent bystander could be shot." 15

But Johnson says people in the community can't ignore the social problems that quickly become school problems. "We have kids who get in trouble with gang-related activity," he says. "So they get scared and hide over the weekend, but they show up at school on Monday. Sometimes, the easiest target is school grounds."

Before the school board's vote, he adds, many teachers expressed support for having armed guards during school hours. "If I'm unarmed and something happens, I'm going to have to hit the deck like everyone else," Johnson says. "I don't want that to happen. I want to have the tools to do what I need to do."

WHAT WOULD HAPPEN IF . . . ?

School officials across the country raise several questions about arming officers, and most of them have no definitive answers. Would the Baltimore kid have been afraid to use a gun if he knew the officer was armed? How about the boy in Portland? Should teachers and other school employees be expected to risk their lives when confronted by students brandishing weapons? Will gun-toting police officers really prevent violence?

In Baltimore, the school board has grappled with those questions. Armed teams of school police officers respond to problems every day, says John Wallace, assistant chief of the city schools police force. But security officers based at the schools carry only handcuffs, mace, and radios—not guns.

"Almost every day, we have to call in armed teams," Wallace says. 20 "But it was felt by the school board and the superintendent that it was best to keep guns away from the officers on site during school hours."

In the Houston Independent School District, it was the students, parents, teachers, and administrators at each school who made the call on whether to arm or not to arm. This year, Houston central office administrators gave each school the choice of arming its security guards, one of the many choices schools have made under site-based management.

Les Burton, chief of the Houston school police, says 80 percent of the district's 69 middle schools and high schools chose to employ armed guards in full police uniforms during the day. The decision did not mean hiring additional guards, however: All of the district's 128 security officers (86 of whom patrol the schools during the day) were already trained to use firearms. Burton says school security officers go through the same kind of training as regular police. In fact, many have retired from traditional police departments.

"I don't see that there was an option," Julie Shannon, principal of Houston's Furr High School, told the Associated Press. Furr chose to use armed guards. "You can't take fists to a gunfight. I'd rather be safe than sorry."

Last year, Houston school police arrested 174 students who carried weapons into school buildings. And school officials know there are many times that hidden in school lockers without the knowledge of teachers or principals. A few years ago, Burton says, a high school student brought a .25 caliber automatic to school without being caught, then accidentally dropped the gun in one of his classes. The gun discharged, a bullet pierced the boy's throat, and he died.

"We know there are an awful lot of weapons out there," Burton says. "The kids carry them around in their backpacks. But legally, we can't search them." (Two Houston schools don't let students carry backpacks around during the day, he adds.) 25

Not all the weapons are concealed: At the beginning of this school year, a middle school student was standing on a corner near his school waiting for a ride home. A group of gang members drove by the corner and shot and killed the boy.

Despite such incidents, some Houston schools have decided arming officers is not the solution. Walter Day, principal of Lamar High School, polled his faculty, senior class members, and several members of the high school's parent-teacher association before choosing not to arm the school's guards.

The 2,600-student high school has one security guard in plain clothes, who wears a badge and carries a walkie-talkie. The school posts teachers at exits and entrances during lunch, and students cannot leave the campus or classes without an authorized pass. The school also has an unarmed security guard in the parking lot, and Day says he relies heavily on information from students, who are usually the first to know if another student has brought a weapon to school. "They're really our only source," he says.

"The faculty was leaning toward [arming security officers]," Day adds. "but the kids didn't feel it was necessary at this point. And the parents didn't want to see us get to the point where we had to resort to those means.

"Unfortunately," he concedes, "when we have a dance or a football game, I hire a good number of armed security guards." 30

Burton says the Houston schools also have a "rover" program that sends armed officers on patrols of district elementary schools. The officers go to schools identified as trouble spots—usually buildings surrounded by high concentrations of apartments. They are not assigned to be at the schools all day. But an incident that happened this year raises questions about whether elementary schools will need on-site armed guards, too.

A man who worked as a volunteer in a Houston elementary school charged into the principal's office one day carrying a gun, Burton says. The man was upset about his son's progress report and demanded to see the principal and the boy's teacher. When he learned neither were in the building, he fired the gun around the office. Teachers pushed their students into classrooms and locked the doors when they heard the gunshots. The man went back to his car, and returned, carrying another gun. A Houston police officer happened to be in the building and confronted the man, who shot the officer in the hip and shoulder and fled the grounds. The man shot another police officer in the back before being arrested.

According to Burton, the man was supposed to be taking medication for depression but wasn't. His son's progress report might have triggered the anger, Burton surmises. "We might have had more injuries had the officer not been there," Burton adds.

So far, none of Houston's new armed officers have had to draw weapons. "They're only supposed to draw their weapon to protect their life or someone's else's life," Burton says. "Not to scare or use for warning shots."

Even so, Lamar Principal Day says he hopes to fight off the trend to   35
arm school security guards. But the way society is changing, he says, that might be a difficult task: "We're going to do everything we can not to get to that point. I'm crossing my fingers."

─────────── ◆ **QUESTIONS FOR DISCUSSION AND WRITING** ◆ ───────────

1. *Ethical question:* What if, at your son's or daughter's school, metal detectors weren't doing the job—students were still able to get guns into the school, even after the metal detectors were installed. Would you then consider guards as a possible answer to the problem? Why or why not?

2. How might you feel if you were a student in a high school that had guards patrolling its halls? What if you were a teacher? Would it matter if the guards were armed? Why?

3. When you were in high school, what would the reaction have been if, one day, armed guards had appeared and begun patrolling your campus?

───

✳ Standing Up to Violence

R. Craig Sautter

The premature death of young James Darby, the 9-year-old New Orleans boy who was shot in the head during a drive-by shooting as he walked home from a Mother's Day picnic last spring, was, at the time, just the latest in a long progression of heartbreaking stories marking an American childhood world that seems to have gone mad with vicious and random violence.

"I want you to stop the killing in the city," the youngster had desperately pleaded in a letter to President Clinton just nine days before his murder. "I think someone might kill me. I'm asking you nicely to stop it. I know you can do it."

Young James was both prophetically right and understandably wrong in his plea. He was right that violence in his city, indeed in almost every U.S. city and in many suburbs and towns as well, threatens tens of thousands of children and teenagers with bodily and psychological harm. And he was right that this societal sickness would soon claim him as well. As we all know, danger and fear stalk too many of our homes, streets, and schools, and—more than any other group—children and teenagers are its victims, as well as its perpetrators.

But James was wrong in thinking that the "most powerful man in the world"—even acting with the full force of government—could stop the scourge of violence that is cutting short so many young lives. It will take a far more profound and widespread response than any President can muster to end this latest social plague that deprives so many young people of life, liberty, and the pursuit of happiness.

Following James' death, President Clinton wrote his classmates, try- 5 ing to console them: "I am deeply saddened to learn of his tragic death, and I assure each of you that I'm determined to answer James' plea with tough and smart solutions to the crime problems in America."

The President then invoked James Darby's tragic tale as he pressed the Congress to end six years of partisan bickering and pass his omnibus crime bill. The final version of the bill included $5 billion for youth programs. But two-thirds of the "pork" cut in the final congressional debate came from funds that would have been directed to youth.

Even with the President's signature on this bill, though, the task of once more making the world safe for and from young people will be a long and arduous one. Many law enforcement officials, while pleased to get additional help, are skeptical about the ultimate impact of the law on crime—and particularly on youth crime.

"The current crime bill and its 'more police on the streets and more prisons' approach is not likely to have the effects that they are selling," confides an FBI agent who works with the public schools and young people in Washington, D.C. "Congress has been passing similar crime bills since Nixon was in office more than 20 years ago, and it obviously hasn't had much impact. There are already three times as many people in jail as 15 years ago. The problem starts at home and in the community. Not enough people care about the things they should care about," he argues.

CARNAGE IN THE STREETS

Every two days, guns kill the equivalent of a class of 25 youngsters and injure 60 more, according to the Children's Defense Fund, which has a memorable way of presenting statistics. Adolescents between the ages of 10 and 19 are killed with a gun at a rate of one every three hours. In fact, an American child today is 15 times more likely to be killed by gunfire than was a child in war-ravaged Northern Ireland before the recent peace talks.

Every year since 1950, the number of American children gunned   10
down has doubled. Today homicide is the third leading cause of death for
all children between the ages of 5 and 14, the second leading cause of
death for all young people between the ages of 10 and 24, and the leading
cause of death among African Americans of both sexes between the ages
of 15 and 34. Teenagers are more than 2½ times as likely to be victims of
violent crime as are those over 20 years of age.

Although no long, black granite wall commemorates them in our nation's capital, more U.S. young people have been killed by guns in their
own homeland during the last 13 years than lost their lives in Vietnam
during that quarter-century war! (The closest thing to a monument for
these youngsters was the chilling collection of 80,000 empty shoes spread
across the Capitol Hill mall this fall [1994], relics of adult and youthful victims of gun violence.)

Yet the American public—numbed by decades of television, radio,
newspaper, and real-life images of dehumanizing violence—has not responded to the loss of so many children and teenagers with the same sorrow, anger, or grief as was roused by Vietnam. Fortunately, that situation
may be changing, as some adults are beginning to say, "Enough is enough,"
and candle-light vigils and marches are becoming more common as communities grope for solutions.

JUVENILE VICTIMIZATION

Anthropologically speaking, violence seems almost endemic to the
human species, something civilization is constantly struggling to suppress.
(Violence is generally defined as injurious or homicidal action toward others.) "History is a slaughterhouse," the 19th-century German philosopher
Hegel declared. Our own century has done little to prove him wrong. In
the contemporary world, over a million people are murdered or commit
suicide each year.

In the U.S. more than 20,000 people die each year from violent acts,
while another 2.2 million are injured. Incredibly, more than 10,000 young
people between the ages of 10 and 24 are murdered or commit suicide (violence against themselves) each year. Over half of the people arrested for
murder in the U.S. in 1991 were under the age of 25.

Still, our culture of violence is romanticized in our history and in our   15
entertainment. In the midst of a youth murder epidemic, a film like *Natural Born Killer* becomes a nationwide sensation, and its soundtrack blares
from teenagers' boom boxes. Our culture of violence has spawned the
children of violence, even child murderers, and suddenly we seem
shocked.

In July 1994 the U.S. Department of Justice released a report noting
that the number of violent crimes perpetrated *against* juveniles between
the ages of 12 and 17 had risen nearly 24% between 1988 and 1992. "Although juveniles accounted for one-tenth of the population age 12 and

over," the report observed, "nearly one in four violent crimes involved a juvenile victim in 1992—up from one in five in 1987." About one in 13 youngsters is now victimized. Compare that to a ratio of one in 35 for adults over 35 years of age. During the same years the raw numbers rose from 5.8 million to 6.2 million young victims. Six out of 10 crimes against young people were assaults.

The problem is complicated by the 211 million firearms circulating among the American public. There are more gun dealers in the United States (284,000) than gas stations. Youth gangs have discovered that it isn't too difficult to go into the arms business along with the drug business. Just as the U.S. government is the biggest arms merchant on the world scene, so the nation's youth gangs now see the enormous profits in the small arms business.

Most observers agree that the easy availability of firearms is clearly a contributing factor to the unacceptable level of youth murder that haunts our communities. "Back in the 1970s when I defended kids in court, I wouldn't have five kids with guns in a year," says Judge Susan Larabee of the Bronx Family Court in New York City. "Now almost every single case I see involves not just a gun, but a loaded gun."

Although public opinion is shifting, legislative moves against guns are decried as unconstitutional. While more laws may help and strict enforcement would help even more, new laws are clearly not the answer. Most states already prohibit juveniles from carrying handguns and automatic weapons, but these laws have made little difference in the past. To solve this problem, society must devise strategies to find and disarm kids with guns.

Meanwhile, some children who become violent are not safe in their own homes and are regularly victimized by the adults entrusted to care for them. There is a direct and indisputable connection between violence in the home or against children in the home and subsequent violent behavior by those children. Psychologists confirm that children exposed to violence are sometimes as traumatized as children in war zones. For many youngsters, their American childhood has literally become a war zone in which they are entrapped—forced to run for cover and to avoid playgrounds, front yards, neighborhood streets, and even their own homes. . . .

20

SCHOOLS IN THE CROSSFIRE

Over three million assorted crimes—about 11% of all crimes—occur each year in America's 85,000 public schools. That compares with one million crimes each year in America's workplaces. In fact, a school crime takes place every six seconds. Some critics charge that figures for school crime are significantly underreported, because schools treat many incidents as discipline problems rather than as crimes.

While the popular perception is that school crime is primarily an urban problem, a 1991 report from the U.S. Justice Department, *School Crime: A National Crime Victimization Survey Report,* indicates otherwise. It found that suburban and urban students are about equally victimized. The report concluded that 2% of students from both settings and 1% of rural students were victims of violent crime, such as assault, robbery, and rape. The study polled 10,000 students between the ages of 12 and 19. Projecting those figures to the entire student population meant that approximately 430,000 students were victims of violent crime. The Justice Department also found that 13% of high school seniors had been threatened with a weapon.

The similarity in crime statistics between cities and suburbs might be attributed to the fact that urban districts have dealt with the problem for some time and have some workable intervention strategies in place. For example, urban schools are more likely to use hall monitors and metal detectors, so some problems are kept in the neighborhoods and out of the schools. Many urban school districts, such as San Diego and Houston, have adopted "zero tolerance" on guns and weapons. And in late October, President Clinton announced an executive order directing the states to require all school districts to enact the "zero tolerance" policy by expelling for one year any student who brings a gun to school. A conference committee had cut the measure out of the legislation reauthorizing the Elementary and Secondary Education Act. Federal funds can be cut off from states that fail to comply.

While schools secure their buildings and grounds, it is essential to understand that violent youths who are expelled must be reached in other ways or they will simply wreak havoc somewhere else. In the big cities, where dropout rates are high, the violence against students is often perpetrated by nonstudents. Turning more students out on the streets without providing the intensive help they need will not solve the larger problem.

Metal detectors seem prudent because national estimates are that more than 200,000 students pack weapons along with their school lunches and bring them into the learning environment every day, destabilizing classes, terrorizing teachers and peers, and often killing teachers, administrators, and other students. According to the National School Safety Center, last year guns led to 35 deaths and 92 injuries in the schools. Moreover, other lives are ruined in the cluster of social ramifications that any death brings to those associated with both the victim and the killer.

A Justice Department study found that 22% of inner-city boys own guns. According to researchers at the University of Michigan, 9% of eighth-graders nationally carry a gun, knife, or club to school at least once a month. The Michigan researchers estimated that students carry 270,000 guns to school each day. And the National Education Association calculates that on any given day about 160,000 students stay home because of fear of violence in or on the way to school. Indeed, their fear may be warranted: firearms are the fourth leading cause of accidental death among children between the ages of 5 and 14.

"Guns just make it too easy to kill people," explains Judge Larabee. "There is no personal involvement between [the killer] and the victim. It's between them and the gun and has almost nothing to do with the other kids. That's why so many kids 'accidentally' kill their best friends. The semi-automatics makes it easier because you hardly have to aim."

GETTING WORSE

While the rate of juvenile arrests may be down from two decades ago, school violence is worse now than it was five years ago, according to 75% of the 700 school districts that participated in a 1994 national survey of suburban, urban, and rural schools, conducted by the National School Boards Association (NSBA). The group concluded that two factors—the disintegration of the family and the increasing depiction of violence in the media and in popular music—are the leading causes of violence in public schools. Other contributing causes, according to the NSBA, are alcohol and drug abuse, easy access to guns, and poverty.

"The problem of school violence cannot be solved by schools working alone," said Thomas Shannon, NSBA executive director. "It will require intensive efforts by the entire community to reduce the epidemic of violence in the nation's schools."

The NSBA survey found that student assaults against other students, students bringing weapons to the classroom, student attacks on teachers, racial and ethnic violence, and gang-related problems were the top five types of violent incidents reported in schools during 1993. Nearly 40% of urban districts reported shootings or knife attacks, while 23% experienced drive-by shootings. 30

It is not just individual victims who suffer from school crime. All students are victimized by the fear, the anger, the guilt, the anguish, and the sense of helplessness that follow an act of school violence. A 1994 Gallup poll found that two-thirds of all teenagers said their "best friends" had been physically harmed in the last 12 months. However, another study by the National Center for Education Statistics found that only 8% of high school sophomores feel unsafe in their schools, down from 12% in 1980.

"Many of the youth we surveyed are being denied a fundamental sense of security," says Mark Singer, associate professor at the Mandel School of Applied Social Sciences, Case Western Reserve University. Singer surveyed 3,700 teenagers in Ohio and Colorado. More than half of the Cleveland high school students in the survey had witnessed knife attacks or stabbings. One-third of the students in a small Ohio town had witnessed the same behavior. Over half of the boys in the survey had perpetrated some form of violence during the preceding year, such as punching, hitting, or slapping someone. Among girls, sexual abuse was higher in the small towns than in the big cities in the survey.

"Many individuals in this survey have been exposed to significant levels of violence and are at risk of developing serious, long-term problems as a result," Singer concluded.

SOURCES OF YOUTH VIOLENCE

Seventeen hundred years ago, the Roman emperor and Stoic philosopher Marcus Aurelius observed that "poverty is the mother of crime." His insight endures because it is at least partially true. For the past 25 years, child welfare experts have warned that the grinding poverty, inequitable educational opportunity, latchkey homes, child abuse, domestic violence, and family breakups, as well as the general abandonment of children to a constant barrage of televised mayhem, would result in escalating real-world violence. Those predictions were pretty much ignored, while everyone blamed everyone else and the condition of children and teenagers continued to decline.

Others warn that today's problem is just the beginning. "Unless we fix our schools and give these kids opportunities, this current wave of violence will look like a picnic in comparison to the gangs and violence we will have in the future," predicts Joe Kellman, co-founder of the innovative Corporate/Community School in Chicago. He sees little inclination toward or progress in developing social supports because he believes that those in control of national resources are indifferent to the problem, if not cynically racist about who is getting killed.

Despite our sophistication, despite a pledge to end poverty 25 years ago, and despite the nation's more recent commitment to get children "ready to learn" before they enter school, U.S. society continues to allow nearly a quarter of its young people to grow up in such desperate and degrading material conditions that the struggle of daily survival can warp the human spirit and deaden moral consciousness. Year after year this psychic destruction of children goes on, waylaying more and more millions of young people.

Obviously, not all poor children respond to the conditions of their lives with destructive anger and aggression. Many use poverty as a motivation for success. And it is unfair, indeed prejudicial, to characterize urban youth as violent youth. In face, much of today's mayhem is the unexpected and nihilistic work of troubled middle-class youngsters. But that's no surprise either. The typical U.S. child of any ethnic or economic group has witnessed more than 8,000 murders and hundreds of thousands of acts of violence on television by the time he or she leaves eighth grade. One recent study by Sen. Byron Dorgan (D-N.D.) recorded 1,000 violent acts on television each week. Without critical lenses to filter this barrage of antisocial behavior, children begin to have unreal and destructive social expectations and desires.

Yet in more and more urban and suburban neighborhoods, kids are afraid to ride their bikes lest they become victims of a drive-by shooting or an assault. In the course of writing this article, I interrupted two separate incidents in which young children were thrown to the ground and viciously kicked in the head by youths their own age or a little older. One took place on a city street next to a decrepit school, the other in an affluent schoolyard far from the threat of urban street gangs.

No wonder many mothers are forced to keep their children cooped up in apartments or homes. Unfortunately, as a result, most youngsters spend their time watching the cartoon violence on their television sets. In fact, Americans spend 97% of their time indoors. Many do so because they are afraid to go outside.

PSYCHOLOGICAL ROOTS

The reduction of youth crime in general may be partially the result of the thousands of anti-violence and mediation courses that have been in place in America's schools since 1972. But the new kind of violence we are seeing suggests that real remedies need to be more specialized and better focused than is generally acknowledged. Teaching students mediation skills, for example, although a good strategy to help many kids cope socially, is not likely to prevent the worst kinds of crimes by children who show early signs of violent behavior. These young people need to be identified quickly and given professional help to learn how to work out their problems in socially permissible ways.

In response to the disturbing and complicated problem of youth violence, the American Psychological Association (APA) has launched a number of studies, new programs, and media outreach efforts that will continue over the next few years. Its first report, *Violence & Youth: Psychology's Response,* is an overview of the APA's findings and provides a number of useful insights for teachers, parents, and communities working to confront the frightening situation of children killing children.[1] The report reflects 50 years of research on child and teenage aggression and other related phenomena. For educators, many of its implications will suggest strategies for action that can be added to new or current school antiviolence plans.

The APA lists domestic violence, hate crimes, sexual violence, and peer violence as the leading threats to the safety of today's children and teenagers. But what causes a person to become violent? According to APA researchers, the causes are many and complex, ranging from "biological factors, child-rearing conditions, ineffective parenting, emotional and cognitive development, gender differences, sex role socialization, relations to

---

[1] *Violence & Youth: Psychology's Response,* vol. 1 (Washington, D.C.: American Psychological Association, 1993).

peers, cultural milieu, social factors such as economic inequality and lack of opportunity, and media influences, among others."

The APA concluded that it is difficult to sort out the roles of heredity, biology (e.g., head trauma), and learned behavior. Indeed, some recent research by neuroscientists suggests that genetic "defects" that produce abnormal levels of two brain chemicals, serotonin and noradrenaline, may account for some violent behavior. The biology of violence is a subject that will be debated often in years to come.

On the positive side, the APA is confident that much of the social violence we are witnessing today is learned behavior. That leads to the APA's optimistic conclusion that, if violence is learned, it can be unlearned.

THE STRONGEST PREDICTOR

The APA found that "the strongest developmental predictor of a child's involvement in violence is a history of previous violence." That includes having been a victim of abuse. (About 70% of men who come through the criminal justice system were abused or neglected children.) The APA also found that "children who show a fearless, impulsive temperament very early in life may have a predisposition for aggression and violent behavior."

That is why the APA says that early childhood intervention to prevent future violence is "critical." Children who show signs of antisocial behavior need to be targeted early for school and family intervention, not only to teach them new ways to resolve social conflicts, but also to ensure that their aggressive tendencies do not interfere with their potential for educational achievement and so contribute to even greater social and learning problems later.

Preschools, Head Start programs, and the early elementary years are times when educators must have the skills and resources, as well as the assistance of psychologists and social workers, to thwart future problems of violence during the difficult years of adolescence. If we are serious about reducing violence, it is ridiculous to ignore the causes insofar as we know them. Therefore, early action is imperative.

Nor should popular remedies such as instruction in nonviolence and mediation be confined to the middle and high school years, when the problem has grown serious. The early years are the best time for schools to teach these skills, particularly if they are not being taught in the home.

ADULT ABANDONMENT

The APA confirms the popular notion that a "breakdown of family processes and relationships" contributes to "the development of antisocial behaviors, including violence." Poor families are not the only ones involved in this situation. Increasingly, families in all economic strata exhibit these problems. The APA found that "lack of parental supervision is one of the strongest predictors of the development of conduct problems and delinquency."

However, supervision does not mean overzealous punishment. The APA warned that "harsh and continual physical punishment by parents has been implicated in the development of aggressive behavior patterns." Conversely, it found that positive interactions by parents and other adults can lessen the risk of developing violent behavior. This is a conclusion also reached by "resilience researchers," who have found that the involvement of just one caring adult can make all the difference in the life of an "at-risk" youth. The first step toward creating real opportunities for young people is reintroducing adults from the community and other places into the lives of these youngsters.

50

NEGATIVE SCHOOL FACTORS

As all teachers know, aggressive and disruptive behavior in the classroom often leads to poor performance and destructive peer relationships, which in turn contribute to the "trajectory toward violence." The APA didn't blame schools, but it did find that several aspects of school organization "help create a milieu that is conducive to aggression." These include "high numbers of students occupying a small space"; the "imposition of behavioral routines and conformity" that may contribute to feelings of "anger, resentment, and rejection"; and poor building designs that "may facilitate the commission of violent acts."

Schools that are serious about reducing violent behavior need to analyze the dynamics of their own cultures to identify both sources of friction and ways in which children and teenagers are permitted—even encouraged—to express their emotions. For example, University of Minnesota researchers David Johnson and Roger Johnson argue that cooperative learning, in addition to contributing to academic improvement, also teaches social and mediation skills that enable young people to live in greater harmony.

Violence is not an inevitable response on the part of children and teenagers. The APA urged that, "on the positive side, early exposure to cultural influences that enable the child to build a positive ethnic identity and a sense of belonging to a group with shared traditions and values may help buffer the child against social risk factors for the involvement in violence."

SEARCHING FOR SOLUTIONS

But what can schools that are caught in the crossfire of youth violence do to protect their students and to get at fundamental psychological and behavioral habits? A 1994 Honeywell survey of teachers and students, titled *Keeping Our Schools Safe*, found that 82% of teachers believed that parenting classes could help reduce violence, while 78% recommended smaller classes, 77% called for stricter discipline, 72% called for more student involvement in discipline procedures, and 76% said that schools need family support systems. Only 30% of the teachers surveyed thought that metal detectors or more security guards could help the situation.

According to the NSBA, many schools are standing up to violence by trying everything from enacting new school suspension policies to using closed-circuit television on school buses and adopting "zero tolerance" policies for possession of weapons or for any kind of violent behavior. More than 70% of the districts in the NSBA survey collaborate with social service agencies to address underlying causes of violence. About 60% of the districts teach students the skills of conflict resolution and peer mediation. (Nationwide, more than 2,000 schools conduct conflict resolution programs.) Half of the districts surveyed reported that they search lockers, 41% have established dress codes, and 24% use drug-sniffing dogs on occasion. But only 15% of the districts in the NSBA survey use metal detectors in their schools. Other studies show that more than 45% of urban school systems use metal detectors.

The debate rages over whether or not metal detectors do the job. "There is little evidence that metal detectors work," says Ronald Stevens, president of the National School Safety Council. But 10% more of the nation's 100 largest districts are using metal detectors this year than did so last year. Detroit schools installed them in 1985, New York City schools in 1987, and Kansas City, Missouri, schools in 1993.

The federal Centers for Disease Control and Prevention advise that metal detectors may reduce but won't eliminate gun violence. The centers concluded that the detectors "have no apparent effect on the number of injuries, deaths, or threats of violence" at schools. And they don't address long-term problems.

The Dallas Independent Schools have introduced a multifaceted strategy to reduce violence. The program has placed new campus safety teams at every school, consisting of specially trained teachers, counselors, and security people. Other components of the program include a crisis planning guide for principals, 24-hour hotlines for students to call in with confidential information, and peer mediation projects. The state of North Carolina started a Scholastic Crime Stoppers program that pays rewards of up to $1,000 for crime tips. The schools in Dade County, Florida, adopted the nation's first gun awareness program.

Indeed, hundreds of schools across the nation have also tried to confront the issue of violence by introducing anti-violence curricula, conflict resolution, and conflict management. Students learn a variety of options they can resort to instead of turning to violence. Some schools train as many as 50 student mediators to conduct hundreds of mediation sessions to resolve everyday disputes.

A five-year study by the National Institute on Drug Abuse and the National Institute of Mental Health found that one program—Anger Management for Youth: Stemming Aggression and Violence—did a good job

One Bullet's Impact on Sullivan High

Not every youth murder makes the national headlines. In fact, most don't. But each is a terrible tragedy that brings deep sorrow to many people and psychological scars to children. The sad fact is that youth murder has become a daily occurrence that threatens places that once seemed immune. In early November 1993, for example, a murder at Sullivan High School rocked a quiet Chicago neighborhood. And the school hasn't been the same since.

Sullivan is a small, stable, and respected general high school with 1,400 students. It is part of the Coalition of Essential Schools and offers the Paideia Program. It is located in one of the most multiethnic neighborhoods in the city. About 55% of Sullivan students are African American, 25% are Hispanic, 15% are Asian, and the rest are white or members of other groups.

A noontime gang dispute across the street from the school ended in the shooting of Kati Faber, a 15-year-old freshman at Sullivan. A 16-year-old pulled the trigger of a .380 semiautomatic handgun that had been held for him during school by a female student. Faber died 1½ hours after the incident, and several lives were wrecked by that lone bullet. The young girl who had kept the gun was convicted in juvenile court of murder (under a law that holds the accessory accountable). The case of the 16-year-old is still pending.

"The shooting shook our school to its very foundation," says principal Patricia Anderson, who has been at Sullivan since 1984 but had only become principal a few months earlier."The impact of the murder was so far-reaching. There were waves of reactions, feelings, and thoughts from all members of the school community."

Ironically, at the exact moment of the killing, Anderson and other school officials were meeting with local police and community members on how to deal with gang problems and danger spots in the surrounding community. "I wanted to make contact with them so they knew our needs and we knew their needs, so we could work together," recalls Anderson. "We wanted to develop relations and develop strategy. We had no sense of the immediate danger that struck Sullivan."

The crowded school has an open campus, and the shooting took place across a narrow street. Financial problems that beset the Chicago Public Schools at the start of the year had held up funding for a full security force. Nor did Sullivan have metal detectors in place at the time, something Mayor Richard Daley has pushed for in all Chicago high schools. The detectors had been rejected by a previous local school council, which did not want to disrupt the academic atmosphere or make the school feel like a maximum-security prison.

"The idealistic side of me agrees with that," says Anderson. "Usually, we are a very quiet, settled place. Yes, there are occasional outbursts, but that is typical of any school these days in this society. But the realistic side of me says that we must do more."

So Anderson had new metal detectors installed, but "as unobtrusive as possible," she says. "We decided not to use handheld detectors that are taken into classrooms, for example. I refused to take class time for security and impose that kind of feeling. We try to make it feel like no more than getting on an airplane. Once youngsters are in the building safely, we will keep that sense of security.

"If I am going to err," she adds, "I am going to err on the side of safety for all my students. The school attracts a variety of people with different home situations, problems, and values, and I have to make sure everyone is safe. In this job I am often torn between both sides of issues."

In addition to detectors, Sullivan introduced a policy that requires students to wear photo IDs at all times when they are in the building, so that monitors can identify any nonstudents, who have occasionally come into the school and created problems. Sullivan also boosted its security force and instituted a hotline on which any student can give information on other students confidentially. That's an idea the Los Angeles schools are using. So far, it hasn't been used a lot at Sullivan, but it is there. The number is well-posted and adds to the sense of security.

"The students were split on these issues," Anderson recalls, "with the majority in favor of these measures because they want their school to be safe and secure. But students have reacted very well to it. They realize that we are not doing this against them, but for them.

"The students also have learned that they have a responsibility to keep the school safe and that it is not up to some outside force," Anderson notes. "Schools are not designed with the kind of staffing that can put security everywhere. Teachers have not been trained to do that. It is not what they chose to do. They need the time to prepare their lessons. So students must be there first. Students also know what gang incidents happened over the weekend that might have repercussions in school. I have gotten the message to them that they need to help us and inform us of danger.

"In the long run," Anderson says, "this unfortunate event reawakened the idea that our society, each community, and, more important, each family must take more responsibility for what is going on with children and youth. It made us realize that we may be even more responsible than other units. Despite the fact that we know crime is in the community and despite the fact that our mission is primarily one of education, we must strongly consider those issues of safety that are out there in the neighborhoods. We have to protect the school and its students against those threats."—RCS of teaching ways to reduce anger. The study tracked 1,200 at-risk teen-agers from Washington, D.C. After just five months, the students had fewer problems with anger, less depression, and fewer feelings of hopelessness and stress.

Many schools use the Resolving Conflict Creatively Program, which began as a partnership between the New York City schools and Educators for Social Responsibility. Forty schools in New York City participate in Project STOP (Schools Teaching Options for Peace).

Students who become mediators learn to listen, to act as role models, to initiate discussions, to channel feedback, to change personal habits, to be vigilant, to deal with their fear, to guide others, and to become learn-ers. In general, teachers who work with students using mediation and res-olution approaches feel that their students have more respect for one another, are more at ease, know alternatives they can pursue, and are able to think about the consequences of their actions. Adults say these pro-grams get kids to take responsibility for maintaining behavioral standards.

But if they are to succeed, good mediation programs require lots of training for teachers and students. And they need to give authority to stu-dents to nominate the people they think will make the fairest mediators. Schools must make that commitment, or their efforts will be diluted from the beginning.

Conflict resolution training is now mandated by the state of Illinois. Minnesota has allocated nearly $2.5 million for violence prevention edu-cation and has developed a progressive statewide plan for integrating its violence reduction program into the general curriculum. At Coventry El-ementary School in Cleveland Heights, Ohio, peace is a unifying theme of learning and living together. Even first-graders are taught mediation skills.

THINKING THE PROBLEM THROUGH

Counteracting youth violence requires more than a criminal justice approach, and scores of new anti-violence curricula have been developed over the past decade. One new approach comes from Ronald Slaby, a se-nior scientist at the Education Development Center in Newton, Massa-chusetts, who is also a member of the APA Commission on Youth and Violence. Along with colleagues Renée Wilson-Brewer and Kim Dash, Slaby developed a new middle school curriculum called *Aggressors, Victims, and Bystanders: Thinking and Acting to Prevent Violence.* The 12-session cur-riculum, funded by a grant from the federal Centers for Disease Control and Prevention, will be one of the teaching modules for teenagers that are distributed through the health departments of all 50 states.

"Violence is learned, so it can be unlearned, or not learned at all," Slaby asserts. "You can change your habits of thinking. The truth is that kids can do it easier than adults." But young people have to be taught how to think of alternatives, clearly and specifically, Slaby reasons. Then they have to practice their new behavior. His curriculum is designed "to teach a think-first model," in which students go through four steps.

1. *Keeping cool.* They talk about being cool-headed versus hot-headed. (The terms were chosen based on feedback from the participants.)

2. *Sizing up the situation.* This step is important because the way young people define a problem influences the solutions they pick. Slaby explains that violent offenders define a problem in hostile ways and automatically treat other people as adversaries when that may not be warranted.

3. *Thinking it through.* Kids learn to think of alternative solutions, as well as to think about the consequences. "Violent juvenile offenders simply do not think things through," says Slaby. "Ironically, our jails are filled with youngsters and even adults who are in for premeditated murder, when they, of all their cohorts, are the least likely to be premeditators who think about consequences. They had a gun, they threatened with the gun, then they hardly know how it happened that they shot the gun, because they were not thinking through to the consequences."

4. *Doing the right thing.* Students are taught to pick the response that is most likely to succeed and be effective in solving the problem and preventing violence.

70

Slaby's research reveals that most youngsters in middle school want to hang out with individuals who know how to solve problems nonviolently, although they may not be consciously aware of this fact. This means that the classroom teacher can teach these skills and ways of thinking. Some youngsters know them already, but even those students profit from more practice. But some youth are at high risk and need to be taught how to prevent violence. "When kids do learn these skills and challenge the superficial beliefs that support violence," Slaby says, "their behavior changes."

PICKING PREVENTION PROGRAMS

Several researchers have called into question the effectiveness of some of the most popular anti-violence programs currently used by schools, charging that most schools are responding to the violence issue with "off-the-shelf" curriculum packages squeezed into the already-crowded curriculum.[2] For example, Daniel Webster of the Injury Prevention Center at Johns Hopkins University found "no evidence" that three of the leading curriculum packages "produce long-term changes in violent behavior or risk of victimization." Webster concluded that the programs were a way for school officials and politicians to find "political cover" in the violence debate.

---

[2] See Marc Posner, "Research Raises Troubling Questions About Violence Prevention Programs," *Harvard Education Letter,* May/June 1994, pp. 1–4.

Standing Up to School Violence: A Resource Guide for Action

Reports and Studies

- *Aggressors, Victims, and Bystanders,* by Ronald Slaby et al., Education Development Center, Inc., 55 Chapel St., Newton, MA 02158. Ph. 800/225-4276.
- *BiblioAlert: Focus on Firearms, New Resources for Preventing Injury and Violence,* Children's Safety Network, National Center for Education in Maternal and Child Health, 2000 15th St. N., Suite 701, Arlington, VA 22201-2617. Ph. 800/899-4301.
- *Call for Violence Prevention and Intervention on Behalf of Very Young Children, Zero to Three,* National Center for Clinical Infant Programs, 2000 14th St., Arlington, VA 22201. Ph. 800/899-4301.
- *Children and TV Violence* and *The Influence of Music and Rock Videos,* Facts for Families Series, American Academy of Child & Adolescent Psychiatry, 3615 Wisconsin Ave. N.W., Washington, DC 20016. Ph. 202/966-7300; include stamped, self-addressed envelope.
- *A Comprehensive Strategy for Serious, Violent, and Chronic Juvenile Offenders,* U.S. Department of Justice, Office of Juvenile Justice and Delinquency Prevention, Washington, D.C., 1993. Ph. 800/638-8736.
- *Early Violence Prevention: Tools for Teachers of Young Children,* by Roland Slaby et al., Education Development Center, Inc., 55 Chapel St., Newton, MA 02158. Ph. 617/969-7100, ext. 2215.
- *Educational Resources for Violence Prevention,* a list of curricula, videos, and other materials, CSN Adolescent Violence Prevention Resource Center, Education Development Center, Inc., 55 Chapel St., Newton, MA 02158. Ph. 617/969-7100, ext. 2374. The cost is $3.
- *Gang/Violence Prevention Material,* Midwest Regional Center for Drug-Free Schools and Communities, 1900 Spring Rd., Oak Brook, IL 60521. Ph. 708/571-4710.
- "Juveniles and Violence: Juvenile Offenders and Victimization Fact Sheet," U.S. Department of Justice, Washington, D.C., July 1993. Ph. 800/638-8736.
- National Victim Center INFOLINK Program, an information and referral center for victims of violent crime. Ph. 800/FYI-CALL.
- *The Prevention of Youth Violence: A Framework for Community Action,* U.S. Department of Health and Human Services, Centers for Disease Control and Prevention, 4770 Buford Highway N.E., F36, Atlanta, GA 30341-3724. Ph. 404/488-4400.
- *Reducing Youth Violence,* U.S. General Accounting Office (GAO/T-RD-92-22). Ph. 202/512-6000.

- *Safety Initiatives in Urban Public Schools,* Council of the Great City Schools, 1301 Pennsylvania Ave. N.W., Suite 702, Washington, DC 20004. Ph. 202/393-2427. The cost is $10.

- *School Crime: A National Crime Victimization Survey Report,* U.S. Department of Justice, Washington, DC, 1991. Ph. 800/638-8736.

- *Schools Respond to Gangs and Violence,* by Joan Gaustad, Oregon School Study Council, May 1991; also available through the Midwest Regional Center for Drug-Free Schools and Communities, 1900 Spring Rd., Oak Brook, IL 60521. Ph. 708/571-4710.

- *Teaching Tolerance,* Southern Poverty Law Center, 400 Washington Ave., Montgomery, AL 36104. Fax 205/264-3121.

- "The Unconvincing Case for School-Based Conflict Resolution Programs for Adolescents," *Health Affairs 12,* Winter 1993.

- *Understanding and Preventing Violence,* A. Reiss and J. Roth, eds., National Research Council, National Academy Press (2101 Constitution Ave. N.W., Washington, DC 20055), 1993. Ph. 800/624-6242.

- *Violence and Youth: Psychology's Response,* American Psychological Association Commission on Violence and Youth, American Psychological Association (750 First St. N.E., Washington, DC 20002), 1993. Ph. 202/336-6046.

- *Voices from the Future: Our Children Tell Us About Violence in America,* Susan Goodwille, ed., Children's Express, Crown Publishers (201 E. 50th St., New York, NY 10022), 1993. Ph. 212/572-6117.

- *Violence in the Schools: How America's School Boards Are Safeguarding Our Children,* National School Boards Association, 1680 Duke St., Alexandria, VA 22314. Ph. 703/838-6722. The cost is $15; $12 for NSBA members.

- *Violence Prevention: A Curriculum for Adolescents,* by Deborah Prothrow-Stith, Education Development Center, Inc., 55 Chapel St., Newton, MA 02158. Ph. 800/225-4276.

- *Violence Prevention for Young Adolescents: A Survey of the State of the Art,* Carnegie Council on Adolescent Development (2400 N St. N.W., Washington, DC 20037-1153), 1991. Ph. 202/429-7979. Also available through the Midwest Regional Center for Drug-Free Schools and Communities, 1900 Spring Rd., Oak Brook, IL 60521. Ph. 708/571-4710.

- *Violence Prevention for Young Adults: The State of the Art of Program Evaluations,* by Stu Cohen et al., ERIC Clearinghouse (ED 356 441). Ph. 800/443-3742. The cost is $10.59.

- *Youth Gang Bibliography,* U.S. Department of Health and Human Services, Washington, D.C., 1991; also available through the Midwest Regional Center for Drug-Free Schools and Communities, 1900 Spring Rd., Oak Brook, IL 60521. Ph. 708/571-4710.

(continued)

Organizations

- Center for Research and Development in Law-Related Education, 2714 Henning Dr., Winston-Salem, NC 57106-4502. Ph. 800/437-1054.
- Children's Defense Fund, 1520 New Hampshire Ave. N.W., Washington, DC 20001. Ph. 202/628-8787.
- Community Board Program, 1540 Market St., Suite 490, San Francisco, CA 94101. Ph. 415/552-1250.
- Educators for Social Responsibility, School Conflict Resolution Programs, 23 Garden St., Cambridge, MA 02138. Ph. 617/492-1764.
- National Associates for Mediation in Education (NAME), 425 Amity St., Amherst, MA 01002. Ph. 413/545-2462.
- National Conference on Peacemaking and Conflict Resolution, George Mason University, 4400 University Dr., Fairfax, VA 22030. Ph. 703/993-3635.
- National Council on Child Abuse and Family Violence, 1155 Connecti-cut Ave. N.W., Suite 400, Washington, DC 20036. Ph. 202/429-6695.
- National School Safety Center, 4165 Thousand Oaks Blvd., Suite 290, Westlake Village, CA 91362. Ph. 805/373-9977.
- Resolving Conflict Creatively, New York City Public Schools, 163 Third Ave., #239, New York, NY 10003. Ph. 212/260-6290.

Renée Wilson-Brewer and her colleagues at the Education Development Center in Newton, Massachusetts, examined the claims of 51 programs and found that only half even *claimed* to be able to affect violent behavior.

The APA suggests intervention to counteract and deflect the forces that contribute to violent behavior. But the proliferation of new anti-violence programs requires parents, schools, and communities to make wise choices. The APA notes that many new programs have not been adequately tested or were not research-based in the first place. In short, the APA recommends that schools use only programs that share two basic characteristics:

- an understanding of developmental and sociocultural risk factors that lead to antisocial behavior; and
- the inclusion of theory-based intervention strategies with known effectiveness in changing behavior, tested program designs, and validated objective measurement techniques to assess outcomes.

The APA also recommends that programs "begin as early as possible," that they "address aggression as part of a constellation of antisocial behaviors in the child or youth," that their "multiple components reinforce each other across the child's everyday social contexts: family, school, peer 75 groups, media, and community," and that they "take advantage of developmental windows of opportunity" when they are most needed or are most likely to make a difference.

The programs that the APA found to be most effective included home visitation components. School programs that "promote social and cognitive skills seem to have the greatest impact on attitudes about violent behavior among children and youth." Such skills include "perspective taking, alternative solution generation, self-esteem enhancement, peer negotiation skills, problem-solving training, and anger management." The APA encourages schools to differentiate between programs aimed at children already exhibiting violent behavior and those aimed at a more general audience.

A SCHOOL SAFETY PLAN

In the end, every school needs to adopt a broadly conceived and well-coordinated strategy to confront violence perpetrated against and by its students. The effort has barely begun in most communities and schools across the nation, even though the levels of concern are high.

A comprehensive plan to prevent school violence should start with issues of school safety and set concrete goals and objectives that will have immediate impact. Schools also need to be prepared for a crisis. The plan must decide how to train teachers, parents, and students in violence prevention. It should investigate curricula for violence prevention that match the real problems at the individual school. It must also find ways to make anti-violence a school expectation and theme. In addition, the plan should enlist the entire community in an effort to see that students can travel confidently to and from school through "safe" neighborhoods where businesspeople and parents constantly look out for their protection.

The school safety plan should chart ways to identify early those violent youths who need help, and it should specify how to arrange professional care for such children and teens. Perhaps the hardest part of a valid plan is finding ways to open up opportunities for these young people by making sure that every child and teen is in contact with adults who care about them, who mentor them, and who help them connect to their society through outside cultural or economic institutions. The plan should also find after-school alternatives for kids who have nowhere to go.

THE SIXTH EDUCATION GOAL

In addition to protecting youth from assaults, each local school/community plan should stand as the first step toward fulfilling the sixth of our national goals for education, which calls for safe schools where learning is not disrupted. Students, teachers, principals, parents, police officers, and

80

community members must be brought into the effort. And since the sixth goal is also a political goal—endorsed by two Presidents, by the Congress, and by all 50 state governors—schools should be given political support when they reach out for help. Moreover, if that support is not forthcoming, these politicians should be held responsible.

If the nation is ever to reach this all-important goal, which is a prerequisite for learning; if it is to spare its children from victimization, injury, psychic and physical pain, and potential death, even as they walk down a school hall or to and from the school; if it is to redeem the real promise of an American childhood, then it must, through its individual communities, launch some kind of campaign to prevent youth violence in order to make life safer for young people. Each person, each family, each community member, each teacher, and each student must take some of the responsibility for standing up to this devastating violence.

A truly effective campaign for the prevention of youth violence may require even more than the implementation of programs and campaigns. The radical reduction of youth violence probably will not happen until the entire society seeks and practices a more nonviolent way of resolving problems and emphasizes an ethic of valuing people. If we want children to learn nonviolent behavior, it seems reasonable that we need to exhibit nonviolent solutions to our social, economic, and even international problems. We must find ways to explain the consequences of violence more clearly to the nation's youth, as well as ways to enforce higher standards of personal behavior and responsibility. We need to set norms of nonviolent expectation and teach skills of social respect for ourselves and for our children.

"If we are going to have an impact on the schools, we're going to have to deal with all the other environmental issues, too," warns Donna Shalala, U.S. secretary of health and human services. Violence prevention "can't be seen simply as trying to make schools safe—because we have to try and make the streets safe as well." She is right. But intensifying the anti-violence message in schools is an important place to begin.

◆ **QUESTIONS FOR DISCUSSION AND WRITING** ◆

---

1. Sautter reports in "Standing Up to Violence" that "only 30% of the teachers surveyed thought that metal detectors or more security guards could help" prevent violence on campus (paragraph 54). Of the teachers surveyed, large numbers suggested other approaches: 82% believe that parenting classes can help; 77% think that stricter discipline can help; and so on (paragraph 54). There are additional suggestions in paragraphs 58–62 of the article. Do you agree with these other kinds of approaches—and therefore think that Dr. Jensen's approach at Westwood High is wrong? If so, what would you do at Westwood?

2. How effective is the presentation of statistical information in "Standing Up to Violence?" Why?

3. In terms of controlling school violence, what is the most effective idea in Sautter's essay? Why?

4. Which of the readings your instructor asked you to work through for this scenario helped you most in determining what you believe about the issues? Why?
5. How much responsibility do high school students have for keeping their campuses safe? What should students do to increase campus safety?

TAKING ACTION

Your Written Appeal to the Governing Council

You've now finished your reading, and you may also have done additional research about specific aspects of the Westwood High scenario, just as you would have if you really were involved with the problems at this high school. The next step is to outline your group's position on Dr. Jensen's proposals to the entity that has control over the situation. In this case, the Winterhaven Valley Governing Council hired Principal Jensen and now will determine which, if any, of his ideas should be implemented at Westwood High.

The elected members of the council usually focus on civic issues, but because of the incidents last year at Westwood High, they've turned their attention to the safety of students in the local schools. Principal Jensen and his administration fully expect the council to support his proposals because its members hired him believing he would know what measures to implement to make Westwood a safe school. Because the council ultimately answers to the public, it also has asked for public comment from parents and students. This is your chance to present your group's ideas to the council.

Principal Jensen has made four main recommendations:

• All cars coming onto campus will be searched.
• All students, staff, and faculty will wear a photo ID badge at all times.
• Each morning, school administrators will search all bookbags.
• Metal detectors will be installed at all school entrances to ensure that weapons are not brought onto campus.

In addition, other approaches to campus safety have been discussed: armed guards, a fence around the school, video surveillance cameras, and locked parking lots. Your group might consider these as it composes its statement.

How do the members of your group respond to each of these suggestions? If the council provides funding and allows Dr. Jensen to implement his recommendations, how will you and the members of your group be affected? Will these ideas increase safety at Westwood High? Do you have any other ideas on what should be done to make Westwood a safer campus?

For the sake of this exercise, assume that you will send your group's statement to the council for its consideration, using this address: Winterhaven Valley Governing Council, 16565 South Timberline Road, Winter-haven, WA 98322-2201.

Asking the Right Questions

It's always useful to begin wrestling with a problem or an issue that affects you by first analyzing what you already know about the subject. This gives you an idea of what you'd like to learn more about. You can begin by asking some questions. Questions lead to other questions that can help your group decide on the best solution for the issues the scenario presents. So, as you draft your statement to the Winterhaven Valley Governing Council, consider the scenario from a reporter's perspective, focusing on the who, what, when, where, and why of the scenario. Try to answer the following questions:

- What perspectives do each of the groups have? What are the strengths and weaknesses of those points of view?
- Can you make your statement to the council stronger by aligning your group with another group and its position? Would it have a greater influence on the council if more than one group shared the same ideas about several of the issues, problems, or possible solutions?
- What events in the Westwood High School scenario can be controlled? In what ways? What cannot be controlled?
- What are some of the positive and negative consequences to Westwood High and its students if Principal Jensen's proposals are put into place?
- If you are a member of the administration group, how can you demonstrate that Dr. Jensen's ideas will be effective? What information can you provide from other high schools that have implemented approaches similar to those Dr. Jensen has proposed?
- If you are a member of the teacher's group, how would you feel about having to deal with Dr. Jensen's proposals each day at school? How effective do you think his ideas would be at stopping dangerous weapons from getting onto campus? How far are you willing to go to help implement his proposals, or would you simply refuse to participate? Why?
- What other solutions to the problems at Westwood can your group offer, and how can you demonstrate that they would be more effective than Dr. Jensen's ideas?
- What are the consequences if your group does nothing to try to change the situation? What actions might make the Westwood situation more problematic?
- How do the problems and issues in the Westwood High School scenario relate to the larger national concern with school violence?

Which group you represent and the approach you decide to take will determine the position you propose. You might, for example, argue in favor of or against all of Jensen's proposals, you might argue against only some of them, or you might suggest ideas of your own to make the campus safe.

Constructing a Collaborative Text

Work with the members of your group to draft a letter to the Winterhaven Valley Governing Council that expresses your views on Dr. Jensen's proposal. It's important that you read through and revise your draft several times, so that your group's ideas are articulated as clearly as possible to the council.

One way to start to construct your group letter is for each group member to compose his or her own letter, listing what each considers to be the most important issues and problems. Then, working together, your group can draw on those initial comments to compose the group letter.

Another approach is to take the notes that each of you has made, designate one group member to record the group's ideas, and then collaboratively compose an initial draft of what your group thinks. At first, this process might be a bit hectic, with several group members offering suggestions on what to write and how to write it, but with time, you'll find that working together is an interesting and useful way to get your collective ideas onto paper.

When you've completed a first draft of your collaborative letter, each group member should read through the draft, marking any sections that are unclear. Work together to clarify those parts. Then, each group member should read the letter once more, this time looking for places in the text where your argument might need more evidence. Then, again working together, decide what pieces of evidence gathered during your research (facts, data, testimony, statistics) might provide additional support for your argument.

Your instructor might ask you to read and comment on the other groups' letters. Working together in such a manner gives you the chance to help your classmates become better writers, as you act as real readers for one another. Indicate the places in the text where more information is needed, or where the writing is confusing, or where some elaboration might help. Follow the procedure in Box 5.2: Using Your Classmates' Suggestions to apply the feedback you receive to improve your composition.

SPEAKING YOUR PIECE
Presenting Your Ideas to the Council

After the Winterhaven Valley Governing Council members have read the letters from the various interested groups, the chairperson of the

BOX 5.2 APPLYING WHAT YOU READ
Using Your Classmates' Suggestions (Written Peer Review)

Once you have a brief (no longer than two pages) collaborative text that outlines your message to the Winterhaven Valley Governing Council, trade your draft with that of another group. Read that group's statement carefully, and look for (and indicate in marginal notes) its strengths and weaknesses. What suggestions can you make on how the group might improve its position?

What are the strengths of the draft? The weaknesses? Where was the group's argument confusing? Did the group address each aspect of Principal Jensen's proposal? What is clear? Unclear? How could the group better articulate its position to the council? What suggestions might you offer to improve the letter?

Once your group receives feedback from your classmates, work together as a group to revise your letter to the council. What suggestions did you receive that make sense? Where does your text need clarification, or further explanation, or more evidence? What facts or other data have group members collected that you can add to your letter to make it more convincing?

council, Nancy Druckett, makes a suggestion. "Because the community feels that there is a growing problem at Westwood High," she says to the other council members, "and because these groups have so many good ideas," she continues, pointing to the letters spread out on the desk in front of her, "I think we ought to let them speak to each other. These statements are good, but they are all addressed to us. I want to bring everyone together, so we all can learn from one another. Then we'll decide what to do about Principal Jensen's proposal."

Accordingly, the Winterhaven Valley Governing Council decides to hold an open meeting to permit all interested parties to voice their concerns and to ask questions about Principal Jensen's ideas. This is a chance for the various groups to find ways to work together and to really understand what everyone involved believes ought to be done at Westwood High School.

This is also your opportunity to question Dr. Jensen and his administration about his proposal: What will his ideas cost? How does the administration group know that these measures will be effective? Are there other ways of solving the weapons problem? What happens if the council funds Dr. Jensen's proposals and they don't work? What if the Westwood situation grows worse?

This meeting is also your group's chance to exchange information with members of the other groups. You can learn something about their perspectives on the problems at Westwood. How can you use the information you'll learn to strengthen your position? What arguments do the other groups make that weaken your position, and how might you refute those arguments? Do the other groups' arguments convince you that yours are weak?

Just as your group will be allowed to question the other groups, those groups will be able to question you. So, during the meeting, listen carefully to all questions, and, when a question is addressed to your group, take a moment to talk among yourselves and determine a suitable answer.

During this open meeting, you and the members of your group need to remember that your comments and behavior will influence the council's decisions. Unreasonable, unprepared group members or groups that represent themselves poorly will probably damage their credibility with the council. On the other hand, group members who ask relevant and thoughtful questions and express an interest in cooperation are more likely to be looked on favorably.

From Written Preparation to Public Speaking

With the members of your group, decide how to modify your written statement so that it forms the basis for an oral presentation in front of the Winterhaven Valley Governing Council. Even though you don't know what the other groups plan to say, you probably have a reasonable idea of their positions, based on the reading and discussions your group has completed. What are likely to be their strongest ideas? Their weakest? How can you clearly articulate your own position?

As an example, let's say that the spokesperson for a group that represents the sophomores at Westwood wants to argue against one of Dr. Jensen's proposals: the installation of metal detectors. Let's also say that this group wants to make two main points:

- Metal detectors won't eliminate all weapons from campus.
- The use of metal detectors constitutes an invasion of student privacy.

If this group were preparing a written statement, members might list these points and the support they have for them. They could assume that readers would return to each one if anything in the statement was unclear.

In an oral statement, however, the spokesperson for the sophomores not only has to be organized, but he or she must make all connections and conclusions clear and explicit. That is, the spokesperson has to provide the audience with a clear and understandable road map to follow throughout the speech. The spokesperson might arrange the oral presentation like this:

I. Metal detectors won't eliminate all weapons from our campus.
  A. Students can find other ways to smuggle weapons onto campus, such as passing them through windows.
  B. Not all weapons are made of metal, so the equipment might not detect everything.
  C. Therefore, the council should not support the installation of metal detectors.

II. This approach constitutes an invasion of student privacy.

    A. Metal detectors and their operators are not perfect; it's likely that students who are not concealing weapons will be forced to undergo a search of their clothing and possessions. That might prove embarrassing to some students.

    B. If students feel they have lost their right to privacy, their learning might suffer. They'll be more concerned about being watched than they are about their education.

    C. Therefore, the council should not support the installation of metal detectors.

This brief example illustrates that everything the spokesperson says needs to connect to and support the group's main position, which is that Dr. Jensen's proposal to install metal detectors will not work.

Speaking in Front of the Council

The spokesperson for each group will address a full-class open meeting (each speaker will be given a time limit) as if he or she were addressing the Winterhaven Valley Governing Council. As the spokespeople explain their groups' ideas on Westwood High, take careful notes of what they have to say. Those ideas may help you in the individual writing you'll soon be asked to do.

Whatever your group's viewpoint (administrator, student, parent, teacher), the spokesperson for your group may want to focus on the consequences and costs to your group's members, if Principal Jensen's proposals are funded:

- How will Dr. Jensen's ideas affect your group's members? Will the effect be positive or negative?

- Will your group's members lose any personal rights if Dr. Jensen's ideas are implemented?

- What other approaches might be more effective or cost less than Principal Jensen's proposal?

- How would your group propose to make Westwood High safe for all students? What alternatives might you offer to Dr. Jensen's ideas?

INDIVIDUAL WRITING
Essay Options

Your instructor will ask you to construct one or more individual writing projects: an informative essay, an evaluation essay, an analytic essay, and/or a proposal essay. Although each project has its own focus and audience, they all allow you to explore your thinking and to use the reading and other research you've done so far. Sit down with the notes you made during your reading and research, during your group's discussions, and during the oral presentations as you begin constructing your individual writing.

The Informative Essay

For this assignment, assume that you've been asked to construct an informative essay about the situation at Westwood High. The larger context for your essay is the issue of weapons on school campuses. Assume that your essay will appear as an article in the Sunday *Seattle Daily News*.

What is happening in schools around the United States? Are students really bringing increasing numbers of weapons onto their campuses? Are more students and teachers being shot? Is school more dangerous than it used to be, and if so, in what ways? What are schools doing to ensure campus safety? These are some of the questions you'll want to ask yourself and perhaps answer for your readers.

Your audience for this informative essay is the readers of the *Seattle Daily News*. They want to know more about the Westwood situation, of course, but they also want to consider the issue from a wider perspective, so you need to inform them about what's happening nationally. This means that although you can use Westwood High as an example, you'll want to focus on some of the larger issues:

- How safe are America's schools?
- In terms of gun violence, are our schools becoming safer — or less safe?
- What trends can we identify in terms of guns, violence, and schools?
- How do schools around the country maintain safe campuses?
- Does campus violence occur more often in rural or in urban settings?
- Does being a student cause someone to lose some of the rights guaranteed by the Constitution?
- What trends in school safety are apparent from national studies?

The Evaluation Essay

This assignment is to construct an evaluation essay about Dr. Jensen's proposal to make Westwood High a safer school. For this essay, write as a member of one of the interested groups (students, parents, administrators, teachers), and assume that your audience is the Winterhaven Valley Governing Council.

As you recall, Dr. Jensen advised the Council that his administration should be allowed to:

- Search every car that enters campus.
- Force all students, staff, and faculty to wear a photo ID badge.
- Search all bookbags every morning.
- Install metal detectors at all school entrances to ensure that no weapons are brought onto campus.

In your evaluation essay, you'll want to address questions like these: How effective is Principal Jensen's proposal likely to be? Are there better or less expensive ways to accomplish the same goals? You'll examine the strengths and weaknesses of each section of Principal Jensen's proposal and then, based on your analysis, explain its overall effectiveness to the governing council.

What facts, data, testimony, or evidence do you have to support the claims you plan to make about Dr. Jensen's proposal? For example, if you argue that the installation of metal detectors will not do what Dr. Jensen claims, can you present data from other schools that use metal detectors to show that the detectors aren't effective? If you hope to convince the council that it is useless to search student bookbags every morning, what information can you provide that shows how ineffective such a search is, that it takes too much time, that it will cost too much, or that it violates student rights?

If you agree with Dr. Jensen's proposal that all faculty, students, and staff members should wear a photo ID badge, what information can you present that supports your position that wearing ID badges has cut down on weapons problems at schools like Westwood High?

The Analytic Essay

The analytic essay involves constructing an analysis of the situation at many high schools (of which Westwood is one example) in an effort to explain why students feel the need to bring weapons with them to school. For this assignment, assume that you're writing an essay that will appear in the *American High School Journal*. This academic journal is read regularly by those who serve on school boards (or, as in this scenario, on school governing councils).

If you could address an audience of the people from around the country who control schools, what would you try to persuade them to do about school safety? How would you convince them that your ideas are the right ones? In what ways would you support your ideas?

Unlike an informative essay, in which the writer maintains a neutral, nonpartisan stance, in an analytic essay you want to take a stand, state a position, and argue for a specific point. You might want to focus on issues such as these:

- These are the causes of school violence, and these are some ways to reduce it.

- These are the reasons that more and more students feel unsafe at school, and these are some ways we can alleviate their concerns.

- School administrations have become too large and unwieldy. This is how we can shrink them so that they become more responsive to student needs.

- These are some of the causes of violent behavior in our society, and here is how we might keep that violence out of our schools.

- These are the only rights students have, and this is how we can respect those rights while keeping weapons off campus.

The Proposal Essay

The purpose of a proposal essay is just what its title suggests: to propose something, usually a solution to a problem of some kind. In this scenario, your proposal should acknowledge the problems you see with school safety at Westwood High and propose your solution as the best way to remedy those problems. You'll also want to demonstrate in what way(s) your solutions will solve the problems you see at the school. If you recommend the installation of metal detectors, for example, you'll need to provide evidence that metal detectors at schools like Westwood High have cut down on the number of weapons on campus. If part of your solution is to use armed guards to patrol Westwood's hallways, can you point to the success of guards in reducing weapons at other schools?

A proposal, then, does not simply say, "Here are the problems, and here is the answer." Rather, it provides sufficient evidence to prove that what is recommended will solve the problem.

For this essay, your audience is the Winterhaven Valley Governing Council, which, if it agrees with you, will provide the money to implement your ideas. If Dr. Jensen and his staff were writing this essay, they would attempt to convince the council that the principal's solution is the best approach; you may choose that perspective from which to write. Alternatively, you can write your proposal from the perspective of a student, a teacher, or a parent.

Once you've explained what the problem is, the next step in the proposal essay is to provide an outline for a solution: What would you do at Westwood? How can you demonstrate the effectiveness of your solution? How much might your proposal cost? How does what you propose compare with what other high schools have done? In what ways is the situation at Westwood different from that at other schools?

> ✳ **BOX 5.3   APPLYING WHAT YOU READ**
> *Reflections on the Westwood High School Scenario*
>
> You've done a lot of reading, discussing, and writing about the problems at Westwood High School and their potential solutions. Now take a few minutes to look back at the first writing you did for this scenario, when you discussed your thoughts about safety, weapons, and your high school after considering the photographs and First Impressions questions that introduce this chapter. Then jot down your answers to these questions:
>
> - Now that you've worked your way through the scenario, have any of your ideas changed? If your viewpoints have changed, in what ways have you modified them? What caused you to do so?
> - Now that you know a great deal about some of the problems and issues in the Westwood High scenario, what strikes you as the most important? Why?
> - Has your writing process changed as you wrote your way through the Westwood High scenario? If so, describe that change.
> - What was the most important thing you learned as you read, discussed, and wrote about the Westwood High scenario?

To conclude this scenario, your instructor may ask that you follow the instructions in Box 5.3: Reflections on the Westwood High School Scenario. The process of writing about ways in which your attitudes may have changed helps clarify your thinking.

FOR FURTHER RESEARCH AND WRITING

This scenario offers many opportunities for further exploration, especially if you consider some of the larger and broader issues and problems you've encountered. One of these is the area of personal property rights, and whether a person gives up some of those rights while attending school. No police agency can come into your home without a search warrant, but can school lockers be searched because they are school property? Does a school's right to search lockers extend to a student's backpack or car? Should it? Where should the line be drawn?

Another area to consider centers on the issue of what a school ought to be and what it should do. Our society expects its schools to teach the basics: reading, writing, and arithmetic. But we also expect our schools to assume responsibility for how well students drive, for whether they can use computers, for providing sex education, for teaching moral and ethical values, and perhaps even for teaching students how to care for a newborn child. On top of that, we expect our schools to transport our children safely and efficiently from home to school, and back. Some schools provide day care for children who are not of school age; others provide after-school and Saturday programs for students . . . and the list goes on.

Do we expect too much of our schools? Do we provide enough funding to enable schools to perform all the work that society expects of them?

You might also explore the issue of how our society regards its teachers. How do you see your teachers? Are they competent? Are you learning? Are teachers paid fairly, in terms of their education and responsibilities? Are teachers given the resources they need to do the job?

Another area to consider is how schools are funded in your county or state. Where does the money come from to build new schools and to maintain existing schools? Are sufficient funds available or is more money needed? How do schools in your state compare with those in other states: does your state spend more or less per student than do other states? Is the quality of education in your state improving or is it growing worse?

Finally, what are your thoughts on standardized testing in schools? Schools are often compared by standardized test scores. Is that comparison fair? What factors might influence student performance on standardized tests? Should teachers in a school with higher test scores be rewarded financially because their students test better than those from other schools? Or does such a reward system force teachers to "teach to the test," ignoring other, perhaps more important, subjects?

You now have read, discussed, and written about some of the problems at Westwood High School. Each day, teachers, parents, administrators, and students at other schools around the country face problems like these. We hope that working through this scenario has helped you improve how you read and write; we also hope that you better understand how to work effectively with others. The skills you used in this scenario will aid you in the work you've yet to do in this and your other college classes. Ultimately, these skills will also help you in your career.

Work Cited

ABCNews.com. "Fear in the Schoolyard: Survey Finds Fewer Students Feel Safe." 10 Aug. 1999 <http://www.abcnews.go.com/sections/us/DailyNews/youthsurvey990809.html>.

CHAPTER 6

Guns for Sale

RECYCLING YOUR POLICE DEPARTMENT'S WEAPONS

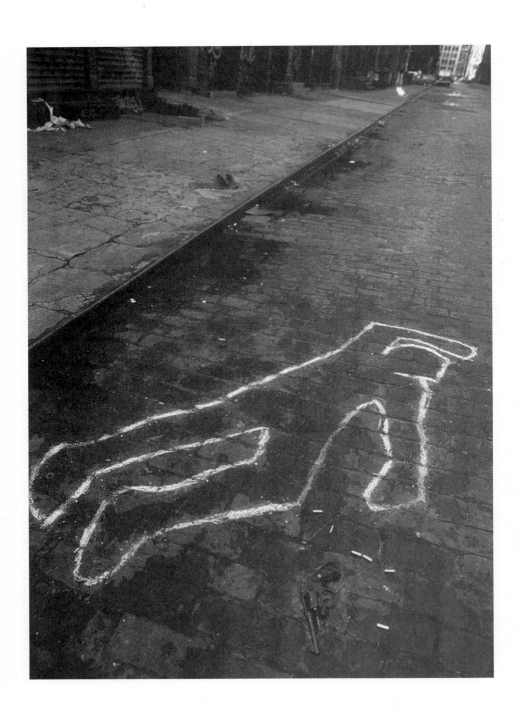

◆ FIRST IMPRESSIONS ◆

Be sure to look at and think about the photographs that introduce this chapter. Then spend a few minutes jotting down answers to these questions:

- Does examining the first two photographs change your thinking about guns and gun control? Does the last photograph change your thinking in any way? Why or why not?
- Do you believe in background checks for firearms purchasers? Why or why not?
- Do you believe there is a relationship between guns and crime? In what way(s)?
- Law enforcement agencies confiscate weapons from criminals: what should they do with those guns? A police department's firearms become outdated: what should they do with their old weapons? Police officers retire, and their firearms often "retire" along with them: what should the department do with those handguns and rifles?
- Would it bother you if your police department or sheriff's office sold weapons it had confiscated or no longer needed to a local gun dealer? At an annual firearms show? Why or why not?
- Would it trouble you if your local police department traded in its firearms on the purchase of new weapons . . . and the company with which the department did business then sold those used firearms? Why? Would such trades be more acceptable if the company promised to sell the used police weapons only overseas? Why?
- How might your community react if a gun that had been confiscated by your police department at a crime scene and then sold to a gun dealer was later used to shoot one of your community's police officers?
- If your law enforcement agencies sell their confiscated and used weapons, does what they do with the funds from those sales make a difference in how you feel about the sales? That is, would you be in favor of weapons sales if the funds they generated supported worthwhile community projects? Why or why not?

When you're done, your instructor may ask you to share your comments with your classmates.

Some law enforcement agencies sell their confiscated or outdated firearms to private gun dealers. These agencies then use the funds they receive to support community programs. The departments that do this have decided that the benefits to the community of the money generated by these gun sales outweigh the possible dangers of putting these firearms on the streets. The projects communities fund through gun sales often include organized youth activities, which are designed to keep young people out of trouble. By funding wholesome activities for youths who might be at risk, these gun sales help to reduce crime. Communities that sell confiscated or outdated guns might argue that these sales not only raise needed money, but are also relatively safe. Because the guns are sold to licensed firearms dealers, anyone buying one of these weapons must undergo a background check. So what's the harm?

In some cases the only way in which a police department can afford to upgrade its firearms is to trade them in to a gun manufacturer, who resells the weapons. Again, the police or sheriff's department benefits by having newer firearms, but this approach also increases the number of weapons on the street.

Other agencies simply destroy or melt down extra firearms. These agencies have decided that the monetary benefit they might receive from the sale of those weapons isn't worth the problems caused by having more weapons on their streets. These communities might suggest that putting guns back on the street, however legal it might be, is not the way to cut down on crime. Sooner or later, someone will use those weapons to commit a crime.

What do you think law enforcement agencies ought to do with their old and confiscated weapons? Here's what some communities around the country are doing:

- In 1998, the New Orleans, Louisiana, police department traded more than 700 "used" Beretta pistols for 1,700 Glock pistols. As part of the trade agreement, the police also included the firearms they'd confiscated. New Orleans traded more than 8,000 confiscated firearms—and more than half of them were then distributed commercially (many were sold in other states) (National Center for Policy Analysis).

- In Colorado, police agencies have supplied the consumer market with hundreds of used guns equipped with high-capacity magazines—weapons that were banned by the 1994 federal assault-weapons law. These banned weapons were sold by police agencies to gun stores and distributors, and they ranged from pistols with 15-round clips to SWAT-team assault rifles. One Colorado agency sold handguns confiscated from criminals for as little as $5 each (Olinger 1).

- Evidently hoping for a change in the 1994 Minnesota law banning the sale of confiscated guns, the sheriff of Otter Tail County has been stockpiling confiscated guns.

- Some law enforcement agencies interpret the laws that ban them from selling confiscated weapons as applying only to sales within the United States. For example, since 1994, San Francisco police agencies have not sold confiscated handguns in this country; instead, they have sold them overseas. The Boston, Massachusetts, police department melts down guns that were used to commit a crime, but trades used police guns to dealers who promise to sell them overseas.

- East Palo Alto, California, which once was known as the "homicide capital of the United States," traded its confiscated weapons to a firearms manufacturer, who agreed to resell them only to other law enforcement agencies. Unfortunately, East Palo Alto had no way to monitor or enforce this agreement.

- Detroit, Michigan, has been labeled the "leader" in sales of used police guns: since 1992, Detroit has sold more than 6,000 police handguns and shotguns to private gun dealers.
- King County, Washington, insists that certain types of confiscated guns—mostly cheap "Saturday night specials"—be destroyed. A 1997–98 audit revealed, however, that the sheriff's office sold more than 900 of those firearms to gun dealers—and received more than $50,000 for those weapons (Slivka and Johnson 1).

There is an ironic twist to many of the gun sales these cities record. Some of the same cities that sell to private gun dealers are suing gun manufacturers and gun distributors for producing and selling an unsafe product. Cities currently involved in such lawsuits include Boston, Detroit, New Orleans, and San Francisco.

Not all law enforcement agencies believe that their departments should sell confiscated weapons, even if the monies raised serve a good purpose. For example:

- In Kentucky, police fought a 1998 law that ordered them to stop melting down their confiscated weapons and instead forced them to sell those guns—even though the law required that the money from such sales be used to purchase bulletproof vests for police officers.
- The Aurora, Colorado, police department no longer sells its confiscated weapons.
- A judge stopped the sheriff's office in Rockdale, Georgia, from selling the guns it confiscates.
- In 1998, the International Association of Chiefs of Police passed a resolution urging police departments to stop selling used and confiscated guns.
- The federal government is also involved in the selling of guns by cities: in September 1999, the *Los Angeles Times* reported that the Department of Housing and Urban Development (HUD) "will provide $14 million in grants to police departments and public housing authorities in at least 20 cities, enabling local officials to buy back and destroy as many as 280,000 guns. . . . Since some cities have drawn criticism for reselling guns purchased in buy-back programs, the HUD initiative will require municipalities to agree to destroy any weapons they buy, officials said. Only stolen guns—which will be returned to their legal owners—or guns needed for police investigations will be exempted" ("Federal" 1).

What does your local police department or sheriff's office do with the weapons it confiscates? What do you think cities and other government agencies should do with weapons retired by their police departments and with the firearms those police agencies confiscate? Does it matter if the firearm is a handgun, a shotgun, a rifle, an assault weapon, or a Saturday night special? Why?

Even though this scenario is situated in an eastern state, the issues and problems you and your classmates will encounter as you work through the story are common to many communities, including, perhaps, your own. Pretend now that you're a New Jersey resident. . . .

For as long as anyone in town can remember, the Maple Plains, New Jersey, Police Department has sold its confiscated firearms at its annual Firearms Show and Sale, using the money it makes for several youth-outreach programs. The guns from the city's retired police officers are also added to the mix.

The sale gives the department the funds it needs for "Saturday Mid-night Basketball," an attempt to keep young men and women in the gym and off the streets. The money is also used to pay for an officer to speak about crime prevention at each local school on a regular basis. Best of all, perhaps, the funds raised by selling confiscated guns pay for fifteen neighborhood outreach programs in which officers come into daily contact with citizens in areas identified as "high risk" based on crime statistics. Assigning extra police officers to spend more time in these dangerous areas is making a difference: the crime rate for these neighborhoods is down. In fact, what the police department is doing appears to be working throughout Maple Plains: overall crime is down, and statistics for juvenile crime are even better, dropping some 17 percent.

Maple Plains earns about $160,000 per year from its sale of confiscated guns. To ensure that these firearms don't fall into the wrong hands, the police department conducts a background check on everyone who purchases a gun at the annual firearms show. Guns that aren't sold at the show are traded in on new weapons through a gun manufacturer, who has agreed to resell those guns only overseas.

Through these sales avenues, Maple Plains has generated much-needed funds for worthwhile community projects, and, through the trade-in program, it provides newer weapons for its officers to use on the streets of the community. So far, it's been a win-win situation.

Things may be changing in Maple Plains, however: recently elected Councilperson Earl Larkin has, in his words, "declared war on our city making a profit from selling guns" and is demanding that the city end the practice immediately.

"We cannot," Larkin says, "continue to contribute to the proliferation of firearms on our neighborhood streets. I call on the Maple Plains Police Department to immediately terminate such sales. Some of those guns, after all, might be used to shoot at our own police officers! I know that stopping gun sales will be a hardship for the police—it will be difficult for the town to replace the money the sales produce. But isn't safety more important than a few dollars?"

Imagine that:

- You are a Maple Plains police officer: how would you react to Councilperson Larkin? Through the firearms trade-in program, your sidearm has been upgraded several times, and you feel safer because of the modern weapon you carry. You also know that the cash the department has received from gun sales has supported some good programs in the community. In fact, you know a number of young men who probably would be in jail right now if not for those programs.

- You live in Maple Plains, and you're proud of your police department. The decreasing crime statistics indicate that they're doing a good job. You know the programs funded by the sale of weapons are worthwhile, so you'd hate to see them cut. You're especially concerned about eliminating the neighborhood policing program, which has allowed more officers to patrol your neighborhood. You also realize that if the city wants to continue these programs and it can't fund them through gun sales, your taxes might increase.

- You're a Maple Plains teenager who participates in Saturday Midnight Basketball almost every week. When you first heard about the idea of the police sponsoring a weekly basketball game—and at midnight!—you thought it sounded silly. But you went, with some of your friends, just to see what was happening. You became involved, and now it's part of your routine. You're wondering what you and your friends will do on Saturday nights if there is no more money for midnight basketball.

- You're the chair of the Maple Plains Hunting and Fishing Club. As part of your volunteer duties, you give several speeches each year outlining your group's position on gun control. The club's position is that the "right of the people to keep and bear arms" is protected by the Constitution. Do you see any relationship between the Maple Plains Police Department's sale of guns at its yearly gun show and what your group believes? If the city were to stop selling those guns, as Councilperson Larkin suggests, would that go against your basic belief that weapon sales should not be restricted in any way? If the Maple Plains Police Department had to halt its gun sales, would that in some way infringe on your own right to "keep and bear arms"? In what way?

- You and several others are partners in Larry's Sporting Goods in downtown Maple Plains. In the past, you've purchased some of the police department's old weapons and resold them. You're always careful to follow federal law in terms of paperwork and to run a background check on anyone who buys a gun from your business. You and your partners wonder how the media might portray Maple Plains if word of the city's gun sales were publicized. Maybe it wouldn't matter—after all, law enforcement agencies in many other cities do the same thing. Do you worry that if

Maple Plains stops its police department from selling guns, its next stop might be to stop you from doing the same?

In this scenario we explore some issues related to our country's ongoing debate about gun control, but from a slightly different perspective. Our scenario doesn't focus on whether guns should be banned; it isn't about who should be able to own a firearm, or even whether those purchasing guns should undergo background checks. Instead, we concentrate on a local aspect of the issue—one that your community might one day face as it, along with many cities, attempts to decide what it should do with its confiscated or outdated weapons. You can see the Maple Plains scenario as a microcosm of the larger, national discussion about firearms.

It initially might seem wrong for Maple Plains to sell its confiscated and used firearms, but the money those sales generate is used for worthy purposes. As a citizen of Maple Plains, how do you weigh one side of this issue against the other? As with many civic and ethical issues, the specifics may differ from city to city, but the basic problem remains the same: how to balance civic needs against possible civic risks.

You and your classmates will form teams that represent the groups most interested in the Maple Plains debate. You'll work within these teams, collaboratively and individually, on a number of activities that address the issues you might face if Maple Plains were a real place.

This scenario can also provide a starting point for further research and discussion on a variety of topics. These include questions of whether it's ethical for a city that sells guns to sue gun manufacturers, the gun laws in your state, the national debate about gun control, the effectiveness of the Brady Bill, background checks for gun purchasers, and limiting the number of weapons someone can buy during a given period of time.

THE SCENARIO

Selling Guns Is Legal, Isn't It?

Due in part to a drop in its local crime rate, Maple Plains, New Jersey, has again become a good place to live. Only five miles from the Atlantic Ocean and twelve from Atlantic City, the town has worked hard to build its reputation as an all-American community, and much of that work is paying off. A number of clean industries are locating nearby, the town's tax base is increasing, and, although the city's budget has run a small deficit for several years, the outlook for Maple Plains's future is bright.

One reason that the city's budget is close to balancing is because the city sells its guns: the weapons it confiscates from criminals, the guns left by retired police officers, the firearms it owns that are outdated. For the past five years, the city has earned more than $160,000 yearly from its gun sales and trades.

The members of the town council have read, of course, about other cities that melt down or otherwise destroy the firearms they have, but Maple Plains has chosen a different path. Simply put, Maple Plains needs the money: over the past ten years, firearms sales have added more than $1.5 million to the city's available funds. Many of the programs these dollars pay for simply wouldn't exist without the gun sales. The city's improved cash flow is one of the reasons for its bright future.

Or perhaps it would be more accurate to say the city's future was bright . . . before the Bowden incident. It's unfortunate that the shooting happened the day after Councilperson Larkin made his emotional appeal to ban the city's sale of firearms. Those comments only fanned the flames ignited by the incident.

Edward "Bud" Bowden was born in Maple Plains, played high school football for the Maple Plains Bulldogs, and attended the local community college for two years without earning a degree. He joined the Marines and came back from Vietnam as something of a local war hero.

Bud was hired by the Maple Plains Police Department two days after his Marine discharge became official. Over the years he advanced rapidly through the ranks, to assistant chief, before retiring in 1996.

With his background, one might have expected Bud to react as he did that day in Larry's Sporting Goods. Bud and Larry were shooting the breeze when, for only the second time since Larry had owned the place, a man in a ski mask walked in and tried to rob the store. There was a scuffle, with Bud, right in the middle of things, wrestling the would-be thief to the ground. In the end, Bud was shot in the leg—but Bud and Larry held the robber until the police could arrive.

That same evening, the *Maple Plains Town Crier* reported that Bud would be fine (although he'd probably always walk with a limp)—and that the weapon the robber had used had been purchased, just last year, at the city's annual gun show. The Maple Plains Police Department had sold the gun that had injured one of its own! Fortunately, the firearm involved was a .25 automatic—a cheap, inaccurate gun without much firepower. However, even a .25 can kill if the bullet hits a vital organ.

ENTERING THE SCENARIO: YOUR TOWN AS GUN MERCHANT

Now that you've read the scenario, it's time to meet the groups that are most affected by what has happened in Maple Plains. Your instructor will ask you to join with several of your classmates to form one of these groups. Although your central concern is for the group to which you belong, reading the descriptions of the other groups should help you understand all of the issues in this scenario. The next step involves working with the members of your group to tailor your group description and perspective based on your ideas about your community's selling weapons.

Residents of Maple Plains

You've lived in Maple Plains for some time, and you love the town. Until you read about Bud Bowden in the *Town Crier* last night, you didn't know that your city sold its confiscated and used firearms. The piece in the newspaper also outlined, in some detail, all the worthwhile activities the proceeds from the gun sales fund. You'd noticed more police officers in your neighborhood, and now you know why: increased neighborhood police patrols, funded by the city's gun sales. And the drop in Maple Plains's crime statistics reported in the *Town Crier* is a comfort to you, too. Are you uneasy that your city is in the gun-selling business, especially after the shooting? Are you concerned that your taxes might increase if the city wants to continue its programs but stops the gun sales that fund those activities?

Maple Plains Police Officers

You and the members of your group are directly involved with several of the projects funded by firearms sales: midnight basketball, school safety speeches, more neighborhood policing. You personally know three young men who you're sure would be serving time today were it not for the department's youth programs.

Like many police officers, you enjoy hunting and target practice and, of course, you're required to maintain proficiency in the use of department weapons. The annual city gun sales have made it possible for you to afford high-quality firearms for leisure use.

But now a gun the department sold has hurt one of your own, and you know it could have been *you* that day in Larry's Sporting Goods. Do you think the city should continue selling its guns?

Maple Plains Teenagers

As a teenager who lives in Maple Plains, you enjoy the city-sponsored Saturday night basketball games with your friends; you love playing, and it's safe in the gym. You've read the article in the *Town Crier*, which made it clear that youth basketball and other programs didn't exist before the city began selling its old and confiscated guns. According to the reporter who wrote the story, these programs will disappear if the city stops selling guns. Is putting firearms back onto the street worth the benefits you and your friends receive from those sales?

Members of the Maple Plains Hunting and Fishing Club

You and the other members of the Hunting and Fishing Club represent the sportsmen and sportswomen of the community, who like to spend time outdoors. Although you belong to the National Rifle Association (NRA), you don't always agree with everything that organization stands for. On the other hand, you do read two NRA magazines and have your Internet browser set to display the NRA home page, at http://www.nra.org/, each time you start your computer. You know that the NRA sees any attempt to halt legal gun sales as a threat to every citizen, so the organization works vigorously against any move to halt such sales—and you feel the same way. What Maple Plains does at the annual firearms show is perfectly legal. In fact, the city takes the extra step of requiring a background check on all firearms purchasers at the show—something not required under federal laws for sales at gun shows. You see no reason for the city to stop selling firearms.

You base your beliefs on the Second Amendment to our Constitution: "A well regulated Militia, being necessary to the security of a free State, the right of the people to keep and bear Arms, shall not be infringed."

The Maple Plains Safety-First Coalition

Although you and the other members of Maple Plains's Safety-First Coalition (SFC) are not formally allied with a national organization, you subscribe to the newsletter published by Handgun Control, Inc., and you've attended some of the organization's conferences in Atlantic City. You enjoy reading the information posted on Handgun Control's Web site, and you generally learn a lot from what the group has to say. For example, the Web site recently listed these informative articles:

News Alert: Statement on Governor Bush's Failure to Prosecute Gun Felons. Read the report on Texas Felons with Firearms by clicking here.

News Alert: More Americans Killed by Guns Than by War in the 20th Century.

News Alert: Statement of Sarah Brady: Illinois Senate, NRA Give Victory to Gun-Toting Criminals.

News Alert: Statement of Jim and Sarah Brady Re: Guns, Felonies, and Misdemeanors.

You're not compulsive enough to have Handgun Control Inc.'s Web site set to display each time you start your browser, but you do have its home page (http://www.handguncontrol.org/) bookmarked.

Every few months, several SFC members get together at someone's home to discuss gun control issues, but there haven't been any local issues for your group to become involved in—until now. When you heard about

Bud Bowden's shooting and where the gun came from, your initial reaction was shock, both at the shooting in your downtown and at the fact that your city was selling firearms. That's something your group might want to discuss.

PARTICIPATING IN YOUR INTEREST GROUP

Now that you've read through the Maple Plains scenario and understand some of the interests and perspectives of the various groups, it's time for you to become actively involved. Your instructor will ask you to work with several of your classmates as a member of one of the groups.

In this activity, you role-play an interested party, pretending that you are a member of the group you represent and considering the issues related to Maple Plains's gun sales from that group's perspective. Working with several of your classmates, you'll discuss and answer questions like these:

- What issues in the Maple Plains scenario do you find especially interesting? What issues might concern your group more than they concern the other groups? Do all the members of your group have the same views on whether Maple Plains should continue selling firearms?

- What other groups might share at least some of your beliefs and ideas about the situation in Maple Plains? With which other groups might you align yourselves, to make each of your positions stronger?

- Which groups might oppose your point of view on gun sales? What objections might they have to your ideas? How might you counter those objections?

For ways in which your group can encourage members to explore their positions on the Maple Plains scenario, read Box 6.1: Representing the Range of Opinion.

TAKING A POSITION: REMAINING IN THE GUN-SELLING BUSINESS?

For this scenario, assume that the Maple Plains City Council asks for public input following Bud Bowden's shooting and Councilperson Larkin's comments. Mayor Bradley and the council want to "get a sense of what the people think about this gun-selling issue. They need to have a voice here. After all, they're the ones whose programs will be cut if we don't have the money those sales generate."

This opportunity to comment on whether your city should continue its gun sales allows your group to make its views part of the record, to at-

---

❋ BOX 6.1   APPLYING WHAT YOU READ
Representing the Range of Opinion

To better understand the various perspectives on the recent developments in Maple Plains, assume that all perspectives exist within your group. To help your group generate a fuller range of ideas and viewpoints about a city's selling firearms, each member of your group should adopt the persona, or role, of someone within that group.

For example, one member of the police officers' group might represent an officer who feels that selling and trading guns is the only way the department can upgrade its weapons. Another member might role-play an officer who disagrees. Yet another group member might represent a member of the force who is uncertain, with many more questions than answers.

For the first part of this activity, work with the members of your group to brainstorm a list of all possible positions that might exist within your group. Assign these positions to group members. Then think for a bit about the position that's been assigned to you. How would someone in your position feel? How might the weapons sales affect you, personally, both today and in the future?

As a group, list all the problems, concerns, advantages, and observations that your members can come up with. Make sure everyone receives a copy of this list: it's valuable invention work that you can all draw on later in the Maple Plains scenario.

When you've finished, your instructor may ask you to share your "personas" with other members of the class.

---

tempt to influence the others involved, and especially to influence the city council members. They are the ones who ultimately will decide whether the city should continue its current practice.

RESOURCES: GUNS, CITIES, AND MONEY

With an issue such as this, it's important to learn what other cities and towns have done in similar situations—after all, they also confiscate weapons, and they also have police departments whose firearms need upgrading.

Therefore, before you and the members of your group construct your brief statement to the city council, you might find it useful to consider what other groups have experienced as they confronted issues similar to those you face in the Maple Plains scenario. You might also want to talk to local law enforcement officers and perhaps to local government officials to identify what is done with confiscated weapons in your community.

The readings that follow provide background on the larger debate over the control of weapons, with some of the selections focusing more narrowly on the issue exemplified by the Maple Plains scenario. The writers of these pieces explore a number of important issues, and each has a different perspective on the subject of whether cities should sell guns. Following each reading you'll find a series of probing questions that will help you better understand the issues involved. These readings should also be useful to you after completing your group statement, when you'll be asked to construct an individual writing project. Remember to interact actively with these readings, using the reading strategies you learned earlier (prereading, annotating, summarizing, and so on).

Our readings begin with a cartoon by Mike Keefe that captures one view of the issue at the heart of our scenario. It's followed by a collection of newspaper and Internet articles from around the country. In the *Denver Post*, reporter David Olinger outlines what happens when "Cops Put Guns Back into Circulation." CNN reports, in "Police Re-think Policy of Trading In Their Weapons," that not every law enforcement agency approves of weapon sales. Finally, two sheriffs who are at odds on the issue have the opportunity to explain their views in separate newspaper articles: "Rockdale's Sheriff Won't Sell Off Guns" (from the *Atlanta Journal-Constitution*) and "Sheriffs Ready to Sell Confiscated Guns" (from the *Brainerd* [Minnesota] *Daily Dispatch*).

These readings place in perspective the problem of cities selling firearms and provide a sense of how widespread the practice is. They're followed by an in-depth analysis of this issue by Jake Tapper that appeared in the online journal *Salon.com*. *Time* magazine journalist Roger Rosenblatt explains his strong feelings about guns and gun control in an editorial, "Get Rid of the Damned Things," and Robin West reinforces Rosenblatt's position in "Gun Rights."

"Cold Comfort," the final reading, is perhaps the most provocative. In an interview with Jacob Sullum and Michael W. Lynch, economist John Lott, a senior research scholar at Yale Law School, defends the view he expresses in a number of academic articles—that if more citizens carried firearms, there would be less crime. And Lott cites statistics he claims support his position.

As you read the pieces your instructor asks you to consider, think about how the group you belong to might react to the arguments presented in them:

- From your group's perspective, what are the most important points each writer makes?
- What ideas, facts, or data in each reading might your group use in your statement to the city council?
- What elements in the readings might work against your group's position? How might you counter those ideas?

As you read, takes notes on any issues, ideas, or facts you think might help or hurt your position so you can address them in your written presentation to the council members.

 **READINGS**

✳ Cartoon
Mike Keefe

Mike Keefe, *The Denver Post*

1. What was your initial reaction to this cartoon? Did you find it funny, or did it disturb you? Why did you react the way you did?
2. In your view, what message does this cartoon convey?

✳ Cops Put Guns Back in Circulation

David Olinger

Colorado police agencies have supplied the consumer market with hundreds of used guns equipped with high-capacity magazines banned from manufacture by the 1994 federal assault-weapons law.

The banned weapons delivered to gun stores and distributors by recent police sales range from pistols with 15-round clips to SWAT team assault rifles. One agency also sold handguns confiscated from criminals for as little as $5 apiece. Another agreed to sell 10 rifles classified as machine guns, then canceled the deal upon receiving a request to ship them to a Miami gun wholesaler.

"I didn't realize they were selling things that were considered to be assault weapons," said Colorado House Minority Leader Ken Gordon, a Denver Democrat who has called for stricter gun controls. "I have a problem with that. They shouldn't be putting them in the stream of commerce."

But Robert Delfay, president of the Connecticut-based National Shooting Sports Foundation, the largest lobbying organization for gun manufacturers, said police departments commonly trade used firearms for newer models, and "it's just logical that guns being traded in right now are going to be pre-ban."

He sees nothing wrong with that. "Those firearms are sold through firearms dealers to individuals who have to pass a background check," he said.

And even if criminals eventually acquire some of those used police guns, "in the average criminal shooting, 3.6 shots are fired," Delfay said. "That would seem to indicate that the magazine capacity is not really an issue."

Police sales of assault weapons and high-capacity magazines are not unique to Colorado. Law-enforcement agencies throughout the country have traded used semiautomatic pistols and SWAT weapons, getting new guns at little or no cost.

That's because Congress created an unusual gun market when it voted five years ago to outlaw production of selected assault weapons and all large-capacity magazines—defined as holding more than 10 bullets—but allowed existing supplies to be owned and resold. To get their hands on "pre-ban" guns, firearms manufacturers turned to the people who could supply them with what they could no longer make for the general public.

The police.

"The gun dealers and the gun manufacturers have recognized that there is going to be a very big market in high-capacity firearms," said Larry Todd, a firearms committee member of the International Association of Chiefs of Police. "There's not a police agency in the country that hasn't been contacted, I suspect, by a manufacturer offering to accept those weapons in trade for new weapons."

The police chiefs' association adopted a resolution last year urging police departments to destroy their used guns, as well as those seized from criminals, to avoid the risk that police guns will end up in the hands of criminals. Earlier this month, President Clinton announced a $15 million program to help police departments buy and destroy as many as 300,000 used guns from private owners throughout the country.

At the same time, however, some law-enforcement agencies are selling weapons that have been illegal to make for five years.

Today, gun magazines holding more than 10 rounds and certain types of assault weapons are manufactured only for law-enforcement agencies and cannot legally be resold to the public. Firearms experts say nobody knows how many police guns with "pre-ban" magazines have been traded back to manufacturers and redistributed to gun dealers since the assault-weapons law took effect.

But "there's absolutely no question, after the assault-weapons ban, police weapons were a huge source" of high-capacity magazines, said Violence Policy Center analyst Tom Diaz, author of a book on the gun industry.

Aside from some imports, "it's the only legal source left," he said.

Colorado actually ranks as one of the smaller players in the national trade of police guns and magazines made before the assault-weapons ban. Most of Colorado's large police departments require officers to purchase their own pistols from an approved list, and therefore have no handguns to sell.

Yet a *Denver Post* survey of law-enforcement agencies around the state found that at least six have sold or traded assault rifles or pistols with high-capacity magazines in the past three years: the police departments in Aurora, Lakewood and Littleton, the Jefferson County Sheriff's Department, the Colorado Department of Corrections and the Colorado State Patrol. A seventh, the Colorado Division of Wildlife, plans to trade its pre-ban pistols for another model.

The largest gun trade involved the State Patrol. It switched from one pistol model to another last year, creating a supply of almost 1,800 used 15-round magazines with 596 used pistols, all made before the magazines were banned.

State Patrol Chief Lonnie Westphal said that trade was made without considering its contribution to the market for "pre-ban" weapons.

"We've always traded them in to a firearms dealer and let them resell them. I've always pretty much supported that policy," he said. 20

But by trading in pistols that can fire 15 bullets in seconds, "we are allowing those magazines to continue to be available," he acknowledged. Today, "I would do that differently as far as the magazines are concerned."

The State Patrol, like many police agencies across the country, switched from six-shot revolvers to semiautomatic pistols a decade ago. In theory, the pistols had decided advantages over the standard police gun. They were easier to load in stressful situations—just slip a clip into the gun—and they let police officers keep up with the increasingly potent firepower that gun manufacturers were supplying to the general public.

In 1991, Colorado state troopers began carrying more firepower of their own: 9 mm Smith & Wesson pistols, each equipped with three 15-round magazines.

In 1998, the State Patrol followed the latest trend in police pistols, switching from the 9 mm model to a larger caliber semiautomatic. The rationale: the 9 mm bullet proved too small and swift, too likely to pass through an intended target and strike a bystander, and not heavy enough to stop an attacker instantly.

This trend was encouraged by the two leading police gun suppliers, Smith & Wesson and Glock, which both introduced a pistol with a larger, slower .40-caliber bullet. Both offered to take police pistols with "pre-ban" magazines in trade, at prices that let law-enforcement agencies get new guns almost for free. 25

The State Patrol, for example, paid $388,000 for 710 new pistols last year. But that cost was offset by a credit of more than $300,000 for its old pistols.

"It's not like we're taking them to a gun show or advertising them in the Yellow Pages," State Patrol spokesman Capt. Steve Smee said of the trade. "I think it's only frugal that we do that with the taxpayers' money."

The State Patrol's used pistols and magazines went to Tuxall Uniforms, a Denver police supply company serving as the middleman in the trade. About two-thirds were bought back at the discounted price of $347 each by state troopers, who are free to resell them to anyone in Colorado who can legally own a gun.

Doug Smith, a Tuxall employee, said a Smith & Wesson representative boxed the rest, putting two 15-round magazines with each pistol and the remaining magazines in a separate box, and shipped them all to a wholesale gun distributor in Alabama.

Westphal recalls no debate about the merits of selling high-capacity magazines to a gun manufacturer. "Quite honestly, at the time that issue was not even brought to my attention. Of course since that time it's been a very hot topic," he said. 30

Westphal grew more uncomfortable with the second part of the Smith & Wesson deal: trading away 10 M-16 military rifles for $500 each.

The State Patrol had converted the M-16s from automatic weapons to semiautomatic rifles, which fire one bullet with each squeeze of the trigger. But because they could be easily reconverted to automatic weapons, they had to be sold to someone with a special license to own machine guns.

The patrol kept the M-16s while Smith & Wesson hunted for a buyer. Recently a Smith & Wesson representative called to say a buyer had been found. Could the State Patrol ship the M-16s to a wholesale gun distributor in Miami?

The chief bought the M-16s back. "I just didn't like the feel of that," he said.

Two events made the market for assault weapons in general, and police pistols in particular, a hot topic this year [1999]. In April, Dylan Klebold used a TEC-DC9 assault pistol made just before the assault-weapons ban to attack his classmates at Columbine High School. Last month, Buford Furrow used a Glock pistol sold by a police department in the state of Washington to shoot children at a Jewish community center in Los Angeles and kill a postal worker.

In Colorado, the Columbine High shooting led the Aurora Police Department to reverse a longstanding policy permitting the sale of used and confiscated guns. 35

But first, the department decided to go ahead with one last sale.

On July 15, Aurora police took 206 guns to a local gun store, Dave's Guns, and received a $19,575 credit toward the purchase of future police supplies.

The department sold six Jennings, Lorcin, Phoenix and Raven pistols—all cheap, California-made pistols commonly called Saturday night specials—for $5 each.

It got $250 apiece for a Glock pistol and a Norinco rifle with high-capacity magazines. It got $65 for an Intratec TEC-22, a smaller version of the assault pistol Klebold took to Columbine High, and $300 for a MAC-10, an assault weapon banned in 1994 that was notoriously easy to convert to a machine gun.

Aurora police spokesman Bob Stef said the department later reclaimed the MAC-10, deducted the $300 credit and destroyed the gun. 40 "We just felt it was in the best interest of the community to get that one back," he said.

Until this year, the Aurora department routinely sold guns it confiscated from criminals. "Almost exclusively, it helped to equip the SWAT team," Chief Verne Saint Vincent said. "It helped us buy some very expensive weaponry, as well as bulletproof vests, ballistic shields, those types of items."

But after the Columbine High tragedy, Saint Vincent decided the risk of putting guns back on the street outweighed the economic benefits to his department.

By then, "we had already in my mind made a commitment to make that deal" with Dave's Guns, he said. But "I told my executive staff—this is the last one. We're not going to be in the business of doing this anymore."

Dave Anver, owner of Dave's Guns, has a good reputation with law-enforcement agencies. He buys police guns, sells police supplies and maintains police weapons. Posted inside his front door is a newspaper article on the Denver police gang unit.

The article explains that almost half the guns seized by the gang unit   45
were cheap Saturday night specials. Beneath it, Anver posted a pledge not to sell 10 brands of "trash" guns at any price. Five brands—Intratec, Jennings, Lorcin, Phoenix and Raven—were on the list of handguns Aurora police sold to his store for $5 to $65.

Anver said a gunsmith paid him $5 each to strip parts from the cheap pistols, and he then returned the receivers with serial numbers to Aurora police.

"I think all of the garbage weapons were destroyed," he said. "I'll be damned if I ever support somebody's right to have a piece of 'Saturday Night' crap like that."

Dave's Guns served as a middleman in several of Colorado's police gun trades.

In the three years, the Department of Corrections has shipped 80 semiautomatic pistols, some with pre-ban magazines, to Anver's store. Denver police sent him 197 used Remington shotguns in a 1996 trade for new shotguns.

Some police guns stay in his shop. But most are shipped to whole-   50
salers, who in turn distribute them nationally to retail gun stores.

"There is no way on God's green earth to sell a thousand of the same pistols" at a single retail store, Anver said.

About 50 of the pistols sold by the Corrections Department to three different gun dealers in the last three years came with magazines banned from manufacture in 1994.

"The reason for trading is economics: You save a lot of taxpayer money," said Liz McDonough, a DOC spokeswoman.

She emphasized that the Corrections Department sells pistols only to federally licensed firearms dealers. "We're relying on that system to work and believe that it does," she said.

The Jefferson County Sheriff's Department, the agency investigating   55
the Columbine High massacre, sold a few AR-15 assault rifles—a sale Sheriff John Stone said will not be repeated. Two cities in Jefferson County, Lakewood and Littleton, also sold AR-15s made before the assault-weapons ban.

To sell or not to sell: For law-enforcement agencies throughout Colorado, the gun-disposal question has created a powerful dilemma, pitting fiscal vs. moral concerns. In Mesa County, it keeps Sheriff Riecke Claussen in a quandary.

Claussen destroys sawed-off or unsafe guns, but he said he can't decide what to do with confiscated guns that are in good condition. So he keeps them—indefinitely—in evidence. He guesses he has several thousand in his evidence vault, including a few collector's items worth thousands of dollars each.

"I am loath to destroy them, but I'm also cognizant it's not the most popular thing to do, to put guns back on the street," Claussen said. "I guess you could say I'm in a position of analysis paralysis."

The sales of used police guns in Colorado have been dwarfed by some trade-ins on the East Coast and in California, where most large police departments purchase handguns for their officers.

In Washington, D.C., for example, Glock obtained nearly 5,600 guns and 17,000 "pre-ban" magazines in a single pistol trade with the city police department.   60

In New York state, a scandal erupted from a gun trade involving the law-enforcement branch of its Department of Environmental Conservation that enabled Glock to get back more than 700 "pre-ban" pistols just three years after it sold them. That trade, like the Colorado State Patrol exchange, involved a switch from 9 mm to .40-caliber models and allowed officers to buy back their weapons at a discount.

In December 1996, the New York state inspector general reported that many conservation officers had resold pre-ban pistols for profit, in some cases to people ineligible to buy them. Three of the guns traded in by a law-enforcement agency switching gun models twice in three years had been traced to people arrested in Miami and Los Angeles.

Days later, New York Gov. George Pataki ordered all state agencies to stop trading in used police guns and destroy them instead.

In Colorado, the state wildlife agency is proposing a similar trade with the same gun manufacturer.

For about seven years, Division of Wildlife officers have carried .40-caliber Smith & Wesson pistols, Model 4026. "The problem we've got is they don't make the 4026 anymore," said John Bredehoft, the agency's law-enforcement chief.   65

In January, the division of wildlife plans to buy new .40-caliber pistols from Glock. Under terms of the proposed trade, Glock would get all 250 of the division's Smith & Wesson pistols, along with its "pre-ban" 11-round magazines, and Colorado wildlife officers would have an opportunity to buy those used pistols at a discount.

"It makes a lot of fiscal sense to trade these handguns," Bredehoft said. "Of course, it would bother me if the handgun ended up someplace where it wasn't supposed to be."

The continuing sales of used police weapons with "pre-ban" magazines troubles U.S. Sen. Dianne Feinstein, the California Democrat who introduced legislation, now in a conference committee, to stop all imports of high-capacity magazines.

"One of our main goals is to dry up the supply of those magazines," said Howard Gantman, Feinstein's spokesman.

"Having police agencies resell them to firearms dealers has the opposite effect. It's keeping them available."   70

1. Is Olinger's opening paragraph effective? What in this paragraph draws you into the text? Why?
2. As you read the article, did your opinion change about the kinds of gun sales that Olinger describes? In what ways?
3. What contradictions become apparent when police agencies sell weapons that are banned by federal law?
4. What facts or statistics in Olinger's article strike you as important? In what ways are they significant? Do any of them support your opinion about cities that sell guns?
5. After reading Olinger's article, do you think law enforcement agencies should resell the weapons they confiscate, or should they destroy those firearms? Why?

✳ Police Re-think Policy of Trading In Their Weapons

CNN

It's common practice for police to take guns they no longer use and trade them in to licensed gun dealers who can resell them. But it's a procedure some local governments were rethinking even before it backfired in the case involving white supremacist Buford Furrow.

The police department in Cosmopolis, Washington, once owned the 9 mm Glock semiautomatic pistol Furrow is accused of using to kill Joseph Ileto. The Philippine-born postal worker was shot repeatedly August 10 [1999] about an hour after five people were wounded at a Los Angeles area Jewish community center.

Furrow is charged with murder and attempted murder in the two incidents.

Gary Eisenhower, Chief of Police in Cosmopolis, said the U.S. Bureau of Alcohol, Tobacco and Firearms had tracked the gun to his five-man department, which had traded it to a local gun shop in 1996.

"We're just devastated," Eisenhower said. "This is not something that we'd like to have notoriety for." 5

DILEMMA FOR SOME DEPARTMENTS

The Furrow case prompted California Gov. Gray Davis to order the destruction of old state law enforcement weapons, and those confiscated from criminals.

Local governments must decide for themselves what to do about used and unwanted weapons—and some have a dilemma.

Police Re-think Policy of Trading In Their Weapons

Twenty-seven cities and counties are suing gunmakers, demanding reform on the sales of handguns. But some of those same cities and counties have traded in guns to licensed dealers—guns that have ended up back on the streets.

East Palo Alto, California, once known as the homicide capital of the United States, is one of the cities suing the gun industry. Police there trade their guns back to the manufacturer with the agreement the guns will only be sold to law enforcement agencies.

But, city officials admit, there's no way to enforce that.   10

"THEY WERE ADVERTISED AS FORMER POLICE RIFLES"

In nearby San Francisco, the practice of trading in weapons to local gun dealers was stopped in 1994. After a street battle that year that left an officer dead, police complained of being outgunned.

The San Francisco Police Department responded by trading in 1,600 handguns overseas, instead of locally.

Until last year, however, used rifles were still traded to gun dealers.

That policy also was changed after someone spotted an ad placed by a dealer with an alarming sales pitch. "They were advertised as former (San Francisco Police Department) rifles," Sgt. Mickey Griffin told CNN.

As a result, San Francisco police ordered that all used police weapons   15
and confiscated guns be destroyed.

The gun industry should stop encouraging police departments to trade in old weapons, says San Francisco City Attorney Louise Renne. Police departments should take a stand as well. "Don't accept those inducements anymore," Renne said.

It was such an inducement that had the Cosmopolis Police Department regretting that one of its old weapons ended up in the wrong hands.

———————◆ **QUESTIONS FOR DISCUSSION AND WRITING** ◆————————

1. Does it really matter that a resold firearm used to kill someone was once owned by a police agency? Why?
2. This article reports that "twenty-seven cities and counties are suing gunmakers, demanding reform on the sales of handguns. But some of those same cities and counties have traded in guns to licensed dealers—guns that have ended up back on the streets" (paragraph 8). Do you think cities or counties should be allowed to do both—to sue gun manufacturers while also selling guns? Why or why not?
3. Is it more acceptable for a community to sell confiscated handguns than assault weapons? Why or why not?

✳ Rockdale's Sheriff Won't Sell Off Guns

Henry Farber

A Rockdale County judge has rejected the Sheriff's Department's practice of selling confiscated guns.

Instead, Superior Court Judge Sidney Nation wants the weapons destroyed.

"We don't want guns to get back in criminal hands again," Nation said.

Sheriff Jeff Wigington said he understands Nation's viewpoint and will go along with his decision, even though it could cost the department up to $5,000 a year.

"But I personally think if someone's going to get a gun, they're going to get one by whatever means they want to," Wigington said.   5

In recent years, law enforcement agencies nationwide have reversed the practice of selling confiscated guns to raise money. The agencies have found that some guns sold lawfully later ended up in the wrong hands.

Georgia law allows sheriff's departments to sell guns confiscated during arrests and criminal investigations, and the practice has become traditional in Rockdale, Cobb and Cherokee counties in metro Atlanta. The guns are sold only to licensed dealers.

The law does not require judges to sign off on the sheriffs' sales, but the chief judge's approval has been sought routinely in Rockdale.

His rejection of the latest request came last month, when he was given a list of about 50 weapons, half of them handguns. There were no assault weapons, officials said.

Rockdale's Sheriff's Department had been selling guns about three times a year, along with confiscated or stolen goods. The county unloaded about 20 or 30 guns at each sale and could net $1,500 or more in profits, deputies said.   10

Rockdale's practice has been to destroy guns if the court determines they were fired during a crime or aimed at someone during a stickup. Wigington said illegal guns or "Saturday night specials" also are routinely melted at the GBI Crime Lab.

The ones that have been sold were found in traffic stops, taken from felons or confiscated in other situations in which the guns were not actually pointed.

Some guns confiscated in Rockdale are cleaned up and kept by the department if they can be used for patrolling or target practice. "We'll just have to look at different ways of funding weapons purchases," Wigington said. "We agree certainly we don't want a revolving door on guns, and it would be unthinkable for a law enforcement officer or a citizen to be injured or killed by a gun that had been previously confiscated and later sold."

─────────◆ **QUESTIONS FOR DISCUSSION AND WRITING** ◆─────────

1. Farber reports that "Rockdale's practice has been to destroy guns if the court determines they were fired during a crime or aimed at someone during a stickup . . . [while t]he ones that have been sold were found in traffic stops, taken from felons . . ." (paragraphs 11–12). Does this policy make sense to you? Is it acceptable for a community to sell a gun if it has not been used in a crime?

2. What is the most important point made in "Rockdale's Sheriff Won't Sell Off Guns"? Why?

✳ Sheriffs Ready to Sell Confiscated Guns
NEW LAWS TAKING EFFECT TODAY
WILL ALLOW THEM TO DO JUST THAT

Ashley H. Grant

Law enforcement leaders—especially those in cash-strapped, smaller communities—are eager to start selling confiscated guns, and a law taking effect today will allow them to do just that.

Otter Tail County Sheriff Gary Nelson has been stockpiling confiscated guns since a 1994 law outlawed selling them. Recently, Otter Tail deputies seized 57 guns in one raid.

"There's $30,000 worth, roughly," he said. "We're not in a position out here to throw away $30,000."

Nelson is organizing a gun sale for five central Minnesota counties that want to empty their gun lockers. The sale will be open only to invited, licensed gun dealers. The department is likely to use the money for training, Nelson said.

The law is one of several passed in the 1999 session that take effect today. Others deal with underage drinking, tracking sex offenders and identity theft. 5

For some smaller enforcement agencies, the gun sales could bring in more than $5,000 a year, said Blue Earth County Sheriff Brad Peterson. That will allow the department to buy some needed equipment.

"It's not like we bring in piles of guns, but once in a while, a raid might produce 35," he said.

The department has gotten special court orders in the past to trade guns to Plymouth-based Streicher's Police Equipment for new guns, uniforms and badges.

The new law allows police to sell confiscated firearms only to federally licensed gun dealers. It prohibits the sale of assault weapons. Only guns made before 1899 can be sold to the general public. Those older guns are considered antiques.

Police agencies in large metropolitan areas are more likely to destroy   10
weapons, either because the money they earn from sales isn't worth the
bother or they don't want the guns falling into the wrong hands.

"We don't want to put guns back into circulation that have been taken
off the street," said Anoka County Sheriff's Lt. Larry Klink.

Officials in the Minnesota office of the federal Bureau of Alcohol, Tobacco and Firearms said no statistics exist on how many guns police agencies confiscate.

But Fred Tonne, co-owner of Streicher's, expects the new law to be
"widely noticed" around the country because only five states allow sales
of confiscated guns.

"I would suspect as the word gets around to states and municipalities
where it is not yet known, they will ask how they can do it," he said. . . .

◆ **QUESTIONS FOR DISCUSSION AND WRITING** ◆
---

1. The previous article by Farber and this article by Grant depict differing approaches to what law enforcement agencies should do with confiscated
   weapons: one sheriff argues that these firearms should not be sold; another
   thinks they should be. With whom do you agree? Why?

2. Which of the two articles—Farber's or Grant's—is the more effectively written?
   Support your argument with quotes from the articles.

❊ City Slickers

**NEW ORLEANS, BOSTON, DETROIT AND ALAMEDA
COUNTY, CALIF., ARE SUING GUN MANUFACTURERS
AND DEALERS FOR DISTRIBUTING WHAT THEY
DEEM A DANGEROUS PRODUCT—AND THEN
TURNING AROUND AND SELLING GUNS THEMSELVES.**

Jake Tapper

When Paul Jannuzzo, the vice president and general counsel of Glock
Inc., the Smyrna, Ga., gun manufacturer, heard that the city of New
Orleans was preparing to sue the gun industry, he couldn't believe the
hypocrisy.

Jannuzzo, after all, had been working with New Orleans, to help the
city swap around 10,000 guns in its possession—most of which had belonged to criminals—in exchange for 1,700 new Glock .40-caliber pistols
for its officers. The deal was worth $613,000.

Thus the city of New Orleans was dumping onto the street the same
allegedly "unsafe" product that it was now suing Glock and several other
companies—including some New Orleans pawn shops—for distributing.

Since last October, more than 20 U.S. cities and counties, copying the states that sued the tobacco industry and won, have filed lawsuits against gun dealers and manufacturers for various forms of negligence and irresponsibility. The NAACP joined the action on Monday.

One small glitch in the agreement, however: Some of these cities and counties have been more than willing to engage in quiet deals with these same manufacturers to trade in their old police weapons—and sometimes even confiscated criminal weapons—for new guns for their officers.

In essence, these cities served as gun distributors themselves. In order to save a buck, they're dumping thousands of firearms, despite the fact that many of them are publicly trying to get guns off the street. New Orleans isn't the only city with the contradictory gun policy: Boston, Detroit and Alameda County, Calif., which includes the high-crime city of Oakland, have also sold confiscated guns while suing the industry. By contrast, the federal government, as well as cities like San Francisco and Los Angeles, destroy criminals' guns.

"It's unfortunate because some of them are beautiful guns," says a spokesman for the LAPD, which eventually melts down all of its confiscated weapons. "But if a gun's been used to kill someone, they don't want it out there where it could kill someone else."

In the New Orleans swap—which is believed to be the largest police trade-in of criminally used weapons—Kiesler Police Supply and Ammunition in Jefferson, Ind., worked as the broker between New Orleans and Glock. The city traded 7,300 weapons seized in crimes as well as 700 Berettas that at one point belonged to New Orleans cops.

Included among the 7,300 criminals' guns that the city of New Orleans was willing to see dumped back out on the street: 230 semiautomatic assault weapons—including TEC-9s, AK-47s, Cobray M11s, an Uzi and a Fabrique National, a self-loading military rifle. The manufacture and importation—though not the sale—of all of these weapons were banned by Congress in 1994.

Dennis Henigan, legal director of the Center to Prevent Handgun Violence, which is co-counsel for many of these lawsuits, says that the gun industry's outrage over this perceived hypocrisy is "part of an overall strategy to change the subject." (Full disclosure: I worked at the Center for six months in 1997.)

"Ever since we filed the case on Oct. 30 of last year," Henigan says, "the gun industry wants to talk about gun swap programs, they want to talk about how greedy trial lawyers are. What they don't want to talk about is how dangerous their products are. You'll notice: They're not defending their products."

But Henigan didn't defend the merits of the gun swaps themselves. Assuming that these products are unsafe and the companies should be held liable, which is what Henigan is arguing though lawsuits, cities that engage in gun swap programs would seem to have some liability as well.

So many cities have engaged in the practice that the International Association of Chiefs of Police was moved to pass a resolution last October condemning police gun swaps. "The re-circulation of these firearms back into the general population increases the availability of firearms which could be used again to kill or injure additional police officers and citizens," the IACP resolution read. It urged "all law enforcement agencies to adopt a mandatory destruction policy," like the federal government has.

But despite the IACP resolution, and federal law enforcement's example, police departments—often short on cash for new weapons—continue to cut financial corners by dancing with the very devil their friends at city hall are suing.

Take the city of Boston, which is the most recent city to file a suit against the gun industry, on June 3. The Boston suit argued that "The defendants employ a strategy which couples manufacturing decisions, marketing schemes, and distribution patterns with a carefully constructed veil of deniability regarding point of sale transactions." 15

But according to a Boston Police Department administrator, the city has for years traded its old guns with the Interstate Arms Corporation, a Massachusetts gun dealer that refused to comment.

William Casey, deputy superintendent of the Bureau of Administrative Services for the Boston Police Department, says that thousands of guns belonging to uniformed Boston cops and detectives were swapped one-for-one for new guns. A few years ago, the Boston PD traded 3,000 to 4,000 .38s for the same number of 9 mms, says Glock's Jannuzzo. Then just a few weeks ago, the Boston PD traded around 4,000 9 mms for .40-caliber Glocks, a deal that could be worth up to $1.7 million to the city.

"I just got mine two weeks ago," Casey said in an interview with *Salon News* on Friday. "We did this with the caveat that the guns would be sold outside of the United States, so as to prevent them from being circulated in the U.S."

But according to Jannuzzo, Boston's previous gun swap—when it traded .38s for 9 mms—had "no such caveat. There were no restrictions on that first deal whatsoever."

Talk about a "veil of deniability." And this from a city now suing the gun industry for, among other things, "willful blindness." 20

Police departments—in order to pay for much-needed equipment—have sometimes turned to creative ways to find money for new weapons.

The city of Detroit filed its lawsuit against the gun industry on April 26. But when Detroit sought to buy new Glock .40-caliber pistols in the mid-'90s, amid a budget crisis, the city looked to sell the 9,000 guns it had in its inventory, says Jannuzzo. "Those were old guns, dating back to when Teddy Roosevelt charged up San Juan Hill," he says. Detroit didn't swap its inventory, however, as New Orleans, Boston and Alameda County did. According to Jannuzzo, Detroit put out word that the inventory was for sale, and then accepted the highest bid, from a private gun dealership in northern Vermont. Then, with that money, Detroit purchased its new weapons from Glock. A spokesman for the Detroit Police Department could neither confirm nor deny where the funding came from, though he did say the department uses relatively new .40-caliber Glock pistols.

Just a few weeks ago, on May 25, San Francisco filed its lawsuit against the gun industry on behalf of several jurisdictions, including Berkeley, Sacramento and nearby San Mateo and Alameda counties.

According to Jannuzzo, however, just last year the Alameda County Sheriff's Department traded 500 9 mm Glocks for roughly the same number of Sigs. "About two years ago we did have the Glocks and we did trade them for Sig Sauers," said Deputy Sheriff R. Glen, who added he didn't know the process by which the guns were traded.

This stands in marked contrast with the San Francisco Police Department, which destroys all of its old weapons. "I got the guy right here who cuts them up with a saw, puts them inside wrecked cars and watches them go through a conveyor belt and get shredded," said San Francisco Police Office Charlie Lyons of the property clerk's division.

But by far the most extreme example of this practice can be seen in the Big Easy. New Orleans, it should be noted, isn't just one of some 20-odd cities and counties to sue gun manufacturers and distributors. When it filed its suit last October, New Orleans was the first city to do so—which Mayor Marc Morial is fond of reminding voters and reporters and fellow mayors and anyone within earshot.

The New Orleans gun swap was similarly groundbreaking, says Doug Kiesler, who brokered the deal. He calls it "the largest confiscated deal ever to happen in the U.S."

(Morial refused comment; a spokesman said that his office was investigating the deal with Glock and would make no comments until that investigation was concluded.)

Rafael Goyeneche, the president of the Metropolitan Crime Commission of New Orleans, a private watchdog group, says he was offended when he heard of the mayor's double-dealing. "In many cases, police officers had put their lives on the line in order to get those guns," Goyeneche says. "To put them back out there through commerce we felt was really the wrong message."

Especially when you consider Morial's own rhetoric. "We have been so focused here in New Orleans on getting guns off the street and protecting our citizens," he said at the press conference announcing the Oct. 30 lawsuit.

Something about New Orleans' gun policy seems markedly out of focus, of course, and not just the surface irony of its putting more guns on the street while trying to "get guns off the street."

The New Orleans suit, for instance, takes a consumerist approach to the issue of guns, arguing that the industry has the technology to make its guns safer, but it refuses to do so. The guns should have locks, the lawsuit states, and the guns should be making use of the high-tech options that use fingerprint ID and computer-chip technology to make sure that no one but the approved user can pull the trigger.

"Guns are sold without the means to prevent their use by unauthorized users, without advance warning which would prevent such shootings by alerting users of the risks of guns, and of the importance of proper storage of guns, and without other safety features," the suit reads.

Gun dealer Kiesler observes that "one of the reasons they said they were going to sue us was that we weren't providing gun locks." But on the 8,000 guns the city sent to Kiesler's company in Indiana, he says, only two were equipped with locks.

To hear Jannuzzo tell it, there's little difference between what Glock 35 does and what New Orleans did. "We're an importer," he says, explaining that the Georgia office of Glock assembles, test-fires and conducts all warranty work on Glock firearms, but the guns are actually manufactured in Austria. "We distribute our guns to make money; [Morial] did it to save money. What's the difference?"

"That was kind of hypocritical," says Paul Bolton of the International Association of Chiefs of Police. "To say that 'guns are bad and terrible, guns are unsafe' and then they turn around and instead of destroying they sell them—it does seem to lean in that direction, of saying one thing in a lawsuit and then turning around and doing another thing."

The story first came out during a Jan. 27 confrontation between Jannuzzo and Morial on NBC's "Today" show. After a discussion of the New Orleans lawsuit, Jannuzzo—in a last-minute snarky aside—mentioned the gun swap.

Morial, for his part, tried to justify the deal by mentioning that, as part of the agreement, Glock had "agreed not to sell them in Louisiana."

And that was, in fact, part of the deal. Morial was apparently fine with these guns returning to the streets, as long as none of the streets had a Louisiana ZIP code.

Still, even that minimal pledge means little in reality. The April 8 New 40 Orleans Times-Picayune contained an ad from a local gun shop advertising the sale of Beretta 9 mms formerly belonging to members of the New Orleans Police Department.

"Own a piece of New Orleans history," the ad said. "All are original duty weapons and are numbered and stamped N.O.P.D." The guns came with two 15-round "pre-ban clips."

Goyeneche says that the gun swap—even with the Not-in-my-bayou promise not to resell in Louisiana—was a joke. "Some of the weapons resurfaced at gun shops in the New Orleans area," he says. "They were sold from Kiesler to someone in Texas, who sold them to a shop in New Orleans. That's the folly of thinking you can stop these weapons from re-entering your community."

Kiesler says that the five or so gun distributors that broker these deals offer different trade-in values for the guns depending on to whom they're permitted to resell them. "Say it's a Smith & Wesson model 686 revolver, which is a very popular gun," he explains. "We pay $200 if we can sell them to any lawful buyer. Now, New Orleans put in this thing with Glock so that the weapons could not be sold in Louisiana, so they would have gotten probably $175 on trade. Then the next level is if you can only sell the guns to other police departments, that would drop the value to $100."

After taking heat from the local press on this issue, Morial suspended the gun swap; according to Jannuzzo, New Orleans still owes Glock around 1,500 to 2,000 guns.

"Let's get to the bottom of it," Morial said in a news conference he 45 called when local criticism of the gun swap grew deafening. "Were any weapons that should not have been traded, in fact, traded?" he asked. In March, Morial told the *Times-Picayune*, "Do you know whose idea [the gun swap] was? The Police Foundation's. But when the controversy came, they hid and left me to defend a controversy that basically started at the Police Department."

But the gun swap had all been done according to an agreement that Morial signed on Feb. 5, 1998. "It is our understanding your representatives [have] determined, based on a preliminary inspection, that we have a sufficient number of confiscated firearms to make this an even exchange, resulting in no monetary obligation to the City of New Orleans," reads the document, which bears the signatures of both Morial and Richard J. Pennington, the New Orleans superintendent of police.

Meanwhile, the practice continues.

In 1997, the New Hampshire State Police signed a contract with Smith & Wesson to trade its 9 mms for .45s, a deal worth about $236,000, according to the state police. "It saved the taxpayers an enormous amount of money," says Sgt. Patrick Pouirier. The concern that the guns might fall into the wrong hands "is always there," he adds, "but Smith & Wesson is only going to sell them to a dealer, and the dealer is only going to sell them to a qualified person. And now we've got top-quality firearms so we can protect citizens of New Hampshire. And I guess it's good advertising [for Smith & Wesson] to have a state police agency carrying their weapons."

Like free Nike shoes for NCAA basketball teams.

In the last few months, the Charleston, W. Va., Police Department 50 traded 175 or so Smith & Wesson service pistols for 200 Glocks. "We had to make a decision on what to do, ethically," says Maj. Pat Epperhart: "The other option was to destroy them. But without getting into the ethical arguments, we did it." Bottom line, says Epperhart. "If it had not been for the swap program we would not have been able to afford new weapons."

New Jersey's Bergen County Sheriff's Department and the Alaska State Troopers have also recently engaged in gun swaps. And according to a Glock document, the following law enforcement agencies are not only trading old law enforcement weapons but confiscated criminal weapons as well: Alabama State Troopers; the Mobile, Ala., and Biloxi, Miss., police departments; the Dayton and Lima police departments in Ohio; the Clayton County Sheriff's Department in Georgia; the Gary, Ind., Police Department; Virginia's Mecklenberg County Sheriff's Department; the

Oklahoma City Police Department and Washington state's Yakima County Sheriff's Department.

One big difference between the above law enforcement agencies and those of New Orleans, Boston, Detroit and Alameda County: The former are, of course, not suing the gun industry for marketing an unsafe product; the latter group is.

The New Orleans gun swap has caused more problems than just a local embarrassment for Morial. In one instance, as the *Times-Picayune* reported in February, a 9 mm Beretta used in a January 1997 shootout had accidentally been traded to Glock through Kiesler, which was only able to recover the gun's barrel and slide.

What's more, Goyeneche says that the gun industry has an interesting strategy in the works in the event that any of the swapped firearms turn up at the scene of a crime.

"I've heard that the defendants are going to [name as a] third-party the city of New Orleans, so the city will be named as a defendant," Goyeneche says.   55

New Orleans suing New Orleans. It's easy to see a certain poetic justice in that.

————————◆ QUESTIONS FOR DISCUSSION AND WRITING ◆————————

1. What prereading or other strategies (annotating, summarizing, and so forth) did you employ to help you understand Tapper's essay?
2. How might you learn whether your community sells its confiscated firearms? Whether your community is suing gun manufacturers? What action would you take if you found out your community is doing one or the other or both?
3. What factual information stands out in Tapper's article? Why do those facts or statistics seem important?
4. What information from Tapper's article supports your beliefs?
5. Make a list of the communities that Tapper reports are selling or trading in confiscated firearms, the number of weapons involved, and the money the communities have received. Do any of the figures surprise you? Why?
6. Some of the communities that sell their confiscated weapons claim to do so only with the understanding that the guns be "sold outside of the United States, so as to prevent them from being circulated in the U.S." (paragraph 18). Does selling confiscated weapons overseas make such sales acceptable to you? Why or why not?
7. Is Tapper's article well written? What can you cite from the article to support your opinion?
8. Did reading Tapper's article change your beliefs about communities that sell firearms? In what way(s)?

✳ Get Rid of the Damned Things

Roger Rosenblatt

As terrible as last week's shooting in Atlanta was, as terrible as all the gun killings of the past few months have been, one has the almost satisfying feeling that the country is going through the literal death throes of a barbaric era and that mercifully soon, one of these monstrous episodes will be the last. My guess, in fact, is that the hour has come and gone—that the great majority of Americans are saying they favor gun control when they really mean gun banishment. Trigger locks, waiting periods, purchase limitations, which may seem important corrections at the moment, will soon be seen as mere tinkering with a machine that is as good as obsolete. Marshall McLuhan said that by the time one notices a cultural phenomenon, it has already happened. I think the country has long been ready to restrict the use of guns, except for hunting rifles and shotguns, and now I think we're prepared to get rid of the damned things entirely—the handguns, the semis and the automatics.

Those who claim otherwise tend to cite America's enduring love affair with guns, but there never was one. The image of shoot-'em-up America was mainly the invention of gunmaker Samuel Colt, who managed to convince a malleable 19th century public that no household was complete without a firearm—"an armed society is a peaceful society." This ludicrous aphorism, says historian Michael Bellesiles of Emory University, turned 200 years of Western tradition on its ear. Until 1850, fewer than 10% of U.S. citizens had guns. Only 15% of violent deaths between 1800 and 1845 were caused by guns. Reputedly wide-open Western towns, such as Dodge City and Tombstone, had strict gun-control laws; guns were confiscated at the Dodge City limits.

If the myth of a gun-loving America is merely the product of gun salesmen, dime-store novels, movies and the National Rifle Association (NRA)—which, incidentally, was not opposed to gun control until the 1960s, when gun buying sharply increased—it would seem that creating a gun-free society would be fairly easy. But the culture itself has retarded such progress by creating and embellishing an absurd though appealing connection among guns, personal power, freedom and beauty. The old western novels established a cowboy corollary to the Declaration of Independence by depicting the cowboy as a moral loner who preserves the peace and his own honor by shooting faster and surer than the competition. The old gangster movies gave us opposite versions of the same character. Little Caesar is simply an illegal Lone Ranger, with the added element of success in the free market. In more recent movies, guns are displayed as art objects, people die in balletic slow motion, and right prevails if you own "the most powerful handgun in the world." I doubt that any of this nonsense causes violence, but after decades of repetition, it does invoke boredom. And while I can't prove it, I would bet that gun-violence entertainment will soon pass too, because people have had too much of it and because it is patently false.

Before one celebrates the prospect of disarmament, it should be acknowledged that gun control is one of those issues that is simultaneously both simpler and more complicated than it appears. Advocates usually point to Britain, Australia and Japan as their models, where guns are restricted and crime is reduced. They do not point to Switzerland, where there is a gun in every home and crime is practically nonexistent. Nor do they cite as sources criminology professor Gary Kleck of Florida State University, whose studies have shown that gun ownership reduces crime when gun owners defend themselves, or Professor John R. Lott Jr. of the University of Chicago Law School, whose research has indicated that gun regulation actually encourages crime.

The constitutional questions raised by gun control are serious as well. In a way, the anti-gun movement mirrors the humanitarian movement in international politics. Bosnia, Kosovo and Rwanda have suggested that the West, the U.S. in particular, is heading toward a politics of human rights that supersedes the politics of established frontiers and, in some cases, laws. Substitute private property for frontiers and the Second Amendment for laws, and one begins to see that the politics of humanitarianism requires a trade-off involving the essential underpinnings of American life. To tell Americans what they can or cannot own and do in their homes is always a tricky business. As for the Second Amendment, it may pose an inconvenience for gun-control advocates, but no more an inconvenience than the First Amendment offers those who blame violence on movies and television.

Gun-control forces also ought not to make reform an implicit or explicit attack on people who like and own guns. Urban liberals ought to be especially alert to the cultural bigotry that categorizes such people as hicks, racists, psychotics and so forth. For one thing, a false moral superiority is impractical and incites a backlash among people otherwise sympathetic to sensible gun control, much like the backlash the pro-abortion rights forces incurred once their years of political suasion had ebbed. And the demonizing of gun owners or even the NRA is simply wrong. The majority of gun owners are as dutiful, responsible and sophisticated as most of their taunters.

That said, I am pleased to report that the likelihood of sweeping and lasting changes in the matter of America and guns has never been higher. There comes a time in every civilization when people have had enough of a bad thing, and the difference between this moment and previous spasms of reform is that it springs from the grass roots and is not driven by politicians or legal institutions. Gun-control sentiment is everywhere in the country these days—in the White House, the presidential campaigns, the legislatures, the law courts and the gun industry itself. But it seems nowhere more conspicuous than in the villages, the houses of worship and the consensus of the kitchen.

Not surprisingly, the national legislature has done the least to represent the nation on this issue. After the passage of the 1994 crime bill and its ban on assault weapons, the Republican Congress of 1994 nearly overturned the assault-weapons provision of the bill. Until Columbine the issue remained moribund, and after Columbine, moribund began to look good to the gun lobby. Thanks to an alliance of House Republicans and a prominent Democrat, Michigan's John Dingell, the most modest of gun-control measures, which had barely limped wounded into the House from the Senate, was killed. "Guns have little or nothing to do with juvenile violence," said Tom DeLay of Texas. Compared with his other assertions—that shootings are the product of day care, birth control and the teaching of evolution—that sounded almost persuasive.

A more representative representative of public feeling on this issue is New York's Carolyn McCarthy, whom gun violence brought into politics when her husband was killed and her son grievously wounded by a crazed shooter on a Long Island Rail Road train in 1993. McCarthy made an emotional, sensible and ultimately ineffectual speech in the House in an effort to get a stronger measure passed.

"When I gave that speech," she says, "I was talking more to the American people than to my colleagues. I could see that most of my colleagues had already made up their minds. I saw games being played. But this was not a game with me. I looked up in the balcony, and I saw people who had been with me all along on this issue. Victims and families of victims. We're the ones who know what it's like. We're the ones who know the pain."

Following upon Columbine, the most dramatic grass-roots effort has been the Bell Campaign. Modeled on Mothers Against Drunk Driving, the campaign plans to designate one day a year to toll bells all over the country for every victim of guns during the previous year. The aim of the Bell Campaign is to get guns off the streets and out of the hands of just about everyone except law officers and hunters. Andrew McGuire, executive director, whose cousin was killed by gunfire many years ago, wants gun owners to register and reregister every year. "I used to say that we'd get rid of most of the guns in 50 years," he tells me. "Now I say 25. And the reason for my optimism is that until now, we've had no grass-roots opposition to the NRA."

One must remember, however, that the NRA too is a grass-roots organization. A great deal of money and the face and voice of its president, Charlton Heston, may make it seem like something more grand and monumental, but its true effectiveness exists in small local communities where one or two thousand votes can swing an election. People who own guns and who ordinarily might never vote at all become convinced that their freedoms, their very being, will be jeopardized if they do not vote Smith in and Jones out. Once convinced, these folks in effect become the NRA in the shadows. They are the defense-oriented "little guys" of the American people, beset by Big Government, big laws and rich liberals who want to take away the only power they have.

They are convinced, I believe, of something wholly untrue—that the possession of weapons gives them stature, makes them more American. This idea too was a Colt-manufactured myth, indeed, an ad slogan: "God may have made men, but Samuel Colt made them equal." The notion of guns as instruments of equality ought to seem self-evidently crazy, but for a long time Hollywood—and thus we all—lived by it. Cultural historian Richard Slotkin of Wesleyan University debunks it forever in a recent essay, "Equalizer: The Cult of the Colt." "If we as individuals have to depend on our guns as equalizers," says Slotkin, "then what we will have is not a government of laws but a government of men—armed men."

Lasting social change usually occurs when people decide to do something they know they ought to have done long ago but have kept the knowledge private. This, I believe, is what happened with civil rights, and it is happening with guns. I doubt that it will be 25 years before we're rid of the things. In 10 years, even five, we could be looking back on the past three decades of gun violence in America the way one once looked back upon 18th century madhouses. I think we are already doing so but not saying so. Before Atlanta, before Columbine, at some quiet, unspecified moment in the past few years, America decided it was time to advance the civilization and do right by the ones who know what the killing and wounding are like, and who know the pain.

◆ QUESTIONS FOR DISCUSSION AND WRITING ◆

1. Do you agree with the assertion in Rosenblatt's opening paragraph that recent gun violence is causing a change in the way in which our society views firearms and that we are now "prepared to get rid of the damned things entirely—the handguns, the semis and the automatics"? Why or why not?

2. Reread paragraph 2. Do the statistics Rosenblatt cites surprise you? Does this information change your view of gun ownership in the United States? Why or why not?

3. Rosenblatt writes that the National Rifle Association (NRA) "was not opposed to gun control until the 1960s, when gun buying sharply increased . . ." (paragraph 3). Why do you suppose the NRA changed its stance on gun control at that time?

4. Are you more convinced by Rosenblatt's argument or by the information that Jake Tapper presents in "City Slickers"? Why? Cite from the articles to support your comments.

5. Does Rosenblatt present a fair representation of the issues and groups involved? Cite examples from his text to support your position.

6. What issues does Rosenblatt raise that relate directly to the issues in this scenario?

7. What positions does Rosenblatt articulate that support or run counter to your group's perspective?

✳ Gun Rights

Robin West

The NRA, right-wing militias, gun sellers, owners, their lawyers, and assorted political pundits all now quite routinely argue, and with growing success, that every individual has a constitutional right to own guns under the Second Amendment. This argument, which ten years ago was regarded as the rantings of the lunatic fringe, is now widely accepted not only by gun owners and advocates but also by a handful of respected liberal constitutional scholars and, more ominously, by at least one federal district court judge.

The claim has serious consequences. First of all, simply as a matter of law, were the courts ever to accept the proposition that an individual has a constitutionally protected right, under the Second Amendment, to possess firearms (as a lower federal district court in Texas has), such a right could invalidate even limited gun control legislation. Like all rights, the "right to bear arms," if it exists, expresses a constitutional commitment to protect the ownership of guns regardless of the severity of social consequences or costs: rights exist, fundamentally, to protect the rights holder against precisely the sort of emotional and political intensity occasioned by events like Columbine. Although rights are never absolute, nevertheless it is the nature of a constitutional right to "trump" laws that unduly infringe upon it, and to do so even if that law represents perfectly sound policy desired by solid majorities. In other words, if the right to own guns is pitted against nothing but a policy in favor of laws that control gun ownership, the policy will very likely lose.

But there is a deeper, less visible cost exacted by this new controversial right, and it is a cost borne directly by our politics of meaning. Asserted constitutional rights—even contested rights—create as well as rest on a cross-generational social consensus about the meaning of civic and individual life, a consensus that runs so deep that it trumps conflicting democratic judgments of policy. A claim that a right exists, then, essentially claims the existence of such a meaning, and such a consensus. The "right to bear arms" is no different. When gun advocates assert a right to own guns, and the courts, the pundits, scholars, and the public listen, something profound has occurred: gun ownership has been invested with constitutional authority, and hence constitutional meaning. The gun owner becomes, by virtue of the claimed constitutional right, the embodiment of a mythic-constitutional vision of our nature, ourselves, our community, and our state. We must protect his rights, because he has become, in essence, a symbol; he represents a way of being in the world—lone, idiosyncratic, and self-sufficient, defiantly bucking the ties of community and state control that in our wisest and longest vision of ourselves, we can and should ideally be. The gun owner becomes an ideal, and an ideal which is constitutional. Her defiance defines us. Even if their legal claim ultimately fails, in other words, the NRA's depiction of our nature, and of what it means to be an American, remains, with respect to guns and gun ownership, the only constitutional story being told.

But is the NRA's the only constitutional story that should be told, or that could be told? Of course, one can without difficulty find, in American mythology and constitutional history both, support for the social vision implied by the community of gun advocates now urging a Second Amendment right to bear arms; one can find in our histories plenty of support for the proposition that we are, fundamentally, a loose confederation of borderline, anti-social, and paranoid individuals, united only in our shared perpetual rage against the demands of community life, each and all of us bent on protecting our individual rights against the smothering embrace of social obligation. Indeed, as "rights critics" have argued over the past thirty years, it is fair to say that this is only a slight exaggeration of the hyper-individualistic constitutional rhetoric that monotonously repeats itself in volumes of utterly mainstream constitutional case law, scholarship, and folklore, and it is for precisely that reason that they urge us to abandon talk of individuating rights altogether, if we wish to create a world of connection. Rights talk, however, is not the only mythology, the only meaning, or the only social history compatible with our constitutional language and history. There are other stories to be told as well, and other constitutional visions to paint. Rather than abandon rights, rights-talk, and the constitution to the monopolistic rhetorical powers of free marketeers, rugged individuals, and gun zealots, we should be telling those other stories and filling in the details of the visions they suggest. The gun debate is an opportunity to do so.

Rights stem, minimally, from our constitutional history, as read   5 through the lens of our highest political ideals, and as informed by our best understanding of our human and social nature. All three sources strongly imply the existence, not of an individual right to bear arms, but, to the contrary, of a right to mutual disarmament. First, as an historical matter, the Reconstruction amendments in general, and the Fourteenth Amendment's Equal Protection Clause in particular, were written in part to ensure that all citizens (not just whites) received the state's protection against private acts of violence. The Amendments' framers understood that unless the freed slaves were granted a right to enjoy this "first duty of government"—the duty to protect citizens against violence—the promise of equality and liberty, given the reality of persecution, threats, and lynchings, would remain illusory. Second, that we have such a right to protection against violence flows directly from the liberal, Hobbesian, and Lockean political ideals that underlie our constitutional framework. The Leviathan exists, so said Hobbes, to protect us against the violence of others, in exchange for our agreement to give up "self help" and enter civil society. A right to that protection, then, and to the private disarmament required to achieve it, is at the very heart of even a "minimalist" understanding of the liberal state.

But most important, a right to disarmament, and the gun control legislation that would require it, would affirm something true and important about both our individual and our civic nature. We cannot forge loving connections between people, or reward ecological and spiritual sensitivity, when we simultaneously, through our shared constitution, valorize the gun owner and his "rights" and disparage the victim of gun violence. More to the point, we cannot ourselves connect with people, live in awe and wonder, or nourish our own spirit, when we live in fear of each other; many of us—disproportionately poor people and women and children— live with that fear daily. Fear destroys trust—it is its antithesis—and pervasive distrust destroys the spirit. As every battered woman, rape survivor, or harassed school child knows, one can neither spiritually grow nor form loving connections when one lives in fear of intimates, neighbors, or co- citizens: the inner self deadens, precisely so as to ward off attack. A right to the equal protection of the state against the lethal violence that triggers that spirit-deadening fear, as well as the state's affirmative obligation in- deed, its "first duty"—to legislate in such a way as to control the flow of private weapons that threatens the right's enjoyment, can be readily de- rived from our constitutional sources. Rather than turn our backs on these constitutional sources of political and moral meaning—as left and pro- gressive rights critics have urged us to do—we should embrace and seek to transform them.

◆ QUESTIONS FOR DISCUSSION AND WRITING ◆

1. The abstract (or summary) for this essay reads: "No 'right to bear arms' exists in the US Constitution, but over the past ten years it has been concocted by the gun lobby. Simply asserting a right does not mean that the concept is support- able in constitutional law, nor that it is a sensible result of social consensus." Do you agree—that is, did West convince you? Provide citations from "Gun Rights" to show which passages you found especially persuasive—or which were unconvincing.

2. Did you find West's essay easy or difficult to read and understand? Support your position with examples from West's text.

3. West writes, "When gun advocates assert a right to own guns, and the courts, the pundits, scholars, and the public listen, something profound has occurred: gun ownership has been invested with constitutional authority, and hence consti- tutional meaning" (paragraph 3). What other rights are you aware of that share such "constitutional authority"?

4. What ideas do Tapper, Rosenblatt, and West share? On what issues might they disagree? Use citations to illustrate your opinions.

✳ Cold Comfort

ECONOMIST JOHN LOTT DISCUSSES THE BENEFITS OF
GUNS—AND THE HAZARDS OF POINTING THEM OUT

Jacob Sullum and Michael W. Lynch

Until recently, when he bought a 9-mm Ruger after his own research impressed upon him the value of gun ownership, John Lott had no personal experience with firearms, aside from one day of riflery in summer camp when he was 12. That fact did not stop a reviewer of Lott's 1998 book, *More Guns, Less Crime* (University of Chicago Press), from labeling him a "gun nut." Writing in *The American Prospect,* Edward Cohn also identified Lott as "a leading loon of the Chicago School of Economics, known for its ultra-market ideology." But that was gentle—a backhanded compliment, even—compared to the attacks from anti-gun activists, who accused Lott of producing his landmark study at the behest of the gun industry.

Lott, now a senior research scholar at Yale Law School, used to be the John M. Olin Law and Economics Fellow at the University of Chicago. That position, like similar ones at other major universities, was endowed by a foundation based on the personal fortune of the late John M. Olin, former chairman of the Olin Corporation. Among many other things, the Olin Corporation makes Winchester ammunition. These facts led Kristen Rand of the Violence Policy Center to conclude that "Lott's work was, in essence, funded by the firearms industry"—a charge that was echoed by other gun control advocates, including Charles Schumer, then a Democratic representative from New York and now a senator.

Never mind that assuming the Olin Foundation takes orders from "the firearms industry" is like assuming the Ford Foundation does the bidding of automakers. Never mind that Olin fellows are chosen by faculty committees, not by the foundation (with which Lott never had any contact). Proponents of gun control were desperate to discredit Lott, because his findings contradicted their dark predictions about what would happen if states allowed law-abiding citizens to carry concealed handguns.

Analyzing 18 years of data for more than 3,000 counties, Lott found that violent crime drops significantly when states switch from discretionary permit policies, which give local officials the authority to determine who may carry a gun, to "shall issue" or "right-to-carry" laws, which require that permits be granted to everyone who meets certain objective criteria. That conclusion, first set forth in a 1997 paper that Lott co-authored with David Mustard, now an economist at the University of Georgia, heartened defenders of gun ownership and dismayed their opponents. Arguing that "shall issue" laws are beneficial, while other gun laws are ineffective at best, Lott quickly became one of the most widely cited—and reviled—scholars in the gun control debate.

Though it was the gun issue that brought Lott notoriety, it hasn't been the focus of his career. The 41-year-old economist, who earned his Ph.D. 5

at UCLA, has published papers on a wide variety of topics, including professional licensing, criminal punishment, campaign finance, and public education. Last summer he published *Are Predatory Commitments Credible?* (University of Chicago Press), a skeptical look at theories of predatory pricing, and he is working on a book about the reputational penalties faced by criminals, a longstanding interest. In addition to his positions at Yale and the University of Chicago, Loss has served as chief economist at the U.S. Sentencing Commission and taught at UCLA and the University of Pennsylvania, among other schools. He lives in Swarthmore, Pennsylvania, with his wife and four children. [*Reason*] Senior Editor Jacob Sullum and Washington Editor Michael Lynch talked to Lott at his Yale Law School office in mid-October [1999].

REASON: How did you become interested in guns?

JOHN R. LOTT JR.: About six years ago, I was teaching a class dealing with crime issues at the University of Pennsylvania, and it dawned on me that my students would be interested in some papers on gun control. It forced me to look at the literature systematically to decide what papers to assign to the class. I was shocked by how poorly done the existing research on guns and crime was.

You had very small samples. By far the largest previous study on guns and crime had looked at just 170 cities within a single year, 1980. Most of the rest looked at, say, 24 counties or 24 cities within a single year. No one had tried to account for things like arrest rates or conviction rates or prison sentence lengths. And the studies were all very limited in the sense that they were purely cross-sectional, where you look at the crime rates across jurisdictions in one year, or [purely longitudinal], where you pick one city or one county and look at it over time.

It was basically because of that class that I saw the benefit to going out and trying to do it right. So I put together what I think is by far the largest study that's ever been done on crime. The book has data on all 3,000-plus counties in the U.S. over an 18-year period. And simply having that large a data set allows you to account for hundreds of factors, thousands of factors, that you couldn't have accounted for in those smaller data sets.

REASON: What has been the most gratifying response to the book? Do you know of any criminologists whose views have been changed by your research?

LOTT: Some well-known people like [University of Pennsylvania criminologist] John DiIulio and [UCLA political scientist] James Q. Wilson have said very nice things about the study. I think it's caused DiIulio to look at these issues differently, and there are other criminologists I know of who have been amazed by how strong the data are. I've done lots of empirical studies, and the

10

regularities that you see here, in terms of the drops in violent crimes right after these laws go into effect, are very dramatic.

The intensity of the issue on both sides is something I wouldn't have expected before I got into it. I've been involved in a lot of debates, and people tell me, "You should have anticipated this before you did the study." But I've written about 80 academic articles, and the interest in this has been so outside the range of experiences I've had before. With the vast majority of articles, you're happy if you can get 10 people to read it.

REASON: The thrust of your argument in *More Guns, Less Crime* is easy enough to understand. But the details of the evidence you cite are hard to follow for anyone who is not trained in econometrics. Does it bother you that people who support the right to keep and bear arms are apt to accept your conclusions at face value, while those who are inclined to support gun control will tend to reject your findings, even though few people in either group are equipped to evaluate the evidence?

LOTT: My guess is that [my critics] assume that the vast majority of people who hear their claims are not going to even look at the book. So they say "Lott didn't account for poverty." Or they say, "Lott didn't account for other types of gun laws." Those are things that are easy to evaluate: Either I did, or I didn't. But I think they feel that they can get away with making those claims, because it'll be only a tiny fraction of 1 percent who will go and buy the book or get it from the library. I've never been involved in a debate like this, because in your normal academic debate, where there are 10 people involved and they've all read the paper, if somebody says, "Professor X didn't account for other gun laws," everybody else in the room would laugh, because they would know it was an absurd claim.

I don't think that most of the comments [the critics] are making are really that difficult to understand. One of the claims, for instance, is that I'm assuming that when these laws are passed there will be a one-time drop in violent crime rates, and it should be the same across all places that adopt these laws. That's absurd. I don't know how much time I spend in the book saying that the level of deterrence is related, according to the data, to the probability that people are going to be able to defend themselves, and the rate at which people get permits changes over time. When you pass these laws, not everybody who eventually is going to get a permit does it the first day. Fifteen years after these laws go into effect, you're still seeing an increasing percentage of the population getting these permits and a decreasing rate of violent crime because of the additional deterrence.

I spend lots of time in the book talking about why you don't expect the drop in crime to be the same in all places. . . . In more urban areas [of states with discretionary permit laws], public officials were especially reluctant to issue permits. So when you change to a nondiscretionary rule, the biggest increases in permits tended to be in these urban areas, and that is where you observe the biggest drops in violent crime.

REASON: Your analysis shows that liberal carry permit policies are associated with lower crime rates even after controlling for a variety of factors that might also have an impact on crime. In the book you concede that some other variable that you did not consider could be responsible for this association. Yet at the end of the book, you write, "Will allowing law-abiding citizens to carry concealed handguns save lives? The answer is yes, it will." Do statements like that go too far?

LOTT: I don't think so. That's one of the last sentences in the book, and at that point the evidence is pretty overwhelming. There are different types of information, and they're all pointing in the same direction.

After these laws are adopted, you see a drop in violent crime, and it continues over time as the percentage of the population with permits increases. If I look at neighboring counties on either side of a state border, when one state passes its right-to-carry law, I see a drop in violent crime in that county, but the other county, right across the state border, in a state without a right-to-carry law, sees an increase in its violent crime rate. You try to control for differences in the legal system, arrest and conviction rates, different types of laws, demographics, poverty, drug prices—all sorts of things. You look at something like that, and I think it's pretty hard to come up with some other explanation. I think you're seeing some criminals move [across the state line].

You find the types of people who benefit the most from these laws. The biggest drops in crime are among women and the elderly, who are physically weaker, and in the high-crime, relatively poor areas where people are most vulnerable.

There are five or six things that one could point to that confirm different parts of the theory. I haven't heard anybody come up with a story that explains all these different pieces of evidence. . . . Since you have all these states changing their laws at different times, it becomes harder and harder to think of some left-out factor that just happened to be changing in all these different states at the same time the right-to-carry law got changed.

REASON: A review of your book in *The American Prospect* claims that "his results are skewed by the inclusion of data from tiny counties with trivial rates of violent crime. In fact, when you consider only large counties and exclude Florida from the sample, his case completely falls apart." How do you respond?

LOTT: When you drop out counties with fewer than 100,000 people, if anything it actually increases the size of the effect. What [the reviewer is] saying is that if you not only drop out counties with fewer than 100,000 people—which is 86 percent of the counties in the sample, so it's not just a few small counties that we're talking about—but also drop out Florida, then the changes in two of the violent crime categories, when you're just looking at the simple before-and-after averages, aren't statistically significant. But the results still imply a drop, and for robberies and aggravated assaults you still get a drop that's statistically significant.

Now, I think it's somewhat misleading to look only at the simple before-and-after averages. Take the case where violent crime rates are rising right up to the point when the law goes into effect and falling afterward, and let's say it was a perfectly symmetrical inverted V. If I were to take the average crime rate before the law goes into effect and the average afterward, where the point of the V is when the law changed, they're going to be the same. Does that mean the law had no impact? When you drop Florida from the sample, [the results] look more like this inverted V than they do when Florida is in there. So I would argue that it strengthens the results, if what you care about is the change in direction.

In any case, the bottom line to me is this: I wanted all the data   25 that were available. . . . I didn't pick and choose, and when somebody drops out 86 percent of the counties along with Florida, you know they must have tried all sorts of combinations. This wasn't the first obvious combination that sprang to mind. And it's the only combination they report. . . . If, after doing all these gymnastics, and recording only one type of specification, dealing with before-and-after averages that are biased against finding a benefit, they still find only benefits, and no cost, to me that strengthens the results.

REASON: University of Florida criminologist Gary Kleck recently told *The Salt Lake Tribune* that "Lott has convincingly demonstrated there is no substantial detriment" from "shall issue" laws. But he questioned whether these laws could have as substantial a deterrent effect as you suggest. Kleck provided a blurb for your book, and his work is often cited by opponents of gun control. Why do you think he has trouble buying your conclusions?

LOTT: Gary has had a strong opinion for a long time that, on net, guns neither reduce or increase crime. He thinks it's essentially a wash. And I'm not sure I understand how he comes to that conclusion, particularly given the survey data that indicate that many more violent crimes are stopped with guns than are perpetrated with guns. But it is something that he has written and felt strongly about for a long time. Now Gary may think that there's something else that's being left out that maybe could explain these changes in crime rates. If he can tell me what that factor is, I'd be happy to try to test it.

REASON: Do you still hear the argument that you're in the pay of the gun industry, or has that been discredited?

LOTT: I think the gun control people are going to continue to bring it up. I've been in debates this year with people from Handgun Control Inc. and other gun control groups in which they asserted flat-out that I've been paid by gun makers to do this study.

REASON: When they raise this charge, how successful are you in making the point that people should be able to assess evidence and arguments on their merits and that your motives don't matter?

LOTT: Well, most people aren't going to look at the data. They're not going to have the data in front of them. The credibility of the data and the message depends on whether or not they believe that the person who's telling them about the data is credible. And I think the gun control groups feel that it's a win to the extent that they even divert three minutes of a show to talking about this issue. Even if it doesn't stick in people's minds, it's still three minutes that I couldn't talk about something else.

REASON: In a working paper you wrote with University of Chicago law professor William Landes [available at papers.ssrn.com/paper. taf?abstract_id=161637], you conclude that "shall issue" laws are especially effective at preventing mass public shootings. Given that the people who commit these crimes seem to be pretty unbalanced, if not suicidal, how does the deterrent work?

LOTT: Most of these attacks do end in the death of the attackers themselves, frequently from suicide, but also because they're killed by others. But part of what's motivating them is the desire to harm other people, and to the extent that you can take that away from them, I think you reduce their incentive to engage in these attacks. Whether they do it just because they intrinsically value killing people or whether they do it because of the publicity, the fact that there might be a citizen there who can stop them well before the police are able to arrive takes away, in their warped minds, some of the gain from the crime, and stops a lot of them from doing it.

REASON: You often say, based on surveys, that Americans use guns to fend off criminals more than 2 million times a year. But in the book, you note that people who report incidents of armed self-defense could be mistaken or lying. How big a problem is that, and how confident can we be that the true number is more than 2 million?

LOTT: Well, 2 million is the average of the various surveys. Differ-   35
ent problems may plague different surveys, and the problems can
go in both directions. You may have questions that weed out
people who shouldn't be weeded out.

REASON: Like "Do you own a gun?"

LOTT: Or it could be you ask them "Has a crime been committed
against you?" before you ask them whether they've used a gun
defensively.

REASON: And they might not consider it a crime if it wasn't
completed?

LOTT: Right. And so, we have errors that can exist on both sides.
. . . But that's the only type of evidence that we have on this. . . .
The most striking thing to me is the comparison between the results from these surveys and [survey data on] the number of violent crimes that are committed with guns each year. You see
many more crimes that are averted by people who defend themselves with guns. I think that difference—even though both sets
of numbers can be tainted for all the same reasons—is what's
striking.

REASON: You say that resistance with a gun is the safest op-   40
tion when confronted by a criminal. What's the basis for that
conclusion?

LOTT: You hear claims from time to time that people should behave passively when they're confronted by a criminal. And if you
push people on that, they'll refer to something called the National
Crime Victimization Survey, a government project that surveys
about 50,000 households each year. If you compare passive behavior to all forms of active resistance lumped together, passive
behavior is indeed slightly safer than active resistance. But that's
very misleading, because under the heading of active resistance
you're lumping together things like using your fist, yelling and
screaming, running away, using Mace, a baseball bat, a knife, or
a gun. Some of those actions are indeed much more dangerous
than passive behavior. But some are much safer.

For a woman, for example, by far the most dangerous course
of action to take when she's confronted by a criminal is to use her
fists. The reason is pretty simple: You're almost always talking
about a male criminal doing the attacking, so in the case of a female victim there's a large strength differential. And for a woman
to use her fists is very likely to result in a physical response from
the attacker and a high probability of serious injury or death to
the woman. For women, by far the safest course of action is to
have a gun. A woman who behaves passively is 2.5 times as likely
to end up being seriously injured as a woman who has a gun.

REASON: Why does the mainstream press seem to downplay the value of armed self-defense?

LOTT: One question is, Why don't they report people using guns defensively? If I have two stories, one where there's a dead body on the ground vs. another where, say, a woman has brandished a gun and a would-be rapist or murderer has run away, with no shorts fired and no dead body on the ground, it's pretty obvious to me which one of those is going to be considered more news-worthy. It doesn't require any conspiracy. Now if we care about policy, if we care about what types of actions are going to save the most lives, or prevent the most crimes, we want to look at both of those cases: not only the newsworthy bad events but the bad events that never become newsworthy because they don't occur.

But I don't think that explains everything. One example is gun deaths involving children. My guess is that if you go out and ask people, how many gun deaths involve children under age 5, or under age 10, in the United States, they're going to say thousands. When you tell them that in 1996 there were 17 gun deaths for children under age 5 in the United States and 44 for children under age 10, they're just astounded. There's a reason why they believe these deaths occur much more frequently: If you have a gun death in the home involving a child under age 5, you're going to get national news coverage. Five times more children drown in bathtubs; more than twice as many drown in five-gallon water buckets around the home. But those deaths do not get national coverage.

This type of news coverage has consequences, because it af-fects people's perceptions of the benefits and costs of having guns around. Concentrating on gun deaths in the home, exaggerating the risks of that, creates a false impression. People are going to die because of that false impression. They're not going to have guns in the home, even though that's by far the safest course of action for them to take when they're confronted by a criminal. You may prevent some of the accidental deaths, but you're going to create other types of deaths because people won't be able to defend themselves.

I think the debate would be so different now if, even once in a while, some of the life-saving uses of guns got some attention in the news. A couple of the public school shootings were stopped by citizens armed with guns well before the police were able to arrive. Or take the case of the day trader shooting in Atlanta, which got huge attention. Within 10 days after that, there were three separate attacks in the Atlanta area that were stopped by citizens with guns, in two cases permitted concealed handguns. They got no attention outside of the local media market.

REASON: You've said that if Chicago Mayor Richard Daley, who filed one of the first city-sponsored gun lawsuits, really believes guns are so bad, he ought to take them away from his bodyguards. Explain that comment.

LOTT: Daley has been arguing that there's no benefit from owning guns. Yet he has a whole set of full-time bodyguards following him every place he goes. He won't even think about visiting some of the more dangerous areas in Chicago without his bodyguards. But there are poor people who have to live in those areas, who live there at great risk, and he's not willing to let them own guns in order to protect themselves. . . . I view it as very hypocritical, that Daley can understand the defensive benefits of guns when it comes to himself, but he's not willing to afford that same level of protection to the poorest, most vulnerable people in his city.

REASON: You've pointed out that somebody who gets turned 50 down for a gun purchase after a background check may simply get the gun by other means. That's a legitimate point, but don't you also have to consider the possibility that people are deterred from even trying to get a gun because they know there's going to be a background check and they know they won't pass it?

LOTT: They may just try to get it the illegal way to begin with. Personally, I don't believe the claims that the Clinton administration makes about the number of people who are stopped from buying a gun. My guess is that to the extent that people are stopped, the vast majority of them are people who may have something on their record from 30 years ago, and they don't realize that it prevents them from buying a gun. These are people who may pose no risk to anybody. In fact, that's one of the reasons why I think there's such a low prosecution rate of those people.

REASON: The feds say they don't have the resources to prosecute.

LOTT: I don't think that's it at all. I think you have prosecutorial discretion. I think that you have a case where somebody who's 50 years old may have done something as an 18-year-old that was wrong. The prosecutor looks at it and says, "This guy has been an upstanding member of the community for 30 years, and he had this one run-in as a teenager. We don't really think that he intended to violate the law. We're not going to send the guy to jail for doing this."

REASON: The National Rifle Association criticizes the Justice Department for not prosecuting enough of these cases.

LOTT: I think that's a mistake. They're also talking about prosecut- 55 ing cases where guns were brought onto school property. My guess is that a prosecutor would bend over backwards to bring a case against a juvenile who had brought a gun onto school property. He doesn't want to not bring the case and then have something bad happen later on. That would be disastrous for his career.

But let's say a kid's gone hunting in the morning before school. He has the gun in the trunk of his car, parks it in the school parking lot, and goes into school. Somebody finds out that he has a gun there. The prosecutor looks at the case and says, "This is a good kid, never done anything wrong. He probably just didn't realize he shouldn't have done this. Do I really want to send this kid to jail for three years for this type of violation?" It's wrong to think that these prosecutors are making the types of mistakes that are being assumed.

REASON: You've criticized the NRA for doing a poor job of making its case. What should it be doing differently?

LOTT: My biggest complaint with the NRA is that they're too defensive. It seems to me that some of the [mass shootings] that have occurred are a result of gun laws that are already on the books. Rather than talking about what new law should be put in place, we should ask to what extent have well-intentioned laws in the past caused us to get to the point where we are right now.

It's only been since the end of 1995 that we've banned guns within 1,000 feet of schools by federal law. Right after the Columbine attack, a friend of mine dropped off his kids at a public school in Seattle, and he e-mailed me afterward, because there was a big sign in front of the school that said, "This is a gun-free zone." The question I had was, if I put a sign like that in front of my home, would I think that people who are intent on attacking my home would be less likely, or more likely, to harm my children and my wife? You may be trying to create a safe area for your family, but what you've ended up accidentally doing is creating a safe zone for [criminals], because they have less to worry about.

The thing that I'd like to see the NRA try to do is to say, when attacks occur, since we can't have the police every place all the time, why not let these people defend themselves? The people who get permits for concealed handguns tend to be extremely law-abiding. They've never done one of these attacks in the 70 years that we've had these types of permits. When these people lose their permits, and it's only a tiny fraction of 1 percent who do, it's usually for reasons that have nothing to do with posing a threat to other people. Laws [like the Gun-Free School Zones Act] are obeyed by honest, law-abiding citizens, not by people who are intent on carrying out attacks. And to the extent that you disarm the law-abiding citizens in certain areas, you increase the probability of these attacks, which perversely leads to calls for more regulations.

Another example is gun locks. If I were with the NRA, I would emphasize the cost of constantly talking about this issue. You're actually endangering people's lives, for two reasons. One, you're exaggerating in their minds the risks of having guns in the home. And two, I would say it's not in everybody's interest to have a lock on their gun. If you live in a safe area and maybe have young kids, that might be fine. But if you live in a city, even if you have kids, I don't think it's really the wisest thing to have the gun locked up, because you're not going to be able to quickly access it to defend your family. And when you compare probabilities, accidental gun deaths in the home are trivial compared to the rate at which other types of deaths occur from crimes where innocent victims are attacked and a gun would benefit them.

REASON: Some advocates of gun rights base their claims mainly on the Second Amendment, while others offer a more utilitarian argument. Which approach is more effective?

LOTT: I understand the constitutional arguments, but I think for the vast majority of people the bottom line is whether the presence of guns, on net, saves lives or costs lives. They may be able to understand in the abstract that having guns owned by civilians is some type of restraint on government, but I don't think most of them view that as a problem that they're facing any time soon. For them the bottom line is, What will save lives? And so I think that's where you have to argue.

──────── ◆ **QUESTIONS FOR DISCUSSION AND WRITING** ◆ ────────

1. Reread paragraph 4. What is your reaction to the results of John Lott's research that Sullum and Lynch outline there?

2. What data or statistical information in this interview affects your views of gun control issues? Why?

3. Researcher Lott claims that his work is based on "data on all 3,000-plus counties in the U.S. over an 18-year period" (paragraph 9). In what ways does this make his claims more or less convincing?

4. One could argue that Lott's research indicates that the greater the availability of guns to people, the safer our society will be. In fact, at the end of his book he writes, "Will allowing law-abiding citizens to carry concealed handguns save lives? The answer is yes, it will" (paragraph 17). Do you agree? Why or why not? Point to passages in this interview or in other readings in this chapter that support your position.

5. The interviewers outline a challenge to Lott's research made in a book review in *The American Prospect* (paragraph 22). How do you interpret this challenge and Lott's answer to it?

6. Download the article mentioned in paragraph 32 (note that there is no "www." in the address: http://papers.ssrn.com/paper.taf?abstract_id=161637). In what

ways does the information in this new source strengthen or weaken Lott's position in the interview?

7. Lott suggests that his "biggest complaint with the NRA is that they're too defensive" (paragraph 58). Do you agree or disagree? Why?

TAKING ACTION

Persuading the City Council

You've now completed your reading and perhaps you've also done additional research into specific aspects of the Maple Plains situation, just as you would if you really were a resident of that community. In this scenario, the Maple Plains City Council has asked for a two-page statement from each interested group indicating how each feels about the city's gun sales. It's time for your group to construct its collaborative statement for the city council.

Asking the Right Questions

It's often a good idea to begin wrestling with a problem or issue that affects you by first discovering what you already know; this gives you a sense of what you'd like to learn more about. The questions you ask lead to others that can help your group arrive at a consensus on the best solution for the Maple Plains scenario. As you draft your statement to the city council, consider the scenario from a reporter's perspective, focusing on the who, what, when, where, and why of the scenario. Try to answer the following questions:

- What perspectives might each of the Maple Plains groups have? What are the strengths and weaknesses of those viewpoints?

- In what ways can you make your group's statement stronger by aligning your group with others? Will it help to let the council know that more than one group shares your ideas concerning some of the issues, problems, or possible solutions?

- What events in the Maple Plains scenario can be controlled? How? What events cannot be controlled?

- What are some of the consequences to the members of your group if the firearms sales are halted?

- What are the consequences for your group if you do nothing to try to change the situation in Maple Plains?

- What actions that you propose might make the situation more difficult?

- In what way do the issues and problems in the Maple Plains scenario relate to the broader national perspective on gun control issues?

Which group you represent and the approach you decide to take will determine the position you propose. You might, for example, argue that all gun sales should stop, you might propose limiting these types of transactions to trade-ins of used police weapons for new ones, or you might argue that things should continue pretty much as they now are.

Constructing a Collaborative Text

Working with the members of your group, compose a draft of your comments to the city council expressing your views on the issues facing Maple Plains. Read through and carefully revise your draft several times, to ensure that your group has articulated its ideas as clearly as possible.

One way to start composing your group statement is for every group member to write his or her own statement, listing the most important issues and problems as he or she sees them. Then, working together, your group can draw on those individual ideas to compose the group statement.

Another method for constructing a group statement is to take the notes that each of you has made, designate one group member to record the group's ideas, and then collaboratively compose an initial draft of what your group thinks. At first, this process might be a bit chaotic, with several group members offering suggestions on what to write and how to write it, but with time, you'll find that working together is an interesting and useful way to get your collective ideas onto paper.

When you've completed a first draft of your collaborative text, each group member should read through the draft, marking any sections that are unclear. Work together to clarify those parts. Then, each group member should read the statement once more, this time looking for places in the text where your argument might need more evidence. Then, again working together, decide what pieces of evidence gathered during your research (facts, data, testimony, statistics) might provide additional support for your argument.

Your instructor may ask you to read and comment on the other groups' statements. Working together in that way gives you the chance to help your classmates become better writers, as you act as real readers for one another. Indicate the places in the text where more information is needed, or where the writing is confusing, or where some elaboration might help. Follow the procedure in Box 6.2: Using Your Classmates' Suggestions to apply the feedback you receive to improve your composition.

BOX 6.2   APPLYING WHAT YOU READ
Using Your Classmates' Suggestions (Written Peer Review)

Once your group has completed a brief, collaborative text that outlines your message to the Maple Plains City Council, exchange your draft with that of another group. Read their comments, and identify (and indicate in marginal notes) the strengths and weaknesses. What suggestions can you make for how the group might improve its comments? What are the strengths of the draft? The weaknesses? Where was the argument confusing or unclear? How might the group clarify its position? What suggestions might you offer to improve the group's statement to the city council?

Even if you disagree with the position the group is taking, it's important to help your classmates by suggesting where they can improve their statement of that position.

Once your group receives feedback from your classmates, work together as a group to revise your statement. What suggestions did you receive that make sense? Where does your text need clarification, or further explanation, or more evidence? What facts or other data have group members collected that you can add, to make your text more convincing?

SPEAKING YOUR PIECE
Making an Oral Presentation to the City Council

Because Bud Bowden's shooting has caused an uproar in the community, and because of the statements received from various groups about that incident and the annual gun show, the Maple Plains City Council has decided to hold an open council meeting. The meeting is intended to give all interested parties the chance to voice their concerns and to ask questions. Because the open meeting allows direct interaction between groups, it offers a valuable opportunity for identifying and finding solutions for the issues in question.

Mayor Bradley also promises that "once we've heard from our citizens, the council will publicly discuss and then vote on whether Maple Plains should continue its policy of selling and trading guns. This meeting is a chance, too, for members of various groups to question one another. In the end, we'll do what's right for the citizens of Maple Plains."

From Written Preparation to Public Speaking

For the sake of illustration, let's assume that your group represents some of the residents of Maple Plains, and you've decided that all gun sales must stop. Your group's spokesperson might state your main idea in this way: "Our group's main point is that although the gun sales Maple

Plains has held might be legal, we should halt them at once. There are several reasons for our view. . . ." Then your spokesperson would explain, with specific examples, why your group thinks as it does. Just as in your written presentation, it's vital to provide specific evidence—facts, testimony, examples of what other cities have done—in your oral presentation.

Remember, too, that another major difference between speaking and writing is that when you speak, your audience is in the same room and can question you. As your group plans what its spokesperson will say, it's a good idea to consider the questions your group might be asked, and the questions you'd like to ask of the other speakers.

Speaking at the Open City Council Meeting

In a full-class discussion, representatives of each group will speak (speakers will be given a time limit). While your classmates present their information, take notes on what they have to say; their perspectives on the issues might help you in the individual writing you'll soon be asked to do. Those notes can also help you respond to any questions your group is asked.

Once each group has presented its side of the issues involved in the Maple Plains scenario and has indicated what it feels is a workable solution, members of each group will be allowed to question members of the other groups. Your instructor might assign one or more students to act as moderators (a function that the Maple Plains mayor might perform in real life), to ensure that everyone who wishes to speak is given the opportunity to do so.

INDIVIDUAL WRITING
Essay Options

You've worked with your group to construct a collaborative written statement of your perspective; your group might also have made an oral presentation. Now it's time for you to write your personal views on whether Maple Plains should continue in the gun sales business.

Your instructor will ask you to construct one or more individual writing projects: an informative essay, a persuasive essay, and/or an analytic essay. Each writing project has an individual focus, but they all allow you to make use of the notes you've taken, your reading, and the collaborative writing and speaking you've done with your group. Before completing these individual writing assignments, you might want to do additional research to better understand the issues or to find support for something you want to say.

The Informative Essay

Your instructor may ask you to compose an informative essay in which you supply the facts concerning how other communities are handling the same issues that now confront Maple Plains.

For this assignment, write from the point of view of the police chief. Construct an informative essay for the city council, outlining what other communities are doing with the weapons they confiscate or otherwise have. As the chief, it's important that your biases not appear in your essay, or city council members might feel that you're attempting to influence their decision.

The Persuasive Essay

Your instructor may ask you to write a persuasive essay in which you convince the Maple Plains City Council to go along with your recommendations concerning the sale of firearms. For this assignment, write from the perspective of a citizen of Maple Plains. You can adopt the persona and perspectives of:

- Someone who has, over the years, purchased several guns from the police department. You're a person who feels strongly about your "right to keep and bear arms," and you're writing to the city council to explain your reasoning. Your purpose is to persuade the council that gun sales should continue in Maple Plains.

- A resident who dislikes the notion of the community's acting as a gun merchant and who thinks that Maple Plains should stop selling weapons. You know that some worthwhile city programs might have to be eliminated, so you'll want to explain to the council members why the potential dangers (and perhaps even liability) of selling guns outweigh the positive benefits of such programs.

The Analytic Essay

Your instructor may ask you to construct an analysis of cities that sell guns: why they do so, as well as the benefits and problems involved. In an analytic essay, you'd first explain what other communities do, then list the pros and cons of the issues, and then detail why the benefits outweigh the costs (or why the costs seem to outweigh the benefits).

Assume that your essay will appear in the journal *Funding Your City Government,* which is read by city council and staff members from around the country. You comments will appear with several other essays in a special report titled "Your City as a Gun Merchant?"

✳ **BOX 6.3   APPLYING WHAT YOU READ**
Reflections on the Maple Plains Scenario

By this point in our scenario, you've done a lot of reading, discussing, and writing about whether Maple Plains should continue to sell old and confiscated firearms. Take a few minutes now to look back at the first writing you did for this scenario, after you'd thought about the photographs that introduce this chapter and read the First Impressions questions. Then jot down your answers to these questions:

- In what ways do you look differently at law enforcement agencies and their firearms sales than you did earlier?
- Are such sales a gun control issue? If so, in what ways?
- How can you measure the dangers of firearm sales by communities against the value of the community activities those sales support?
- What have you learned about your writing as you worked through the Maple Plains scenario?
- In terms of your writing, what might you do differently for your next assignment?

To conclude this scenario, your instructor may ask that you follow the instructions in Box 6.3: Reflections on the Maple Plains Scenario. The process of writing about ways in which your attitudes may have changed helps clarify your thinking.

FOR FURTHER RESEARCH AND WRITING

The situation in Maple Plains, New Jersey, isn't unusual. Communities around the country struggle to balance the dangers of selling firearms against the funds those sales provide for worthwhile projects.

One idea you might explore further and write about is current trends in city firearms sales. Are more communities beginning to halt gun sales, or are more setting up such programs?

As we mentioned at the start, it seems ironic that some of the same cities that sell firearms to private gun dealers are also suing gun manufacturers and gun distributors, arguing that they produce and sell an unsafe product. You might write about this apparent conflict, and the ethical issues it involves.

You can expand the Maple Plains scenario to the larger issue of gun control in this country. You might consider questions such as these:

- Should we have any form of gun control in this country? If so, what should it be?

- Should everyone be required to carry a gun? Would that make society safer? How? (This reverses the usual way of addressing the issue, but looking at a question from a new perspective can produce fresh insights.)
- How effective is the Brady Bill (a federal law requiring background checks of everyone who purchases a firearm from a licensed gun dealer)? What changes might be made to strengthen or weaken it?
- How effective are background checks for potential firearms purchasers?
- Should those buying a weapon at a gun show be required to undergo a background check? (Maple Plains insists on this procedure, but it's not a federal law.)

You now have read, discussed, and written about some of the benefits and potential problems weapon sales pose for one community. Each day, public servants like those on the Maple Plains City Council face issues such as this one. We hope that working through this scenario about weapons sales has helped you improve how you read and write; we also hope that you better understand how to work effectively with others. The skills you used in this scenario about how guns are distributed in our society will aid you in the work you've yet to do in this and your other college classes. Ultimately, these skills will also help you in your career.

Works Cited

"Federal Government to Start Gun Buyback Effort." *Michigan Daily* 9 Sept. 1999. 31 Dec. 1999 <http://www.pub.umich.edu/daily/1999/sep/09-09-99/news/news20.html>.

National Center for Policy Analysis. "Crime and Gun Control: A City Trafficking in Guns Sues Gun Makers and Sellers." 2 Feb. 1999. 13 June 2000 <http://www.ncpa.org/pi/crime/pd020299e.html>.

Olinger, David. "Cops Put Guns Back in Circulation." *Denver Post* 19 Sept. 1999. 13 June 2000 <http://www.denverpost.com/news/gun0919.htm>.

Slivka, Judd, and Tracy Johnson. "Sheriff Broke Law Selling Guns, Audit Says." *Seattle Post-Intelligencer* 29 Sept. 1999. 31 Dec. 1999 <http://www.seattle-pi.com/local/guns292.shtml>.

CHAPTER 7

Suburban Sprawl

THE FUTURE OF SAGUARO FLATS

Now, this is a neighborhood.

Higley Groves at Morrison Ranch will make you feel like you stepped back in time. Here, tree-lined streets wind through friendly, intimate neighborhoods reminiscent of a small town. There is a green belt between the curb and the sidewalk as well as old-town lampposts and mailboxes. And open spaces wind through the community. To add to the special neighborhood charm, you can choose from features such as front porches, courtyards, cultured stone and exterior shutters. **Higley Groves.** It's the kind of community that reminds you of how neighborhoods used to be. Come experience it for yourself.

HIGLEY & ELLIOT / MASTERPLANNED BY SHEA HOMES / WWW.SHEAHOMES.COM

Heritage at Higley Groves	Farmington at Higley Groves	Summerfield at Higley Groves
From the low 170s	From the low 120s	From the mid 130s
480-503-0363	480-503-2356	480-503-0693

◆ **FIRST IMPRESSIONS** ◆

Be sure to look at and think about the photographs that introduce this chapter. Then spend a few minutes jotting down your answers to these questions:

- The first two photographs show new housing developments growing into rural areas. Do you think such activity will improve those areas? Why or why not?
- The advertisement illustrates a community most people would like to live in, one in which "tree-lined streets wind through friendly, intimate neighborhoods reminiscent of a small town." Do you think it is worthwhile to give up rural areas so people can live in such developments? Why or why not?
- How have things changed in your neighborhood in the time you've lived there? How do you feel about those changes? Have they improved or hurt your neighborhood? How?
- How much of a voice should you have in what your neighbors do with their property?
- What do you think of environmental protection laws? Should property owners have to obey them even if it means that the value of their property will be reduced?
- If someone were proposing to build something that you considered undesirable in your neighborhood, how might you react?
- How important is it to preserve a rural lifestyle in the face of urbanization? Is the rural lifestyle outdated?
- When a community is faced with changes that some residents consider improvements and others interpret as detriments, how can people work to resolve their differences? Is resolving those differences important? Why?

When you're done, your instructor may ask you to share your comments with your classmates.

M any areas of our country are experiencing what is called urban sprawl: unmanaged rapid growth and development. In just one Arizona county last year, for instance, about 80 new homes were completed every day, for a total of more than 30,000 for the year. Nationwide in 1998, nearly 900,000 new single-family houses were constructed. Each month, Salt Lake City, Utah, converts 1,000 acres from farmland and open areas to roads and buildings. By 2020, the Salt Lake metropolitan area is expected to double in size, to more than 800 square miles.

There are some signs of change, however. Led by its mayor, Milwaukee, Wisconsin, is working to demolish its Park East Freeway: what is now pavement will become new homes and small businesses. Many cities and towns are imposing growth limits. Voters in Portland, Oregon, put in place a controversial slow-growth measure to manage and control the city's growth until the year 2040.

What's happening where you live in terms of population growth and development? What does it mean in terms of:

- *Your way of life:* Is the air you breathe getting cleaner or dirtier?
- *Traffic:* Is traffic getting heavier and more congested, or is it becoming easier to get around by car?
- *Public transportation:* Is public transit improving or deteriorating?
- *Your freeway system:* Are the highways improving or declining?

Issues related to growth and development and urban sprawl are not confined to any one part of the country, of course, and different locations may grow (or shrink) in spurts. Rapid changes make it difficult for government bodies to keep up with shifting populations and their need for services: Does our city need to expand utility (water, sewer, electric, and such) capacities on the south side of town? Does our county need a new road to the north? Does our state need more freeways, and, if so, where should we build them?

Although the scenario we present in this chapter is situated in the desert Southwest, the issues and problems you and your classmates will encounter as you work through the story are common to many places around the country—including, perhaps, your own community. Pretend now that you live in a small Arizona town. Recently, a large contracting firm purchased a tract of land near the small rural community we call Saguaro (pronounced *suh-WAR-oh*) Flats, Arizona. This developer plans to build a number of homes and apartments, a strip mall with a modern supermarket, a health center, an eighteen-hole golf course, and perhaps even several buildings to house light industry. The development will radically alter the area's rural lifestyle. There will be more traffic and pollution, certainly, but the development will also bring to the area new jobs, increased services, a broader tax base (which should mean lower taxes for everyone), and perhaps even lower prices for consumer goods such as food and clothing. Imagine that:

- You live in Saguaro Flats and you love the lifestyle: clean air, small-town environment, little traffic, and you can see a million stars at night. How would you react to news of the development?
- Three generations of your family have owned and operated a ranch near Saguaro Flats. Now you learn that the developer plans to build a golf course where you've always driven your cattle to summer grazing on the national forest property. How would you react to news of the development?
- You're a member of one of Saguaro Flats' historic preservation groups: you learn that the land the developer bought includes a large hill covered with Native American petroglyphs. How would you and other members of the group react?

- You're the owner of the land development company that recently purchased the tract of land near Saguaro Flats. What kind of new community do you hope to create in this rural area? Do you plan to optimize your profits, or are you willing to settle for less if local concerns demand it? What are some of the benefits your development will bring to Saguaro Flats?
- You're involved with several environmental organizations, including the Audubon Society and the Sierra Club. What concerns might you have for the local environment, including desert plants and wildlife, if the area is developed?

In this scenario we explore some of the issues that arise as urbanization expands into rural communities. Sometimes referred to as urban sprawl, this type of growth can spark heated debate, as ideas about progress and economic expansion come into conflict with questions about community self-determination and lifestyle. As cities grow and absorb the surrounding countryside, they bring with them the urban problems many rural residents sought to escape: overpopulation, crime, noise, and pollution. Although it's easy to think of rural areas as blank slates awaiting development, these undeveloped regions are often sites for recreation or agriculture, or perhaps they have historical significance—and many of these areas also provide important habitat for native plants and wildlife.

Although our scenario is set in a sparsely populated area in the desert Southwest, population growth and expanding urbanization are issues in many parts of the country—and, indeed, the world. As the population in an area grows or shifts, dramatic changes can occur. In a few short months what was once desert can be covered with businesses and houses, including amenities such as golf courses or artificial lakes. Although we highlight some issues of particular importance to the region in which our scenario is set, questions about the uses of private property, the pace and nature of change, the preservation of the environment, and the protection of historical sites can arise anywhere. The particulars may differ from region to region, but the basic problem remains the same: how best to balance the conflicting desires and needs of a diverse and growing population.

We will ask you and your classmates to divide into teams that represent the various groups most interested in helping to determine the future of Saguaro Flats. You'll work within these teams, collaboratively and individually, on a number of exercises that address the issues and situations that you might experience if Saguaro Flats were a real place.

This scenario can also provide a springboard for further research and discussion on a variety of topics, ranging from the significance of prehistoric Native American art to the history of private access by ranchers to land that is held in the public trust. It invites you to think about urban planning, local politics, zoning, environmental issues, civic involvement, and more. To give you a starting point, we provide a selection of readings from a variety of sources: newspapers, magazines, the Internet, and so on. The readings offer a sampling of the type of information you'd find if you were really involved in the Saguaro Flats scenario.

THE SCENARIO

The Future Arrives at Saguaro Flats

Saguaro Flats is an unincorporated, sparsely populated, rural area in Arizona's Valley of the Sun. At the center of the valley lies Phoenix, with more than two million residents, surrounded by a number of suburban communities. Because of an expanding economy, the entire region is experiencing rapid population growth. Saguaro Flats sits on the edge of this advancing urban sprawl in an area of picturesque desert beauty. Most people who live in the area own five or more acres and like the relative seclusion the area offers. Many own horses, and a few are full-time ranchers who lease nearby national forest land on which they graze their cattle. These long-time residents bought their land years before the arrival of the strip malls, whose parking lot lights now illuminate the horizon at night. Lately, the area has attracted more elderly residents, who are drawn to its healthy air and slow-paced lifestyle. At the same time, many younger residents feel they need to leave Saguaro Flats to find attractive and well-paying employment.

Bisecting this area of scrubland and cactus is Gila Creek, a seasonal watercourse through which flash floods rage during the infrequent summer rains. Big Thumb Butte towers over the other rock formations that give the community its distinctly Western character. There is no convenient freeway access, and municipal services are limited. The area is not connected to Phoenix water and sewer lines (residents have their own wells and private septic systems), and the locals haul their garbage to the dump themselves. Area children ride nearly thirty miles round-trip to school, and the nearest retail shopping of any kind is ten miles away.

Despite its secluded location, Saguaro Flats has seen several waves of immigration. Its earliest inhabitants were prehistoric native tribes who left sacred rock carvings (petroglyphs) and the nearly indistinguishable remains of a small village when they disappeared centuries ago. Anglo occupation didn't come until late in the 1800s, when settlers were attracted to the promise of valuable minerals beneath Big Thumb Butte. Prospectors met with limited success in finding silver and eventually abandoned their claims, but their pits and mine shafts still dot the butte. In the early part of the twentieth century the natural splendor of Saguaro Flats served as the backdrop for a few silent film Westerns and a matinee serial of the 1940s called *Russ Cole, Frontier Sheriff*. For a brief time Saguaro Flats bustled with the activity of moviemaking. Now, however, a few collapsing buildings are all that remain of Hollywood's fleeting interest.

The area has also become a favorite of hikers and bird watchers, both locals and tourists. Trails crisscross the flats, winding partway up Big Thumb Butte and down the length of Gila Creek, which is dry most of the year but supports an amazing diversity of plant and animal life. In addition to the increasingly scarce roadrunners, gila monsters, and rattlesnakes that are nearly synonymous with Arizona, Saguaro Flats is home to the elusive yellow-necked gnat darter, a bird that is not yet classified as endangered, but is listed as "threatened."

Saguaro Flats finally came face to face with the future when its residents learned that a development company plans to create a new community that will offer a range of living and working opportunities. The corporation feels that the scenic qualities of the area will attract new home buyers. The announcement of these plans has caused an uproar in normally sleepy Saguaro Flats.

Local residents, some of whom fear that development signals the beginning of the end for their lifestyle, have mobilized to fight the changes. They were quickly joined by the ranchers' association, which has indicated its opposition to the development plans. The ranchers are especially concerned that they could lose access to important grazing land. A number of small environmental groups have organized under the umbrella of a coalition to voice their concerns over important ecological issues. Most recently a number of environmentally concerned citizens have formed a group whose express purpose is to defend the area's archaeologically significant prehistoric sites.

Although many local residents oppose development of the Saguaro Flats area, others welcome the increased employment opportunities, access to improved health care, introduction of public transportation, and promise of lower taxes for everyone that development should bring. And there is a feeling among members of some of the other groups that a bit of development and more access to conveniences would help Saguaro Flats —and that more local jobs might allow some of the young people to remain close to their families.

The future of Saguaro Flats is far from clear. The developer's plans require changes in current zoning regulations, which restrict population density to no more than two homes per acre. Issues of waste disposal and other services, including police, fire, and education, must be decided. Even so, Maricopa County has traditionally been pro-development, and chances are good that some zoning changes will be made. Because the struggle pits a number of powerful interest groups against one another, however, the development company probably shouldn't expect to get everything it wants.

ENTERING THE SCENARIO: THOSE WERE THE GOOD OLD DAYS . . .

Now that you've read the scenario, it's time to meet the groups that are most interested in helping to determine the future of Saguaro Flats. Your instructor will ask you to join one of these groups along with several of your classmates. Although the profile of the group to which you belong will be your central concern, the descriptions of the other groups will help you understand all of the issues involved in this scenario. These descriptions are only a beginning: each group will work to develop its description and perspective based on its members' ideas about development.

The Saguaro Flats Residents

Quite simply, you live in Saguaro Flats for a reason. You want to avoid all the hazards and hassles of life in the city or suburbs, but somehow now these have managed to find you. For the past few years you've watched the city creep steadily closer, swallowing up communities like your own and replacing the local feed and tack store with a strip mall where you can buy a sixty-four ounce soft drink twenty-four hours a day. Although you hoped otherwise, you knew that someday Saguaro Flats might suffer the same fate. That day seems to have arrived.

Nothing that the development has to offer interests you at this point. The long drives to schools and shopping are inconvenient, but not seriously so, and you love the clean and clear air and the stars at night. To you, development means more traffic, more noise, and more crime. In addition to these lifestyle changes, you have real fears about the potential economic impact of high-priced housing in the area, which is likely to drive up property taxes, including your own. Even if some residents refuse to sell their land to developers, the tide of development may sweep around them and, in time, over them.

In addition to these concerns, you face the loss of control of your future: a rapidly increasing population will give new residents a strong voice in local matters, making you and other old-timers a minority. The impending development seems to signal the beginning of a long slide into just the kind of life you moved here to Saguaro Flats to avoid.

The Ranchers' Association

Until recently the ranchers' association was little more than an excuse for the dozen or so ranch families to get together every year for one heck of a barbecue. With the impending development, however, the association has become political. The area ranchers who hold grazing rights in the national forest north of the proposed development rely on a road that runs through the property. Without that road, access to good grazing would be virtually impossible, or at best prohibitively expensive. But realistically, you can't expect developers—and wealthy homeowners—to allow you to herd several thousand head of livestock over their golf course twice a year.

You are all small-time independent ranchers who survive on modest profit margins. The end of nearly free grazing might mean selling your stock to larger industrial ranching interests. In your view this would be a loss not only to your families, but also to the state, and to the West in general. You believe that you represent a way of life that embodies what is left of American frontier ideals: hard work, independence, and connection with the land. Many of you have been on your land for generations and are willing to work extremely hard to maintain your chosen lifestyle.

The Historic Preservation Coalition

The historic preservation coalition includes representatives of a number of historic preservation societies and of the Gila River, Salt River, and Fort McDowell Indian nations. These tribes trace some of their heritage to the Hohokam, an ancient tribe that left behind sacred petroglyphs before disappearing mysteriously around 1450 AD.

The Hohokam were a prehistoric Native American culture who migrated into the desert Southwest of what is now the United States in the third century BC. Making extensive use of sophisticated irrigation canals to establish large-scale agriculture, the Hohokam spread their culture through the Sonoran Desert. Although the Hohokam custom of cremating their dead has left archaeologists with limited information about the people themselves, excavations have revealed that the Hohokam excelled in the creation of ceramics and jewelry. The Hohokam traded extensively with other native tribes, and the influence of their neighbors to the south, the Maya, can be seen in the many ball courts archaeologists have discovered. The Hohokam culture reached its zenith in the fourteenth century, but disintegrated during the fifteenth century for reasons that remain unclear (changing climatic conditions may have played a role).

The historic preservation coalition is concerned about preserving and protecting the prehistoric Hohokam petroglyph sites within the development area. Current Arizona law provides no protection for such sites on private property: in past developments (by other corporations) many petroglyphs have been destroyed during construction; some were ground into gravel with other rocks, and others were moved to decorate residents' front yards.

Because the geographic location of the site is considered as sacred as the objects themselves, relocation of the petroglyphs is unacceptable. The Hohokam have disappeared, but their early settlement of the Valley of the Sun has influenced recent history. For example, the modern irrigation canals that make intensive agriculture possible in this area of sparse rainfall largely follow the Hohokam's ancient irrigation systems. If you are to succeed in achieving your goals, the coalition must help the other groups understand the critical importance of these sites while you insist on their respectful treatment by the developers.

The Environmentalists

Your group represents a number of environmental organizations, including the Audubon Society, the Sierra Club, and several smaller groups. Your primary concern is for the desert wildlife that inhabits the Saguaro Flats ecosystem. The area is home to more than three hundred species of native plants and nearly one hundred animal species, including some birds that are on the threatened, though not the endangered, species list. Many of these threatened birds live in the twisted trunks that line Gila Creek, and a few live in the ruins of the old movie set.

Your group is concerned that development of the area will increase environmental pressures beyond what the ecosystem can handle. Although many people think that desert plants and animals are hearty (surviving as they do in a harsh climate), in fact they are quite fragile. Desert plants take a long time to grow, and many desert animals require extensive areas in which to forage. You fear that development will inevitably disrupt this ecosystem's delicate balance. Indeed, possible dangers include damage to the water table, an event that could have far-ranging effects on the area's plant, animal, and human inhabitants.

Also, the area that is to be developed has long been favored by valley hikers and birders, with trails crisscrossing the landscape and winding up the butte. In fact, hikers and birders from across the country and even from abroad travel to Saguaro Flats to enjoy its natural beauty. You would like to see it stay that way.

The Development Company

As owners and employees of the development company, you see yourselves as responsible businesspeople doing what you think is right for the whole community. You have no intention of destroying the beauty of Saguaro Flats. After all, that setting is what will attract home buyers and allow you to demand premium prices for lots and houses. Of course, things will change somewhat, but that's progress. Better facilities help everyone in the long run, right? The initial plans for development of the area are sketchy because they depend on what the county board of supervisors will allow. You'd like to build several separate communities, in different price ranges; a medium-sized strip mall that offers basic support businesses, such as a supermarket, a bank, and a video store; some office space for small, service-oriented companies like insurance or real estate; and maybe even a light industrial site. You have no plans to introduce smokestack industry into the area, but perhaps some small-scale manufacturing or assembly companies could be accommodated. Over the past few years, the tourist industry has become the real growth business in Arizona, and the rugged terrain and hiking trails of Saguaro Flats are ideal for the outdoor types who frequently visit. Perhaps the development of a large guest ranch would be a profitable investment for your company.

The area's remote location may pose some problems at first, but nothing that you feel can't be overcome with careful planning. You hope to maintain a good relationship with all the local groups as you move toward development, because you realize that bad feelings on the part of any of the groups could cause expensive delays. The bottom line, however, is that you own the land and are entitled to all the rights that ownership conveys.

JOINING AND NAMING YOUR INTEREST GROUP

Now that you've read through the scenario and understand some of the interests and perspectives of the various groups, it's time for you to become actively involved. Your instructor will ask you to work with several of your classmates to role-play. In this activity, you pretend that you're a member of one of the interested groups and consider the issues from a group member's perspective. Working with several of your classmates, you'll discuss and answer questions like these:

- What issues in this scenario do you find especially interesting? What issues might concern your group more than they concern the other groups?

- What issues do you and members of your group feel less interested in?

- What other groups might share at least some of your beliefs and ideas? That is, with which other groups might you ally yourselves?

- Which groups might oppose your point of view? What objections might they have to your ideas? How might you counter those objections?

To increase your involvement with the Saguaro Flats scenario and your identification with your group, follow the instructions in Box 7.1: Naming Your Interest Group (page 282).

TAKING A POSITION: CONTACTING THE BOARD OF SUPERVISORS

For this scenario, assume that the Maricopa County Board of Supervisors has invited all interested groups to submit a two-page written statement presenting their positions on the proposed land development. The board, which is elected by the citizens of Maricopa County, is the government body that will determine exactly what the development company will be allowed to do with the land it has purchased in Saguaro Flats. It's

BOX 7.1   APPLYING WHAT YOU READ
Naming Your Interest Group

Thus far we've referred to the Saguaro Flats interest groups by generic labels: the environmentalists, the ranchers' association, and so on. Although those labels may be enough to give you a sense of each group's perspective on the Saguaro Flats situation, to really become part of the scenario, your group needs to give itself a name.

The name you decide on for your group should convey the image your group hopes to project. Naming your group also helps you control how others respond to your group's ideas. Keep in mind the associations that words have. For example, a developers' group that chooses the name Bulldozer Incorporated comes across differently from one calling itself The Sparrowhawk Company. A ranchers' group that calls itself Drive and Slaughter conveys a different image than one named Families of the Old West.

Discuss with other group members the feelings you associate with the names of real groups, and then brainstorm a list of possibilities for your scenario group. Once you've reached a consensus, share your group's new name with the other groups.

important to remember that the development company already owns the land, so some development and building will occur. It's up to the board of supervisors, with input from interested local groups, to determine exactly what that development can consist of.

RESOURCES: THE SPRAWLING OF AMERICA

As with any issue, it's important to learn what others have done in similar situations. Therefore, before you and the members of your group construct your position statement, you'll find it useful to consider what others have experienced as they confronted issues similar to those in this scenario. You may also want to interview those in your local government who are responsible for zoning regulations, to get their perspectives on the issues on which this scenario focuses.

It's important to interact actively with the selections your instructor asks you to read, and to keep in mind the reading strategies you learned earlier (prereading, annotating, summarizing, and so forth).

The readings that follow provide background information on the larger debate of which Saguaro Flats is just a small part. The debate over suburban sprawl is not new; these readings enter into an ongoing conversation about the subject. The writers explore a number of important issues, and each has a different perspective on development.

Peter Gordon and Harry W. Richardson, both planners and economists, examine the costs and benefits of sprawl, in search of a balance.

Professor of architecture Roger K. Lewis and building-industry writer David F. Seiders both look at the underlying factors that drive sprawl, whereas Linda Baker's article from the *Utne Reader* focuses more narrowly on the trend toward bigger and more opulent homes.

Brian Tokar's article explores how environmental politics shape the decisions that in turn shape development. Tokar writes regularly on environmental issues, in this instance for *Z Magazine*, which bills itself as a journal of critical thinking on political, cultural, social, and economic life in the United States.

It should be no surprise that Reed McManus's article from *Sierra* magazine addresses many of the same environmental issues as the other readings, but from a different perspective. *Business Week* outlines some new ways to combat sprawl. We again hear from planner/economist Peter Gordon in Rick Henderson and Adrian T. Moore's interview with him, in which he expands on his thoughts about market forces and urban sprawl. Finally, Bruce Katz and Jennifer Bradley's "Divided We Sprawl" from the *Atlantic Monthly* goes beyond exploring the causes of sprawl to offer a new way of thinking about the issue and an agenda to help moderate development.

As you read these articles, consider how they represent voices in a larger conversation, all presenting their interpretations of the facts and circumstances before them. Think about how you might use what these writers and others say to help shape the future of Saguaro Flats.

Following each reading you'll find a series of questions that encourage you to probe the reading and better understand the issues involved. You'll draw on what you've read later, after you complete your group statement, when you'll be asked to construct an individual writing project. As you read, think about how the group you represent might react to the arguments presented in the articles:

- From your group's perspective, what are the most important points this writer makes?
- What ideas, facts, or data in this reading might your group be able to use in your statement to the board of supervisors?
- Are there issues in any of the readings that might work against your group's position?

As you read, make note of any issues, ideas, or facts that you think might help or hurt your position so that you can address them in your writing. That information will be useful as your group composes its written statement to the board of supervisors.

◆ READINGS

 Prove It: The Costs and Benefits of Sprawl

Peter Gordon and Harry W. Richardson

Cities have been generating suburbs for as long as records have existed. Most of the world's large cities are growing outward now, and very likely the pace will accelerate in the new age of information networking. Unpopular as the word is in some quarters, it is hard to avoid concluding that "sprawl" is most people's preferred life-style. Because no one wants to appear to contradict popular choices and interfere with the principle of consumer sovereignty, the critics of sprawl instead blame distorted prices, such as automobile subsidies and mortgage interest deductions, and claimed but unregistered costs of sprawl, such as unpaid-for infrastructure, lost agricultural output, congestion, and dirty air.

The cost position, however, is encumbered with at least two problems. First, most of us are not cost minimizers. Rather, we trade off costs for perceived benefits. And second, the costs argument is empirically shaky. Traffic "doomsday" forecasts, for example, have gone the way of most other dire predictions. Why? Because suburbanization has turned out to be the traffic safety valve. Increasingly footloose industry has followed workers into the suburbs and ex-urban areas, and most commuting now takes place suburb-to-suburb on faster, less crowded roads. The last three surveys by the Nationwide Personal Transportation Survey (NPTS) show increasing average work trip speeds—28 mph in 1983, 32.3 mph in 1990, and 33.6 mph in 1995.

The alleged loss of prime farmlands is, in the words of the late Julian Simon, "the most conclusively discredited environmental-political fraud of recent times." U.S. cropland use peaked in 1930. Each year American farmers grow more crops using less land and labor.

As for the "compactness equals efficiency" argument, technological change takes us in the direction of efficient small-scale provision, weakening the old idea that scale economies of utility generation are there to be exploited by more compact urban forms. Large retail establishments, for example, can now keep low-kilowatt natural gas turbines on the premises.

U.S. public policies do not have a singular spatial thrust. Some policies, such as subsidized downtown renewal, subsidized and downtown-focused transit, subsidized downtown convention centers, sports [stadiums], and similar facilities, favor centralized settlement. Others, including inflexible zoning codes and the deductibility of mortgage interest and real estate property tax, favor dispersal.

The much vaunted subsidies to the auto-highway system consist mainly of decisions by government policymakers not to tax drivers to recover the cost of such externalities as congestion and environmental damage. And that issue recedes in importance as highway speeds increase and internal combustion engines become cleaner. The mortgage interest tax deduction raises land values throughout the metropolitan region. It has contributed much less to central-city decline than have suburban minimum lot size restrictions and poor central-city amenities. In any event, reducing subsidies makes more sense than equalizing them, as, for example, through trying to equate automobile and transit subsidies.

The evidence that has been assembled on the difficult issue of infrastructure services costs is, at best, mixed. Even if it could be conclusively demonstrated that suburban and ex-urban infrastructure costs are higher than central-city costs, the solution is not to ban suburbanization and low-density development or introduce strict growth management controls. A better approach is to use developer impact fees (fees per residential unit imposed on new development) to recoup any difference between the fiscal costs and revenues from residential development.

THE NEED FOR CLARITY

The sprawl discussion is distorted by a high degree of misinformation. To take one example, state and local growth management, "smart growth," and anti-sprawl protagonists frequently cite Los Angeles as the sprawl capital of the United States, with a land use pattern to be avoided at all costs. In fact, the urbanized area of the Los Angeles metropolitan region has the highest residential densities in the United States—higher even than the New York urbanized region—largely the result of its high land prices.

Casual observers have been deceived by looking at only the gross densities based on all the land area, much of which consists of vast unbuildable areas such as mountains and peripheral deserts. Another false conception is that suburban areas are dominated by single-family homes on large lots. In fact, the suburban and ex-urban "attached house" share of the metropolitan housing stock is about 50 percent. Of the nation's presumably higher-density attached housing, then, half is located outside central cities.

Increasingly, the attack on sprawl is being justified by the need to achieve the goal of "sustainable urbanization." But no one has defined the term satisfactorily. Rather, the talk is of recycling, increasing densities, and promoting transit as instruments for preserving resources for future use. The concern for future generations that sustainability implies gives insufficient weight to today's problems of poverty and inequality. In the words of Nobel Prize–winning economist Robert Solow, "There is at least as strong a case for reducing contemporary inequality (and probably stronger) as for worrying about the uncertain status of future generations." In our view, these problems cannot be alleviated significantly via the social engineering of urban space.

Some observers see compact and high-rise development as an accommodation to inferior forms of transportation that have been eclipsed by the automobile. The universal choice is for the freedom and flexibility that come only with personal transportation. Collective transportation loses in any head-to-head contest, as the widespread operations of large numbers of clandestine "gypsy" cabs and vans above one of the world's premier subway systems in New York City make clear. Even in New York, many origins and destinations are too dispersed to be serviced by fixed-route systems. The record of conventional transit throughout the United States is the same theme writ large. After hundreds of billions of dollars of public subsidy, transit use per capita is now at a historic low. The evolution of American cities and life-styles has outgrown 19th-century-style urban transit. Ironically, the mass transit favored by anti-sprawl activists—street cars, subways, and urban rail systems of earlier days—was the prime instrument of suburbanization. The automobile merely diversified its radial pattern.

And though mass transit supporters argue for higher densities to reduce congestion and improve air quality, in fact the relationship between density and traffic congestion is positive rather than negative, and the link between congestion and air quality is very complex and highly technical.

In the end, the goals of the anti-sprawl position are unattainable. Opportunities for in-fill development in central cities exist, but they are limited. There is a small, if growing, scattering of compact new developments in the suburban and, more often, ex-urban environments, but their impact on anti-sprawl goals is minimal. There is, for example, no evidence that they reduce off-site trips. Any reasonable assumptions about the extent of future compact developments must yield the conclusion that their influence on tomorrow's urban landscape is minuscule.

Proponents of the New Urbanism claim the ability to design community-friendly neighborhoods, thus joining the movement to revive communitarianism. While there is a lively debate over the current state of civil society (as the contributors to this Review's fall 1997 issue make clear), the case of the New Urbanists is much less clear. Residential developments and whole neighborhoods are being supplied by market-savvy builders attentive to the trade-offs that their customers are eager to make. People in compact communities live as privately as those in low-density suburbs. Were people to demand cozier spatial arrangements, they would soon get them. Moreover, the public's demand for "community" is being met in other ways, facilitated by the auto and even Internet access. In terms of transportation, we know that the overwhelming amount of travel is non-work travel. About one-fifth of person-trips are for work-related purposes, one-fifth are for shopping, and three-fifths are for "social" reasons (including the NPTS categories "other family and personal business," "school/church," "visit friends or relatives," and "other social or recreational" purposes).

DEALING WITH THE COSTS OF SPRAWL

We are not advocating a "laissez-faire" approach to the development of our cities. Cities are, almost by definition, the cause of myriad unintended costs. Many problems (not all) can, and should, be resolved by low-cost negotiation between the affected parties (for example, developers and environmentalists) or by the exchange of expanded property rights (using such measures as emission fees, congestion prices, and development credits). The more radical measures proposed by critics of American cities—maximum densities, restrictions on automobile use, and mandatory fees and taxes to pay for transit—are grounded in misconceptions and are unlikely to achieve their stated goals.

The principle of consumer sovereignty has played a powerful role in the increase in America's wealth and in the welfare of its citizens. Producers (including developers) have responded rapidly to households' demands. It is a giant step backward to interfere with this effective process unless the benefits of intervention substantially exceed its costs. Bans on the amount of land that individuals can consume, or even worse, on driving, are extremely difficult to justify. In fact, when households purchase a single-family home in the suburbs, they are not consuming land per se. Rather, they are buying a number of attributes—good public schools, relative safety from crime, easy access to recreation and shopping opportunities, low taxes, responsive public services. Lot size is rarely crucial to the decision. In any event, lot sizes are becoming smaller as a result of rising land prices, and there may be opportunities for developers through creative design to reduce lot sizes still further while preserving privacy. But smaller lots are not going to revive the central city or alter significantly the consequences of suburban and ex-urban development.

Paradoxically, as the U.S. political system increasingly emphasizes deregulation and market processes at the federal, and sometimes the state, level, command-and-control restrictions and interest-group impositions at the local level are growing and are frequently being reinforced by actions in the courts. Much of this shift, exemplified by the expansion of land use regulations, reflects a retargeting of regulatory activity from economic sectors to such social concerns as education, health, and the environment. But for the cost-benefit calculus advocated by the anti-sprawl protagonists to prevail, the quality of their empirical evidence must be improved.

◆ **QUESTIONS FOR DISCUSSION AND WRITING** ◆

1. Gordon and Richardson reason that many of the traditional arguments against sprawl are unfounded. Is their reasoning convincing? Why or why not?
2. Were you surprised to learn that Los Angeles has a higher residential population density than New York? If that statement leaves you skeptical, what would it take to convince you?
3. What is New Urbanism, and what role does it play in the urban sprawl debate?
4. The article's title indicates that its authors see at least some benefits of sprawl. According to Gordon and Richardson, what benefits does sprawl bring? Do you agree or disagree that these are in fact benefits?

❋ A Call to Stop Buying Into Sprawl

Roger K. Lewis

"Gore Proposal Aims to Tame Urban Sprawl" reported the *Washington Post* headline early last week [February 1999] after the vice president announced the "Better America Bonds" initiative to be included in the fiscal 2000 federal budget. The proposed $10 billion bond program is intended "to help communities preserve green space, reduce traffic congestion, protect water quality and clean up abandoned industrial sites."

According to the *Post* report, 15-year Better America Bonds, issued by local governments after review and approval by the Environmental Protection Agency and other authorities, would be bought by investors who would receive tax credits instead of interest payments. Thus, state and local governments would be able to borrow funds for open-space acquisition and environmental preservation projects without incurring interest costs.

But take a close look at what sprawl really is all about and what this budget proposal—and the political tide on which it is riding—really mean.

Sprawl is a code word. It refers generally to patterns of land development, mostly appearing since World War II, either surrounding traditional cities and towns established in the 19th century or constituting substantially all of the fabric of America's newer, 20th-century cities. No matter where you look, metropolitan sprawl has several distinct and common characteristics:

- Sprawl around a city consists primarily of hundreds of separate, physically autonomous residential subdivisions developed at relatively low densities, rarely exceeding four dwellings an acre.

- These low-density residential neighborhoods are made up almost exclusively of single-family, detached homes on lots with frontage along local, discontinuous streets or cul-de-sacs. Sprinkled here and there at slightly higher densities may be enclaves of apartments or town houses.

- With a few exceptions, sprawling subdivisions are accessible only by way of a branching system of local feeder roads, primarily collectors and arterial highways. Such a hierarchial system of roads, offering few alternative routes between point A and point B, is unable to absorb all the vehicles crowding each year onto its fixed number of travel lanes.

- Normally occurring after residential development has taken root in an area, commercial growth forms "strips" along arterial and collector roads. Each parcel along a strip, like each residential subdivision, typically is developed independently, with little or no physical, functional or aesthetic relationship to adjoining developments. Surface parking lots engulf the buildings. When there are enough residential "rooftops" within reasonable driving distance, a regional shopping mall or office park appears.

- Automobiles are the only practical mode of transportation. Amid sprawl, almost no one travels by foot, even for short trips to local destinations. Sidewalks, crosswalks and pedestrian walk lights are rare.

- In Sprawlsville it is difficult, if not impossible, to formulate a cohesive physical image or picture of the community, to identify tangible elements—public spaces, buildings, civic landmarks, streets and recognizable street-scape patterns—that make a place recognizable and unique. A community of people and activities exists, but not of form.

But what we pejoratively call sprawl didn't occur by accident or neglect, nor is it something malevolently propagated by land developers and 5 home builders. It is entirely market-driven, the direct consequence of a majority of Americans making choices about how they want to live, choices facilitated by economic, physical and social circumstances.

Sprawl couldn't occur without inexpensive gasoline, affordable automobiles, extensive road and highway building, cheap and ample supplies of land, readily available mortgage financing and favorable zoning ordinances. Sprawl reflects public will and public policy.

Above all, sprawl happens in response to the aspirations of American families seeking what they perceive to be the individualist, utopian ideal: owning a house on a piece of land—a small estate, but still an estate. This aspiration, rooted in our agrarian history, remains deeply engrained in our culture and psyche.

Therefore, America is confronted with a paradox. On the one hand, the physical product sought by the majority of the market, America's home buyers, generates sprawl. On the other hand, homeowners in America's suburbs, finally recognizing and suffering from the negative effects of sprawl, are searching for antidotes. Among the antidotes frequently proposed is to close the door, as if to say to those with the same aspirations: "We've got ours, but you can't have yours." And one way to close the door is to stop growth by preserving open space that might otherwise be developed.

Thus the real question is how to resolve this paradox, this conflict between aspirations, in a manner that is both fair and cost-effective. Across a continent, how much can $10 billion for open-space acquisition ultimately contribute to taming urban sprawl?

Preserving natural open space is a very desirable goal for a number 10 of valid reasons other than curtailing sprawl. It safeguards wetlands and watersheds, geological and soil resources, vegetation, wildlife habitats, scenic landscapes and the atmosphere itself. In the form of public parks, it provides places for diverse recreational activities.

Yet preserving open space should be but one part of more comprehensive national and local strategies. In the long run, the only real solution lies in convincing the market, through a combination of education, persuasion and wiser land-use planning and regulation, that there are viable and desirable alternatives to conventional, sprawl-generating patterns of development.

Increasing numbers of Americans must come to understand that the utopian ideal is not so ideal after all. They must learn that higher density is not intrinsically bad and that residing in cities and towns can be the most civilized way to live. Of course, such cultural and psychic shifts will occur only if people perceive that critical urban problems that historically drove them into sprawling suburbs—poor schools, crime, lack of employment—have diminished significantly.

The Better America Bonds initiative is at best a Band-Aid. America's environment cannot be protected, or growth pressures relieved, just by buying privately owned parcels of open space piecemeal.

But the public, whether or not it buys open space, must be willing to stop buying into sprawl. This is the great challenge in creating a "better America."

1. Lewis argues that sprawl is a result of Americans' "utopian" desires to own a house and a piece of land. In what ways is this a utopian dream? Does home ownership fulfill this dream?
2. Outline what you see as the most important of Lewis's ideas, and discuss whether they will work.
3. After reading Lewis's ideas, do you think people will act in the interest of others, or will they pursue their own interests regardless of the cost to others' well-being? Why?
4. The author believes that one solution to sprawl is to educate potential home buyers about it. What incentives might help to convince people to accept higher density housing?

✳ McMansion Mania

WE'RE SUPERSIZING IN THE SUBURBS, AND WE CAN'T SEEM TO STOP

Linda Baker

On Northwest Skyline Boulevard overlooking Portland, Oregon, a French country manor sits majestically atop a 25-acre hillside, offering 360-degree views of the mountains and the Willamette Valley. The 6,000-square-foot house features a two-story entryway, copper roof, four bedrooms, six bathrooms, and a "great room" boasting a 25-foot ceiling. "We wanted to be able to accommodate all the features we needed in a house," says the Portland home owner.

If you continue along Skyline to Thompson Road, you'll come to Phase Seven of the Forest Heights Development. Rising from the steep hillside are several dozen contemporary mansions with five bedrooms, five baths, multiple decks, and price tags ranging from $600,000 to $800,000. "These are people's dream homes," says Lydia Dobranski, a Forest Heights resident who owns Edgewater Homes, a building company.

Not everyone has the same vision of the American Dream. Whether they're McMansions or architect-designed estates, megahouses are ostentatious symbols of America's class divide. Their proliferation and the decline of affordable housing in the United States are simultaneous trends that underscore the polarization of the American class structure in the year of the 10,000-plus Dow. But megahouses do more than reflect inequitable division of wealth. As noted by critic James Howard Kunstler, author of *The Geography of Nowhere: The Rise and Decline of America's Man-Made Landscape* (Touchstone, 1994), supersized homes reflect a fundamental problem with American culture: impoverishment of the public sphere and glorification of the private. "In these large houses people are compensating for the lack of a meaningful public realm or public places," Kunstler says. "It's especially characteristic of suburbia that the private realm is luxurious and the public realm is squalid."

Wealthy home owners and palatial residences always have been a part of the American mystique. But at the end of the millennium, the megahouse has gone mainstream. Over the past 50 years, average house size has gone from 1,100 square feet (the size of homes in Levittown, New York, the original carburb) to 2,200 square feet. And that's just the average. Thirty percent of new homes in the United States are more than 2,400 square feet, compared to 18 percent in 1986. These huge homes, which often sell for more than $750,000, have become a trend mostly in suburban areas of large cities. So prevalent are megahomes that the Campbell-Ewald Reference Center put "McMansion Mania" at the top of its list of 10 social change indicators for 1998.

At the far end of the megahouse spectrum are the mansions that rival the temples to commerce built for '20s-era business barons: Bill Gates' $50 million, 40,000-square-foot palace, for example, or Amway distributor Terry McEwen's 25,000-square-foot estate. "There's more wealth in big cities today than there has been since the turn of the century," says Pat Ritz, president of Oregon Title Company, who also helps write quarterly reports on housing trends. "People don't want to just get in the bathtub with it. They want new homes, country estates with whips and spurs. That's what megahouses are all about." 5

Bill Schweinfurth, chief operating officer of Vedder Community Management, a mobile-home-park management company based in Burbank, California, and his wife, Maggie, are a typical megahouse family. After moving to Portland from Los Angeles two years ago, the Schweinfurths built a 4,200-square-foot home on their 2-acre lot off Skyline Boulevard. Admitting that they hardly ever use the living and dining rooms, Maggie Schweinfurth says owning a four-bedroom, five-bathroom home is about the little luxuries space affords. Big closets mean she never has to put away off-season clothes; a second laundry room makes washing a breeze. And the bathrooms? "One for the kids, one for the master bedroom, a powder bath for entertaining, and one for the guest room." The only superfluous not-quite-bathroom, she muses, is off the mud room—the area leading to the backyard. The shower for the dog, she adds, was her husband's idea.

This unabashed materialism makes large homes an easy target for class grievance. The size of the megahouse is especially difficult to stomach given that average U.S. family size continues to decline. Yet a far more complex issue is the relationship between the rise of the megahouse and the decline of affordable housing—dual trends set in motion by gentrification, inequitable housing subsidies, and exclusionary zoning laws. "The people willing to spend the kind of money these mansions cost inflate land values," says Tasha Harmon, an affordable-housing advocate and member of the steering committee of the Coalition for a Livable Future in Oregon. "The people who want to do the right thing—build smaller, more affordable homes—can't afford the price of land."

Consider the striking disparity between housing subsidies for wealthy and low-income households. According to the National Low Income Housing Coalition, an estimated 18 percent of this fiscal year's total housing subsidies will go to households with an average annual income of just under $9,000. By contrast, an estimated 63 percent of total housing subsidies will go to households with an average income of $123,000 or more. Many suburban municipalities also favor large homes; zoning codes in most wealthy suburban neighborhoods establish minimum lot sizes with two-car garages and limit or outlaw smaller houses and multifamily dwellings.

These policies, in effect, have made affordable housing obsolete. Demolition, gentrification, and sprawl reduced the number of affordable, low-cost unsubsidized housing units available by 19 percent between 1996 and 1998. Subsidized housing suffered a similar fate. In 1998 alone, 13,000 subsidized units were lost as private landlords quit the project-based Section 8 program in search of higher, market-rate rents. As a result, waiting lists for subsidized housing increased by as much as 25 percent between 1998 and 1999. Today, more than 2 million families wait an average of two and a half years for subsidized housing—seven to ten years in major cities such as New York, Houston, and Los Angeles.

The detrimental effect megahouses have on affordable housing is symptomatic of larger problems of livability in suburbia. If suburban zoning codes encourage megahouses, they also encourage auto-based sprawl and decimation of green space by restricting pedestrian-friendly, mixed-use development. The Congress for the New Urbanism (CNU), a San Francisco–based organization that pushes for changes in development policy, puts it this way: "Disinvestment in central cities, the spread of placeless sprawl, increasing separation by race and income, loss of agricultural lands and wilderness, and the erosion of society's built heritage [are] one interrelated community-building challenge."

In the past decade, the relationship between community and public space has become a recurring theme in architecture and urban planning. There is no "third place" in contemporary American life, wrote critic Ray Oldenberg 10 years ago, "no public places that host the regular, voluntary, informal, happily anticipated gatherings of individuals beyond the realms of home and work." So sterile is the contemporary subdivision, he wrote, that it "cries out for something as modest as a central mail drop or a little coffee counter at which those in the area might discover one another."

New urbanist architects Andres Duany and Peter Calthorpe have tried to revitalize suburbia by designing compact residential/retail developments organized around clear public centers: parks, libraries, and town squares. The new urbanist logic is compelling, as it sheds light on super-sized homes as the product of both cultural and economic forces. To understand the distinction, says Shelley Poticha, CNU executive director, compare today's big houses with the wealthy neighborhoods built around the turn of the century. "Areas like the Country Club District in Kansas City and Forest Hills Gardens in New York were built on the model of a classic American neighborhood. They had a beautiful sense of civic infra-structure," Poticha says. "There are mansions, but more modest houses are also interspersed. All the houses faced onto the street, and you could walk to shops and parks, in many cases even catch a train into the city." By contrast, she says, the dominant feature of today's megahouses is that they are inwardly directed: "They don't qualify as neighborhoods. Every-one just wants a piece of the rock."

Opulent residences have existed in various forms throughout his-tory, Kunstler argues. What is truly characteristic of our age is that luxury homes represent the demise of "the part of our everyday world that be-longs to everybody." This distinction between community-driven turn-of-the-century affluence and sterile megahouse developments may strike some as elitist or merely nostalgic. Yet today's architecture of isolation undeniably shapes and reflects the lifestyles of the people who live in the megahouses, shop in the strip malls, and work at the business parks. "Most of my neighbors are corporate executives who will have to relocate in a couple of years. There's not a real strong sense of neighborhood," says Phil Bennett, a lawyer who lives with his wife, Laurie, in a brand-new megahouse development in Portland. COO Bill Schweinfurth spends only half of each month in his Portland residence; the other half he's in Cali-fornia on business.

The megahouse distorts two cherished American ideals: privacy and property. As the logical outgrowth of policies that have eroded public and green spaces, the megahouse is a fortress standing guard in a wasteland. This begs several questions: What form will U.S. housing patterns assume in the next century? Will land scarcity compel policy makers and planners to perfect evolving models of cluster housing and encourage both smaller houses and smaller lots? Or will housing policies continue to reflect con-temporary divisions between rich and poor, public and private?

One thing is certain: The megahouse ideology won't be easy to dis- 15 mantle. Gesturing toward the 3,500-square-foot, four-bedroom, four-bath home she and her husband bought a couple of years ago, Portland retiree Judy Lawrence explains the purchase this way: "We downsized," she says seriously. "The house we raised our children in was much bigger."

◆ QUESTIONS FOR DISCUSSION AND WRITING ◆

1. By simply describing a house, what point does Baker make in her opening paragraph?
2. What specific word choices does Baker make that help you to identify her feel-ings about her subject? How effective is her use of words?
3. Baker argues that the rage for large houses distorts the American ideals of pri-vacy and property. How might the purchase of a house, which seems to embody ideals of privacy and property, be a distortion of them?

4. What does Baker's final paragraph convey about her feelings about mega-houses? How does Baker convey those feelings without including her own observations?
5. How do you feel about the "mania" for big houses?

✳ Questioning Official Environmentalism

Brian Tokar

Seven years ago in these pages, we launched an in-depth investigation of the mainstream environmental movement. The occasion was the widely publicized 20th anniversary of the original Earth Day, an event which in many ways helped institutionalize the widespread corporate co-optation of environmental themes.

The year 1990 was an auspicious one for environmental activists in the United States. The widespread popularity of environmental concerns was reflected in the rapid growth of environmental organizations, the appearance of new publications, and some of the first glossy catalogs of environmental products. Expressions of concern for the environment adorned politicians' stump speeches, both in the U.S. and overseas. Environmental scientists and activists widely agreed that the 1990s were a critical decade to stem the course of environmental degradation, and political and cultural trends offered many people a renewed hope that this was possible.

Still, the coming Earth Day celebrations aroused a curious mixture of hope and cynicism on the part of longtime activists. The cynicism was fueled by much of the literature emanating from the official Earth Day organizations that had been established throughout the country. They had apparently decided that Earth Day was going to be a politically safe event, with almost no attention toward the institutions or the economic system responsible for ecocide, nothing about confronting corporate polluters, nothing about changing the structures of society. The overriding message was simply, "change your lifestyle": recycle, drive less, stop wasting energy, buy better appliances, etc. Celebrations in several major U.S. cities were supported by some of the most notorious corporate polluters—companies like Monsanto, Peabody Coal, and Georgia Power, to name a few. Everyone from the nuclear power industry to the Chemical Manufacturers' Association took out full-page advertisements in newspapers and magazines proclaiming that, for them, "Every day is Earth Day." The now-familiar greenwashing of Earth Day had clearly begun.

Activists across the country began exploring the origins of Earth Day and also mainstream environmental groups that were making the most hay of this anniversary. What they found was a mixed message: while Earth Day had for many come to symbolize the emergence of environmentalism as a social movement in its own right, it was dominated from the very beginning by those who hoped to dilute the movement's political focus. In 1970, *Ramparts* magazine, one of the New Left's leading journals of opinion, called Earth Day, "the first step in a con game that will do little more than abuse the environment even further." Journalist I. F. Stone, in his investigative weekly, took a significantly harsher view: ". . . just as the Caesars once used bread and circuses so ours were at last learning to use rock-and-roll idealism and non-inflammatory social issues to turn the youth off from more urgent concerns which might really threaten the power structure."

Many activists responded by organizing more politicized local Earth   5
Days of their own. These events focused on local environmental struggles, inner city issues, the nature of corporate power and other concerns that had been largely excluded from the official Earth Day events. The most ambitious was a demonstration in New York City called by members of the Youth Greens and Left Greens, with the aid of environmental justice activists, Earth First!ers, ecofeminists, urban squatters, and many others. Early Monday morning, April 23, 1990, the day after millions had participated in feel-good Earth Day commemorations, several hundred people converged on the nerve center of U.S. capitalism, the New York Stock Exchange, with the goal of obstructing the opening of trading on that day. New York *Daily News* columnist Juan Gonzalez told his 1.2 million readers, "Certainly, those who sought to co-opt Earth Day into a media and marketing extravaganza, to make the public feel good while obscuring the corporate root of the Earth's pollution almost succeeded. It took angry Americans from places like Maine and Vermont to come to Wall Street on a workday and point the blame where it belongs."

CHALLENGING THE MAINSTREAM

The events around Earth Day 1990 helped provoke an unprecedented scrutiny of the habits and institutions of environmental politics in the United States. Growing numbers of activists began to see the best-known national environmental organizations, which had long dominated media coverage, fundraising and public visibility—the voices of "official environmentalism"—as hopelessly out of step with the thousands of volunteers who largely define the leading edge of locally based ecological activism.

Throughout the 1970s and 1980s, representatives of environmental groups, from the National Wildlife Federation to the Sierra Club, had become an increasingly visible and entrenched part of the Washington political scene. As the appearance of success within the system grew, organizations restructured and altered their personnel so as to enhance their ability to play the insider game. The environmental movement became a stepping stone in the careers of a new generation of Washington lawyers and lobbyists, and official environmentalism came to accept the role long established for other public regulatory advocates: that of helping to sustain the smooth functioning of the existing political system. Environmentalism was redefined, in the words of author and historian Robert Gottlieb, as "a kind of interest group politics tied to the maintenance of the environmental policy system."

The mainstream groups grew especially rapidly during the late 1980s. The Sierra Club grew from 80,000 to 630,000 members, and the conservative National Wildlife Federation reported membership gains of up to 8,000 a month, totaling nearly one million. The World Wildlife Fund, best known for its efforts to establish national parks on the U.S. model in Third World countries, grew almost tenfold, while the Natural Resources Defense Council (NRDC) had doubled its membership since 1985. The total budget of the ten largest environmental groups grew from less than $10 million in 1965, to $218 million in 1985 and $514 million in 1990. Journalist Mark Dowie discovered that of the approximately $3 billion contributed to environmental advocates each year, the 25 largest organizations get 70 percent, while the remaining share is divided among some 10,000 smaller, more local groups. Many groups have become extremely dependent on direct mail, using each new environmental disaster to gain members for their organization, whether the organization was meaningfully addressing the issue or not.

In light of these developments, activists began to investigate environmental movement using the tools of corporate research. An examination of the Annual Reports of the major environmental organizations revealed an extent of overt corporate influence upon the leading national environmental groups that surprised all but the most jaded activists. Almost all of the leading groups were receiving substantial contributions from the most polluting corporations. Many had restructured their operations so as to become more attractive to such donors, and the National Wildlife Federation, in particular, saw "dialogue" with "key industrial leaders" as a central part of its mission. Few were surprised when NWF later became the first U.S. environmental group to support the North American Free Trade Agreement.

Others began examining the boards of directors of the leading environmental groups. *The Multinational Monitor* found that 23 directors and council members from Audubon, NRDC, the Wilderness Society, the World Resources Institute, and World Wildlife Fund were associated with 19 corporations cited in a recent survey of the 500 worst industrial polluters. These companies included such recognized environmental offenders as Union Carbide, Exxon, Monsanto, Weyerhaeuser, DuPont, and Waste Management, Inc. Furthermore, some 67 individuals associated with just 7 environmental groups served as CEOs, chairpersons, presidents, consultants or directors for 92 major corporations.

Feminist environmentalist Joni Seager surveyed 30 leading environmental groups and found that only three (the National Audubon Society, Earth Island Institute, and WorldWatch Institute) had even 30 percent

10

female members on their boards. Women, in most mainstream groups, remain relegated to traditionally female administrative roles, and none of 30 groups she surveyed had more than 5 staff members from any racial minority. Seager described the widening schism in the environmental movement as "increasingly between a mostly male-led professional elite and a mostly female-led grassroots movement." A widely quoted 1990 letter, initiated by Richard Moore of New Mexico's Southwest Organizing Project and signed by 100 leading community activists, criticized the dearth of people of color on the boards and staff of the major environmental groups, as well as these groups' growing reliance on corporate funding.

THE SAGA CONTINUES

Today, analyses of the political and financial ties that have corrupted mainstream environmentalism have become almost commonplace. Mainstream journalists, business schools, and even anti-environmental "wise use" organizations have published their own studies of environmental groups' finances, and have used the data to support their own often questionable political agendas. As the largest environmental groups came to resemble the corporations they opposed, this kind of research found uses well across the political spectrum. While grassroots activists view corporate contributions as a symbol of co-optation, and of the dangers inherent in a strategy of working entirely within the existing political system, those seeking to discredit environmental protection see these contributions as evidence for simple corruption, greed, and a cynical response to changing public opinion. Anti-environmental advocates have articulated a rather distorted theory of the decline of mainstream environmentalism, asserting despite all evidence to the contrary that the mainstream groups are bound to an "extremist" agenda which is at odds with the views of a majority of the public.

For example, the Washington-based Environmental Working Group reported in July of last year on the annual lobbying week of the virulently anti-environmental Alliance for America. Amidst presentations by oil industry lobbyists, property rights agitators, and House Speaker Newt Gingrich, was a talk by Jonathan Adler of the well-endowed anti-environmental think tank, the Competitive Enterprise Institute. Adler described his own version of a split between "Big Green" and the "grassroots," in which dependence on direct mail, foundation support, and government grants are signs of dwindling "grassroots" support for an environmental agenda.

In 1994, the Center for the Study of American Business at Washington University in St. Louis examined the established environmental groups' stock portfolios, ostensibly developed as a hedge against fluctuating memberships, and found that the Wilderness Society, for example, held stock in Dow Chemical, Kerr McGee, and General Motors, and the

NRDC in Dow, Westinghouse, and General Electric. For organizations committed to protecting the environment and combating pollution to become financially dependent on the stock values of major polluters may represent the ultimate corruption of ecological values. The same study confirmed that membership dues represented an ever declining share of the income of groups like the Wilderness Society and National Audubon. But while the political influence wielded by these groups has fallen considerably since the early 1900s, income and membership levels have in most cases only leveled off, or continued to rise at a slower rate.

Though corporate contributions rarely represent a very large overall share of the budgets of the best known environmental groups, they have conferred influence and political results well beyond their statistical measure. As Brian Lipsett, a leading researcher and editor for the environmental justice movement has written, "The corporations get a good return from their contributions to environmental causes. . . . Beyond public relations dividends and tax deductions, and even increased business opportunities, corporate sponsorship fractures internal consensus within recipient groups, divides grantees from other environmental groups, blunts criticism from grantee groups, and creates openings for future influence by securing corporate representation on the groups' boards of directors." This helps explain why corporations give to environmental organizations at nearly two and a half times the rate of overall public charitable donations to the environmental movement. Environmental giving amounts to 6 percent of corporate philanthropy, while it only accounts for 2.5 percent of all charitable donations.

My review of the 1993 and 1994 Annual Reports of some of the best known environmental groups revealed a generally higher level of corporate influence than existed five years earlier. For example, the National Audubon Society, with similar budget totals and share of member contributions as in 1988, had expanded its list of corporate donors to include large gifts from Bechtel, AT&T, Citibank, Honda, Martin Marietta, Wheelabrator, Ciba-Geigy, Dow, and Scott Paper, with smaller donations (less than $5,000) from Monsanto, Mobil, and Shell Oil. The Audubon Society's major capital project, the conversion of an historic building in New York's Greenwich Village to a new Society headquarters—and a showcase of energy efficiency and recycled materials use—was supported by grants of over $100,000 each from WMX (formerly Waste Management, Inc.) and Wheelabrator. The former is the world's largest processor of toxic chemical waste, and has been the subject of numerous bribery and antitrust convictions, as well as countless environmental violations. The latter is a leading supplier of incinerator technologies that have been widely opposed by activists across the country due to serious environmental and public health concerns.

The World Wildlife Fund's corporate contributors are now led by the likes of the Bank of America, Kodak, and J. P. Morgan (over $250,000), with the Bank of Tokyo, Philip Morris, WMX, DuPont, and numerous others playing supporting roles. Its budget grew from $17 million in 1985 to

$62 million in 1993, with roughly half of its revenues coming from individual contributions. The National Wildlife Federation's budget had increased by more than 50 percent since 1988, to $96 million in 1994. Major corporate donors included Bristol Myers Squibb, Ciba-Geigy, DuPont, and Pennzoil, and an additional 161 companies participated in the federation's matching gift program, in which individuals' gifts to the organization are matched by their employer. Other organizations, such as the Sierra Club, have made contributor information more difficult to obtain, but it is noteworthy that their annual budget had leveled off at $39 million, after peaking at $52 million in 1991. Membership dues had fallen to 32 percent of the Sierra Club's annual budget, half of the 1988 figure.

THE MONEY CHASE

One consistent factor in the institutionalization of official environmentalism has been the role of influential foundations in helping to frame the agendas of the leading organizations. Large foundations like the Ford Foundation and the various Rockefeller funds played a forceful role in the development of environmental organizations since the 1940s, leading some 1960s activists to dismiss environmental concerns as a mere creation of corporate philanthropists.

Foundations often play a controversial role in movements for social change. Organizations that wish to sustain themselves over time, initiate new projects, and offer salaries to staff members invariably need to attract large donations, and the established foundations have long been the most available source of these. Political scientist Joan Roelofs has demonstrated the role of foundations in the decline of 1960s-era activism, arguing that grants were systematically allocated to assure "that radical energies were being channeled into safe, legalistic, bureaucratic and occasionally profit-making activities." This pattern has been repeated in anti-poverty groups, women's groups, and in the African American, Latino, and Native American communities, as well as in the environmental movement.

In the 1990s, large donors have begun to intervene more directly to set the course of environmental activism. For example, a $275,000 grant to the Sierra Club in 1990 to support work on population issues made population advocacy the highest-funded program in the Club's budget. This raised concern among activists who feared the effort would inadvertently support the rising wave of anti-immigration sentiment that was just beginning to sweep the country. In 1993, officers of the Pew Charitable Trusts brought together representatives from some of the leading regional and national forest protection groups in an effort to create a unified nationwide forest campaign. While the participants initially seized the opportunity to help develop such a unified effort, they soon learned that Pew had a very particular agenda in mind.

"Pew was only interested in funding a campaign focused on legislation that would be passed by a Democratic Congress and that Clinton would sign," explains Andy Mahler of the Indiana-based Heartwood organization, who served as an interim chair of the effort. Pew expressed little interest in aiding ongoing efforts at grassroots organizing, public education, or legal intervention by the member groups, suggesting to many that the potential effectiveness of the campaign was merely a secondary concern.

Ultimately, Pew put its resources into a series of regional, rather than national efforts. One of these was in the Northeastern states, where a two-year Congressional study had failed to raise sufficient political momentum for the protection of the endangered Northern Forest region. Representatives of mainstream environmental groups and leading foundations created the Northern Forest Alliance, with a stated mission of protecting the forests of northern New England and New York, while promoting economic diversification. Groups in the region that depend on foundation grants were subsequently pressured to join the Alliance, and mute their criticisms of its rather bland, non-controversial, and rather piecemeal approach to the environmental health of a region that is threatened with significant, short-term increases in destructive logging and commercial development.

The 1994 Annual Report of the Pew Charitable Trusts, describes the strategy behind these efforts. A "team of professionals," the report declares, stands behind the Trusts' environmental programs. This team, consisting of lawyers, scientists, and outside consultants, will "play a key role in generating many of the ideas behind the programs we support, participating with colleagues from the environmental community in defining the goals and objectives of these programs, designing their operating structures, hiring key staff and, in some cases, being directly involved in program execution."

Investigative journalist Stephan Salisbury of the *Philadelphia Inquirer* described the strategy of a growing sector of leading environmental funders when he described Pew's having "created and funded dozens of programs and independent organizations to carry out agendas determined by the foundation and its consultants. It has promoted its own causes, pursued its own initiatives, bankrolled its own research and imposed its own order." Salisbury, writing in Pew's home city of Philadelphia, examined the Trusts' increasingly controversial activities in areas from journalism and school reform to tourism marketing and restructuring local arts organizations, as well as in the environmental movement. He described Pew's overall philosophy as "professionalized, self-promoting corporate liberalism."

In 1995, Northwest forest activist and journalist Jeffrey St. Clair joined with Alexander Cockburn to investigate the stock holdings of the three foundations that play the largest institutional role in supporting mainstream environmentalism. The three foundations, each the product of leading transnational oil fortunes, are the Pew Charitable Trusts (Sun Oil Co.), W. Alton Jones Foundation (Cities Service/CITGO), and the Rockefeller Family Fund. St. Clair and Cockburn found that the Pew endowment, with a total of $3.8 billion in holdings, is heavily invested in timber firms, mining companies, arms manufacturers, and chemical companies, as well as oil exploration. Alton Jones' timber investments include a subsidiary of the notorious Maxxam conglomerate, which is attempting to liquidate the largest single expanse of old growth redwood forest that remains in private hands, along with Louisiana Pacific, the largest purchaser of timber from the National Forests. The foundation also holds a $1 million share in the controversial gold mining giant, the FMC Corporation. The Rockefeller fund holds investments in no less than 28 oil and gas development companies, as well as timber giants Weyerhaeuser and Boise Cascade. St. Clair and Cockburn traced a number of instances in which environmental compromises engineered by the Clinton administration, and by groups such as the Wilderness Society, directly benefited these foundations' holdings.

THE NATIONALS RESPOND

The mid-1990s saw the beginnings of a shakeup at the top among some of the largest Washington-based environmental groups. In some cases it was a response to persistent grassroots criticism; more often it was a reflection of the persistent decline in the influence of the environmental movement in Washington. This loss of influence began well before the Republican takeover of Congress in 1994, and has been exacerbated by the Clinton administration's often duplicitous approach to environmental policy. Some of the mainstream groups have made concerted efforts to cast their efforts in more grassroots terms. For example, when environmental lawyer Mark van Putten assumed the position of CEO of the National Wildlife Federation in 1996, he described his mission as one to "reinvigorate the real roots of the conservation movement."

The Wilderness Society also chose a new top officer in 1996, and the Sierra Club elected a 23-year-old activist and founder of the Sierra Student Coalition as its new president. The Sierra Club has gradually, though often reluctantly, strengthened its positions on some issues of primary concern to grassroots Club members. A five-year campaign by Sierra Club members to press the Club to take a stand against all commercial logging in the National Forests culminated in a 1996 membership referendum that passed by a margin of 2 to 1 in favor of the proposal. This despite the opposition of some notable Sierra Club board members, including Earth First! co-founder Dave Foreman, who condemned the Club's "true believers who hold onto some idealistic notion of no compromise," apparently with little intended irony. Spurred in part by widespread outrage at the devastating effects of expanded "salvage" logging during the past two years, the referendum may have added some much needed teeth to the Club's efforts to recast itself in more grassroots terms.

The mainstream environmental movement also played a more visible role in the 1996 congressional elections than ever before. The League of Conservation Voters targeted a dozen members of Congress for defeat, highlighting their role in promoting a virulently anti-environmental agenda. Of these, six were defeated in their re-election bids, most significantly Larry Pressler of South Dakota, who was the only incumbent U.S. Senator to be defeated in 1996. A seventh, Rep. Steve Stockman of Texas, was defeated in a December runoff. The Sierra Club spent ten times as much as ever before in support of pro-environment candidates, a total of $7.5 million. However, such efforts have proved far from sufficient to alter the terms of environmental debate in official Washington circles. The most noticeable result may have been to encourage candidates on both sides of the issues to drape their campaigns in green cloth, advancing the corporate greenwash by promoting environmental images over substance.

Bill Clinton's various high-profile environmental proclamations during the campaign season—from Yellowstone Park to Utah to the California redwoods—not only affirmed the trend toward image over substance, but each featured measures to handsomely compensate corporations for not fully exercising their "property rights" to expand mining and timber cutting on corporate-owned lands. Last year, the federal government offered trades of federal land with a combined value of several hundred million dollars to mining companies in Arizona, timber companies in the Northwest, and the Houston-based conglomerate Maxxam, in exchange for the protection of their California redwood forest holdings. A subsidiary of the Canadian mining conglomerate Noranda was offered nearly $65 million in federal property to withdraw its proposal for a massive gold mining operation just north of Yellowstone National Park. The Environmental Defense Fund, which has been the leading proponent of an unabashedly "market-oriented" approach to environmentalism, described tradeoffs of federal land as the best "source of revenue on the horizon that is going to enable us to protect these sensitive areas as quickly as we have to," according to the *New York Times.* This despite a large reserve of unspent federal funds designated specifically for conservation-related land purchases.

To challenge the hegemony of the voices of official environmentalism on the national level will ultimately require more active and diverse networks of grassroots activists, organized and coordinated from the ground up. Such networks have begun to appear in the environmental justice movement, as well as among grassroots forest activists. Activists working on similar issues and facing an increasingly unified corporate agenda need to find ways to join forces across boundaries of geography, ethnicity, class, and specific-issue focus. Local groups may have ties to several regional and national networks, sometimes sharing legal and technical resources with larger, better-funded organizations. However, it is essential that they retain the prerogative to set their own agendas and speak to their own communities' priorities, while steadfastly resisting the pressures of cooptation that the existing larger organizations so frequently succumb to—sometimes unwittingly but often with unabashed enthusiasm.

In 1995, the long-awaited 25th anniversary of Earth Day came and went with considerably less fanfare than five years earlier. Controversies over corporate contributions largely derailed plans for the biggest—and the most utterly compromised—Earth Day ever. Earth Day organizers hired a corporate public relations firm, Dorf & Stanton, to coordinate program development and communications, and established a short-lived "Earth Day Corporate Team" to actively solicit corporate participation. The organization was rocked with dissent and underwent two complete reorganizations before a revived Earth Day organization raised $6.5 million in corporate contributions.

The official Earth Day 1995 petition, addressed with a puzzling forthrightness to House Speaker Newt Gingrich, began, "With major polluters such as Texaco and Monsanto attempting to 'sponsor' Earth Day, and every politician in the nation claiming to be 'for the environment,' it is getting hard to figure out who is really protecting the planet and who is poisoning it." The corporate co-optation of Earth Day, an idea that provoked intense controversy in 1990, and brought hundreds of people to demonstrate on Wall Street, had become conventional wisdom by mid-decade. Will activists in 1997 begin to chart a different path?

◆ **QUESTIONS FOR DISCUSSION AND WRITING** ◆

1. Tokar describes environmental activists converging on Wall Street to disrupt trading on Earth Day. How effective is this kind of tactic? What impact might it have?

2. Were you surprised to learn that people at the upper levels of the large environmentalist groups are associated with corporations cited as major polluters? What effect does this knowledge have on your understanding of environmental issues?

3. Some of the problems that Tokar cites are the result of the large size of the major environmentalist organizations; at the same time, size increases lobbying power. How might this apparent conflict be resolved?

✸ Taking It to the Streets

AL GORE WADES INTO THE SPRAWL DEBATE

Reed McManus

Ronald Reagan battled a distant Evil Empire, but presidential contender Al Gore is taking on an enemy right here at home: suburban sprawl. In January [1999], the vice president outlined the Clinton administration's "livability agenda," whose centerpiece is a "Better America Bonds" program that would use $700 million in federal tax incentives to generate $9.5 billion. States and cities could use that money to reclaim polluted land, protect green space from development, and create urban parks. The same week, the administration proposed the largest-ever federal budget for public transportation, and $1 billion for a "lands legacy initiative" to preserve parklands.

Why would the federal government wade into issues that are traditionally local matters, carried out by planning commissions and zoning boards in endless hearings? Gore has never shied away from arcane topics, but in deciding to make sprawl a theme of his presidential bid all he had to do was pay passing attention to the last election. In November, there were some 240 state and local measures on ballots coast-to-coast to preserve parks, open space, farmlands, and watersheds. More than 70 percent of them passed, many with the help of the Sierra Club.

State politicians caught on even before the V. P. In 1996, Maryland Governor Parris Glendening (D) unveiled an initiative to discourage development in rural areas and channel funds into urban areas. In November, Republican Governor Christine Todd Whitman won voters' approval to dedicate about $1.4 billion to help preserve half of New Jersey's remaining 2 million acres of undeveloped land over the next decade. Newly elected Georgia Governor Roy Barnes (D) has proposed a regional transportation authority to unclog Atlanta's gridlocked suburbs. Twelve states have adopted growth-management plans, and seven more plan major land purchases to protect open space and farmland.

Compared with the effort it takes to educate voters about issues like global warming, convincing people of the ills of haphazard development is a walk in the park. Sprawl is an issue that hits suburban voters every time they find themselves stuck in traffic trying to buy a half-gallon of milk, or spend their weekend looking for open space in which to recreate. Those frustrations mean plenty to candidate Gore: about half of American voters live in suburbs.

But anti-sprawl efforts resonate because they affect more than just the residents of Willowbrooke Estates. Cities stand to gain if tax dollars that might be spent on new infrastructure in expanding suburbs were redirected to the needs of already developed areas. Farmers find new allies and resources that enable them to keep farming. (According to the American Farmland Trust, the outward growth of metropolitan areas consumes one million acres of farmland each year.) And government agencies struggling to control pollution have a new way to address seemingly intractable issues. In an effort to reduce auto pollution, for instance, in February the EPA began its own anti-sprawl campaign in New England.

There are even signs that real-estate interests might join the coalition. It's easier and cheaper to build on undeveloped land beyond the cities than it is to rebuild older areas, which usually have stricter rules regarding development. Yet in February the National Association of Home Builders agreed to construct a million new homes in the nation's cities and "close-in" suburbs over the next ten years in exchange for a federal pledge to streamline building-approval processes. On this issue, Charles Ruma, the builders' association president, beams like an energetic big-city mayor: "Once housing returns, commerce, retail, jobs, and the deli down the street will follow. Step by step, block by block, we will begin to see the rebirth of our nation's urban centers." Ruma's cheerleading ends, however, when the discussion shifts to new construction on the urban fringe. He

5

is "leery" of government efforts to keep farmlands out of the hands of developers.

The administration's anti-sprawl message is also designed to assuage conservative fears of federal intrusion in local issues. The bond program, Gore says, will simply deliver money to state and local governments to spend as they see fit, not cast the federal government as "beauty commissar." Still, detractors worry that Gore is peddling "social engineering," exemplified on-screen by Seahaven, the mind-numbing planned community that Jim Carrey's Truman Burbank eventually flees in *The Truman Show.*

Government involvement in land-use decisions is hardly new. Since the end of World War II, federal subsidies and spending (particularly on the interstate highway system) have encouraged growth outside urban areas. In many cities, zoning laws mandating large-lot "ranchettes" have contributed to sprawl by forcing developers to look to remote areas for developable land. According to Sierra Club Executive Director Carl Pope, the administration's proposal "reverses a 50-year trend that helped create sprawl."

In the end, Gore's sprawl program provides more options than restrictions. No homebuyers who crave a three-car garage and a half-acre lawn are going to be herded against their will into "cluster" housing within—gasp—walking distance of a grocery store and public transit. But for suburbanites who want to spend less time shackled to automobiles, city dwellers who hope to revitalize once-flourishing neighborhoods, farmers who want to continue working their land, and activists and government officials striving to reduce air pollution and protect parkland, Gore's attention gives national shape to issues they've been struggling with locally for years.

───────◆ **QUESTIONS FOR DISCUSSION AND WRITING** ◆───────

1. What new ideas does McManus add to the debate on sprawl? Compare what McManus has to say with the ideas presented by Roger Lewis.
2. Reread McManus's final paragraph. How does the tone of his writing reinforce his feelings?
3. This selection is from the Sierra Club's official magazine. How might that affect the way in which you read it?

✳ Stressed Out on Growth

David F. Seiders

The housing boom of the past five years has fueled the "smart growth" debate now raging in so many communities around the country.

WHAT'S THE PROBLEM?

Heated discussions of farmland preservation abound, and NIMBY feelings are deepening in many areas. Yet, only a small proportion (about 3 percent) of the nation's land mass is urban or built-up space, the total volume of farmland is not actually shrinking, and the United States is in no danger of running short on food.

The problem is that the bulk of recent development has occurred in areas that lie within or close to those that already house the majority of Americans. It's the incumbent residents who are agitated, not the cows in the fields. Both native-born citizens and immigrants are streaming into areas in and around metro centers.

METRO FRINGES

A recent report by the Joint Center for Housing Studies of Harvard University examined the geographic pattern of housing development in the 1990s. The report says that in 17 states more housing permits were issued last year than during the peak production years of the 1980s. Moreover, the lion's share of new construction has been occurring in medium- and lower-density counties at metropolitan fringes or beyond.

The Joint Center report noted that between 1990 and 1997 home building activity exceeded 200,000 units in eight metropolitan areas, and 100,000 units in 21 metropolitan areas, and that most of this development was around the metro fringes. Nearly one million building permits issued in nonmetropolitan areas during the 1990s have been in counties bordering metro areas. This phenomenon fits common perceptions of urban sprawl.

In addition, the report pointed out, increasing numbers of Americans are bypassing metropolitan areas altogether in choosing where to live. Population growth in nonmetropolitan areas is approaching the growth level in metropolitan areas for the first time since the 1970s. However, the surge in nonmetropolitan growth has been in counties adjacent to metro areas, not in far-flung places.

FUTURE PRESSURES

It's likely that home building activity will remain concentrated around the metropolitan fringes in the foreseeable future, because that's where most of the baby boomers and their children prefer to live. Thus, medium-density counties are likely to continue to undergo the most dramatic changes in the next few years, exacerbating farmland preservation and related NIMBY efforts that will be part of the "smart growth" debate in next year's political campaigns. It remains to be seen whether or not local growth controls or federal government incentives will be able to direct more of the inevitable housing growth toward the central cities or toward rural areas where developable land is plentiful.

───────◆ **QUESTIONS FOR DISCUSSION AND WRITING** ◆───────

1. Seiders mentions "NIMBY feelings," in paragraph 2. What are they, and what role do these feelings play in the sprawl debate?
2. "Stressed Out on Growth" originally appeared in *Builder* magazine, which is published for the home-building industry. In what way does this information influence your thoughts about what Seiders has to say?
3. What useful information does this article provide that supports your point of view?

✳ New Neighborhoods Can Combat Urban Sprawl

Business Week

Kendall is a prime example of sprawl. What passes for the downtown of this south Florida suburb, a few miles southwest of Miami, is a hodge-podge of office buildings, a mall, parking lots, auto dealerships, and a dingy canal. But over the next 40 years, Miami-Dade County planners hope to pack Kendall with people, creating a European-flavored town center with romantic canal-side walkways, tree-lined boulevards, trolleys, colonnaded sidewalks, and stylish condominiums and apartment houses. The theory is that the best way to keep people from spreading out all over the landscape is to give them a good reason for working, playing, shopping, and living close together. A dream? Maybe. But as the new century approaches, many Americans are disturbed by the relentless expansion of the suburban frontier. Right now, 1,000 to 3,000 acres of farmland, forest, and other unbuilt-upon land are developed every day. In once-bucolic Loudoun County, Va., outside Washington, "all of a sudden, people are sitting in traffic jams, with crowded schools and higher taxes—and wondering how the hell development is good for them," says Scott K. York, chairman of the county's Board of Supervisors. Says Carol M. Browner, administrator of the U.S. Environmental Protection Agency: "People want a different kind of future." Glimpses of such a future exist. Stockholm, Sweden, a city of islands and winding streets, is one of many in Europe that are meccas for walkers and paragons of mass transit. Stockholm is surrounded by compact satellite communities connected by trains. More than half of the residents of the suburban town of Vallingby commute by mass transit. The area's beauty proves that clusters of development around rail lines don't have to be ugly.

SCHMOOZING ON PORCHES

In the 1970s, metropolitan Portland Ore., drew a line around its core, severely limiting development outside of a 230,000-acre area. That, coupled with an expanded rail and bus system, has enabled the metro area to accommodate a 50% increase in population since the 1970s with only a 2% increase in developed land area and only a moderate rise in the number of trips by car. Communities built by anti-sprawl planners, such as Seaside, Fla., and Kentlands, Md., make it easy for people to schmooze on front porches and walk to stores. Seaside is so popular that one-bedroom cottages can go for more than $500,000. Far bolder plans are on the drawing boards. The five counties in South Florida, already home to 5.5 million people, are expected to swell to 7.5 million by 2020. Three-fourths of the growth is taking place west of the I-95 corridor, where there's more open land. That's costing the state billions for new roads, while threatening the Everglades just to the west. So the region has launched an Eastward Ho! initiative to funnel growth into the eastern section. A key part is attracting people back to places such as Kendall. "People are realizing it's dumb to throw away parts of our communities," says Isabel Cosio Carballo, Eastward Ho! coordinator at the South Florida Regional Planning Council. Atlanta, so choked with traffic that companies are deciding to leave or not relocate there, has also decided to make changes. The Metro Atlanta Chamber of Commerce has recommended creating a regional superagency to build new transit lines and redirect development. BellSouth plans to move 13,000 employees from the suburbs to offices in the city near transit stops. Employees who work on the train ride home will be able to zip off faxes and E-mails from facilities at the station before hopping in their cars. Trying to create neighborhoods and downtowns where residents can walk to shopping or catch a streetcar to work is an echo of America's own past. In Silicon Valley, high-tech CEOs see transportation bottlenecks and housing costs as barriers to economic growth, so they're pushing clustered developments and transit. "It is a return to the communities that we had in America in the 1940s," says Carl Guardino, president of the Silicon Valley Manufacturing Group, an industry-backed organization. Making a real dent in urban sprawl is an enormous challenge. "Americans are accustomed to cheap gas, weak land-use controls, and subsidies for roads," says Columbia University historian Kenneth T. Jackson, author of *Crabgrass Frontier*. And people don't like the idea of cramming more homes and apartments into high-density pockets for the sake of controlling sprawl elsewhere. It's a dilemma, says Ohio developer Charles J. Ruma: "Americans hate two things: sprawl and high density." Local ordinances often help cause sprawl by mandating big lots and too-wide roads. "We worked with a township that had an ordinance requiring that roads on the interior of a subdivision be at least 34 feet wide. That's enough room for three semis to have a race," says

Keith Charters of the Traverse City (Mich.) Area Chamber of Commerce. He figures an 18-foot road is plenty wide enough. But attitudes are changing. Vice-President Al Gore has made sprawl a bogeyman of his Presidential campaign. Last November [1998], voters passed more than two-thirds of 240 ballot initiatives, authorizing $7.5 billion in new spending, to preserve open space or otherwise tackle sprawl. "We can redirect development patterns anywhere we want," says Robert W. Burchell, professor of urban policy at Rutgers University in New Brunswick, N.J. As traffic jams worsen and farms disappear around our cities, we may be willing to begin a profound reshaping of the American landscape.

◆ QUESTIONS FOR DISCUSSION AND WRITING ◆

1. How does this article reflect some of the concerns the other readings in this chapter examine?
2. Do you agree that Americans might be ready to change their housing patterns? Based on what you read in this article, how might you support your answer?
3. Mass transit is a recurring theme in the sprawl debate. How might mass transit affect the kind of settlement patterns that lead to sprawl?

✳ Plan Obsolescence

URBAN PLANNING SKEPTIC PETER GORDON ON THE BENEFITS OF SPRAWL, THE WAR AGAINST CARS, AND THE FUTURE OF AMERICAN CITIES

Rick Henderson and Adrian T. Moore

Life in America's suburbs is under attack. In journals ranging from *The Nation, The Atlantic Monthly,* and *Utne Reader* to *The American Enterprise* and *The Weekly Standard,* critics of suburbia argue that policies implemented since World War II—from the home-mortgage income tax deduction to subsidies for automobile operation to inflexible zoning laws—have lured Americans away from traditional downtowns and urban neighborhoods into soulless suburbs, where a landscape littered with strip malls and tract housing makes it nearly impossible for people to form genuine communal bonds with their neighbors. Contemporary suburbanites are condemned, in the words of the left-leaning *L.A. Weekly,* to "a future of endless sprawl and equally endless commutes."

To save suburban dwellers from this hellish existence, urban planners have devised massive subway construction projects, controls on the development of neighborhoods with single-family homes, "mixed-use" zoning districts that allow commercial operations to coexist with residences, and "urban growth boundaries" that have made it illegal to build homes or locate businesses on the outskirts of such cities as Portland, Oregon.

Enter Peter Gordon, a professor of planning and economics at the University of Southern California's School of Urban Planning and Development. For nearly three decades, Gordon, along with his USC colleague Harry Richardson, has challenged conventional views about gridlock and sprawl, finding that the data don't match the received wisdom: "Suburbanization" is not an artifact of late 20th-century America but a process that has unfolded as long as people have possessed the means to travel and relocate. Commute times are no longer than they were 15 years ago. Individuals are finding the types of living arrangements they prefer. And while Los Angeles–style sprawl is vilified in the traditional planning literature, as well as in most popular accounts of urban life, Los Angeles has the highest population density of any major metropolitan area in the country.

Gordon, who received his Ph.D. from the University of Pennsylvania, has published dozens of articles in popular publications and peer-reviewed journals. He is co-editor of *Planning and Markets,* a new online publication that focuses on land-use and transportation issues (www~pam.usc.edu). While he may be considered a lightning rod in the planning community, in person he's gentle and patient, hardly the sort of firebrand his heretical views suggest.

Reason Managing Editor Rick Henderson and Adrian T. Moore, director of economic studies at the Reason Public Policy Institute, interviewed Gordon at his Brentwood home in March [1998]. 5

> **REASON:** There is a pervasive argument among traditional planners that compact cities built around a traditional downtown are intrinsically good. While cities once developed around transit centers, raw materials sites, or natural harbors, contemporary cities seem to be more the artificial creations of planners. What has happened?

> **GORDON:** Compact cities are archaic forms, and they are not coming back. When you study the economics of location, all the textbook models say a firm wants to locate near the urban core or other advantageous sites, and workers must make their living arrangements so that they are close to their jobs. That may be the way it was once upon a time.

> But all these firms have become much more footloose. And they go where the workers want to live. The orientation has flip-flopped. Even manufacturing businesses are no longer locked into specific sites, so they have more locational choices. They want to go where the labor force wants to go. The workers and their families want to live where the land is cheap and the air is clean and the schools are good and there are high amenities and so forth.

There's a lot more spatial flexibility than ever before, and the consequences are pretty benign.

People don't have to live near work. They can be near good schools if they want to be without paying the price in longer-duration commutes. If you make travel less expensive, there will be more travel.

REASON: You've shown that the average-duration commute has stayed the same over the past 15 years or so. Why does everyone believe that traffic congestion is getting worse?

GORDON: What's interesting is how little congestion there is. If you take a resident of any large foreign city like Tokyo and transplant him or her to Los Angeles, they think they've died and gone to heaven, because the commutes are less than half, on average, here than they are there. Something like 10 percent of the people nationwide commute more than 40 minutes one way. There is a lot of self-correction going on. For 1995, the average automobile commute in L.A. was 23.5 minutes one way.

People are part of a spontaneous order. I think it's not only pessimistic but even ignorant to believe that people are going to sit tight while their lives go to hell. That's never happened. Even where the commuting distances have increased, the trip durations have not, which means commuting speeds are up. It is the opposite of impending gridlock, and it means people can have their cake and eat it, too.

REASON: So why don't people in Tokyo correct in the same way Angelenos do?

GORDON: Many Japanese choose long train commutes because they have a much smaller scope of trade-offs available. Automobile travel is much more expensive [in Japan]. Land doesn't change hands as frequently. There are all kinds of things standing in the way of the fluidity that we're used to.

REASON: You're a critic of the New Urbanism, which is the hot thing in the planning profession. Here's how Alan Ehrenhalt describes the principles of New Urbanism in *Governing* magazine: "The automobile, and four decades of building homes, streets and suburbs for the automobile's convenience, were draining American places of the community and intimacy that human beings naturally desire." The New Urbanists claim that people want neighborhoods with tree-lined streets, and parks and shops all within walking distance of homes. What's wrong with that?

GORDON: I think the development of neighborhoods by private developers is driven by markets, not by public policy. People are getting the neighborhoods they want. And I trust that competing developers are reading the trade-offs that you and I are willing to

10

15

make and that those trade-offs include our demand for community. Our demands for community are met in many ways. We can use the automobile [to meet those demands], or we can even use the Internet.

People are getting a sense of community in the neighborhoods we have. We know that 20 percent of all trips by automobile are for work, 20 percent are for shopping, and 60 percent are for things I would call social. The U.S. Department of Transportation uses categories like family/personal business, school, church, visits to relatives, and other social or recreational uses, but you could easily call all these social or "community" trips.

New Urbanism is heavy on intervention, and it's tied into the "civil society," or communitarian, discussion. It dances around defining whether there's a problem with the way we live and says, "There's a problem—automobile use—and we have a solution." I'm not sure we all agree there's a problem. And it's a long shot to say that there's a design fix and we know what that design fix is.

REASON: Conservatives such as Karl Zinsmeister at the American Enterprise Institute have become big boosters of New Urbanism. They argue that the fatal conceit of traditional planning and zoning has led to these soulless suburbs. But aren't the conservatives substituting their own fatal conceit, that everyone wants to live in Small Town, USA?

GORDON: That's the weak link in the New Urbanism. If there were   20 a grain of truth in their view, we would soon see people demanding it, and developers would strive to provide it. Builders are not ideologues.

New Urbanists say there are land use configurations that will lead to lower trip frequency. And if we object to the use of the automobile, then we can develop a land use solution. They have advanced all kinds of street designs, and hypothesized how to lay out homes and neighborhoods more compactly, and say if people can walk to all the places they need to go, presto, there will be less automobile use. The smallest introspection will show that trip frequency isn't fixed.

The New Urbanists certainly haven't done their homework. They certainly don't look at the facts a lot, so I keep going back to the international comparison. We've all traveled, we've all seen suburbanization in other parts in the world. There's clearly a universal demand for and use of automobiles that's reflected in the data.

International studies, like those from the Organization of Economic Cooperation and Development, are always funny to read, because the authors prejudge everything. At the beginning you have all these conclusions articulated that the automobile is the problem, what are we going to do with the automobile, how can we keep people out of automobiles, and so on. But what's revealing is that the authors lament automobile use in all these places. You have a tough time blaming American policy for automobile use [in other countries], and when you get rid of that explanation, you have to end up saying the reason people drive is consumer preference. Preference is a pretty powerful explanation compared to the one suggested by the New Urbanism.

Not just that, but the New Urbanists claim suburban development, which they call "sprawl," is something that people are using against their better judgment. One of the favorite themes of planners is that people haven't got enough choices, and builders are restricted by zoning codes to give people stuff that they don't really want. That's of course inconsistent with the other story the New Urbanists tell: that planners are beholden to builders. Well, if that's true, and just one of these greedy builders would figure out that people wanted to live in neotraditional settlements, then that greedy builder would overcome political barriers and we'd have the neotraditional developments.

REASON: Aren't there private attempts to create the type of places the New Urbanists want? 25

GORDON: I don't know of a lot of success stories. A lot of these developments are too new to judge. A lot of attention has been paid to the Disney-built community in Florida [Celebration], but the reviews of it have been mixed. Even that refers more to opinions of reviewers and less to the judgment of the market.

REASON: *The New York Times Magazine* has suggested it's more like living in a Disney-built theme park than in a real community.

GORDON: But social arrangements that are provided in the marketplace are constantly evolving. We would expect that savvy builders are evolving and experimenting in providing new things. It's a wonderful process.

If the New Urbanists have something to contribute to that evolution, that's wonderful. But instead they want to make a clean break and say that society is marching one way and we know the way it ought to go instead.

REASON: What's good about suburban living? 30

GORDON: Those of us who believe in markets place a lot of value on living arrangements that are an expression of consumer preferences. People are voting for spacious living, so by all means let them have what they are voting for. They're voting for access to their schools, they are voting for clean air and those kinds of things. By any measure, suburban living has to be a success story.

Americans run to [visit] Europe because, hell, those are *cities*. Now, that doesn't mean we choose to live there; it's just a nice place to visit. Traditional cities are fun for tourists. [That has] nothing to do with whether you want to live there.

There is the presumption that suburbanites are living these lives of quiet desperation and isolation, and they really hate being there. You see trotted out ideas about community being missing. And to have community, you've got to be in Manhattan. There are a lot of ex-Manhattanites that would challenge that theory very seriously.

REASON: A lot of people seem to think that auto travel is heavily subsidized but mass transit isn't.

GORDON: Federal transit subsidies go back to the 1960s, and for the first 10 years they were capital subsidies only. You had all this overbuilding of rail transit and a lot of people wrote articles that said overbuilding occurred because the feds subsidize only one part of the activity, and that's building. In 1974 the feds began subsidizing operation as well as building of transit systems. The whole idea of a federal transit policy may be silly, but as long as all this money is funneled through Washington, locals want to get in line to get theirs.

Whether you [do] it per mile or per trip, transit subsidies are hugely greater than any subsidies to the automobile. Per passenger mile, transit subsidies are 50 times what auto subsidies are. And the L.A. experience suggests that we spend a lot of money and get less transit use. We're spending more to get rid of riders. Back-of-the-envelope calculations show that about $7 billion has been spent on rail so far, and we know that they've lost an aggregate of about 1 billion riders over a 10-year span. So they've spent $7.00 for every transit rider eliminated.

REASON: How does that loss of ridership compare to the national average?

GORDON: There have been market-share losses in all of the new rail cities. The other thing you want to control for is background growth. So this is over a period where L.A. County added 12 percent to the population, and a lot of those were lower-skilled immigrants, who are sort of a natural constituency for mass transit. So to spend that much money and lose that many riders, that's not simple. You've really got to work at it.

REASON: Is any public transportation economically viable?

GORDON: At best, a *maybe* if you legalized vans. There's a big fight in New York City over them right now. Los Angeles legalized airport vans, and now Super Shuttle wants to get in the way of new entrants. But whatever [form of public transit] you come up with

35

40

would be running neck and neck with large numbers of used cars. The transportation mode of choice of low-income people is used cars.

REASON: The communities that are held out as almost utopian by the New Urbanists—Portland, Oregon, or the Kentlands in suburban D.C.—have intensely politicized almost every private land use decision. Is putting every decision about painting your roof before a plebiscite the way people really want to live?

GORDON: That scares off a lot of people because they fear that their own property rights are up for grabs. If their own property rights are subject to being put in a common pool, a lot of people will say, "No, thank you."

On the other side, we have the growth of community associations, or what some people are calling entrepreneurial communities. When everything is contractual, then you're not going to have these surprises. So people are making ever more such choices, and it puts them in the category of getting out of harm's way and providing insurance for my property rights, because my property rights are ever more up for grabs, [depending upon what] judges are doing or not doing, or what the zoning board is doing in response to organized groups, and all that. The entrepreneurial communities—or whatever you want to call them, community associations—are a mechanism that fits very well.

REASON: But can't community associations become political organizations that have as much power as zoning boards?

GORDON: If everything is covered by contract, there are no misunderstandings and no surprises. We either bargain for the contract that we want or we go look for another one somewhere else. 45

REASON: But contracts can't anticipate everything. An entrepreneurial community established 20 years ago could have never anticipated the development of 18-inch satellite dishes, which might well be banned in such a place.

GORDON: More adaptive forms will have to come on the market. My friend Spencer MacCallum, an anthropologist who writes on these issues, says that we may see the development of leasehold arrangements rather than traditional contract arrangements. The model he uses is that of hotels and shopping malls, where entrepreneurs provide services that people want. Leaseholds may provide much more flexible property arrangements than we typically imagine.

REASON: You mean the neighborhood association may renegotiate parts of its contract every year? We won't let you build a deck on the back of your house this year, but next year we'll think about it? Or people could decide to live in rigidly defined communities with extremely inflexible contracts if there's a demand for them?

GORDON: Right. All in the direction of increasing competition. People are more mobile than ever, and they have an easier time moving from one place to another as their requirements change.

   The downside of these entrepreneurial communities, of course, is that as more affluent people withdraw from cities the interest groups that are left behind become ever more powerful. The people who are victims are the people who are least likely to move. We condemn the poorest to the worst public schools and the worst public services.

REASON: So are decaying urban cores part of an evolutionary process that no planning can overcome?

GORDON: The best thing that's happening to old urban cores is the immigrants, and immigrants have almost nothing to do with the planners except for the fact that planners often give them a hard time when they want to get occupational licenses. The infusion of capital and entrepreneurial skills in the core areas is coming entirely from the immigrants. If we make it our business to chase them out, then we may be hastening the decay of those urban cores.

REASON: You don't fit the profile of the typical urban planner, advocating top-down remedies. How did you arrive where you are? Are you indeed atypical?

GORDON: Planning is so eclectic it draws people from everywhere: architecture, the social sciences, the natural sciences. You really get an odd stew. I have a very Hayekian view of the world, and given the way that I view the evolution of the built environment, the Hayekian view has a lot to say. I teach about markets, so I'm less suspicious of market mechanisms than most of my planning colleagues.

   And even when I speak with like-minded colleagues, I have to ask if market-friendly planning is realistic or plausible. Is there any mileage in doing market-friendly planning, or are spontaneous orders or spontaneous adjustments going to outdistance what planners try to do all the time? And that's why it's interesting to look at the migrations that are going on into the exurbs and into private communities, because those are going on in spite of any planning or any policy.

   If we have local policy interests, and we have an understanding of the role of markets, then I think you reach the conclusion that a lot of the conventional, command-and-control stuff is disastrous. Spending $7.00 per rider to lose a billion transit riders is disastrous. So I think we have a huge case study which does not offer us any cause for optimism for traditional planning.

What can we, as researchers, really do? We can quit, or we can keep believing—let's unearth some of these facts and ideas, present them as best we can, and maybe somebody will learn something.

REASON: How are you perceived in the planning community? Are you on the fringe?

GORDON: I'm at the edge of the fringe.

REASON: So when you go to the American Planning Association's convention, do you drink alone? 60

GORDON: Well, I don't go very often. When I'm invited to speak at certain places, I think it's as a curiosity. There's the usual handful of people who thank you. God knows if they thank you because they've been informed or entertained or whatever.

But the intent is to uncover some facts, support them as best you can, put them in context, because there are all sorts of unfounded assertions out there.

REASON: Even so, the traditional planning community doesn't seem to shun you completely. In the Winter 1997 issue of the *American Planning Association Journal,* you and your USC colleague Harry Richardson engaged in a fascinating debate with Florida International University planning professor Reid Ewing. Your article, "Are Compact Cities a Desirable Goal?," was a straightforward exposition of the case against traditional planning and for consumer preferences. Ewing's "Is Los Angeles–Style Sprawl Desirable?" directly challenged your arguments. How did that come about?

GORDON: We sent them our article, and they wrote back and said, "We can run this if we run it with a counterpoint." There wasn't even the suggestion that they would run ours alone. I'm happy they did run both, because I want that discussion to be out there. Nevertheless, the editors of the journal of the APA felt they needed the safety of a counterpoint before even letting us present our side. But Harry and I were pleased to find out that the editors awarded us honorable mention for feature article of the year.

I was asked to address the L.A. City Planning Commission two years ago because there was a draft of their plan which favored transit-oriented development. And I said, "Here are the various reasons why it will not work." The response I got was a big yawn. There was zero interest in that, either [from] the commissioners who for some reason invited me, or [from] a lot of the staff people who were there. I just said their document was full of holes, but there was no interest as to asking why, or can you tell us what's wrong, or anything like that. 65

REASON: Is traditional planning becoming inconsequential? Are today's academic planners comparable to the slide-rule designers of 20 years ago, preparing to offer a product which has no market?

GORDON: We are trending away from planners in the traditional form, who primarily serve the interests of municipalities. But property arrangements are coming on line which require the developer to wear the planner's hat or the planner to wear the developer's hat. You could call this role "planning," but it's not traditional or public-sector planning.

People who are savvy enough to see the opportunities may be called planners, but they are less likely to operate in city hall and are more likely to operate in a development group, to arrange the types of developments that are successful. They will need a more sophisticated range of skills.

Maybe the world is changing so fast that what's coming out of the academy will lag behind [what the real world demands]. Maybe students will come out of the academy being trained in one way and find, once they leave, they need skills that direct them in another.

But that may be true of any number of other disciplines. It may be a problem professional schools in general face. We know universities are having a hard time keeping up. That's why we have think tanks [laughs].

70

―――――◆ QUESTIONS FOR DISCUSSION AND WRITING ◆―――――

1. In what ways do Henderson and Moore establish Peter Gordon's credibility?
2. Gordon argues that people are getting the neighborhoods they want through market forces. If this is the case, what accounts for the nationwide outcry about urban sprawl, especially the perspectives of Linda Baker and Reed McManus?
3. What are the effects, positive and negative, of community associations that regulate what people can do with the property they own?

✳ Divided We Sprawl

Bruce Katz and Jennifer Bradley

By many accounts Baltimore is a comeback city. It has a beautiful piece of calculated nostalgia in the Camden Yards baseball stadium, which draws tens of thousands of visitors throughout the spring and summer. It has a lively waterfront district, the Inner Harbor, with charming shops and hot snacks for sale every hundred yards or so. But although it may function well as a kind of urban theme park (and there are plenty of cities that would love to achieve that distinction), as a city it is struggling. For twenty years Baltimore has hemorrhaged residents: more than 140,000 have left since 1980. Meanwhile, the surrounding suburbs have steadily grown. The population of Howard County, a thirty-minute drive from the city, has doubled since 1980, from 118,600 to 236,000. The people who have stayed in Baltimore are some of the neediest in the area. The city has 13 percent of Maryland's population but 56 percent of its welfare caseload. Only about a quarter of the students who enroll in a public high school in the city graduate in four years.

And Baltimore is not unique. The image of America's cities has improved greatly over the past few years, thanks to shiny new downtowns dotted with vast convention centers, luxury hotels, and impressive office towers, but these acres of concrete and faux marble hide a reality that is in many cases grim. St. Louis, Cleveland, Philadelphia, and Washington, D.C., lost population throughout the 1990s. These cities are also losing their status as the most powerful economies in their regions. Washington started the 1990s with a respectable 33 percent of the area's jobs. Seven years later it had only 24 percent. The rate of population growth in the nation's suburbs was more than twice that in central cities—9.6 percent versus 4.2 percent—from 1990 to 1997. In just one year—1996— 2.7 million people left a central city for a suburb. A paltry 800,000 made the opposite move. In the major urbanized areas of Ohio 90 percent of the new jobs created from 1994 to 1997 were in the suburbs. The central business districts of Ohio's seven largest cities had a net gain of only 19,510 jobs from 1994 to 1997; their suburbs gained 186,000. The 1990s have been the decade of decentralization for people and jobs in the United States.

Not even cities that are growing—southern and western boom cities —are keeping pace with their suburbs. Denver has gained about 31,000 people in the 1990s (after having lost residents during the 1980s), but the counties that make up the Denver metropolitan area have gained 284,000 people—about nine times as many. In Atlanta and Houston central-city growth is far outmatched by growth in outlying counties. And these cities, too, are losing their share of the jobs in their respective regions. In 1980, 40 percent of the jobs in the Atlanta region were in the city itself; by 1996 only 24 percent were.

Meanwhile, the poor have been left behind in the cities. Urban poverty rates are twice as high as suburban poverty rates, and the implementation of welfare reform appears to be a special problem for cities. Although welfare caseloads are shrinking in most cities, in general they are not shrinking as quickly as they are in the states and in the nation as a whole. Often cities have a disproportionate share of their states' welfare recipients. Philadelphia County, for example, is home to 12 percent of all Pennsylvanians but 47 percent of all Pennsylvanians on welfare. Orleans Parish, in which the city of New Orleans is located, has 11 percent of Louisiana's population but 29 percent of its welfare recipients. This hardly adds up to an urban renaissance.

Cities—both the lucky, booming ones and the disfavored, depleted ones—are losing ground for two reasons. First, they push out people who have choices. Urban crime rates have fallen, but they are still generally higher than suburban rates. Some urban school systems are improving, but in most of the nation's twenty biggest urban school districts fewer than half of high school freshmen graduate after four years. City mayors have cut taxes, but urban tax rates (and insurance rates, too) are often higher than suburban ones. Second, suburbs pull people in. This is not a secret. What is less well known—in fact, is just beginning to be understood—is how federal, state, and local policies on spending, taxes, and regulation boost the allure of the suburbs and put the cities at a systematic, relentless disadvantage. People are not exactly duped into living in detached houses amid lush lawns, peaceful streets, and good schools. Still, it is undeniable that government policies make suburbs somewhat more attractive and affordable than they might otherwise be, and make cities less so.

Federal mortgage-interest and property-tax deductions give people a subtle incentive to buy bigger houses on bigger lots, which almost by definition are found in the suburbs. States also spend more money building new roads—which make new housing developments and strip malls not only accessible but financially feasible—than they do repairing existing roads. Environmental regulations make building offices and factories on abandoned urban industrial sites complicated and time-consuming, and thus render untouched suburban land particularly appealing.

Together these policies have set the rules of the development game. They send a clear signal to employers, householders, builders, and political leaders: build out on open, un-urbanized, in some cases untouched land, and bypass older areas. These policies were never imagined as a coherent whole. No individual or committee or agency wrote the rules of development as such. No one stopped to consider how these rules, taken together, would affect the places where people live and work. The rules are simply the implacable results of seemingly disparate policies, each with unintended consequences.

When the policies that made it easier for people to flee the cities and move to the suburbs hurt only urban neighborhoods, the people who chose or had to stay behind suffered. Now, however, these policies, together with the problems of decay and decline in the cities and rapid suburban development, are causing problems for suburbanites, too—most notoriously the problem known as sprawl.

Thus much of the unhappiness of the cities is also the unhappiness of the suburbs. The familiar image of a beleaguered urban core surrounded by suburban prosperity is giving way to something more realistic and powerful: metropolitan areas in which urban *and* suburban communities lose out as a result of voracious growth in undeveloped areas and slower growth or absolute decline in older places. The idea that cities and suburbs are related, rather than antithetical, and make up a single social and economic reality, is called metropolitanism.

Metropolitanism describes not only where but also in some sense how   10
Americans live—and it does this in a way that the city-suburb dichotomy

does not. People work in one municipality, live in another, go to church or the doctor's office or the movies in yet another, and all these different places are somehow interdependent. Newspaper city desks have been replaced by the staffs of metro sections. Labor and housing markets are area-wide. Morning traffic reports describe pileups and traffic jams that stretch across a metropolitan area. Opera companies and baseball teams pull people from throughout a region. Air or water pollution affects an entire region, because pollutants, carbon monoxide, and runoff recognize no city or suburban or county boundaries. The way people talk about where they live reflects a subconscious recognition of metropolitan realities. Strangers on airplanes say to each other, "I'm from the Washington [or Houston or Los Angeles or Chicago or Detroit] area." They know that where they live makes sense only in relation to other places nearby, and to the big city in the middle. Metropolitanism is a way of talking and thinking about all these connections.

The old city-versus-suburb view is outdated and untenable. We can no longer talk about "the suburbs" as an undifferentiated band of prosperous, safe, and white communities. There are two kinds of suburbs: those that are declining and those that are growing. Declining suburbs, which are usually older and frequently either adjacent to the city or clustered in one unfortunate corner of the metropolitan area, are starting to look more and more like central cities: they have crumbling tax bases, increasing numbers of poor children in their schools, deserted commercial districts, and fewer and fewer jobs. For such suburbs to distance themselves from cities makes about as much sense as two drowning people trying to strangle each other.

Growing suburbs are gaining, sort of. They are choking on development, and in many cases local governments cannot keep providing the services that residents need or demand. Loudoun County, a boom suburb in northern Virginia, epitomizes this kind of place. The county school board predicts that it will have to build twenty-three new schools by 2005 to accommodate new students. In February of this year the board proposed that the next six new schools be basic boxes for learning, with low ceilings, small classrooms, and few windows. "We cannot ask the voters to keep voting for these enormous bonds," a county official told *The Washington Post* earlier this year, referring to a $47.7 million bond issue in 1988 for the construction of three new schools. "Nor can we continue to raise taxes every single year to pay for school construction." Predictably, parents complained about the cutbacks in amenities—after all, they had moved there for the schools. "I just think they have to maintain their standards," a disgruntled parent told *The Washington Post.* But these suburbs cannot maintain their standards. There are simply too many new people who need too much new, expensive infrastructure yesterday—not just schools but also sewer and water lines, libraries, fire stations, and roads.

Whether they moved to these places for rural tranquillity, lovely views, and open space, or for good schools, or for the chance to buy a nice house, or just because they wanted to get away from urban hassles, residents of growing suburbs sense that frantic, unchecked growth is undermining what they value and want to keep. The old paradigm of cities and suburbs as opposites, or partisans in a pitched battle, doesn't explain the relationship between these gaining suburbs and their declining older cousins a few exits back on the highway.

Suburbs are not the enemies of cities, and cities are not the enemies of suburbs. That is the first principle of metropolitanism. Cities and suburbs have a common enemy—namely, sprawl. The cycle described above, of draining the center while flooding the edges, is familiar to almost anyone who has driven from one edge of a metropolitan area to another. It is endlessly repeatable, at least potentially: the center just gets bigger, and the edges move out. Metropolitanism is a way of thinking that might break this cycle.

Alas, the city-suburb dichotomy is alive and well in law and in policy. 15 The result is a tangle of regulations and programs that are excellent at throwing growth out to the edges of metropolitan areas and ineffectual at bringing it back to or sustaining it in the metropolitan core. One reason the problem of growth has not been solved is that the city-versus-suburb analysis doesn't properly describe it. The metropolitan reality requires different kinds of policies—ones that take connections and the varying impact of growth into account.

The metropolitanist policy agenda has four basic elements: changing the rules of the development game, pooling resources, giving people access to all parts of a metropolitan area, and reforming governance. These are interlocking aspects of how to create good places to live; they are closely related and can be hard to distinguish. To understand the cascade of consequences that policies can have, consider the policy chain reaction that would begin if the rules of the development game were changed to fit the metropolitanist paradigm. Those rules are mainly the policies that guide transportation investments, land use, and governance decisions, all of which are themselves entangled. Start at one end of the knot: transportation. Major highways, built by federal and state dollars, act as magnets for new development. This has been clear ever since the 1950s, when the interstate-highway system made the suburbs widely accessible and hugely popular. A metropolitanist viewpoint recognizes that these highways will probably pull lots of investments and resources away from the metropolitan core. New development, spawned by highways, will necessitate expensive state-funded infrastructure, such as sewer systems, water pipes, and new side roads. Meanwhile, existing roads, pipes, and sewers, which already cost taxpayers plenty of money, are either not used to the fullest or starved of funds for repair.

A metropolitanist transportation policy might eschew a new beltway and instead direct federal transportation dollars to public transit, which draws development toward rail stations rather than smearing it along a highway, or to repairing existing roads rather than building new ones. That is what Governor Parris Glendening, of Maryland, and Governor Christine Todd Whitman, of New Jersey, have proposed for their states, and what elected officials are working on or have accomplished in the metropolitan areas of Boston, Chattanooga, and Portland, Oregon. New businesses and housing developments will be steered toward where people already live and public investments have already been made.

At this point land use comes into play. "Land-use planning" may sound a little soporific, but it is simply a brake on chaos. It allows communities to prepare for growth in a way that avoids gridlock and preserves public resources. It connects the basic places of life: where people work, where they live, where they play, drop off their dry cleaning, check out a library book, buy a box of cereal. A metropolitanist land-use scheme would preserve open spaces and create parks and other public areas, thereby taking big parcels of suburban land off the development market. Where, then, would all the new development go? An enormous amount of vacant land already exists inside the boundaries of metropolitan areas, which generally have developed in leapfrog fashion, with big gaps between one subdivision or strip mall and the next. Parks and open spaces will not fill all those gaps, which could support development—as could the abandoned urban properties known as brownfields.

Land-use decisions can affect how as well as where things are built. Zoning policies can call for transit-oriented development—clusters of shops, apartment buildings, and offices around bus or rail stops, so that people will drive a little less. They can require or at least encourage varied housing near office buildings and supermalls, so that everyone who works there, from the receptionist to the escalator repairer to the middle manager to the chief financial officer, can live near his or her workplace.

Pooling resources is the second element of a metropolitanist agenda.   20 In most metropolitan areas a new office complex or amusement park or shopping mall tends to confer benefits on a single jurisdiction by adding to its property-tax coffers. Meanwhile, neighboring communities are stuck with some of the burdens of development, such as additional traffic and pollution and the loss of open space. Pooling resources—specifically, a portion of the extra tax revenue from development—means that development's benefits, like its burdens, are spread around. The Twin Cities area has a tax-base-sharing scheme whereby 40 percent of the increase in commercial and industrial property-tax revenues since 1971 is pooled and then distributed so that communities without substantial business development are not overwhelmed by needs and starved of resources. In other parts of the country regional jurisdictions have agreed to tax themselves to support cultural and sports facilities; this makes sense, because the entire region benefits from those facilities.

The third element of a metropolitanist agenda is giving everyone in the metropolitan area access to all its opportunities. Access is easy for people with decent incomes and decent cars. They can live where they wish, and they can get from their houses to their jobs without enduring extraordinary hassles. Poor people do not have this kind of mobility.

There are three ways to solve the access problem: make it easier for urban workers to get to suburban jobs; provide affordable housing (through new construction or vouchers) throughout a metropolitan region; or generate jobs in the metropolitan core or at least near public-transportation routes. State and federal governments are now implementing programs that help people to overcome core-to-edge transportation problems, and through housing vouchers are giving low-income people more choices in the metropolitan housing market. Across the country churches and nonprofit organizations are running jitney services and private bus lines to get people to work. A group of Chicago business leaders has called on major employers to weigh affordable housing options and access to public transit in their business location and expansion decisions. Businesses and nonprofit groups are also trying to bring jobs and people closer together. Housing vouchers administered by nonprofit organizations with a metropolitan scope allow low-income families to move into job-rich municipalities. The nonprofits counsel families about their options and develop relationships with landlords. In the Atlanta region BellSouth will soon consolidate seventy-five dispersed offices, where 13,000 people have worked, into three centers within the Atlanta beltway, all of which are easily accessible by mass transit. After studying where employees lived, the company picked locations that would be of roughly equal convenience for commuters from the fast-growing northern suburbs and from the less-affluent southern suburbs.

The final element of the metropolitanist agenda has to do with governance. Whereas markets and—more important—lives operate in a metropolitan context, our governmental structures clearly do not. They hew to boundaries more suited to an eighteenth-century township than to a twenty-first-century metropolis. Chicago's metropolitan area, for example, encompasses 113 townships and 270 municipalities. This fragmentation works against sustainable metropolitan areas and facilitates segregation by race, class, and ethnicity. Welfare-to-work programs are hindered when public transportation stops at the city-suburban border, for example. Issues that cross jurisdictional borders—transportation, air quality, affordable housing—need cross-jurisdictional solutions and entities that bring together representatives from all the places, small and large, within a metropolitan area to design and implement these solutions. Some such entities already exist: In every urban region in the country a metropolitan planning organization coordinates the local distribution of a chunk of federal transportation funds. Oregon and Minnesota have established metropolitan governments for their largest urban areas, Portland and the Twin Cities. But informal metropolitan governance, in which local governments coordinate their policies and actions, is possible and efficacious. Also, it's necessary.

Metropolitanism is a genuinely different view of the American landscape, and politicians from both parties are beginning to think that a majority of voters might find something to like in it. Like Governor Glendening and Governor Whitman, Governor Thomas Ridge, of Pennsylvania, has laid out land-use objectives for his state that include linking new development to existing infrastructure and encouraging metropolitan co-operation. Governor Roy Barnes, of Georgia, has proposed a strong metropolitanist transportation authority for Atlanta, and in March [1999] the state legislature approved it. Governors and state legislators are central to the metropolitanist agenda, because states control an important array of tax, land-use, governance, transportation, work-force, and welfare issues.

Vice President Al Gore clearly recognizes the political potential of this   25
issue and is trying to establish it as one of his signature issues. "We're starting to see that the lives of suburbs and cities are not at odds with one another but closely intertwined," he said in a speech last year. "No one in a suburb wants to live on the margins of a dying city. No one in the city wants to be trapped by surrounding rings of parking lots instead of thriving, livable suburban communities. And no one wants to do away with the open spaces and farmland that give food, beauty, and balance to our post-industrial, speeded-up lives." For more than a year Gore has been talking about America's growing "according to its values," and has even implied that development is not always welcome.

Of course, the idea of cities and suburbs coming together to solve common problems has been around for decades. No one ever before thought of using it to propel a presidential campaign, because the idea of metropolitanism had yet to prove its appeal, in referenda or in elections or in state legislatures. This is no longer the case.

These ideas are only just beginning to penetrate a recalcitrant real-estate-development industry, however. Christopher Leinberger is a managing director of one of the nation's largest real-estate advisory and valuation firms and a partner in a new urbanist consulting company. He has thought a lot about how the industry works, and he has concluded that sprawl is extremely attractive to the industry, because the kind of development it involves is simple and standardized—so standardized that it is sometimes hard to tell from the highway whether one is in Minneapolis or Dallas or Charlotte. These cookie-cutter projects are easy to finance, easy to build, and easy to manage. Builders like the predictability of sprawl. They know how much a big parking lot is worth, but they aren't sure how to value amenities in older communities, such as density, walkability, and an interesting streetscape. More or less the same can be said of big retail chains. For example, they often overlook the fact that although people in core neighborhoods may have low incomes, they are densely concentrated, which works out to a significant amount of purchasing power. Developers and retailers will have to be willing to think differently if development is to come back to the core. There are encouraging signs. Magic Johnson Theaters, Rite Aid pharmacies, and Pathmark supermarkets are all recognizing that the people left in core communities need places to earn money and to spend it; each of these companies has opened outlets in central cities in recent years. The National Association of Home-builders has joined with Gore, the U.S. Conference of Mayors, and the U.S. Department of Housing and Urban Development to encourage the development of a million new owner-occupied homes.

Of course, for the politicians' plans to work and the developers' projects to take off, urban core communities will have to win people over. Unless these places have good schools, safe streets, and efficient governments, people will not move from the edge back toward the center. Some mayors have realized this and are trying to make their cities better places to live. Richard Daley, of Chicago, and Stephen Goldsmith, of Indianapolis, are finding innovative ways to address issues that have bedeviled cities for decades: schools, crime, public services, and taxes. It is hard and often unpleasant work; it means privatizing some services, eliminating others, and ending wasteful patronage. But cities must be ready to take advantage of the opportunities that metropolitanist policies offer them.

Academics, architects, and bohemians may decry the soullessness of sprawl, but people seem to like it. Why put up such a fight to save dying places, whether they are called cities or older suburbs or metropolitan cores? After all, as people who see no harm in sprawl like to point out, Americans are living on a scant five percent of the land in this country. Why not just keep sprawling?

There are several reasons to defend not cities against suburbs but centeredness against decentralization, metropolitanism against sprawl. One reason to encourage development in metropolitan cores is a familiar one: the people who live there are among the poorest in their regions—indeed, in the country—and they need these opportunities and this investment. It is not fashionable to talk about having a moral obligation to poor people, but that doesn't mean that the obligation has disappeared. John Norquist, the mayor of Milwaukee, is fond of saying "You can't build a city on pity"; but disinvestment and the resulting lack of good schools, good jobs, and good transportation options is also impractical. The U.S. economy needs workers, and there are people in the metropolitan cores who are not getting into the work force. The need for workers will only increase as the average age of the population rises. By 2021 almost 20 percent of the American people will be over sixty-five, as compared with about 12.7 percent today. Whatever Social Security and Medicare reforms are enacted, these elderly people will need an abundance of payroll-tax-paying workers to support them.

The aging of the U.S. population will soon make it clear that sprawl is of no benefit to people who cannot drive. For a seventy-five-year-old without a car, sprawl can be uncomfortably close to house arrest. But metropolitan core communities where public transportation is available and distances are shorter between homes, pharmacies, doctors' offices, and libraries are navigable for older people in a way that settlements on the metropolitan fringe are not. Apartment buildings for the elderly are being built in the suburbs, with a variety of services under one roof, and vans to get people from here to there. But there should be choices for elderly men and women who do not want to be segregated from neighborhoods where babies and teenagers and middle-aged people also live.

Unlimited suburban development does not satisfy everyone. Metropolitanism will probably provide a greater range of choices, for the elderly and for everyone else. Policies that strengthen the metropolitan core lead to safer, more viable urban neighborhoods for people who prize the density and diversity of city life. These policies can reinvigorate older suburbs, with their advantages of sidewalks and public transit and a functioning Main Street. And, of course, they allow for brand-new, sizable single-family houses with yards.

It is also possible to argue against sprawl because of a commitment to community. Throughout this essay we have used the word "community" interchangeably with "township," "suburb," "municipality," "jurisdiction," "city," and "place." But "community" also designates a feeling, an ideal—as in "a sense of community," which many people worry that they have lost and would like to re-create. And they are trying to re-create it. Newspaper dispatches from the suburbs of Detroit and Washington, D.C., report that developers are trying to build what people left behind in older places: town centers, with wide sidewalks and big storefronts, where a person can perhaps run into a friend or an interesting stranger and have a place to hang out in public. In a 1998 essay titled "The City as a Site for Free Association," the political philosopher Alan Ryan writes, "If people are to be self-governing, they must associate with each other in natural and unforced ways from which their political association can spring." By "political association" Ryan means involvement in public life and public decision-making. The underlying assumption of a democracy is that this involvement is a wonderful thing. Yet it is unclear whether the new town centers can generate the unforced interactions that make municipalities feel like communities. For all the good intentions of the developers who build them and the government officials who support them, they are not natural centers. They are places where people are invited to go and be social or civic-minded, but, as Ryan says, "Telling people to go to such and such a café in order to promote political cohesion and political activity is like telling people to be happy; there are many things they can do that will make them happy, but aiming directly at being happy is not one of them."

These town centers are actually some of the few places where suburban people might mingle with crowds and see people who are not like themselves. They are, along with shopping malls, the public spaces of sprawl. Free association, in the sense of unexpected, unplanned encounters that draw us out of ourselves, is hard to come by in decentralized environments. Driving alone or with family members or close friends from one destination to another leaves little opportunity for spontaneity. Sprawl can create a kind of cultural agoraphobia that depletes public life.

Certainly, the outer edges of metropolitan areas are not the only 35 places that are finding public life difficult to sustain. The most depleted neighborhoods of metropolitan cores, with their forlorn "community centers," dingy streets, and empty sidewalks, are not fertile ground for free association either. And yet the architecture and layout of these places are at least supposed to facilitate interaction. Moreover, Ryan writes, there are still "galleries and concert halls, city parks, monuments, and other such places" in our urban cores for

> communities to come together, group by group and interest by interest. . . . To the degree that this is irreplaceable by seeing and hearing it all on television or on the stereo system, it encourages people to understand themselves as members of one society, engaged in a multitude of competing but also cooperative projects. A society that does not understand this about the basis of its cultural resources is a society in danger of losing them. At present, we seem to be such a society.

Suburbs are not new. They have been in existence in the United States since the nineteenth century. But hypersuburbanization, decentralization, and sprawl are new—less than two generations old. Americans are now discovering how hard it is to live without a center. In a typical attempt to move simultaneously in opposite directions, they are moving out but also trying to come back. This is not merely nostalgia for some dimly remembered era of civility and good cheer. People are honestly trying to balance the frantic privacy of the suburbs with some kind of spontaneous public life. By now it seems clear that continued sprawl will make this public life very hard to achieve—at the edges of metropolitan areas, where there are no places to gather, and at the cores of metropolitan areas, where the gathering places are unsafe or abandoned. Is this really a good trade for a big back yard?

◆ QUESTIONS FOR DISCUSSION AND WRITING ◆

1. Katz and Bradley discuss "metropolitanism." How well does their definition apply to the area in which you live?

2. How do some of the arguments about sprawl made in this article relate to those in other readings in this chapter? Of the pieces you've read, which are you the most inclined to believe? Why?

3. Katz and Bradley identify the traditional conceptual split between city and suburb as being part of the problem of urban sprawl. What other differences of definition complicate the sprawl issue?

4. This article sets up a template for a policy agenda. How successful do you think such an agenda might be in the Saguaro Flats scenario? How might it be applied to Saguaro Flats?

5. The article points out that, for an aging population, sprawl can present major mobility problems. Why might this point be particularly important to the article's readers?

6. How effective is the last line of the article? Why?

TAKING ACTION

Getting Your Message Across to the Board of Supervisors

You've now completed your reading, and perhaps you've done some additional research about specific aspects of the situation, just as you would have if you really were a resident of Saguaro Flats. In this scenario, the next step is to explain your group's position to the entity (government agency, school board, city council) that has control over the situation. In this case, the Maricopa County Board of Supervisors handles all planning and zoning ordinances and regulations, so your group must contact and attempt to influence that body.

For some time now, the Maricopa County Board of Supervisors has been considering the fate of the Saguaro Flats area. Before it approves anything, the board must assure itself that all development plans conform to existing laws. Although the developers have not yet submitted detailed plans, they have notified the board of their desire to change the current zoning standards for the area to allow both single- and multiple-family housing, retail and office space, a golf course, and light industrial buildings. There will be no smokestack industries, but businesses such as shipping companies or light assembly facilities might be included. Part of the decision process includes soliciting input from interested groups or individuals.

The board invites all interested parties to submit a two-page position statement in the form of a letter. The board will also consider impact studies and will hold open meetings, but this brief letter is your group's opportunity to make a strong first impression. Your group plans to submit a position statement to make its concerns part of the record.

Your letter really has several purposes. It will introduce your group to the board and make it aware that you expect your views to be considered in the decision process. This letter is your group's chance to present a brief statement about what it thinks should be done with Saguaro Flats. Your group need not oppose all development, or even this one, to prepare a letter for the board. What is important is that the members of your group determine what the group's goals are. Those goals will define what you say to the board in your letter. Another possible purpose for your letter might include making the board aware of issues it may not have considered.

BOX 7.2   FOR EXAMPLE
Formal Letter Format

A formal letter is a specific kind of document that has its own set of conventions. Readers expect that a formal letter will:

- Be in block format, with a return address, date, address, salutation, body, close, and signature.
- Use formal language, avoiding slang, contractions, and other informalities.
- Be clear, concise, and focused on the writer's main point.
- Maintain a courteous and professional tone.

Because the board is busy, and the Saguaro Flats issue is only one of its current agenda items, your letter should be no longer than two pages. For this exercise, prepare your letter as if you were actually planning to mail it. This means, among other things, using a suitable formal letter format. You can find models of several acceptable formats in any good writing handbook. Box 7.2: Formal Letter Format provides some suggestions for preparing a formal letter. Address your letter to the board as a whole rather than to a particular member, using this fictional address: Maricopa County Board of Supervisors; 2112 Central Plaza, Suite 318; Phoenix, AZ 85434.

As you write your letter, consider the purpose of the board of supervisors. The board is an elected body that answers to many constituencies (including you). Part of its mandate includes responsibility for Maricopa County's tax base: the money that allows the county to maintain its roads, fund the county hospital, pay the sheriff, stage local elections, and so on. Because the board is responsible for the county's fiscal health, it generally wants to encourage business activity, development, and building—all of which add to the county's tax base. If there is more developed land to tax, individual tax rates can sometimes be decreased—a wise political strategy.

At the same time, the board is aware of environmental and other issues, including the lifestyle that is so important to the residents of Saguaro Flats. Because board members are elected, they are conscious not only of what their decisions may mean to your group, but also of how their decisions will affect other voters within the county.

Asking the Right Questions

As we've mentioned, it's often a good idea to begin wrestling with a problem or issue that affects you by first discovering what you already know and then determining what you'd like to learn more about. One way to do this is to ask questions—questions that will lead to other questions that will help your group agree on the best solution for the problems the scenario presents. As you draft your statement to the board, consider the scenario from a reporter's perspective, focusing on the who, what, when, where, and why of the scenario. Try to answer the following questions:

- What perspectives might each of the interested groups have? What are the strengths and weaknesses of those perspectives?
- Can you make your position statement to the board stronger by aligning your group with others? Will it help to let the board know that more than one group feels the same way about several of the issues, problems, or possible solutions as your group does?
- What events in the Saguaro Flats scenario can be controlled? In what way(s)? What events cannot be controlled?
- What are some of the consequences to the Saguaro Flats area if the proposed development takes place? What specific effects will development have on the members of your group?
- What are the consequences if you do nothing to try to change the situation? What action might make the situation more difficult?
- How do the issues and problems in the Saguaro Flats scenario relate to the broader national perspective on urban growth and sprawl?

Which group you represent and the approach you decide to take will determine the position you propose. You might, for example, argue against any development, you might try to restrict the extent of the development, or you might work to circumscribe the nature of the development.

Constructing a Collaborative Text

Work with the members of your group to draft a letter to the board of supervisors that expresses your views on the issues outlined in the scenario. Read through and carefully revise your draft several times, to ensure that your group's ideas are articulated as clearly as possible.

One way for your group to start constructing its statement is for each group member to compose his or her own statement, listing what each considers to be the most important issues and problems. Then, working together, your group can draw on those initial comments to compose the group statement.

Another approach is to take the notes that each of you has made, designate one group member to record the group's ideas, and then collaboratively compose an initial draft of what your group thinks. At first, this process might be a bit hectic, with several group members offering suggestions on what to write and how to write it, but, with time, you'll find that working together is an interesting and useful way to get your collective ideas onto paper.

BOX 7.3 APPLYING WHAT YOU READ
Using Your Classmates' Suggestions (Written Peer Review)

Once you have a brief, collaborative text that outlines your message to the board of supervisors, exchange your draft with that of another group. Read that group's letter, and look for (and indicate in marginal notes) its strengths and weaknesses. What suggestions can you make on how the group might improve its position?

What are the strengths of the draft? The weaknesses? Where was the group's argument confusing? What is clear? Unclear? How could the group clarify its position? What suggestions might you offer to improve the letter?

Once your group receives feedback from your classmates, work together as a group to revise your letter. What suggestions did you receive that make sense? Where does your text need clarification, or further explanation, or more evidence? What facts or other data have group members collected that you can add to make your text more convincing?

When your group has completed a first draft of its collaborative text, each group member should read through the draft, marking any sections that are unclear. Work together to clarify those parts. Then, each group member should read the statement once more, this time looking for places in the text where the argument might need more evidence. Then, again working together, decide what pieces of evidence gathered during your research (facts, data, testimony, statistics) might provide additional support for your argument.

Your instructor may ask you to read and comment on the other groups' statements. Working together in such a manner gives you the chance to help your classmates become better writers, as you act as real readers for one another. Indicate the places in the text where more information is needed, or where the writing is confusing, or where some elaboration might help. Follow the procedures in Box 7.3: Using Your Classmates' Suggestions to apply the feedback you receive to improve your composition.

SPEAKING YOUR PIECE
Saguaro Flats Open Meeting

Because of the widespread attention focused on the development of Saguaro Flats, the board of supervisors has decided to hold an open meeting to permit all interested parties to voice their concerns and to ask questions. This is a rare opportunity: an open meeting allows direct interaction between groups, which can make it easier to identify and find solutions to the various conflicts.

This meeting is an opportunity to exchange information. The audience will consist not only of the board but also of the members of the other interested groups. During the meeting, it's important to listen carefully to all questions. If a question is addressed to your group, take a moment to confer among yourselves and determine a suitable answer. During the meeting itself, you and the other members of your group must remember that your comments and behavior may influence the decisions the board will make. Unreasonable, rude, or unprepared groups who represent themselves poorly can hurt their positions. Groups that ask insightful and relevant questions and express an interest in cooperation are more likely to be looked on favorably.

From Written Preparation to Public Speaking

For the sake of illustration, let's say that the spokesperson representing the ranchers' association wants to be sure the board recognizes the effect that losing their access to grazing land would have on ranchers. The speaker intends to make four points:

- If their cattle can no longer graze, ranchers will have to spend more on feed for them.
- Therefore, the cost of beef will increase for the consumer.
- An important part of the ranching way of life will be lost if there are no more cattle drives.
- Those visiting the forests where ranchers now graze their cattle will lose the benefit of seeing the animals in their natural habitat.

In a written argument, the ranchers' group could probably simply list these points and assume that readers could reread them if they needed clarification or became confused. In an oral presentation, however, the spokesperson for the ranchers' association would want to make each connection explicit, explaining how each point relates to the development's negative effects. To make these connections, the spokesperson might say something like this: ranchers will be negatively affected by the proposed development for these reasons:

- We will have to spend more on feed for our cattle because we won't be able to graze them. Our costs will increase, which means some of us might have to go out of business. That would put us—and those who work for us—out of our homes and our jobs, a negative consequence of the development.
- The cost of beef will increase for the consumer if we have to pay more to feed our cattle. We'll have to pass along some of our increased costs to stay in business, so all of you will pay more for beef—another negative consequence of the development.
- An important part of the ranching way of life will be lost if there are no more cattle drives. The ranching way of life is part of our

heritage. Once it's lost, we can't recover it—another negative consequence of the development.

- Those visiting the forests where we now graze our cattle will no longer be able to see the animals in their natural habitat if the development blocks our access to those lands. That real benefit to campers and hikers and other citizens who enjoy the woods will be lost if the development is allowed.

This brief illustration emphasizes the importance of making each oral example clear and complete and of connecting each example to the larger issue—in this case, the negative consequences of development to the ranching community.

Speaking at the Open Meeting

In a full-class open meeting, representatives of each group will speak (you will be given a time limit), just as you might to the board of supervisors. While your classmates present their viewpoints on Saguaro Flats and the proposed development, take notes on what they have to say. You'll find that their viewpoints on the issues will help you in the individual writing you'll soon be asked to do.

Whatever your group's perspective (homeowner, rancher, environmentalist, and so on), your spokesperson will want to explain your position on the issues you consider important. One way to focus your ideas is in terms of consequences:

- What are your main concerns about the proposed development?
- What consequences will the proposed development have on the members of your group?
- What are the major problems the proposed development will bring to Saguaro Flats?
- What benefits, if any, might the development bring? Are there other or better ways to gain these benefits without allowing the development?
- What ideas can your group offer for containing the development? From your point of view, what constraints should be placed on the developer?
- What alternatives can you offer to the proposed development?

Once each group has presented its viewpoint and has suggested what it feels is a workable solution, members of each group will be allowed to question members of the other groups. Your instructor may assign one or more students to act as moderators.

INDIVIDUAL WRITING
Essay Options

Your instructor will ask you to construct one or more individual writing projects: an informative essay, a persuasive essay, a proposal essay, and/or an analytic essay. Each project has its own focus and audience, but they all allow you to use what you've learned so far about the issues and problems in the Saguaro Flats scenario. It's now up to you to work with your invention notes, your group's written statement to the board of supervisors, your group's oral presentation at the town meeting, the questions that were asked and the answers that were given at that open meeting (by all groups), and the evidence you've collected from your reading.

The Informative Essay

Your instructor may ask that you compose an informative essay in which you explain the issues and problems in the Saguaro Flats scenario. The purpose of such an essay it *not* to take a position on the issues or to suggest solutions to any of the problems. It's simply to inform your readers.

For this writing project, assume that your audience is readers of the local newspaper. Your essay will not appear on the editorial pages, but in a special section devoted to local issues. Your goal is not to persuade the newspaper's readers that development should or should not take place, but rather to inform them of the effects and consequences of such development—both positive and negative.

Your readers, the citizens of Saguaro Flats and the surrounding area, will use the information you provide to decide how they feel about the proposed local development. As the writer of an informative essay, you'll want to present information in a neutral manner—or in as neutral a way as possible. This means you should focus on facts and data that indicate the real effects of development:

- Who is helped when a rural area is developed? In what ways?

- Who might be harmed when a rural area is developed? In what ways?

- What are the costs of such development? Are there any hidden costs, and if so, who pays them? What are the possible future costs?

- What happens to a county's tax base when development takes place?

- What kind of a community can its residents expect Saguaro Flats to be in five years if the development is built? In ten years?

- What might happen to the local water supply over the next ten or twenty years if the development is built?

The Persuasive Essay

A persuasive essay seeks, by its nature, to make its audience react as the writer wishes them to react. For this essay, assume that you're writing as a member of one of the interested groups (the Saguaro Flats residents, the ranchers' association, the historic preservation coalition, the environmentalists, or the development company) and that your audience is the Maricopa County Board of Supervisors.

In this persuasive essay you'll take a stand on the development of Saguaro Flats: Should it be allowed? Why or why not?

You already know a good deal about the board from your group position statement, and you've read and perhaps heard in an open meeting what other groups think should happen in Saguaro Flats. Remember that the board must balance as many conflicting concerns as possible. In this case it will examine, discuss, and decide which proposal is best for all the interested parties. Keep in mind, too, that the board is an elected body whose members (usually) want to win reelection. Therefore, the board will be looking for a solution that will satisfy the largest number of people.

What facts or data or other information do you have that will support your position? What similar situations have you found in other locations, and how have those developments turned out? What are the general feelings of those who will be affected by the board's decision? Whether you argue in favor of or against development, what good arguments are there on the other side, and how might you answer those objections to your point of view?

The Proposal Essay

Your instructor may ask that you construct a detailed proposal for the board of supervisors in which you put forward a plan for the development of Saguaro Flats. Your proposal should attempt to satisfy the needs of as many of the interested groups as possible, to give it the greatest likelihood of being adopted and accepted.

A proposal presents a solution to a problem. In this scenario your proposal essay should focus on what sort of development should be allowed in Saguaro Flats. For this assignment, assume that the board of supervisors has taken into consideration the initial statements of the groups concerned with the development of Saguaro Flats, and the board has decided to let development move forward, but with some restrictions. What do you think those restrictions should be?

Think about creative solutions to the apparent conflicts among the interest groups and how those solutions might help to resolve differences. Your proposal might include a map of your planned development to help your audience visualize your ideas, and it might also include a timeline for development to help the board understand how things should progress.

Your audience is the Maricopa County Board of Supervisors, because they're the ones who will ultimately determine the future of Saguaro Flats. The board has already made some decisions, which your proposal for development must take into account. Those decisions include:

- Access for ranchers through the developed area for biannual cattle drives.
- Access to hiking trails.
- Improved access to highways and expansion of services to meet the needs of a larger population.
- Protection for petroglyph sites both within and near the development.
- Protection for the nesting areas of the yellow-necked gnat darter and other threatened species.
- Protection of existing waterways.
- Concessions to protect the rural lifestyle.

Keep in mind that the more specific you are, the more persuasive you'll be. Your proposal should include some sort of detailed planning structure for the development, including when and where development will begin. You may want to turn the map into your primary visual aid, create a key for the map, and then link your proposal to the map.

Don't feel limited by the list of decisions the board has made. There are many other issues involved, and you may want to address some of them: services such as schools, mail, utilities, fire and police protection, or whatever else seems important.

The Analytic Essay

An analytic essay focuses on one or more local issues and works to move the discussion to a wider audience, which may have a broader— even national—perspective.

For this assignment, you've decided that it might be helpful to gain support for your position from those who live outside of Saguaro Flats. To that end, you've decided to write an essay and submit it to a national newsmagazine, such as *Time* or *Newsweek*.

Because defining the terms of the argument are so important, you've decided to elaborate on the meaning of either "sprawl" or "development," (your choice, depending on your goals and position).

As you develop your extended definition of the term you select, you might want to provide examples, make comparisons, contrast your definition with how others might define the term, and so on. Pay close attention to the feelings that are associated with words, and try to employ those associations in support of your position.

BOX 7.4   APPLYING WHAT YOU READ
Reflections on the Saguaro Flats Scenario

By this point in the scenario, you've done a lot of reading, discussing, and writing about the development of Saguaro Flats. Take a few minutes now to look back at the first writing you did for this scenario, after you'd thought about the photographs that introduce this chapter and read the First Impressions questions. Then jot down your answers to these questions:

- Has your initial reaction to the introductory photographs changed, now that you've worked your way through the scenario? If so, in what way? If not, why not?
- What issue or problem in the scenario do you feel the strongest about? Why?
- What was the most important thing you learned as you worked through this scenario?
- Did your writing process change at all as you "wrote your way through" this scenario? If so, in what way(s)?
- What might you do differently for the next scenario project you work on? Why?

When you're finished, your instructor may ask you to share your thoughts with your classmates.

Your audience will be the general reading public—something of a national audience. They'll have somewhat broader concerns than just what happens to Saguaro Flats, Arizona.

What are the bigger issues that the Saguaro Flats scenario brings to mind? How might you adapt what you've learned about urban development or rural living or historic artifacts or the need for city conveniences or quality of life to a broader national discussion? In what way(s) can you move beyond the specific issues that surround Saguaro Flats to a national conversation about growth and development and what ought to be important to this country?

To conclude this scenario, your instructor may ask that you follow the instructions in Box 7.4: Reflections on the Saguaro Flats Scenario. The process of writing about ways in which your attitudes may have changed helps clarify your thinking.

FOR FURTHER RESEARCH AND WRITING

This scenario presents a number of opportunities for further writing, especially if you decide to explore broader national issues and problems. One area to consider is the continuing role of ranching in the American

West. Is the ranching way of life still important to this country, or is it simply a historic artifact that modern society no longer needs and should discard? Have rugged individualism and the rural way of life been supplanted by society's urban, technologic focus?

You could also examine the importance of zoning laws in developing communities. What happens to a small town that grows without a master plan of some kind? And, if there should be a master plan, who ought to design it, and how should it be implemented? You've read about various approaches to limiting urban sprawl: what approach to limiting growth make the most sense to you, and why?

Another area of interest might be the current status of the Endangered Species Act and whether it functions effectively. What are the main provisions of the act? Does wildlife still need protection in this day and age? Should the act be strengthened and, if so, in what ways?

Another question to ask is what responsibility society has to protect historic and prehistoric artifacts and sites. Who decides what is important, historically? What if such sites stand in the way of important growth and development?

Several years ago there was a widespread movement known as The Sagebrush Rebellion, in which a number of western states argued with the federal government over land rights. In broadening the focus to how government works, you might explore the ability of grassroots political movements to change or influence decisions made by political bodies. Which populist, grassroots movements have proven effective and why? Which movements succeeded only in raising issues that the political bodies in charge more or less ignored? Why?

You now have read, discussed, and written about some of the problems with urban sprawl, as exemplified by the situation at Saguaro Flats. Every day, people from many parts of this country face the same questions about urban growth and development: What development and changes are beneficial to an area, and which ones are not? What kinds of growth should be allowed and, indeed, encouraged, and which types should be restricted? We hope that working through this scenario has helped you improve the ways in which you read about and understand issues and problems. We also hope you're learning how to work more effectively with others and how to revise your written work more efficiently. The skills you worked to develop in this scenario will help you in your other college classes, as well as throughout your career.

CHAPTER 8

Pornography on the Internet

CYBERPORN AT YOUR LOCAL LIBRARY?

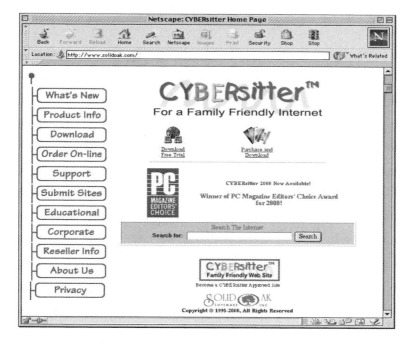

◆ **FIRST IMPRESSIONS** ◆

Be sure to look at and think about the photographs that introduce this chapter. Then spend a few minutes jotting down answers to these questions:

- Does the *Time* magazine cover sensationalize the issue of Internet censorship? Why or why not?
- Is controlling Internet access the same kind of censorship as book burning, or is it different in significant ways? Explain.
- How do you define these terms: *pornography, censorship, obscene, offensive content*?
- At your local bookstore, are some sections blocked off, to keep those who are underage from viewing the material they contain? Is a public library different from a commercial bookstore? Do you think that a library should restrict access to what some of its patrons can read or see? Why or why not?
- Does your local library impose access restrictions (such as making some areas off-limits to children)? Do you agree with those restrictions?
- Do you think that your local or college library should have a filtering system on its computers to block certain Web sites? Why or why not?
- Would you consider such a system to be censorship? Why or why not?
- Do you consider the V-chip, which is installed in some newer televisions and allows certain shows to be blocked, to be a form of censorship? What about mandatory CD labels to warn the purchaser of offensive content?
- As a college student doing Internet-based research, do you believe your Web access should be restricted in any circumstances? Why or why not?

When you're done, your instructor may ask you to share your comments with your classmates.

W hen patrons in the public library in Loudoun County, Virginia, tried to view sexually explicit material on a computer linked to the Internet, their computer screen flashed "VIOLATION!! VIOLATION!! VIOLATION!! Access to this site has been blocked." The library had installed a computer program to prevent access to information and images the software identified as pornographic.

But library users complained that they were denied access to information about important topics such as sex education, breast cancer, and gay and lesbian rights because the library's software couldn't differentiate between "obscene" information and material containing language or illustrations related to the sex organs. Some filtering programs block out discussions about breast cancer or abortion because of the language they contain. Automated software filters see no difference between "XXX-rated" and "Superbowl XXX" because they are designed to recognize controversial words or even suffixes ("www.oneplace.sex?").

In November 1998, a federal judge ruled that Loudoun County public libraries could not limit their patrons' use of the Internet. The ruling forced librarians to disconnect the filtering software they had been using.

Similar disputes are taking place in communities from Austin, Texas, where all fifty-two of the public library's computers use software filters, to rural Kern County, California. The Kern County libraries, under threat of a lawsuit by the American Civil Liberties Union (ACLU), agreed to provide two computers in each branch library, one with an activated filter program and one without such a program. Other libraries around the country have emulated the Boston Public Library, which after public outcry, installed filter programs only on computers in children's rooms (Harmon).

It is not only materials viewed as pornographic that are targeted: the Anti-Defamation League recently unveiled an Internet filter that it labeled the ADL Hatefilter. The Hatefilter screens out sites that preach anti-Semitism, racism, homophobia, and other forms of bigotry. Off-limit sites include Ku Klux Klan sites and the white supremacist Aryan Nations site (Mendels).

How are such problems handled at your local library? In your community:

- Does your library offer unlimited access to the Internet?
- Can library patrons send and receive e-mail?
- Does your library have an Internet filtering system to protect children? How effective is it?
- If you have a college or university library, does it handle Internet or e-mail restrictions differently than does your public library?
- Should libraries serve as "morality police" for their communities? Why or why not?
- How would you respond to a taxpayer's comment that he or she "won't foot the bill for putting pornography on my library's computers"?

Although our scenario is set in the fictitious town of Derry, New Hampshire, the issues you'll read about, discuss, and write about are universal. Is viewing or reading whatever you wish a right American citizens have, or should that right be restricted in certain instances? Can public libraries, supported by public funds, limit what someone is allowed to read or to view on the library's computers?

Pretend for a moment that you live in Derry, New Hampshire. As a young mother checks out a book from the downtown library, her ten-year-old comments on a picture he sees on a nearby computer screen. It's not the sort of image you would see on your home television set.

The woman is offended and complains to the reference librarian. She's told that library patrons have the right to view and print whatever they wish. "Even if my son can see it?" the mother asks.

Catherine Grimme, reference librarian of the Derry Public Library, walks over and looks at the offending screen. She is none too pleased with what she sees. "I don't like it either," she says, "but, after all, we don't have censorship in the library. All one has to do is click the little X, to close the screen."

But when Ms. Grimme presses the mouse button, the screen suddenly fills with several brightly colored windows of various sizes, each showing a picture of a scantily dressed woman in a suggestive pose.

Quickly, Ms. Grimme clicks again, this time pressing hard on the mouse button—but each time she does so, more windows pop up on the screen. Each window somehow generates more windows, all showing the same types of images.

As the two women stare at the computer screen, things take a turn for the worse: Pastor and Mrs. Walter Roger Kohl and their four children walk by, on their way to the Children's Reading Room.

"Why, Walter, look at *that*!" Mrs. Kohl says, pointing at the computer screen, which is happily creating even more windows.

"What's that, Daddy?" one of the Kohl's sons asks.

Because no one has the presence of mind to simply turn off the computer, they all stand there—the young mother, her child, Ms. Grimme, and the whole Kohl family—watching the computer screen continue to generate windows, each with an image seemingly more offensive than the last.

Of course, there was quite a fuss after that—and, one month later, all of Derry Library's computers had Internet filtering software designed to stop viewers from logging on to offensive Web sites.

In a public library, can patrons use the library's computers to access whatever they wish? Can the library—and should the library—censor what its patrons can view? Should patrons be allowed to view any screen they wish, even if those images can also be seen by others in the library?

Is Internet access in some way different from access to printed texts? Does the library already limit access to certain texts? Who decides which texts should be restricted? Who should determine what constitutes pornography? The library? Its patrons? And if a library wishes to restrict on-line access, how should it go about it? Imagine that:

- You're the parent of small children, and you don't want them to see images that you consider offensive. You especially don't want your children to see those pictures at the local library. And you certainly don't want to give up your family's Saturday morning visits to the library, when a guest reader—often a local author— comes in and reads children's books to Derry's youngsters. You value your local library, but, at the same time, you won't tolerate exposure to "electronic pornography" on your way to the Children's Reading Room.

- You're part of the library administration, and you've always been a strong proponent of free speech: citizens should be able to read what they choose. But this Internet problem presents a new sort of challenge. The library has always been able to restrict access to certain texts by placing them in a separate room. The check-out process made it easy to control what certain patrons could read: children weren't allowed to take home books that were considered inappropriate for them. But the Internet is puzzling. Although the Derry Library bought and installed net-filtering software, that software has been too restrictive—and yet not powerful enough to prevent access to all of the sites and images it was intended to stop. You've considered putting all the computers in a special room, but none is available. Even if one were, you don't have enough staffers to monitor the activity in that room. And e-mail, which once contained only text, now can include pictures and Web links, which causes other problems. What do you think should be done?

- You're one of the local authors who reads to children at the Derry Library every Saturday morning. You've always been a strong proponent of free and unrestricted speech—you certainly wouldn't want anyone telling you what you could write! You're a member of the Author's Guild, and you often participate in peaceful demonstrations during "Banned Book Week," during which many bookstores showcase famous books that were once banned (and sometimes burned). You've always worked hard to support everyone's right to write and to read what he or she sees fit.

- You write for the *Derry Daily News,* and any threat of censorship concerns you. You worry that once people's rights are restricted at the local library, the newspaper could be next. But you also realize that the *Daily News* already has certain restrictions concerning the words its writers can use and the kinds of photographs it will print. Are such self-imposed restrictions the same as library censorship?

In this scenario, we focus on some of the issues and problems that new technology brings to the table: Do people have the right to look at everything they wish to (or stumble across) on the Internet, especially in a tax-supported and public area? Do materials available through electronic media differ in some way from printed texts? Is using public money to purchase artwork or texts that some might consider pornographic or obscene the same as using it to pay for library computers that can be used to access sites that some consider obscene or pornographic? How great a voice should the public have in the ways in which its tax dollars are used? Are some levels of censorship acceptable? If so, who should decide how much censorship is appropriate? As technology advances, so do the problems that society will have to address regarding information access.

We will ask you and your classmates to divide into groups that represent the parties most interested in and involved with Derry's Internet issues. You'll work within these groups, collaboratively and individually, on a number of activities that address the issues you might face if you really lived in Derry, New Hampshire.

This scenario can also provide a springboard for further research and discussion on a variety of topics, ranging from the history of the Internet, to the future directions of technology, to free speech rights, to a discussion of the ways in which electronic images are different from (or the same as) textual material.

THE SCENARIO

What's Showing on Your Library's Computer?

As in many small communities, much of the life of Derry, New Hampshire, centers around its downtown area. In the very middle of town, Derry boasts a small grassy park with an obelisk at its center. That pillar list the names of Derry residents who died while fighting for their country. Derry's list reaches as far back as the War of 1812 and includes servicemen and -women from the Civil War, World Wars I and II, the Korean conflict, and a single casualty from the Vietnam War.

On one side of the small park are Derry's block-granite municipal buildings, with their large windows facing east, to catch the morning sunlight. Next to the city hall is Derry's public library. Unlike libraries in some communities, over the past few years Derry's library has become more, rather than less, active—perhaps because Derry is somewhat isolated. The library now boasts a Children's Room, where Saturday readings by well-known authors are a regular event, a large current periodicals room, and ten computers, all connected to the Internet. The library also has a joint arrangement with Derry Community College, which houses its text collection at the public library. That saves both the library and the college money.

So far, Derry's library patrons have shared resources amicably with Derry Community College students, except for those times when a paper is due in the college's first-year composition classes. "You always know when those kids have a paper due," Becky Reese, the Derry librarian, likes to relate. "There's a million of them here the day before, doing their research!"

On a cold Saturday morning in February, Heidi Ernst and several of her classmates walked into the Derry Public Library, sat down at the computer terminals, logged on, and began their research. Heidi's plan (which her composition teacher had approved) was to write an informative paper on the exploitation of women who work as professional dancers. She tried several search terms, using different search engines. Heidi collected some useful information, but then she typed in the words "private dancing."

Heidi's screen filled with line after line of search results, some promising "XXX girls girls girls!" "WOMEN! PHOTOS! XXX," and other, more explicit offerings. When Heidi clicked on one of these links—just out of curiosity—her screen turned bright red and flashed VIOLATION!! OFFENSIVE WEB SITE!! At the same time, Heidi's computer emitted a loud series of beeps.

Everyone turned and looked at Heidi—and librarian Grimme bolted from her chair and ran over to Heidi's computer.

"Didn't you see the sign?" Ms. Grimme shouted over the beeping, pointing to a sign taped above the computer screen that read, "Filtering software installed on this PC."

Heidi answered, "No, I guess I didn't—"

"Well, it's important to pay attention," Ms. Grimme admonished. She'd learned a lesson from the earlier incident, and this time reached to the rear of Heidi's computer and switched it off.

"What's this filtering stuff?" Heidi asked.

"It's software we've installed on the library's computers that blocks offensive Web sites, pictures, and so on."

"You're censoring my access to the Internet?" Heidi asked.

"Well," Ms. Grimme answered, "these *are* the library's computers. . . ."

One thing led to another—and some strong words—and the next day, there was a demonstration in front of Derry Community College's administrative offices. More than a hundred students protested what they called "Internet censorship," but the librarians held their ground, and the filtering software remains on the library's computers.

ENTERING THE SCENARIO: WHAT CAN I LOOK AT ON THAT COMPUTER SCREEN?

Now that you've read through the scenario that focuses on Derry's public library and understand some of the issues it raises, it's time for you to become actively involved. Your instructor will ask you to join several of your classmates to role-play as a member of one of the groups involved in the Derry situation. Although your main interest lies in the group of which you're a member, the descriptions of the other groups will help you understand all of the issues involved in this scenario. Note that the group descriptions that follow are only a starting point: your group (and the others) will work to tailor your descriptions and perspectives to fit your ideas about Internet access.

We ask you to pretend that you are a member of the group you represent and to consider the issues from your group's perspective. Working with several of your classmates, you'll discuss and consider issues and questions such as these:

- What kind of Internet access should a public library provide its users? Should that access be restricted in any way?

- Viewing an Internet site is a passive activity; sending e-mail is an active event: one can inadvertently look at an "offensive" Web site, but one cannot accidentally send an offensive e-mail. In terms of possible restrictions, then, is looking at Internet sites different in some way from sending e-mail?

- If your group agrees that a library should monitor what can be seen on its computers, how can the library exercise that control?

- What issues in this scenario does your group find especially interesting? What are some of the issues that might concern your group more than they concern the other groups?

- What part of the Derry scenario especially troubles the members of your group? What are some of the issues you feel less interested in?

- Are the issues confronting the Derry Library more complex because it shares facilities with the local community college? Do the free speech rights of college students differ from those of other citizens?

- What other groups might share at least some of your beliefs and ideas about the Derry Library situation? With which other groups might you align yourselves?

- If you were the head librarian at Derry's public library, what might your views on censorship be? Should a public library decide what its patrons are allowed to read or see?

Derry Library Patrons

You and the others who use the library visit there for many reasons: to borrow books, of course, but also sometimes just to sit and read. Lately, you've taken advantage of the library's new computers, and you've enjoyed "surfing the Web," looking up stock prices, browsing the *New York Times* online, and so on.

Some members of your group are parents with young children, and you enjoy introducing your children to books and reading. Many of you are well read, and you want books to be a part of your children's lives, too. Derry is a small community, and word of the "Heidi Incident" has spread rapidly. You're concerned about free speech rights and censorship issues, but those of you with children certainly don't want them exposed to some of the adult materials that are available on the Internet.

How do the parents among you define *offensive* or *pornographic*? Do those in your group who are not parents define those terms differently? How might other groups define those terms? Are you concerned that once some form of censorship begins, it will be impossible to control how far it goes?

Reporters for the *Derry Daily News*

Most reporters favor free speech and are opposed to censorship, but you have to admit that you're concerned with the text and images your newspaper prints. There are certain words that will never appear in your newspaper, and the photo editor takes great care to ensure that offensive photos are not published. Aren't you being somewhat duplicitous, then, if you object to Internet restrictions at the Derry Library? Or do you consider self-censorship acceptable, but believe that restrictions imposed from outside are different in some way?

Like most businesspeople, reporters spend a great deal of time sending and reading e-mail. At the Derry Library, they're talking about censoring e-mail use. You remember reading, not too long ago, about several employees of some large company who were fired for sending inappropriate e-mail messages. What if that kind of e-mail monitoring spilled over into your workplace?

What would your group do if it were in charge of the Derry Public Library?

Derry Community College Students

You and other community college students use Derry's library to do research for many of your classes. The library is convenient, after all, and you know that Derry CC has managed to keep tuition low partly by combining its library resources with those of the local public library. Sometimes, especially when a paper is due, the library is a little crowded, but that's to be expected.

What do you and the others in your group think about library censorship? How might you define *offensive, obscene,* or *pornographic*? Would your definitions be the same as, say, those a group of parents might provide? Do you believe that certain things—certain words, photos, paintings—will always offend someone, so to censor anything is, in effect, to censor everything?

Do you and the members of your group worry that if your Internet access is restricted in some way, you might not be able to locate all the information you need to write an effective paper on certain topics?

Derry Librarians

Librarians generally feel very strongly that censorship in any form is wrong, but at the same time you have to be realistic about who uses the library's resources. The library already controls, to some extent, the texts on its shelves; should there be a separate limited-access Internet area? As librarians, do you want to become the "Internet police"? Is this a role you'd have to assume if a decision were made to monitor e-mail and other Internet activities?

How do you feel about the installation of software "filters" on your library's computers? Should the library build a special room or cubicles where adults could go and view anything on the Internet they choose to? Or would such cubicles be too much like what you visualize an adult bookstore as having?

JOINING YOUR INTEREST GROUP

Now that you've read through the Derry Library scenario and understand some of the interests and perspectives of the various groups, it's time for you to become actively involved. Your instructor will ask you to work with several of your classmates as a member of one of the groups, to role-play.

In this activity, you take on the role of an interested party, pretending that you are a member of the group you represent and considering the issues related to Internet filtering from that person's perspective. Working with several of your classmates, you'll discuss and decide on answers to the following questions:

- What issues in the Derry Public Library scenario do you find especially interesting? What are some of the issues that might concern your group more than they concern the other groups? Do all the members of your group have the same views on whether Internet access at the library ought to be restricted?

- What other groups might share at least some of your beliefs and ideas about the situation in Derry? With which other groups might you align yourselves, to make each of your positions stronger?

- Which groups might oppose your point of view on Internet filtering or other forms of Internet protection? What objections might those groups have to your ideas? How might you counter those objections?

Before beginning your group discussion, read Box 8.1: Representing the Range of Opinion for suggestions your group can apply to encourage members to explore their positions.

BOX 8.1   APPLYING WHAT YOU READ
Representing the Range of Opinion

To better understand the various perspectives on the recent developments in Derry, assume that all perspectives exist within your group. To help your group generate a fuller range of ideas and viewpoints about Internet filtering, each group member should adopt the persona, or role, of a person who would belong to the real group.

For the first part of this activity, work with the members of your group to brainstorm a list of all the positions that might exist within your group. Assign these positions to group members. Now, think about the position you're representing. How would someone in your position feel? How might Internet filtering affect you, today and in the future? How would you define the terms *pornography, censorship, obscene,* and *offensive content*?

As a group, generate a list of all the problems, concerns, advantages, and observations that your members can come up with. Decide how your group would define the terms *pornography, censorship, obscene,* and *offensive content.* Be sure all group members receive a copy of the list: it's valuable invention work that all can draw on later in the Derry Public Library scenario.

When you've finished, your instructor may ask you to share your "personas" with other members of the class.

TAKING A POSITION: WRITING TO THE COMMUNITY LIBRARY OVERSIGHT PANEL

Because its funding comes from two sources—the city of Derry and Derry Community College—the public library is overseen by Derry's Community Library Oversight Panel (CLOP). For this scenario, assume that CLOP asks each interested group to submit a two-page written statement presenting that group's position on what, if anything, the library should do to limit its patrons' Internet access.

RESOURCES: EXAMINING CENSORSHIP IN A TECHNOLOGICAL AGE

Before your group constructs its statement to CLOP, you'll find it useful to consider what others have experienced as they've confronted issues similar to those you find in this scenario. You might want to interview your local or college librarian to learn what restrictions, if any, there are on Internet access.

The readings that follow provide you with background information on the larger debate of which the Derry Public Library controversy is just an example. These writers explore a number of important free speech and censorship issues, and each has a different perspective on the subject. Following each reading you'll find questions that will increase your understanding of the problems and issues these writers address—and of how technology is changing the ways in which we view censorship. Remember to interact actively with these readings, and use the reading strategies you learned earlier (prereading, annotating, summarizing, and so forth).

As you read, think about how the group you represent might react to the positions outlined in these readings:

- From your group's perspective, what are the most important points in each reading?
- What ideas, facts, or data in each reading might your group use in your statement to the Community Library Oversight Panel?
- Do any of the readings offer insights on free speech or censorship that might work against your group's position?

As you read, make note of any issues, ideas, or facts that you think might help or hurt your position, so that you can address them in your writing. This information will be useful as your group composes its written statement to Derry's Community Library Oversight Panel.

These selections begin with a provocative cartoon by Gary Brookins, followed by a brief history of "the sex trade," as writer N. R. Kleinfield describes it, in New York City. Kleinfield demonstrates the impossibility of protecting anyone from exposure and access to pornography.

An editorial that appeared in the *San Jose Mercury News* aims at the heart of this scenario: regulating Internet access. Then, columnist Leonard Pitts argues that parents are ultimately responsible for what their children see on a computer screen and suggests that no amount of legislation can successfully halt the flow of Internet material.

Two articles from the *New York Times* examine what took place when two separate libraries attempted to filter "pornography" from their computers, as did the fictitious Derry Public Library. A pair of editorials follows. The first, "X-Rated" from the *Wall Street Journal,* criticizes the stand taken by the American Library Association concerning the use of public library computers to access the Internet. The second, "Porn May Have Place, But It's Not in Class," was written by a first-year journalism student, Meghan Gaynor, for her campus newspaper.

Finally, we include three readings that focus on the Communication Decency Act (CDA) and its connection to the First Amendment to the Constitution. Joshua Quittner in *Time,* "@ the Supreme Court," focuses on the Court's view of the CDA. For his part, William Bennett Turner asks in *Wired* magazine, "What Part of 'No Law' Don't You Understand?" In a longer essay written for an academic audience (readers of the education weekly *Chronicle of Higher Education*), Lawrence Biemiller and Goldie Blumenstyk center, as did Quittner, on the Supreme Court's thoughts on the CDA.

◆ READINGS

✳ Cartoon

Gary Brookins

Gary Brookins, *Richmond Times-Dispatch*

1. What message does this cartoon send? Do you find it humorous? What in the cartoon makes you feel as you do, do you suppose?
2. Would your reaction to the cartoon be different if the person pictured in it were a woman instead of a man? Why or why not?
3. How would you react if your son or daughter were caught looking at "pornographic" Web sites at your local library?
4. Is the cartoon a fair depiction of a real Internet danger? Why or why not?

It's Not Easy to Push Sex into the Shadows

N. R. Kleinfield

As early as the 1840's, dauntless pushcart vendors and stationery stores hawked lewd postcards of women in considerably less than full attire. It was only a matter of time before there was a topless shoeshine parlor in Times Square.

In one form or another, the sex trade has always had a durable X-rated visibility in New York City. It is a stubbornly resilient industry that has stumbled and rebounded under the force of the law and changing tastes and technologies. But it has never gone away—not nearly.

The city's peep shows and topless bars, however, now face the most formidable test of their bare-bodied, multimillion-dollar buoyancy, with Mayor Rudolph W. Giuliani's administration seeking to enforce zoning regulations that could severely limit the city's lineup of sex shops.

Last week [February 1998], the State Court of Appeals upheld zoning rules that bar sex-oriented businesses from operating within 500 feet of residential areas, schools, churches, day-care centers or one another. On Friday, a Federal judge issued a temporary restraining order preventing the city from acting on the zoning rules, pending a hearing.

How radically the sex trade will be revamped by this fresh campaign   5
remains to be seen, but it is hard to imagine the city barren of a sex industry, for the very reason that it never has been.

Prostitution and the sale of erotic material trace back to the early days of the city. Before the end of the 19th century, even respectable vendors sold lascivious postcards and photographs.

During the Depression, Times Square began its steady descent from a thriving theater district into seediness. While it continued to be a center for a wide range of entertainment—movie premieres and burlesque shows, taxi dance halls and dime museums—many theaters were transformed into "grinder" houses that offered continuous showings of nudist films and, eventually, sexually explicit movies.

In the 1960's, the face of an explicit sex shop industry emerged as Times Square coalesced into the nation's capital of retail sex. It was a ripe place for Martin J. Hodas. In the early 1960's, he hatched the notion of putting pornographic movies in nickelodeon machines. The public enthusiasm for his innovation amply enriched him and gained him notoriety as the "King of the Peeps."

The 1970's were boom times for the sex industry. Dozens of massage parlors staffed with prostitutes lined Eighth Avenue in midtown. Show World opened its doors in Times Square, a glitzy multistory sex emporium that came to be known as the McDonald's of the sex industry. Richard Basciano, one of Show World's owners, came to control an empire of sex-oriented businesses that made him the emperor of Times Square smut.

By the mid-1970's, more than 100 sex shops and topless bars plied their trade in Times Square, and politicians had begun their long, exhausting dance with the sex trade. Virtually every city administration would undertake at least one campaign to clean up Times Square. Unsuccessful attempts to thwart the businesses through zoning go back decades.

The sex industry was a major issue in the 1969 mayoral election, during which Billy Graham denounced Times Square and exhorted the candidates to stamp out pornography. After winning the election, Mayor John V. Lindsay set up a task force to tackle the issue and began cracking down on peep shows and sex-oriented magazine stores.

During the administration of Abraham D. Beame, in 1976, the Mayor's Office of Midtown Enforcement was created to attack vice in Times Square. A new measure, the Nuisance Abatement Law, took effect in the summer of 1977, making it far easier to close illegal sex businesses.

"We used the law extensively and were able to essentially close down all the massage parlors," said William Daly, who is now the director of the Office of Midtown Enforcement. Much of the prosecution under that statute took place under Mayor Edward I. Koch, who once proposed moving all the sex-related businesses to city-owned piers on the Hudson River.

The new enforcement tactics and the fact that the industry had acquired a certain maturity sent it into decline in the 1980's. Increasingly, people favored watching sex tapes on their own VCR's. Between 1975 and 1986, according to the Office of Midtown Enforcement, the number of sex shops and pornographic movie houses in central Manhattan plunged to 44 from 147. Massage parlors and topless bars all but vanished.

But the sex business gathered momentum again in the early 1990's. The upscale strip club arrived as conventional nightclubs that were losing business reinvented themselves. The advent of low-priced sex films led to a resurgence in pornographic video stores rarely vulnerable under the nuisance statute.

Yet the elaborate redevelopment of Times Square has brought about a pronounced dispersion of the industry. The depressed real estate market in the early 1990's led landlords elsewhere in the city to rent to sex businesses they previously spurned. Only about 20 sex businesses, including

Show World, are believed to be operating in midtown today, but the city appears to have more sex shops than ever—in neighborhoods like Chelsea, the Upper West Side and Greenwich Village in Manhattan, Forest Hills, Queens, and Sunset Park, Brooklyn.

A 1994 study by the city's Planning Department concluded that the number of sex-oriented businesses rose 35 percent, from 131 in 1984 to 177 by the end of 1993, a number the department feels has held steady over the last few years. The study found that video stores and peep shows had tripled in number, while topless bars increased by 26 percent. The number of theaters showing pornographic films, however, fell by more than 50 percent. More material is now available at bargain prices. Videos that sold for more than $100 a few years ago can now sell for less than $5.

These days, technology has made the industry even more mobile and mutable. Telecommunications and the Internet allow customers to bypass storefronts and partake of a virtual sex industry beyond zoning constraints. "With the Internet, the sex shops are going to be obsolete in a few years anyway," said an executive with *Stripper* magazine, a trade journal, who insisted on anonymity.

The new zoning push will allow the city to close legally operated sex businesses and thus could have an impact unlike any previous effort. Herald Price Fahringer, a lawyer who represents 107 of the city's sex businesses, said the new rules would put 85 percent of the industry out of business. Show World, which is less than 500 feet from Holy Cross Roman Catholic Church, would be among those forced to close.

Mitchell Moss, director of the Urban Research Center at New York   20
University, imagines that the zoning rules will bring additional changes to the industry but will hardly trigger its demise.

"It's going to be less visible in certain parts of the city," he said. "There will be darkened windows and less signage. We're going to go back a hundred years. We're going to put it back in the home and on the side streets and in the pushcarts."

───────◆ **QUESTIONS FOR DISCUSSION AND WRITING** ◆───────

1. In what ways can you relate the information N. R. Kleinfield presents to today's Internet? In what ways does the Internet resemble the sex trade Kleinfield describes? In what ways does it differ from it?

2. Do you agree with the title of Kleinfield's essay? Why or why not?

3. In paragraph 18 Kleinfield suggests that Internet access will "allow customers to bypass storefronts and partake of a virtual sex industry." Do you agree? Why or why not?

✳ www.oneplace.sex?
INTERNET PORN WOULD BE EASY TO FILTER (OR FIND)

San Jose Mercury News *Editorial*

Sex is not a noun, the wisecrack goes, it's a proposition.

Well, maybe the time has come to make it a suffix as well, as in .sex. Then pornography can join .com, .gov and .org in its own corner of the Internet—one that's easy for consenting adults to find and, as importantly, one that's easy for parents to avoid.

Paul Saffo, director of the Institute for the Future in Menlo Park, has observed that many new media, from "Canterbury Tales" to cable TV, have gone through a pornography stage, a period of growth he likens to "intellectual acne."

Pornography certainly is propelling the popularity of the World Wide Web. And not only porn stars from the San Fernando Valley are cashing in. It's cheap and easy to put a camera in your bedroom, build a home page and start charging for peeps by the minute.

As chronicled in the June 28 [1998] *Mercury News,* one enterprising Sunnyvale woman's site even flaunts risque poses beside Silicon Valley landmarks.   5

Such ingenuity is not going unrewarded. Zona Research of Redwood City estimates that Net users will spend $560 million this year on sex—from books and hard-core videos to real-time sex shows.

Clearly, the stuff is there because people want it. But such a profusion of sexually oriented sites is turning the Internet into a minefield for parents. They're finding that their children are intentionally searching for or inadvertently being exposed to the raunchy and the profane. Even word searches for seemingly innocuous terms can trigger ads for erotica.

That's why .sex or maybe .prn for porn would be useful. It would provide a location on the Internet for those who want to profit from sex. It would be like a virtual adult bookstore, which must be allowed but can be restricted to certain parts of town.

Our bet is that most peddlers of the obscene would welcome .sex as a marketing tool. At the same time, a suffix for pornography would make site-blocking simple and unambiguous. The problems with the current software filters, like Net Nanny, Cyber Patrol and SurfWatch, have been well documented. They are overreaching. Some block out discussions about breast cancer. Some can't tell the difference between XXX and Superbowl XXX. And others have an ideological edge, excluding sites about gays and abortion. That's because their largely automated programs target largely constitutionally protected speech—controversial words—instead of pornographic images or, in this case, a suffix.

The .sex domain would be a perfect solution if everyone could agree   10
on what's obscene and if the purveyors of smut voluntarily requested it. But we're not naive; neither will likely happen.

There will be legitimate disagreements as to what's pornographic, targeting prurient interests. Should a Web site on condoms, with an illustration on how to put one on, be in .sex? Should an artist who posts his portraits of nudes be there as well? Probably not, but views would differ.

Some sex merchants would choose to avoid .sex, either for perversity or for profit. They prefer stealth to lure people. One common trick is to use misleading codes, so that their sites pop up on search engines under unrelated topics.

So who should be the arbiter to compel the resisters and decide disputes over .sex? There's no easy answer. The administration of the Internet is not a government function. It's been done by a loose band of computer gurus.

A non-profit company, Network Solutions, Inc., currently oversees the common top domain names. It prevents duplication and ensures that companies end up under .com and non-profits get .org. In theory, it or its successor could decide .sex as well.

But deciding a domain designation has never been based on a site's content. And you can bet that it would take a lot of persuading for the libertarian Internet chiefs to start doing it. Then there's the question of whether courts would view a forced labeling of .sex as an unconstitutional form of involuntary association or as censorship.   15

We're under no illusion: .sex would not end the contentious and messy First Amendment debate over free speech on the Internet. It would not displace the need for parental supervision or maybe a system of third-party rating.

But it would keep many sex sites from kids' and disinclined adults' eyes. And, better yet, it might dampen Congress's enthusiasm for passing bad laws that encroach on the First Amendment.

—————◆ QUESTIONS FOR DISCUSSION AND WRITING ◆—————

1. Is the editorial "www.oneplace.sex" written satirically, or is it a real argument? Why do you think so? What can you cite from the editorial to support your position?

2. What is this editorial writer's position on pornography and the Internet? Do you agree with the position outlined? Why or why not?

3. If some entity (as Network Solutions currently does—see paragraph 14) were to decide that certain Internet sites should have an .xxx or a .sex extension on their domain name, on what basis could the entity make that determination?

❋ Parents, Not Legislation, Save Kids from Smut

Leonard Pitts

I was on my way to the White House when I encountered the topless woman. I'm bopping merrily along and suddenly she's just . . . there, before my eyes, engaging in a rather intimate act of self-gratification, if you catch my drift. And I realize—hey, I don't need a house to fall on me— that I've taken the mother of all wrong turns.

Wasn't difficult to figure out what had gone wrong: I had mistyped the Web site address of the real White House by three measly letters. So my computer delivered me instead to this ersatz "White House" of carnality and capitalism where naked women are "First Ladies" and for $19.99 a month, I'm promised access to all the "young teens, hot lesbians and hard-core nymphomaniacs" I can handle.

I've had this happen before. Once, I ran a search for Stan Lee, the comic book writer. Stumbled upon a pornographic Web site run by some guy with a similar name.

One can hardly turn around in cyberspace without accidentally tripping over naked people doing naughty things. You don't even want to talk about how easy it is to find such stuff on purpose, especially for a determined, computer-literate kid. It is, well . . . child's play to find smut on the Internet.

So you'd think I'd be cheering the new legislation designed to make   5
cyberspace child-safe. Actually, I'm ambivalent, even skeptical.

The Child Online Protection Act, which passed the House of Representatives last week [October 1998], mandates up to six months in jail and fines of up to $50,000 for anyone who makes sexually explicit material available to young Web surfers.

An earlier attempt to restrict online smut was rejected by the Supreme Court last year. Too broad an infringement on the First Amendment, it said. Assuming it's signed into law, I wouldn't be surprised to see this latest effort suffer the same fate. But it's not the free speech aspects of the bill that make me dubious. Rather, it's this sense I have that the whole thing is a wasted effort.

See, I have a healthy respect for the ability of a computer-savvy young person to get around online restrictions. And an even healthier respect for the youngster's willingness to disregard legal ones.

Granted, it should not be so easy to inadvertently cross paths with porn. If there's a reliable way to discourage that, I'm all for it. But let's say a sex Web site requires a customer to verify that he is 18 or older before entering.

Does anyone really think that your average hormonal adolescent,   10
having come this far in search of dirty pictures, is going to balk at lying about his age? Can a site's managers be held liable for making bad stuff available to minors if the minors in question sought the stuff out and then

lied to gain access? And what of those sites that originate beyond American borders?

The medium, I suspect, will always be several steps ahead of the law.

The thing we keep failing to take into account is that we're dealing with a construct unlike any that's ever come before, one which theoretically allows virtually anyone on Earth to reach, or be reached by, virtually anyone else on Earth, under cover of mutual anonymity. The Net may be a godsend for research and communication, but it's also, by its very nature, tailor-made for the dispensation of dirt.

So you'll forgive me if I'm doubtful of Congress' ability to regulate cyberspace. I'm reminded of the V-chip, the new technology that's supposed to censor what children watch on TV, and it strikes me as troubling the way law and technology are finding it necessary to step into a breach once occupied by parents.

Of course, parents are often absent now—working too hard, or just flat uninterested. So I guess we do what we can.

But I'm glad to say that in my house, federal law is still superseded by   15 paternal law.

Meaning that the computer is kept in my office. And any kid caught ogling a "First Lady" better make darn sure her name is Hillary.

◆ QUESTIONS FOR DISCUSSION AND WRITING ◆

1. In your own words, what stand does Pitts take regarding access to pornography on the Internet? Support your comments with quotations from the editorial.
2. How would you define *smut*?
3. How well argued is Pitts's editorial? What, specifically, in his column do you find persuasive? What is less persuasive?
4. What ideas do Pitts and Kleinfield have in common? On what aspects of the issue do they disagree? Provide citations to show what you mean.

✳ Reviews Follow Ban on Library Internet Filter

Amy Harmon

A ruling by a Federal judge on Monday [November 1998] that barred public libraries in Loudoun County from limiting how patrons use the Internet is binding only in eastern Virginia, but it seemed sure to have national implications as librarians across the country began to review their own Internet policies in the wake of the decision in the closely watched case.

The judge, Leonie M. Brinkema of Federal District Court in Alexandria, Va., is a former librarian herself and wrote that the county library's decision to install computer programs that seek to block sexually explicit material on the Internet "offends the guarantee of free speech in the First Amendment."

Such "filter" programs have been widely criticized by civil libertarians as ineffective because they fail to screen out all material that might be harmful to minors and in the process block a wide spectrum of material that is not inappropriate.

The plaintiffs in the Loudoun case, represented by the American Civil Liberties Union, included the proprietors of sites on the World Wide Web about safe sex, banned books and gay and lesbian teen-agers. All claimed to have been blocked by the software.

In striking down the Loudoun County Library board's policy, which required that all library computers connected to the Internet be equipped with a filtering program, Judge Brinkema cited Reno v. A.C.L.U., the 1997 Supreme Court decision that upheld a ruling that overturned a Federal law that sought to prohibit the distribution of indecent material to minors over the Internet.   5

"It has long been a matter of settled law that restricting what adults may read to a level appropriate for minors is a violation of the free speech guaranteed by the First Amendment," she said.

The ruling comes as a Federal judge in Philadelphia last Thursday issued a temporary restraining order on a new Federal law intended to protect children from Internet pornography. And several Congressional efforts to require schools to install filter programs failed to pass in the last session.

But particularly because public libraries provide free access to the Internet to those who may not have any other means of using it, they have been seen as a crucial site of the struggle over how the medium will be regulated. In the absence of any precedent, librarians and patrons have cobbled together various compromises in an effort to strike a balance between providing access to the vast array of information on the Internet and protecting children from portions of it that may be harmful.

On Tuesday, several librarians in communities where the decision to use filters has been particularly controversial said they were carefully reviewing the Loudoun decision.

"This will be helpful for decisions in the future," said Mike Harris, interim director of the Medina County District Library in Ohio, where last year community members organized an unsuccessful campaign to cut the library's funding unless it installed filters. "We've been flying a little bit blind here and this gives us a good referral point."   10

Brenda Branch, director of the Austin Public Library, where the decision to install filters has endured sustained protest from civil libertarians over the last year, said she had asked the city attorneys to review the Virginia court's decision.

Dorothy Field, director of the Orange County Library system in Orlando, Fla., said she would not consider removing the filtering system there. "We have exercised our role as librarians to choose the material for our selection," Ms. Field said. "What happens in Loudoun County is not going to change anything here."

The Virginia decision raised the possibility that less restrictive methods, like using privacy screens or installing filters on terminals that are set aside for children, might be acceptable under the First Amendment.

"We're very pleased with the decision, and we are hopeful that the library board will now put a constitutional policy in place and that this will be the end of the issue," said Jeri McGiverin, a retired schoolteacher who helped organize the group of Loudoun residents who initially filed the complaint.

Loudoun librarians cut off the Internet connections on Tuesday pending a library board meeting next week where a decision will be made on whether or not to appeal. 15

"I would expect to win on appeal," said John J. Nicholas Jr., the former chairman of the library board who helped install the old policy. "This is an issue of the library following its historical mandate, which is to select material which is appropriate to the community at hand."

But Mr. Nicholas said that the composition of the board had changed since the policy was instituted, and that he did not expect a vote to appeal to pass.

───────◆ **QUESTIONS FOR DISCUSSION AND WRITING** ◆───────

1. Now that you've read about some of the problems with software designed to block access to certain Web sites, do you think it's a good idea to use filtering software if it isn't completely effective? What can you cite from the articles you've read that supports your position?

2. Is it reasonable, do you think, for others to have to give up access to some Internet sites to protect young people from viewing pornographic material on the Web? Why or why not?

3. Because libraries already prevent young people from borrowing certain materials, can they do the same with Internet access? Why or why not?

───

✳ Library Grapples with Internet Freedom

Katie Hafner

Just inside the entrance of the public library here hangs a photograph of the building's namesake, John Henry Faulk, a radio performer and humorist famous for his uncompromising defense of free speech.

Faulk, who was blacklisted in the McCarthy era but sued his blacklisters and won, died in 1990. Were he alive today, Faulk would no doubt shake his head at the tangle over free speech in which the Faulk Central Library and the Austin Public Library branches now find themselves.

The Austin Public Library is one of hundreds of public libraries around the country grappling with the question of whether to keep objectionable material on the Internet from reaching computers intended for public use, and, for those libraries that have decided on blocking, how much blocking to do. After much soul-searching, the Austin library installed filtering software on most of its computers, a decision that divided the community, as it has many others.

In Loudoun County, Va., a group of library patrons who object to the county library's filtering software on its computers, along with the American Civil Liberties Union and Web publishers, have filed a court case challenging the constitutionality of the practice. On the opposite side of the continent—and the debate—in Livermore, Calif., a parent is suing the public library, accusing it of failing to restrict minors' access to pornographic Net content. Similar conflicts are taking place across the country.

The First Amendment issues raised by Internet filtering may seem clear enough when public debate is at full tilt. But people's positions are less clear in private as they struggle with their commitment to free speech and their desire to protect children.   5

Austin's two-year struggle, which is still unresolved, reflects the national debate in all its complexity. At every step of the way, librarians around the nation have watched Austin in search of guidance, confirmation or any hook on which to hang a policy of their own.

Like her counterparts across the nation, Brenda Branch, the energetic, high-spirited director of the Austin library, has been at the center of the discussion. Like many other librarians, she has always considered the defense of free speech to be part of her job description. For most of the 23 years she has been at the Austin library, that stand has presented her with no personal conflict.

Ms. Branch's problems began in the summer of 1996, when computers with unrestricted access to the Internet were placed in the main library and its 19 branches. "Upholding freedom of speech becomes so second nature to librarians that unrestricted access was our natural fallback position," Ms. Branch said. "We almost didn't question it."

When staff members saw children looking at questionable sites, they resorted to an ad hoc method of control—cajoling them to move elsewhere. They suddenly felt thrust into the role of parents.

But things remained relatively quiet until a branch librarian happened to walk past the library's printer one day and saw a graphic depiction of child pornography emerging. "One look at this and you knew it was illegal stuff," Ms. Branch said. As the librarian was pulling the offending document out of the printer, whoever had sent the print command disappeared.   10

Coincidentally, a few days later, another library employee shot off an angry letter to the local newspaper, the mayor, the City Council and the city manager, charging the library with making pornography available, in violation of the state's "harmful to minors" statute. Texas is one of several states with a law prohibiting an adult from knowingly displaying material considered harmful to anyone younger than 18.

"All of a sudden, it was like the dam broke," Ms. Branch said. She met with her staff members, she said, and many of them broke down and told her how uncomfortable they felt with unfettered Internet access. Ms. Branch's employees, it turned out, were worried that they could be arrested if they were thought to be exposing children to pornography, however inadvertently.

Lawyers for the city reinforced those fears. One option, which the library swiftly rejected, was to remove Internet access from the libraries altogether, Ms. Branch said. The lawyers then recommended strongly that the library install software to filter objectionable material.

Within two weeks, the library had installed Cyber Patrol, a filtering program popular among parents but much maligned among civil libertarians, on the 52 public computers with Internet access. In its haste, the library installed the software at full throttle. The product was set up at its most restrictive so it blocked Web sites promoting "intolerance," "alcohol and tobacco" and "illegal gambling."

Filtering products like those sold by Cyber Patrol often work by searching Web sites for strings of what appear to be unseemly text. Such a method can cause the words "Essex County," for example, to be blocked, or "chicken breast." The company also maintains a proprietary list of site addresses that it chooses to block, and it updates the list regularly. 15

Within a week, a stack of written complaints two inches thick had arrived on Ms. Branch's desk. Many library patrons objected to being subject to any censorship. Others complained about the software's hamhanded blocking, which censored harmless sites while giving ready access to others filled with obscene language and images.

One library user conducted an Internet search for "toys." At the top of the search results was "Toys 4 Lovers." At the same time, patrons trying to retrieve Web sites dedicated to Georgia O'Keeffe and Vincent Van Gogh were confronted by a computer screen flashing a yellow Cyber Patrol police badge. An H.I.V. Information Center was also found to be off limits.

"It's operating like the K.G.B.!" one person complained.

Another wrote, "Incensed that you would tell me as a parent what my child should see and what they should not see." People even complained that sites containing the name John Henry Faulk were banned, presumably because of the proximity to one another of the letters F, U and K.

But Cyber Patrol says its software would not exclude those kinds of sites. 20

Ms. Branch's office in the Faulk Central Library in downtown Austin is playfully decorated with stuffed animals and dishes of candy. On her door frame is a magnet that reads: "Don't rush me. I'm making mistakes as fast as I can." Inspired more by Gidget than gravitas, Ms. Branch's office betrays no trace of the somber situations in which the librarian has found herself.

Ms. Branch, 51, was named director of the Austin public library system in 1991. She said the only previous experience that foreshadowed the current debate occurred in 1992, when Madonna's graphic book *Sex* sparked an outcry from some parents and church groups.

During the Madonna incident, as Ms. Branch refers to it, she was in frequent touch with the American Library Association. "The A.L.A. was an incredible source of support," she said. "I really depended on them for information and legal advice."

When the issue of filtering Internet content arose, however, the A.L.A. left Ms. Branch trapped squarely between library science and local politics. In late 1996, a few months after the library introduced Internet access, Ms. Branch sought guidance from the A.L.A. about whether to install filters. She was surprised to get a sharp letter in reply, in which the A.L.A. endorsed the idea of unrestricted Internet access for adults and minors alike. In July 1997, the A.L.A. issued a formal resolution condemning the use of filtering software that blocks access to constitutionally protected speech and recommended parental discretion.

According to the A.L.A.'s Office for Information Technology Policy, 25 11,600 of the nation's nearly 16,000 libraries offer Internet access, and some 15 percent of those have installed filtering software. Most libraries, including many with filters, have an "acceptable use" policy in place, which urges patrons to use the Internet responsibly.

"Our policies are very carefully considered," said Richard Matthews, deputy director of the Office for Intellectual Freedom at the A.L.A. "We certainly have addressed the First Amendment implications of our stance against filtering, and to take any position accepting something less than that ideal stance would be unacceptable."

Ms. Branch said she found the A.L.A.'s policy frustrating because it fails to take into account the practical considerations of exposing children to what she calls "some of the horrifying stuff out there."

That horrifying stuff is precisely what has given rise to the pro-filtering position among a number of Austinites. "If we live in a society that requires one to be 21 to drink, 18 to smoke, and last I understood, 18 to purchase porno magazines, why is it free and acceptable to view porno on the Internet at a public library?" one Austin parent wrote to Ms. Branch.

"My biggest dilemma," Ms. Branch said, "is how to balance the rights of adults with the need to protect youth."

Shortly after Austin installed filters, the A.C.L.U condemned the new 30 practice. A.C.L.U. lawyers investigated the possibility of filing a lawsuit to challenge the constitutionality of the library's action.

Austin has long been known as a city more liberal than the rest of the state. For nearly eight years, the city has been home to Electronic Frontiers-Texas, a small but active group of civil libertarians who focus on the rights of those who travel in cyberspace. When members of the group heard about the library's filters, they joined forces with the A.C.L.U. and complained to the City Council, which controls the financing for the library. Invoking an analogy often used when discussing library filtering, Jon Lebkowsky, an EF-Texas member, said, "It came down to a fundamental question: Are you taking books off the shelves, or are you exercising the library's prerogative to select some books and not others?"

In March 1997, city officials convened a community roundtable, with Ms. Branch and other librarians, EF-Texas, the A.C.L.U., the city, and Jennifer Padden, a representative of the local P.T.A.

After several weeks of debate, the library disabled the keyword blocking and reduced the number of categories being filtered out to four: "gross depictions," "sexual acts," "partial nudity" and "full nudity."

Now there are four unfiltered computers scattered around the library system, with plans to have one unfiltered computer at each branch by this time next year. The screens for the unfiltered machines are in specially built recessed tables that keep the computer screens well out of public view. Only patrons 18 and older may use an unfiltered machine, and they must present proof of age. Minors cannot use the machines even if they have parental permission slips or are accompanied by parents.

Now that fewer categories of Web sites are blocked and unfiltered   35
computers are available to adults, Ms. Branch said, complaints about the filtering have diminished sharply. A library customer who objects to the blocking of a certain site can complain to the library staff, who can ask Cyber Patrol to stop blocking the site.

Everyone agrees that the current setup in Austin is a fragile compromise. From the point of view of EF-Texas and the A.C.L.U., which calls filtering "censorship in a box," it is an unacceptable one. "The least filtering we're likely to get is still more filtering than any of us want," said Jim Robinson, an EF-Texas member who opposes filters.

But EF-Texas members aren't completely in unison. While Mr. Robinson is unwavering in his stance against any and all filtering, others, like Mr. Lebkowsky, are less so. "There's the potential for libraries to become like adult arcades if access to hard-core porn isn't somehow restricted," said Mr. Lebkowsky. He said "minimal filtering" might be the solution.

Ms. Padden of the P.T.A. spoke passionately at the community roundtable in favor of filtering, yet the computer she has at home is unfiltered. When her children go on line, she goes with them. "I'd like to think I've raised my kids with my values, and they respect them," she said. "But there are probably 10 times more kids whose parents don't have the time or the computer capability to understand what their kids are looking at or doing at the library."

Ultimately, legislation or a court ruling may set boundaries. Some version of mandatory-filtering legislation for public libraries and schools may become law as part of the appropriations bill being constructed this week in Congress.

Librarians in Austin and elsewhere are also watching the Loudoun   40
County case.

Ann Beeson, an A.C.L.U. lawyer who spends much of her time on Web cases, said: "We hope the decision coming out of Loudoun will heavily influence how other jurisdictions proceed. If we get a strong decision in our favor, we'll feel even more confident in challenging other jurisdictions trying to impose mandatory filtering."

Eugene Volokh, a law professor at the University of California at Los Angeles, speculated that a court might be more likely to accept Internet filtering that, like Austin's, would affect only children. "Then again," he added, "it's conceivable that a court will say the library has a completely free hand, that blocking the Internet is more like not buying the book in the first place."

Ms. Beeson, who is monitoring the struggles over filtering in several cities simultaneously, said the A.C.L.U. continues to watch Austin closely. "It's still not off the radar screen," she said. "We've just been eminently patient with Austin."

Ms. Beeson said she approved of the plan to place an unfiltered machine in every library branch, but she objects to the library's uncompromising restrictions on minors, particularly older teen-agers.

But Ms. Beeson said she also sympathized with Ms. Branch. "Like many librarians, she's been caught between a rock and a hard place," Ms. Beeson said. "Her instincts are in all the right places, but she's in a very awkward position." 45

◆ QUESTIONS FOR DISCUSSION AND WRITING ◆

1. What is your initial response to "Library Grapples with Internet Freedom?" What is the author's attitude toward the use of library computers to access pornography? Cite evidence from the article to support your analysis.

2. How do you feel about the Austin library's plan to allow "unfiltered" access to all Web information only to adults? Should this kind of solution be implemented in your college library? Why or why not?

3. If you were to compose a position paper addressed to your local library in favor of filtering software, what data or other information from the readings included with this scenario would you use to support your argument?

❋ X-Rated

Wall Street Journal *Editorial*

While Tallie Grubenhoff stood at the checkout counter of the Selah, Wash. (pop. 5,000), library with her toddler daughter, she noticed a rowdy group of preteens around a computer. Her other kids drifted over to see what all the fuss was about. The six-year old came back with the answer: They'd been watching "a lady bending over with something in her mouth going up and down and she was a naked lady."

But the worst was yet to come. The librarian informed Mrs. Gruben-hoff that she was powerless to prevent children from accessing Internet porn because the word from her boss was that doing so would violate their free-speech rights. And that informing their parents, she added, would violate their privacy rights.

Welcome to the American library, where Marian the Librarian is fast making room for the Happy Hooker.

Mrs. Grubenhoff isn't the only one with a horror tale; most American parents are understandably disturbed by the terrors that lurk on the free-wheeling Internet for their children. And their fears have reached the politicians; in at least two presidential debates, Sen. John McCain came out for the mandatory installation of blocking software in libraries. All the more reason to wonder why, as the American Library Association's mid-winter conference begins today, the subject hasn't even made it onto the group's agenda.

"We think filters is a simplistic approach," ALA President Sarah Ann Long told us. Indeed, the most the ALA will do this weekend is to issue a lowly fact sheet that states that "the American Library Association has never endorsed the viewing of pornography by children or adults." 5

Problem is, it's never endorsed their not viewing it, either. Quite the opposite. Virtually all the ALA's energies appear directed toward a highly politicized understanding of speech. As one ALA statement puts it, libraries "must support access to information on all subjects that serve the needs or interests of each user, regardless of the user's age or the content of the material." One gets the sense that the activists at the ALA consider Larry Flynt less of a threat than Dr. Laura, who's complained about ALA opposition to efforts to ensure that minors are protected from pornographic Web sites on library computers.

Maybe blocking software is not the solution. We do know, however, that there are answers for those interested in finding them, answers that are technologically possible, constitutionally sound and eminently sane. After all, when it comes to print, librarians have no problem discriminating against *Hustler* in favor of *House & Garden*. Indeed, to dramatize the ALA's inconsistency regarding adult content in print and online, blocking software advocate David Burt three years ago announced "The *Hustler* Challenge"—a standing offer to pay for a year's subscription to *Hustler* for any library that wanted one. Needless to say, there haven't been any takers.

Our guess is that this is precisely what Leonard Kniffel, the editor of the ALA journal *American Libraries,* was getting at last fall when he asked in an editorial: "What is preventing this Association . . . from coming out with a public statement denouncing children's access to pornography and offering 700+ ways to fight it?"

Good question. And we'll learn this weekend whether the ALA hierarchy believes it worthy of an answer.

──────── ◆ **QUESTIONS FOR DISCUSSION AND WRITING** ◆ ────────

1. What might this editorial mean when it says that the American Library Association (ALA) "consider[s] Larry Flynt less of a threat than Dr. Laura" (paragraph 6)? Analyze how the *Wall Street Journal* seems to feel about the ALA.

2. The *Wall Street Journal* editorial suggests that perhaps "blocking software is not the solution. We do know, however, that there are . . . answers that are technologically possible" (paragraph 7). Do you agree or disagree? What are those "solutions"?

 Porn May Have Place, but It's Not in Class

Meghan Gaynor

Something very disturbing happened during group discussions in my political science class. As my group, consisting of roughly five women and one man, commenced discussion, I noticed the man fumbling around in his backpack. After a short amount of time he found what he was looking for—a large envelope—and joined the conversation.

As he spoke, I couldn't help but notice he wasn't actually looking at any of us. Rather, his eyes were suspiciously focused on the interior of the envelope. He seemed to be thoroughly engrossed in whatever it was he was reading. It was about this time that the outside of the envelope captured my attention.

I noticed a black-and-white cutout photograph of a scantily clad woman. In fact, it would have been quite difficult not to notice her. She was bent over, exposing the majority of her large breasts. Next to the woman was a caption written in red. While I can't recall exactly what the caption said, it was something to the effect of "you know you want it" or "come and get it." Basically, it said something incredibly disgusting and offensive. Some text on the bottom of the envelope also grabbed my attention. "Warning: sexually oriented material enclosed. Adults Only!" It became pretty clear what was inside the envelope.

I was dumbfounded. This kid had a lot of nerve leering at porn in the middle of class—surrounded by a group of women, no less. So I waited. I waited for one of these intelligent women to go ballistic, to tell this jerk where he and his crappy porn could go. Only, no one said a thing. They must have noticed! He was so completely arrogant; he wasn't even trying to hide his perverseness. Yet, no one said a word.

I began to grow more uncomfortable as my group continued to talk 5 politics, the offender actively participating in the conversation (with one eye in his dirty little envelope, of course). Finally, I decided to oh-so characteristically speak up.

"I don't think it's appropriate for you to be looking at that during class, (pervert)." Actually, I didn't call him a pervert, but I wish I would have.

"Oh, um . . ." he stuttered. He looked like a deer caught in the headlights. Pardon the cliché. "Well, I didn't know what was in here," he fumbled as he tried to explain himself, "so thought I'd take a look. That's all." He appeared completely tense, awkward and uncomfortable. Good. That's exactly how I had felt up until that moment.

Now this is where my sisters were supposed to back me up. This would have been the perfect opportunity to lay into this guy, to call him on his slimy, abhorrent behavior. Once again, no one said a word. Instead, the women looked at me as if I was screwy. With all of that nasty business out of the way, politics resumed, as if nothing had been said.

I don't know which I find more upsetting: that this guy thought it was "OK" to look at pornography during class, or that the women were totally apathetic to the situation. I've heard horror stories of people standing in long lines at the Computing Commons, anxiously waiting to type an important paper, while an inconsiderate few monopolized the computers in search of Internet porn. As far as I'm concerned, pornography doesn't have any place in a university, an institution that supposedly promotes the expansion of people's minds, not the primitive limitations of pornography.

Of course, I do not think pornography should fall victim to censorship. We cannot overlook the many women who support themselves through work in pornography and other areas of the sex industry. These are women who, perhaps, do not have enough skills to secure "mainstream" employment that would sufficiently support not only them, but their families, as well. 10

Naturally, if women are to make money in this industry, there needs to be consumers. So, is it selfish of me to not want to see any evidence of this consumption of goods in my classroom? Perhaps. But I digress.

As I sat in class that day, watching him look at porn with no regard for me or the other women in the group, something became painfully clear. Pornography truly does promote the dehumanization of women. Otherwise, this man who appeared to be quite the consumer would not have felt comfortable looking at such degrading material right in front of our faces. To him, we were less than human, lacking the emotional responsiveness, intelligence and character to stand up for ourselves when being humiliated. I only wish we could have proven him wrong.

◆ QUESTIONS FOR DISCUSSION AND WRITING ◆

1. In what way(s) is the personal story that Meghan Gaynor tells an example of effective writing? Support your opinion with quotes from her editorial.
2. Do you agree with Gaynor's argument? Why or why not?
3. Gaynor "waited for one of these intelligent women [in her small group] to go ballistic" over the pictures a classmate was "leering at," but "no one said a

word" (paragraph 4). If you found yourself in a similar situation, what would you do or say? Why?

4. Could allowing others to view the "pornographic" images on your computer screen be considered sexual harassment? Why or why not?

@ The Supreme Court

SOME SURPRISINGLY WIRED JUSTICES HEAR
AN ANTIPORN CASE THAT WOULD RESTRICT
FREE SPEECH IN CYBERSPACE

Joshua Quittner

Deputy Solicitor General Seth P. Waxman went before the U.S. Supreme Court last week [March 1997] to praise the Communications Decency Act, not to bury it. That was his first mistake.

The CDA, as it is known by everyone who has followed its tortured history, is the controversial antiporn bill passed by Congress and signed into law last year by President Bill Clinton. The act makes it a federal crime to put online, where children might see it, not just the obscene or the pornographic but any "indecent" word or image—a prohibition so vague that it might criminalize an AIDS-awareness lesson. Proponents argue that without such strictures, any child cruising the Net would have, as Waxman told the court, "a free pass into the equivalent of every adult bookstore and video store in the country."

That may have been his second mistake. The government's lead counsel got exactly 201 words into his argument when the first Justice cut in, asking for a citation. Waxman recovered, mustered an additional 111 words about how it's technologically feasible for Websites to screen users by age, when Justice Sandra Day O'Connor interrupted. "Does that technology require use of something called cgi?" she asked, referring to a complex protocol for changing what users see on a Web page. "It does," agreed Waxman, thereby opening the door to a line of argument in which he found himself suggesting—apparently in all seriousness—that U.S. citizens might have to purchase a government-issued, Maxwell Smart–like "cone of silence" before making a speech in a public park.

And so it went for an extraordinary 70 minutes that showed not just how wired this bench has become but also how important a test of constitutional principles it believes this case to be. The CDA, once feared and reviled by civil libertarians, is now seen as so flawed ("dead meat" is how Wired News described it last week) that its opponents are eagerly looking forward to a ruling. A clear judgment against it by the Supreme Court could end up extending First Amendment protection for all media into the

21st century. It could also help douse anti-Net brush fires that have sprung up at state and county levels in the months since the bill was signed.

That isn't to say that Bruce Ennis, lead counsel for a coalition of 20 plaintiffs that included the American Civil Liberties Union and the American Library Association, didn't suffer his share of interruptions. The Justices were particularly unimpressed by his argument that the law was worthless because it could not stop naughty bits from flowing to the U.S. from overseas. But at least Ennis managed to do something Waxman never did: forcibly state his case. "For 40 years," he said, "this court has repeatedly and unanimously ruled that government cannot constitutionally reduce the adult population to reading and viewing only what is appropriate for children. That is what this law does." The court did not argue with that.

Clearly, the judges had done their homework. The most-wired-Justice award went to Antonin Scalia, who pointed out that technology is changing so rapidly that what's unconstitutional today might be constitutional next week. Said Scalia: "I throw away my computer every five years." At another point, when Ennis was arguing that parents should chaperone their kids online, Scalia cracked, "If I had to be present whenever my 16-year-old is on the Internet, I would know less about this case than I know today."

Of course, whether it's good or bad for the A.C.L.U. that some Justices know a Website from a legal cite probably won't be known for months. The Justices will rule sometime before the court's summer recess—usually by July 4. Meantime, in the absence of any clear constitutional law in cyberspace, at least 17 states have passed or are considering their own legislation to regulate the Net. New York enacted a law last year that resembles the CDA. In Virginia it's now illegal for state employees—including state-college professors—to access "sexually explicit" materials online. That law might prevent English professors from running an online discussion of *Lady Chatterley's Lover.* In Georgia it's a crime for people to communicate anonymously over the Net, which could come as a surprise to 8 million America Online users, most of whom use pseudonyms.

And here's more bad news for Georgians: if the Supreme Court finds the CDA is indeed unconstitutional, the ruling would not automatically void those state laws, says Ann Beeson, a national staff attorney for the A.C.L.U. It would, however, make it easier for the courts to strike down local statutes. "Unfortunately," says Beeson, "state legislatures pass unconstitutional laws all the time, and you still have to go to court to fight them."

Of course, the U.S. Congress also has a history of passing unconstitutional laws, and several conservative legislators have already promised that if the Supreme Court rules against this law, they will try again with a more carefully crafted "Son of CDA." "Some way, somehow," says Republican Senator Charles Grassley of Iowa, a fierce supporter of the CDA, "we will have to find a constitutional way of protecting kids from porn."

──────── ◆ **QUESTIONS FOR DISCUSSION AND WRITING** ◆ ────────

1. Based on what Quittner writes, do you think that the Communications Decency Act (CDA) can be effective? Why or why not?

2. If you were a Supreme Court justice, what questions would you have asked the attorneys (Seth Waxman for the government and Bruce Ennis for the American Civil Liberties Union and others)?

3. According to Quittner's essay, what are the main problems with the Communications Decency Act?

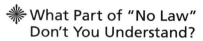

✳ What Part of "No Law" Don't You Understand?

William Bennett Turner

It's hard to imagine that our antique First Amendment, written in 1789, is up to the task of dealing with 21st-century digital communication. James Madison would have had a hard time getting his mind around instant worldwide electronic communication. The Supreme Court has said, ominously, that "differences in the characteristics of new media justify differences in the First Amendment standards applied to them." In light of this, some thoughtful observers of new technology have proposed constitutional amendments to ensure that government does not censor, manage, or restrict electronic communications.

The truth, however, is that we don't need a new First Amendment for digital communication. All we need is adherence to the bedrock principles of First Amendment interpretation that have grown up with us over the first two centuries of the republic. Madison's 18th-century framework is flexible enough to protect our freedoms in any century.

REALITY CHECK: FREE SPEECH IS NOT ABSOLUTE

The First Amendment speaks in seemingly absolute terms: "Congress shall make no law . . . abridging the freedom of speech or of the press." This has never meant, however, that people can say *whatever* they want *wherever* they want. Freedom of speech does not mean speech totally uninhibited by any legal restraint. It has always been true that some forms of speech can be outlawed or penalized—and many have been. Common examples include fraudulent advertising, child pornography, obscenity, "fighting words," help-wanted ads that discriminate on the basis of race, words used in a criminal transaction ("I'll kill your husband for US$10,000), unkept promises, unlicensed broadcasts, libel, speech that infringes a copyright, and unauthorized disclosure of data used to make atomic weapons.

Correctly interpreted, the First Amendment does not prohibit all restrictions on speech. It doesn't prohibit private restrictions at all. Our constitution is a series of constraints on government, not on individuals or even powerful corporations. It is not a violation of the First Amendment for the Microsoft Network, if it so desired, to forbid postings that criticize Bill Gates. Microsoft is not the government, at least not yet. Similarly, CompuServe's censorship of sex newsgroups may offend freedom lovers but does not violate the First Amendment.

The amendment prohibits government restrictions on "the freedom of speech," not on all speech, and it's a mistake to argue that no speech can be restricted. In every case, the question is whether the particular "speech" is within the "freedom" comprehended by the amendment.

NO FINE PRINT

The First Amendment means what the courts say it means. Since the amendment's words themselves don't tell us what falls within its "freedom," it is up to the courts, faced with the necessity of deciding particular cases, to spell out the rules for deciding exactly what speech is free, in the sense that it cannot legally be prohibited or penalized. While the courts sometimes go astray, it remains true that Americans have freer speech than any other people because our freedoms have been forthrightly defined and enforced by the courts.

In every case in which government tries to restrict speech, some high-minded—or at least plausible—reason is offered. When the Nixon Administration tried to suppress publication of the Pentagon Papers, it was argued that their publication would undermine national security. When Congress acted to prohibit phone sex, it said that such action was necessary to protect children from exposure to indecent material. When state governments forbid publication of the names of rape victims, they say it is necessary to protect privacy and encourage the reporting of sex crimes. And so on. In each new case, a court has to decide whether the government's justification prevails over the interest in free speech.

FUNDAMENTAL FREE SPEECH PRINCIPLES

In deciding free speech cases, the courts have elaborated some bedrock principles that inform First Amendment decision-making. What the First Amendment "freedom" means, in fact, is basically this set of principles. We should remind ourselves of them and ask whether they need adjustment for the 21st century. Here are some of them:

- Government may not restrict or penalize speech because of its content or its viewpoint. It must remain neutral in the marketplace of ideas.

- There is no such thing as a "false idea." This principle rests on the belief that bad ideas will be driven out not by censorship but by good ideas, that the remedy for offensive speech is not suppression, but more speech.

- Restrictions on speech must not be vague or uncertain but sufficiently precise so that everyone understands exactly what is unlawful. No overly broad meat-axe regulation is allowed—any restriction must be a sensitive tool that cuts no more than is necessary to serve the precise government interest involved.

- "Journalism" is not a licensed, credentialed profession. Under our legal system, the "lonely pamphleteer" has the same First Amendment rights as the publisher of the *New York Times*.

- The press cannot be ordered to print statements it does not wish to print.

- "Prior restraints" on speech—government orders that certain information not be published—are prohibited.

- Penalties (like damages in libel suits) may not be imposed for innocent mistakes that happen to defame someone.

- Advocacy—including advocacy of the overthrow of the government—cannot be outlawed, so long as it does not amount to inciting people to imminent lawless action. Speech short of incitement cannot be banned because of the anticipated adverse reaction of the audience.

- Punishment for "seditious libel"—scathing criticism of government—is not tolerated under the First Amendment.

- No one can own or control facts or ideas (though a person can copyright the unique way he or she expresses those facts or ideas).

These are all great protections that allow us to call ourselves free people. And these principles apply regardless of the means of communication: via big newspapers, small magazines, telephones, television, radio, or the street-corner orator. There is no reason to fear that these principles will not apply with full force to all forms of digital communication.

On the other hand, one must recognize that some of these principles—like the First Amendment itself—are not absolute. There can be exceptions. For example, government can restrict certain speech because of its content, if it proves that there's a "compelling" government interest (like protecting national security or shielding children from sexual exploitation) and there's no less onerous means of protecting the government interest. Even a "prior restraint" on certain speech may be warranted if the government proves, say, that disclosure of the locations of

10

strategic missiles in wartime would sabotage the war effort or endanger troops.

The question, then, is whether anything about the nature of digital communication would justify exceptions to the basic principles of our longstanding First Amendment freedom.

NEW MEDIA, NEW RULES?

The Supreme Court spoke too loosely when it said that differences in new media justify different First Amendment standards. The notion first surfaced in a 1949 case (*Kovacs v. Cooper*) involving restrictions on the use of sound trucks in congested cities. The court not surprisingly ruled that cities could keep the "new medium" from disrupting sleep and drowning out all conversation by blaring slogans at all hours and decibel levels. Such a regulation is a reasonable "time, place, and manner" restriction that does not forbid any speech based on its content. Government can more easily justify regulating the way the message is delivered rather than the message itself.

Unfortunately, the Supreme Court retrieved the thought about new media years later, reformulated it, and unthinkingly applied it to a case in which the issue was government regulation of content. In 1969, the court handed down *Red Lion*, the most important decision ever on broadcasting.

The Court upheld the FCC's "Fairness Doctrine," which required licensed broadcasters to cover important public issues and to give voice to contrasting views on the issues. In other words, broadcasters were required to air information they would otherwise have chosen not to air, including views with which they vehemently disagreed. For example, a broadcaster strongly in favor of constructing a nuclear power plant would have to air the anti-nuke point of view as well as his or her own.

The Court's rationale in *Red Lion* was that the airwaves were a public resource, and those licensed to monopolize one of the scarce frequencies could be required to use this government-bestowed benefit in the public interest. Scarcity of frequencies justified both government allocation of frequencies and regulation of content. The court said that requiring broadcasters to air diverse views enhanced rather than hobbled our First Amendment marketplace of ideas.

Just five years later, people concerned about the increasing concentration of media power in large corporations owning newspapers tried to get a similar concept applied to the world of print. They asked the Supreme Court to uphold a Florida law giving political candidates a "right of reply" to newspaper attacks against them during campaigns. The law was a lot like the FCC's "personal attack" rule (part of the Fairness Doctrine), one that the court had enforced against broadcasters in Red Lion. But in the *Miami Herald* case, the Court rejected the argument as completely inconsistent with the First Amendment right of newspapers to exercise editorial discretion in deciding what to publish and what not to publish. The result left one rule for print and another for broadcast—the most prominent illustration to date of the different-media, different-standards rule.

Now that print is becoming electronic, will it lose its preferred status? Certainly not. There is far less need for a government-enforced right of reply regarding digital communication than there is for print. There is no "scarcity" problem. You can reply instantly without permission, and you don't have to worry about economic or license barriers to entry. Your ability to respond, virtually free of charge, makes it silly to think that government should strive for some kind of "fairness" or balance in digital communication.

Whatever the merits of the Fairness Doctrine (it was abandoned by the FCC in 1987, though the *Red Lion* precedent stands), the Supreme Court should not extend the broad statement that new media justify different First Amendment rules. Former Justice Robert Jackson's original statement in the sound-truck case was that "the moving picture screen, the radio, the newspaper, the handbill, the sound truck, and the street-corner orator have differing natures, values, abuses, and dangers. Each, in my view, is a law unto itself." In *Red Lion*, the Court gave too much emphasis to the "law unto itself" part. If all the Court meant to say is that the law must reflect the "differing natures, values, abuses, and dangers" of each medium, that's fine—the unique characteristics of computer-mediated communication favor greater freedom.

NOT BROADCAST, NOT PRINT

Computer-mediated communication should have much greater freedom than, for example, broadcast. Instead of being one-way—from a broadcaster with a government license to a captive audience—it's interactive and from many to many. Its decentralization and user control are vastly different from the monopolistic control of scarce frequencies by powerful broadcasters.

Nor is the medium "intrusive" in the sense that our kids might be surprised and "assaulted" by hearing dirty words, such as when they scan radio stations. (This is what led the Court, in the 1978 *Pacifica* decision, to uphold the FCC prohibition of "indecency" on the radio.) User control means you need to work at it in a fairly sophisticated way to participate, and you have an incredible range of choice about exposing yourself to communication. Parental control should not be a thing of the past.

Of course, the fact that digital communication is cheap means anybody can become a publisher. There's no built-in preference for speech by the rich and powerful—those who own printing presses, tons of newsprint, or broadcast licenses—or for speech whose main appeal is to generate paid advertisements. It's far more democratic even than print.

Unfortunately, the Supreme Court has repeated the new-media new-rules statement in recent cases. In 1994, for example, the Court quoted the line from the *Red Lion* decision in deciding a case (*Turner Broadcasting v. FCC*) on whether cable television operators could be required to carry local broadcast and public television channels. I hope the Court, when it gets its first digital communication case, does not woodenly recite the same slogan.

The idea that there should be special First Amendment rules for new media makes little sense. The basic principles of First Amendment jurisprudence apply to all media. And, to the extent that digital communication is different—because it is fast, cheap, interactive, and controlled by decentralized users—the differences call for less regulation than traditional media, not more. The application of the basic principles should reflect these characteristics of the new technology.

NEW WINE INTO OLD VESSELS

So how would First Amendment principles established for older media apply to digital communication? Check out the bedrock principles already listed. They ought to resolve just about any restriction on digital communication that you can imagine.

Yes, the new technology will present different kinds of issues. It has   25 occurred to many people that libel or "indecency" on the Internet presents novel problems, and that hate speech and the invasion of privacy will have to be dealt with. Cases involving the liability of access providers and bulletin board operators already have appeared in the lower courts. And issues about anonymous speech and encryption have been hotly debated, though not decided by the courts.

In my view, none of these problems requires alteration of any of the fundamental First Amendment principles. Deciding cases involving these new issues should be done the old-fashioned way: by looking to precedent, reasoning by analogy, and considering the policy implications of ruling one way or another.

The most immediate example is the impending telecommunications law prohibiting "obscene" or "indecent" speech on the Internet. Like it or not, this is a no-brainer. Material that is so gross as to fall within the Supreme Court's strict definition of obscenity, which is really hardcore material that has no artistic, political, or social value, is unprotected by the First Amendment regardless of the medium in which it appears. So, for better or for worse, we have to accept that Congress can make a law outlawing obscene speech on the Internet. To be sure, there are knotty issues involving whose "community standards" are being used to judge obscenity when an alleged dirty picture is uploaded in libertine San Francisco and downloaded in Logan, Utah, by a recipient with no geographic address.

This is a rule that could profit by reexamination in light of the new manner of communication. And maybe there should be a new, nongeographic definition of "community" that prevents federal prosecution of, for example, those who wish to discuss safe-sex options for preventing AIDS. But there's no basis for arguing either that obscene speech is now legal because it's communicated by computer or that obscenity must now be judged by the standards of the most prudish community a prosecutor can find.

Indecent material—dirty words or pictures that the government can't prohibit adults from seeing but can keep from children—is treated differently from obscene material. The ban on "indecent" communications on the Internet is plainly invalid under the recognized principles that forbid vague, overly broad, content-based restrictions promoting interests that can be served by less restrictive means. The Supreme Court threw out, on those grounds, the comparable prohibition of "indecent" speech on the telephone in the Sable Communications case in 1989—it must do the same with the new law. The availability of less restrictive means, like filtering technology, will allow parents to control their children's access instead of reducing all communication to the level of what is fit for children.

Consider also what adjustments need to be made in the law of libel. 30 More people will be "publishing" all over the country and presumably saying false and defamatory things about more people, and it won't be long before defamation cases work their way up the court system. Since *New York Times v. Sullivan* in 1964, all libel cases are governed, at least in part, by First Amendment rules. A public figure can't sue for an innocent mistake but basically has to prove that the publisher deliberately lied. Whether you are a public figure depends on whether you have ready access to the media to combat an untruth published about you, and whether you inject yourself into a particular controversy.

Well, if you are actively participating in a chat room or posting material on a bulletin board, you probably ought to be considered a "limited purpose" public figure and you will have to shrug off false—but not deliberately false—statements made about you in that forum. And because it's within your power to respond to statements instantaneously and to the very same audience that saw the falsehoods, any damages should be limited. Digital libel ought to be harder, not easier, to prove.

But what about the system operator, the one who allows "indecent" or libelous speech to be published on his or her system? The rule ought to be that the operator is not liable as a "publisher" unless the operator actually knows that the system is being used for plainly unlawful speech. The operator cannot be a guarantor of the accuracy of all posted information. He or she cannot reasonably be expected to monitor all postings, to screen for possible torts or even dirty words. The analogy is to a bookstore owner, not a magazine publisher.

Hate speech and harassment can be found on the Internet, just as they can be found on college dormitory bulletin boards or over the telephone.

They may wreck one's enjoyment of the digital conversation but they don't present any unique First Amendment problems that can't be dealt with by the established principles. Again, we have to remember that private regulation is not unconstitutional and there is no First Amendment prohibition against expelling those whose speech is abusive or unwelcome from your digital circle. If you want government to do it for you, you're asking that First Amendment principles be diluted. Remember, we don't protect speech because it can cause no harm but because we don't trust government to decide what expression is acceptable in our discourse.

———————◆ **QUESTIONS FOR DISCUSSION AND WRITING** ◆———————

1. Is Turner effective in the arguments he makes in the "Reality Check" section of his essay (paragraphs 3–5) concerning Internet restrictions? Cite evidence from the article to support your view.
2. In paragraph 6, Turner suggests that "the First Amendment means what the courts say it means." Does Turner offer details to support this claim? What are they?
3. In paragraph 8, Turner outlines a number of "free speech principles." Do these principles share a common theme? Can you provide examples of the ways in which Turner uses those principles to support his argument?
4. Based on what Turner writes about the Internet and "broadcast rules" (paragraphs 19–23), is the Internet a broadcast medium like television? Why or why not?

❋ Supreme Court Strikes Down Law on Internet Indecency

MANY PROFESSORS OPPOSED THE STATUTE
AS INFRINGING ON ACADEMIC FREEDOM

Lawrence Biemiller and Goldie Blumenstyk

Faculty members, college computing administrators, and university lawyers and presidents breathed a collective sigh of relief last week [June 1997] when the U.S. Supreme Court struck down the parts of the Communications Decency Act that had threatened to wreak the most havoc on the Internet and the campus computer networks connected to it.

The 1996 law, which has never been enforced, was said by backers to be aimed at protecting children from pornography on the Internet. But in doing so, it appeared to put at risk a wide variety of materials available in one way or another through college computers, such as students' personal home pages on the World-Wide Web, images stored on college servers for art-history classes, and discussion lists for faculty members in the humanities.

The law also seemed to some to call into question the future of the Internet as a medium for distance-education courses and other higher-level academic pursuits, which will depend upon an unfettered exchange of ideas.

Most college lawyers and computing managers had expected the Court to reject the law, but many had discussed what actions to take if it were upheld. "Had it not been overturned, we were prepared to cut off access to our Web site from the outside world," said William Doemel, director of computer services at Wabash College.

If the law had passed muster with the Court, he said, Wabash would have had to create a "firewall" within which ideas could be freely discussed. Computer users outside that wall would have been able to see only materials that had been reviewed and approved by the college—itself a daunting task. Dr. Doemel said such measures would have sharply limited the Internet's usefulness to faculty members—infringing, for example, on "the exchange of ideas on course work" now taking place among scholars at many colleges. "The inhibition of learning would have been substantial." 5

Steven J. McDonald, an associate legal counsel at the Ohio State University, said the law would have forced colleges to consider creating password systems to limit access to some materials. They might also have had to deny Internet accounts to students under the age of 18, who would have been considered minors under the law.

"I don't think the government was about to go out and prosecute things that have redeeming social value," he said. But as long as the law was on the books, he said, colleges would have been on uncertain ground with all kinds of on-line materials, from artistic images to Chaucer. "The Miller's Tale," Mr. McDonald noted, "is pretty raunchy."

The court's decision, he said, "makes it clear you have the same First Amendment and academic-freedom rights on the Internet as you have anywhere else." But the ruling's language also makes clear that the government has an interest in protecting children from obscenity, he added, suggesting that colleges should help create software to let parents control what their children encounter on line. "I would like to see us beat the legislative solution to the punch," he said.

The Communications Decency Act, which President Clinton signed into law in February of last year, would have prohibited any display of "patently offensive" material "in a manner that is available to a person under 18 years of age." In a provision particularly worrisome to the operators of campus computer networks, the law also made it illegal for a person to let "any telecommunications facility under such person's control" be used for an activity the law proscribed. At many universities, students and faculty members can create their own home pages, which administrators are loath to review for fear of violating academic freedoms.

Justice John Paul Stevens, writing for the Court's seven-member majority, said that "the breadth of the C.D.A. is wholly unprecedented," and 10 that the law would confer on any on-line opponent of indecent speech a sort of "heckler's veto," which could be exercised merely by claiming that a 17-year-old child had logged on. "In order to deny minors access to potentially harmful speech," Justice Stevens wrote, "the C.D.A. effectively suppresses a large amount of speech that adults have a constitutional right to receive and to address to one another." He also noted that the law's "general, undefined terms 'indecent' and 'patently offensive' cover large amounts of non-pornographic material with serious educational or other value."

Justice Sandra Day O'Connor wrote an opinion that concurred with some parts of the majority ruling and dissented from others. She was joined by Chief Justice William H. Rehnquist. The case is known as *Reno* v. *American Civil Liberties Union*. The A.C.L.U. represented a variety of challengers to the law, including the American Library Association and the Health Sciences Library Association.

Not everyone in academe applauded the decision, however. Dan R. Olsen, a professor of human-computer interaction at Carnegie Mellon University, said the majority opinion failed to take into account how fast computer technology can change. The Justices, he said, were too quick to accept the claim that it is not technically feasible to require users to insure that offensive material is kept away from minors. The Court "took a snapshot in time of what the technology could do," he said.

Dr. Olsen, who testified in favor of the law during federal appeals-court hearings in Philadelphia last year, said that a workable age-verification system for Internet exchanges does not exist today, but that he expects that such systems are not far off.

Another academic who participated in the case, Jonathan Green, said he was delighted by the ruling, adding that "the proliferation of all kinds of words and images on the Net guarantees the widest possible discussion and dialogue on the broadest range of issues and concepts." Mr. Green, who is director of the California Museum of Photography at the University of California at Riverside, said that even if the law had been upheld, he would not have removed from the museum's Web site photographs by Edward Weston and Robert Mapplethorpe that some might consider indecent. The museum signed a friend-of-the-court brief opposing the law.

Lloyd K. Stires, a professor of psychology at Indiana University of Pennsylvania, teaches a course called "Pornography: Critical, Behavioral, and Legal Approaches," in which he uses an e-mail distribution list to forward materials to students, "occasionally" including "samples" collected from the Internet. The course became part of the Court's deliberations when it was described in the same friend-of-the-court brief that the photography museum signed. Had the law been upheld, Dr. Stires said, the class "might have been weakened" and the law "might have forced me to teach it in a different way."

Graham B. Spanier, president of Pennsylvania State University, said administrators there "have had concerns about the act and what it would

15

have meant for us." The Penn State system, he said, currently has 107,000 people with active e-mail accounts. "The challenge of policing more than 100,000 people would have been immense," he said.

Dr. Spanier said Penn State "has had incidents where people have differed about what's in good taste, and it's only a matter of time till that would have played out over some electronic issue."

"As a parent of teen-aged kids," he added, "I'm not exactly crazy about them having access to some of the material in question. But I am strongly in favor of holding up the right to free speech."

◆ QUESTIONS FOR DISCUSSION AND WRITING ◆

1. Authors Biemiller and Blumenstyk note that if the Supreme Court had confirmed the 1996 Communications Decency Act, colleges would have had to create a "'firewall' within which ideas could be freely discussed" (paragraph 5). In what ways might such a "firewall" restrict your college research activities?

2. Biemiller and Blumenstyk quote Supreme Court Justice John Paul Stevens, who argued that "in order to deny minors access to potentially harmful speech," the Communications Decency Act "suppresses a large amount of speech that adults have a constitutional right to receive and to address to one another" (paragraph 10). Do you agree with Stevens? Why or why not?

3. Several writers in this chapter focus on the Communications Decency Act, including Quittner, Turner, and Biemiller and Blumenstyk. Which essay do you find the most convincing? Cite evidence from several essays to support your opinion.

TAKING ACTION

Your Collaborative Statement to the Community Library Oversight Panel

Now that you've read, discussed, and written about some of the issues and concerns and perspectives involved in the Derry Library scenario, it's time for you to construct your group statement. You'll contact those who will decide what, if anything, will be done about the filtering software that's now limiting Internet access at the Derry Public Library. That group is the Derry Community Library Oversight Panel. Your group might want to focus on questions and issues such as these:

- Should Derry's library be taking any steps to restrict access to any of its sources of information (text, films, magazines, newspapers, videotapes, the Internet, e-mail, and so on)? Why or why not?

- If you believe it's appropriate for the library to restrict what a person is allowed to read or see, what should those restrictions be? Where will the funds come from to implement your ideas? How should your constraints on Internet viewing be enforced?

- Do the members of your group think that Derry Community College students need freer access to information sources than do other library patrons? Why or why not? Should Derry Community College simply build its own library, or do you think that library might have restrictions, too?

Asking the Right Questions

As mentioned earlier, it's useful to begin wrestling with a problem or issue that affects you by first thinking about what you already know; then you'll have a sense of what you'd like to learn more about. Start by asking questions; those questions will lead to others that will help your group determine the best solution for the problems the scenario presents. As you draft your group's statement to CLOP, think of the issues from a reporter's perspective, focusing on the who, what, when, where, and why of the scenario. Try to answer the following questions:

- What perspectives might each of the interested groups have about free speech and censorship? What are the strengths and weaknesses of those perspectives?
- Can you make your statement to CLOP stronger by aligning your group with others? Might it help to make CLOP aware that several groups share your views concerning some of the issues, problems, or possible solutions?
- What events in the Derry Library scenario can be controlled? How?
- What are some of the consequences to the various groups of library patrons from the Internet access limitations now in effect at the Derry Library? How is this type of censorship affecting the members of your group?
- What are the consequences if you do nothing to try to change the situation? What action might make the situation more difficult?
- How do the issues and problems in the Derry Public Library scenario relate to the broader perspective concerning free speech and censorship in libraries?

Which group you represent and the approach you decide to take will determine the position you propose. You might, for example, argue against any form of censorship, or you might recommend specific types of access limitations.

Constructing a Collaborative Text

Work with the members of your group to draft a statement to Derry's Community Library Oversight Panel that expresses your views on the issues in this scenario. Read through and carefully revise your draft several times, to ensure that your group's ideas are articulated as clearly as possible.

One approach to constructing a group statement is for every group member to compose a brief individual statement listing what each considers to be the most important issues and problems. Then, working together, draw on those individual comments to compose your group statement.

Another technique is to take the notes that each of you has made, designate one group member to record the group's ideas, and then collaboratively compose an initial draft of what your group thinks. At first, this process might be a bit frenzied, with several group members offering suggestions on what to write and how to write it, but you'll find that working together is an interesting and useful way to get your collective ideas onto paper.

Here's an example of how you might begin composing your statement to CLOP. Perhaps your group has decided that some censorship of Internet material and other information makes sense, but you still want the library and its computers to remain as open as possible. E-mail, for example, should be completely unrestricted and unmonitored, you believe. If this is your group's view, you might introduce your collaborative statement with something like this: "Facts and statistics from around the country indicate that unlimited Internet access in libraries leads to problems with children viewing inappropriate material. . . ." You'd follow this introduction with specific examples to illustrate your ideas.

At this point, also consider possible objections to your plan and how you might answer them:

- Does your group's plan violate anyone's rights? How?
- How does your plan differ from the way in which the library handles other material (texts, videos, and so forth)?
- Who is likely to disagree with your plan, and what concerns might they express? How will you answer their objections to your proposal?
- How do you know that the monitoring you're proposing will be more effective than the software that's now available to restrict access to certain parts of the Internet?
- How will the community pay for your proposal?
- What might current library patrons have to say about your proposal?

When you've completed a first draft of your collaborative text, each group member should read through the draft, marking any sections that are unclear. Work together to clarify those parts. Then, each group member should read the statement once more, this time looking for places in the text where your argument might need more evidence. Then, again working together, decide what pieces of evidence gathered during your research (facts, data, testimony, statistics) might provide additional support for your argument.

BOX 8.2 APPLYING WHAT YOU READ
Using Your Classmates' Suggestions (Written Peer Review)

Once you have a brief, collaborative text that outlines your message to CLOP, exchange your draft with that of another group. Read that group's comments, and identify (and indicate in marginal notes) their strengths and weaknesses.

What suggestions can you make to help the group improve the way in which it states its ideas? What are the strengths of the initial draft? The weaknesses? Where are the comments confusing? What is clear in the statement? Unclear? How might the group clarify its position? What suggestions might you offer to improve the group's comments to CLOP? It's important to understand that you should help your classmates improve their statement, even if you disagree with their position.

Once your group receives feedback from your classmates, work together as a group to revise your statement. What suggestions did you receive that make sense? Where does your text need clarification, or further explanation, or more evidence? What facts or other data have group members collected that you can add, to make your text more convincing?

Your instructor may ask you to read and comment on the other groups' statements. Working together that way gives you the chance to help your classmates become better writers, as you act as real readers for one another. Indicate the places in the text where more information is needed, or where the writing is confusing, or where some elaboration might help. To apply the feedback you receive to improve your composition, follow the procedure in Box 8.2: Using Your Classmates' Suggestions.

SPEAKING YOUR PIECE
Addressing the Community Library Oversight Panel

Because of the attention that the "Heidi Incident" and the peaceful protests at Derry CC have focused on the Derry Public Library, the Community Library Oversight Panel has decided to hold an open meeting to permit all interested parties to voice their concerns and to ask questions. New Hampshire residents are familiar with local political town hall meetings, so it makes perfect sense for CLOP to hold such a meeting.

Because it permits direct interaction between groups, this type of meeting should help interested parties develop solutions for local conflicts. For this public discussion, your audience consists of the Derry Community Library Oversight Panel, members of other interested groups, and the general public (much of what is said at this meeting will be printed in the *Derry Daily News*).

The sharing of information at the meeting also provides the opportunity for each group to question members of the other groups. This should help each group refine its position.

From Written Preparation to Public Speaking

Here's an example of how your group might organize its oral presentation. Let's say that your group represents some concerned parents. The main point your group wants to make is that the public library is *not* the place for people to view whatever "obscene materials are out there on the Internet." Your spokesperson plans to begin by making that clear. Then, your group will make several recommendations:

- Derry Library should keep the filtering software it's installed on all its computers.

- The library should position its computers so that children cannot see the screens as they walk by.

- The library should have a staff member monitor what users are viewing on library computers, so that they can stop people from visiting "those obscene Web sites" that the filtering software fails to block.

Of course, just as in your written presentation, it's vital to provide specific evidence—facts, testimony, examples of what other communities and libraries have done—in your oral presentation, to support your views. Each example, piece of evidence, fact, or statistic that you supply should support your main point and be clearly connected to it. Don't assume your audience will make the connections for you.

Speaking at the Open Meeting

In a full-class open meeting, representatives of each group will have the opportunity to state their group's position on what the Derry Public Library ought to do about Internet access. Speakers will be given a time limit, as if they were actually speaking in front of CLOP. When each group has presented its statement on what the library should do, all groups will be allowed to ask questions.

Your instructor might ask one or more students to act as moderators (much as the CLOP chairperson would do), to make sure that everyone has an opportunity to contribute to the discussion.

INDIVIDUAL WRITING
Essay Options

Your instructor will ask you to construct one or more individual writing projects: an informative essay, a proposal essay, and/or an analytic essay. Although each project has its own focus and audience, they all allow you to use the reading, class discussion information, and notes you've taken. You may decide that you want to do additional outside research to better understand the issues or to find support for a point you want to make before you begin these writing assignments.

The Informative Essay

For this assignment, assume that the Community Library Oversight Panel has asked you to prepare an informative essay detailing what other libraries around the country are doing about Internet access and censorship. An informative essay transmits facts and information, so that its readers can make up their own minds. A good way to start an informative essay is with a complete summary of what you've read.

In your essay for CLOP, you might focus on questions such as these:

- Are libraries nationwide providing Internet and e-mail access to their patrons? Are librarians aware of and concerned about censorship issues? In what ways are librarians addressing these problems and issues?

- Are libraries reporting significant problems with computer users viewing materials that some might consider inappropriate? If so, how widespread is the problem?

- What steps have libraries taken to address the issue that seem to work? Why do they work? What approaches don't seem to be very effective? Why are they ineffective?

- What are the costs (both monetary and in terms of free speech) associated with some of the solutions being tried?

- What are the local reactions to some of the solutions that libraries are implementing?

The Proposal Essay

If you were responsible for deciding what the Derry Public Library should do, what would you suggest be done, if anything, about Internet access? A proposal essay gives you the opportunity to state in precise terms your position on what should be done.

For this assignment, assume that you are the library director and that you've been asked to write an essay for the editorial page of the *Derry Daily News*. Assume also that your audience comprises the citizens of Derry, who pay your salary. If this audience agrees with you, they'll provide the money to implement your ideas.

You might begin your proposal essay with a sentence such as this: "As the person the citizens of Derry have hired to manage their library, this is what I propose we do about Internet censorship. . . ."

A proposal, remember, does not simply state problems and solutions. Instead, it provides sufficient evidence to prove (1) that there is a problem and (2) that what's being proposed will solve that problem.

To construct your proposal essay, you'll need to address questions like these from your point of view: What are some of the Internet and e-mail problems at libraries around the country? What specific examples illustrate these problems? How serious are the problems? How widespread are they? How have librarians reacted to them?

Once you've explained what the problem is, you propose your solution by responding to questions like these: What would you do at the Derry Public Library? How can you demonstrate that your solution will be effective? Where might the money come from to fund your proposal? How does what you propose compare with what other libraries have done? In what ways is the situation at Derry similar to or different from that at other libraries?

The Analytic Essay

In an analytic essay on the issue of libraries and Internet access, you analyze what's happening in this arena and why. For this assignment, assume that your essay will appear in *Public Libraries Today: Problems and Solutions,* an academic journal read regularly by those who manage public libraries (or, as in this scenario, serve on a community library oversight panel).

If you could address an audience of those from around the country who manage public libraries, what would you attempt to persuade them to do about Internet and e-mail access and censorship? How would you convince them that your ideas are the right ones? In what ways would you support your ideas?

Unlike in an informative essay, in which you maintain a neutral, nonpartisan stance, in an analytic essay you take a stand, state a position, and argue for a specific point. In this essay, you might focus on national issues such as these:

- Definitions of *obscenity, pornography,* and *censorship.*
- Ways in which libraries around the country have restricted access to their print collections.
- How technology is redefining the question of censorship.
- Ways in which some libraries are addressing issues involving censorship and technology.
- Methods for limiting Internet access: what has worked, what has not, and why.

To conclude this scenario, your instructor may ask you to follow the instructions in Box 8.3: Reflections on the Internet Access Scenario. The process of writing about ways in which your attitudes may have changed helps clarify your thinking.

FOR FURTHER RESEARCH AND WRITING

This scenario presents a number of opportunities for further writing. This is especially true if you work to explore broader national issues and problems.

✳ **BOX 8.3   APPLYING WHAT YOU READ**
Reflections on the Internet Access Scenario

By this point in our scenario, you've done a lot of reading, discussing, and writing about the issues facing the Derry Public Library. Take a few minutes now to look back at the first writing you did for this scenario, after you'd thought about the photographs that introduce this chapter and read the First Impressions questions. Then jot down your answers to these questions:

- Have your initial definitions of the terms *pornography* and *censorship* changed, now that you've worked your way through the Internet access scenario? If so, in what way? If not, why not?
- If you had to state your position on Internet censorship in one sentence, what would you say?
- About which issues or problems related to the Internet and the Derry Library do you have the strongest feelings? Why?
- What was the most important thing you learned as you worked through this scenario?
- Did your writing process change at all as you worked through the Derry Library scenario? How?
- What might you do differently in the next scenario project on which you work? Why?

When you're finished, your instructor may ask you to share your thoughts with your classmates.

You might consider how terms are defined, and who defines them. In this scenario, terms like *pornography, obscenity,* and even *censorship* are critical to discussion of the issues involved. The Supreme Court has generally argued that these terms are subject to local interpretation; if so, who in any given community should determine how terms like these are defined?

You might also examine the history of censorship in this country, especially that involving public libraries. Should there be a difference between what a person can keep in his or her personal library and what is available in a public library? What might that difference be? You might broaden this examination to include the role and the history of censorship nationally.

You might also consider how technology has changed—and will continue to change—the ways in which we gain access to information. What problems are associated with these changes?

Many people agree that pornography should not be allowed on the Internet. However, what about "virtual" pornography—where what we see on the screen appears to be real, but no humans are involved?

You might also explore the roles libraries have played, historically, in American communities, and how their roles are changing. Are libraries becoming more or less popular? How are they funded? Is funding for libraries increasing or decreasing? Are libraries the only place in which a citizen can log on to the Internet free of charge? Will there ever be such a thing as a purely electronic library? What might that mean to those who cannot afford a home computer with Internet access?

You might consider whether college or university students and professors have a greater right to view whatever they wish to on the Internet than do other citizens. Do they? If so, why?

You now have read, discussed, and written about some of the problems that become apparent when access to the Internet is restricted, as exemplified at the Derry Public Library. Every day, library patrons and administrators all over the country face problems such as these: What should people be allowed to read or view? Who makes those decisions?

We hope that working through this scenario has helped you improve how you read and learn about issues and problems. We also hope you're learning how to work effectively with others and to revise your written work efficiently. The skills you employed in this scenario will help you in your other college or university classes, as well as throughout your career.

Works Cited

Harmon, Amy. "Library Suit Becomes Key Test of Freedom to Use the Internet." *New York Times* 2 Mar. 1998: Business/Financial Desk.

Mendels, Pamela. "Filter to Block Hate Speech on Internet." *New York Times* 12 Nov. 1988: National Desk.

"www.oneplace.sex? Internet Porn Would Be Easy to Filter (or Find)." *San Jose Mercury News* 5 July 1988: 6C.

CHAPTER 9

Living Wills

DECISIONS ABOUT LIFE AND DEATH

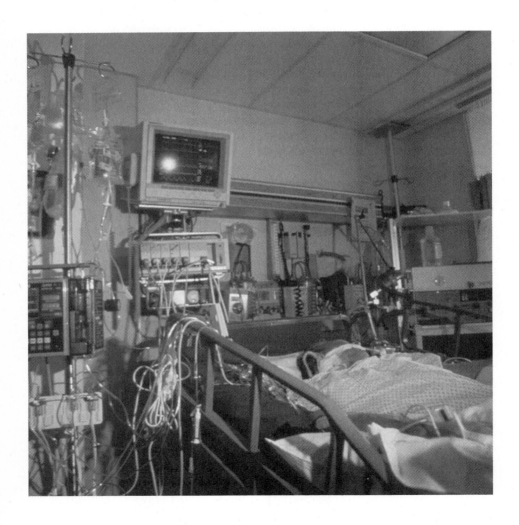

LIVING WILL

If I should have an incurable and irreversible condition that has been diagnosed by two physicians and that will result in my death within a relatively short time without the administration of life-sustaining treatment or has produced an irreversible coma or persistent vegetative state, and I am no longer able to make decisions regarding my medical treatment, I direct my attending physician, pursuant to the Natural Death Act of California, to withhold or withdraw treatment, including artificially administered nutrition and hydration, that only prolongs the process of dying or the irreversible coma or persistent vegetative state and is not necessary for my comfort or to alleviate pain.

If I have been diagnosed as pregnant, and that diagnosis is known to my physician, this Declaration shall have no force or effect during my pregnancy.

I authorize the reliance upon photocopies of this completed document as though they were originals.

Signed this _____ day of _____ , _____
                (day)   *(month)*   *(year)*

Signature _____
Print Name _____
Address _____

STATEMENT OF WITNESSES

Note: *This document will not be valid unless it has been signed by two qualified witnesses. The following may not serve as witnesses: (1) a health care provider or employee of a health care provider, including doctors, nurses, and others who work in health care facilities; and (2) an operator or employee of an operator of a community care facility or residential care facility for the elderly (sometimes called board and care homes). In addition, your second witness cannot be someone who is named in your will or who otherwise stands to inherit anything from you.*

Special Requirement: *If you are a resident of a long-term care facility (such as a nursing home) at the time you are completing this document, one of your witnesses must be a patient advocate or ombudsman designated by the State Department of Aging.*

First Witness

The declarant voluntarily signed this writing in my presence. I am not a health care provider, an employee of a health care provider, the operator or an employee of an operator of a community care facility, or the operator or an employee of an operator of a residential care facility for the elderly.

Signature _____ Date _____
Print Name _____
Address _____

Second Witness

The declarant voluntarily signed this writing in my presence. I am not entitled to any _____ or her death under any will or codicil thereto of the declarant now existing or by oper_____ an employee of a health care provider, the operator or an employee of an operator of a _____ employee of an operator of a residential care facility for the elderly.

Signature _____
Print Name _____
Address _____

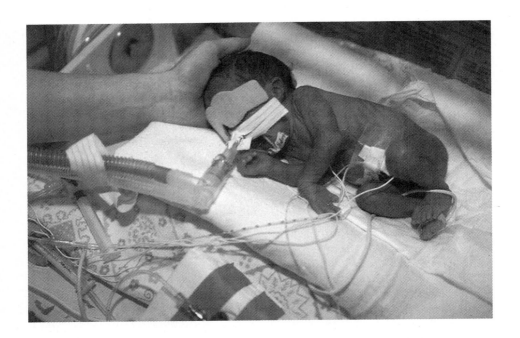

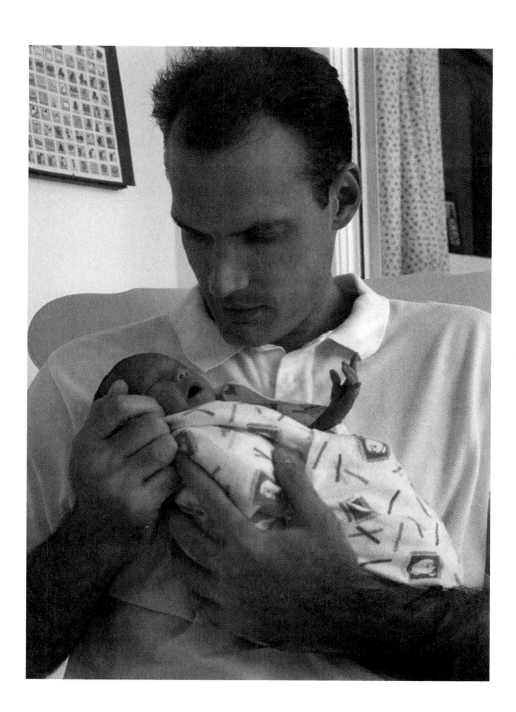

◆ **FIRST IMPRESSIONS** ◆

Be sure to look at and think about the photographs that introduce this chapter. Then spend a few minutes jotting down your answers to these questions:

- Do the first two photographs in this chapter disturb you? Why?
- Do you ever wonder whether, in some cases, the cost of our medical technology outweighs its benefits? When?
- How do you define the term *ethics*?
- How do you define the term *abortion*? *Euthanasia*?
- Is abortion, according to your definition, ever acceptable? Under what circumstances?
- Is euthanasia, according to your definition, ever acceptable? Under what circumstances?
- Can an ethical person be involved in an abortion? In euthanasia? When?
- What are some of the issues and problems that the terms *abortion* and *euthanasia* bring to mind?
- How would you describe/define a *living will*?

When you're done, your instructor may ask you to share your comments with your classmates.

As the twenty-first century started, a number of public and ethical debates remained unsettled. Many promised to increase in intensity.

In this scenario, we combine aspects of several of those debates to focus on issues and problems that perhaps you have not yet considered. To help you begin to understand them, we ask you to think about the definitions of four terms: *death, euthanasia, living will,* and *abortion.* You'll find them in Box 9.1: Definitions.

Do you generally agree with the definitions in Box 9.1? How do they compare with your definitions of those terms? If a person loses all "vital functions," for example, do you consider that person to have died? Is euthanasia "mercy killing"? Is a living will what you thought it would be? Would you modify the definitions in Box 9.1 in any way?

As food for thought and to set the stage for the scenario, Box 9.2: Real Cases tells the stories of two people who attracted national attention. As you read these stories, ask yourself: In these situations, how were the terms defined in Box 9.1 applied? Did the families involved act correctly? Did the doctors and other health care professionals act properly? How well did the state or government or court do its job, in your view? How do your definitions of the terms in Box 9.1 relate to the situations in these cases?

Do you agree with the way in which the parties involved handled the Quinlan and Fiori cases? Would you, as a family member, a doctor, or a

✳ **BOX 9.1**
Definitions

Death   "The cessation of life; permanent cessations of all vital functions and signs. Numerous states have enacted statutory definitions of death which include brain-related criteria" (Black).

Brain Death   "Characteristics of brain death consist of: (1) unreceptivity and unresponsiveness to externally applied stimuli and internal needs; (2) no spontaneous movements or breathing; (3) no reflex activity; and (4) a flat electroencephalograph reading after 24 hour period of observation" (Black).

Euthanasia   "1. an easy or painless death. 2. the practice of deliberately ending the life of a person or animal suffering from an incurable and often painful condition or disease" ("Euthanasia," 21 June 2000).

Living Will

"To My Family, My Physician, My Lawyer, and All Others Whom It May Concern

"Death is as much a reality as birth, growth, maturity, and old age—it is the one certainty of life. If the time comes when I can no longer take part in decisions for my own future, let this statement stand as an expression of my wishes and directions, while I am still of sound mind.

"If at such a time the situation should arise in which there is no reasonable expectation of my recovery from extreme physical or mental disability, I direct that I be allowed to die and not be kept alive by medications, artificial means or 'heroic measures.' I do, however, ask that medication be mercifully administered to me to alleviate suffering even though this may shorten my remaining life.

"This statement is made after careful consideration and is in accordance with my strong convictions and beliefs. I want the wishes and directions here expressed carried out to the extent permitted by law. Insofar as they are not legally enforceable, I hope that those to whom this Will is addressed will regard themselves as morally bound by these provisions" ("Death").

Abortion   "The expulsion of a fetus from the uterus before it has reached the stage of viability (in human beings, usually about the 20th week of gestation). An abortion may occur spontaneously, in which case it is also called a miscarriage, or it may be brought on purposefully, in which case it is often called an induced abortion.

"Spontaneous abortions, or miscarriages, occur for many reasons, including disease, trauma, or genetic or biochemical incompatibility of mother and fetus. Occasionally a fetus dies in the uterus but fails to be expelled, a condition termed a missed abortion.

"Induced abortions may be performed for reasons that fall into four general categories: to preserve the life or physical or mental well-being of the mother; to prevent the completion of a pregnancy that has resulted from rape or incest; to prevent the birth of a child with serious deformity, mental deficiency, or genetic abnormality; or to prevent a birth for social or economic reasons (such as the extreme youth of the pregnant female or the sorely strained resources of the family unit). By some definitions, abortions that are performed to preserve the well-being of the female or in cases of rape or incest are therapeutic, or justifiable, abortion" ("Abortion").

  Real Cases

The Karen Ann Quinlan Case

After mixing alcohol and sedatives at a party in April 1975, Karen Ann Quinlan went into cardiac arrest and stopped breathing for at least two 15-minute intervals.

She was taken by ambulance to a nearby hospital, where on examination her pupils were unreactive, and she was unresponsive to deep pain. She also needed a respirator to help her breathe. An electroencephalogram (EEG) reading of her brain activity was abnormal, but showed some activity.

Expert physicians characterized Ms. Quinlan's condition as a "chronic persistent vegetative state," but one in which she could "maintain vegetative parts of neurological function without cognitive function." They explained that the brain works in essentially two ways. Internal vegetative regulation controls the body's temperature, breathing, blood pressure, heart rate, chewing, swallowing, sleeping, and waking. This aspect of Ms. Quinlan's brain activity was functioning partially. Sapient function is more highly developed and uniquely human, controlling our relationship with the outside world. This controls the capacity to talk, see, feel, and think. This aspect of Ms. Quinlan's brain activity was not functioning.

For a person to be considered brain-dead, both of these functions must cease. Because Ms. Quinlan's vegetative functions continued, she could not be considered brain-dead.

Joseph Quinlan, her father, sought to be made guardian over his daughter and also sought to authorize the discontinuation of life-sustaining processes. Mr. Quinlan said his decision to discontinue treatment was in accordance with his beliefs as a Catholic. The request was opposed by Ms. Quinlan's doctors, the hospital, the court-appointed guardian, the Morris County Prosecutor, and the State of New Jersey.

After receiving permission from the court, Mr. Quinlan had his daughter's respirator removed. Karen Ann Quinlan lived for almost nine years thereafter, dying of an infection in 1985.

The Daniel Fiori Case

Daniel Fiori was first injured in 1971 when he was thrown from a motorcycle. When he awoke from a nearly year-long coma, he was paralyzed and was able to articulate only the words *itch* and *eye*. Fiori suffered a second head injury in a veteran's hospital in 1976, which left him comatose. A feeding tube was surgically implanted in his stomach.

In February 1992, Fiori's mother, Rosemarie Sherman, decided that her son's treatment should be terminated, and she sought to have his feeding tube removed. Upon Daniel's death, Mrs. Sherman was due to receive approximately $100,000 from her son's insurance policy. The nursing home refused to comply without a court order.

The court ruled that life support could be terminated, saying that without a clear expression of the patient's wishes, any decision to remove life support must "take into account such factors as the relief of suffering, the preservation or restoration of functioning, and the quality as well as extent of life sustained."

This case was distinguished from another case, In re. Doroe, 452 A. 2d.127 (Pa. Super. 1985), where a blood transfusion was given to an accident victim despite proof that he did not want it because of his religious beliefs. In the Doroe decision, the Pennsylvania Superior Court ruled that the victim might have changed his mind had he been conscious and aware of the probability of his recovery ("Euthanasia," 8 April 2000).

member of the court, have done anything differently? How do you react to the notion that Mr. Doroe "might have changed his mind" about accepting a blood transfusion after his accident? That is, can a doctor or someone else *overrule* what he or she knows to be an individual's specific health request?

Although our scenario focuses on an accident victim in Denver, Colorado, its implications have national importance and are subject to debate. The issues presented here focus on *who* should make life-or-death decisions.

Consider the situation of a woman, four months pregnant, who has been in an automobile crash. She is in a coma and has been connected to life-support systems; her unborn child is still alive. The doctors say that there is a 50 percent chance of saving the child if they're allowed to keep the mother on life-support systems for two months. At that time it will be safe to perform a cesarean birth. The woman recently signed a valid living will.

Would removing the mother from life-support systems be euthanasia? Would terminating life support to the mother be the same as aborting the child? Imagine that:

- You are the woman's husband. You desperately want your wife and child to survive. When you're told that your wife will die unless she's kept on life support, you know she would not want to live that way. After all, you both recently signed living wills, documents indicating that neither of you wanted to be kept alive artificially, no matter what the circumstances were. Would you go against your wife's wishes if there was a chance of saving your unborn child?

- You are the young woman's mother or father. How would you react? Should the doctors and hospital respect the living will your daughter signed, or should they ignore her wishes, at least for the next two months, so that your grandchild has a chance to survive?

- You are one of the four grandparents-to-be. If the doctors are able to deliver a healthy child, would you be willing to help the father raise it? How would you feel if the child—because of the accident—were born with severe physical problems? Would you still be willing to help raise that child?

- You are a nurse at the hospital. If the young woman is kept on life support, she will be your patient. You will have to care for her and manage your own emotions. What do you think should be done? Is it ethical to keep a person alive in this way, against that person's wishes?

- You are a member of the clergy who serve the hospital. How do you feel about euthanasia? Does this instance meet your definition of the term? Do you think that removing the woman from life support is the same as aborting her unborn child? If so, how would you react in this situation?

- You are a member of the hospital's legal team. How do you interpret the woman's living will? That is, even if her will is legally valid, can you *delay* removing her from life support in an effort to save her unborn child? How would you respond if the woman's husband interpreted his wife's wishes differently and told you he'd sue the hospital if it didn't adhere to the terms of her living will?

THE SCENARIO

Who Has the "Right" to Live?

John Scott III and Helen Sumner were married five years ago in what the local paper termed the "event of the year" at the Saguaro Flats Church of the Resurrection. John and Helen are the oldest children in their respective families and were not only the first to go away to college but also the first to get married. John is now a second-year student at the University of Colorado College of Law, and Helen is four months pregnant. In a few months, the young couple will deliver the first grandchild to the Sumner and Scott families. The rumors are that if the child is a boy, he will be named John Scott IV, but John and Helen will not reveal their name choices to anyone.

On a Tuesday in late November, as Helen and John drive home from a visit to the doctor's office, the couple's car is blindsided by a drunk driver who ran a red light. Although the driver of the truck receives only minor injuries (and, it turns out, has no automobile insurance), both John and Helen end up in intensive care at Denver's Mercy Hospital. John's injuries are serious but not life-threatening. Helen is in a coma, and the doctors place her on life-support equipment. Their assessment is that if Helen is removed from life support, she will die. For the moment, all tests indicate that the fetus has survived the accident and is healthy.

Relatives are called (both sets of parents fly together in a tearful journey from Saguaro Flats, Arizona). They rush from the airport to the hospital, where they meet briefly with Dr. William Frasier, chief of surgery at Mercy. Dr. Frasier details the extent of the couple's injuries to the parents, and they spend as much time with their children as the nurses will allow.

After a week John is released from the hospital. Helen's condition, however, has deteriorated. Dr. Frasier spends an hour with John and the four parents, explaining the medical options.

"There may come a time," Dr. Frasier quietly puts it, "when we need to consider removing Helen from life support. Right now, there is no brain activity at all. And then, of course," Dr. Frasier notes, "there is the matter of the unborn child. None of us would suggest removing Helen from life support while there is any chance that we might save the child."

Dr. Frasier assures the Sumners and the Scotts that the doctors feel confident that if they can keep Helen on life support for the next two months, it will be safe to perform a cesarean section and bring the child into the world.

"There's no way to be certain our efforts will be successful," Dr. Frasier says. "Any number of unforeseen problems can develop. But," he says, "we want to try to keep Helen alive so we can save the child. It's simply the right thing to do."

"What are the chances that the baby will be . . . alright?" John asks.

Dr. Frasier responds, "We have perhaps a 50 percent chance at best of saving the child. The technology that's keeping Helen alive is wonderful, but it cannot give the fetus everything a mother can. So, there is a real chance that he will be born with significant birth defects. The whole idea is risky, John. But we feel it's a chance we have to take."

Dr. Frasier pauses for a moment and then goes on, in a softer voice. "And you need to understand that once the child is born, if we get to that point, we will have to let Helen go."

But there are questions to be answered. Is it ethical for the doctors to keep Helen alive on life support in an attempt to save her unborn child's life, even though Helen is clinically dead? Is keeping Helen alive so much different than, say, artificially maintaining a corpse so that its organs can be harvested for transplant? These questions seem to be forgotten as the focus shifts to Helen's unborn child.

And then, as the discussion seems to be drawing to a close, John blurts out something that complicates things. "I think you all ought to know something," John says, pausing and then looking at his parents. "Only a few weeks ago, Helen and I signed living wills. Neither of us wanted to be kept alive artificially." He sighs. "And, of course, Helen knew she was pregnant at the time she signed her living will. I'm convinced that Helen knew exactly what she was doing when she signed it."

"But John," Mrs. Scott asks, "surely she couldn't have anticipated this situation. And this is your own child that would . . . would be lost," she sobs.

Can, and should, Mercy Hospital keep Helen alive against her wishes? Aside from the legal issues (the courts can settle those), what responsibilities does the hospital have? What rights and responsibilities does John have? What about the other family members?

ENTERING THE SCENARIO: WHO SHOULD LIVE? WHO DECIDES?

Now that you've read through the scenario and understand some of the issues, it's time for you to become actively involved. Your instructor will ask you to work with several of your classmates to role-play as one of the interested parties. The group descriptions that follow are only a beginning: your group (and the others) will work to tailor your descriptions and perspectives to reflect your ideas about the ethical questions in this scenario.

We ask you to pretend you're a member of the group you represent and to consider Helen Scott's case from that group's perspective. Working with several of your classmates, you'll discuss and decide questions like these:

- How do the terms you defined earlier—*death, euthanasia, living will,* and *abortion*—relate to Helen's situation? Can you reach a consensus within your group on how to define those terms? Can you collectively decide how those definitions apply in Helen's case?

- What are the issues in this scenario that your group finds especially interesting? What are some of the issues that might concern your group more than they concern the other groups?

- What part of Helen's situation especially troubles your group? What are some of the issues that your group feels less interested in?

- What other groups might share at least some of your beliefs and ideas about Helen's situation? With which other groups might you ally yourselves?

- Which groups might oppose your point of view on whether Helen should be kept on life support? What objections might they have to your ideas? How might you counter those objections?

Family Members

You and the members of your group represent Helen's family: her husband, John, both sets of grandparents-to-be, and others in the immediate family. Your conversations center on whether the doctors at Mercy Hospital should keep Helen on life-support systems to try to save her unborn child.

Your group comprises two sets of family members, of course: the Sumners (Helen's family) and the Scotts (John and his family). Each set might have differing views about whether the doctors and the hospital should try to keep Helen alive artificially. The unborn child must be considered—

but so must Helen's wishes. Might Helen's parents feel differently about her wishes than do John's parents?

Mercy's Nurses

Dr. Frasier and his medical team are the ones who must consider the ethical implications of keeping a mother-to-be on life support—not to save her life, but to save the life of her unborn child. You and the other members of the hospital's nursing staff, however, will bear most of the responsibility for caring for Helen and will have the closest contact with her family. You'll also need to control the emotions you feel as you work with Helen and her family.

Helen's case is unusual but not unique. Complications could arise over the next two months that might require those involved to reconsider the decisions they are making now. What if something goes wrong during the next sixty-odd days—and the fetus's body or mind is harmed in some way? Who would be responsible? Should the nursing staff, whose job it will be to carry out the decisions that are made, have a say in the matter?

The Clergy Who Serve Mercy Hospital

You and the other ministers who visit sick parishioners at Mercy Hospital also have an interest in Helen's case, and you expect to have a voice in the decision about Helen and her unborn child. Your group is likely to have strong feelings concerning abortion. Some members may argue that removing Helen from life support is the same as aborting her unborn child. Is it?

Mercy Hospital's Legal Team

You and the other members of the hospital's legal team participate in all medical decisions involving termination-of-life issues, and you must consider the hospital's possible liability if things go wrong with Helen's case. From a legal perspective, your first reaction might be to ask a court to decide whether to keep Helen on life support. Although Colorado is one of the states that honors living wills, you know that there is nothing in state law concerning a pregnant woman and her living will. Taking this issue to court means making a de facto decision to maintain life support until the court hands down its decision. Is this what your group wants?

Your group also might consider the consequences if the health of the unborn baby is compromised over the next sixty days. What potential liabilities might Mercy Hospital have?

The costs of keeping Helen on life support for two months and then caring for her preterm infant are estimated to be about $500,000. Is this expense justified, or could the money be spent in better ways? What if something goes wrong and the child is born with birth defects serious enough to require institutionalization? Who will bear that expense?

PARTICIPATING IN YOUR GROUP

You've read the scenario and the group descriptions, so now you're ready to participate actively. Your instructor will ask you, along with your classmates, to role-play—to put yourself in the place of someone in the group you've joined and explore how that person might feel. Use the group descriptions as starting points to help you get into character. Remember, though, that the issues involved are more complex than the descriptions can portray.

None of the groups in this scenario is likely to be completely unified. There will be a range of opinions within each group because of the diversity of members' backgrounds and experiences. Before beginning your group discussion, read Box 9.3: Representing the Range of Opinion for suggestions your group can apply to encourage members to explore their positions.

TAKING A POSITION: CONVINCING THE COMMITTEE FOR ETHICAL DECISIONS

Administrators at Mercy Hospital want to do what's right for everyone involved. They therefore ask that each interested party submit a brief written statement of its views concerning Helen, for consideration by the hospital's Committee for Ethical Decisions (CED). This gives your group an opportunity to make its views part of the record and to try to influence the others involved, particularly the members of the hospital CED, who will decide whether Helen remains on life support.

RESOURCES: REAL LIVES AND ETHICAL ISSUES

If you and your classmates were facing a situation like the one this scenario outlines, you might try to learn more about the issues involved at the library or on the Internet. You'd want to learn how other hospitals, spouses, parents, and families grappling with similar problems had handled them. You might also want to interview physicians and others who make life-and-death decisions at your local hospital.

The readings selected for each scenario provide context, background information, and sometimes specific examples of how those who have wrestled with similar issues have responded. Many of the readings that accompany this scenario are lengthy and complex, reflecting the life-and-death issues on which the scenario focuses. These readings are drawn

BOX 9.3   APPLYING WHAT YOU READ
Representing the Range of Opinion

To better understand the issues that Helen Scott's situation raises, assume that all perspectives exist within your group. Adopting the persona, or role, of someone within the group to which you belong can help you generate a fuller range of ideas and viewpoints. For example, someone in the family members' group might represent a grandparent who feels that life support must be provided for Helen; another might role-play one of Helen's siblings who feels that Helen's living will should be respected. Another group member might feel unsure, with more questions than answers.

For the first part of this activity, work within your group to brainstorm a list of all possible positions those in the real group might take. Then assign those positions to group members. Think about the position you've been assigned to represent. How would someone in your position feel? How would Helen's situation affect you?

As a group, list all the problems, concerns, advantages, and observations that your members can identify. Be sure that everyone receives a copy of this list—it represents valuable invention work that you can draw on later in the scenario.

When you've finished, your instructor may ask you to share your "personas" with other members of the class.

from a variety of sources—including newspapers, scientific journals, and the Internet.

The first two readings—"Are Living Wills Honored?" and "New Living Will Puts Legal Issues in Plain English"—discuss the benefits of these documents, and the problems they can prompt. The second article, especially, outlines one opinion of what a living will should contain.

The American Dietetic Association provides its perspective on "feeding" unconscious patients. This technical article contains the guidelines that dietitians follow when caring for those who are permanently unconscious. Some of the dangers that arise when hospitals and health care professionals do *not* pay attention to a patient's living will are the subject of Tamar Lewin's essay in the *New York Times*. Anne E. Weiss, in a thoughtful essay, questions whether anyone has the "right to die."

Julian Savulescu, of Oxford University, wonders whether physicians aren't better equipped than lay people to make life-and-death decisions. This study, from the *Journal of Medical Ethics*, is one of the more demanding readings in this text. In "The Sanctity of Life: An Analysis of a Concept," K. Danner Clouser discusses the meaning of life and notions of who should control its ending.

Finally, noted philosopher Peter Singer invites us all to "rethink" life and death. In his remarkable essay "In Place of the Old Ethic," Singer challenges us to consider questions we may not yet have thought about.

As always, try to interact actively with these readings, remembering the reading strategies you learned earlier (prereading, annotating, summarizing, and so forth).

◆ READINGS

✳ Are Living Wills Honored?

PBS-Online

Having an advance directive is no guarantee that end-of-life wishes will be honored. A 1995 Robert Wood Johnson Foundation–funded study of 4,300 critically ill patients found that only 49 percent who requested do not resuscitate (DNR) orders actually got them; 70 percent of those patients were never asked their preferences. There have been many cases in which individuals who have taken all the right steps have been deprived of seeing their loved ones' wishes carried out because of physician, family, or institutional resistance.

Julie Kurnitz' mother had a living will with a DNR order on it. But when 84-year-old Sylvia Kurnitz, an Alzheimer's patient, was moved from the nursing home to the hospital for a respiratory problem, the emergency medics put her on a ventilator to help her breathe. Julie says she didn't think much about it because she thought it would be temporary. But her mother wound up depending on the ventilator. When Julie and her sister, who was her mother's health proxy, asked the hospital to remove it based on her living will, they were rebuffed by her mother's physician.

"They were not about to take her off the respirator. My sister said, 'We should unplug her and see if she can breath on her own,'" says Julie. The physician was more interested in curing an infection Julie's mother had acquired. Julie and her sister began to challenge him; their mother had Alzheimer's disease and she was 84 years old. The doctor said to Julie's sister: "So, you are asking me to put a pillow over her face?" Julie and her sister prevailed, but only after they threatened to seek legal action. Another doctor took over the case and her mother was removed from life support after being tethered to it for more than a month. Julie admits the first impulse "was to plug it back in." But she knew this is what her mother wanted. Sylvia died two days later.

SENDING A MESSAGE

Karen Kaplan of Choice in Dying acknowledges that "a sufficient number of physicians have not been trained to regard [living wills] as a document of law." But she says that is changing. Hospitals are beginning to step up their efforts to educate staff as more courts make providers suffer the consequences.

Last year [1996], a Michigan jury awarded $16.6 million to the family of 34-year-old Brenda Young because the hospital ignored her living will wishes. Brenda Young, who suffered a series of strokes tied to a blood vessel disorder in her brain, had appointed her mother as a health care proxy. She made clear in writing and via her mother that she did not want to be saved if she could not be restored to her former state. But those wishes were not complied with because of a breakdown in hospital bureaucracy. Brenda now lives with her 70-year-old mother in a complete state of disability and constant pain. She screams for hours at a time; her screams are so relentless that her mother can't place her in a long-term care facility. She can't feed herself, control her bodily functions, or sit up in a chair without being tied.

Gordon Hoy, a lawyer who represents Brenda's estate, says the verdict should send a powerful message to the medical community about the meaning of advance directives. "When these documents exist, you are to follow [them] and consult with patients or their advocates before you undertake treatment. . . . If you disregard the rights of patients, then you are going to be held accountable."

——————◆ **QUESTIONS FOR DISCUSSION AND WRITING** ◆——————

1. This article employs brief vignettes about real people and real problems for illustration or to help convince readers. Are these short stories an effective writing strategy? In what ways?

2. Now that you know more about "advance directives," should you prepare a living will? Why or why not?

3. "Are Living Wills Honored?" notes that only about half of living wills are honored. Do you think that all living wills should be taken at face value? Why? If a doctor refuses to honor a living will, should he or she be held liable for damages of some kind? How would you assess such damages?

❊ New Living Will Puts Legal Issues in Plain English
LAWYERS QUESTIONING "FIVE WISHES"

Maureen West

In a family setting, what's the only thing that's harder to talk about than sex?

How about planning for incapacitating illness and death?

Because it's so difficult, yet important, a new way to handle the subject gracefully has been developed by a Florida-based nonprofit organization, Aging with Dignity.

Called "Five Wishes," it was launched Thursday in 33 states, including Arizona. But some Arizona attorneys have concerns about the approach.

The do-it-yourself "living will" covers five key areas where family members should make advance decisions about medical care and dying. Most living wills focus on medical matters. The "Five Wishes" living will goes beyond that. 5

The fill-in-the-blanks legal document includes questions such as, "The person I want to make care decisions for me when I can't make them is ———." A checklist of medical treatments that would be acceptable or unacceptable is provided.

LEAVING MEMORIES

Preferences regarding pain relief, family relationships, even prayer and forgiveness are included with open questions such as: "How comfortable I want to be," "How I want people to treat me" and "What I want my loved ones to know."

"This document allows families to decide if they want someone by the bedside praying for them," said Jim Towey, president and founder of Aging with Dignity, which is distributing the document free via the Internet or for $4 postage and handling via regular mail.

He said it also allows people to leave "memories," not just material things.

"People love it because it speaks to them in their own language, not in 'doctor speak' or 'lawyer talk,'" said Towey, a former Florida Health Department secretary who also worked for 12 years as a legal counsel for Mother Teresa. 10

Towey announced the development of the new living will last spring [1998] when he was a speaker in Prescott at the Arizona Town Hall on aging issues.

He believes the medical communities will welcome this document.

"They don't want to play God—they want families to help them," he said.

Five Wishes

The five decisions a person should make in the new living will are:

1. The person I want to make care decisions for me when I can't.
2. The kind of medical treatment I want or don't want.
3. How comfortable I want to be.
4. How I want people to treat me.
5. What I want my loved ones to know.

FORM EASY TO FOLLOW

One Valley expert on end-of-life care welcomes an easy-to-understand form.

"I'm constantly talking to patients who are bringing their documents in and not understanding what they say," said Dr. Kenneth Levine, medical director of Odyssey Hospice in Tempe. "It's very distressing to them."

He welcomes anything that will help people plan for their final days, before they are incapacitated or in emotional distress.

Towey agrees.

"The document allows these discussions to take place in the living room, not a hospital room," he said.

Only one in four people has advanced directives, according to Towey.

Legally valid living wills must be signed in the presence of two witnesses over the age of 19.

Operators of new statewide Elder Law Hotline, however, have concerns about the simple approach Five Wishes recommends.

NOTHING BLACK AND WHITE

"Too much is at risk here to have people fill in the blanks and think they have accomplished their objectives," said Paul Julien, executive director of Southern Arizona Hotline, which operates the elder hotline.

"Nothing in the law is that clear and easy and black and white," said his associate, Sharon Rauseo, managing attorney with the hotline.

In some areas, she believes it is inconsistent with Arizona law.

"This is better than nothing," Julien said. "But if you are interested in doing complete planning, they should do more than this."

Whatever you do, they both advise, don't replace the medical power of attorney or living will that you have written after consulting with your lawyer.

Living wills that they know comply with Arizona's law are also available through the area agencies on aging, private attorneys or the Dorothy

Garske Center in Phoenix. The hotline lawyers also said to call on them at 1-800-231-5441. No matter what form you choose, you ought to talk to your family and your doctor in very clear terms about what your final wishes are, well in advance of when you are sick, Rauseo said.

Five Wishes is free on the Internet at www.agingwithdignity.org or by mail for $4 from Aging with Dignity, P.O. Box 1661, Tallahassee, FL 32302-1661.

───────── ◆ **QUESTIONS FOR DISCUSSION AND WRITING** ◆ ─────────

1. Maureen West includes in a small box "Five Wishes" a person needs to make in his or her living will. What would you specify for each of these decisions?
2. Do you think that members of your family might have a difficult time "planning for incapacitating illnesses and death" (paragraph 2)? Why or why not?
3. Do you have or wish to have a living will? Why or why not? Is there anything that would stop you from signing one?

❋ Position of the American Dietetic Association: Legal and Ethical Issues in Feeding Permanently Unconscious Patients

American Dietetic Association

Dietitians' unique education in nutritional, medical, psychosocial, and behavioral sciences as well as in philosophy and ethics provides them with expertise in feeding people and determining their nutrition needs. In the United States, 14,000 to 35,000 persons, 4,000 to 10,000 of which are children, are in a permanently unconscious state (1). This number is expected to increase as the population ages and acute trauma care improves. Feeding these patients creates ethical dilemmas; the meaning of nutrition and hydration and the definition of death are central to the dilemma. The dietitian, as a member of the health care team, has the responsibility to identify and implement the nutrition needs of each patient on an individualized basis and to develop ethical feeding guidelines for when nutrition and hydration may or may not be essential medical therapy. This position complements ADA's position on issues in feeding the terminally ill adult (2).

Various ethical principles are seemingly in conflict in the care of patients who are permanently unconscious: the sanctity of life, the health care professional's duty to provide life-sustaining care, and respect for personal autonomy. In general, for a competent patient the principle of autonomy supersedes the other two principles. If a person's choice is known, this also holds true for a patient who is permanently unconscious or in a persistent vegetative state (PVS). However, a patient in a PVS does not have the ability to request or to refuse treatment.

POSITION

It is the position of the American Dietetic Association that dietitians serve an integral role with other members of the health care team in developing and implementing ethical guidelines for feeding permanently unconscious patients.

DEFINITION OF PERMANENTLY UNCONSCIOUS

The American Academy of Neurology defines a patient in a PVS as one who "at no time is aware of himself or his environment" and has a ". . . total loss of cerebral functioning" (3, p 125). Persons in a PVS have lost the function of their cerebral cortex and thalamus, although the brain stem is relatively intact (4). Thus, after trauma:

"The patient will begin to breathe spontaneously, the eyes will open and 'wander' and respond normally to light, and periods of sleep will occur. The protective gag, cough and swallow reflexes are usually normal and hand-feeding is possible by placing food at the back of the throat thus activating the involuntary swallow reflex. All voluntary reactions or behavioral responses reflecting consciousness volition or emotion at the cerebral cortical level are absent." (5, p 71)

Although patients in a PVS can be hand-fed, most are tube-fed because it is safer and more practical.

Lack of progressive improvement for a prolonged period is essential to the diagnosis of a PVS. The possibility of a positive outcome should be assumed until the patient has not shown progress over time. The Multi-Society Task Force on Persistent Vegetative State defines the persistent vegetative state "as a vegetative state present one month after acute traumatic or nontraumatic brain injury or lasting for at least one month in patients with degenerative or metabolic disorders or developmental malformations" (1, p 1499). In the Task Force's judgment, a PVS is only one form of being permanently unconscious. Alternatively, Freeman suggests categorizing "a person as in prolonged coma between 2 weeks and 3 months after trauma, vegetative state from 3 to 12 months, and persistent vegetative state after 12 months" (6).

The diagnosis of PVS is determined through the clinical judgment of the attending physician. The results of imaging technology and laboratory tests are not helpful in confirming the diagnosis. Rappaport et al (7) suggested a coma/near coma scale to systematically determine early changes in the patient's clinical status to predict whether further improvement is likely. The Multi-Society Task Force report provides a thorough review of the status of diagnostic tests and cautions against a diagnosis of PVS when

there is any "degree of sustained visual pursuit, consistent and repro-
ducible visual fixation, or response to threatening gestures" (1, p 1501).
However, much still needs to be known about PVS, especially to determine beyond a reasonable doubt whether a person is permanently unconscious.

LEGAL DECISIONS

The past two decades have seen landmark judicial decisions addressing the question of when life-sustaining medical procedures can be withdrawn. The question of whether nutrition and hydration are medical
procedures has been debated in the medical and legal arenas. The following cases explore some of the ethical, medical, and legal issues related to
feeding patients who are permanently unconscious.

The Cruzan Case

The Nancy Cruzan case provides the current US legal framework for
care of a patient in a PVS. Five US Supreme Court Justices wrote opinions
on the case (8). After their daughter had been in a PVS for 5 years, the
Cruzan family requested removal of her feeding tube. Hospital employees
refused to honor the request without a court order. The Missouri Trial
Court found that Nancy Cruzan had the fundamental right to ask for the
removal of death-prolonging procedures (8). The Supreme Court of Missouri reversed the decision because it was skeptical that the right to refuse
treatment was applicable in this case. The Court decided that the state's
policy to preserve life should govern because there was insufficient evidence to support the parents' claim of Nancy Cruzan's wishes. The US
Supreme Court agreed to hear the case to determine whether the US Constitution protects Nancy Cruzan's right to withdraw life-sustaining treatment and, thus, whether the hospital is required to stop treatment (8). In
1990, the five-to-four decision of the US Supreme Court affirmed the
state's right to determine its requirements for "clear and convincing evidence" and affirmed the right of the patient in a PVS to discontinue
nutrition and hydration when sufficient evidence is available (8). The definition of "clear and convincing evidence" set by each state could require
oral or written evidence from another person affirming the patient's
wishes regarding life-sustaining treatment.

In the opinion, the US Supreme Court stated that the "principle that
a competent person has a constitutionally protected liberty interest in refusing unwanted medical treatment may be inferred from our prior decisions . . . [so] we assume that the United States Constitution would grant
a competent person a constitutionally protected right to refuse lifesaving
hydration and nutrition" (8, pp 13–14). The various opinions also mentioned that the decision of life or death is a deeply personal issue.

The concurring opinion by Justice Sandra Day O'Connor stated that the Cruzan decision "does not preclude a future determination that the Constitution requires the States to implement the decisions of a patient's duly appointed surrogate" (8). Justice John Paul Stevens' dissent stated that "the best interests of the individual, especially when buttressed by the interests of all related third parties must prevail over any general state policy that simply ignores those interested . . . To deny the importance of these consequences is in effect to deny that Nancy Cruzan has interest at all and thereby to deny her personhood in the name of preserving the sanctity of her life" (8).

Six months after the US Supreme Court decision, three new witnesses testified of Nancy's desire not to continue with life-sustaining medical treatment. The court case was subsequently dismissed, and the court granted permission for the feeding tube to be removed. The decision of the Court emphasizes the need for patients to have written directives. The use of health care proxies would have made the court case unnecessary.

The Wanglie Case

The issue of futility of care was raised in the Helga Wanglie case (9). While she was in a nursing home, 86-year-old Wanglie suffered severe brain damage after a stroke. After rehospitalization she was diagnosed as permanently unconscious. During the initial hospitalization, Wanglie had not completed an advanced directive. Her physicians stated that her respirator and feeding tube were of no benefit to her in restoring consciousness. The physicians described her care as nonbeneficial and medically inappropriate. The family argued that Wanglie believed in the intrinsic value of life. The Minnesota District Court decided the best decision maker was Wanglie's husband. Before a decision could be made, Wanglie died with the respirator and tube in place. Tong (10, p 387) points out that "Because the Wanglie case ended as it did, no court has yet ruled whether, in the presence of clear and convincing evidence that a patient in a PVS wants life-sustaining treatment, physicians may nonetheless withhold or withdraw treatment on the grounds that it is medically inappropriate or nonbeneficial." The issue of futility of care is further discussed in the section on ethical considerations.

The Bland Case

In February 1993, the British House of Lords determined that it was lawful to withdraw medical treatment and support, including nutrition and hydration, from Anthony Bland, a patient in a PVS. Using the Bolam principle, which states that the decision to provide care should be based on a responsible body of medical opinion and that care is not required when a case is hopeless, the House of Lords stated that health professionals can act on what they believe is in the best interest of the patient and,

15

thus, may start or curtail treatment considered inappropriate (11). The Bland decision, however, is not legally binding in the United States.

Self-Determination

The Patient Self-Determination Act, which took effect on December 1, 1991, requires all Medicare/Medicaid health care providers to inform patients of their right to prepare advance directives and to refuse treatment (12). The Act is based on the principle, which was affirmed in an 1891 case, that "[N]o right is held more sacred, or is more carefully guarded by the common law, than the right of every individual to the possession and control of his person, free from all restraint or interference of others, unless by clear and unquestionable authority of the law" (13, p 411). The crucial ethical responsibility is to ensure that the patient, not the family or institution, makes the decision about medical treatments.

ETHICAL CONSIDERATIONS

Health care professionals have an inherent ethical obligation to respect the sanctity of life and to provide relief from suffering. Beneficence, autonomy, and justice are accepted moral principles governing the behavior of health care professionals within society. Technological and medical advances have created a conflict between application of these moral principles and use of certain types of medical treatment. The decisions of which moral principle takes precedence in what situation creates the conflict. Guidelines on the ethical considerations to forego or discontinue hydration and nutrition support have been written by numerous organizations including The American Dietetic Association (2), the American Medical Association (14), The American Nurses Association (15), and the Hastings Center (16).

Ethics in Patient Care Delivery

Two diverse ethical theories affect attitudes toward health care delivery and services: the utilitarian, or consequentialist view and the formalist or deontological view. The utilitarian viewpoint, expressed by John Stuart Mill (17), sees ethical decisions as those that produce the greatest positive balance of value over negative balance of value for all persons affected. The deontological viewpoint of ethics, which was expressed by Immanuel Kant (18), states that some acts are wrong and others are right independent of their consequences. American society highly values tolerance of conflicting moral values. It also values the right of the individual to control or govern himself or herself according to his or her own reasoning and ethical values.

Guidelines for feeding a permanently unconscious patient support the patient's right to self-determination as the overriding principle. Within

American society, the individual's right to self-determination generally takes precedence over the beliefs or wishes of health care providers. According to ADA's position on feeding the terminally ill:

Each patient approaches that universal, common end called death [20] with different religious, philosophical, and personal attitudes and values. For some, every moment of life—no matter how painful and limited in quality—is of inestimable value. . . . On the other hand, because of their circumstances and values, competent, informed patients may seek to forego various medical procedures—which may include nutrition support (2, pp 996–997).

Some patients may wish to forego aggressive medical care, such as withdrawal of antibiotics or ventilators, but may wish to continue nutrition support.

ADA's position on feeding the terminally ill further states: "Attempting to establish the preferences for treatment or nontreatment of the legally 'incompetent' patient is a complicated and often perplexing process" (2, p 998). Surmising what the patient would have wanted can be done through living wills, durable power of attorney for health care, or family discussions depending on the laws within the state. A 1992 conference brought together families involved in "right to die" cases. All of them "stressed the abysmal quality of life of their loved ones, how 'personal' such a decision is and how they would support another's decision not to terminate treatment under the very same circumstances that caused them to do so" (10, p 389).

Religious Viewpoints

Roman Catholic and some Protestant church authorities have rejected the notion of prolonging life regardless of quality. In 1977, Archbishop of Canterbury Coggan concluded that extending life by artificial means was distinct from euthanasia, and that removal of life support was acceptable if it would be better for the patient to be allowed to die (19). However, persons who believe that a PVS is a God-mandated fate may think they are benefited rather than burdened by life-prolonging treatment (10).

In 1992, the National Conference of Catholic Bishops released a paper opposing all willful suicides but stating that Roman Catholics are not obliged to use extraordinary or disproportionate means when there is no hope for recovery, only burden of care (20). Roman Catholic theologians agree that an unconscious patient must be treated with value and dignity, but disagree on the proper medical care for permanently unconscious patients. The debate centers on the issue of moral obligation. The argument is that if there is no benefit, the procedure cannot be obligatory. Hence, the decision to omit nonobligatory care is to avoid burden for the patient. Although the Roman Catholic bishops expressed the need for further reflection on the issue of care for patients in a PVS, their statement concludes:

"We are concerned that withdrawal of all life support, including nu- 25
trition and hydration, not be viewed as appropriate or automatically indicated for the entire class of PVS patients simply because of a judgment that
they are beyond the reach of medical treatment that would restore consciousness. . . . Recognizing that judgments about the benefits and burdens of medically assisted nutrition and hydration in individual cases have
a subjective element and are generally best made by the patient directly
involved, we also affirm a legitimate role for families' love and guidance,
health care professionals' ethical concerns, and society's interest in preserving life and protecting the helpless" (20, p 20).

Orthodox Judaism does not accept the concept of "brain death" and
defines death as the absence of respiration, cardiac function, and brain
function. The PVS state is not clearly discussed by Jewish religious authorities, but their belief that the soul is present in a comatose patient suggests a need to maintain life (21). Other religions practiced in the United
States hold different points of view regarding the sanctity of life and the
appropriateness or inappropriateness of withholding or withdrawing nutrition and hydration.

Futility of Care

The Hippocratic Corpus encourages physicians to recognize when
medicine has reached its limit of usefulness. Mitchell et al note that Plato
emphasized the "inappropriateness of persisting with treatment which
leaves the surviving patient with a useless life" (5, p 73). When there is dis-
agreement on futility of care, the question of benefit enters. The question
is whether nutrition and hydration are morally obligatory or morally optional. A common method of distinguishing between obligatory and optional is to consider the effects, both benefits and burdens. Nutrition and
hydration can be effective in that they maintain life, but alone they can
rarely restore consciousness. Hence, nutrition may be considered futile
as a medical treatment "because the ultimate goal of any medical intervention should be improvement of the patient's prognosis, comfort, well-
being, or, general state of health" (5, p 73). Conversely, one may be
reluctant to withdraw feeding because it is morally obligatory, the patient
is neither terminally ill nor dead, the family wishes to continue feeding, or
withdrawal of nutrition and hydration appears to be intentional killing (5).

If care providers decide that there is an obligation to feed a permanently unconscious patient, does that obligation ever stop? Can it be over-
ridden when health care professionals are certain that the condition is
irreversible? Does moral obligation change to a moral option after a time
frame suggests that the patient's state will be permanent whether that
time frame be 1 month, 12 months, or more? Because the patient cannot feel pain and suffering, the burden cannot be physical. Can the burden, however, be emotional or financial? Can treatment be medically
futile but of emotional benefit? Arguments that feeding is a benefit be-

cause of the sanctity of life can be countered with arguments about the dignity of death.

According to Tong (10), a singular goal of prolonging a patient's life is not an independent goal but a dependent goal. The physician's responsibility is restoring and correcting. Although there is general agreement patients have the right to refuse treatment, the question is whether they have the right to demand treatment if it is nonbeneficial or medically inappropriate. The Wanglie case started to examine this. As yet, there is "no official consensus among physicians that it is inappropriate to aggressively treat PVS patients or that prolonging life is not an 'independent' and 'overriding' goal of medicine and such a consensus may be long in coming" (10, p 387). In addition, such a consensus may not be desirable. Even if physicians agreed, society might be foolish to give the health care provider unilateral say over what is best for the patient. The debate on the definition of futility is in the early stages. Public values and standards of care for patients in a PVS will evolve. Angell states that "any solution must be a principled one that applies generally and is established by consensus, in the same way that death was redefined as brain death" (22, p 1524).

Justice and Scarce Resources

An additional issue in the treatment of patients in a PVS is the "need to ensure a just and fair allocation of scarce resources" (5). The question of whether cost should be a factor in clinical ethical decision making is intensifying as resources become more scarce. It is widely accepted that nutrition support may be withdrawn when the burden of feeding outweighs the benefit. A patient in a PVS is said to experience nothing; thus, there is no benefit or burden to the patient. This raises the question of whether nutrition support without benefit or burden is futile.

The issue of justice and the patient in a PVS may intensify. Should decisions be different for children, older adults, or pregnant women in a PVS? Tong (10) and Angell (22) provide some interesting points to consider. Tong (1) suggests that with respect to patients in a PVS, legislative and social changes may be the solution. For instance, if the definition of death were changed to be the death of higher brain functions, a patient in a PVS would be considered dead. This change would mean that society rather than the physician would decide when a patient is dead; however, the lack of diagnostic certainty complicates this approach. Further, as the debate over the rationing of health care intensifies, it could be required, as a principle of justice, that people who would want to live in a PVS purchase special insurance or pay for their care and feeding. Angell (22) suggests that the presumption be that the patient in a PVS would not want to be alive when permanently unconscious. Thus, the health care team needs to establish guidelines of when to stop artificial feeding based on when the irreversibility of a patient's condition is virtually certain. Families could object to ending feeding and document the patient's earlier wishes to be sustained in a PVS. Because of their knowledge about the ethical, social, and legal principles of feeding patients in a PVS, dietitians are invaluable participants with the health care team and society in the debate and development of these principles and standards of care.

Guidelines for Feeding a Patient in a PVS

The nutritional concept of "when in doubt, feed" is essential for the patient in a PVS. The Multi-Society Task Force on PVS states that a patient must have no sign of consciousness for a minimum of 1 month before a PVS diagnosis may be established; other professionals encourage a longer period of time. Feeding should start for a patient in a coma or an unconscious state as soon as he or she is medically stable and should continue at least until a diagnosis of PVS is established. During this time, it is essential to provide adequate nutrients and fluids generally via tube feeding. The tube feeding may have nasal or gastric placement and should contain sufficient energy to maintain or achieve a reasonable weight and adequate fluids to maintain hydration. Protein intake should be determined according to stress level and individual need. Adequate vitamins and minerals are needed. Fiber-containing formulas may prevent bowel irregularity. Feeding should only be stopped after the patient is diagnosed as permanently unconscious and the team has evidence of the patient's wish to stop nutrition and hydration.

SUMMARY

Health care team members, including the dietitian, must set patient-centered treatment goals that are handled individually and that respect the unique values and personal decision of the patient. The patient's expressed desire is the primary guide for determining the extent of nutrition and hydration once the patient is diagnosed as being in a PVS. Within the extent of the law, the family should share decision making when the patient's preference is not stated and the family is in agreement about medical care. The health care team will need to discuss with the family as needed the issues of ethics, values, religious guidelines, and pastoral advice. If the patient's choice is feeding, the dietitian will ensure that the composition of the feeding promotes nutritional health. If the patient's choice is cessation of feeding, the dietitian should explain what is known about the duration of time between cessation of feeding and death. Sensitivity to the family's needs and responsiveness to their questions are imperative in both scenarios.

Within institutions, the ethics committee should help establish and implement defined written guidelines for care of the permanently unconscious. The dietitian should be required to be a member of or consultant to such a committee and should serve an integral role in development of institutional policy. The dietitian must provide education about nutrition and hydration issues, serve as a patient advocate, and participate in the legal and ethical issues regarding feeding. The dietetics community is involved in the legislative arena at the state and local level to promote the use of advanced directives and to affect legislative and societal changes that result in appropriate care for patients in a PVS.

References

1. The Multi-Society Task Force on PVS. Medical Aspects of the Persistent Vegetative State. *N Engl J Med.* 1994; 330: 1499–1506.
2. Position of The American Dietetic Association: issues in feeding the terminally ill adult. *J Am Diet Assoc.* 1992; 92: 996–1005.
3. American Academy of Neurology. Position on certain aspects of the care and management of the persistent vegetative state patient. Adopted by the Executive Board, American Academy of Neurology. April 21, 1988. Cincinnati, Ohio. *Neurology.* 1989; 39: 125–126.
4. Kinney H, Korein J, Panigraphy A, Dikkes P, Goode R. Neuropathological findings in the brain of Karen Ann Quinlan. *N Engl J Med.* 1994; 330: 1469–1475.
5. Mitchell KR, Kerridge IH, Lovat TJ. Medical futility, treatment withdrawal and the persistent vegetative state. *J Med Ethics.* 1993; 19: 71–76.
6. Freeman EA. Protocols for vegetative patients. *Med J Aust.* 1993; 159: 428.
7. Rappaport M, Dougherty A, Kelting D. Evaluation of coma and vegetative states. *Arch Phys Med Rehab.* 1992; 73: 628–634.
8. *Cruzan v Missouri Dept of Health,* III L Ed 2d 224 (110S Ct 1990).
9. *Wanglie v Minnesota,* PX91 283 (Dnt Ct 1990).
10. Tong R. An exercise in futility: Are we bidden to "treat" the untreatable? *NC Med J.* 1993; 54: 386–391.
11. Brahams D. Persistent vegetative state. *Lancet.* 1993; 341: 428.
12. LaPuma J, Orentilicher D, Moss RJ. Advanced directives on admission: clinical implications and analysis of the Patient Self-Determination Act of 1990. *JAMA.* 1991; 266: 402–405.
13. White M, Fletcher J. The Patient Self-Determination Act. *JAMA.* 1991; 266: 410–412.
14. Council on Scientific Affairs and Council on Ethical and Judicial Affairs. Persistent vegetative state and the decision to withdraw or withhold life support. *JAMA.* 1990; 263: 426–430.
15. New ANA guidelines on withdrawing or withholding food and fluids. *Nurs Outlook.* 1988; 36(3): 122–123, 148–150.
16. *Guidelines on the Termination of Life-Sustaining Treatment and the Care of the Dying. A Report by the Hastings Center.* Briarcliff Manor, NY: Hastings Center; 1987.

17. Mill JS. *On Liberty.* New York, NY: WW Norton and Co; 1975.
18. Friedrick CJ, ed. *The Philosophy of Kant: Immanuel Kant's Moral and Political Writings.* New York, NY: The Modern Library; 1977.
19. Coggan F. On dying and dying well: spiritual and moral aspects. *Proc R Soc Med.* 1977; 70: 75–81.
20. Committee for Prolife Activities. National Conference of Catholic Bishops. *Nutrition and Hydration: moral and pastoral reflections.* Washington, DC: US Catholic Conference Office of Publishing and Promotion Services; 1992. No. 516-X.
21. Levin F. *Halacha Medical Science and Technology.* Brooklyn NY: Maznaism Publishing Corp; 1987.
22. Angell M. After Quinlan: the dilemma of the persistent vegetative state. *N Engl J Med.* 330: 1524–1525.

------------◆ **QUESTIONS FOR DISCUSSION AND WRITING** ◆------------

1. *Ethical question:* If you were in a persistent vegetative state (PVS), as defined in the first few paragraphs of this essay, would you want to be kept alive? Why or why not?
2. The last sentence in paragraph 8 reads, "However, much still needs to be known about PVS, especially to determine beyond a reasonable doubt whether a person is permanently unconscious." If this is true, then would you wish to be kept alive in a persistent vegetative state?
3. In reporting on the case of Helga Wanglie, in paragraph 14, the position paper notes "No court has yet ruled whether, in the presence of clear and convincing evidence that a patient in a PVS wants life-sustaining treatment, physicians may nonetheless withhold or withdraw treatment on the grounds that it is medically inappropriate or nonbeneficial." In paragraph 23, we learn that "in 1977, Archbishop of Canterbury Coggan concluded that extending life by artificial means was distinct from euthanasia, and that removal of life support was acceptable if it would be better for the patient to be allowed to die." Which of these points of view do you believe is correct? Why?
4. Reread the series of questions in paragraph 28. How would you answer each one? Why?

❋ Ignoring "Right to Die" Directives, Medical Community Is Being Sued

Tamar Lewin

For the last four years, Brenda Young has spent her days in torment, rhythmically screaming and thrashing in her mother's modest house in Flint, Mich.

Since a seizure in 1992, Ms. Young, now 38, has needed total care. She must be fed, bathed, diapered and, at night, tied into bed so she does not push herself over the padded bed rails. Sometimes she manages a few intelligible words: "Water" or "Bury me." But mostly she screams, over and over.

It is precisely the kind of existence that Ms. Young sought to avoid by signing an advance directive, on her doctor's advice, one month before the seizure that left her so disabled. Warned that the seizures she had been having were likely to worsen, Ms. Young gave her mother, Ramona Osgood, power of attorney to stop treatment if she became incapacitated. But to no avail: After her next seizure, Ms. Young was put on a ventilator, tube-fed and maintained through a two-month coma, despite her mother's insistence that she did not want life support.

In a lawsuit against the hospital, Genesys St. Joseph, Ms. Young and her mother and daughter won a $16.5 million verdict this year [1996]. Sue Zitterman, the lawyer representing the hospital, declined to discuss the case, except to say that the judgment had yet to be formally entered, and that the hospital would seek to have it modified or overturned. At trial, the hospital argued that the family had authorized the treatment Ms. Young received, that her doctors believed that they were doing what was best for her and that they could not predict how disabled she would be.

Although the Michigan case is apparently the first of its kind in which a jury awarded substantial damages, hospitals, lawyers and right-to-die advocates say there is a new wave of lawsuits seeking to hold hospitals, nursing homes and doctors liable for ignoring living wills and other advance directives. 5

"The Michigan case is one of these jolts in the field that sets off waves of discussion and reminds us how vulnerable we are, because we are human beings whose training and background are in saving lives," said Richard Wade, a spokesman for the American Hospital Association. "So it's going to take us a while to learn to deal with these end-of-life issues."

The legal theories in such cases vary, with some based on charging negligence and others on intentional infliction of emotional, physical and financial distress. But increasingly, lawyers are arguing that treatment given against a patient's will is a form of battery, an illegal attack on the patient's body.

"This is a new area of law, and the legal theories are still developing," said Anna Moretti, a lawyer with Choice in Dying, an advocacy group that tracks the cases. "But most people are using a theory of medical battery. The idea is that patients have a right to refuse treatment, so if the patient has expressed a wish not to have a particular treatment or procedures, and the doctors and hospitals do it anyway, it's legally like an assault on the patient."

SUITS SEEK TO SWAY CULTURE OF MEDICINE

Advance directives do not always resolve what to do in an emergency, doctors and hospital administrators say, both because patients and families often waver when confronted with imminent death and because it is often hard to predict whether an emergency intervention will improve the patient's quality of life or consign him to a long, painful process of high-tech dying.

"No one acts out of malice but these are very complicated issues, and except in the most clear-cut cases, everyone following an advance directive has some doubts," said Mr. Wade, the association spokesman. "Even if you're sure this is what your relative wanted, you have some doubts, too. It's all a confluence of human judgments around a traumatic situation, and everything becomes different when it comes right down to it. No piece of paper tells you exactly what to do."

But right-to-die advocates argue that hospitals still do not pay enough attention to patients' wishes. And, they say, the new lawsuits provide useful pressure to change a medical culture that too often insists on extending life, without regard to the patient's wishes or to the cost in pain and suffering.

The pending lawsuits cover a wide variety of situations. Among them are the following:

An Arkansas woman whose husband collapsed from end-stage heart disease, and was resuscitated, filed suit this year, saying she was forcibly ejected from his hospital room when she protested that, as her husband's legal proxy, she wanted to stop the resuscitation effort. The complaint charges battery of both husband and wife, and intentional infliction of emotional distress.

A California man whose wife had a degenerative and fatal genetic disease had her admitted to the hospital in 1994, when she was having seizures and seemed to be dying, with the understanding that she was to receive only comfort measures. But two days later, the hospital, over his objections, inserted a feeding tube, strapped her to the bed and provided antibiotics to threat the pneumonia she was developing. She is still alive, and in need of full-time nursing care; her husband has sued the doctor and the hospital.

Four days after an Indiana woman suffered a massive stroke that left her in a persistent vegetative state, the hospital where she was treated removed her feeding tube, after consultation with her family, including the son who held her power of attorney. She was then sent back to her nursing home, where she was to be allowed to die naturally, receiving only intravenous fluids. But less than two weeks later, the nursing home put a feeding tube into her stomach and restarted nutrition, keeping her alive five more months. The family is suing for fraud and negligence.

An Ohio man, Edward Winter, told his doctors and his children that he would not want resuscitation, after watching the slow death of his wife, who suffered brain damage after being resuscitated through electric shock following a heart attack. But a few months later, when Mr. Winter, 82, had a heart attack himself, he was shocked back to life at a hospital. He then suffered a stroke that left him partly paralyzed, barely able to speak and mostly confined to bed in a nursing home.

The lawsuit he filed in 1989, the year before he died, was initially dismissed on the ground that keeping someone alive against his will is not a legal wrong. But in an appeal argued to the Ohio Supreme Court in May, Mr. Winter's lawyer, William Knapp, argued that the case was based on negligence and battery, not a claim of "wrongful life."

MEDICAL EXPERTS DEFEND DECISIONS

In most of the cases, the doctors and hospitals defend their actions, asserting that saving a life is never against the law.

Deborah Lydon, the lawyer representing the Ohio hospital, said: "We don't think it's appropriate to say you can recover damages for living, and we're concerned that an adverse decision would cause health practitioners to be terribly confused about which way to proceed if there was an emergency health-care decision. It's terribly difficult to know one way or another what the outcome is going to be, in many cases."

And the decision must often be made very quickly. 20

"A good bit of the urgent care hospitals offer must start literally in minutes, so we've developed the mentality that if you don't intervene and the patient dies, maybe you will be liable," said Dr. Nancy Dickey, chairwoman of the board of the American Medical Association. "The thinking has been that if you do intervene and you shouldn't have, the worse that will happen is that the patient will live a little longer and that you'll never be held accountable if you keep the patient from dying. Of course, that's not true anymore."

Dr. Dickey and others say doctors and hospitals are slowly changing their attitudes and talking more with patients about their desires on treatment.

"This goes very deep in hospital culture, and it's going to take a lot to change it," said Daniel Callahan, an expert on end-of-life medical care who is president of the Hastings Foundation, which specializes in issues of biomedical ethics. "One way that may happen is through legal pressure and jury verdicts. If doctors get worried that they'll get sued if they don't do what the patient directed, it's bound to affect their behavior."

ADVANCE DIRECTIVES FOUND INEFFECTIVE

The lawsuits come at a time when patients' end-of-life decisions are getting new attention. Over the last two decades, every state has provided mechanisms for people to declare, in advance, what measures they want taken if they are incapacitated, or to name a proxy who will make such decisions, or both.

Since 1990, the Federal Patient Self-Determination Act has required 25 hospitals and nursing homes to tell patients, on admission, of their right to file an advance directive, and to refuse treatment. And just this year, two Federal appeals courts—in New York and California—have struck down laws prohibiting physician-assisted suicide.

Despite all the legal momentum, advance directives have done little to change end-of-life medical care, according to a study financed by the Robert Wood Johnson Foundation and made public late last year [1995].

The study, which has generated criticism and debate in the medical community, found that fewer than half the doctors knew when patients wanted to avoid resuscitation, that half the patients who died in the hospitals were in moderate to severe pain at least half the time, and that more than a third of those who died spent at least 10 days in intensive care, comatose or on a ventilator.

What stunned the medical community even more was another finding, that intensive efforts to improve matters, using nurses to talk to families and doctors and encourage planning, had no influence on how much the patients' wishes were followed or how much aggressive treatment they received before dying.

"IT'S A LIVING HELL," ONE MOTHER SAYS

Brenda Young's case, in Michigan, is a good example of how decisions are made on the spot, even when the patient has an advance directive.

Ms. Young was in good health until 1977, when she suffered a brain hemorrhage, and her doctors found that she had abnormal vessels in her brain. She began having bad headaches and increasingly severe seizures. Her doctor warned her that at some point the seizures would be so severe that she would emerge profoundly disabled, if at all. It was that warning that sent Ms. Young to the lawyer, to make her mother her health proxy.

On Feb. 3, 1992, when Ms. Osgood found her daughter in the midst of a seizure, she called the ambulance, and took her to Genesys St. Joseph, taking the power of attorney with her. Ms. Young was found to be in critical condition by the time she arrived at the hospital, and doctors repeatedly came out to seek her mother's permission for the procedures they wanted to begin.

Clark Shanahan, the lawyer representing the family, described the back and forth: "The doctors would come out and say, 'Can we have your consent to put your daughter on a ventilator,' and she'd say, 'That ain't life support, is it? She doesn't want life support,' and they'd say, 'No, we're just trying to make her more comfortable,' so she'd agree."

Ms. Shanahan continued: "Then it was dialysis, then dopamine, then blood transfusions. Ms. Osgood has a fifth-grade education, and she had no idea what she was consenting to. And no one really explained it."

At trial, witnesses for the hospital testified that they had tried to explain their treatment decisions and that Ms. Osgood had seemed conflicted, but had agreed to the treatment. An outside hospital-ethics expert testified, however, that the records show the doctors never fully explained

Ms. Young's situation to her mother and she never understood enough to give genuine consent.

Either way, the results have been disastrous. Ms. Young's father, unable to stand it, abandoned his wife and home after more than 30 years of marriage, and her daughter, Chastity, married and moved out of state at the age of 17. Ms. Osgood has tried to place her daughter in a convalescent home, but none has been willing to cope with the screaming. 35

And it may be years before Ms. Osgood gets enough money to pay for round-the-clock nursing as the verdict makes its way through the appeals process.

"It's a living hell, really a living hell," Ms. Osgood said in a videotape of her daily life made two years ago for the lawsuit. "I get no rest, no sleep. The girl hollers constantly. She screams very, very loudly, for five or six hours at a time. I don't know how she does it, but she does it. It's got to me, physically and mentally."

◆ QUESTIONS FOR DISCUSSION AND WRITING ◆

1. What do you think should happen to the doctors and/or Mercy Hospital if they decide not to honor Helen Scott's living will? Considering the real-life story Lewin tells, who should be held liable for the catastrophic consequences of incorrect decisions?

2. How effectively do real-life stories, such as the one with which Lewin begins this piece, set the stage for what follows and draw the reader into the piece?

3. According to Lewin, "lawyers are arguing that treatment given against a patient's will is a form of battery, an illegal attack on the patient's body" (paragraph 7). Do you agree or disagree with this argument? Why?

4. In paragraphs 13 through 17, Lewin relates some real cases. Suppose that you were a judge. Based solely on the evidence presented here, how would you rule on each case? Why?

❋ A Right to Die?

Anne E. Weiss

The young man, barely out of his teens, had been injured in an auto accident. Rushed to a local hospital, he was placed on a respirator and connected to other life-support systems.

That was on a Thursday in early 1984. By the next Monday, although machines continued to pump the man's blood and move his lungs, his brain and body had lost all ability to function on their own. Doctors declared the man dead.

On Tuesday, they saw a muscle ripple in his foot.

How could it happen? Is it so difficult for a doctor to tell when someone has died?

It didn't use[d] to be. Traditionally, doctors have defined death as "a total stoppage of the circulation of the blood, and a cessation of the animal and vital functions consequent thereon, such as respiration, pulsation, etc." As recently as 1968, this was the definition of death in *Black's Law Dictionary,* considered an authority by legal and medical professionals alike.

But medicine has changed since the 1960s, and many of the old definitions must be discarded. Sophisticated equipment and new techniques now permit HCPs [health care professionals] to resuscitate and save the lives of patients who would have had no chance of survival only a few years ago. Many of these people have almost literally "come back from the dead." Aware that a new definition of death was needed, the President's Commission for the Study of Ethical Problems in Medicine and Biomedical and Behavioral Research began to review the subject in 1978.

"BRAIN DEATH"

The commission submitted its report in 1981. It recommended that each state adopt a "definition of death" law, and that these laws be the same throughout the country. The commission's proposed statute reads in part: "An individual who has sustained . . . irreversible cessation of all functions of the entire brain, including the brain stem, is dead."

This amounts to a definition of death as brain death. Under it, a person who is maintained on artificial life-support systems may be declared dead when doctors can no longer detect any measurable brain-wave activity. In other words, people die when their brains die, despite what machines may be doing to maintain breathing or circulation. By 1984, thirty-seven states and the District of Columbia had passed brain-death legislation.

However, laws and definitions by themselves are not enough to solve thorny bioethical problems like those that surround the matter of death and dying. By the brain-death standard, the road accident victim *was* dead. Yet how could his doctors ignore that twitch?

What's more, bioethical questions are rarely limited to one clear-cut issue. Any individual case may be complicated by a variety of factors. The accident victim's doctors, for instance, had special cause for caution in determining his state. The man's family had agreed to allow his organs to be donated to people in need of transplants.

WHO LIVES? WHO DIES?

One such person was waiting in a Memphis, Tennessee, hospital. He was Phillip Cockerham, a twenty-six-year-old carpenter with a failing liver. On Monday night, as soon as doctors had declared the accident victim dead, physicians in Memphis began preparing Cockerham to receive a transplant.

Then the "dead" man moved. Both operations were hastily cancelled. Cockerham left his hospital bed and went home. Gone, at least for the time being, was his chance for a life-saving transplant.

Was the doctors' decision to cancel right? That decision seemed likely to cost Cockerham his life. Nor did it seem probable that it would do much to benefit the accident victim. Even after doctors saw his muscle move, they still considered him clinically dead. In any case, they knew that the damage to his brain—he had suffered head injuries—was so severe that he would never think, or feel, or sense anything ever again. By contrast, Cockerham had every reason to hope that given a healthy liver, he would live a full, normal life.

Tough as the decision not to operate may have been ethically, in practical terms it was the only decision possible. If the public ever came to suspect that doctors might hurry to declare people dead in their eagerness to obtain needed organs, it would surely mean an abrupt end to donations.

Ironically, of course, the accident victim's life—if he *was* alive on Tuesday—was actually extended by his having been intended as a donor. Had he not been, he would not have remained on life-support systems hours after his "death." Besides, it may have been largely because he was scheduled to become a donor that doctors were so sensitive to the possibility that he was still living. Such a tiny sign of life as that twitch might have been overlooked had the physicians not been so aware of their ethical responsibility regarding the use of cadavers as sources of transplantable organs. Without that awareness, the man might have been given up for dead days earlier. That is because in hospitals around this country HCPs do sometimes take people who are still technically alive off life-support machinery under certain circumstances.

At first, this seems a direct violation of the Hippocratic oath and of other codes of medical ethics. HCPs are enjoined by their oaths to preserve life. Over the ages, resisting death has been regarded as medicine's ultimate goal.

But HCPs point out that their professional oaths also require them to relieve suffering. In modern American hospitals, they stress, the two promises are frequently at odds with each other. To preserve life, it may be necessary to impose terrible suffering. To relieve that suffering may require doing something that ends a life. The conflict presents HCPs with an agonizing bioethical dilemma: When, if ever, does a patient have the right to die?

KAREN QUINLAN AND THE "RIGHT TO DIE"

One of the first cases to bring this dilemma before the public involved a young New Jersey woman named Karen Quinlan. In 1975, Karen, then age twenty-one, slipped into a deep coma. At a hospital near her home, Karen was attached to a respirator. Then began a time of waiting.

Waiting—for what? Karen's doctors warned the Quinlans that their daughter was never going to wake up from her comatose state. Her brain was too badly damaged for that to happen. But neither would she necessarily die, doctors added. Kept on life-support systems, Karen might live for many years. An Illinois woman, thrown from a horse in 1956, survived in a coma for eighteen years before dying.

Eighteen years! The prospect seemed unbearable to the Quinlans. After days of anguished prayer and discussion, they asked the doctors to turn the machinery off and allow Karen to die. The doctors refused, and the case went to court.   20

There, the Quinlans presented their view: Karen had a right to die. In this, they had the backing of their parish priest and of the Roman Catholic Church itself. Death is a natural process, Catholic theologians argue, one rightfully governed by God alone. Although human beings may seek to save lives through surgery, medicine, and so on, they are not required to use "extraordinary" means—like those being used on Karen—to prolong life to the last possible moment.

The judge in the Quinlan case disagreed and ruled against Karen's parents. They appealed the decision, and finally, on March 31, 1976, they won the right to have their daughter's respirator turned off.

Contrary to most people's expectations, however, Karen proved to be able to breathe on her own. Eventually, she was moved from the hospital to a nursing home. She died there, still off the respirator, in June 1985.

In most cases, though, "pulling the plug"—turning off a respirator or other life-support systems—does result in death. Is that death a merciful release? Or a form of murder? In part, the answer depends on where you are.

PULLING THE PLUG ON THE TERMINALLY ILL

In 1981, two California doctors were charged with murder after they removed life-support systems from a comatose man. The doctors acted at the request of the man's wife, who contended that her husband would not have wanted to survive in a vegetablelike state. (Later, however, the wife said that the doctors had not fully discussed the case with her before they pulled the plug. She filed a malpractice suit against them.)   25

First, the doctors turned off the comatose man's respirator. Two days later, they removed the IV tubes through which he was being fed. Not along afterward, the man died.

The district attorney who brought the murder charge against the doctors apparently did so at the request of Right-to-Life groups. His charges were quickly thrown out by a California appeals court. The judges ruled that the doctors' action had been justified by the medical facts in the case. Physicians, they said, have no obligation to continue treatment "once it has proved to be ineffective." Furthermore, removal of life-support machinery "is not an affirmative act but rather a withdrawal or omission of further treatment." In other words, the doctors did not *do* anything that caused their patient to die. He died because of what they did *not* do.

Not everyone accepts the distinction. In a New Jersey case, a court came up with a ruling that runs counter to the one in California. Here, the patient was an eighty-three-year-old woman. She was not comatose, but she was considered mentally incompetent, since she could not communicate and appeared to have little awareness of what was going on around her.

In 1982, the woman's foot and leg became severely ulcerated, the result of diabetes. Doctors asked her legal guardian for permission to amputate, but the guardian refused to give it. At the same time, the guardian asked the doctors to remove the tube through with the patient was been fed.

Although a lower court granted the guardian's request, the appeals court later denied it. (In the meantime, the patient had died, feeding tube still in place.) Unlike the California court, the one in New Jersey decided that disconnecting a feeding tube is a positive action. With the tube in place, the woman might have died of blood poisoning, or heart failure, or any one of a number of already-existing ailments. Removing it would have subjected her to an entirely new condition—starvation. "Thus," the court concluded, "she would have been actively killed by independent means."

What all this adds up to is that while the California court saw no difference between removing a feeding tube and turning off a respirator, the New Jersey court did. To the New Jersey judges, denial of nourishment would have been murder.

The AMA echoes the New Jersey court's stand. According to official AMA policy, it can be ethical for a doctor to cause a patient's death by stopping treatment in some cases. Taking a positive action that will hasten death, on the other hand, is "contrary to the most fundamental measures of human worth and value."

But what is the measure of human worth and value? To the parents of a girl named Andrea, whose case is cited in a Hastings Center publication, it seems to involve more than a simple choice between life and death.

Andrea was nine when she died of complications arising from cystic fibrosis. In the previous twelve months, she had been hospitalized eight times. Besides having breathing problems, Andrea was poorly nourished and weak. She showed no interest in anything and would speak only to her mother. Andrea's parents, knowing how desperately ill she was, asked the doctors not to subject her to extraordinary life-prolonging measures. The doctors agreed.

But avoiding extraordinary measures was not enough, the parents de-   35
cided as Andrea lay slowly dying. Obviously, the child was suffering hor-
ribly. Couldn't the doctors "do something," give Andrea a massive dose of
some pain-killer that would speed up her death and end her agony? The
doctors answered that they could but that they would not. State law, the
AMA code, their professional oaths—all forbade it.

After forty-eight terrible hours, Andrea died. Her doctors had done
nothing to hasten her death, but neither had they done all that they could
have done to prolong her life. Had they acted according to "the most fundamental measures of human value and worth"?

Commenting on this case, James Rachels, professor of philosophy at
the University of Alabama, calls the doctors' action "inconsistent." Clearly,
by agreeing not to use life-prolonging equipment, they indicated that they
thought it would be better for Andrea to die quickly. But if they thought
that, Dr. Rachels asks, why would they refuse to shorten her life a little
further? "If it was pointless for her to endure, say, a four-day period of dying, why would we choose a course that requires her to endure a two-day
period of dying?" he demands. Dr. Rachels' conclusion: Giving Andrea a
drug overdose "seems more consistent with the reasoning that motivates
us not to prolong life in the first place."

The argument seems logical. If it is ethical to relieve suffering by omission (failing to use every means possible to prolong life), why isn't it
equally ethical to relieve suffering through a positive action? Or turn the
argument around. If it is ever wrong to permit a terminally ill person to
die, isn't it always wrong? How can medicine and the law insist on a sharp
distinction between passively allowing patients to die and actively helping
them to do so?

Some say that the answer is that such a distinction is rooted in the
past, in a time when medicine was simpler and HCPs did not have the
elaborate life-sustaining technology they possess today. In those days,
doctors could not bring people back from the dead. Death, when it came,
was certain and final.

Not so today. Such is the effectiveness and potency of modern medi-   40
cal technology that it has already altered the very meaning of the word
"death." Now it is forcing us to think anew about the meaning of "life,"
too, and about what gives life its value. At the same time, it is causing society to reevaluate some old ideas about the right to die and the ethics of
euthanasia.

EUTHANASIA, PRO AND CON

Euthanasia means good death. Another phrase for it is mercy killing.

Over the ages, many people facing slow and painful deaths have
sought euthanasia. Charlotte Perkins Gilman, the American feminist and
social reformer, chose it when she was dying of cancer in 1935. In her last

message, Gilman defended her decision. "When all usefulness is over," she typed, "when one is assured of an imminent and unavoidable death, it is the simplest of human rights to choose a quick and easy death in place of a slow and horrible one. . . . I have preferred chloroform to cancer."

But to many people, what Gilman and others like her have done is not "chosen a quick and easy death," but "committed suicide." When a patient who decides on euthanasia succeeds in getting the cooperation of an HCP, a murderous action compounds the suicidal one.

The Catholic Church is outspoken in its opposition to euthanasia. In 1980, Pope John Paul II issued a declaration in which he rejected mercy killing as objectively and universally wrong. Like the AMA, however, Catholic theologians distinguish between "active" and "passive" euthanasia. The Church does condone the disconnecting of life-support systems in certain situations, such as the one faced by Karen Quinlan.

Catholics and others who oppose euthanasia have a number of specific reasons for the position they take. Many regard euthanasia as yet another slippery slope. First doctors take the comatose patients off respirators. Then they refuse to feed them. After that they try to starve those who aren't even in comas—just unable to talk or feed themselves. Who will be next? The blind? The middle-aged? 45

And what about HCPs who may be corruptible? One might agree to end the life of a patient whose continued stay in the hospital is a financial burden to his family. Another might accept a bribe to do the same to someone's rich aunt or grandmother. The idea that hundreds of people may come to rely on euthanasia as a legal way to do away with unwanted relatives seems a real threat to many.

Another threat is that euthanasia could be turned into something with no resemblance at all to killing out of mercy or pity. Forced euthanasia might be used to eliminate whole groups of people considered to be undesirable. That is how Adolf Hitler used it during his twelve-year dictatorship in Nazi Germany. Jews, gypsies, Catholics, scholars, homosexuals —all were ordered into the death chambers. In this country, mass forced euthanasia might be a possibility for elderly people on welfare or for the retarded, those who oppose euthanasia warn.

Some people contend that permitting euthanasia would be a death-blow to modern medicine. "Legalized euthanasia would be a confession of despair in the medical profession," a Jesuit priest wrote nearly forty years ago. "It would be the denial of hope for further progress against presently incurable maladies." Since doctors and scientists would no longer be confronted with the suffering of the terminally ill, the argument goes, they would no longer feel impelled to develop cures or treatments for serious illnesses.

Currently, scientists do devote themselves to medical research, and that raises another argument against euthanasia. At any time, a new discovery could save the lives of hundreds of the terminally ill. "Cures can come down the pipeline at any hour of the day," says Dr. Marshall L.

Bruner, of Fort Lauderdale, Florida. How would family members feel if they had okayed a mercy killing just days before a new drug became available?

Finally, there are those who argue that no human being has the right   50
to decide that he or she—or anyone else—no longer has a life worth living, or that "all usefulness is over." That is what Charlotte Perkins Gilman thought about her life, but was she right? If nothing else, she could have offered herself as an experimental research subject, allowing anticancer drugs or painkillers to be tested on her body. That way her life would have continued to have a purpose, some say.

On the other side of the euthanasia debate are the people who argue that an individual's life belongs to that individual and to him or her alone. "What gives a physician the right to keep alive a patient who wants to die?" one man—burned, blinded, and crippled in a fire—demanded bitterly. He had begged in vain to be permitted to die. A woman dying of a painful cancer has no obligation to suffer for months just to enable researchers to test a new drug, say those who favor making euthanasia legally available. A comatose man should not be forced to stay "alive" just to prove to society that he has not committed suicide. If a particular religion condemns euthanasia, that is fine—for members of that religion. But people of other faiths must not be compelled to abide by its moral dictates.

There is a puzzling inconsistency in the way our society regards mercy killing, say some who think euthanasia ought to be available to those who honestly want it. Society says euthanasia is wrong because it involves the taking of life. But society permits the taking of life in other ways. It sends people off to kill and be killed in wars. Over half the states allow criminal executions. Ethicist Joseph Fletcher sums this paradox up eloquently in his book *Morals and Medicine:*

> We are, by some strange habit of mind and heart, willing to impose death but unwilling to permit it; we will justify humanly contrived death when it violates the human integrity of its victims, but we condemn it when it is an intelligent voluntary decision.

What if the law were changed to allow euthanasia—or at least passive euthanasia—in certain circumstances? Could any precautions be taken to protect those who want to continue living?

PROTECTING THE TERMINALLY ILL

One precaution could be "living wills." A living will is signed by a person while he or she is in good health. It gives permission for that person's doctor to turn off life-support systems in the case of terminal illness or permanent coma. The purpose of a living will is to give those who have signed them some measure of control over their final days and weeks. At the same time, by *not* signing one, people can indicate their desire to be maintained on artificial support systems until every flicker of life is gone. In 1985, living wills were legal in twenty-two states and the District of Columbia.

Another obvious precaution would be to set up hospital euthanasia review boards, similar to the Institutional Review Boards that rule on human experimentation. Such boards would be required to approve any euthanasia request before it could be honored. 55

Euthanasia review panels would have to work closely with patients and with their families. They would have to help the terminally ill to clarify their own thoughts and desires, and to make sure that patients who request euthanasia are expressing their sincere wishes. They would have to guard against selfish family members who might have reasons of their own for encouraging a mercy killing, and be alert to overprotective families who, through love, urge euthanasia on a patient who is in pain, yet still wants to live. Finally, they would have to steer a cautious middle course between HCPs who do not want to admit that they have "failed" and that death is inevitable, and those who hope to obtain transplantable organs or to make a hospital bed available for a new patient.

EUTHANASIA AND THE FUTURE

Back in 1935, when Charlotte Perkins Gilman chose chloroform over cancer, she predicted that euthanasia would soon be a common practice. "The time is approaching when we shall consider it abhorrent to our civilization to allow a human being to live in prolonged agony which we should mercifully end in any other creature," she wrote.

She was wrong. The idea of legalized euthanasia continues to horrify many people today. The moral objections to it are deep and strong, and the possibilities for abuse clear and terrifying.

Yet, in a way, Charlotte Perkins Gilman was right. As modern medicine has extended the barriers of life— and death—doctors have won a greater and greater measure of control over both. More and more, they and their machines have the power to determine the precise moment of death.

―――――◆ **QUESTIONS FOR DISCUSSION AND WRITING** ◆―――――

1. Weiss cites both a traditional definition of *death* (paragraph 5) and a more recent definition (paragraph 7). Which makes the most sense to you? Why?
2. In the section titled "Pulling the Plug on the Terminally Ill," Weiss compares what is often called "passive euthanasia," in which treatment of a patient in a vegetative state is stopped, to "active euthanasia," in which something is done to end the patient's life. Do you see a real difference between these two types of euthanasia? Explain your answer.

3. How would you answer these questions, both from paragraph 38? "If it is ethical to relieve suffering by omission . . . , why isn't it equally ethical to relieve suffering through a positive action?" "If it is ever wrong to permit a terminally ill person to die, isn't it always wrong?"

❋ Rational Non-Interventional Paternalism
WHY DOCTORS OUGHT TO MAKE JUDGMENTS OF WHAT IS BEST FOR THEIR PATIENTS

Julian Savulescu

It is almost universally accepted that doctors ought to make judgments of what is medically best for their patients. However, the view that doctors ought to make judgments of what is, all things considered, best for their patients has fallen into serious disrepute. It is now widely believed that it is up to patients, not their doctors, to judge what they ought to do, all things considered. I will argue that doctors ought to make value judgments about what is best for their patients, not just in a medical sense, but in an overall sense.

In the bad old days of paternalism, doctors did make judgments about what patients ought to do, all things considered. They also compelled patients to adopt what they judged to be the best course of action. Over the last twenty years, this approach has received much criticism. Liberal societies are founded upon a belief that we each have a fundamental interest in forming and acting on our own conception of what is good for us, what direction our lives should take, what is, all things considered, best for us. Forming a conception of what is best for oneself and acting on that conception is being an autonomous agent. By taking away from patients the ability to make and act on conceptions of what they judged was best, paternalists frustrated the autonomy of their patients.

There is a second problem with the old approach. Paternalists were making value judgments (often under the guise of what was "medically or clinically indicated" (1)) which would have been more properly made by the patients who were going to be affected by the treatment. Consider one example. Joe is about to have an operation to remove a tumour from his diaphragm. An anaesthetist visits him pre-operatively to discuss his anaesthetic. She then discusses post-operative analgesia. This, she explains, is very important because the major complication after his operation will be the development of lung collapse and pneumonia. If he does not receive adequate analgesia, and is unable to breathe deeply and cough comfortably, this will be much more likely. She informs him that there are two forms of analgesia available after his operation: thoracic epidural analgesia and intravenous narcotic infusion. The analgesic effectiveness of the thoracic epidural is greater. Joe will more easily be able to cough and breathe deeply, so better preventing the development of pneumonia. She explains that the risk of nerve damage from any epidural is around 1/15,000. There is an additional risk with thoracic epidurals in particular: a very small risk of spinal-cord damage from the procedure (damage from the needle) or complications that arise after it (epidural haematoma or abscess). In some of these cases, spinal-cord damage could result in paraplegia. There have only been isolated case reports of these complications so it is not possible to put a figure on how great the risk is but it is certainly very small. Overall, the risk of nerve damage is very small and the risk of developing pneumonia much greater. The anaesthetist explains the significance of developing pneumonia. In some cases, it results in respiratory failure requiring artificial ventilation. Such infections are sometimes very difficult to treat and patients stand a reasonable chance of dying if they develop respiratory failure. The overall risk of serious morbidity and mortality is greater if one has the narcotic infusion than if one has the epidural. She recommends having a thoracic epidural. (If she had been a paternalist, she would have simply inserted a thoracic epidural at operation.)

Joe, having understood all this information, chooses to have the narcotic infusion. He is an active sportsman and the risk of spinal-cord injury is very significant for him. He also claims that he is willing to put up with more pain, and still attempt to cough and breathe deeply, if in this way he will avoid the potential for harm to his spinal cord.

TWO REASONS

In this case, which treatment Joe ought to have is not simply determined by facts related to Joe's health (the medical facts). There are two reasons why Joe's doctor ought not make a decision about what is, all things considered, best for Joe. Each has to do with a different sense of 'value'. Firstly, Joe's decision is based on his values, that is, what he is valuing. It is an essential element of self-determination that people construct a notion of what is important in their lives (their values) and act on these. Joe values independence and an active physical life. His choice reflects these values.

Secondly, the question of whether Joe ought to have the thoracic epidural is a value judgment, a judgment of what is of value. Judgments of what is of value, all things considered, are different from judgments of fact. It is a fact, let us assume, that a thoracic epidural is associated with better analgesia and a lower risk of developing pneumonia, but a greater risk of spinal-cord damage than a narcotic infusion. However, it is not a fact that this makes thoracic epidural overall better for Joe. That is a value judgment. Value judgments must be based on all the relevant facts. These include the medical facts but also facts about the significance of the medical procedures for Joe's own life, and facts about his values. Since no one but Joe knows his plans, his hopes, his aspirations and his values, the argument goes, Joe is better placed than his doctor to evaluate the significance of the various benefits and complications of each treatment. Joe is in a privileged position to judge what is best, all things considered. Joe's doctor, ill-placed to know these other relevant facts, ought to stick to judgments about the medical facts.

For these reasons, medical practice has moved away from the old paternalistic model of 'Doctor knows best' or 'Doctor's orders' to the currently fashionable 'shared decision-making' model.

"Physicians bring their medical training, knowledge, and expertise—including understanding of the available treatment alternatives—to the diagnosis and management of the patients' conditions. Patients bring a knowledge of their own subjective aims and values, through which the risks and benefits of various options can be evaluated. With this approach, selection of the best treatment for a particular patient requires the contributions of both parties" (2).

On one widely held interpretation of this account, doctors bring medical knowledge, medical facts, to the patient who makes a judgment of what ought to be done on the basis of his or her values. Doctors give up making judgments of what is, all things considered, best for the patient and stick to providing medical facts. This approach has found considerable favour in the literature and in practice. Many informed general practitioners and medical students whom I have taught tell me that doctors ought not make tricky value judgments about their patients' lives.

This model of doctor as fact-provider has some serious shortcomings.   10

Firstly, it is not clear that doctors *can* avoid making value judgments about what patients ought to do, should do, or what it is best for them to do. Sometimes these value judgments are difficult to spot. Consider the oncologist whose patient has lung cancer. "Chemotherapy is medically indicated," he says. This appears to be a purely descriptive, factual statement. But it is really also a prescription to have chemotherapy. If we were to ask this oncologist why chemotherapy was medically indicated, he might offer this argument: 1. chemotherapy will prolong your life; 2. longer life is better than shorter life; 3. so you ought to have chemotherapy. Premise 2 is clearly a value judgment.

It is difficult to see how doctors, as persons, could avoid making judgments like 2. The content of these value judgments varies from person to person, but it is difficult to imagine a person with no values. Most people have some norms which they apply to their behaviour. It is also difficult to imagine that these values do not come into play when a doctor is asked to perform a procedure on a patient.

'FRAMING EFFECT'

Perhaps doctors cannot avoid making value judgments, but they should keep these to themselves. According to the fact-provider model, doctors should just provide facts such as, "Chemotherapy will prolong your life."

However, it is not clear that facts can be communicated free of value. Psychologists have described how the way information is presented can determine the significance of that information for people. This is called the 'framing effect'. When choice is framed in terms of gain, we are risk-averse. When choice is framed in terms of loss, we are risk-taking (3). For example, lung cancer can be treated by surgery or radiotherapy. Surgery is associated with greater immediate mortality (10 per cent v 0 per cent mortality), but better long term prospects (66 per cent v 78 per cent five-year mortality). The attractiveness of surgery to patients is substantially greater when the choice between surgery and radiotherapy is framed in terms of the probability of living rather than the probability of dying. This effect still occurs whether the evaluator is a physician or someone with statistical knowledge (4).

The manner in which physicians present information is influenced by their values. Surgeons present the probabilities of the outcome of surgery in terms of survival, not death. It is not clear that framing effects can easily be overcome. Even if we present probabilities in terms of both survival and mortality, people are 'loss averse'. They focus myopically on the loss associated with events (5). Subtle nonverbal cues also influence the impact of information. Indeed, information seems ineluctably to bring with it a message. It is not difficult to recognise what someone values, even if they do not tell us. Far better, I think, to bring the practice out into the open, and argue explicitly for what we believe in.

But let's assume that doctors can give up either making value judgments or communicating them. Should they?

Medicine as a practice is founded on commitment to certain values: pain is bad, longer life is usually better than shorter life, and so on. A part of learning to practise medicine is learning to take on these values. These implicit evaluative assumptions rarely surface because they are a matter of consensus. 'Ethical dilemmas' arise when patient values diverge from medical values (6).

Should medicine give up a commitment to certain values? To be sure, we might believe that some of medicine's values are mistaken. Some ought to be changed or refined. But medicine should have a commitment to *some* values. Otherwise what would direct research effort, provide a standard of care or a framework for the organisation of practice? Mass consumer choice, a thin reed which bends to the prevailing winds, is sometimes irrational and even chaotic, at other times immovably apathetic, and seems ill-suited to provide such direction alone. This may be slightly hyperbolic, but it does seem true that medicine needs a set of values, no doubt shaped by informed public attitude, which guides practice. Those values must be more substantial than a commitment to do what every individual patient desires.

MORAL STAKES

The second serious shortcoming of the doctor as fact-provider model is that medicine differs from many other professional practices in that the doctor is often called upon to do very serious things to his patient. In deciding to ablate a patient's bone marrow prior to bone-marrow transplantation, a doctor is going to make his patient very sick. There is unavoidable serious harm associated with medical practice that is far greater than in engineering or tax consultancy. The moral stakes are much higher. Since medical practice involves serious harm to others, as well as benefit, doctors ought to form a judgment of what ought to be done, all things considered. In the extreme case of assisted suicide, a patient asks her doctor to help her die. Should a person do this without making a decision whether it is for the best? Surely not. It is at least generally true that good moral agents reflect upon and form judgments concerning what they ought to do. The same applies to less spectacular, every-day instances of medical practice. Prescribing an antibiotic may cause renal failure. A good doctor must form a judgment about whether prescribing that antibiotic is really justified, even if the patient has an informed desire to have it.

Thirdly, and most importantly, patients can fail to make correct judgments of what is best, just as doctors can. Patients can fail to make choices which best satisfy their own values (7). They can make choices which frustrate rather than express their own autonomy (8). The mere fact that a competent patient makes an informed choice does not imply necessarily that that choice reflects what he values.

Patients can also make incorrect value judgments. They can fail to give sufficient weight to relevant facts, just as the old paternalists did when they concentrated on the medical facts. Consider an example.

Joan is 35 years old and has a one cm cancer of the breast without clinical evidence of lymph node metastasis. Her mother and sisters had cancer of the breast. Her surgeon argues, based on her history and the cytology of the tumour, that she has a very high chance of developing a second carcinoma. He recommends a bilateral mastectomy. This, he argues, will give her the best chance of survival. Joan replies that this will be very disfiguring. She would prefer to have a lumpectomy followed by yearly mammography. This, she argues, will give her a better quality of life.

Joan's surgeon inquires further. It turns out that by better quality of life, she means that she will retain her present physical appearance. Her husband would be shocked if she had a bilateral mastectomy, even if she were to have breast implants. "He is very attached to my breasts," she says. Her marriage is difficult at present, and she does not believe that it would survive the shock of such operation.

These are of course relevant facts to which the surgeon was not originally privy. Previously, he believed she ought to have a mastectomy. Are these new facts of sufficient importance to cause him to change his judgment? In some cases, they might be. If survival with lumpectomy and mammography was roughly the same as that after mastectomy, then he might change his mind. If Joan's life was really going to be miserable after a mastectomy, and much happier after a lumpectomy, then this would be a good reason not to have the mastectomy.

However, in some cases, the surgeon might retain his original judg- 25 ment. He might believe that, if the risk of dying from not having the mastectomy was significant, that it was not worth risking death to conform to her husband's and society's expectations of her physical appearance. Moreover, he might believe that if her relationship would be destroyed by her having a mastectomy, it was not likely to survive or was not worth dying for. He might believe, not necessarily without basis, that Joan will be unhappy in her marriage whether she has a lumpectomy or a mastectomy. He might believe that Joan is mistaken in attaching so much weight to her husband's attachment to her breasts. He might continue to believe that she ought to have the mastectomy, despite the revelation of new facts. Indeed, even in the presence of *all* relevant facts, if these could be discovered, he might believe that Joan ought to have a mastectomy. Despite having access to the same facts as Joan, such a doctor might continue to differ with her about what is best and he may continue to try to convince her that she is wrong.

Some value judgments are wrong. To claim that one's life is not worth living because one's bunion is painful is mistaken, no matter how well-informed the judgment. To be sure, doctors make wrong judgments of what is best. But so do patients at times.

It is of course easier to turn the decision over to Joan and just provide some medical facts. It is easier to avoid making an all-things-considered value judgment. It is difficult to discuss with a patient why she holds the views she does. It is difficult to provide an argument for why she is wrong which is convincing to her. But such discussion and argument can help patients to make better decisions for themselves. Good advice, which we should expect from our friends and doctors, consists in more than information.

SHARED DECISION-MAKING

There has been a movement away from paternalism. There are, however, two ways of responding to the problems which have thrown paternalism into disrepute. The first is for doctors to give up the practice of making judgments about what is, all things considered, best for their patients. They should stick to providing medical facts to competent patients who then make choices as to what is best based on their values. This is the model of 'shared decision-making'.

The second approach agrees that in the past doctors concentrated too much on medical facts. Other facts are also important in determining what is best. These include facts about the patient, his values, his circumstances and so on. But this approach denies that the patient has sovereign access to the relevant facts, though in many cases she knows them better than anyone else. Doctors can, and ought to, try to discover these other facts and form for themselves an all-things-considered judgment of what is best. Doctors need not give up making value judgments; they can try to make better value judgments. If a doctor's value judgment differs from that of her patient, she ought to engage her patient, find reasons for their differences, and revise her own views. Or, if her view still appears justified, she ought to continue to attempt to convince her patient that she is wrong.

Does attempting to convince a patient that he is wrong in choosing   30
some course threaten his autonomy? It may. One can argue coercively or non-coercively. There are many ways in which a doctor might get a patient to come around to agreeing with him that do not involve rational convergence between the two parties. I am not discussing these ways of arguing. What I am discussing is attempting to convince a patient by rational argument that he is wrong. Far from frustrating a patient's autonomy, this enables a patient to act and choose more autonomously. There are at least three ways in which this is so.

1: To be autonomous, one must be informed. A doctor, in attempting to convince his patient, will appeal to reasons. Some of these reasons will draw attention to relevant facts. He will be asking his patient to reconsider the significance of these facts for her life. Thinking about these facts in a new light, her choice will become more active, more vivid and so more an expression of her autonomy (8).

2: The second point I cannot argue for in detail here. For a choice to be autonomous, one must be informed. But one must not only be informed of the facts, but also of what is of value. (Or, a relevant fact is what other people have rationally valued or thought to be of value.)

3: As a result of a patient rethinking her choice and giving reasons for that choice in the process of arguing for it, that choice will become a more rational choice and one which she really does value.

So a doctor ought not to be merely a fact-provider but also an argument-provider. In this way, he enables his patient to make a more autonomous choice.

Paternalists went wrong not in forming judgments about what was   35
best for their patients, all things considered. They went wrong in concentrating too much on only medical facts. Moreover, they went wrong in *compelling* patients to live according to their, the doctors', evaluations of what was best. That often does violate patient autonomy. If Joan continues to want a lumpectomy despite her surgeon's attempts to convince her that she is wrong, he ought not to compel her to have a mastectomy (though in some cases, he might believe that her judgment is so wrong that he cannot provide what she asks and withdraws from the case). We ought not to compel competent people to do what is best, even if what they desire is substantially less than the best. However, allowing compe-

tent people to act on their judgment of what is best for their own lives does not imply that those judgments are right. Nor does it imply that doctors should not form for themselves judgments about what is best. Nor does it imply that doctors should not try to convince their patients by rational argument that what they are advocating is the best course. Indeed, a doctor ought to form such judgments for his own sake as a moral agent and the patient's sake as an autonomous agent. We can retain the old-style paternalist's commitment to making judgments of what is, all things considered, best for the patient (and improve it) but reject his commitment to compelling the patient to adopt that course. This practice can be called rational, non-interventional paternalism. It is 'rational' because it involves the use of rational argument. It is 'non-interventional' because it forswears doing what is best.

Medicine is entering a new era. Doctors are now required not only to have medical knowledge, but knowledge of ethics, of what constitutes a value judgment, of the fact/value distinction, of how to make value judgments and how to argue rationally about what ought to be done. This requires new skills. It is relatively easy to be a fact-provider (though how to present facts itself presents a problem). It is easy to turn decision-making over to patients and say: "There are the facts—you decide." It is difficult to find all the relevant facts, to form evaluative judgments, and critically examine them. It is even more difficult to engage a patient in rational argument and convince him that you are right. If doctors are to avoid the shortcomings of being mere fact-providers, if they are to function properly as moral agents, if they are to promote patient autonomy, they must learn these new skills. They must learn these skills for another reason: gone are the days when they could make uninformed judgments of what was best for their patients and act on these. Gone too are the days when they did not have to provide a justification for the position they were advocating. And that justification goes beyond the fiction of a 'purely medical' justification.

References

1. Hope T, Sprigings D, Crisp R. Not clinically indicated: patients' interests or resource allocation? *British medical journal* 1993; 306: 379–381.
2. Brock D W, Wartman S A. When competent patients make irrational choices. *New England journal of medicine* 1990; 322: 1595–1599.
3. Tversky A, Kahneman D. The framing of decisions and the psychology of choice. *Science* 1981; 211: 453–458.
4. McNeil B J, Pauker S G, Sox Jr H C, Tversky A. On the elicitation of preferences for alternative therapies. *New England journal of medicine* 1982; 306: 1259–1262.

5. Kahneman D, Varey C. Notes on the psychology of utility. In: Elster J, Roemer J E, eds. *Interpersonal comparisons of well-being.* Cambridge: Cambridge University Press, 1991: 127–163.

6. Thanks to one referee for expanding this point.

7. See reference (3), and also: Kahneman D, Tversky A. Choices, values, and frames. *American psychologist* 1984; 39: 341–350.

8. Savulescu J. Rational desires and the limitation of life-sustaining treatment. *Bioethics* 1994; 8: 191–222. Savulescu J. *Good reasons to die* [doctoral dissertation]. Monash University, Jun, 1994.

◆ QUESTIONS FOR DISCUSSION AND WRITING ◆

1. In the end—and now that you've read and discussed Helen Scott's situation—who should make advance directive decisions? Put another way, is Savulescu's argument convincing? In what ways?

2. Are the real-life stories in "Rational Non-Interventional Paternalism" as effective and as compelling as some of the real-life stories you read about at the beginning of this chapter? Support your comparison with examples.

3. There is a good deal of discussion in "Rational Non-Interventional Paternalism" about "patient autonomy." What does this term mean in Helen's situation?

4. Is it really "paternalism" when doctors attempt to influence their patients? Doesn't a physician, in the end, know better than anyone else what is the right thing to do?

※ The Sanctity of Life
AN ANALYSIS OF A CONCEPT

K. Danner Clouser

My task is to analyze a concept—the concept of "the sanctity of life."[1] One would like to know more precisely what it means, when it should be used, what it commits us to, whether it can be defended. What makes sense must be sorted out from what does not. My main hope is to stimulate thinking about this issue. To that end I want my analysis to remain more on the suggestive and broad level than on the narrow and definitive.

I will first make some general observations about the concept—its ordinary connotations and its immediate muddles. Then I will try out other possible interpretations of its meaning and logic. The fallout from that effort will then constitute my main claims about the concept. Anticlimactically, I will consider two counterexamples.

It is always helpful to know from the start what an author will be concluding; knowing the end product, one can be far more alert to the author's mistakes as they occur. Hence: I find the sanctity of life concept to be impossibly vague and to be a concept that is inaccurate and misleading, whose positive points can be better handled by other well-established concepts.

CONNOTATIONS OF RELIGIOUS ORIGIN

The first thing that must be said about this concept is that it is clearly religious in origin. It is found more explicitly in Eastern religions (Hinduism in particular). But it also appears throughout our Judeo-Christian traditions. There its theological status may not be clear, but in a variety of ways it surfaces. Basically it bespeaks life to be God's creation, over which we have no authority; life is a gift-in-trust from God, and we are pledged to practice good stewardship of it; it is for our use, but it is only on loan.

Much work could be done on explicating the religious conception of life's sanctity: its origin, its basis, its meaning. But that is *not* the focus of this article. Such an approach would be far too limiting, given my concern with ethics; that is, it would be appropriate only to those who accept the religious viewpoint. But in ethics we must seek that to which all rational men could agree. Our world is too pluralistic to derive its rules from a limited set of metaphysical commitments to which only a smaller subset of persons subscribe.

This is by no means to disparage the religious; it is only to say that these are not the commitments around which we could expect or require all men to rally. Generally, religious requirements are more stringent than what could be expected of all rational men. They go beyond the reasonable obligation, beyond the call of duty; they require you to go the second mile. Generally, religious practices will be in accord with, but more stringent than, whatever we find binding on all men.

Although "sanctity," after all, is a religious concept, refusing to discuss the religious meanings of "sanctity of life" does not cut us off from meaningful discussion of the concept, simply because the concept has been taken over by the world at large. It is used by the religious and the nonreligious, and in both cases with "religious" fervor. It is used and appealed to by almost everybody, and those who use it seem to think that all their fellow men should agree, at least in principle. It is this ordinary secular use that we shall look at more closely, insofar as it relates to human life in particular.

GENERAL CONNOTATIONS AND RELATED MUDDLES

Treasuring of life. In the very general sense, it would seem that the concept means the treasuring of all human life, no matter what. It is being used to argue that wherever there is human life, nothing can count against it; life can never be taken. It thus is posed as a conclusive reason instead of just a reason to be weighed with other reasons and arguments;

that is, it is feigned to be conclusive rather than being simply one point among many to be considered. Furthermore, the connotations are that this concept applies to *all* human life, including fetal life and comatose life. "Sanctity of life" is often appealed to as though it settles the abortion question as well as the question of the artificial support of unconscious life. In effect, this proposition says that where there is life, it would be inconsistent with "the sanctity of life" for us to interfere.

Surely, on closer examination we would find that this is simply not a defensible use of the sanctity of life concept. "Sanctity of life" should not be interpreted as defining what is human life and what is not, although it frequently is. One could say, with consistency, that he accepted both "sanctity of life" and abortion, because he did not happen to believe fetal life was human life. In short, "sanctity of life" leaves the definition of human life undetermined. It just does not say.

So it seems a mistake to think that "the sanctity of life" is a conclusive   10
judgment, rule, or principle that, if accepted, solves the problem, leaving nothing more at issue. Rather, it is just one consideration among many that enter the argument. For example, there are times when we have believed it was justified to commit suicide, to put to death, to withhold lifesaving therapy, or to kill. In short, "sanctity of life" is not the decisive consideration; it is not a conclusive argument. At best, it is one consideration among many, and it is at times outweighed by these other considerations.

Quality of life. It is unclear whether "sanctity of life" means that life must be protected at all costs or whether it means that the *quality* of life must be protected at all costs (even if it requires the sacrifice of other life). The argument based on the quality of life is used for permitting abortion, for allowing badly deformed infants to die, for determining government medical priorities as to where money will go (say, to the elderly rather than to the young). This is frequently thought to be in opposition to the "sanctity of life" argument. Yet its proponents could claim the "sanctity of life" as their basis, contending that human life is so very special that it should not be degraded, that there are some forms and conditions of life not worth living. Thus the ambiguity of the "sanctity of life" argument allows it to be used against itself.

We have glanced superficially at some ordinary connotations of the concept. We have seen, surrounding it, ambiguities, contradictions, and a general lack of clear direction; at least we have seen enough to realize that it is not as clear, decisive, and helpful as many seem to believe. Now we must try even harder to find its meaning.

ITS MEANING: SOME POSSIBILITIES

A property of life? At least on the surface, in speaking of the "sanctity of life" it would seem we are attributing some property to human life. It would seem to be an attribute that comes into being and exists with each individual life, something that attaches to each life. (To define "individual life" would require a separate entourage of metaphysical distinctions, claims, and maneuvers.)

But our ordinary criteria for a property's existence are not fulfilled in this case. Our senses do not detect any such attribute, nor can we be led by an expert to "sense" some more mysterious and illusive property that might inhere in or hover about life. There is the possibility of a "derived" property, that is, a property that, although unperceived, "must" exist within the phenomenon of life because it happens to follow from some theory about life. It could be derived, for example, from the religious sense of sanctity. That is, it might follow from certain other propositions that are held—such as "God created life," "man is God's creation," "man is God's steward," and so on. But this is not our present point of focus. There is no universally accepted theory—if any at all—that entails a property called "sanctity."

There is another reason for believing sanctity is not some sort of property that adheres to life. If it were a "good," a treasured something or other, there surely would be a feeling of obligation to create as much human life as possible. Yet none of us feels the obligation to reproduce without ceasing! This realization gives us an important clue: "sanctity of life" does not seem to be telling us to *do* something (create as much life as possible); it seems more to be telling us what *not* to do (do not take life). This point will be elaborated later.

A feeling? Of course, all this is not to say that we do not have special *feelings* about life—all the way from treasuring it to feeling a deep sense of mystery about it. We may experience awe at being alive. This is important to the ordinary concept of sanctity, as I shall show later; but it could hardly be the meaning of sanctity. That is, it simply would not do the work generally presumed to be done by appealing to the sanctity of life principle.

For one, "sanctity" seems more objective than simply feelings we have about life, however deep. It suggests something to be acknowledged, rather than a description of things felt. For another, neither command nor obligation follows from the fact that we feel a certain way about life. For example, the fact that we may sense the mysteriousness of existence does not imply anything about how we should treat life—our own or others. If we sometimes find life exhilarating it does not follow that we must "protect life at all costs" or "never allow a life to cease." On the other hand, it may very well be why we value life and establish certain rules for its protection.

A value? A right? One way of locating more precisely the ordinary meaning of "sanctity" would be to substitute some possible synonyms, and "listen" to the result. "The value of life" or "the importance of life" obviously do not have the same ring as "sanctity of life." For example, "because life is important, abortion cannot be legalized" or "we cannot allow respirators to be turned off because of the value of life." These phrases

15

seem much weaker; they seem to be saying a lot less than is connotated by "the sanctity of life." The ring of "sanctity" has the strength of a quality-in-reality that attaches to a life principle; it sounds much more inviolable. There may be many reasons why the substitutions seem to have less force. Among them is that both "value" and "importance" sound too subjective; they sound more like something we impute to life than something it has in itself. They do not have the overtones of being facts that command acknowledgment. "Sanctity of life" seems to have this objective connotation, although, as was suggested earlier, this "inherent property" idea is hardly defensible.

The phrase "right to life" comes closer precisely because it suggests something somewhat more objective, something out there and given, and hence something to be acted in accord with. For example: "The fetus has a right to life"; "The comatose patient has a right to life." "Right to life" seems much closer to the thrust and intent of "sanctity of life." This is, at least partially, because both expressions imply an obligation binding on us, an obligation not to violate that particular life. This point will be elaborated later.

An overall life orientation? Perhaps we have been pressing too hard for 20 a precise meaning. It may well be that the sanctity of life concept is simply not intended to be exact, to settle issues, to give direction. Rather, it might simply bespeak a very general orientation toward life, a kind of world view. As such we should not expect rigorous differentiations, decisive exclusions, and definitive direction. We should rather expect a pervading awareness, a gentle suasion, nudging our views and actions in one way or another. Widely diverse views and actions would be compatible with this world view, since the meaning (and hence criteria, implications, and applicability) would be so vague. Although this interpretation would concern the concept's use rather than its meaning, I have some sympathy with it. It is consistent with a point I think important, that "sanctity of life" is more something we pledge ourselves to, a commitment, than it is an objective property that demands acknowledgment.

Nevertheless, one particular aspect of this "world view" interpretation is very disconcerting. That is its indeterminateness; as it stands it seems impossibly vague. It involves believing life has value, that it should be treated as important, that it should be preserved—all other things being equal. But, given this interpretation, it is not at all clear who would disagree. Is it even a helpful distinction? Does it separate anyone from anyone else? Wouldn't everyone—save wanton, whimsical killers—subscribe to this world view? As such, it hardly bears talking about, let alone appealing to for settling arguments.

Of course not everyone believes life is equally important; there would be widely discrepant ideas of what constitutes "adequate justification" for taking life. But that would be so even among those who were pledged to the sanctity of life world view. Surely nearly everyone agrees that life should be protected and not taken without a reason. And the sanctity of life world view is no more precise about life than that. What counts as a reason is not specified by the concept itself; so this world view is no more exacting about life than is the world at large.

What, precisely, does this sanctity of life world view come to? What would it mean to have this as one's general life orientation? If asked, a believer might respond with a variety of statements:

1. Life is precious.
2. I have respect for life.
3. Life should be caringly nurtured.
4. Life should not be taken without adequate justification.
5. Every living thing has a presumptive right to live.

All these in effect boil down to statements 4 and 5, and for our purposes statements 4 and 5 are equivalent. Feelings and attitudes about life ("precious," "respect") are really not to the point, except insofar as they affect one's behavior. What difference does "respect for life" make in one's actions? The most likely manifestation would be urging and practicing the principle that life not be taken except for very good reasons, and that is equivalent to 4, above. "Respect" would have to imply at least that, if it is to make any sense at all. Also, statement 3—caringly nurturing life—could be reduced to 4, or simply be deleted as a viable interpretation of "sanctity of life." That is, the sanctity of life principle is not ordinarily called on to justify or insist on humane treatment of individual lives (unless lack of such treatment is a threat to life itself). Usually it is cited only in decisions between life and death, not in a call for loving treatment.

If I have not gone astray in these reduction maneuvers, we are left with something like: urging and practicing that life not be taken without adequate reason. This is the heart of a world view committed to "sanctity of life." It means that life has a presumptive right to exist, and that the burden of proofs sits on him who would take life, not on him who would preserve it. "Do not take life without adequate justification." This is at least more precise, but again almost everyone would agree because it leaves the crucial issue undetermined: namely, when is taking life justified? *That* is where all the disagreements are, and that is what is left undetermined by "sanctity of life."

SOME FALLOUT FROM OUR INQUIRY

From our "world view" considerations, there are four significant results:

1. The concept now seems to be saying nothing more than "don't kill" or "don't deprive of life." And, as in all moral rules, it is a general prohibition to which there can be exceptions, but the exceptions must be justified.

2. Notice that it is now stated in the negative: "do not take life." It is now a prohibition. It is not making an ambiguous command like "treat life as sanctified" or "regard life as sanctified" or even the straight claims, "life is sanctified" or "life is precious." You do not have to figure out what "sanctity" is, or "precious" or "important" or "valuable"; the command is much more straightforward. *Whatever* human life is, in any case, do not take it.

3. It follows that an important shift in the grounding of this admonition has also taken place. It does not depend on a quality or property called "sanctity"; it does not depend on the presence of this attribute which may or may not be there; it does not depend on people acknowledging the existence of this "property." It now depends more securely on our own self-interest and our concern for friends and family. That is, it is to the advantage of each of us that we honor this directive. We would be foolish not to urge everyone to do so; by advocating it, we enhance the safety of ourselves, our friends, and our family.[2] This is not to say that most of us would not act on it anyway, but, if we are looking for universal acceptance, this kind of self-interest is as strong a basis for it as we can hope to find.

4. The fourth advantage of this formulation is that it focuses the attention where the action really is, namely, on the *exceptions*. As with all moral rules, there is a general prohibition to which there can always be exceptions, provided the exceptions are justified. This puts the burden of proof on those who would disobey the moral rule. Then the interesting arena of debate becomes: What constitutes justifiable exceptions? This is an improvement over subscribing to "sanctity of life" principle, which seems to hide the fact of exceptions; "sanctity of life," when taken as the conclusive consideration rather than as one among many, obfuscates the vital role of exceptions and their justification. Consequently, the really crucial questions are much less apt to surface: What life is to be protected? What is human life? Is a fetus human life? Is allowing to die different from taking a life? Is extreme suffering a reason for allowing to die?

Just to sharpen this point a bit, compare being told "treat life as sanctified" and being told "do not take a life." Being told the first, it would never be clear where and if you transgressed it. *Whatever* you did—as long as you were remembering that life was precious—you might feel you were treating life as sacred. But under the admonition, "do not take life," anytime you were about to help die, let die, or turn off the respirator, you would immediately be forced to the real issue—what justifies it in this case? You are immediately pushed to give reasons, and you are thus in the area where the real debate is: When and why is it justifiable to take a life?

Proclaiming "sanctity of life" can keep one from ever directly facing up to these hard questions. In short, when you are transgressing the rule "do not kill," it is immediately apparent in a way that is not apparent when you are told "treat life as sanctified." In the former case the focus immediately shifts to where the issues really are. In the "sanctity" case, we bog down in the fat of ambiguity, imprecision, and hidden reasoning.

SUMMARY

Before raising two niggling puzzles, I will summarize where we have been.

We began by noticing some of the misleading aspects of the "sanctity of life" concept, such as the assumption that it solved the question of what was and was not human life in those notorious borderline cases and the assumption that it was a conclusive consideration against which nothing could count.

We found muddles concerning exceptions. Even though we believe ourselves to accept the sanctity of life principle, we do tolerate many exceptions, even though we may see no reason for them.

We questioned the sense of regarding "sanctity" as a property embedded in life itself or as a feeling about life. And, even if these views could somehow be defended, we still saw no way to derive what we *ought* to do from what is the case.

Our final foray into its territory considered the possibility that "sanctity of life" was a very general orientation toward life. This nonspecificity seemed to wash it out completely. But we learned some things in the process: that the command "don't kill" provides more precise guidance; that the "thou shalt not . . ." form of admonition is more helpful because the burden of justification is thereby placed on the transgressor (which, in turn, considerably sharpens the ingredient issues); and that a foundation is provided for advocating and defending the rule, namely, self-interest and concern for friends and family.

For most readers this is an appropriate stopping place. What follows is an attempt to deal with some of the related fine points.

LINGERING DOUBTS

I do think that most of what is valuable, understandable, and defensible in the sanctity of life concept can be more clearly and helpfully handled by the moral rule, "do not take life." But after my reduction maneuvers are over there may be an irreducible remainder. I can find two instances not provided for here that may be accounted for by "sanctity of life." These issues are complicated; I can but sketch them here, but this will at least serve to initiate reflection on them.

One worry concerns future generations and our obligations to them. ³⁵ Intuitively, we may feel that we owe something, namely, continuation of the human race. Yet acting in accord with our moral rule, "Do not kill," would not necessarily guarantee future generations. And, for that matter, none of our moral rules (which essentially proscribe us from depriving others of life, pleasure, and freedom) or our moral ideals (which basically enjoin us to prevent suffering) would ensure the future of the human race. In fact, the moral ideal of preventing suffering might actually advise us *not* to perpetuate the race. Yet don't we feel a deep sense of obligation for continuing human life? Of course this may be caused by other than moral factors, but on the surface it seems to be a moral commitment. How do we account for this? Is this perhaps what sanctity of life really means? Is this the principle behind our felt commitment to create future generations? Life is precious; so keep it going.

Look at the "felt commitment" more closely. It seems more a commitment to keep the race going than simply to create life. That is, there is no obligation to create as much life as we can but only to see that human life continues—not this life, nor that life in particular, nor all the life possible—but life ordered and selected so as not to have undue suffering and to contribute to the progress of life. In short, we see even here that "sanctity of life" (if that's what we choose to call it in this instance) is not an unqualified commitment to the creating and survival of all life in any way, shape, or form. It is not all life that is precious, but only the continuation of *some* life rather than none.

We feel a commitment to preserve the life of the species, yet there seems to be no standard moral principle that underlies this felt commitment; we cannot reduce it to a more ultimate principle. So here is a plausible meaning for "sanctity of life," although it would be a struggle to restrict it to *just* that meaning; it would soon overflow this rigid boundary and assume some of its old misleading and indefensible senses.

Even in this case, however, the sanctity of life concept does not give wholesale endorsement to life but is quite compatible with modifying and restricting judgments about how much life, what quality of life, what qualifies as human life, and so forth. So this felt commitment is really a commitment to seeing that human life continues, but it leaves undecided the specific conditions under which it may continue.

It might be more helpful to speak of this as a commitment to *potentiality* rather than "sanctity" of life. Our obligation would be to realizing potential. This at least would tie it in with the deep-seated obligation we feel to actualize potential or at least preserve it, thus allowing it to develop. But, like "sanctity of life," this potentiality principle obviously does not mean any and all potentiality should be realized. There must be other guidelines for what should be realized and what should not. Once again our attention is directed to the real concerns: which potentials should be allowed to develop, which not, and why. (Thus the stage is set for the whole cast of ethical problems involved in genetic engineering.)

The second puzzle has to do with the rational basis of ethics. Very roughly, it is this: the rational basis for urging us to follow the moral rules is that it is for our own good (and that of family and friends) if others follow these rules. It would be irrational of us not to advocate these rules; we run a risk of being hurt if we do not. But there *are* forms of life that could never represent any threat to us; they could not retaliate directly nor would we ever find ourselves in their situation. Hence why should we practice or urge morality with respect to them? There are not many such; a fetus would be one and perhaps a severely retarded child. Why should we urge concern toward these forms of life? We cannot be harmed by them, nor can we ever become them and hence eventually be harmed by attitudes and actions we have allowed and engendered. So why should we urge concern? The difficulty in answering this question is reflected in the moral ambiguity encompassing these cases. Why do some people respect life in these forms? The moral ideal of preventing suffering may account for some concern, but these lives *could* be snuffed out without anyone suffering pain or apprehension. So why protect them? Yet many of us feel a commitment to give these forms of life some protection. We might agree that there could be considerations that would *outweigh* their right to life, but there at least seems to be felt obligation to grant them a prima facie right to life. This question is too complicated to pursue here. But, for the purpose of this discussion, have we raised a point that cannot be accounted for by the rational foundation of ethics? If so, then this may be the one place where the concept is finally applicable, because many feel it strongly in this case. Maybe it is here that there is a difference between those who espouse "sanctity of life" and those who do not. In the case of the fetus and the severely retarded child there seems to be, in some people, a deeply felt obligation to preserve the life. Yet it does not seem to be required on a rational ethical basis. So perhaps "sanctity" does stand by itself as a principle or commitment clear and distinct from others. Nevertheless, it is far more limited than is usually believed, with far less applicability than to the broad range of actions for which it is usually cited as the basic principle. Although I will not attempt it here, there might be a way to reduce even this small reminder. Such a move would at least have the advantage of conceptual economy, and it would place this felt obligation on firmer, more defensible ground than the sanctity of life concept, which is unclear, indefensible, and applicable only to this particular case. The reduction would show that for important, pragmatic reasons this felt obligation was an extension of the standard moral rule, "do not deprive of life," even though the beings in question are neither rational nor capable of retaliation, and we will never find ourselves in their place. It has to do with the importance of maintaining general respect for *all* human life by honoring it even in the borderline cases. That is, it might be argued that if we are to honor life in the clear-cut cases, we cannot allow disrespect to creep in on the borders. This would rid us of the need for the "sanctity" concept even in this limited, last-ditch stand. But I suggest it only as a possibility, the development of which I will spare you.

CONCLUSION

Many discussions within medical ethics appeal to and pivot on the sanctity of life concept. Yet the really critical issues are hidden by the hulking darkness of that concept. It has been my purpose to bring these submerged structural elements to the surface where they can be explicitly focused on and examined. To this end I discussed the meaning and use of this concept; my arguments were meant to be more suggestive than conclusive. My conclusion is this: the sanctity of life concept as it is generally used—not in its original religious sense—is only a slogan. It not only gives no clear guidance, but it can be positively misleading. There is no place for it in the formal structures of ethics, and what good emphases we can find within the concept are already taken care of by clearer, more defensible rules within ethics. Its best use as a slogan would be as a rhetorical reminder, urging us to weigh life heavily when it is balanced against other goods. And of course we are all for that on solid rational grounds.

There may be another benefit accruing from these reductionist efforts. By showing the secularized sanctity of life concept to be ineffectual, the way has been cleared for the religious meaning of that concept to be reinstated. Freed from the dilution of secular adaptation, this concept can more forcefully assume its pivotal role in the religious stance on these life and death issues.

Notes

1. Although it might be worthwhile, I am not in this paper distinguishing between "the sanctity of life," "the concept of the sanctity of life," and "the sanctity of life principle." These will be used interchangeably, except where context makes it clearly not so.
2. For an excellent account linking "rationality" and "publicly advocating" in the justification of moral rules, see Bernard Gert, *The Moral Rules: A New Rational Foundation for Morality,* Harper and Row, Publishers, Inc., New York, 1970.

───────── ◆ **QUESTIONS FOR DISCUSSION AND WRITING** ◆ ─────────

1. How do you define the term *sanctity of life*?
2. How do you relate your definition of *sanctity of life* to your definitions of the terms *euthanasia* and *abortion*?
3. Clouser works hard at defining terms; do you find this approach to writing an essay useful? Why or why not?

4. In the next-to-last paragraph, Clouser suggests that "the sanctity of life concept . . . is only a slogan. It not only gives no clear guidance, but it can be positively misleading." Do you agree or disagree? Why?

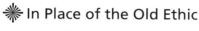

In Place of the Old Ethic

Peter Singer

THE STRUCTURE OF ETHICAL REVOLUTIONS

Four hundred years ago our views about our place in the universe underwent a crisis. The ancients used a model of the solar system devised by Ptolemy, according to which the earth was the centre of the universe and all the heavenly bodies revolved around it. Even the ancients knew, however, that this model did not work very well. It did not predict the positions of the planets with sufficient accuracy. So it was assumed that, as the planets moved in great circles around the earth, they also moved in smaller circles around their own orbits. This helped to patch up the model, but it didn't fix all the problems, and further adjustments were required. These adjustments were again an improvement, but still did not quite get it right. It would have been possible to add yet another modification to the basic geocentric model—but then Copernicus proposed a radically new approach. He suggested that the planets, including the earth, revolve around the sun. This remarkable new view met stiff resistance, because it required us to give up our cherished idea that we are the centre of the universe. It also clashed with the Judeo-Christian view of human beings as the pinnacle of creation. If we are the reason why everything else was made, why do we have such an undistinguished address?

The resistance to the Copernican theory was not, however, simply due to human pride, hidebound conservatism, or religious prejudice. The truth is that, in predicting the movements of the planets, Copernicus was not really any more accurate than the latest patched-up version of Ptolemy's old system. For Copernicus too had made a mistake. He clung to the idea that the heavenly bodies move in perfect circles, when really, as Kepler was later to show, the orbits of the planets are slightly elliptical. So there were some who continued to believe in the ancient model of the universe, and looked for better ways of making it fit the facts. The Copernican theory nevertheless triumphed, not because it was more accurate than the old one, but because it was a fresh approach, full of promise.[1]

Like cosmology before Copernicus, the traditional doctrine of the sanctity of human life is today in deep trouble. Its defenders have responded, naturally enough, by trying to patch up the holes that keep appearing in it. They have redefined death so that they can remove beating hearts from warm, breathing bodies, and give them to others with better prospects, while telling themselves that they are only taking organs from a corpse. They have drawn a distinction between 'ordinary' and 'extraordinary' means of treatment, which allows them to persuade themselves that their decision to withdraw a respirator from a person in an irreversible coma has nothing to do with the patient's poor quality of life. They give terminally ill patients huge doses of morphine that they know will shorten their lives, but say that this is not euthanasia, because their declared intention is to relieve pain. They select severely disabled infants for 'non-treatment' and make sure that they die, without thinking of themselves as killing them. By denying that an individual human being comes into existence before birth, the more flexible adherents of the sanctity of life doctrine are able to put the life, health, and well-being of a woman ahead of that of a fetus. Finally, by putting a taboo on comparisons between intellectually disabled human beings and nonhuman animals, they have preserved the species boundary as the boundary of the sanctity of life ethic, despite overwhelming evidence that the differences between us and other species are differences of degree rather than of kind.

The patching could go on, but it is hard to see a long and beneficial future for an ethic as paradoxical, incoherent and dependent on pretence as our conventional ethic of life and death has become. New medical techniques, decisions in landmark legal cases and shifts of public opinion are constantly threatening to bring the whole edifice crashing down. All I have done is to draw together and put on display the fatal weaknesses that have become apparent over the last two or three decades. For anyone who thinks clearly about the whole range of questions I have raised, modern medical practice has become incompatible with belief in the equal value of all human life.

It is time for another Copernican revolution. It will be, once again, a revolution against a set of ideas we have inherited from the period in which the intellectual world was dominated by a religious outlook. Because it will change our tendency to see human beings as the centre of the *ethical* universe, it will meet with fierce resistance from those who do not want to accept such a blow to our human pride. At first, it will have its own problems, and will need to tread carefully over new ground. For many the ideas will be too shocking to take seriously. Yet eventually the change will come. The traditional view that all human life is sacrosanct is simply not able to cope with the array of issues that we face. The new view will offer a fresh and more promising approach.

REWRITING THE COMMANDMENTS

What will the new ethical outlook be like? I shall take five commandments of the old ethic that we have seen to be false, and show how they need to be rewritten for a new ethical approach to life and death. But I do not want the five new commandments to be taken as something carved in stone. I do not really approve of ethics carved in stone anyway. There may be better ways of remedying the weaknesses of the traditional ethic. The title of this book suggests an ongoing activity: we can rethink something more than once. The point is to start, and to do so with a clear understanding of how fundamental our rethinking must be.

First Old Commandment:
Treat All Human Life as of Equal Worth

Hardly anyone really believes that all human life is of equal worth. The rhetoric that flows so easily from the pens and mouths of popes, theologians, ethicists and some doctors is belied every time these same people accept that we need not go all out to save a severely malformed baby; that we may allow an elderly man with advanced Alzheimer's disease to die from pneumonia, untreated by antibiotics; or that we can withdraw food and water from a patient in a persistent vegetative state. When the law sticks to the letter of this commandment, it leads to what everyone agrees now is an absurdity, like Joey Fiori's survival for almost two decades in a persistent vegetative state, or the continuation of respirator support for the anencephalic Baby K. The new approach is able to deal with these situations in the obvious way, without struggling to reconcile them with any lofty claims that all human life is of equal worth, irrespective of its potential for gaining or regaining consciousness.

First New Commandment:
Recognise That the Worth of Human Life Varies

This new commandment allows us frankly to acknowledge—as the British judges did when presented with the facts about Tony Bland's existence—that life without consciousness is of no worth at all. We can reach the same view—again, as British judges did in considering the condition of Baby C—about a life that has no possibility of mental, social or physical interaction with other human beings. Where life is not one of total or near total deprivation, the new ethic will judge the worth of continued life by the kind of balancing exercise recommended by Lord Justice Donaldson in the case of Baby J, taking into account both predictable suffering, and possible compensations.

Consistent with the first new commandment, we should treat human beings in accordance with their ethically relevant characteristics. Some of these are inherent in the nature of the being. They include consciousness, the capacity for physical, social and mental interaction with other beings, having conscious preferences for continued life, and having enjoyable experiences. Other relevant aspects depend on the relationship of the being to others, having relatives for example who will grieve over your death, or being so situated in a group that if you are killed, others will fear for their own lives. All of these things make a difference to the regard and respect we should have for a being.

The best argument for the new commandment is the sheer absurdity 10 of the old one. If we were to take seriously the idea that all human life, irrespective of its capacity for consciousness, is equally worthy of our care and support, we would have to root out of medicine not only open quality of life judgments, but also the disguised ones. We would then be left trying to do our best to prolong indefinitely the lives of anencephalics, cortically dead infants, and patients in a persistent vegetative state. Ultimately, if we were really honest with ourselves, we would have to try to prolong the lives of those we now classify as dead because their brains have entirely ceased to function. For if human life is of equal worth, whether it has the capacity for consciousness or not, why focus on the death of the brain, rather than on the death of the body as a whole?

On the other hand, if we do accept the first new commandment, we overcome the problems that arise for a sanctity of life ethic in making decisions about anencephalics, cortically dead infants, patients in a persistent vegetative state, and those who are declared to be brain dead by current medical criteria. In none of these cases is the really important issue one of how we define death. That question has had so much attention only because we are still trying to live with an ethical and legal framework formed by the old commandment. When we reject that commandment, we will instead focus on ethically relevant characteristics like the capacity for enjoyable experiences, for interacting with others, or for having preferences about continued life. Without consciousness, none of these are possible; therefore, once we are certain that consciousness has been irrevocably lost, it is not ethically relevant that there is still some hormonal brain function, for hormonal brain function without consciousness cannot benefit the patient. Nor can brain-stem function alone benefit a patient, in the absence of a cortex. So our decisions about how to treat such patients should not depend on lofty rhetoric about the equal worth of all human life, but on the views of families and partners, who deserve consideration at a time of tragic loss. If a patient in a persistent vegetative state has previously expressed wishes about what should happen to her or him in such circumstances, they should also be taken into account. (We may do this purely out of respect for the wishes of the dead, or we may do it in order to reassure others, still alive, that their wishes will not be ignored.) At the same time, in a public health-care system, we cannot ignore the limits set by the finite nature of our medical resources, nor the needs of others whose lives may be saved by an organ transplant.

Second Old Commandment: Never Intentionally Take Innocent Human Life

The second commandment should be rejected because it is too absolutist to deal with all the circumstances that can arise. We have already seen how far this can be taken, in the Roman Catholic Church's teaching that it is wrong to kill a fetus, *even if that would be the only way to prevent both the pregnant woman and the fetus dying.* For those who take responsibility for the consequences of their decisions, this doctrine is absurd. It is horrifying to think that in the nineteenth and early twentieth century it was probably responsible for the preventable and agonising deaths of an unknown number of women in Roman Catholic hospitals or at the hands of devout Roman Catholic doctors and midwives. This could occur if, for example, the head of the fetus became stuck during labour, and could not be dislodged. Then the only way of saving the woman was to perform an operation known as a craniotomy, which involves inserting a surgical implement through the vagina and crushing the cranium, or skull, of the fetus. If this was not done, the woman and fetus would die in childbirth. Such an operation is obviously a last resort. Nevertheless, in those difficult circumstances, it seems appalling that any well-intentioned health-care professional could stand by while both woman and fetus die. For an ethic that combines an exceptionless prohibition on taking innocent human life with the doctrine that the fetus is an innocent human being, however, there could be no other course of action. If the Roman Catholic Church had said that performing a craniotomy is permissible, it would have had to give up either the absolute nature of its prohibition on taking innocent human life, or its view that the fetus is an innocent human being. Obviously, it was—and remains—willing to do neither. The teaching still stands. It is only because the development of obstetric techniques now allows the fetus to be dislodged and removed alive that the doctrine is no longer causing women to die pointlessly.

Another circumstance in which the second old commandment needs to be abandoned is—as the British law lords pointed out in deciding the Bland case—when life is of no benefit to the person living it. But the only modification to the absolute prohibition on taking human life that their lordships felt able to justify in that case—to allow a life to be taken intentionally by withholding or omitting treatment—still leaves the problem of cases in which it is better to use active means to take innocent human life. The law found Dr. Nigel Cox guilty of the attempted murder of Mrs. Lillian Boyes, despite the fact that she begged for death, and knew that she had nothing ahead of her but a few more hours of agony. Needless to say, no law, no court, and no code of medical ethics, would have required Dr. Cox to do everything in his power to prolong Mrs. Boyes' life. Had she suddenly become unable to breathe on her own, for instance, it would have been quite in accordance with the law and the traditional ethical view not to put her on a respirator—or if she was already on one, to take it away. The very thought of drawing out the kind of suffering that Mrs. Boyes had to endure is repugnant, and would have been regarded as wrong under the traditional ethic as well as the new one. But this only shows how much weight the traditional ethic places on the fine line between ending life by withdrawing treatment, and ending it by a lethal injection. The attitude of the traditional ethic is summed up in the famous couplet:

> Thou shalt not kill; but need'st not strive
> Officiously to keep alive.

These lines are sometimes uttered in revered tones, as if they were the wisdom of some ancient sage. One doctor, writing in the *Lancet* to defend the non-treatment of infants with spina bifida, referred to the lines as "The old dictum we were taught as medical students."[2] This is ironic, for a glance at the poem from which the couplet comes—Arthur Hugh Clough's "The Latest Decalogue"—leaves no doubt that the intention of this verse, as of each couplet in the poem, is to point out how we have failed to heed the spirit of the original ten commandments. In some of the other couplets, this is unmistakeable. For example:

> No graven images may be
> Worshipped, except the currency.

Clough would therefore have supported an extended view of responsibility. Not killing is not enough. We are also responsible for the consequences of our decision not to strive to keep alive.[3]   15

Notes

1. The classic account of the shift from the Ptolemaic to Copernican models is Thomas Kuhn, *The Structure of Scientific Revolutions,* University of Chicago Press, Chicago, 1972.
2. Dr. L. Haas, from a letter in the *Lancet,* 2 November 1968; quoted from S. Gorovitz (ed)., *Moral Problems in Medicine,* Prentice-Hall, Englewood Cliffs, NJ, 1976, p. 351.
3. Clough's "The Latest Decalogue" can be found in Helen Gardner (ed.), *The New Oxford Book of English Verse,* Oxford University Press, Oxford, 1978.

◆ QUESTIONS FOR DISCUSSION AND WRITING ◆

1. Singer's "first new commandment" is to "recognize that the worth of human life varies" (paragraph 8). Do you agree? Why or why not?
2. Singer reports a British case in which judges ruled that "life without consciousness is of no worth at all" (paragraph 8). Does this match your personal definition of death? Should someone "without consciousness" be allowed to die? Be put to death? Why or why not?
3. How effective is Singer's introduction? Does his discussion of changing science convince you that it's time for a new revolution in ethics?
4. In paragraph 3, Singer writes that the "defenders" of the "traditional doctrine of the sanctity of human life":
   - ". . . have redefined death so that they can remove beating hearts from warm, breathing bodies, and give them to others with better prospects, while telling themselves that they are only taking organs from a corpse."

- ". . . give terminally ill patients huge doses of morphine that they know will shorten their lives, but say that this is not euthanasia, because their declared intention is to relieve pain."
- ". . . select severely disabled infants for 'non-treatment' and make sure that they die, without thinking of themselves as killing them."

Do you find any of Singer's comments to be provocative or disturbing? Why or why not?

5. How do you reconcile your definition of *sanctity of life* (from Clouser's article) with the situation Singer describes in paragraph 12 of this essay?

TAKING ACTION
Your Collaborative Statement to the Committee for Ethical Decisions

Now that you've read, discussed, and written about some of the issues and concerns involved in this scenario, consider who the decision makers are in this case. Whom should you and the members of your group seek to persuade that your approach offers the best solution?

You might, for example, write a letter to the editor of your local newspaper in an attempt to sway public opinion, you might contact the government body that manages your city or county, or you might communicate with your state or national representatives. In our scenario, the authority rests with Mercy Hospital's Committee for Ethical Decisions; its members are the ones your group must influence.

Mercy Hospital convenes what it calls a critical care meeting at which all parties can discuss and come to conclusions about the critical situations every hospital faces. Now, Dr. Mary Theresa, the hospital's administrator, and Mercy Hospital's Committee for Ethical Decisions must decide what to do about Helen Scott and her unborn child. They have asked the family members to submit brief written statements; they also expect to hear from the hospital's nurses, the clergy who regularly attend the sick, and Mercy Hospital's legal team. Each interested group has been asked to prepare a two-page written statement for the CED.

At the moment, Helen's condition appears to be stable. Several machines monitor her condition and help her breath, and she is being fed by tube. The doctors also continually monitor the condition of the fetus.

Asking the Right Questions

When addressing a problem that affects you or those close to you, it's often a good idea to first determine what you already know and what you'd like to learn more about. Begin by asking questions; those questions will lead to others that will help your group identify the best solution for the problems the scenario presents.

As you draft your statement to Mercy Hospital's Committee for Ethical Decisions, think about the issues and problems from a reporter's perspective, focusing on the who, what, when, where, and why of the Mercy Hospital scenario. Try to answer the following questions:

- How do the members of your group feel about Helen's being on life support? Can you reach a consensus on whether these systems should remain in place? Or will your group have to issue a "minority report" because one or more members disagree with the others?
- How does your group interpret the key terms in this situation? Is Helen *dead*? Would removing her from life support *abort* her fetus? Would you call that act *euthanasia*? Which is more important: Helen's *living will* or the life of her unborn child?
- What perspectives might the other groups have on Helen's situation? What are the strengths and weaknesses of those points of view?
- In what ways can you strengthen your group's comments about Helen by aligning with another group? Will it help your group's position to let the CED know that others share your ideas on some of the issues, problems, or possible solutions?
- Can you identify the consequences for your group if Helen is kept on life support? What if she is removed?
- What are the consequences if you do nothing to try to change Helen's situation? What action might make the situation more difficult?
- How do the issues and problems in this scenario reflect broader national discussions about euthanasia, abortion, and the validity of living wills?

Constructing a Collaborative Text

Work with your group to draft a brief statement to the Committee for Ethical Decisions that expresses your views on the issues just outlined.

Consider the audience for your brief statement: the members of the Committee for Ethical Decisions of Mercy Hospital. Serving on the committee are Dr. Mary Theresa, the hospital's administrator; Marjorie Holmes, Mercy Hospital's head nurse; and a physician who has operating privileges at the hospital: this month, that is Dr. Rebecca Tussey, a local obstetrician-gynecologist (physicians serve on a rotating basis). After reviewing all statements, committee members will meet to discuss the issues and decide what to do.

One way to prepare a group statement is for each group member to compose a statement listing what he or she considers to be the most im-

BOX 9.4 APPLYING WHAT YOU READ
Using Your Classmates' Suggestions (Written Peer Review)

Once you have a brief collaborative text that outlines your message to the hospital's Committee for Ethical Decisions, exchange your draft with that of another group. Read that group's statement and indicate in marginal notes what you see as its strengths and weaknesses. What suggestions can you offer the group for improving or clarifying its statement? What are the strengths of the draft? The weaknesses? Where was the argument confusing? What is clear or unclear?

It's important to provide help in this manner to your classmates even if you disagree with the positions they take in their statement.

Once your group receives feedback from your classmates, work together as a group to revise your statement. What suggestions did you receive that make sense? Where does your text need clarification, or further explanation, or more evidence? What facts or other data have group members collected that you can add, to make your text more convincing?

portant issues and problems. Then, working together, your group can draw on those initial comments to compose its group statement.

Another method is to take the notes that each of you has made, designate one group member to record the group's ideas, and then collaboratively compose an initial draft of what your group thinks. At first, this process might be a bit hectic, with several group members offering suggestions on what to write and how to write it, but, with time, you'll find that working together is an interesting and useful way to get your collective ideas onto paper.

When you have completed a first draft of your collaborative text, each group member should read through the draft, marking any sections that are unclear. Work together to clarify those parts. Then, each group member should read the statement once more, this time looking for places in the text where your argument might need more evidence. Working together, decide what evidence gathered during your research (facts, data, testimony, statistics) might provide additional support for your argument.

Your instructor may ask you to read and comment on the other groups' statements. Working together in that way, you can help your classmates become better writers as you act as real readers for one another. Indicate the places in the text where more information is needed, or where the writing is confusing, or where some elaboration might help. To apply the feedback you receive to improve your composition, follow the procedure in Box 9.4: Using Your Classmates' Suggestions.

Carefully revise your draft several times, to ensure that your group's ideas are articulated as clearly as possible.

SPEAKING YOUR PIECE
A Debate before the Committee for Ethical Decisions

Because Mercy Hospital is a public hospital and because Dr. Mary Theresa generally follows the recommendation of the Committee for Ethical Decisions, she wants the people of Arapaho County to understand exactly what is happening in the Helen Scott case. In earlier critical care situations like this one, when Mercy Hospital did not explain to the taxpayers what the hospital was doing and why, a number of highly critical letters in the local paper called for more openness from the hospital. Dr. Theresa and the members of the CED hope to avoid this sort of negative publicity by holding an open forum.

Once the Committee for Ethical Decisions has received and read the statements provided by the interested groups, Dr. Theresa supplies copies of all statements to each of the groups. She also invites the interested parties to attend an open forum at which they can voice their concerns to the CED and ask questions of the other groups. This is a unique opportunity to go beyond a paper exchange of ideas. This public forum allows for intense discussion and interaction between groups, which can help facilitate solutions to the conflicts inherent in any controversy.

For this public discussion, your audience consists of the members of the Committee for Ethical Decisions, members of other groups, as well as the general public. Reporters are expected, and much of what is discussed at this forum will appear in the local newspapers.

The CED has indicated that the groups may question one another, following their prepared statements.

From Written Preparation to Public Speaking

To prepare for the open meeting before the CED, your group must adapt its written position statement for oral presentation.

Let's say that your group represents Mercy Hospital's legal team. You've decided that the hospital should follow the spirit of the law: it must honor Helen Scott's living will. Your group's oral presentation might begin like this: "Our main concern is that the hospital follow Helen Scott's written wishes and immediately remove her from life support." Then you'd supply evidence—facts, statistics, testimony, examples of what others have done—supporting your argument or thesis, to persuade your audience that your position is the correct one.

Speaking at the Public Forum

In a full-class discussion, representatives of each group will speak (you will be given a time limit). Just as in your written presentation, it's important to provide specific evidence—facts, testimony, examples of what other hospitals have done—in your oral presentation. Take careful notes while your classmates make their presentations. The perspectives you hear in these presentations will help you in the individual writing you'll soon be asked to do.

Once each group has presented its views, others will be allowed to ask questions. Listen carefully to questions addressed to your group, take a moment to confer with the others in your group, and determine a suitable answer. Your instructor might ask one or more students to act as moderators (much as the Committee for Ethical Decisions would do), to ensure that everyone has an opportunity to contribute to the discussion.

INDIVIDUAL WRITING
Essay Options

Your instructor will ask you to complete one or more of the following writing assignments: an informative essay, a persuasive essay, and/or an analytic essay. Each project has its own focus and audience, but they all prompt you to think and write about the issues and problems this scenario raises.

You'll approach the subjects of euthanasia, abortion, and the legality of living wills from different perspectives, but each assignment requires that you make use of the thinking, writing, and speaking you've done so far in this scenario. Look over the notes you've taken, think about the group discussions you've had, and consider the statements the other groups made during the public forum. You might want to do additional research to better understand the issues or find support for something you wish to say.

The Informative Essay

For this assignment, assume you've been asked to construct an informative essay to provide Mercy Hospital's Committee for Ethical Decisions with the information it needs to decide the Helen Scott case. Write from the perspective of an interested but detached outsider. Write as if Mercy Hospital had hired you to research the decisions that other hospitals have made in cases like this one. What similar scenarios can you discover? What parties were involved? What decisions were made? Were precedents established? Box 9.5: A Basic Report Format explains how to structure your essay.

Your audience for this informative essay, the members of Mercy Hospital's CED, are already familiar with Helen Scott's situation. They have asked for this report to help them examine the issues from a wider, national perspective. You'll want to focus on the larger issues, such as these:

- How frequently have cases like Helen's occurred? How similar were those cases to Helen's?

✳ **BOX 9.5 FOR EXAMPLE**
A Basic Report Format

- Your first page is a title page.
- Your second page provides a one-page summary of the main points in your report.
- The body of your report follows. Use as many pages as you need to thoroughly explain what you've discovered through your research.
- Finally, provide a works-cited page showing the CED the sources of the information in your report.

- Can removing Helen from life support be considered euthanasia? Has the term *abortion* been applied in similar situations? In cases such as this, what other issues have been raised?
- What decision has most often been made in situations similar to this one? Can you determine the effects of that decision on the parties involved?

The Persuasive Essay

Assume that the Committee for Ethical Decisions has reviewed the written statements and has listened to the public debate. It has determined that the best course of action—what it feels "is right for everyone involved"—is to ignore Helen Scott's living will and to attempt to keep "the woman alive, by whatever means, until the child can be born. We will continue to constantly monitor the health of the unborn child," the CED's statement continues, "and if it becomes compromised in some way, we will reconsider terminating the situation."

Because of the public interest in the CED's decision, Marcia Keaton, a reporter from the *Denver Courier*, writes a series of opinion pieces, in which she argues against the hospital's decision. Box 9.6: Keaton's Editorial contains an excerpt.

As Keaton's pieces appear, the local media are filled with stories, letters to the editor, and television and radio commentaries offering differing perspectives on what should be done about "Baby Johnny," as the unborn child is now being called. Pictures outlining the development of a fetus between 18 and 26 weeks of age have appeared in the newspapers. The national media have discovered the story: both ABC's *20/20* and *Dateline NBC* have called, requesting interviews with John, members of his family, Helen's mother and father, members of the hospital's Committee for Ethical Decisions, and hospital staff.

❋ **BOX 9.6 FOR EXAMPLE**
Keaton's Editorial

This is an excerpt from one of *Denver Courier* reporter Marcia Keaton's early editorials on the position Mercy Hospital's Committee for Ethical Decisions has taken on the Helen Scott case:

. . . First, the amount of money that will be spent in the slim hope of saving one child seems out of proportion to me. Can this county really afford to gamble half a million dollars and go against the wishes of a young woman, all with only a 50–50 chance of success in saving her fetus? Remember that we are gambling—Mercy Hospital cannot promise a healthy baby boy. Rather, we have the real chance that the child will suffer severe birth defects and, even if he is born alive, be unable to survive on his own. More county monies will be required for extended care, for however long he lives.

I think that the half a million dollars (at least) would be much better spent in other places—including aiding poor Denver residents who cannot afford the kind of health care that Mrs. Scott is receiving. Surely Mrs. Scott would want the greater good for the greater number of Denver residents, and in fact she so indicated in her living will.

Come on, folks. The woman did not want to be kept alive artificially, and she knew she was pregnant when she signed her living will. If we do keep her alive against her will, her child is likely to suffer from severe problems, which will cost us even more money.

Yes, this is a sad situation. In a perfect world, we would want both to keep Mrs. Scott alive and to save her child. But that is simply not possible. I think that Mercy Hospital should immediately remove Helen Scott from the mechanical support systems that are keeping her alive.

Some of the more inflammatory letters to the editor have used the word *murder* to describe removing Helen's life-support systems. Several local residents have offered to adopt "Baby Johnny" if that would keep Helen's life-support systems in place. Several national religious leaders have publicly condemned the "purportedly legal living will as a 'will of death.'"

You wish to add your voice to this discussion, so you decide to write an essay to persuade others that your ideas are the correct ones. Remember, a persuasive essay seeks, by its nature, to make its audience react as its writer wants them to. For this persuasive essay, respond to Keaton's editorial in the *Courier,* either agreeing or disagreeing with the CED decision. As with any persuasive writing, the more evidence you supply to support your points, the more convincing your case will be.

This essay represents an opportunity for you to have your say, but keep in mind the views that others have expressed. Draw on everything you've learned from working with your group, as well as what you've read and heard from the other groups.

The Analytic Essay

Your instructor may ask you to compose an analytic essay in which you outline and explain the ethical decisions (similar to those in Helen Scott's case) that face hospitals today. Your analysis should explain why hospitals deal with those situations in the ways they do.

For this assignment, assume that your essay will be published in *Hospitals and Ethics: Conflicts and Resolutions*. This national academic journal is read regularly by hospital administrators as well as by those who serve on hospitals' ethics committees.

If you could communicate with a national audience of those who make ethical decisions for hospitals, what information would you supply to help them make those decisions? Unlike an informative essay, in which the writer maintains a neutral, nonpartisan stance, or a persuasive essay, in which the writer takes a stand, an analysis seeks to explain why something has happened. An analytic essay about the Helen Scott scenario should explain the reasoning behind the type of ethical decision the CED made in Helen's case. You might want to consider issues such as these:

- What does the CED's decision in the Helen Scott case say about the committee's definition of *euthanasia* (or *abortion*)? How might the CED's definitions of those terms have influenced its decision about Helen?

- Is the hospital's most important duty to those who cannot speak for themselves: the comatose? the unborn? Why or why not? In what way(s) have other hospitals handled similar mother-child situations? On what criteria have they made their decisions?

- Some might suggest that by keeping Helen alive for two months, the hospital is not going against her wishes in her living will but is simply delaying carrying them out. What have other institutions done in similar instances? How has time affected decisions of this sort?

To conclude this scenario, your instructor may ask that you follow the instructions in Box 9.7: Reflections on the Situation at Mercy Hospital. The process of writing about ways in which your attitudes may have changed helps clarify your thinking.

FOR FURTHER RESEARCH AND WRITING

This scenario offers many opportunities for further exploration, especially if you consider some of the issues and problems you've encountered from a broader, national perspective.

For example, this scenario introduces several terms that are defined differently by different people. Euthanasia, for example, is often thought

BOX 9.7   APPLYING WHAT YOU READ
Reflections on the Situation at Mercy Hospital

You've done a lot of reading, discussing, and writing about Helen Scott's situation. Take a few minutes to review the first writing you did for this scenario, in which you commented on the photographs that introduce this chapter and the terms highlighted at the beginning of it. Jot down your answers to these questions:

- Have you changed your mind about any of the images or how you define the terms? If so, in what ways?
- How well do the definitions at the beginning of this chapter apply to Helen Scott's situation?
- Now that you understand more about this scenario, what images would you add to those at the beginning of this chapter? Would you alter the definitions in any way?
- Now that you have investigated the problems and issues in this scenario, what strikes you as the most important? Why?
- Did your writing process change as you wrote your way through this scenario? If so, describe that change.
- What was the most important thing you learned as you worked on the scenario about Helen, her unborn child, and her living will?

of as "mercy killing" or "an easy or painless death." Do such definitions apply to Helen's situation? Who has the power to determine how terms like these are defined? Who should be able to define the terms involved in a debate?

Another area to consider is that of individual rights: Does a person have the right to control the end of his or her life, as a living will purports to do? What if another life (in this case, Helen's unborn child) is involved? Do the rights of the mother supercede those of the child? Do the rights of a fetus outweigh the expressed wishes of the mother? Why or why not?

You might examine how physicians are perceived in this country and whether they should have the power to overrule a living will. Can a doctor, who takes an oath to "do no harm," make a reasoned decision on the life or death of Helen's unborn child? Is it fair to ask a physician to make such a decision? Should living wills be abolished and all such decisions left to the discretion of physicians?

In your research on euthanasia, you undoubtedly came across the name and activities of Dr. Jack Kevorkian, the Michigan doctor who has become a national advocate for mercy killing. How do you think Kevorkian would handle Helen's situation? Why?

What rights do family members have in situations such as the one this scenario describes? Should a family's interests and rights come before an individual's wishes specified in a living will? Why or why not?

What role might your writing and discussions in this scenario play in the national debates about euthanasia or abortion? Can they contribute to discussions on whether a living will is binding—and if so, how binding—on those involved?

You've now read, discussed, and written about the issues surrounding Helen, her unborn child, and her living will. Hospitals, doctors, nurses, and patients and their families from around the country sometimes face problems like these. We hope working through our scenario has helped you improve your reading and writing skills; we also hope you understand how to work more effectively with others.

The skills you used in this scenario will aid you in the work you've yet to do as you continue your education. Ultimately, these skills will also help you in your career.

Works Cited

"Abortion." *Encyclopaedia Britannica.* 23 June 2000 <http://www.britannica.com/bcom/eb/article/0/0,5716,3410+1+3376,00.html>.

Black, Henry Campbell. *Black's Law Dictionary.* 5th ed. St. Paul, MN: West, 1979.

"Death and Dying." 23 June 2000 <http://hlthed.sask.com/cni/units/10.3.1/ap_1will.html>.

"Euthanasia." *Academic Press Dictionary of Science and Technology,* 1996. 21 June 2000 <http://www.apnet.com/inscight/07161997/euthana1.htm>.

"Euthanasia." Aish HaTorah. 8 Apr. 2000 <http://www.aish.edu>.

APPENDIX A

Preparing a Writer's Portfolio

After some or all of the writing projects you complete, your instructor might ask you to reflect on your writing process. The reflective thinking you do on paper may become part of your writer's portfolio—a collection of your writing that you assemble for a particular purpose. Most portfolios you'll put together in your college writing classes, for example, begin with a reflective letter setting the stage for and discussing the writing you included.

Reflection helps you learn from your writing mistakes as well as your successes. Recording your reflective comments helps you to see and understand what parts of your writing "worked," as well as which sections might be improved. When you face a similar writing task, you'll have a good sense of how to complete it successfully.

We begin this appendix by discussing strategies for reflecting on your work. Then we explain why you should assemble a writer's portfolio and what you might include in it.

GETTING STARTED: REFLECTING ON YOUR WORK

Reflection forces you to think about your working and writing processes. Knowing what worked well and what you could improve will help you with future writing projects.

The reflections you're asked to compose after you work through each scenario in this text can serve as the basis for a more complex composition. For example, your instructor might ask you to construct an end-of-semester reflection in which you review and comment on all the writing activities you completed for your class.

To construct a reflective piece, you work through the same steps you follow in composing any piece of discourse: you consider your rhetorical situation (the occasion for writing, your purpose, your audience, the topic, and you, the writer).

Brainstorming on Your Own

To begin reflecting on the work you did for a scenario, jot down notes about your writing process. Start by considering the opening discussions in class. Review the written comments you and the members of your group made, the questions that were asked (and those that should have been, but were not) at the "open meeting" (if your class conducted one), and the way in which you composed your individual writing for the scenario. You might want to draw on some of the invention techniques you've worked with, including brainstorming, freewriting, and clustering. As you reflect, you might ask and answer questions such as these:

- What "writerly habits" did you develop or hone during this writing project?
- If you were to do this project again, how would you change it or the ways in which you tackled it?
- How did peer readers help you during this project? Give some examples of peer comments that were useful. Give examples of what you did with your text in response to your peers' suggestions.
- As the project emerged, how could you have made better use of your peers' responses?
- How could your peers have been more helpful?
- What was the best response you received from a peer? How did you use that advice in your revision?
- What did you and the members of your group do that was effective? What was ineffective? What might you do differently next time?
- What did you learn about yourself as a writer as you wrote your way through this scenario?
- What are the strongest and the weakest parts of your writing for this scenario? Why? How can you further develop the strengths you've found and eliminate the weaknesses?

Remember that weaknesses in writing are nothing to be ashamed of. Each of us has strengths as well as areas that require more attention. Only by recognizing both aspects and working on them can we improve our writing.

Considering Your Audience

Reflective writing has two audiences. Because your audience includes your instructor, you want to demonstrate that you've given your writing serious critical thought. Your reflective writing should provide a sense of what you've learned in working through the scenario.

Because reflective writing is an exercise in self-examination, your audience also includes yourself. To satisfy that audience, you need to assess your writing performance and your attitudes toward and thoughts on everything that you've done. Reflection involves identifying what you've learned about yourself as a writer.

How do I do this? you might ask. Let's look over the shoulder of a fictitious student, Sharon, as she works through several versions of her reflective comments, receives criticism and advice from her classmates, and then works to revise her comments so that she says exactly what she wants to say. Sharon's work might serve as a model for your reflective activities.

For the sake of this illustration, we'll assume that Sharon is writing about the scenario outlined in chapter 5, which involves weapons on a high school campus. Here is part of the list Sharon created as she brainstormed about her work in that scenario:

Sharon's Brainstorming

1. We got along well in our small group.
2. I wish we'd spent more time getting to know each other; that would have helped when we later disagreed on things.
3. We all needed to be more open and honest about what we thought, but that was hard to do, especially at the beginning.
4. We needed to write down more things—we all liked to talk, but we didn't spend enough time getting our ideas onto paper, so we forgot some stuff.
5. We could have been more active during the class discussions.
6. I wish our instructor had asked us to read more—I could have used more research time and information because other schools have the same kinds of problems, and I would have liked to have learned more about possible solutions.
7. I really liked the open meeting where we could question each other.
8. I shouldn't have tried to do my first draft the night before it was due —and I should have—well, we all should have—been more critical when we did peer review. It didn't help me much when someone told me my "paper is perfect."

Composing a First Draft

Sharon, like most of us, was not accustomed to spending time think-ing about and then writing about a "writing activity." Therefore, she be-gan by jotting down what were useful activities for her, as she worked her way through this scenario. Then Sharon spent some time thinking about the problems she had and the challenges she and the members of her group faced in trying to express their ideas. Finally, Sharon listed the things she might do differently the next time she finds herself in a similar writing situation. Sharon knows that by thinking about the good as well as the less effective parts of her work, she can learn from her mistakes (and learn to build on her strengths), so that she won't have to start from scratch next time. Here is the first version of Sharon's reflective thoughts, in which she's transformed her brainstormed list into an essay:

Sharon's Reflective Comments

As I look back on my writing for this scenario, I can see that I should have done a few things differently.

First, I wish I'd become more involved early in the process, when our group was figuring out what to propose. I was one of the students who felt that perhaps the situation at the school wasn't as bad as some of the others thought it was. I wish I'd thought about what it might be like to be a student whose bookbag was searched or how it might feel to go through metal detectors just to get to class (another "role" it would have been useful for me to play!).

Second, I wish I'd listened a bit more to, and also had taken better notes on, all the different things we discussed. That information would have helped me a lot when I had to write my own paper.

Finally, I should have done more than two drafts—because I can now see how much work it takes to really do a good job of writing about something. I also could have used more research about what other high schools have done with the issue, and I wish I'd found a real example of someone else's approach and reasoning.

As to what I did well, it seems to me that the best thing I did was to speak out during the "open meeting." That forced me to decide what I really believed, and why I believed it. I also had several good ques-tions from my classmates, questions that were hard to answer—and they made me see what I needed to do when I sat down to write my paper.

Our teacher asked us to keep a journal in which we listed what we were learning and our questions and problems; I did okay with this part. But I wish now that I had written something every day—that would have helped me.

I also learned that we (our class) can work well together, both in figuring out what's important (our teacher kept asking, "What's at stake here?") and in gathering information. I could have done more research; now I know that next time I want to spend <u>a lot</u> of time in the library!

Using Your Classmates' Suggestions (Written Peer Review)

Sharon wants others to read her reflective work. She's looking for slightly different advice from that she needed when she was writing her essay for the scenario. Then, Sharon wanted to know whether her ideas were clear and logical, whether she had supported her main points, and so on. Now, though, Sharon wants to know whether her writing is clear and whether she's covered everything her instructor asked her to address. Sharon's peer readers should indicate whether Sharon has reflected and commented on all the invention work she did, whether she has identified the effective (and less effective) parts of the early drafts of her group's collaborative statement, and what she learned from the verbal presentations and arguments her group made. Peer comments are in italic following each section of Sharon's essay.

Sharon's Reflective Comments with Peer Suggestions

As I look back on my writing for this scenario, I can see that I should have done a few things differently.

First, I wish I'd become more involved early in the process, when our group was figuring out what to propose. I was one of the students who felt that perhaps the situation at the school wasn't as bad as some of the others thought it was. I wish I'd thought about what it might be like to be a student whose bookbag was searched or how it might feel to go through metal detectors just to get to class (another "role" it would have been useful for me to play!).

Good start. Now can you provide some examples to illustrate what you mean?

Second, I wish I'd listened a bit more to, and also had taken better notes on, all the different things we discussed. That information would have helped me a lot when I had to write my own paper.

Finally, I should have done more than two drafts—because I can now see how much work it takes to really do a good job of writing about something. I also could have used more research about what other high schools have done with the issue, and I wish I'd found a real example of someone else's approach and reasoning.

Okay, but as above, can you provide some examples to show what you mean?

As to what I did well, it seems to me that the best thing I did was to speak out during the "open meeting." That forced me to decide what I really believed, and why I believed it. I also had several good questions from my classmates, questions that were hard to answer—and they made me see what I needed to do when I sat down to write my paper.

What did you say at that meeting? What questions were you asked, and how did you answer them? How did that activity help your paper?

Our teacher asked us to keep a journal in which we listed what we were learning and our questions and problems; I did okay with this part. But I wish now that I had written something every day—that would have helped me.

I also learned that we (our class) can work well together, both in figuring out what's important (our teacher kept asking, "What's at stake here?") and in gathering information. I could have done more research; now I know that next time I want to spend a lot of time in the library!

Revising the First Version

Sharon now reads through and considers the comments and ideas she's received from her classmates, so she can address what she's learned in the second version of her reflective comments. Here is her revised draft:

Sharon's Second Draft

As I look back on my writing for this scenario, I can see that I should have done a few things differently.

First, I wish I'd become more involved early in the process, when our group was figuring out what to propose. I was one of the students who felt that perhaps the situation at the school wasn't as bad as some of the others thought it was. I wish I'd thought about what it might be like to be a student whose bookbag was searched, or how it might feel to go through metal detectors just to get to class (another "role" it would have been useful for me to play!). Then, I might have better understood some of what I'd read—like the story about Joel, who brought a pocketknife to school to give to another student. The administration found out about it, and they expelled him. I found several stories about incidents that seemed really unfair.

Second, I wish I'd listened a bit more to, and also had taken better notes on, all the different things we discussed. That information would have helped me a lot when I had to write my own paper.

Finally, I should have done more than two drafts—because I can now see how much work it takes to really do a good job of writing about something. I also could have used more research about what other high schools have done with the issue, and I wish I'd found a real example of someone else's approach and reasoning. For instance, I eventually found out about Coleman High's policy requiring that students involved in weapons incidents receive counseling and help: they're not simply expelled from school. I could have argued that we could use the same approach at Westwood High.

As to what I did well, it seems to me that the best thing I did was to speak out during the "open meeting." That forced me to figure out what I really believed, and why I believed it. I also had several good questions from my classmates, questions that were hard to answer— and they made me see what I needed to do when I sat down to write my paper.

I think my comments at the open meeting were especially effective when I brought some emotion into the conversation. That's what happened when I discussed how unfair Joel's case was.

One difficult question had to do with insurance and liability in case a student was hurt by a knife or something that another student brought to campus. Before I wrote my paper, I did more research by calling two insurance agencies, which gave me the exact cost for a liability policy. Because the cost wasn't that high, I was able to answer the objection I'd received in the open meeting.

Our teacher asked us to keep a journal in which we listed what we were learning and our questions and problems; I did okay with this part. But I wish now that I had written something every day—that would have helped me.

I also learned that we (our class) can work well together, both in figuring out what's important (our teacher kept asking, "What's at stake here?") and in gathering information. I could have done more research; now I know that next time I want to spend <u>a lot</u> of time in the library!

Sharon's paper isn't perfect yet, of course, but she's revised it to reflect what her readers said they needed. She may need to rework it several times before she's satisfied with it.

CONSTRUCTING YOUR WRITER'S PORTFOLIO

After you work through each scenario in this text, your instructor may ask you to reflect on the work you and your classmates have completed. A natural extension of this activity is the construction of a writer's portfolio: a collection of your own writing.

There are many reasons to assemble a sample of your "best" writing (writing that illustrates your capabilities). For example, many college composition classes now ask students to collect a representative sample of their writing. Often, graduate schools ask applicants for a writing portfolio—as do potential employers—because they see writing as critical for the work you'll do.

A Writer's Portfolio and Your Rhetorical Situation

Most often, you select the writing samples you include in your portfolio. In making your selection, pay particular attention to the rhetorical situation for which you're preparing the portfolio. Begin with an idea of what your portfolio should do for its audience and in its situation. Who is the audience? What should your portfolio show them about your writing and about you?

This means assembling different documents for a portfolio to accompany an application to law school (which might look for your abilities to construct analytical and persuasive writing) than you'd collect for one you're submitting to a major corporation (which might look for evidence that you can work well with others to solve problems). A portfolio accompanying your application to graduate school (which might want to see how well you work with textual research and integrate it into your writing) would require still other selections. For a college writing class, your portfolio might include copies of your journal entries, invention activities, and so on.

Many instructors also ask that you include in your writer's portfolio several pieces explaining and commenting on your selections:

- A text describing what you've included in your portfolio.
- An explanation of (and perhaps a justification for) the documents you've included in your portfolio.
- Reflective comments about various aspects of the work, including invention activities, various drafts, and perhaps comments from peer reviewers.
- Reflective comments with a broader focus that discuss what you learned from the activities that produced your writing.
- Comments on the steps you plan to take to improve your writing and your writing process in future work.

Examining Your Work

To put together a writer's portfolio for a graduate school application, for example, or for a potential employer, you need to identify what you're trying to accomplish. Answering questions like these should help:

- What examples from my writing show how I focused on a specific purpose?
- What examples show that I can anticipate the needs of different kinds of readers?
- What examples show that I can use the format, organization, language, and conventions appropriate to specific writing situations?
- What examples show that I can use writing to record, explore, organize, and communicate?

- What examples indicate that I can find, evaluate, analyze, and synthesize appropriate research (such as notes I've taken, texts I've read, and Internet sources I've used)?
- What materials should I include and discuss to demonstrate that I can use writing strategies like brainstorming, outlining, and focused freewriting during all stages of the writing process, and especially to revise my drafts?
- In what ways can I show that I can use strategies appropriate to specific writing situations to generate, organize, revise, and edit my compositions?

Using Peer Review to Improve Your Portfolio

As with any other writing you do, the texts you construct to explain your inclusions in your writer's portfolio can benefit from peer review. Peer reviewers can respond with prompts like these:

- Here are the elements I identify with and understand in your draft.
- Tell me more about these sections.
- Here are the parts of your draft that I especially like and why.
- Here are the parts of your draft that need more clarification.
- Here are some suggestions for rearranging your writing.
- These are some questions it's important you address: What did you learn from your work in this course/project? What changes might you make in your writing because of what you learned? You did/didn't address these questions.
- Here are some suggestions for other ways you might you reflect on your work. . . .
- You did/didn't discuss your future goals for writing in the academic, professional, personal, and civic aspects of your life.

You can see that reflective writing serves several purposes. By thinking about and writing about what has worked well for you and what you might improve, you'll be better able to complete future, similar writing tasks. Reflective writing can also help you create a portfolio of your work.

APPENDIX B

Extending the Scenarios to Your Community

SERVICE LEARNING

Many colleges and universities now offer service-learning classes in which students perform a community service of some kind that is connected to the writing they do in a class they're taking. Students might, for instance, tutor grammar-school students and then write, in their college composition class, about their experiences. Students in an introductory science class might teach modified versions of their lab experiments to high school students, and then write about those teaching experiences as part of their class requirements. Service-learning classes ask students to actively use what they've learned in the classroom and then to write about the process. In most cases these activities involve helping others.

There are many definitions of service learning, but composition courses with a service-learning component usually have several common features:

- Students perform some useful community service, almost always in conjunction with a nonprofit agency or an educational institution. They spend time outside of class working with that agency and usually receive college credit for their service work.
- The college or university coordinates and monitors the work students do.
- The work students perform is integrated into class writing assignments.
- Students usually receive reflective writing assignments to help them think about the service work they've done and absorb what they've learned.

SCENARIOS AND SERVICE LEARNING

Because all of the scenarios in this text address problems and issues that colleges or communities face, they offer opportunities for service learning. You might, for example, build on what you've learned to produce documents to help others: for example, pamphlets or brochures that can be distributed to interested students, parents, and community members. A class might construct a brochure outlining solutions to the problems illustrated in one scenario, with various small groups focusing on specific areas of interest. Each scenario in part II lends itself to specific types of service-learning activities.

Chapter 4: Education Today: Who Needs the Classroom, Anyway?

In this scenario, you and your classmates consider, discuss, and write about what constitutes a university education. A logical next step would be for your class to produce a document (a brochure or perhaps a Web page) that could be used in the following ways:

- To help students understand your school's reasoning on whether credit will be given for Internet classes and why some classes (and which ones, perhaps) must be taken on campus.
- To help students understand what types of courses might effectively (or perhaps not so effectively) be offered online.
- To help students and administrators better understand the benefits and limitations of online classes.
- To provide advice to students on how to get the most out of an online class.

Chapter 5: Student Privacy: Bad Times at Westwood High

In this scenario, you and your classmates address a concern shared by many students and parents these days: what to do about weapons (and other potential dangers) on high school campuses. Your class activity lends itself to the construction of a student handbook or set of rules that:

- Outlines the rights of students in your community's schools, perhaps with differing rights for various age groups.
- Guides student behavior in an effort to prevent problems in local high schools.
- Outlines the reasoning behind rules and regulations that are necessary to maintain a safe school environment.
- Might be adapted to other educational issues, such as random drug testing for student athletes.

Chapter 6: Guns for Sale: Recycling Your Police Department's Weapons

In this scenario, you and your classmates consider whether your city should be involved in the sale of the firearms its police department confiscates or no longer needs. As a service-learning project, your class could construct a brochure that:

- Outlines what other communities do with the weapons their law enforcement agencies confiscate; this might be an informational presentation, much like a voter's guide, to help citizens make up their minds on the issues.
- Explains the benefits of firearms sales: what your community does with the funds those sales generate, and how the activities the proceeds pay for benefit the residents of your city or town.
- Uses a cost-benefit approach to analyze whether your city should sell its confiscated guns.

Chapter 7: Suburban Sprawl: The Future of Saguaro Flats

This scenario focuses on land use and development. You might compose a set of rules and regulations concerning the future use and development of almost any piece of property, from small lots to major tracts of land:

- Development of playgrounds, fields, and other areas for youth sports.
- Your own neighborhood.
- Your city or county.
- Riparian or agricultural areas.
- Parks and other recreational areas.
- Transportation systems, including public transportation issues.

The questions you and your classmates might discuss and seek to answer in a set of guidelines or rules include:

- Who should control this land?
- What is the best and most logical use for this land? Why?
- What costs might be involved? Who is responsible for those costs?
- Does the "good of the many" (the residents of your city, for instance) ever outweigh the rights of the few (the landowner)?
- If we allow this land to be developed, what are some of the possible future implications? For example, what rules and regulations should your town or county enact for developments that consume large amounts of water (such as industry or golf courses)? What consideration should be given to an industry with possible toxic

waste or pollution problems? Should current regulations concerning development be changed? Why? How?

Chapter 8: Pornography on the Internet: Cyberporn at Your Local Library?

This scenario asks you to investigate the problem of pornography that can be accessed on your library's computers. Such an examination might produce:

- A brochure that outlines rules and regulations library patrons should follow when using the library's computers for Internet access.
- A pamphlet that explains the reasoning behind the library's rules.
- An informational brochure that explains, as interpreted locally, what "pornographic" means.

Chapter 9: Living Wills: Decisions about Life and Death

Although living wills might seem to be simply a legal concern, human questions are involved, especially about who should make the kinds of decisions these documents address and when those decisions should be made. You might generate:

- An informational brochure outlining the reasoning behind a living will (nonprofit legal aid agencies might welcome the production of such information).
- An educational handout your local hospitals might distribute, explaining what a living will is and does and what a "do not resuscitate" order means.
- A brochure or Web page listing local resources (attorneys who specialize in wills; counseling agencies) to help people who want more information but don't know where to find it.

CONCLUSION

The addition of a service-learning component to the activities you'll do in this text lets you put much of what you learn (through discussing and writing about the issues in a scenario) to good use. In fact, even if your composition class does not have a service-learning component, you can still use what you've learned here: You might want to volunteer to produce a brochure or other handout. You might use what you've learned to help your city or county government. Or you might find a worthwhile project at school in which you can use your skills.

APPENDIX C

Documenting Your Sources

Modern Language Association (MLA) and American Psychological Association (APA) documentation styles allow writers to quickly and accurately acknowledge their sources. Citing sources allows you to support your assertions and demonstrate the rigor with which you've researched your topics. Although source citation might seem like an intimidating and time-consuming task, it is a necessary and relatively painless process once you get the hang of it.

Both MLA and APA styles are parenthetical citation systems. That simply means that the source of information you include in your text— whether you quote the information directly, paraphrase it, or summarize it—is indicated in the text in parentheses. This in-text citation, most often the author's last name followed by either a page number (MLA) or a date (APA) is really just a reference pointer that sends the reader to the list of works cited (or references, as APA calls them) at the end of your paper or article. That list presents alphabetically, usually by the author's last name, all the sources you cite in your paper. Together, the works-cited list and the parenthetical citation send the reader to the precise place in the original source where you found your information. If you keep in mind that your intent is to provide your reader with the information necessary to locate your source, the reasons behind the conventions of documentation become clearer.

For more information on documentation, refer to *MLA Handbook for Writers of Research Papers* (5th ed., New York: MLA, 1999) or the organization's Web site (http://www.mla.org). If you are using APA style, refer to the *Publication Manual of the American Psychological Association* (4th ed., Washington, D.C.: APA, 1994) or the Web site (http://www.apa.org/journals/webref.html).

MLA DOCUMENTATION

IN-TEXT CITATION

As you do in-text parenthetical citation, keep in mind that it isn't necessary to repeat information. Your goal is to let your reader know which of the sources in your works-cited list you've used, and, if necessary, on what page in the source the information can be found. So, that is what you tell your reader in your citation:

> The locating or creating of shelter is "key to survival when lost in the wilderness" (Anderson 43).

The reader then refers to your works-cited list for a work listed under "Anderson." Note that the parenthetical reference is a part of the sentence and thus is within the closing punctuation. Also note that there is no comma between the author's name and the page number.

If your text already identifies the source, then your parenthetical citation doesn't need to repeat it:

> According to outdoorsman Dale Anderson, "Running water doesn't mean it is fit to drink" (112).

Note again that the parenthetical citation is part of the sentence, but because it is not a part of the quote, it is placed outside the closing quotation mark.

These two examples assume that you're referring to a specific piece of information within your original source. If you are making a general reference to an entire source or to ideas that run throughout a work, no page number is necessary:

> Proper preparation is the most important factor in wilderness survival (Anderson).

Citing two authors is no more difficult:

> Certain parrot species can learn to use language--not just mimicry--at the level of a three- or four-year-old child (Howe and Whye 341).

For three authors simply add the third name: (Howe, Whye, and Watt 341), using a series comma before the "and." If your source lists more than three authors, cite only the first author followed by the words *et al.,* literally "and others": (Howe et al. 341). When no author is given, use the first significant word in the title to guide the reader to the proper reference: (Saving 71).

If your works-cited list includes two or more entries by the same author, you will need to distinguish among the entries for the reader. Do this by adding the title, or a shortened version of the title if it is long, to the parenthetical notation: (Evans, Think 221).

PREPARING THE WORKS-CITED LIST

The works-cited list appears on its own page at the end of the paper. Center the words *Works Cited* at the top of the page and double-space between that line and your first entry. Begin the first line of each entry at the left margin. Indent subsequent lines half an inch (or five typewriter spaces) from the left margin. Alphabetize the entries by author (or title if no author is given).

The examples that follow illustrate how to cite many of the most commonly used sources, but you may make use of sources that are not included here. Refer to the *MLA Handbook for Writers of Research Papers* or the MLA Web site for examples of other types of documentation.

Books and Works Treated like Books

To cite books and works treated like books (pamphlets, government documents), include the following information:

Author: List the author's last name first, followed by a comma, and then the first name and middle name or initial if one is given, followed by a period.

Title: Underline the title and subtitle, and capitalize all main words. End with a period.

Publication Information: Give the city of publication, followed by a colon, a single space, and then the publisher's name in shortened form, followed by a comma, the year of publication, and finally a period.

1. One Author

   Bismark, Elaine. <u>Toxic Nightmares: Pollution and the American Suburb.</u> Boston: Boston UP, 1993.

2. Two or Three Authors (note that authors after the first are listed first name first)

   Langley, Aubrey, and Wilson Dynes. <u>Secrets of International Marketing.</u> New York: Ludwig, 1997.

3. Four or More Authors (after the first name add *et al.* ("and others") to indicate the other authors)

   Tanser, Marlena B., et al. <u>Making the Modern City.</u> Chicago: Kingsley, 1984.

4. Corporate or Group Author (alphabetize by the first significant word of the organization's name)

   People for Better Government. <u>Turning Out the Vote.</u> Washington: PBG, 1998.

5. No Author Given (alphabetize by the first significant word of the title)

   <u>Saving on Your Taxes.</u> New York: Barlowe, 1991.

6. More Than One Work by the Same Author (list works alphabetically by the first significant word of the title; use three hyphens to represent the author's name in subsequent entries)

   Evans, Penelope. <u>Understanding Your Child's Mind.</u> New York: Random, 1992.

   ---. <u>What Children Think: Learning and Problem Solving and Toddlers.</u> Berkeley: U of California P, 1992.

7. Pamphlet (treat as a book)

   Underwood, Tyler. <u>Appreciating Opera.</u> Cleveland: Northern Ohio Opera Association, 1988.

8. Government Document

   United States. US Geological Survey. <u>Natural Gas Deposits in the Pacific Northwest.</u> Washington: GPO, 1987.

Articles and Chapters in Books

To cite journal or magazine articles or chapters in books, include the following information:

Author: List the author's last name first, followed by a comma, then the first name and middle name or initial if one is given. End with a period.

Article or Chapter Title: In quotation marks, provide the full title, with all main words capitalized. End with a period inside the closing quotation mark unless the title ends with a question mark or an exclamation point (which also goes inside the quotation mark).

Publication Information: Underline the title of the journal or book, and capitalize all main words. Give the volume (and issue, if applicable) number, year of publication, and page numbers. Introduce page numbers with a colon if a journal and a period if a book.

9. Article in Journal Paginated by Volume

   Verchenko, Alexi. "Rethinking Csarism." <u>Journal of Russian History</u> 112 (1983): 231–44.

10. Article in Journal Paginated by Issue

    Oswald, Maria. "Modern Dance and the Interpretation of Style." <u>Aesthetics</u> 21.3 (1996): 87–99.

11. Article in Weekly Magazine

    Indurain, Hector. "Madagascar Enters Cyberspace." <u>Time</u> 17 May 1998: 84.

12. Article in Monthly Magazine

  Jorgensen, Ellen. "Why Don't We Vote?" <u>George</u> Oct. 1998: 37.

13. Article with No Author Given

  "Eavesdropping." <u>Atlantic Monthly</u> Aug. 1983: 18.

14. Article in Newspaper

  Farmer, Chris. "Cease Fire Broken." <u>New York Times</u> 17 Dec.
  1995: A1.

15. Editorial or Letter to the Editor

  "Making Mistakes, but Learning." Editorial. <u>Cleveland Plain Dealer</u>
  24 May 1993: D14.

  Hughes, Alphonse. Letter. <u>Arizona Republic</u> 15 Jan. 1994: C12.

16. Interview (published)

  Sobcheck, Alanna. "Making Things Work." Interview with Nina
  Papadopalus. <u>City Planner</u> Mar. 1992: 43–47.

17. Article in Encyclopedia

  "Cubism." <u>Encyclopaedia Britannica: Micropedia.</u> 15th ed. 1987.

18. Chapter in Edited Book or Selection in Anthology

  McDevitt, Jack. "Gus." <u>Standard Candles.</u> San Francisco: Tachyon,
  1996. 78–98.

  Frank, Quentin. "Are We There Yet?" <u>Assessing Civil Rights.</u> Ed.
  Janice Brown. New York: Polanski, 1989. 230–42.

Field and Media Sources

19. Interview (unpublished)

  Trujillo, Adelita. Personal interview. 3 Apr. 2000.

20. Film

  <u>Do the Right Thing.</u> Dir. Spike Lee. Perf. Danny Aiello and John
  Turturro. MCA Home Video, 1989.

21. Television or Radio Program

  "Birth of the Blues." <u>Fresh Air.</u> Prod. Cal Turner. Natl. Public Radio.
  7 June 1985.

22. Cartoon

  Yazgur, Maxwell. "Duck, Santa!" Cartoon. <u>Chicago Tribune</u> 30 Sept.
  1995: F14.

Internet and Electronic Sources

To cite material you retrieve from the Internet or another electronic
source, include the following information:

Author, Title and Publication Information: As for print sources, give as much of this information as is available.

Dates: Provide both the date the material was posted or revised and, before the URL, the date you accessed it.

Page Numbers: Include page numbers if they are provided.

23. Individual or Professional Web Site

> Gordon, Simon. <u>Pez Collector's Online Pricing Guide.</u> 15 Nov. 1998 <http://www.pezprices.com>.

24. Article in Online Magazine

> Ehrlich, Regina. "Archetypes of the Hero in Polynesian Journey Tales." <u>Folklore Studies Online</u> 2.1 (1997). 14 Jan. 1997 <http://www.umich.edu/clas/fso>.

25. Article in Online Magazine

> Ingveld, Lawrence. "Using Shadow and Light in Portraits." <u>Ephotographer</u> June 1999. 22 August 1999 <http://ephotographer.com/jun/ingveld>.

26. Article in Online Newspaper

> Preston, Hannah. "Freeway Expansion Moves Forward." <u>San Francisco Chronicle</u> 1 Dec. 1999. 14 Feb. 2000 <http://www.sfchronicle.com/news/metro/01121999/hpreston>.

27. E-mail

> Cardenas, David. E-mail to the author. 14 Nov. 1998.

28. CD-ROM

> Caprioti, Susan. <u>A Visual Guide to Leonardo's Notebooks.</u> CD-ROM. New York: Kingsley Multimedia, 1997.

Works Cited

"Birth of the Blues." <u>Fresh Air.</u> Prod. Cal Turner. Natl. Public Radio.

    7 June 1985.

Bismark, Elaine. <u>Toxic Nightmares: Pollution and the American</u>

    <u>Suburb.</u> Boston: Boston UP, 1993.

Caprioti, Susan. <u>A Visual Guide to Leonardo's Notebooks.</u> CD-ROM.

    New York: Kingsley Multimedia, 1997.

Cardenas, David. E-mail to the author. 14 Nov. 1998.

Evans, Penelope. <u>Understanding Your Child's Mind.</u> New York:

    Random, 1992.

---. <u>What Children Think: Learning and Problem Solving and Toddlers.</u>

    Berkeley: U of California P, 1992.

Frank, Quentin. "Are We There Yet?" <u>Assessing Civil Rights.</u> Ed.

    Janice Brown. New York: Polanski, 1989. 230–42.

Gordon, Simon. <u>Pez Collector's Online Pricing Guide.</u> 15 Nov. 1998

    <http://www.pezprices.com>.

Jorgensen, Ellen. "Why Don't We Vote?" <u>George</u> Oct. 1998: 37.

Langley, Aubrey, and Wilson Dynes. <u>Secrets of International</u>

    <u>Marketing.</u> New York: Ludwig, 1997.

"Making Mistakes, but Learning." Editorial. <u>Cleveland Plain Dealer</u>

    24 May 1993: D14.

People for Better Government. <u>Turning Out the Vote.</u> Washington:

    PBG, 1998.

Preston, Hannah. "Freeway Expansion Moves Forward." <u>San Francisco</u>

    <u>Chronicle</u> 1 Dec. 1999. 14 Feb. 2000 <http://www.sfchronicle.

    com/news/metro/01121999/hpreston>.

Tanser, Marlena B., et al. <u>Making the Modern City.</u> Chicago: Kingsley,

    1984.

Yazgur, Maxwell. "Duck Santa!" Cartoon. <u>Chicago Tribune</u> 30 Sept.

    1995: F14.

Sample MLA Works-Cited List

APA DOCUMENTATION

IN-TEXT CITATION

American Psychological Association in-text documentation style identifies a source by its author's name and the date of publication in parentheses. The parenthetical notation directs readers to further information in a list of references at the end of the paper.

In a standard APA parenthetical notation, the author's name, the publication date, and the page number are separated by commas:

> The locating or creating of shelter is "key to survival when lost in the wilderness" (Anderson, 1994, p. 43).

The reader then refers to your reference list for a work listed under "Anderson." Note that the parenthetical reference is a part of the sentence and thus is within the closing punctuation.

If your text already identifies the author's name, then your parenthetical citation need not repeat it:

> According to outdoorsman Dale Anderson (1994), "Running water doesn't mean it is fit to drink" (p. 112).

Note again that the parenthetical citation is part of the sentence, but because it is not part of the quotation, it's placed outside the quotation mark.

These two examples assume that you're referring to a specific piece of information within your original source. If you are making reference to an entire source or to ideas that run throughout a work, no page number is necessary:

> Proper preparation is the most important factor in wilderness survival (Anderson, 1994).

Citing a work by two authors is no more difficult than citing a work by one:

> Certain parrot species can learn to use language--not just mimicry--at the level of a three- or four-year-old child (Howe & Whye, 1993).

For three to five authors, include all the names, separated by commas, the first time you cite the source; after that, replace all except the first author's name with the words *et al.*, literally "and others":

> According to Howe, Whye, and Watt (1995), many animals "demonstrate remarkable abilities to recognize and respond to human speech" (p. 243). Howe et al. examined a number of species in their research.

If your source lists six or more authors, name only the first author followed by *et al.* on all mentions: (Howe et al., 1997). When no author is given, use the first significant word in the title to guide the reader to the proper reference: (Saving, 1991).

If your list of references includes two or more entries by the same author or authors with the same publication date, you'll need to distinguish the entries for your reader when you refer to them in your text. Do this by adding a lowercase letter to the parenthetical notation after the date (alphabetize the titles in the reference list before assigning the letters): (Evans, 1992a, p. 221).

Letters, unpublished interviews, e-mails, and other sources to which readers will have no access must be cited in the text but should not be included in the list of references. The same applies to entire Web sites:

> Milton Washburn notes that few job applicants have the kind of experience his company needs (personal communication, April 17, 2000).

> Prices for Pez dispensers vary (http://www.pezprices.com).

PREPARING THE REFERENCES

The list of references appears on its own page at the end of the paper. Center the word *References* at the top of the page and double-space between that line and your first entry. Indent the first line of each entry five to seven spaces (the same as your text paragraph indent), and position subsequent lines at the left margin. Alphabetize the entries by author (or title if no author is given).

The examples that follow illustrate how to cite many of the most commonly used sources, but you may make use of sources that are not included here. Refer to the *Publication Manual of the American Psychological Association* or the APA Web site (http://www.apa.org/journals/webref.html) for examples of other types of documentation.

Books and Works Treated like Books

To cite books and works treated like books (pamphlets, government documents), include the following information:

Author: List the author's last name first, followed by a comma, and then the initials only (followed by periods) of the author's first and middle names. Separate the names of multiple authors with commas, and place an ampersand (&) before the final author's name.

Date: Give the year of publication, in parentheses, followed by a period.

Title: Underline the book title and subtitle, and the period at the end. Capitalize only the first word of the title (and the subtitle) and all proper names.

Publication Information: Give the city of publication, followed by a colon, a single space, and then the publisher's name in abbreviated form, including the words *Press* and *Books* but omitting *Publishers, Co.,* and *Inc.*

1. One Author

   Bismark, E. (1993). <u>Toxic nightmares: Pollution and the American suburb.</u> Boston: Boston University Press.

2. Two to Five Authors (note that all author names are inverted)

   Langley, A., & Dynes, W. (1997). <u>Secrets of international marketing.</u> New York: Ludwig.

3. Six or More Authors (after the first name add *et al.* ("and others") to represent the other authors)

   Tanser, M. B., et al. (1984). <u>Making the modern city.</u> Chicago: Kingsley.

4. Corporate or Group Author (alphabetize by the first significant word of the organization's name; note that when the author and the publisher are the same, APA style uses the word *Author* in the publisher position)

   People for Better Government. (1998). <u>Turning out the vote.</u> Washington, DC: Author.

5. No Author Given (alphabetize by the first significant word of the title)

   <u>Saving on your taxes.</u> (1991). New York: Barlowe.

6. More Than One Work by the Same Author (list works chronologically, earliest first; repeat the author's name in each entry; alphabetize multiple works published in the same year by title, then add "a," "b," etc., after the date)

   Evans, P. (1992a). <u>Understanding your child's mind.</u> New York: Random House.

   Evans, P. (1992b). <u>What children think: Learning and problem solving and toddlers.</u> Berkeley: University of California Press.

7. Pamphlet (treat as a book)

   Underwood, T. (1988). <u>Appreciating opera.</u> Cleveland: Northern Ohio Opera Assn.

8. Government Document

   U.S. Geological Survey. (1987). <u>Natural gas deposits in the Pacific Northwest.</u> Washington, DC: U.S. Government Printing Office.

Articles and Chapters in Books

To cite journal or magazine articles or chapters in books, include the following information:

Author: List the author's last name first, followed by a comma, then the author's first and middle initials.

Date: In parentheses, give the publication date. Follow the closing parenthesis with a period.

Article or Chapter Title: Provide the full title, capitalizing only the first word of it and any subtitle, as well as all proper names. Do not underline the title or enclose it in quotation marks. End with a period (unless the title ends with a question mark or an exclamation point).

Journals and Other Periodicals: Capitalize all main words in the name of the publication. Follow the title with a comma, and then the volume number. Continuously underscore both title and volume. The article page span, preceded by a comma, follows the volume number. (The issue number, if any, follows the volume in parentheses.)

Books: Precede the book title with the word *In,* followed by the name of the book's editor. Capitalize only the first words of the title and subtitle and all proper nouns, and underscore the title. Place the page span of the chapter after the title, in parentheses. Conclude with place of publication and publisher, as for book entries.

9. Article in Journal Paginated by Volume

   Verchenko, A. (1983). Rethinking csarism. <u>Journal of Russian History, 112,</u> 231–244.

10. Article in Journal Paginated by Issue

    Oswald, M. (1996). Modern dance and the interpretation of style. <u>Aesthetics 21</u>(3), 87–99.

11. Article in Weekly Magazine

    Indurain, H. (1998, May 17). Madagascar enters cyberspace. <u>Time,</u> 84.

12. Article in Monthly Magazine

    Jorgensen, E. (1998, October). Why don't we vote? <u>George, 3,</u> 37.

13. Article with No Author Given

    Eavesdropping. (1983, August). <u>Atlantic Monthly,</u> 18.

14. Article in Newspaper

    Farmer, C. (1995, December 17). Cease fire broken. <u>New York Times,</u> p. A1.

15. Editorial or Letter to the Editor

    Making mistakes, but learning [Editorial]. (1993, May 24). <u>Cleveland Plain Dealer,</u> p. D14.

    Hughes, A. (1994, January 15). We need more freeways [Letter to the editor]. <u>Arizona Republic,</u> p. C12.

16. Chapter in Edited Book or Selection in Anthology

> McDevitt, J. (1996). Gus. In <u>Standard candles</u> (pp. 78–98). San Francisco: Tachyon.

> Frank, Q. (1989). Are we there yet? In J. Brown (Ed.), <u>Assessing civil rights</u> (pp. 230–242). New York: Polanski.

Media Sources

17. Film

> Lee, S. (Writer/Director). (1989). <u>Do the right thing</u> [Videotape]. MCA Home Video.

18. Television or Radio Program

> Turner, C. (Producer). (1985, June 7). Birth of the blues. In <u>Fresh air.</u> New York: National Public Radio.

Internet and Electronic Sources

To cite material you retrieve from the Internet or another electronic source, include the following information:

Author, Date, Title, and Publication Information: As for print sources, give as much of this information as is available. For the parenthetical date, use the date the material was posted or last revised.

Electronic Source: Conclude the entry with a retrieval statement including the date you retrieved the information, the source of the material (World Wide Web or other), and the path for retrieving it (URL or other). Do not end the retrieval statement with a period.

19. Article in Online Journal

> Ehrlich, R. (1997). Archetypes of the hero in Polynesian journey tales. <u>Folklore Studies Online 2</u>(1). Retrieved January 14, 1997 from the World Wide Web: http://www.umich.edu/clas/fso

20. Article in Online Magazine

> Ingveld, L. (1999, June). Using shadow and light in portraits. <u>Ephotographer.</u> Retrieved August 22, 1999 from the World Wide Web: http://ephotographer.com/jun/ingveld

21. Article in Online Newspaper

> Preston, H. (1999, December 1). Freeway expansion moves forward. <u>San Francisco Chronicle.</u> Retrieved February 14, 2000 from the World Wide Web: http://www.sfchronicle.com/news/metro/01121999/hpreston

Living in America: Modern Troubles   10

References

Bismark, E. (1993). <u>Toxic nightmares: Pollution and the American suburb.</u> Boston: Boston University Press.

Ehrlich, R. (1997). Archetypes of the hero in Polynesian journey tales. <u>Folklore Studies Online 2</u>(1). Retrieved January 14, 1997 from the World Wide Web: http://www.umich.edu/clas/fso

Evans, P. (1992a). <u>Understanding your child's mind.</u> New York: Random House.

Evans, P. (1992b). <u>What children think: Learning and problem solving and toddlers.</u> Berkeley: University of California Press.

Farmer, C. (1995, December 17). Cease fire broken. <u>New York Times,</u> p. A1.

Frank, Q. (1989). Are we there yet? In J. Brown (Ed.), <u>Assessing civil rights</u> (pp. 230–242). New York: Polanski.

Hughes, A. (1994, January 15). We need more freeways [Letter to the editor]. <u>Arizona Republic,</u> p. C12

Ingveld, L. (1999, June). Using shadow and light in portraits. <u>Ephotographer.</u> Retrieved August 22, 1999 from the World Wide Web: http://ephotographer.com/jun/ingveld

Langley, A., & Dynes, W. (1997). <u>Secrets of international marketing.</u> New York: Ludwig.

Making mistakes, but learning [Editorial]. (1993, May 24). <u>Cleveland Plain Dealer,</u> p. D14.

Oswald, M. (1996). Modern dance and the interpretation of style. <u>Aesthetics 21</u>(3), 87–99.

Tanser, M. B., et al. (1984). <u>Making the modern city.</u> Chicago: Kingsley.

Turner, C. (Producer). (1985, June 7). Birth of the blues. In <u>Fresh air.</u> New York: National Public Radio.

Sample APA List of References

CREDITS

TEXT

ACADEMIC PRESS, definition of "euthanasia," *Academic Press Dictionary of Science and Technology,* 1996. Copyright © 1996 Academic Press, Inc. Reprinted by permission.

AMERICAN DIETETIC ASSOCIATION, "Position of the American Dietetic Association: Legal and Ethical Issues in Feeding Permanently Unconscious Patients," *Journal of American Dietetic Association,* 1995, 95:231–234. Copyright © 1995 American Dietetic Association. Reprinted by permission.

LINDA BAKER, "McMansion Mania," *In These Times,* http://www.utne.com/bSocietyPr.tmpl @search?db=dArticle.db&eqheadlinedata =McMansion%20Mania. Reprinted by permission of the author.

LAWRENCE BIEMILLER and GOLDIE BLUMENSTYK, "Supreme Court Strikes Down Law on Internet Indecency," *The Chronicle of Higher Education,* July 3, 1997. Copyright © 2000 by The Chronicle of Higher Education. Reprinted with permission. This article may not be published, reposted, or redistributed without express permission from The Chronicle.

HENRY CAMPBELL BLACK, definitions of "death" and "brain death." Reprinted from *Black's Law Dictionary,* Fifth Edition, 1979. Reprinted by permission of the West Group.

KEVIN BUSHWELLER, "Guards with Guns," *American School Board Journal,* January 1993. Copyright © 1993 National School Boards Association. All rights reserved. Reproduced with permission.

BUSINESS WEEK, "New Neighborhoods Can Combat Urban Sprawl," August 30, 1999. Copyright © 1999 The McGraw-Hill Companies, Inc. Reprinted with permission.

DAN CARNEVALE, "How to Proctor from a Distance," *The Chronicle of Higher Education,* November 12, 1999. Copyright © 2000 by The Chronicle of Higher Education. Reprinted with permission. This article may not be published, reposted, or redistributed without express permission from The Chronicle.

K. DANNER CLOUSER, "The Sanctity of Life: An Analysis of a Concept," *Annals of Internal Medicine,* 1973, Vol. 78:119–125. Reprinted with permission from American College of Physicians and American Society of Internal Medicine.

CNN, "Police Re-think Policy of Trading in Their Weapons," www.cnn.com/US/9908/20/used. police.guns, August 20, 1999. Copyright © 2000 Cable News Network LP, LLLP. All Rights Reserved. Used by permission of CNN.

STEVEN CROW, "Virtual Universities Can Meet High Standards," *The Chronicle of Higher Education,* October 29, 1999. Copyright © 2000 by The Chronicle of Higher Education. Reprinted with permission. This article may not be published, reposted, or redistributed without express permission from The Chronicle.

ROBERT CWIKLIK, "A Different Course," *Wall Street Journal,* November 16, 1998. Copyright © 2000 Dow Jones & Co., Inc. Reprinted by permission of Wall Street Journal via the Copyright Clearance Center.

ENCYCLOPAEDIA BRITANNICA, definition of "abortion." Reprinted with permission.

HENRY FARBER, "Rockdale's Sheriff Won't Sell Off Guns," *Atlanta Journal-Constitution,* November 4, 1999. Reprinted by permission of The Atlanta Journal-Constitution via the Copyright Clearance Center.

JANET FIRSHEIN, "Are Living Wills Honored?" from *Before I Die* at www.pbs.org/wnet/bid/ sb-livingwills.html. Reprinted by permission of the author.

SAN JOSE MERCURY NEWS, "www.oneplace.sex? Internet Porn Would Be Easy to Filter (or Find)," *San Jose Mercury News,* July 5, 1998, Editorial, p. C6. Reprinted by permission.

R. CRAIG SAUTTER, "Standing Up to Violence," *Phi Delta Kappan,* January 1995. Copyright © 1995 Phi Delta Kappan. Reprinted by permission.

JULIAN SAVULESCU, "Rational Non-Interventional Paternalism," *Journal of Medical Ethics,* 1995, Vol. 221, pp. 327–331. With permission from the BMJ Publishing Group.

DAVID F. SEIDERS, "Stressed Out on Growth," *Builder,* September 1999. Copyright © 1999 Hanley-Wood, Inc. Reprinted by permission.

REBECCA MARTIN SHORE, "Personalization," *Phi Delta Kappan,* January 1996, pp. 362–363. Reprinted by permission of the author.

PETER SINGER, "In Place of the Old Ethic," *Rethinking Life and Death: The Collapse of Our Traditional Values.* Copyright © 1995 by Peter Singer. Reprinted by permission of St. Martin's Press, LLC.

MICHAEL J. SNIFFEN, "School Crime up 25%," *Associated Press,* April 1998. Reprinted by permission of The Associated Press.

JACOB SULLUM and MICHAEL LYNCH, "Cold Comfort," *Reason,* January 2000, v.31, i8, p. 34. Copyright 2000 by the Reason Foundation, 3415 S. Sepulveda Blvd., Suite 400, Los Angeles, CA 90034. Reprinted with permission.

JAKE TAPPER, "City Slickers" first appeared on salon.com, July 1999. Reprinted by permission.

BRIAN TOKAR, "Questioning Official Environmentalism," *Z Magazine,* April 1997. Reprinted by permission of Z Magazine, 18 Millfield St., Woods Hole, MA 02543.

WILLIAM BENNETT TURNER, "What Part of 'No Law' Don't You Understand?" *Wired,* May 1998. Copyright 1998 Conde Nast. All rights reserved. Reprinted by permission.

WALL STREET JOURNAL, "X-Rated," *Wall Street Journal,* January 14, 2000, Review & Outlook. Copyright © 2000 Dow Jones & Co., Inc. Reprinted by permission of The Wall Street Journal via the Copyright Clearance Center.

ANNE E. WEISS, "A Right to Die?" from *Bioethics: Dilemmas in Modern Medicine.* Copyright © 1985 Enslow Publishers, Inc. Reprinted by permission.

MAUREEN WEST, "New Living Will Puts Legal Issues in Plain English," *Arizona Republic,* October 24, 1998. Used with permission.

ROBIN WEST, "Gun Rights," *Tikkun,* Vol. 14, No. 5, (September/October 1999) pp. 25–26. Copyright 1999 Institute for Labor and Mental Health. Reprinted with permission from Tikkun: A Bimonthly Jewish Critique of Politics, Culture & Society.

PHOTOGRAPHIC

Chapter 4 p. 77, © Lara Jo Regan/Liaison Agency; p. 78T, © Gary Conner/PhotoEdit; p. 78B, © Bonnie Kamin; p. 79, Courtesy of Canyon College; p. 80, © Paul Conklin/PhotoEdit **Chapter 5** p. 135, © James Kegley; p. 136, © Michael Newman/PhotoEdit; p. 137T, © Eric Gay/AP/Wide World Photos; p. 137B, © Bonnie Kamin **Chapter 6** p. 212, © Steve Kagan/Liaison Agency; p. 213T, © Gifford/Liaison Agency; p. 213B, © A. Ramey/PhotoEdit; p. 214, © David R. Swanson/Liaison Agency **Chapter 7** p. 270, The San Diego-Union Tribune Photo by Scott Linnett; p. 271T, © Jim West/Impact Visuals; p. 271B, © J. Sohm/ The Image Works; p. 272, Shea Homes **Chapter 8** p. 341, © Evan Agostini/Liaison Agency; p. 342, © TimePix; p. 343T, © Tom McCarthy/ PhotoEdit; p. 343B, Courtesy of CYBERsitter, Solid Oak Software, Inc. **Chapter 9** p. 394, © Mark Richards/PhotoEdit; p. 395, © Bonnie Kamin; p. 396T, © States/SABA; p. 396B, © Mark Richards/PhotoEdit; p. 397, © Michael Newman/PhotoEdit

INDEX OF IMAGES

INDEX